1 MONTH OF
FREE
READING

at

www.ForgottenBooks.com

By purchasing this book you are
eligible for one month membership to
ForgottenBooks.com, giving you
unlimited access to our entire
collection of over 1,000,000 titles via
our web site and mobile apps.

To claim your free month visit:

www.forgottenbooks.com/free1049275

ISBN 978-0-331-80000-5
PIBN 11049275

REPORT

OF THE

PUBLIC SERVICE COMMISSION

OF MARYLAND

FOR THE YEAR 1919

BALTIMORE
KOHN & POLLOCK, INC.
1920

COMMISSION

JNO. MILTON REIFSNIDER, *Chairman*,

JAMES C. LEGG,

J. FRANK HARPER.

BENJAMIN T. FENDALL,
Secretary.

WILLIAM CABELL BRUCE,
General Counsel.

JOSEPH S. GOLDSMITH,
Assistant General Counsel.

CONTENTS.

REPORT

OF THE

PUBLIC SERVICE COMMISSION
OF MARYLAND

For the Year Ended December 31, 1919

STATE OF MARYLAND

OFFICE OF THE

PUBLIC SERVICE COMMISSION

BALTIMORE, December 81, 1919.

To the Governor and General Assembly of Maryland:

As required by Chapter 180 of the Acts of the General Assembly of Maryland, Session of 1910, creating the Public Service Commission, report for the year ending this date is respectfully submitted by the Commission.

CHANGES IN ORGANIZATION

On August 1st, 1919, Honorable Albert G. Towers resigned as Chairman and Commissioner, to become president of a large financial institution in Baltimore. Mr. Towers was appointed Commissioner on October 16th, 1913, to fill out the unexpired term of the late Dr. Joshua W. Hering, and upon the expiration of the term on May 4th, 1914, was reappointed for a full term of six years, and upon the resignation of Honorable Philip D. Laird on August 1st of the same year, was made Chairman of the Commission. During his almost six years of service as a member of the Commission, Mr. Towers was always quick to grasp the real point or principle involved in matters in controversy before the Commission, and this keen insight, combined with his forceful power of expression, served to make him a most valuable member of the Commission. On August 4th Commissioner Reifsnider was designated by the Governor to be Chairman of the Commission, and on August 6th Honorable J. Frank Harper was

appointed Commissioner to fill out the unexpired term of Mr. Towers. Mr. Harper qualified on same date and took up his duties on the following day.

On February 15th Mr. Bruce W. Duer, who had been Transportation Expert of the Commission since the organization of the Transportation Department on July 1st, 1915, died after an illness of but a few days. Mr. Duer was a capable and industrious official, and his efforts were constantly directed toward securing better transportation for the people of the State of Maryland. On March 1st, Mr. Joseph L. Wickes was appointed Transportation Expert of the Commission, entering upon the duties of his office on the same day.

Effective the same date, the Commission appointed Mr. Charles G. Edwards Chief Engineer, to fill the vacancy created by the death of the late Mr. Charles E. Phelps, Jr., on December 23rd, 1918. Mr. Edwards had served as Assistant Engineer of the Commission since April 4th, 1911, and on March 1st Mr. W. F. Strouse was appointed Assistant Engineer to fill the vacancy in the Commission's staff resulting from Mr. Edwards' promotion.

Three of the Commission's employees upon being released from the military and naval service of the Country have returned and resumed their former positions with the Commission, while three other former employees of the Commission, upon being discharged from the army, obtained employment elsewhere.

The Commission regrets to state that several of its employees have left the service of the State during the year to accept more lucrative positions in other fields, and it takes this opportunity to commend the loyalty of those members of its staff who have remained at their posts and continued in the discharge of their respective duties. A number of these men, highly trained in technical branches, and skilled in their particular work, have declined alluring offers to enter commercial life, because of their reluctance to give up what has come to be their life work. Some of these men are receiving the same salaries which they received when the Commission was organized nearly ten years ago, and it can truly be said in every instance their compensation is far less than the value of their services. It would be a distinct misfortune if the services of these skilled employees should be lost to the State.

GENERAL WORK OF THE COMMISSION

Cases were entered during the year as follows:

Formal Docket 134
Correspondence Docket ....
Short Notice and Reparation Docket 34

Total 168
Petty Complaints satisfied but not Docketed 562

Grand Total 730

Including cases entered in earlier years and remaining open on the Commission's docket on January 1st, 1919, 121 cases were closed during the year.

CORPORATIONS UNDER JURISDICTION

The following table shows the number of corporations other than automobile transportation companies and toll bridge companies over which the Commission exercises jurisdiction, with their capitalization and other information:

CORPORATIONS UNDER JURISDICTION OF THE COMMISSION.

CLASS.	NUMBER UNDER JURISDICTION.	NUMBER REPORTING.	INCOMPLETE REPORTS.	NOT REPORTING.	CAPITAL STOCK.	FUNDED DEBT.	TOTAL CAPITALIZATION.	INTEREST ACCRUED ON FUNDED DEBT.	DIVIDENDS DECLARED ON CAPITAL STOCK.
Express Companies	5	5			$51,150,000	$19,733,000	$70,883,000	$417,230	$1,235,496
Electric Light Companies	43	35	4	4	12,184,300	16,943,200	29,127,500	702,168	775,137
Gas and Electric Companies	5	4		1	14,782,140	38,190,247	52,972,387	1,787,965	1,152,325
Gas Companies	14	14			2,620,007	6,019,000	8,639,007	352,600	35,480
Electric Railway Companies	24	21		3	60,036,050	102,605,678	162,641,728	1,560,853	2,828,128
Steam Railway Companies	30	26		4	519,827,414	701,217,508	1,221,044,922	27,658,668	23,690,133
Steamboat Companies	9	7	1	1	1,289,650	0	1,289,650	0	52,235
Water Companies	34	20	8	6	1,565,756	1,623,300	3,189,056	78,219	36,275
Telegraph Companies	2	2			110,000	0	110,000	0	0
Telephone Companies	14	10	3	1	1,205,245	2,200	1,207,445	117	600,325
Miscellaneous Companies	2	1	1		1,969,400	479,000	2,448,400	24,300	40,000
Sleeping Car Company (Pullman Company)	1	1			120,000,000	0	120,000,000	0	9,544,016
Totals	183	146	17	20	$786,739,962	$886,813,133	$1,673,553,095	$35,582,110	$39,989,550

IMPORTANT CASES

On January 7, 1919, the Commission filed its opinion and entered its order in Cases Nos. 1568 and 1583, sustaining the reasonableness of the six cent cash fare established by the United Railways and Electric Company of Baltimore on October 1, 1918. After seven months' operation under this increased fare, the railway company in May of the present year filed an application with the Commission for authority to further increase the rate of fare to seven cents, with four tickets for twenty-five cents, with similar increase in commutation fares. The Commission employed Osborne I. Yellott, Esq., former Assistant General Counsel of the Commission, as special counsel, in which capacity Mr. Yellott had also served in the six cent fare case. The railway company's application for the further increase in fares (Case No. 1682) came on for hearing on August 7 and was concluded on September 5, 1919, eighteen days in all having been devoted to hearings and arguments. On August 17, 1919, while the hearings were still in progress, the railway company found it necessary to grant a wage increase to practically all of its employees, resulting in an increase in operating expenses of over $800,000.00 per year, and its application to the Commission was amended so as to provide for this additional expense of operation and also to provide an increased allowance for maintenance and depreciation, which increased allowance the company claimed was essential in order that it might adequately provide for the proper maintenance and replacement of its property. A fare of 10 cents straight with two tickets for 15 cents was claimed to be necessary for the purposes of the company. On September 30, 1919, the Commission filed its opinion and entered its order in this case, permitting the railway company to make effective on the following day a fare of seven cents cash, with four tickets for twenty-six cents, no increase being permitted in children's fares or commutation rates. Subsequently, the company voluntarily established the sale of two tickets for thirteen cents. The Commission's order provides that the increased fare is to remain in effect for the period of one year, and the railway company is required to render monthly reports to the Commission, so that thereby the Commission is kept in constant touch with the situation and is in a position to act promptly should the operating results demonstrate that a further adjustment of the fares is proper. On December 26, 1919, the railway company petitioned the Commission for a further increase in its rate of fare to seven cents straight, and discontinuing the sale of fare checks at the rate of six and one-half cents each, and in support thereof cited increases in taxes, cost of materials, etc., since the previous case which would make it impossible to continue rendering adequate service to the public at the rate prescribed by the Commission. Hearing was had on the petition, and the Commission has on this date filed its opinion and entered its order permitting the seven cent rate to become effective on January 1, 1920.

On January 27, 1919, the Commission filed its opinion and entered its order in the matter of the complaint and protest of The Mayor and Council of Hagerstown vs. The Hagerstown Light and Heat Company, Case No. 1589, in which it sustained the reasonableness of the increased rates for gas established by the respondent company on October 1, 1918. The Commission found that the rates in question were necessary in order to enable the company to meet the increased cost of operation, and by its order permitted such rates to remain effective until December 31, 1920, unless earlier modified or changed by the Commission.

Case No. 1603, complaint of John R. Warfield, J. M. Patterson, et al., vs. Cumberland and Westernport Electric Railway Company, involves the rates charged and service furnished by the railway company. After full investigation and hearing, the Commission, on June 5, filed its opinion and entered its order sustaining the rates of that company and requiring the railway company to make certain changes designed to improve the service and remove the cause of complaint in that respect.

In Case No. 1725 the Terminal Freezing and Heating Company applied to the Commission for permission to suspend the furnishing of steam heating service in certain sections of Baltimore theretofore served by that company. Numerous protests against such suspension of service were filed with the Commission by patrons of the heating company, and after investigation and hearing, the Commission, on October 21, 1919, entered its order refusing to permit the company to discontinue service.

Cases Nos. 1622, 1623 and 1624 are directed against the Washington and Rockville Railway Company, the City and Suburban Railway of Washington, and The Washington Interurban Railroad Company, respectively, suburban lines running from Washington, D. C., to points in Maryland, and have to do with the rates and service of these companies. Hearings and investigations were had in each of these cases, and in each the Commission found that the rates complained of were essential in order to enable the companies to continue to operate, though the Commission found lower rates to be justified for certain school commutation tickets, and its orders so provide. The service was found to be considerably better than it had been at the time the complaints were filed, and the Commission has since kept in touch with the situation through its Transportation Department with the view of further improving the service.

Case No. 1616, being complaint of the Mayor and Councilmen of Lonaconing vs. The Lonaconing Water Company, concerns the reasonableness of increased rates for water established by the respondent on January 1, 1919. In this case it became necessary for the Commission to make a valuation of the property of the water company, and after this had been done and the case heard by the Commission, it was evident to the Commission that the rates in effect prior to

January 1, 1919, would adequately provide for the proper corporate requirements of the water company, and on June 19 the Commission filed its opinion and entered its order requiring the company to restore the former rates, the same to become effective July 1, 1919. Thereafter the water company petitioned the Commission for a rehearing, contending that the rates prescribed by the Commission are not compensatory. Pending such rehearing the rates established by the Commission remain effective.

Cases Nos. 1525 and 1590 primarily involve the reasonableness of the rates charged by The Consolidated Public Utilities Company of Westminster for water furnished in the town of Westminster and environs, and the rules and regulations of said company governing such furnishing of water. In order to reach a satisfactory determination of the question of rates, it became necessary for the Commission to make an appraisal and valuation of the property of the water company. The valuation made by the Commission's Engineering Department proving unsatisfactory to the complainant, the Commission, upon request of the complainant, and in order to have before it the best judgment obtainable before finally passing upon the matter, employed Professor John H. Gregory, of Johns Hopkins University, as consulting engineer to review the valuation work of its staff. Prof. Gregory upheld the findings of the Commission's Engineering Department upon all essential points in controversy. On July 31, the Commission filed its opinion in which it fixed the valuation for rate-making purposes of the water property of the Consolidated Company and the maximum rate of return which might be earned thereon. The rates charged private consumers of water were not changed, the Commission having found that the existing rates produced a net return to the water company considerably less than the return permitted by the Commission. Certain reductions in rates for fire-protection service were made by the Commission, and the rules against which the protests of the complainant were directed were either modified or eliminated entirely.

The Consolidated Gas Electric Light and Power Company of Baltimore made effective on February 1, 1918, rules and regulations governing gas and electric main extensions and service connections, under which prospective consumers were required to pay for gas and electric service connections theretofore made at the expense of the utility, and to make a deposit covering the entire main extension necessary to serve such consumers, this deposit being subject to refund in whole or in part in accordance with the terms of the schedule three years after date of agreement. The Commission on February 15, 1918, on its own motion docketed Case No. 1476, complaining against the rules aforesaid. Owing to the press of other business, the Commission was unable to at once carry this case to a conclusion, but in the spring of the present year it announced its intention of starting hearings at an early date, and on May 20, 1919, the Consolidated Company submitted to the Commission revised rules and charges with respect to gas and electric main extensions and service connections, and offering to adjust all charges and deposits made since February 1, 1918, in conformity with the provisions of the revised rules, and to refund any excess payments or deposits with interest at the rate of 6 per cent. per annum. As the rules submitted tend to largely remove the objectionable features of the schedules against which the Commission complained, the same were permitted to become effective.

The Director General of Railroads has made a number of applications to the Commission during the course of the year for permission to discontinue freight and passenger agencies at various stations on railroads under Federal control. In each case hearing has been had and the Commission has endeavored to dispose of the matter in such way as to safeguard the interests of the shipping and traveling public and at the same time refrain from placing any undue burden upon the railroads. The Commission has in some cases granted the application, in others it has required the railroads to maintain a station-keeper at the station, while in others the applications have been denied and the carriers ordered to continue the points as agency stations.

The control and operation of the telephone and telegraph systems of the United States was taken over by the Federal Government on August 1, 1918, and the Postmaster General was placed in charge of their operation. On January 21, 1919, the Postmaster General made effective numerous changes in the toll rates throughout the nation, and on May 1, 1919, he likewise promulgated and put into effect new exchange rates to govern service through the several Maryland telephone exchanges. The wires were restored to private control and operation on August 1, 1919, and immediately prior to that date The Chesapeake and Potomac Telephone Company of Baltimore City filed with the Commission application to continue in effect the exchange and toll rates promulgated by the Postmaster General of the United States during the period of Federal control, or to charge and collect such other rates as may be found to be just and reasonable, and sufficient to provide for the proper corporate requirements of the company. The Commission thereupon docketed Case No. 1709 and proceeded to gather such information and statistical data as will be necessary in order to intelligently pass upon the question of the reasonableness of the telephone rates throughout the State of Maryland. The Commission hoped to start hearings early in October, but has been compelled to postpone the case from time to time, the present plan being to proceed with hearings on January 5, 1920. The Commission first considered the rates of the telephone company in 1912, at which time it prescribed rates to apply in Baltimore City. Thereafter the Commission entered into an investigation of the rates and charges, property and affairs of The Chesapeake and Potomac Telephone Company of Baltimore City, Case No. 690. On March 8, 1916, the

Commission filed its opinion in this case, wherein it established the fair value for rate-making purposes of the property of the telephone company and found that the earnings of the company under its then existing schedule of rates, taken as a whole, were not excessive.

DISCUSSION

Probably never in the history of this Commission has there been a greater pressure of business before it than has existed this year.

With the signing of the Armistice in November, 1918, it was the belief of practically one and all—the layman, the economist, the leaders of industry—that the then high costs had reached the peak and, while no quick reduction was likely, a gradual decline would be witnessed.

The contrary has actually occurred; the prices of all commodities have materially increased and at the close of the year are higher than at any time before the war.

The public well knows the extent of the increase in wages, particularly of skilled mechanics and day laborers, as well as the increase in the cost of the actual necessities required in its daily life and incidentally of all recreations and amusements.

These known high costs have confronted every business enterprise in the State as they have affected the individual citizen. Most mercantile and manufacturing enterprises were able to pass on the increased cost of production until it was ultimately paid by the consumer.

The same recognized increased costs were experienced by every public service utility under the jurisdiction of this Commission, some, of course, to a greater extent than others, but all to a marked degree, and particularly by those which were large employers of labor and users of coal.

It is obvious that these utilities must meet the increased costs with increased income, or court almost certain bankruptcy.

The increased income could only be secured by an increase in rates, and therefore there were filed either petitions or schedules for increased rates in a seemingly endless number.

Where a schedule of increased rates was actually filed and effective under the law in thirty days, or a hearing on a petition for an increased rate was necessary, protests from the communities involved generally followed, with public hearings in many sections of the State held as rapidly as the various cases could be reached.

This Commission has long since and with frequent reiterations made known that its policy is to permit the utilities under its jurisdiction to earn a fair return on the fair value of their property used and useful in service to the public, where such property is economically and efficiently managed, and in return for this such utilities are required to render adequate service reasonably required by the public.

By the very nature of regulation, utilities are prohibited from earning excessive profits and therefore cannot create a substantial surplus reserve in fat years to tide them over the lean periods, and since 1916, with costs advancing so rapidly, most of· these public utilities have merely struggled for actual existence.

It is this very fact, that public utilities are never allowed to earn more than a very reasonable rate of return, and at this time, when industrial enterprise affords such unusual opportunities for abnormal profits, capital, naturally attracted by these possible large rewards, has made it difficult for public utilities to obtain the necessary credit or new financing to enable them to properly maintain and extend their properties and meet maturing obligations.

Public utilities placed under the jurisdiction of this Commission are those furnishing commodities most essential to the needs of the community—not only the essentials of life itself but the conveniences vital to the actual industrial and social life of the community.

The Commission believes that the vast majority of our citizens realize that any factor that helps these utilities enures even to a greater extent to the public interest and benefit, and further, while the Commission realizes that some individuals have been critical of increases in rates allowed, yet it feels that the general public holds that its interests have been better safeguarded and served by enabling the utilities to continue rendering adequate service.

Reports of the several department heads of the Commission summarizing the activities of such departments during the year are hereto appended.

Respectfully,

JNO. MILTON REIFSNIDER,
Chairman;

JAMES C. LEGG,

J. FRANK HARPER,
Commissioners.

REPORT OF SECRETARY

BALTIMORE, December 31, 1919.

HON. JOHN MILTON REIFSNIDER,
Chairman of the Public Service Commission
of Maryland.

DEAR SIR:

The following·report of the Secretary of the Commission for the year 1919 is respectfully submitted:

During the year 1919, 134 cases were entered on the Formal Docket, of which 119 were closed by formal orders, after thorough investigation; hearings were had in all complaint cases before final disposition unless complainant withdrew complaint or admitted satisfaction therein, thus rendering a hearing unnecessary. On the Short Notice and

Reparation Docket 34 cases were entered and disposed of by final order. Five hundred and sixty-two petty complaints formerly placed on Correspondence Docket, but now handled by the Secretary, were disposed of during this year.

On the Formal Docket 1,751 cases have been entered since the Commission has been in existence, of which 1,712 have been settled and disposed of by final order, or otherwise, leaving 39 formal cases still open on this docket as of December 31, 1919, two of which were filed in December, 1919. During the past year hearings were had in 98 cases. These hearings in several cases extended over periods of from one day to four weeks. Number of orders entered in 1919 is 684. The issue of Stocks and Bonds has been authorized in the following cases:

	Stocks	Bonds
Edison Electric Illuminating Co., of Cumberland	$100,000.00	$200,000.00
Salisbury Light, Heat & Power Co....		92,500.00
The Peninsular Light & Power Co....		2,000.00
Dorchester Water Co.	12,800.00	
Idlewild Electric Light, Heat & Power Co., of Federalsburg, Md..........		6,000.00
Cambridge Gas Electric Light & Power Co.		17,000.00
The Hagerstown & Frederick Railway Co.		100,000.00
The Baltimore & Ohio Railroad Co..		3,000,000.00
Washington, Baltimore & Annapolis Electric Railroad Co.		439,000.00
The Hagerstown & Frederick Railway Co.		40,000.00
The New Taxi Service Co..........	10,000.00	
The Union Bridge Electric Manufacturing Co.		30,000.00
(1) Consolidated Gas, Electric Light & Power Co., of Baltimore..........		10,000,000.00
(2) The Consolidated Power Company of Baltimore.		2,500,000.00
(3) Western Maryland Railway Co......		2,857,000 00
The Baltimore & Ohio Railroad Co...		85,000,000.00
Washington Suburban Sanitary Commission.		750,000.00
Washington, Baltimore & Annapolis Electric Railroad Co.	1,044,250.00	
The Hagerstown & Frederick Railway Co.		85,000.00
Idlewild Electric Light, Heat & Power Co., of Federalsburg, Md.		2,000.00

The Peninsular Light & Power Co...	$4,000.00
Salisbury Light, Heat & Power Co..	22,000.00
Cambridge Gas, Electric Light & Power Co.	6,000.00
The Eastern Shore Gas & Electric Co., of Maryland	$815,000.00
Peninsula Ferry Corporation........	158,750.00

(1) Includes $5,000,000 of 3½-year Convertible Gold Note and like amount of 36-year Gold Bonds for collateral and conversion purposes.

(2) Issued as collateral to secure 3½-year Convertible Gold Notes of Consolidated Gas, Electric Light & Power Company of Baltimore.

(3) Issued as collateral to secure promissory note for $2,000,000.00.

Permission to exercise franchises has been granted to the following corporations and individuals:

The Maryland Electric Railways Company—
(Baltimore City) two franchises.
The New Taxi Service Company.
The Union Bridge Electric Manufacturing Company—
(Taneytown).
The Dundalk Water Company.
Edward C. Yingling—
(Electric Plant, Pleasant Valley, Carroll County).
Fawn Light and Power Company.
Edison Electric Illuminating Company of Cumberland, Maryland—
(Lonaconing).
The Eastern Shore Gas and Electric Company of Maryland.
Potomac Gas and Electric Company.
Peninsula Ferry Corporation.

There has been no abandonment of franchises previously exercised.

B. T. FENDALL,
Secretary.

REPORT OF GENERAL COUNSEL

BALTIMORE, January 2, 1920.

Public Service Commission,
Munsey Building, Baltimore, Md.

GENTLEMEN:

I beg leave to submit the following report for the period from January 1, 1919, to December 31, 1919, in regard to the transactions of my office as General Counsel of the Commission.

I rendered to the Commission 26 opinions in writing touching different questions submitted to me by it. While these opinions, in point of number, fall below the aggregate of opinions rendered by me in 1918, some of them—notably the opinion No. 386 upholding the validity of the Resolution of Congress taking over the telephone and telegraph lines of the country, and the opinion No. 396 asserting the full authority of the Commission to regulate the rates of the United Railways and Electric Company of Baltimore—are of more than usual importance.

In addition to the formal opinions I have been very frequently called upon to give oral and written advice to the Commission and have attended numerous conferences held by it.

The case of the West Virginia and Maryland Gas Co. against the Commission, on appeal from the Circuit Court of Baltimore City to the Court of Appeals of Maryland, was decided favorably to the Commission, and the important point thereby established that the Commission has the authority to regulate the rates for natural gas originating in West Virginia but distributed in the State of Maryland.

The growth of motor vehicle traffic on the improved highways of the State of Maryland gave rise, during 1919, to frequent occasions for advice by me to the Traffic Expert of the Commission, and provoked a considerable amount of litigation. In most of the cases making up this litigation the effort has been to enforce the contention that persons conveying only a special and limited part of the public, pursuant to a special contract or otherwise over the improved highways of the State, require only a hiring license and not a permit from the Public Service Commission. A case that will probably be decisive of some of the points involved in these controversies has been recently argued before the Court of Appeals and is now *sub judice*. I refer to the case of the Public Service Commission *vs.* Charles Wildason appealed by the Commission from the Circuit Court for Harford County. Two other cases which will probably turn on the decision in the Wildason case are now pending in the Circuit Court for Harford County and awaiting the result of the final decision in the Wildason case. Two other cases involving the refusal of motor vehicle owners to apply to the Commission for permits for operating over a State highway are now pending in the Circuit Court for Dorchester County. The case of the Commission against Messrs. Fillinggame and Krastle in the Circuit Court for Cecil County originating in similar circumstances is still pending, but I have not thought it worth while to press the application for an injunction in it to a hearing in view of the fact that the defendants have ceased to operate their vehicles.

An appeal has been taken from the recent action of the Commission in fixing water rates in the matter of the complaint of the City of Westminster against the Consolidated Public Utilities Company of Westminster, and a transcript of the papers in the case is now being made out by the Secretary of the Commission for transmission to the Circuit Court for Carroll County.

Since the decision of the Havre de Grace & Perryville Bridge Company case in the Court of Appeals, the Bridge Company, notwithstanding the vacation of the order of the Commission, has been charging rates not in excess of those prescribed by the order, and consequently for the time being the public has enjoyed the full benefit of the reduced rates prescribed by the order. The Bridge Company, however, has failed to file any new schedule evidencing the lower rates that it has been collecting contrary to the provisions of Section 16 of the Public Service Commission Law which forbids it to charge a greater, or less, or different compensation than that specified in the tariff schedule attacked by the Commission, which is the only one that it has ever filed with the Commission. The attention of the Bridge Company has been called to this provision of the law which it has overlooked, it states, through oversight, merely, and it expresses the intention of filing a new schedule immediately after the beginning of the coming year.

Various matters involving the delay of corporations in filing annual reports have been referred to me, but have all been brought, or are about to be brought, to a satisfactory conclusion.

I have no legislative recommendation to make except that in view of the "high cost of living" the salary of my secretary be increased for the next two fiscal years, say, from $1,500.00, the present amount, to $1,800.00 per annum.

Truly yours,

W. CABELL BRUCE,
General Counsel.

REPORT OF ASSISTANT GENERAL COUNSEL

BALTIMORE, January 5, 1920.

To the Hon. W. Cabell Bruce,
  General Counsel, Public Service Commission.

DEAR SIR:

I beg leave to submit the following report in reference to the duties which I have performed during the period of time from January 1, 1919, to December 31, 1919.

In the course of that year, I appeared as People's Counsel in a number of cases which were heard by the Public Service Commission.

The first of the aforesaid cases was that of the Mayor and Common Council of Westminster against the Consolidated Public Utilities Company of Westminster, which was a controversy regarding water rates that had recently been made effective by the aforesaid company. The case involved some very difficult problems, and the preparation of it consumed a considerable amount of time. The hearing began on

January 21, 1919, and was continued through the succeeding days to and including January 25. On March 26, the Commission being still in doubt about the matter, additional expert testimony was heard, and the argument of the case consumed two days, i. e., April 9 and April 11.

I went with the Public Service Commission to Hyattsville, to appear for the complainants in the case of W. A. Brooks, Mayor of Hyattsville, et al., vs. City and Suburban Railway of Washington. The hearing was not completed in Hyattsville, and I therefore appeared in the same case again at a later date for completion of same in Baltimore.

I went with the Public Service Commission to Bethesda, and there appeared for the complainants in the case of F. C. Heaton, et al., vs. Washington and Rockville Railway Company.

I went with the Public Service Commission to Chevy Chase to appear for the complainants in the case of the Town of Kensington against the Capital Traction Company of Washington. After our arrival there, I took part in a conference which resulted in a compromise of the controversy, and the proceedings before the Public Service Commission were thereafter merely of a formal nature.

I went with the Public Service Commission to Cottage City, and appeared for the complainants in the case of the Citizens of Berwyn Heights, et al., against the Washington Interurban Railroad Company.

I appeared for the complainants in the case of Mrs. J. M. Horner, et al., against the Pennsylvania Railroad.

A complaint was filed by the Mayor and City Council of Havre de Grace against the Havre de Grace Gas Company, on account of increased rates for gas. I carefully investigated the matter and fully prepared it for a hearing, but it was so manifest that the company had lost a large amount of money at previous rates, and would have little or no profit in the rates complained of, that after seeing the statement prepared by the Auditor of the Commission, and the report of the Chief Engineer, the complainant dismissed the case.

A complaint was filed by the Mayor and City Council of Havre de Grace against the Havre de Grace Electric Company, because of unsatisfactory service. I was assigned to that case by the Public Service Commission, and with the approval of the Commission, I thereupon undertook to ascertain whether the company could not be induced to improve its service to such extent as to satisfy the people of Havre de Grace, and so avoid the labor and expense of a formal hearing. The company readily complied with my suggestions, and improved the service to such extent that the Mayor and City Council of Havre de Grace dismissed the complaint.

A complaint was filed by the Mayor and City Council of Havre de Grace against the Havre de Grace Water Company. The preparation of that case involved a great deal of labor, and when it was ready for hearing, the complainant re-considered the matter and concluded that it was not advisable to proceed at that time with the hearing, and therefore dismissed the complaint without prejudice.

On May 23, 1919, the United Railways and Electric Company of Baltimore filed an application for permission to further increase car fares. I appeared as People's Counsel in the aforesaid case, and Mr. Osborne I. Yellott, who had been employed as Special Counsel in the case relating to the increase of fares from five cents to six cents, was again employed in a similar capacity when the latter petition was filed. After a considerable amount of time had been consumed in the preparation of the case, the hearing was begun on August 8, and consumed seventeen days, the argument having terminated on September 5. After the opinion in the above mentioned case had been filed, a petition was filed by the Railway Company for modification of the opinion, and I appeared when the last mentioned application was heard by the Public Service Commission on November 14. I appeared also at the hearing on December 30 of a later application for permission to further increase car fares.

I appeared as one of the counsel for the complainant in the case of the Mayor and City Council of Crisfield against the Crisfield Light and Power Company, the hearing of which consumed two days, and I appeared for the complainant in the case of the Evergreen Lawn Welfare League against the City and Suburban Realty Company.

The drivers of a number of jitney buses were reported to the Public Service Commission as having persistently violated the rules of the Commission. Several of them were summoned to appear in the Traffic Court to answer such charges. I appeared at the hearings. The men accused admitted that they had been guilty of violating the rules of the Commission, but the cases were dismissed, with my approval, when the men promised the Judge of the Traffic Court that they would not again violate the said rules.

During the last part of the year, I devoted a large amount of time to investigation of the affairs of The Chesapeake and Potomac Telephone Company, which had applied for approval, by the Public Service Commission, of the continuance of the telephone rates adopted by the Postmaster General while the telephone system was under Federal control. The hearing of the application of the company was not begun during the year 1919.

I have rendered other services which do not call for special mention herein.

Respectfully submitted,

JOSEPH S. GOLDSMITH,
Assistant General Counsel.

REPORT OF CHIEF ENGINEER

BALTIMORE, December 31, 1919.

Public Service Commission,
Baltimore, Md.

GENTLEMEN:

I beg to submit herewith report of the operations of the Engineering Department for the year ended September 30, 1919.

During the year eighty-eight special trips of inspection were made throughout the entire State, as compared with eighty-three for last year. This does not include many trips to points in the vicinity of Baltimore.

One hundred and fifty-four formal reports made by this department to the Commission may be classified as follows:

SUBJECTS	Steam Railroads.	Electric Railways.	Gas and Electric Companies.	Water Companies.	Steam Heating Companies.	Miscellaneous.	Totals.
Appraisals, New Equipment and Rates......		5	5	13			23
Grade Crossings........	3	2					5
SERVICE:							
Complaints..........	3	13	29	9	7		61
Quality of Gas........			11				11
Additional Facilities...			1	27			28
Miscellaneous..........	2	3	11			10	26
Totals............	8	23	57	49	7	10	154

Many of these reports were voluminous, and required such detailed investigation, that their preparation extended over a considerable period of time.

The increase in the number of investigations and reports resulted in general from the conditions brought about by the war. The difficulties experienced by the operators of the various utilities in the matter of fuel, while not so acute as in the preceding year, have been, nevertheless, very onerous. The prices have continued at a high level, and the purchaser is practically helpless in the matter of selection, from the point of view of the suitability of the fuel for his special purposes.

The labor difficulties have been very difficult; while it is true that the condition is not quite as acute as at the height of the war, nevertheless a new standard of wages and work seems to have been established. These standards militate certainly against any successful effort to approximate the former normal expense and efficiency of operation.

The re-adjustment is gradual, and apparently ineffectual.

These conditions naturally have stimulated the character and number of complaints of service rendered by the utilities of the State.

I. METER TESTING

Routine tests of gas meters to the number of 24,072, and 11,886 electric meters have been made; 12 gas meters, 10 electric meters, and 25 water meters were tested upon complaint of consumers, a total of 36,015. Compared with last year, these figures show an increase of 9.70 per cent. in the total number of meters tested; an increase in gas meters of 2.58 per cent.; an increase in electric meters of 27.5 per cent. The following table gives the number of gas and electric meters tested for each year during the past nine years. The record for water and steam meters is included for the first time:

YEAR.	ROUTINE TESTS.		COMPLAINT METERS.				TOTALS.
	Gas.	Electric.	Gas.	Electric.	Water.	Steam.	
1911..	24,058	5,592	24	24	2	......	29,700
1912..	27,276	8,819	57	30	3	......	36,185
1913..	31,115	10,143	26	10	18	......	41,312
1914..	33,858	9,959	22	4	13	1	43,857
1915..	32,270	9,310	23	8	20	......	41,631
1916..	30,370	11,969	18	12	17	1	42,387
1917..	34,046	13,362	12	13	13	......	47,446
1918..	23,467	9,324	7	7	11	5	32,821
1919..	24,072	11,886	12	10	25	10	36,015
Totals,	260,532	90,364	201	118	122	17	351,354

II. TESTING

Electrical Testing. The laboratory equipment for electrical testing has been improved during the year by some changes of detail, and there is now in process the installation of a method to secure better speed control of the testing set, and consequently more regular condition of the voltage and current during tests.

The activities in the field have been extended. Some of the small companies have been instructed in and brought into the scheme of inspection, which has been gradually heretofore applied to the more important operations.

Gas Testing. The program of testing in the laboratory at Baltimore of the quality of the gas has been maintained on the same plane as in the latter part of the preceding year—that is, more numerous tests are being made. This program is rather onerous with the small staff available. It is hoped that by means of a recording calorimeter, the demands on the time of the inspector may be somewhat relieved.

There has been added this year to the gas laboratory equipment an effusion type of gravitometer, for determining the specific gravity of the gas.

III. SURVEY OF GAS PLANTS

As noted earlier in this report, the conditions in this State, especially in the field of operation of the supply of gas, have been greatly disturbed, as the result of developments due to the war.

This is evidenced not only from the complaints of consumers as to the character of service, but also by the increasing burden of operating expenses experienced by the companies, consequent deficits in their yearly balances, and numerous applications for increase in rates.

It seemed imperative to determine whether, by adopting any reasonable expedient to improve the efficiency of operations, it would be possible to obviate continuous efforts on the part of the various companies to secure relief, by means of higher schedule of rates.

These investigations would require special experience and skill, in order to be accomplished effectively. A general knowledge of the changes and efforts to meet new conditions beyond the confines of this State are essential.

Obviously improvements in efficiency of plant operation tends toward the conservation of fuel. During the war, the Engineering Department had been in close touch with the Bureau of Standards' investigation in the matter of conservation of fuel in gas manufacture. This fact led to conferences with the Bureau directed toward securing their co-operation in a survey of the gas plants of the State.

The Commission has been fortunate in securing their consent to undertake a survey of all of the gas plants in the State, to be followed by reports on each, dealing with their present condition, and pointing out whether improvements might be made in existing operation, leading to greater efficiency.

This program has been started, and is now in active prosecution. Examinations and reports have been made in several instances.

It is hoped that the result from the State-wide study will be beneficial, both to the consumers and to the owners of the gas utilities.

IV. CHANGES IN ENGINEERING STAFF

Mr. Charles G. Edwards was appointed to the vacancy of Chief Engineer, occasioned by the death of Mr. Charles E. Phelps, Jr. He qualified on March 1, 1919. Mr. Wm. F. Strouse was appointed to the vacancy thus occasioned of Assistant Engineer, and qualified on March 1, 1919.

Pursuant to the policy of the Commission, Mr. H. C. Ward resumed the duties of Inspector of Gas upon his return from service in the United States Navy, April 1, 1919, vice Mr. Stanley H. Hays, resigned.

Respectfully submitted,

CHARLES G. EDWARDS,
Chief Engineer.

REPORT OF TRANSPORTATION EXPERT

BALTIMORE, December 31, 1919.

HON. JNO. MILTON REIFSNIDER,
Chairman, Public Service Commission.

DEAR SIR:

You will find herewith the report of the Transportation Department of the Public Service Commission for the year 1919. The question of improving the transportation facilities of the State is one that has occupied our entire attention, and aside from the formal reports which have been made from time to time to the Commission, you have been kept informed verbally of the various activities of this department.

As far as has been practicable, the equipment and service have received personal attention, and matters pertaining to the betterment of existing conditions have been vigorously taken up with the operating officials of the incorporated bodies and with individuals of the various bus lines operating all over the State.

In regard to The United Railways and Electric Co., while much is lacking in the service to make it conform to your rules, yet as compared to 1918 a marked improvement has been noted. A great deal of trouble in obtaining quick service is due to our antiquated traffic laws, and the congestion on certain streets because of the wish of everybody to go to their ultimate destination without the physical exertion of walking a block or two. During the peak of the afternoon rush, many of the streets in the delivery districts are so congested that the movement of the cars is almost impossible, and this can only be remedied by the re-routing of several of these lines, and placing them elsewhere. This matter at present is receiving the very serious attention of the railway officials, and it is believed that in a comparatively short time conditions in this regard will be very much better.

The Garrison Avenue line was re-routed and taken off Park Avenue and put on Madison Avenue and Eutaw Street, which has been a great benefit, not only in the saving of time, but as a convenience to the patrons of this line.

The systematic construction of improved roads, under the supervision of the State Roads Commission, not only the roads comprised in their system, but also State Aid Roads, has, together with the perfecting of the motor vehicle, revolutionized transportation through the country districts of the State. This method of transportation of passengers and freight is in its infancy, but it is satisfactory to note the steady growth of this industry. Like every other innovation, the development of this means of transportation has shown weak points that can be improved. This service is now largely in the hands of individuals, and at the present time the law is not very clear in drawing the line between those who operate as hiring cars and those who operate over a fixed route and on a fixed schedule; and we find many cases of conflict between these two separate services. Because of the personnel of those who operate over a fixed route and for a fixed compensation, full powers and facility in observation should be afforded to the Public Service Commission to enable their proper supervision in the interest of the traveling public. The public who use this means of transportation should be afforded the same protection against loss, damage and accident as is afforded by steam and electric roads and steamboat companies, so that in case of loss or damage they may be afforded some tangible means or method of recovery. There should also be a schedule arranged to enable through passengers to connect from one bus line to another, so that in a small way this service could be worked into one system of transportation.

The same principle could be applied to the freight service and a satisfactory and standard bill of lading devised that would bind the operator to the obligations of a common carrier and set forth the extent of his liability very clearly. It should be designed so as to permit the transfer of goods from one carrier to another.

In addition to the features of the ordinary railroad bill of lading, it should include some of the features of the invoice so as to obviate the need of a large number of forms for a relatively small business. A bill of lading to meet these conditions could be devised and a proper form incorporated and made part of the Motor Vehicle Law, in order that the improvements and extent of this service may be appreciated.

It might be interesting to say that 31 freight lines were operated during the year 1919, covering 381½ miles of road, and 70 passenger lines, covering 784½ miles of road. These lines, both passenger and freight, extend to every portion of the State, and from the fact that most of them have applied for a renewal of their permit for the year 1920, it is believed that this is developing into a lucrative business. The above estimate takes in only the country districts and does not include any of the jitney operation in Baltimore City. It will be seen from the above that motor bus transportation, if properly developed and supervised, has tremendous possibilities for the betterment of communication in the country districts.

During the past year your Transportation Department had devoted a great deal of time and study looking toward the betterment of this service. Much has been accomplished in securing the proper operation of various lines for the public benefit, and while this service has shown a decided improvement, it is far from perfect, but from month to month a gradual improvement has been noted and the various operators are understanding more and more that by operating strictly according to the rules of this Commission, and thereby making their service more reliable, they are not only benefiting the public but benefiting themselves.

The possibilities of this service are almost without limit, and under a wise direction an evolution will gradually take place from the haphazard operating to a reliable system of transportation.

It is not at all improbable that the time will come when the motor bus will, to a large extent, supersede the trolley car for city as well as suburban transportation. The motor bus has many advantages over the trolley.car, and given good streets, reliable operation with economies, which will from time to time be introduced in holding its own in furnishing cheap and reliable transportation. The original outlay is small, having no expensive track system, power stations, or overhead system of construction. Each bus acts as an individual unit, and is not dependent on any other unit as in the case of the trolley car, and provided the streets are in reasonably good condition, they could select their route without waiting for a long and expensive construction.

During the year 1919 this department has issued permits for the operation of motor vehicles for the public transportation of passengers and freight as follows:

For passenger service 302
For freight service 65
                                                    ——
Total permits issued 367

It will be observed that the number of permits issued is far in excess to the number of lines operated. This apparent discrepancy is accounted for in the fact that over many of the lines several vehicles are operated, and additional permits have been taken out for reserved vehicles; also a few have discontinued operating entirely, and a large number of permits have been issued in Baltimore City for jitney service which are not included in the above summary.

CHANGES IN PERSONNEL

The death of Mr. Bruce W. Duer, head of this department, occurred on February 15, 1919, after a short illness, and his loss was very keenly felt. Not knowing Mr. Duer personally, I was nevertheless impressed by the thorough manner in which the matters of this department were handled, as shown by the condition in which he left them.

Mr. Albert L. Dean, who resigned July 1, 1918, to enter the service of the United States, after seeing active service in France, returned and was re-appointed as an inspector, taking effect July 1, 1919.

Mr. James R. Dunlop resigned to accept a better position, his resignation taking effect October 15, 1919. Mr. Dunlop's loss is a very serious one, as he had been here a long time, and was familiar with all the different phases of the work of this department. In addition, he was thoroughly conscientious and was very efficient in everything he handled.

Mr. Gilbert Hagadone resigned to accept another position, resignation taking effect October 1, 1919.

Mr. James E. Yursik was appointed in Mr. Hagadone's place, the appointment taking effect October 22, 1919.

Mr. Dean was promoted to the position held by Mr. Dunlop, and Miss Alice Ashmore was appointed to Mr. Dean's place, her appointment taking effect November 11, 1919.

ACCIDENTS

A comparative summary of the total number of accidents to persons during the last nine years is submitted below, the accidents being tabulated as between those occurring on steam railroads and electric railways:

TOTAL PERSONAL ACCIDENTS COMPARED BY YEARS

YEAR	CLASS OF PERSONS	STEAM RAILROADS		ELECTRIC RAILWAYS		GRAND TOTALS	
		K.	I.	K.	I.	K.	I.
1911	Public	63	190	31	5,670	94	5,860
	Employees	38	677	4	1,192	42	1,869
1912	Public	94	148	33	6,365	127	6,513
	Employees	40	799	2	1,367	42	2,166
1913	Public	96	244	32	3,748	128	3,992
	Employees	70	902	3	1,414	73	2,316
1914	Public	72	233	35	7,213	107	7,446
	Employees	37	1,044	5	1,400	42	2,444
1915	Public	90	257	31	6,395	121	6,652
	Employees	29	813	5	1,249	34	2,062
1916	Public	78	144	29	[6,244	107	6,388
	Employees	35	853	4	1,250	39	2,102
1917	Public	89	195	46	6,398	135	6,593
	Employees	45	866	10	1,560	55	2,426
1918	Public	85	196	69	5,312	154	5,508
	Employees	55	811	2	1,477	57	2,288
1919	Public	63	124	58	6,355	121	6,479
	Employees	37	497	5	1,636	42	2,133
Totals	Public	730	1,731	364	53,700	1,094	55,431
	Employees	386	7,261	40	12,545	426	19,806
Grand Totals		1,116	8,992	404	66,245	1,520	75,237

Out of the above total accidents to persons, those which occurred at grade crossings for each year during the last nine years are as follows:

GRADE CROSSING ACCIDENTS COMPARED BY YEARS

YEAR	COMPANY	KILLED	INJURED	TOTALS
1911......	Steam Railroads............ Electric Railways...........	11	(	18
1912......	Steam Railroads............ Electric Railways...........	12	10	22
1913.......	Steam Railroads............ Electric Railways...........	12	44	56
1914......	Steam Railroads............ Electric Railways...........	8	40	48
1915.......	Steam Railroads............ Electric Railways...........	15	49	64
1916......	Steam Railroads............ Electric Railways...........	18	39	57
1917......	Steam Railroads............ Electric Railwasy...........	44	103	147
1918......	Steam Railroads............ ElectricRailways...........	38	101	139
1919......	Steam Railroads............ Electric Railways........	24	78	102
	Totals...............	182	471	653
	Averages per year......	20	52	72

Those accidents to persons trespassing upon railroad property have been segregated, and are as follows:

FATALITIES AND INJURIES DUE TO TRESPASSING UPON RAILROADS—COMPARISON BY YEARS

YEAR	B. & O. R. R.		Penna. R. R.		W. Md. R. R.		Minor Steam		Minor Electric		Totals	
	K.	I.	K.	I.	K.	I.	K.	I.	K.	I.	K.	I.
1911..........	53	22	30	51	9	20	6	4	10	5	108	102
1912..........	45	45	20	9	9	17	15	7	9	7	98	85
1913..........	42	30	20	26	10	80	16	4	5	16	93	156
1914..........	38	41	15	37	8	25	7	14	9	19	77	136
1915..........	38	28	10	12	12	15	12	12	6	19	78	86
1916..........	36	18	10	9	9	9	4	3	10	1	69	40
1917..........	27	13	10	8	4	9	6	2	10	4	57	36
1918..........	18	15	13	11	4	3	1	....	13	12	49	41
1919..........	16	9	17	14	7	6	3	2	14	7	57	38
Totals.....	313	221	145	177	72	184	70	48	86	90	686	720

	KILLED	INJURED
Total Steam Railroads.........................	600	630
Total Electric Railways......................	86	90
Grand Total (9 years)...................	686	720

During the year the Transportation Department was represented at twenty inquests or investigations, with the view of recommending methods or plans that would prevent loss of life and personal injury.

Respectfully submitted,

J. L. WICKES,
Transportation Expert.

REPORT OF BUREAU OF RATES AND TARIFFS

BALTIMORE, December 31, 1919.

HON. JOHN MILTON REIFSNIDER,
Chairman.

DEAR SIR:

Report upon the work of this bureau during the current year is herewith tendered.

During the war period the routine work of the bureau has been disarranged to a considerable extent, but with the return to pre-war procedure, if not to pre-war conditions, the situation will probably soon readjust itself satisfactorily. The first step in this direction was when the telephone and telegraph lines were returned to private control and operation, which occurred on August 1, 1919, after the wires had been under Federal control for a period of one year, under the immediate direction of the Postmaster General of the United States. The railroads are also to be returned to their corporate owners on March 1, 1920, and the bureau recently has been in communication with officials of some of the carriers with the idea of determining upon some satisfactory method which will enable the Commission to resume its procedure with respect to the handling of tariffs under the system which obtained prior to the taking over of the operation of the railroads by the Federal Government, but this work has been set to naught by recent action of certain of the carriers, to which further reference is made.

As heretofore pointed out to the Commission, the usefulness and accuracy of the Commission's railroad tariff files have been greatly lessened by reason of the fact that during the period of Federal control tariff schedules have been filed with the Interstate Commerce Commission exclusively, without State commission numbers. The United States Railroad Administration evidently has recently come to realize the error it made when it permitted the elimination of State commission numbers from tariff publications, and to correct this Mr. Edward Chambers, director, Division of Traffic of the United States Railroad Administration, on December 12, 1919, issued his Circular No. 12, providing that the proper State commission numbers should be shown on all tariffs thereafter issued, and that numbers should be assigned to tariffs already issued. When this circular was received, the bureau at once got into communication with officials of the more important carriers and suggested that the carriers get together and agree upon some uniform method of procedure to carry into effect the requirements of Mr. Chambers' circular aforesaid, but the carriers have seen fit to disregard the Commission's suggestion, with the result that there has been no uniformity of action among the railroads, or even between different departments of the same railroads. The bureau realized that the Commission was without power to require the matter to be handled in any particular way, but had hoped that the carriers could have consistently met the wishes of the bureau. The result will probably be that the Commission will have to devise its own plans for handling the tariff situation upon the return of the railroads to private control and operation.

The Director General of Railroads at various times during the year has submitted to the Commission for its consideration and advice a number of contemplated rate changes affecting Maryland interests, . all of which matters have been investigated by this bureau, and in a number of instances conferences with interested shippers and their representatives have been held with the idea of gaining the views of others with respect to the matters under consideration.

Owing to the continued unsettled conditions following the termination of actual hostilities, and the absence of any marked downward trend in the costs of labor and materials, there has not yet been any indication of a general readjustment of the rates of public utilities in this State. On the contrary, during the year there have been a number of utilities that have found it necessary to increase further their rates and charges to meet their higher costs of operation. Some of these rate increases have resulted in complaints to the Commission respecting the reasonableness thereof and in several cases the Commission has been able, after investigation, to reduce the rates complained of without jeopardizing the ability of the utilities to continue furnishing service. All such rate increases naturally require the closest scrutiny of the Commission, regardless of whether or not they are the subject of formal complaint and investigation by the Commission. During this period when changes in rates are frequently being made, it is highly desirable that the rate schedules of the utilities should be standardized as to form and as complete as possible with respect to the rates, rules and regulations contained therein, and to this end I would respectfully direct the attention of the Commission to the desirability of adopting and making effective the revised rules to govern the construction, filing and publishing of rate schedules of all classes of public utilities (other than common carriers), tentative form of which revised rules was first submitted to the Commission under date of November 24, 1916, accompanying my Report No. 64.

Eighty-four formal reports have been rendered the Commission during the year. Aside from the complaints and inquiries sent by the Commission to this bureau for investigation and report, an increasingly large number of matters are handled informally through the bureau, with the result that frequently the matter in controversy is settled satisfactorily without the necessity of formal complaint to the Commission. The bureau has also rendered assistance to numerous persons who have called upon it to aid them in constructing rate schedules of both utilities and carriers, so that they might obtain the best rating possible. Sometimes the bureau has been able to offer suggestions respecting either a change to some other rate schedule or some change in the customer's use, thereby producing a better load factor, which when put into operation have had the effect of producing a lower average rate to the particular user.

Under the provisions of Section 15 of the Public Service Commission Law, authorizing changes in rates for good cause shown on less than statutory notice of thirty days, thirty-four orders were entered during the year. The number of orders entered this year in these short notice and reparation cases is somewhat less than the average of those entered in previous years, due largely to the fact that most of the railroads operating in Maryland have been under exclusive Federal control during this period.

Respectfully submitted,

FRANK HARPER,
Chief of Bureau.

REPORT OF AUDITOR

BALTIMORE, December 31, 1919.

HON. JNO. MILTON REIFSNIDER,
Chairman, Public Service Commission,
Baltimore, Md.

DEAR SIR:

The report of the work of the Auditor's office for the year ended December 31, 1919, is submitted herewith.

The general work assigned to this office has been kept up to date and other special work that has been referred to this office has been dispatched as quickly as possible. Statements that have been necessary in a large number of rate cases coming before the Commission have been prepared, and assistance has been given the office of Assistant General Counsel whenever called upon.

The Budget System, adopted by the Legislature at the 1918 session, has been in operation since October 1, 1918, and has proven satisfactory.

The Commission has under its jurisdiction 183 public service corporations; 146 corporations made complete reports, 17 incomplete reports and 20 did not make any reports for the year ended December 31, 1918.

The following statement shows the capitalization of all corporations reporting to the Commission:

COMPARATIVE STATEMENT OF CORPORATIONS UNDER JURISDICTION OF THE
COMMISSION FOR THE YEARS ENDED DECEMBER 31, 1917,
AND DECEMBER 31, 1918

	Dec. 31, 1917 Amount	Dec. 31, 1918 Amount	Increase or Decrease
Capital Stock Outstanding...	$783,953,762	$786,739,962	$2,786,200
Funded Debt	896,310,531	886,813,133	*9,497,398
Total Capitalization	$1,680,264,293	$1,673,553,095	*$6,711,198
Interest Accrued on Funded Debt	$34,798,703	$35,582,110	$783,407
Dividends Declared on Capital Stock	44,829,099	39,989,550	*4,839,549

* Denotes decrease.

During the fiscal year ended September 30, 1919, there was collected
and remitted to the Treasurer of Maryland office fees amounting to
$1,476.51.

Below is a detailed statement of disbursements for the fiscal year
ended September 30, 1919:

OCTOBER 1, 1918, TO SEPTEMBER 30, 1919

Salaries	$80,123.76
Rent	6,000.00
Furniture and Fixtures	995.58
Postage	716.00
Printing and Stationery	4,991.09
Books and Periodicals	457.86
Traveling	3,197.59
Court Costs	26.15
Engineers' Apparatus	899.40
Laboratory Supplies	99.77
Telephone and Telegraph	595.61
Office Supplies	675.83
Special Services	3,791.09
Total Expenses for Year	$102,569.73

The appropriation of the 1918 Legislature available for the year
was $105,670.25, and therefore $3,100.52 reverted to the Treasury of
Maryland.

Respectfully submitted,

JAMES F. DUNN, JR.,

Auditor.

APPENDIX I

RECEIPTS AND DISBURSEMENTS OF THE COMMISSION

FOR THE FISCAL YEAR, OCTOBER 1, 1918, TO SEPTEMBER 30, 1919, INCLUSIVE

SALARIES AND EXPENSES

SALARIES

Jno. Milton Reifsnider, Chairman............	$1,000 00
Jno. Milton Reifsnider, Commissioner........	4,166 67
Albert G. Towers, Chairman................	5,000 00
James C. Legg, Commissioner................	5,000 00
J. Frank Harper, Commissioner..............	766 18
Benjamin T. Fendall, Secretary..............	3,000 00
Wm. Cabell Bruce, General Counsel..........	4,800 00
Jos. S. Goldsmith, Assistant General Counsel..	4,722 50
Jas. F. Dunn, Jr., Auditor..................	3,600 00
Joseph L. Wickes, Transportation Expert.....	2,100 00
Bruce W. Duer, Transportation Expert.......	1,860 71
Charles E. King, Chief Stenographer.........	2,400 00
Edward S. Brittain, Stenographer............	1,500 00
Wm. G. Dawson, Chief Clerk................	1,800 00
G. Archer Hays, Stenographer................	1,500 00
Frank F. Kormann, Sténographer............	2,400 00
Helen J. Lease, Stenographer................	1,200 00
Gertrude C. Cottman, Stenographer..........	660 00
Penelope S. Westcott, Stenographer..........	396 78
Mollye Greenstein, Stenographer............	300 00
Jas. R. Dunlop, Stenographer................	1,500 00
Alice L. M. Tubbs, Stenographer............	900 00
Frank Harper, Rate Clerk..................	2,500 00
Maud Stewart, Stenographer................	900 00
Nellie Ford, Telephone Operator.............	360 00
Nan Delany, Telephone Operator............	270 97
Mary Lortz, Telephone Operator............	60 00
Chas. E. Phelps, Chief Engineer.............	1,200 00
Chas. G. Edwards, Chief Engineer............	2,800 00

Chas. G. Edwards, Assistant Engineer.........	$1,500 00
Wm. F. Strouse, Assistant Engineer..........	2,100 00
Luke Ellis, Assistant Engineer..............	1,960 00
J. Garland Turner, Clerk—Engineering Department	1,100 00
Anna C. Ehrhardt, Clerk—Engineering Department	180 00
Wm. T. Russell, Superintendent Inspector.....	2,040 00
Jas. W. Ebaugh, Meter Inspector............	1,140 00
John H. Marley, Meter Inspector.............	1,000 00
Stanley H. Hays, Laboratory Assistant.......	600 00
H. Clay Ward, Laboratory Assistant.........	600 00
Edna Strouse, Stenographer.................	1,200 00
Benjamin M. Haughey, Transportation Inspector	1,200 00
Gilbert Hagadone, Transportation Inspector...	1,200 00
Henry Hynson, Transportation Inspector.....	1,200 00
Jos. T. Birckhead, Transportation Inspector....	1,200 00
Louis Sellman, Transportation Inspector......	1,200 00
Thomas Shaw, File Clerk...................	1,040 00
Ross S. Hans, Clerk........................	1,000 00
Christian Naumann, Clerk..................	200 00
Albert L. Deen, Transportation Inspector.....	300 00

Total Salaries for the Year Ended September 30th, 1919 $80,123 76

EXPENSES

Rent	$6,000 00
Furniture and Equipment...................	995 58
Postage	716 00
Printing and Stationery.....................	4,991 09
Books and Periodicals......................	457 86
Traveling	3,197 59
Court Costs................................	26 15
Engineer's Apparatus.......................	899 40
Laboratory Supplies........................	99 77
Telephone and Telegraph....................	595 61

Incidentals:

Towels	$114 00
Water	41 90
Ice	37 40
Time Clock.....................	24 00
Inspecting Dictagraphs..........	8 40
Advertising	61 60

Expressage	$12 24
Signs on Doors	15 00
Refinishing Floors	69 20
Dues, National Association of Railway Commissioners	25 00
Notary Fees	2 70
Witness Fees	5 40
Subpœnas	4 95
Sanitary Drinking Cups	27 00
Directory	16 00
Cabinet	16 00
Paper Punch	3 50
Pencil Sharpener	24 00
Numbering Machine	14 00
Repairs	141 31
Sundry	12 23
	$675 83

Special Services:

Robert B. Peter, Attorney—P. S. C. of Md. vs. Kensington Ry. Co	25 00
Osborne I. Yellott, Attorney—County Commissioners of Balto. County vs. P. S. C. of Md. in equity	100 00
Osborne I .Yellott, Attorney—Confederated Civic Improvement Association vs. P. S. C. of Md. in equity	100 00
Osborne I. Yellott, Attorney—Special Counsel in connection with application of The United Railways and Electric Co. of Baltimore to increase fare. Cases Nos. 1568 and 1583	1,000 00
John H. Gregory, Consulting Engineer—Professional services in connection with the valuation of the physical property of The Consolidated Public Utilities Co., Westminster, Md	500 00
Nan Delany, Telephone Operator—Services as telephone operator from February 25 to March 31, 1919	75 00
Osborne I. Yellott, Attorney—Special Counsel in the matter of the application of The United Railways and Electric Co. of Baltimore for increased fare	1,500 00
Expenses	91 09

Chas. G. Edwards, Chief Engineer—Extraordinary expenses in connection with gas survey in the State of Maryland co-operating with experts of the U. S. Bureau of Standards, Washington, D. C.... $400 00

Total Expenses for Year Ended September 30, 1919... $22,445 97

Total Salaries and Expenses for Year Ended September 30, 1919... $102,569 73

Appropriation for Year Ended September 30, 1919, Acts 1918, Chap. 206...................................... $105,670 25
Salaries and Expenses for Year Ended September 30, 1919   102,569 73

Unexpended Balance Returned to State of Maryland... $3,100 52

RESIGNATIONS AND APPOINTMENTS

Albert G. Towers, Chairman, resigned August 1, 1919.
J. Frank Harper, Commissioner, appointed August 6, 1919.
Joseph S. Goldsmith, appointed October 4, 1918.
Joseph L. Wickes, appointed March 1, 1919.
Bruce W. Duer, died February 15, 1919.
Gertrude C. Cottman, resigned April 1, 1919.
Penelope S. Westcott, appointed December 23, 1918; resigned June 1, 1919.
Mollye Greenstein, appointed June 1, 1919.
Nellie Ford, resigned April 1, 1919.
Nan Delany, appointed April 1, 1919; resigned August 17, 1919.
Mary Lortz, appointed September 1, 1919.
Chas. E. Phelps, died December 23, 1918.
Chas. G. Edwards, appointed March 1, 1919.
Chas. G. Edwards, resigned March 1, 1919
Wm. F. Strouse, appointed March 1, 1919.
J. Garland Turner, resigned August 1, 1919.
Anna C. Ehrhardt, appointed August 1, 1919.
Stanley H. Hays, resigned April 1, 1919.
H. Clay Ward, appointed April 1, 1919.
Gilbert Hagadone, resigned September 30, 1919.
Ross S. Hans, resigned August 1, 1919.
Christian Naumann, appointed August 1, 1919.
Albert L. Deen, appointed July 1, 1919.

RECEIPTS FROM OFFICE FEES TRANSMITTED TO THE TREASURER OF MARYLAND FOR THE FISCAL YEAR OCTOBER 1ST, 1918, TO SEPTEMBER 30TH, 1919.

1918:

November	$9 00
December	499 40

1919:

January	63 60
February	208 40
March	64 80
April	43 10
May	3 35
June	15 20
July	23 25
August	141 80
September	394 10

Total Office Fees for Year Ended September 30th, 1919. $1,466 00

MISCELLANEOUS

1918:

Interest on Bank Balance........................... 10 51

Total Receipts for Year Ended September 30th, 1919. $1,476 51

APPENDIX II

OPINIONS AND ORDERS OF THE COMMISSION

ORDER No. 4606

In the Matter of	Before the
The Application of EDISON ELECTRIC ILLUMINATING COMPANY OF CUMBERLAND for Authority to Issue $200,000.00 of Its First Mortgage Five Per Cent. Bonds and $100,000.00 of Its Capital Stock.	Public Service Commission of Maryland. Case No. 1617.

WHEREAS, The Edison Electric Illuminating Company of Cumberland, Maryland, has applied to this Commission for an order authorizing the issue of Two Hundred Thousand Dollars ($200,000) of additional First Mortgage Five Per Cent. Bonds, and One Hundred Thousand Dollars ($100,000) of additional capital stock,

AND WHEREAS, After consideration of the application and the exhibits filed therewith, and after due hearing this day had and testimony at such hearing, the Commission is of the opinion and finding that the use of the capital to be secured by said issue of $200,000 of First Mortgage Five Per Cent. Bonds and $100,000 of capital stock is reasonably required for the purposes of said corporation as in said application set forth, to-wit: the acquisition of property and the construction, completion, extension and improvement of its plant and distributing system and the discharge or lawful refunding of its obligations;

IT IS, THEREFORE, This 7th day of January, in the year Nineteen Hundred and Nineteen, by the Public Service Commission of Maryland,

Ordered, That the Edison Electric Illuminating Company of Cumberland, Maryland, be and it is hereby authorized:

(a) To issue additional First Mortgage Five Per Cent. Bonds in the amount of Two Hundred Thousand Dollars ($200,000) for the purposes aforesaid;

(b) To issue One Hundred Thousand Dollars ($100,000) of additional capital stock for the purposes aforesaid;

AND IT IS FURTHER *Ordered*, That the said Edison Electric Illuminating Company of Cumberland, Maryland, shall make reports, verified by affidavits, to this Commission as follows:

(a) Upon the sale for cash of said bonds authorized and approved as aforesaid, or any part thereof, the fact of such sale or sales and the terms and conditions thereof and the amount realized therefrom;

(b) Upon the sale or issuance for cash of said additional capital stock authorized and approved as aforesaid, or any part thereof, the fact of such issuance or sale or sales, and the terms and conditions thereof, and the amount realized therefrom;

(c) At the termination of every period of six (6) months from the date of this order, the disposition and use of the proceeds of said bonds and stock.

OPINION

In the Matter of

The Petition of the BALTIMORE TRANSIT COMPANY for Permission Under Section 15 of the Public Service Commission Law to File and Publish on Less Than Statutory Notice a Schedule of Rates Changing Its Rate of Fare from Five Cents to Six Cents.

Before the

Public Service Commission of Maryland.

S. N. & R. Docket.

Case No. 547.

By the Commission.   Filed January 7th, 1919.

The complaint in this case involves the reasonableness *vel non* of a recent increase of the fares charged by the Baltimore Transit Company, from five to six cents.

This Company was organized in 1915 for the purpose of operating a motor bus line or lines in Baltimore City, and up to the present time has confined its sphere of operations to a route beginning on the north of the intersection of Charles Street and University Parkway, and running thence southerly along Charles Street a distance of about three miles to the intersection of Charles and German Streets.

The Company is owned and controlled by the United Railways and Electric Company of Baltimore, which is the owner of practically its entire issue of common stock, amounting to $5,000, par value, and holds or has guaranteed the payment of its outstanding notes given to secure equipment or pay losses in operation, said notes aggregating $230,000 on September 20th, 1918.

The Company began operations with twenty motor busses July 25th, 1915, and between that date and September 30th, 1915, a period of about two months, during which it was operating new equipment requiring virtually no repairs or replacements, earned a net profit of $191.20 over and above interest, but without any deduction for depreciation, taxes, or return upon the investment.

During the year beginning October 1st, 1915, and ending September 30th, 1916, the Company's actual operating expenses, exclusive of any allowance for deferred maintenance or depreciation, were $8,912.23 in excess of its income. When to this amount was added the sum of $2,376.80 representing interest, taxes and license charges, the deficit from operation during the year was found to be $11,289.03 over and above whatever would have been proper charges for depreciation and return upon the investment.

In the latter part of the ensuing year ended September 30th, 1917, the Company was obliged to scrap its entire original equipment and purchase twenty new busses of an improved type with greater carrying capacity. During that year the property was operated at a total loss of $30,907.74, including a charge of but $1,087.50 on account of depreciation, and no allowance for any return upon the investment.

During the next year ended September 30th, 1918, with new and improved equipment, the Company operated at a loss of but $4,805.47 after charging off $21,750 for depreciation on its equipment, but making no allowance for return upon the investment. During this year, however, the Company had a bad accident on its line resulting in the destruction of one of its busses and the injury of a number of passengers who were therein. The cost of adjusting the claims for damages arising out of this accident to date has been $31,028.13.

A condensed income and profit and loss statement for the Company's entire period of operations, July 25th, 1915, to September 30th, 1918, is as follows:

Income	$260,000.28
Total Operating Expenses	281,572.28
Operating Deficit	$21,572.00
Total Fixed Charges	25,239.04
Balance—Deficit	$46,811.04
Total Profit and Loss Adjustments (debit)	15,258.54
Profit and Loss Deficit Sept. 30, 1918	$62,069.58
Extraordinary Accident Loss	31,028.13
Total Deficit	$93,097.71

If we were to assume the average investment of the Company during the above period of operation, three and one-sixth years, to have been $100,000, which is approximately correct, and that the Company was fairly entitled during this period to a return of not less than six per cent. upon its investment, or $19,000 in the aggregate, without. interest, it will be seen that its total losses from operation during the above period would have been approximately $112,000, or $12,000 in excess of its entire average investment.

The evidence in the case indicates that the affairs of the Company have been managed as economically and efficiently as the peculiar nature of a new and previously untried venture of the kind would admit. There has never been any serious complaint of the service of the Company since the improved vehicles have been put in operation, the rules of the Commission with respect to the overcrowding of the busses having been carefully observed in the main. The service is recognized as strictly alternative to the service of the United Railways and Electric Company, the lines of which in part parallel only one square away, and in other part traverse, the same route traversed by the vehicles of the respondent Company. While the service rendered by the Company is not as comfortable as service upon the electric railway cars under normal conditions, it is nevertheless a great convenience to those living along or near its route, and particularly to those who are desirous of making the trip up or down town in the shortest time reasonably possible.

In view of the ownership of this Company by the United Railways and Electric Company, and the unity of management which exists in practically all its departments, and in further view of the fact that many patrons of the United Company are now using, and more will eventually use the tickets or pay-checks issued by the latter, it occurs to the Commission that public convenience would be greatly promoted, and the patronage of the Transit Company probably increased during non-rush hours, were such tickets or pay-checks made interchangeable on the two lines. No order will be passed to this effect, but it is hoped that the companies will be able to devise a plan by which this can conveniently be done.

It was suggested in the course of the hearing upon this complaint that the two companies be required to give transfers interchangeably. This would simply mean a considerable reduction in the receipts of the Transit Company, which, as we have seen, are already insufficient to meet its proper corporate requirements, and would moreover result in giving its patrons more service for a single fare than they are now receiving.

The service rendered by this Company is of a special and peculiar nature, especially adapted to the requirements of those who wish to avail themselves of the same, and is well worth the six cents which the Company is charging therefor.

For these reasons an order will be passed dismissing the complaint.

ORDER No. 4607

In the Matter of .	Before the
The Petition of the BALTIMORE TRANSIT COMPANY for Permission Under Section 15 of the Public Service Commission Law to File and Publish on Less Than Statutory Notice a Schedule of Rates Changing Its Rate of Fare from Five Cents to Six Cents. .	Public Service Commission of Maryland. S. N. & R. Docket. Case No. 547.

For the reasons stated in the aforegoing opinion, it is, this 7th day of January, in the year Nineteen Hundred and Nineteen, by the Public Service Commission of Maryland,

Ordered, That the complaint filed in this case be and the same is hereby dismissed.

OPINION

In the Matter of	Before the
The Application of THE UNITED RAILWAYS AND ELECTRIC COMPANY OF BALTIMORE for Permission to Make a Uniform Increase of One Cent in Cash Fares Heretofore Charged.	Public Service Commission of Maryland. Case No. 1568.

In the Matter of	Before the
The Complaint of THE PUBLIC SERVICE COMMISSION OF MARYLAND *vs.* THE UNITED RAILWAYS AND ELECTRIC COMPANY OF BALTIMORE, With Respect to the Fairness and Reasonableness of Its Proposed General Increase in Its Passenger Rates.	Public Service Commission of Maryland. Case No. 1583.

Appearances:
    Messrs. JOSEPH C. FRANCE, EDWIN G. BAETJER and W. H. MALTBIE, representing The United Railways and Electric Company of Baltimore;

Messrs. JOSEPH S. GOLDSMITH, Assistant General Counsel, and OSBORNE I. YELLOTT, Special Counsel, representing the Public . Service Commission of Maryland.

PETER PECK, ESQ., counsel for certain residents of North Baltimore.

J. COOKMAN BOYD, ESQ., counsel for patrons of the Curtis Bay Line.

Hearings:

November 18, December 2, 3, 4, 5, 6, 9, 16 and 17.

Arguments:

December 17, 18 and 19.

By the Commission.   Filed January 7, 1919.

On July 19, 1918, The United Railways and Electric Company of Baltimore filed a petition with this Commission in Case No. 1568, setting forth at length some of the additional expenses to which it had been put and was still undergoing by reason of war conditions, and alleging in substance that it was no longer possible to render adequate service to the public at the existing rates of fare. Upon such statement of facts the Company asked "the approval of the Commission for a uniform cash fare of six cents in lieu of all cash fares now collected except in the case of children between the ages of four and twelve years; and in the case of such children and also in the case of all riders now using commutation tickets a uniform increase of one cent."

Paragraph III of said petition was as follows:

"Your petitioner expressly disclaims any intention to establish by this proceeding any permanent rate of fare. It asks for relief purely as a war emergency and during the period of war conditions. The sole purpose is to preserve its pre-war efficiency and to prevent, as far as possible, injury to its credit and to its organization and the deterioration of its plant, which would otherwise result. To preserve its credit, it must maintain its former margin of profit; and, without such credit, it will be unable to obtain the money over and above amounts now available, for capital expenditures which it will be called upon to make.

"In order to preserve such credit, however, it will not be necessary, and it is not intended that any part of the increased revenue hereby sought should increase the margin of profit which the Company had heretofore earned. An examination will show that, notwithstanding the increased charges which began soon after the outbreak of the European War, the Company was able to set aside a depreciation reserve of five per cent. of the gross revenue, and to pay a sufficient return to security holders to maintain the Company's credit. Since the entry of this country into the war, the situation in this respect has changed greatly, both by reason of the enhanced prices for and the difficulty of obtaining materials because of Government needs and priorities."

At the conclusion of such petition, the Company agreed:

"1. That the new rate shall from time to time and at all times be subject to readjustment and revision by the Commission on its own initiative;

"2. That the resulting increase of revenue shall be applied only to meet the war-produced increases with which it is and may be confronted;

"3. That the surplus, if any there be, shall be used only in accordance with the directions of the Commission upon application duly made."

Owing to the pressure of other matters of great public importance the Commission was unable to promise the representatives of the Company an immediate hearing upon the above petition, and it was uncertain whether the case could be heard and determined before the end of the current year.

Consequently the Company on August 28, 1918, filed with the Commission its revised schedule "P. S. C. Md. No. 8," effective October 1, 1918, in which it provided for a flat increase of one cent in each of its existing adult, children and commutation fares. Subsequently the Company filed a letter giving notice of an increase of $1\frac{1}{4}$c in the case of employees' tickets sold in twenty-trip books to the Maryland Steel Company, thus increasing this rate from $3\frac{1}{4}$c to $4\frac{1}{2}$c, and an increase in its strip tickets sold the Central Foundry Company in lots from $4\frac{1}{6}$c to 5c each. In filing such revised schedule the Company eliminated the three-cent transfer previously issued to patrons of its Curtis Bay line.

In the letter of transmission accompanying the above schedule, the Railways Company, through its president and attorneys, said:

"III. As stated in the petition recently filed, the amount of increased revenue which will result from the proposed increased fares is uncertain, and can be determined only by actual trial; and the Company will keep the Commission advised as to the effect of the increase on its revenues.

"IV. The Company understands that this Schedule of Rates is subject to any action the Commission may hereafter take on the petition heretofore filed."[1]

On September 18, 1918, the Commission, of its own motion, filed a complaint alleging that the proposed increases in fares set forth in the above schedule were "excessive, unjust, unfair and unreasonable," and ordered that the matters complained of be satisfied by the Company or that the charges in said complaint be answered in writing within ten days.

On September 24, 1918, the Company filed its answer setting forth certain facts upon which it relied to show that the proposed increases in its fares were not excessive, unjust, unfair or unreasonable, and stating that it did not know and could not tell, otherwise than by actual trial, how much additional revenue would be derived from the fare increase of one cent to become effective October 1, 1918. It accordingly suggested that the results of the increase after October 1st be checked for use at the hearing before the Commission in such a way as the Auditing Department of the Commission under the direction of the Assistant General Counsel might advise.

On September 26, 1918, the Commission passed its Order No. 4491, setting the issues raised by its complaint and the above answer for hearing on the 18th day of November, 1918, and further directing that the Company keep the Commission advised of the result of the increased fares effective October 1, 1918, and that such result be tabulated in such a way as should be approved by the Accounting Department of the Commission under the direction of the Assistant General Counsel.

On September 30, 1918, counsel for some fifty-one residents of North Baltimore who had filed protests against the Company's application in Case No. 1568, filed a further protest in Case No. 1583, in which they asked the Commission to pass an order notifying the Company to issue excess fare receipts to passengers paying the increased rates to the end that such excess fares might be refunded to such passengers in the event that the same might be declared unlawful by the Commission or by the Courts, the protest alleging further that the action of the Company in increasing its fares in the manner above recited was unlawful. This protest was submitted to the General Counsel of the Commission with a request for his opinion as to the right of the Commission to require such excess fare receipts. On October 2, 1918, the General Counsel filed his Opinion No. 367, in which he concluded that the Commission had no power to pass such an order, and further concluded that Section 768 of Article 4 of the Public Local Laws of Maryland relating to Baltimore City providing that the respondent Railways Company should charge five cents and no more for each passenger over twelve years of age, and three cents and no more for each child between the ages of four and twelve years, respectively, had been repealed by Section 31½ of the Public Service Commission Law.

Numerous other protests were filed in Case No. 1583 against the Company's proposed increases in its rates of fare.

Among these protests was one filed November 18, 1918, on behalf of the Interocean Oil Company, the United States Asphalt Refining Company, the Union Ship-Building Company, the Martin Wagner Company, Swift & Company, the Rasin Monumental Guano Company, the F. S. Royster Guano Company, and the Standard Acid Works, all large employers of labor with plants located at or near Fairfield in what is sometimes referred to as the Curtis Bay district, said district being reached by the Curtis Bay Line of the Railways Company. In this petition the above parties complained both of the increases in fares effective October 1, 1918, and also of the equipment and service of the Company on the lines leading to Fairfield. This complaint was by order of the Commission consolidated with the main complaint of the Commission in Case No. 1583, and set for hearing on the same date.

At the preliminary hearing on November 18th, Special Counsel for the Commission, in his opening statement, made the point that Order No. 1010 entered by the Commission December 24, 1912, in Case No. 96, the Complaint of the Old Frederick Road Improvement Association, et al., vs. The United Railways and Electric Company of Baltimore, and Order No. 1430 of October 20, 1913, in Case No. 579, the Complaint of Louis Knieling, et al., vs. the same Company, in so far as said orders fixed the rates of one way and commutation fares to be charged by the Company over the portions of its lines therein referred to, had been violated by the Company's action in putting in effect its increased fares on said lines pursuant to its revised schedule No. 8, effective October 1, 1918, without the prior consent and approval of the Commission. On November 24, 1918, the Company filed its petition in the case referring to the above contention and praying the passage of an order suspending such prior orders pending the hearing in this case. Inasmuch as the Commission's insistence upon the observance of such previous orders pending the hearing in this case would have resulted in great complication in the charging and collection of fares on many of the Company's lines to the general detriment of the service, and would have resulted in many instances in unjust and unreasonable preferences and discriminations, the Commission on November 25, 1918, passed its Order No. 4547 suspending said Orders Nos. 1010 and 1430 to the extent above stated pending the filing of its conclusions in Case No. 1583. Moreover, the Commission's Order No. 4491 of September 26, 1918, setting the Commission's complaint for hearing, and directing the Company to keep the Commission advised as to the result of the increased fares to become effective October 1, 1918, might well have been taken as an implied suspension of such earlier orders pending the Commission's investigation of the propriety of such fare increases, the Commission's understanding at the time of passing such order being that there was to be a uniform increase of one cent over all the lines in the Company's system as set forth in the schedule filed August 28, 1918, to become effective October 1st.

At the preliminary hearing on November 18th, Special Counsel for the Commission filed as exhibits in the case a number of tabulations of figures showing the earnings and expenses of the Company in the past, such figures having been taken from the Company's books, and also filed a written analysis of these exhibits, which he read as an opening statement. Accompanying this statement he filed a chart and tabulation in which he estimated the number of revenue passengers who might reasonably be anticipated to be transported by the Company each month from November 1, 1918, to October 31, 1919. This tabulation was as follows::

TABLE X

Estimate of Revenue Passengers November 1, 1918, to October 31, 1919

1918.	
November	19,250,000
December	18,750,000
Total, bal. 1918	38,000,000

1919.	
January	17,500,000
February	16,500,000
March	18,000,000
April	18,000,000
May	19,000,000
June	19,500,000
July	19,700,000
August	19,500,000
September	19,000,000
October	19,500,000
Total, 1919	186,200,000

The details of the tabulation become of peculiar importance for the reason that the estimates therein contained were subsequently accepted by the Company as the basis of its own calculations as to its probable net earnings up to October 31, 1919.

The actual number of revenue passengers actually transported by the Company during the month of November, 1918, was subsequently shown to have been 18,642,833, or 607,167 (3.15%) less than the number estimated by Special Counsel. The Commission has carefully considered these estimates in the light of the past experience of the Company and of the various facts bearing upon the probabilities as to the future, and concludes that they can be accepted as a factor in the basis of calculations of probable future net earnings without prejudice to the interests of the general public.

FINANCIAL HISTORY OF THE RESPONDENT COMPANY

The United Railways and Electric Company of Baltimore was formed by articles of Agreement of Consolidation, dated March 4, 1899, which resulted in a combination of all the street railway lines in Baltimore and Vicinity into a single system, the lines so consolidated being as follows:

The United Railways and Electric Company of Baltimore City, a consolidation of the Baltimore City Passenger Railway Company and the Baltimore and Northern Electric Railway Company; The Baltimore Consolidated Railway Company, a consolidation of the Baltimore Traction Company, the City and Suburban Railway Company and the Lake Roland Elevated Railway Company; The Central Railway Company; The Baltimore, Gardenville and Bel Air Electric Railway Company; The Baltimore, Catonsville and Ellicott's Mills Passenger Railroad Company, purchaser under mortgage foreclosure proceedings of the corporate properties of the Baltimore, Catonsville & Ellicott's Mills Passenger Railway Company; The Maryland Traction Company; The Baltimore & Curtis Bay Railway Company, the stock of which was owned by the Baltimore Traction Company; The Gwynn's Falls Railway Company; The Shore Line Electric Railway Company; The Pimlico and Pikesville Railway Company, and The Walbrook, Gwynn Oak and Powhatan Railroad Company, the stock in the last three companies having been owned at the time of the consolidation by the Baltimore Traction Company.

The authorized capitalization of the new consolidated Company at the date of consolidation of March 4th, 1899, was as follows:

1st Consol. Mort. 4% gold bonds	$38,000,000
4% Cumulative pref. stock	14,000,000
Common Stock	24,000,000
Total	$76,000,000

At the time of the consolidation $18,000,000 of the 1st Consol. 4% bonds were sold and the proceeds used as part payment for the Baltimore City Passenger Railway Company and the Baltimore Consolidated Railway Company; $15,366,000 were reserved to retire bonds of the constituent companies, and the remaining $4,634,000 were reserved or sold and the proceeds used for betterments, extensions, expenses of consolidation, etc. Not all of the bonds reserved for funding purposes were issued, but $29,450,000 of the same being in the hands of the public at the date of the hearing in this case, and the remainder of the authorized issue either being in the hands of the trustee to be used for the refunding of some $8,550,000 of the underlying bonds still on the properties of certain of the constituent companies, or in the treasury of the Company.

Shortly after the consolidation, to wit: March 30, 1899, the Company authorized the issue of $14,000,000 of Income Bonds with which to retire the preferred stock originally authorized. At the date of the hearings all but $23,000 of such preferred stock had been retired, and $13,977,000 of these Income Bonds were outstanding in the hands of the public. These bonds are secured by a mortgage covering all the property of the Company, subject to its 1st Consol. 4% bonds.

After the Baltimore Fire of February, 1904, it was found desirable to pass the interest on these Income Bonds for the purpose of securing funds for track reconstruction and repair, improvements to power houses and for the general improvement and betterment of the Company's property. Accordingly such interest was passed in 1904 and 1905, and on July 25, 1906, the Company entered into an agreement with the holders of such Income Bonds under which the latter, to the amount of $13,842,000, agreed to accept the interest due them from 1904 to 1910 inclusive in the shape of 5%, 30 yr. Income Funding Bonds, the Company agreeing unconditionally that the principal and interest on these latter bonds should be paid out of income ahead of the priorities of the Income Bond holders. Funding Bonds to the amount of $3,920,000 were issued under this agreement for the purposes aforesaid, and are still outstanding.

Of the $24,000,000 of Common Stock originally authorized, $20,461,-000 has been issued up to this date. Prior to 1912 no dividends were paid upon this stock, the Company's surplus earnings over operating expenses and fixed charges being put back into the property. In 1912 a dividend at the rate of 3% was paid upon the common stock outstanding. To stockholders of record April 11, 1913, a semi-annual dividend of $1.00 per share was declared, this being at the rate of 4% per annum. Since 1913 dividends at the latter rate have been paid regularly.

The Company's financial plan of 1906 entered into after the Baltimore Fire of 1904 necessitated not only the diversion of income to improvements and betterments through the Income Funding Bonds above referred to, but also necessitated securing additional capital for new property, such as terminal stations, car-houses, equipment, extensions, excursion resorts, etc. The existing property was already heavily encumbered by the outstanding First Consol. Mortgage 4% Bonds, and the underlying bonds of certain of the constituent companies, the income, in turn, being pledged to the holders of the Income Bonds and Income Funding Bonds above referred to. As a comprehensive plan of refinancing did not seem feasible at that time, it was necessary to seek some new source of capital for the acquisition of new property. Accordingly the Maryland Electric Railways Company was formed on August 6, 1906, by the consolidation of the Maryland Electric Railway Company and the Baltimore and Annapolis Short Line, the latter at that time owning and operating a line, since electrified, between Baltimore and Annapolis—a distance by rail of twenty-two miles. The Maryland Electric Railways Company, on September 15, 1906, executed a mortgage to secure an authorized issue of $8,000,000 of First Mortgage, 5%, 25 year Gold Sinking Fund Bonds, the same being a first lien upon the properties of such consolidated company. Thereupon the United Company entered into a contract with the Maryland Company under which the latter agreed to furnish funds for the purchase and construction of such property as the United Company might require, the property so acquired to be leased to the United Company at a rental of 6% per annum on the cost of the same. In addition the United Company agreed to pay, after March 30, 1910, 1½% per annum as a sinking fund, and also to pay to a special sinking fund annually 7½% of the cost of equipment purchased with the bond proceeds until the equivalent of the full purchase price of the equipment had been paid. The United Company moreover agreed to pay all the cost of maintenance, operation, taxes, insurance, etc., and to purchase the property at the maturity of the. bonds, or upon any default thereon, at a sum sufficient to retire such bonds. The Maryland Electric Railways Company continued to operate the Annapolis Short Line. At the date of the hearings in this case, there were $4,946,000 of the Maryland Electric Railways Company bonds outstanding in the hands of the public and $702,000 of the same in the treasury of the United Company, forming a part of its sinking fund securities.

Prior to the above arrangement with the Maryland Electric Railways Company, the United Company had leased from the Baltimore, Sparrows Point and Chesapeake Railway Company all the properties of such company and had guaranteed the principal and interest of the First Mortgage, 50 year, 4½% bonds of that Company amounting to $2,000,000, the whole amount of this issue being outstanding at the date of the hearings in this case.

In addition to the above obligations there were outstanding in the hands of the public at the date of the hearings in this case, the following securities of the Company:

Five Year, 5% gold notes.................	$1,222,000
" " Convertible 5% gold notes.......	1,528,000
" " " 6% " "	3,000,000
Bills payable............................	800,000
Total................................	$6,550,000

These notes were all issued with the consent and approval of this Commission, and the proceeds used for the refunding of outstanding obligations, the acquisition of property or for other proper corporate purposes of the Company, as provided by the Public Service Commission Law.

After deducting from the grand total of the above outstanding interest-bearing indebtedness the $3,710,000 of treasury and sinking-fund securities in the hands of the Company, it was found that the net out-

standing interest-bearing indebtedness of the Company at the dates of
the hearings in this case was $65,683,000, the outstanding common
stock being, as above stated, $20,461,200 and of the preferred stock,
$23,000, a grand total of $86,167,200 for the whole.

FAIR VALUE OF THE PROPERTY NOT AN ISSUE

Section 30 of the Public Service Commission Law relating to valuations of property provides:

> "Every such valuation shall be so made and ascertained by
> the Commission that as far as possible it shall not disturb the
> value of bonds of any of said corporations issued prior to the
> passage of this Act."

In the opinion of this Commission in the Matter of the Complaint
of Davis Bachrach and others vs. The Consolidated Gas Electric Light
and Power Company of Baltimore, decided January 13, 1913, P. S. C.
Md. Vol. 4, p. 39 at 53-5, the Commission concurred in the opinion of
its General Counsel, to the effect that this was a positive direction,
binding upon the Commission, and based its order establishing rates
upon the assumption that the outstanding bonded indebtedness of the
Company at the time of the creation of the Commission in 1910 established the minimum fair value of the property for rate-making purposes as of that date. To this sum was added the amount of the bonds
issued since the Commission was established and under its authority,
these bonds representing actual expenditures for extensions and improvements, and thereby representing actual capital investments which
the Commission in that case held unassailable.

The Commission, as at present constituted, expresses no opinion as
to the legal effect of the above provision of the Public Service Commission Law, and is not to be understood as conceding that in a case
where the bonded indebtedness of a public utility is in excess of the
fair value of its property, the former shall be accepted as the minimum fair value of the property for rate-making purposes. Nevertheless this Commission fully recognizes the justice of the legislative
intent that the actual value of the securities of a public utility outstanding in the hands of the public at the time of a rate-making inquiry should not be unduly prejudiced by any action of the Commission
in the premises, whether such action be by way of arriving at the fair
value of the property for rate-making purposes, or, more directly, by
the actual fixing of rates for service.

This Commission's physical valuation of the property of the Railways Company has never been fully completed, and even if completed,
would be of little or no worth for rate-making purposes at the present
time of abnormal property values and abnormal operating conditions.

As a matter of fact, the whole question of fair value of the Railways Company's property is of little or no relevancy in the present

case, for the reason that the issues have been narrowed down by the Company's petition above referred to, by agreement of counsel, and by understanding between the Company and the Commission, that the sole issue involved is whether or not the increase of one cent in the Company's fares is reasonably required to enable the Company to render adequate service to the public, and yield to the owners of the property a return approximately equivalent to the return received under normal pre-war conditions.

QUESTIONS OF PUBLIC POLICY INVOLVED

The above issue, and the acceptance of the same by this Commission as the real issue in the present case, involves grave and important questions of public policy.

(A) THE RIGHTS OF THE SECURITY HOLDERS

It has been seen in the preceding statement of facts that the respondent Company has almost an absolute monopoly of the street railway business in the City of Baltimore and its immediate vicinity; that the Company is the outgrowth of the consolidation of a large number of previously more or less independent street railway companies which formerly served this community, and the leasing of the properties of the other companies, otherwise independent of the respondent Company; that the properties of said constituent companies were taken over by the consolidated company at valuations arrived at by agreements of the parties consummated long before the creation of the Public Service Commission of this State, and that the securities issued in exchange for such properties at valuations agreed upon nearly twenty years ago are outstanding in the aggregate of many millions of dollars in the hands of the public, who have invested therein upon the faith both of the property believed to be behind such securities and of the earning power of the combined railways system as a whole. Under such circumstances it would require no act of assembly to lead this Commission to the conclusion that the property rights of the holders of such securities should not lightly be impaired by any action of this Commission.

(B) IMPORTANCE OF THE RAILWAYS SYSTEM TO THE GENERAL PUBLIC

In the course of a relatively few years the street railway has become one of the most important adjuncts to life in all thickly populated communities. With water, gas and electricity, it has become one of the prime necessities of life. Without it, business would come almost to a standstill, and social life in our cities and suburban communities would be most radically changed. So dependent have the people of

our cities become upon the street railway, that an interruption of only
an hour or so in the service is almost instantly felt throughout the
length and breadth of the community, and continuous bad or inadequate service is a thing which no community will long tolerate if redress of any kind can be found.

(C) OBLIGATIONS OF THE COMMISSION TO THE PUBLIC

From the above reasons it follows that the prime obligation which
any state regulatory body, such as a public service commission, owes
to the public in connection with the property and affairs of a street
railway corporation is, first, to see that the property of such corporation is at all times so constructed, equipped and maintained as to
enable those in charge of the same to render at all times adequate
service to the public, and, second, to see that such character of service
is at all times rendered.

The former proposition requires that the Company shall at all times
be kept in such a condition, financially, that it can command investments in its property by the investing public, in order that necessary
extensions to meet the demands of a rapidly growing community may
be made promptly when and as required, and that its road-bed, power
houses and equipment may always be of a type and capacity to render
adequate service economically and efficiently.   There is no statutory
law which can be resorted to in order to compel the investing public to
invest its money in a public utility rather than in any other class of
enterprise, and the only laws which can be appealed to are the natural
laws of trade and commerce which lead men to invest their money
where it may reasonably be expected to yield them a fair return for
its use, and forbid the investment of money where there is no reasonable hope or expectation of such a return.

The obligation of a state regulatory body to see that those in charge
of the affairs of a public utility render at all times adequate service to
the public demands primarily that the company be permitted to charge
such rates for its service as will enable it to pay its operating expenses, including the maintenance of its property, its fixed charges,
and a reasonable return upon the fair value of the investment.   For
if less than a reasonable return upon the investment is paid the owners of the property, they could not well be expected to continue the use
of their money in the service of the public.   Where it is questionable
whether or not there is any equity in the investment over and above
the bonded indebtedness, the return should still be sufficient not only
to meet the fixed charges themselves, but should be sufficiently in
excess thereof to serve as a reasonable guarantee to the investing
public that the company will at all times be in a position to meet such
fixed charges promptly when and as due.   Otherwise a relatively short
season of poor business or abnormally heavy expenditures would result
in default in the payment of interest upon the bonded indebtedness,

and the instant destruction of the credit of the company with the probability of an early dissolution of the company itself.

Consequently it follows that a state regulatory body could do no greater harm to a community so entirely dependent upon the service of a street railway company as the public of Baltimore is dependent upon the service of the respondent Company than to refuse to permit it to change such rates for its service as will enable it at all times both to command the investment of money necessary for the making of required extensions and continued maintenance of its property in efficient condition, and also to render such character of service as the needs of the community reasonably require. So to refuse would not only be to render it physically impossible for the company to render adequate service, but would also be to drive the company itself into a position of pecuniary decrepitude which would in the end result in bankruptcy and dissolution, after a long drawnout period of such inadequate service, during which the property and equipment would fall into a condition of disrepair which could only be corrected after the lapse of many years and the expenditure of many millions of dollars.

(D) PRIMARY OBLIGATION OF THE COMPANY TO THE PUBLIC

But neither the rights of the holders of the securities of a public utility, nor the fear of driving such utility into bankruptcy through the withholding of funds deemed necessary for its preservation, should ever be permitted by a public service commission to cause it to lose sight of the primary obligation of the utility to render adequate service to the public. This is an obligation which the utility assumes when it undertakes to serve the public of a given community, and becomes the more absolutely binding both in law and in morals, when it pre-empts the entire field of service, and enjoys such an absolute monopoly in its chosen field as is the monopoly enjoyed by the respondent Company in Baltimore and its immediate vicinity.

(E) THE POLICY OF THIS COMMISSION

In conformity with these principles it has always been the policy of this Commission in its regulation of the affairs of public utilities made subject to its jurisdiction to allow such reasonable rates for their services, and to insist that in return for such reasonable rates the utilities shall render adequate service to the public dependent upon them for such service. And if, under such circumstances, a public utility cannot succeed in its chosen field, then it will be far better in the end both for its security holders and the general public for it to be forced out of such field and required to give way to others who will be only too glad to enter the field and undertake to render adequate service once the original utility is out of the way.

STATUTORY LAW INVOLVED

Section 11 of the Public Service Commission Law of this State provides as follows:

> "Every order of the Commission shall take effect at a time there specified *and shall continue in force for a period therein designated* unless earlier modified or abrogated by the Commission, or unless such order be unauthorized by this Act, or be in violation of a provision of the Constitution of the State or of the United States."

Section 13 provides in part as follows:

> "All charges made or demanded by any such common carrier for the transportation of passengers * * shall be *just and reasonable*, and not more than allowed by law, *or by order of the Commission*, conformably with the law."

Section 23 provides in part as follows:

> "Whenever the Commission shall be of the opinion, after a hearing, upon its own motion, or upon a complaint made as provided in this Act, that the rates, tolls, fares or charges * * by any common carrier * * are unjust, unreasonable * * *the Commission shall determine the just and reasonable rates, tolls, fares and charges to be thereafter observed and in force as the maximum to be charged for the service to be performed, and shall fix the same by order.*"

Section 31½ provides in part as follows:

> "All acts or parts of acts heretofore passed and now exististing, prescribing or limiting the price at which any * * * corporation subject to this Act may furnish, sell or dispose of its * * * produce or utility are hereby repealed, *it being the intent of this Act that the powers of the Commission herein created to ascertain the price of such * * product or utility as provided for herein, shall supersede all such Acts or parts of Acts aforesaid.*"

Section 796 of the Baltimore City Charter provides in substance that the United Railways and Electric Company of Baltimore shall charge five cents and no more as a fare for the conveyance of each passenger over twelve years of age, and three cents and no more for each child between the ages of four and twelve years, from any point on any of its lines to any other point on such lines within the city of

Baltimore, with free transfers at all points of intersection with other lines not forming a route which would permit a passenger to return in the same general direction.

Section 2 of Chapter 82 of the Acts of 1918 provides in substance that all the provisions of the Baltimore City Charter shall be applicable to such portions of Baltimore County and Anne Arundel County as were annexed to and made a part of the City under that Act.

The above several provisions of the law gave rise to a variety of contentions during the course of the argument, all of which contentions will be hereinafter considered.

THE COMPANY'S NEED FOR INCREASED REVENUES

That the Company is reasonably entitled under conditions at present existing to an increase of one cent in each of the fares specified in its schedule P. S. C. Md. No. 8, there would seem to be little or no question.

The exhibits show that during the years 1912 to 1917 inclusive, the average of which may fairly be taken as representing normal conditions, the Company earned over and above its operating expenses, taxes and maintenance expenses, including in the later years an annual appropriation to its depreciation reserve account of five per cent. of the gross revenue, an average of $3,659,609 available for the payment of fixed charges and dividends, any resulting balance going into the corporate surplus account. During the above six years such average net earnings amounted to 6.337% of the average funded debt of the Company, the yearly ratios ranging from 6.134% in 1917, as the lowest, to 6.731% in 1916, as the highest. During the above period the average fixed charges of the Company amounted to $2,810,807, thus leaving an average balance of $848,802 available for dividends and surplus. It will be noted that the above net earnings amounted to approximately one and one-third times the amount of the Company's fixed charges, a ratio by no means excessive in view of the desirability of upholding the credit of the Company, and in fact considerably less than that frequently demanded by reasonably conservative investors.

Assuming the above fairly to represent operating results, under normal pre-war conditions, the Company contented itself at the hearings with merely pointing out the effects which war increases in wages alone would have upon its net earnings in the future, taking no account of any possible increases in the costs of materials and supplies over and above the actual costs of such during the twelve months ended September 30, 1918, in one instance, and October 31, 1918, in another.

Two exhibits were filed upon this theory. In the first the Company took the actual operating income for the year ended September 30, 1918, on the basis of the existing five cent fare, to wit: $11,351,019, and deducted therefrom the total of its actual maintenance and operating expenses during the year, $6,201,242, plus a correction for increased wages alone, not reflected in operating results during that year, $1,479,000, leaving a balance of $3,670,277. From this sum was deducted $1,198,790 paid for taxes during that year and $567,552 for depreciation, leaving a balance of $1,903,935, to which was added non-operating income amounting to $100,101, yielding a total balance available for fixed charges and dividends of $2,004,036. Inasmuch as the fixed charges alone had amounted during the year to $3,047,151, this exhibit showed a deficit in interest of $1,043,115, meaning that upon the theory of this exhibit the Company would have had to exhaust its entire accumulated surplus and borrow funds in addition with which to pay its fixed charges in full had it been obliged to pay throughout the year the labor prices which were current at the end of that year. For further illustration the Company in this exhibit added to the above deficit of $1,043,115 the sum of $905,611, representing the average annual surplus earnings over fixed charges during the four years ended December 31, 1917, thus showing a total deficit in such earnings of $1,940,726 as compared with the preceding four years. The theory of this exhibit was that the Company could not reasonably expect its gross revenues during the year ending September 30, 1919, to be greater than during the year ended September 30, 1918, without a fare increase, and that the prices current for labor September 30, 1918, would remain practically constant during the ensuing twelve months.

In the second exhibit of this series, the Company undertook to prognosticate for the year ending October 31, 1919, upon the basis of the estimates of the Commission's Special Counsel of the number of revenue passengers to be carried during those twelve months as contained in the table set forth earlier in this opinion.

Upon this basis, and assuming that no increase in fares would be permitted, it was shown that the total passenger revenue would amount to $10,929,750. To this sum was added "other transportation revenue" and "other railway revenue" as actually received during the twelve months ended October 31, 1918, amounting to $303,847, there being no reason to assume that these items would be materially different during the next twelve months. From the sum of the above items, to wit: $11,233,597, there was deducted actual operating expenses for the twelve months ended October 31, 1918, $6,347,514, plus a correction for increased wages not yet reflected in the above figures, $1,326,-000, a total of $7,673,514, leaving a balance of $3,560,083. From this balance was deducted the taxes actually charged against earnings during the twelve months ended October 31, 1918, $1,213,413, and depreciation, 5% of gross operating expenses or $561,679, leaving a balance of $1,784,991 to which was added non-operating income amounting to $89,658, being the amount actually received during those twelve months, these computations yielding a total of $1,874,649, out of which to meet the fixed charges and dividends. The fixed charges for the ensuing year were computed upon the basis of twelve times the fixed charges for October, 1918, and amounted to $3,188,904, thus leaving a deficit in interest of $1,314,255. To this sum was added $905,611 representing the average annual surplus for the four years ended December 31, 1917, resulting in a total deficit in net earnings of $2,219,866 as compared with such previous years.

If the actual net earnings during the preceding four years had been disregarded over and above the amount of $818,448 representing the pre-war annual dividends upon the common stock, the deficit would still have been $2,132,703. Or if the average net earnings over fixed charges for the six years ended December 31, 1917, had been used instead of the average for four years only, the deficit would have been $2,163,057.

The above exhibits were designed primarily to demonstrate beyond any question that the Company was badly in need of increased revenues. At the same time they demonstrated quite convincingly that the amount of increased revenues required if the Company were to be kept in the future upon substantially its pre-war basis as to earnings was approximately the amount which might reasonably be expected to be yielded by the one cent increase in the Company's fares as set forth in its revised schedule P. S. C. Md. No. 8.

Upon the estimated basis of 224.200,000 revenue passengers during the year ending October 31, 1919, as originally made by the Commission's Special Counsel, and accepted by the Company for purposes of illustration, the increased revenues from the additional one cent fare would amount to $2,242,000, or but a few thousand dollars more than sufficient to pay the Company's operating and maintenance expenses, taxes, fixed charges and the average annual surplus earned during the four years prior to December 31, 1917.

Both at the hearings and in the arguments made at the conclusion thereof, counsel for the Company contended that the estimates for the Commission's Special Counsel as to the number of passengers likely to be carried during the coming year were excessive, both in that they failed to take sufficiently into account the tendency of the increased fare to diminish traffic and in that they failed to take sufficiently into account the falling off in traffic which would result by the closing down of the munition plants and other war industries which would cease with the coming of peace. Their estimate of the effect of this alleged excess in estimate was $300,000. They also contended that the cost of additional service which the Company would be required to give during the ensuing year would be not less than $400,000 more, and that it was questionable under all the circumstances whether the Company would be able, even with the increased fares, to earn more during the ensuing twelve months than an amount sufficient to pay all its expenses of operation and maintenance and meet its fixed charges.

Granting that there may be merit in the above contentions, it is also at least equally probable that there may be, during the ensuing twelve months, a substantial falling off in the cost of labor and materials in comparison with the peak prices which were made the basis of the above estimates.

The relative or net effects of the various counteracting tendencies resulting both from the increases in the Company's rates of fares and from the cessation of hostilities, it is impossible for this Commission to forecast at this time with any reasonable degree of assurance. Time and experience alone will demonstrate the correctness or incorrectness of the various assumptions made in the exhibits referred to, and in the arguments of counsel.

Meanwhile the Commission is satisfied from the evidence before it, only a very small portion of which has been referred to in this opinion, that if the respondent Company is to be put in a position to render adequate service to the people of this community, it must have a substantial increase in its revenues, and that the amount of such increase required in the immediate future is approximately the amount which may reasonably be anticipated to be yielded by the increase of one cent in practically all the Company's fares.

Ever since it developed early in the course of the hearings that there was such a need for increased revenues, the Commission has given much thought to the possibility of requiring the Company to adopt a form of ticket or check to be sold in small quantities at a reduced rate. The following table shows the extent to which a variety of such reduction would have upon the Company's gross revenues upon the assumption that all passengers would use such tickets. This assumption would have to be modified by the further assumption that relatively few would use the tickets sold at a slight reduction while relatively a great many more would use them if sold at a greater reduction.

		Decrease in Revenue.
10 tickets for	55c	$1,120,000
9 " "	50c	994,560
8 " "	45c	819,840
7 " "	40c	540,640
6 " "	35c	371,840

In view of the very great reductions in the Company's revenues which would result from the sale of tickets at any of the above prices, as compared with the relatively small saving to the individual user of such tickets, and in further view of the Company's apparent need for the whole of the increased revenues which are likely to result in the flat increase of one cent in each of its fares, the Commission has concluded that it would be most unwise at this time to order the sale of tickets in bulk at reduced rates.

The Company will be required by the Commission's order to make regular monthly reports of its operating results under the new rates effective October 1, 1918, and if it appears at any time that a reduction of less than the full one cent increase can be properly required, such reduction will be made through the sale of tickets in small quantities at such prices as may be deemed expedient from time to time.

Meanwhile public convenience can be greatly promoted by the sale of tickets or fare checks in bulk for multiples of six cents by the conductors on the cars, in addition to their sale at the offices of the Company, banks, department stores, etc., as at present conducted, and the Company will be expected to perfect a plan in the near future by which this will be done.

CONDITIONS OF ORDER

Special Counsel for the Commission, who was also representing the public, contended that the order of the Commission prescribing the rates of fare hereafter to be charged by the respondent Company shall be limited to a definite period as provided by Section 11 of the Public Service Commission Law and suggested that such period be one year, after which the fare should be restored to five cents, unless the Commission should conclude at the expiration of that period that the service rendered by the Company has been reasonably adequate throughout the same, and that a continuance of a charge in excess of five cents was reasonably necessary to insure the continuance of such reasonably adequate service in future. Counsel for the Company, on the other hand, contended that the increased fare should be permitted preferably for an indeterminate period, or, if that were not feasible under the law, for a definite period longer than one year, subject to a re-opening of the case at any time by the Commission and a reduction of the fare in the light of the evidence then adduced.

In passing upon the merits of these respective contentions we must bear in mind the statements contained in the Company's petition of July 19, 1918, for such increase, as set out at length in the beginning of this opinion, and also the statements made in the letter of the Company transmitting its revised schedule P. S. C. Md. No. 8, as set out on page four of this opinion. By these statements the Company expressly disclaimed "any intention of establishing by this proceeding any permanent rate of fare," and asked only "for relief purely as a war emergency and during the period of war conditions," further stating that its sole purpose was "to preserve its pre-war efficiency, and to prevent, as far as possible, injury to its credit and to its organization and the deterioration of its plant" which would result without such increase in its fares.

Since the filing of such petition and revised schedule the war has virtually terminated, but the reason underlying the application for increased fares is also applicable to a reasonable period for readjustment following the war. How long that period of readjustment will continue it is impossible for this Commission to determine, but bearing in mind the nature and avowed objects of the application, it seems to this Commission most desirable that the right to charge such increased

it to be its duty to the investing as well as to the general public to declare that it will under no circumstances permit any public utility to charge the public an unreasonable price for inadequate service.

In passing upon the reasonable adequacy of service it has not been this Commission's practice in the past, nor is it its intention in the future, to be unduly captious or over-critical in arriving at its conclusions. This Commission fully realizes that there cannot well be any fixed and arbitrary standard of street railway service applicable to all conditions and under all circumstances. Due allowances have always been made for lapses in efficiency of service due to abnormal conditions and occasions, and it is only in cases where it has been shown that the Company has evinced a clear disregard for the ordinary rights and convenience of the public that this Commission has declared its service inadequate. With the increase in fares which will be permitted by our order in this case, it is not to be expected that the Commission will be as tolerant of the defections of the Company with respect to service as it has been in the past, when it was realized that the Company was operating in the face of difficulties which were enhanced by its lack of sufficient funds to render the highest grade of service. The Company will be expected to make the most efficient use reasonably possible of every dollar of revenue received during the period the increased fare is permitted to remain in effect.

THE SKIP-STOP PLAN

On April 15, 1917, the respondent Company inaugurated upon its North Avenue and Edmondson Avenue lines a new plan of operation, generally known as the "Skip-Stop" plan, under which system of operation the cars skipped each alternate street crossing, there being certain exceptions to the general rule, particularly as respects transit crossings. Owing to the subsequent re-routing of some of the cars on these lines the "Skip-Stop" plan was extended to portions of the Garrison Boulevard line and the Liberty Heights branch of the Linden Avenue line.

Directly after this scheme was adopted the Commission began receiving communications respecting the new system of operation, some of which condemned while others praised the plan. By Order No. 3832 entered on September 10, 1917, (P. S. C. Md. Reports, Vol. VIII, pp. 244-247) the Commission established rules to be observed by the Company in respect to the method of procedure before this Commission in the determination of street intersections at which the Railways Company should not be required to stop its cars to take on or discharge passengers.

After the plan had been in effect several months the Commission, upon its own motion, and in order fully to develop the controversy, filed a complaint respecting the "Skip-Stop" plan, and thereafter held hearings extending over several days, at which opportunity was afforded all persons desiring to testify either on behalf of or against the "Skip-Stop" plan of operations, either as a whole or with respect to particular stops which were skipped under the system. On October 6th the Commission filed its opinion (Vol. VIII, pp. 275-280), wherein it held that the "Skip-Stop" plan of operation as theretofore practiced by the Railways Company was unjust and unreasonable, though the Commission did not require the Company to restore all of the stops formerly in effect. By order No. 3887, entered on the same day, (p. 281) the Commission directed the respondent Company to restore a dozen or more stops which it had abandoned under the aforesaid plan of operation and by subsequent orders required the restoration of still other stops.

Thereafter the Railways Company began formulating plans looking to the adoption of a "Staggered-Skip-Stop" plan of operation on certain of its lines, under which scheme cars stop to take on and let off passengers at alternate street crossings in both directions. That is to say, if the cars stop at a given corner when on the west-bound trip, that corner is skipped on the east-bound trip, subject to the same exceptions respecting transit crossings etc., as in the case of the original "Skip-Stop" plan, the object of the "Staggered-Skip-Stop" plan being to equalize, as far as possible, the inconvenience to the Company's patrons. In April last the co-operation of this Commission was sought by the Special War Committee of the National Association of Railway and Utility Commissioners, by the Conservation Division of the United States Fuel Administration, and by the Fuel Administrator of Maryland in the matter of the conservation of fuel by the respondent Company, it being represented that a great saving of fuel would result were said Company permitted to put into effect the "Staggered-Skip-Stop" plan of operation upon all of its lines. The Commission on April 9, 1918, entered its Order No. 4262, by which the Railways Company was authorized and requested to adopt and put into operation at as early a date as practicable the "Staggered-Skip-Stop" plan of operation. By the terms of this order the Commission reserved unto itself the right, at any time thereafter, to modify or change any particular application thereof when such particular application was found to be an unreasonable exercise of the authority granted the Railways Company by the said order. By the same order the rules of procedure established by Order No. 3832 aforesaid were modified to meet the new conditions. From time to time thereafter the Commission has entered orders requiring the restoration of specific stops when the restoration of such stops was found to be necessary in the interest of the public service, but the "Staggered-Skip-Stop" plan of operation as a whole remained in effect on all lines of the Company until December 23, 1918, when it was abandoned pursuant to an oral order of the Commission given the officers of the Company during the course of the hearings in this case.

During such hearings the plan had been made the subject of attack by counsel for the public, and an opportunity was given the general public to make objections to its abandonment. No such objections

were made, and the President of the Company when on the stand
declared that the plan as such had been a failure in that it had not
saved the money it had been expected to save, that it had not resulted
in any noticeable saving in the running time of the cars, and that the
small amount of money and time-saved by the plan were far more
than outweighed by the general inconvenience to the public resulting
therefrom. The Commission concurs in these conclusions, and a
formal order will be passed in the appropriate case abolishing the
same.

ZONE EXTENSIONS TO NEW CITY LIMITS

During the course of the hearings it was contended by counsel for
certain residents of North Baltimore that the legal effect of that portion of Section 2 of Chapter 82 of the Acts of 1918, providing that all
existing provisions of the Baltimore City Charter should be applicable
to such portions of Baltimore and Anne Arundel Counties as were
annexed to Baltimore City by that Act, was to extend the provisions
of Section 796 of the City Charter prescribing certain fares within the
old limits of the City to such annexed portions of Baltimore and Anne
Arundel Counties, and thereby make uniform the fares within the
limits of Baltimore City as enlarged by such Act. As hereinbefore
stated, this Commission had been advised by its General Counsel
October 2, 1918, that the effect of the enactment of the Public Service
Commission Law was to repeal that portion of Section 796 of the City
Charter above referred to. When the question was raised in a somewhat new form during the course of the argument, it was again referred to the General Counsel, who advised the Commission in his
opinion of December 31, 1918, that by the several sections of the
Public Service Commission Law hereinbefore referred to the whole
matter of the rates of fare proper to be charged by the respondent
Company has been committed by the Legislature in the first instance
to determination by this Commission, subject to review by the courts
as in said Law provided. The Commission concurs in such opinions.

This Commission is not prepared at this time to express any final
conclusion as to the extension of existing fare zones, for the reasons
that this question was not fully presented to it at the hearings in this
case, and that an extension of such zones at the present time and
under existing conditions would so far reduce the gross earnings of
the respondent Company as to render the increase of one cent in the
fares over existing lines entirely inadequate to meet the operating
requirements of the Company.

The general question of fare zones should be made the subject of
an independent study, and this cannot be done until the effect of the
increased fares, on the basis of the existing zones, has been demonstrated by experience over a reasonable period.

For the present no order will be passed upon this point.

THE CURTIS BAY LINE

The Curtis Bay Line of the respondent Company begins at the intersection of Baltimore and Light Streets, in the heart of the city, and runs south along Light Street to a point near the northern end of the Hanover Street bridge, where it is diverted to Hanover Street and crosses the Middle Branch of the Patapsco River over such bridge into what was formerly Anne Arundel County and is now a part of Baltimore City. Thence it passes to the town of Brooklyn, which it leaves by way of Patapsco Avenue and passes into the town of South Baltimore, its southern terminus, a distance of 3.77 miles beyond the old city limits. At Stone House Cove, a point about midway between Brooklyn and South Baltimore, there is a junction, at which at present a jerk-water line runs easterly to East Brooklyn and Fairfield, a thriving community located on the west bank of the main body of the Patapsco River, East Brooklyn also fronting on Curtis Bay. The section served by this jerk-water line is occupied mainly by large manufacturing enterprises employing thousands of laborers, some of the latter having their homes in the immediate vicinity, but the great bulk of the same residing in Baltimore City.

Prior to the filing of the respondent Company's revised schedule, P. S. C. Md. No. 8, effective October 1, 1918, it was the practice of the Company to issue free transfers between its other lines and that portion of the Curtis Bay Line extending from Baltimore and Light Streets on the north to the southern end of the Hanover Street Bridge (south bank of the Middle Branch of the Patapsco) on the south, and then to charge an extra full fare of five cents on the remainder of the line south of the latter point. In the alternative it was the practice of the Company to issue a cash transfer for three cents from either section of this line to the other, where a cash fare had originally been paid on the first. Transfer from the main line to the jerk-water line running to Fairfield was without charge in either event.

Revised schedule, P. S. C. Md. No. 8, eliminated the above three cent cash transfer, with the result that the fare to Brooklyn or Fairfield has been increased from eight to twelve cents.

Without going further into the details of this rather complicated situation, and without undertaking at this time to pass upon the reasonableness or unreasonableness of the fare as it originally stood, the Commission has concluded, in view of the avowed intention of the Company to increase its existing fares but one cent in any instance, that it should hereafter be required to issue cash transfers on said line for four cents instead of three cents previously charged, thus making the full fare ten cents instead of eight as heretofore and twelve as now.

The evidence upon this branch of the case also showed a glaring case of inadequacy of service to the Fairfield District. Three ways were pointed out by which this service could be materially improved without any very great expenses, (1) by side tracking some of the Curtis Bay main line cars at Stone House Cove; (2) by completing the Fairfield extension as originally contemplated in the form of a complete loop over one or the other of the routes suggested, and putting additional cars thereon, or (3) by installing a series of turn-out switches on the existing jerk-water line pending the completion of such loop, and running additional cars over the same. Whichever of these plans the Company may deem it proper and expedient to adopt, the service must be improved within the immediate future.

While the complaint of the Fairfield patrons was heard with the main complaint as a matter of convenience, it is deemed advisable by the Commission to dispose of the same for the present by a separate order.

An order upon this branch of the case will be duly passed pursuant to this opinion.

RECENT STEPS LOOKING TO IMPROVED SERVICE

Something over a year ago the respondent Company employed the firm of A. L. Drum & Company, Consulting and Construction Engineers of Chicago, to come to this city and make a complete survey of the situation with a view of advising the management of as to the propriety of re-routing certain of its lines in order to diminish as far as reasonably possible the rapidly growing congestion of traffic in the central business portion of the city. The investigations of this form covered a considerable period and most of the proposed re-routing has been accomplished, with beneficial results which will no doubt be more evident as time goes on.

More recently the respondent Company has employed Day & Zimmerman, Inc., Engineers of Philadelphia, for the purpose of making an exhaustive study of traffic conditions generally over the entire system and advising the management in the premises. This latter work has not yet progressed far enough for this Commission to speak with any degree of positiveness as to its probable effect upon the service of the Company, but it is nevertheless encouraging to note that the Company is availing itself of expert service of this character in attempting to solve the problems of service which confront it.

It has been largely in view of this attitude upon the part of the management of the Company toward outside advice and assistance in the comparatively recent past, that this Commission has been so sparing in its criticism of the service which has heretofore been rendered, and it is sincerely hoped, for the sake of both the Company and the public, that such attitude will continue to prevail in the future.

An order will be passed embodying the principal conclusions embodied in the aforegoing opinion.

ORDER No. 4608

In the Matter of	Before the
The Application of THE UNITED RAILWAYS AND ELECTRIC COMPANY OF BALTIMORE for Permission to Make a Uniform Increase of One Cent in Cash Fares Heretofore Charged.	Public Service Commission of Maryland. Case No. 1568.

In the Matter of	Before the
The Complaint of THE PUBLIC SERVICE COMMISSION OF MARYLAND *vs.* THE UNITED RAILWAYS AND ELECTRIC COMPANY OF BALTIMORE, With Respect to the Fairness and Reasonableness of Its Proposed General Increase in Its Passenger Rates.	Public Service Commission of Maryland. Case No. 1583.

Pursuant to the conclusions reached in the aforegoing opinion, it is Ordered, this 7th day of January, 1919, by the Public Service Commission of Maryland:

1. That from and after this date and until December 31, 1919, and for no longer, unless such period be extended for a further period as hereinafter provided, or this order be earlier modified or abrogated by further order of this Commission, The United Railways and Electric Company of Baltimore shall be permitted to charge and collect for the transportation of persons over its several street railway lines, in Baltimore City and vicinity, the following rates, fares and charges, to wit:

(a) Six cents fare for the conveyance of each passenger over twelve years of age, and four cents for each child between the ages of four and twelve years, on any of its lines between the points designated under the first general caption in its schedule P. S. C. Md., No. 8, filed with this Commission August 28, 1918, effective October 1, 1918, or between intermediate points, in either direction, on any of such lines; except in the case of its Curtis Bay Line, in which case the fare to be charged shall be modified under the conditions set forth in a separate order of this Commission passed on this date;

(b) Full fare and half fare when paid by continuous trip tickets, on the lines and between the points, on the Company's Gorsuch Avenue, East Monument Street (Orangeville), Third and 8th Streets,

Union Avenue, South Charles Street, Walbrook-Hillsdale, Shore Line and Ferry Bar lines, as designated in said schedule P. S. C. Md. No. 8, otherwise the regular fare to be collected between the points so designated;

(c) Four and one-half cents when paid by commutation tickets sold for use on lines operating over more than one fare zone between the points so designated in the Schedule P. S. C. Md., No. 8, aforesaid, and five cents when paid by commutation tickets sold for use on lines operating over more than one fare zone between the points so designated in said schedule, said commutation tickets to be sold in the manner and subject to the conditions set forth in said schedule with respect thereto;

(d) Four and one-half cents between Sparrows Point and Highlandtown when paid by employee's tickets from 20-trip books sold in lots to the Maryland Steel Company for distribution; five cents between Dundalk and city points, when paid by strip tickets sold in lots to the Central Foundry Company for distribution; and two and one-half cents on the Lakeside line when paid by tickets from 200-trip books sold to the landowners along such line, all such tickets to be subject to the conditions printed thereon and to the rules of the Company governing the use thereof, the full fare in each of said cases otherwise to be paid.

2. That from and after the hour of midnight on the 31st of December, 1919, said Company's right and privilege to charge and collect the increased fares herein authorized to be charged and collected shall cease and determine, and said Company shall thereafter be permitted to charge no fares in excess of those charged by it on September 30, 1918, unless this Commission shall in the meantime, by its order in writing, for such cause as may then seem to it, and be in law, good and sufficient, authorize said Company to charge fares in excess of those which were in effect September 30, 1918;

3. That so soon after the date of this order as may be reasonably practicable, and convenient, and in no event later than January 31st, 1919, said Company shall furnish to this Commission accurate and complete statements under oath, and in convenient form, setting forth the number of revenue and transfer passengers carried, and the number of car-miles operated, the cash receipts from operation and other sources, and the operating and other expenditures of the Company, all set forth in the manner prescribed by the rules of this Commission for accounting by street railway companies, for the calendar months of October, November and December, 1918, respectively; and thereafter, so soon as may be reasonably practicable and convenient after the end of each calendar month during the year 1919, and in no event later than the last day of the next succeeding calendar month, said Company shall furnish this Commission a complete statement as aforesaid covering the operations of the Company during the next preceding month;

4. That the right of the respondent Company to charge and collect the fares in this order prescribed shall be held subject at all times during the period covered by such order, or any extension thereof which may hereafter be granted as aforesaid, to the right and power of this Commission to reopen this case in the light of the facts disclosed by the monthly reports aforesaid, or of other facts otherwise coming to the attention of this Commission and modify the rates of fare by this order authorized to be charged and collected by the respondent Company;

AND IT IS FURTHER Ordered, That a copy of this order be forthwith served upon the proper officers of the respondent, The United Railways and Electric Company of Baltimore, and that said Company, within ten days from the date of the srvice of such copy, advise this Commission in writing whether or not it will accept and abide by the same.

ORDER No. 4609

In the Matter of

The Complaint of THE INTER-OCEAN OIL COMPANY, THE PRUDENTIAL OIL COMPANY, THE UNITED STATES ASPHALT REFINING COMPANY, THE UNION SHIPBUILDING COMPANY, MARTIN WAGNER COMPANY, SWIFT AND COMPANY, F. S. ROYSTER GUANO COMPANY, RASIN MONUMENTAL COMPANY, STANDARD ACID WORKS, and the BALTIMORE CAR FOUNDRY COMPANY

vs.

THE UNITED RAILWAYS AND ELECTRIC COMPANY OF BALTIMORE.

Before the

Public Service Commission of Maryland.

Pursuant to the conclusions reached in the opinion of this Commission on this date rendered In the Matter of the Application of The United Railways and Electric Company of Baltimore for permission to make a uniform increase of one cent in cash fares heretofore charged, Case No. 1568; and In the Matter of the Complaint of the Public Service Commission of Maryland vs. The United Railways and Electric Company of Baltimore, etc., Case No. 1583, it is, this seventh day of January, 1919, by the Public Service Commission of Maryland,

Ordered, 1. That from and after January 19th, 1919, and until

December 31, 1919, unless earlier modified or abrogated by order of this Commission, the respondent, The United Railways and Electric Company of Baltimore, shall issue on its Curtis Bay Line transfers entitling the holder to a continuous ride on such line as such transfers were issued on and prior to September 30, 1918, except that the charge for such transfers shall thereafter be four cents instead of three cents, as heretofore.

2. That the service heretofore and now being rendered by the respondent company over the Fairfield extension of its Curtis Bay Line, and to its patrons generally in the Fairfield and East Brooklyn districts, more particularly during the rush hours on said line, is hereby found and declared to have been and to be unjust, unreasonable, unsafe, unreasonably improper and inadequate; and said company is hereby ordered and directed, within thirty days hereafter, or within such further period of extension as may be granted for good cause shown, to render reasonably adequate and proper service over said line and to its patrons generally in the Fairfield and East Brooklyn district, the means by which such adequate service is to be rendered to be left for the present to the judgment and discretion of the respondent company, subject to more specific orders by this Commission in case the relief hereby ordered is not speedily afforded.

AND IT IS FURTHER Ordered, That a copy of this order be forthwith served upon the proper officers of the respondent, The United Railways and Electric Company of Baltimore, and that said Company within ten days from the date of the service of such copy advise this Commission in writing whether or not it will accept and abide by the same.

ORDER No. 4610

In the Matter of

The Recommendation of UNITED STATES FUEL ADMINISTRATION, by P. B. NOYES, Its Director of Conservation, and F. A. MEYER, Fuel Administrator of This State, That the "Stagger Stop" Be Permitted and Put in Effect by The United Railways and Electric Company of Baltimore as a War Measure for the Conservation of Fuel.	Before the Public Service Commission of Maryland. Case No. 1506.

Pursuant to the conclusions reached in the opinion of this Commission this day filed In the Matter of the Application of The United Railways and Electric Company of Baltimore for permission to make

a uniform increase of one cent in cash fares heretofore charged, Case
No. 1568; and In the Matter of the Complaint of the Public Service
Commission of Maryland vs. The United Railways and Electric Com-
pany of Baltimore, etc., Case No. 1583, it is this seventh day of Janu-
ary, in the year Nineteen Hundred and Nineteen, by the Public Service
Commission of Maryland,

Ordered, That the "Staggered-Skip-Stop" plan of operation inaugurated on the lines of The United Railways and Electric Company
of Baltimore in compliance with the authority and request of this
Commission embodied in its Order No. 4262 entered herein on April
9th, 1918, be and it is hereby abolished, and said The United Railways
and Electric Company of Baltimore be and it is hereby directed and
required to forthwith discontinue operating its cars upon the "Staggered-Skip-Stop" plan of operation.

ORDER No. 4617

In the Matter of

The Application of THE CHESAPEAKE
AND POTOMAC TELEPHONE COMPANY OF
BALTIMORE CITY for the Approval of
an Agreement, Dated December 11th,
1918, Between It and EDGAR H. BENDER
for the Leasing by the Former to the
Latter of Certain Quarters for Resi-
dential Purposes at No. 8 Union
Street, Cumberland, Maryland, Under
the Terms and Provisions of Order No.
2913, Entered June 20th, 1916, in Case
No. 1131.

Before the

Public Service Commission
of Maryland.

Case No. 1621.

The agreement or other written instrument evidencing the transaction in this case having been submitted to this Commission for the
purpose of securing its consent to the consummation thereof and the
Commission having determined that a hearing is unnecessary,

IT IS, THEREFORE, This thirteenth day of January, in the year 1919,
by the Public Service Commission of Maryland,

Ordered, That the consent of this Commission be, and the same is
hereby, given to the disposition of the property described in said
agreement, or other written instrument, evidencing the transaction in
accordance with the terms outlined therein.

ORDER No. 4618

In the Matter of	Before the
The Complaint of GEORGE T. HILL	Public Service Commission
vs.	of Maryland.
THE UNITED RAILWAYS AND ELECTRIC COMPANY OF BALTIMORE.	Case No. 1477.

WHEREAS, This case, involving the adequacy of the service furnished by The United Railways and Electric Company of Baltimore to the north-eastern section of the City of Baltimore, to correct which alleged inadequacy of service this Commission is petitioned to order and require the respondent to divert the cars of its Guilford Avenue Line at North and Guilford Avenues, running said cars eastward on North Avenue to Milton and North Avenues, or eastward on North Avenue to Washington Street and thence south on Washington Street to Preston Street, returning over same route, being at issue upon complaint and answer on file, and having been duly heard and submitted by the parties and full investigation of the matters and things involved having been made by the Commission, and

WHEREAS, It being the opinion and finding of the Commission that it is impracticable at this time to re-route the cars of the Guilford Avenue Line of the respondent over the route aforesaid,

IT IS, THEREFORE, This 15th day of January, in the year Nineteen Hundred and Nineteen, by the Public Service Commission of Maryland,

ORDERED, That the complaint in the above entitled matter be, and the same is hereby dismissed.

ORDER No. 4622

In the Matter of	Before the
The Application of THE UNITED RAIL-WAYS AND ELECTRIC COMPANY OF BAL-TIMORE for Permission to Make a Uniform Increase of One Cent in Cash Fares Heretofore Charged.	Public Service Commission of Maryland. Case No. 1568.

In the Matter of	Before the
The Complaint of THE PUBLIC SERVICE COMMISSION OF MARYLAND *vs.* THE UNITED RAILWAYS AND ELECTRIC COMPANY OF BALTIMORE, With Respect to the Fairness and Reasonableness of Its Proposed General Increase in Its Passenger Rates.	Public Service Commission of Maryland. Case No. 1583.

The United Railways and Electric Company of Baltimore having on this day filed its petition praying certain modifications of Order No. 4608 passed in this cause, and it not being convenient for this Commission to pass upon said petition, it is, therefore, this 16th day of January, 1919, by the Public Service Commission of Maryland,

Ordered, That the time within which said company shall advise this Commission whether or not it will accept and abide by said Order be, and the same is hereby extended for a period of ten days from January 17th, 1919.

ORDER No. 4625

In the Matter of

The Application of THE MARYLAND ELEC-
TRIC RAILWAYS COMPANY and THE
UNITED RAILWAYS AND ELECTRIC COM-
PANY OF BALTIMORE for an Order Per-
mitting and Approving the Exercise of
a Franchise Granted Them by the
Mayor and City Council of Baltimore
Under the Terms and /Provisions of
Ordinance No. 352, Approved May 25,
1918, and to Begin the Construction of
the Tracks and the Operation of Cars
Thereon as Provided in Said Ordi-
nance.

Before the

Public Service Commission
of Maryland.

Case No. 1619.

WHEREAS, The Maryland Electric Railways Company and The
United Railways and Electric Company of Baltimore have applied to
this Commission for its permission and approval of the franchises
granted to said The Maryland Electric Railways Company by the
Mayor and City Council of Baltimore, as set forth in "Exhibit A,"
filed in these proceedings, and for the construction by The Maryland
Electric Railways Company of the railway to be constructed in pursuance of said franchise, and the possession and use thereof by The
United Railways and Electric Company of Baltimore, in accordance
with the terms of the lease and agreement between said corporations,
under date of September 15th, 1906, a copy of which, marked "Exhibit
B," is filed in Case No. 29 of this Commission; and

WHEREAS, This Commission has determined, after due hearing, that
the exercise of said franchise and the construction, possession and use
of said railway is convenient for the public service,

IT IS, THEREFORE, This 17th day of January, in the year Nineteen
Hundred and Nineteen, by the Public Service Commission of Maryland,

Ordered, 1. That the exercise by said The Maryland Electric Railways Company of the franchise granted to it by the Mayor and City
Council of Baltimore, by Ordinance No. 352, approved by said Mayor
and City Council of Baltimore on May 25th, 1918, to wit: "To construct, maintain and operate double electric railway tracks, with the
necessary curves, poles, overhead trolley wires, feed wires and overhead construction and appurtenances, and to operate and maintain an
electric railway on, along and over Columbia avenue from the present
location of the tracks of The United Railways and Electric Company
of Baltimore on Columbia avenue at the eastern end of the city bridge
over Gwynn's Falls to and across the city bridge over Gwynn's Falls to

the western end thereof, and the said company is hereby authorized and empowered to connect the tracks and overhead construction hereby authorized by all necessary appurtenances with the tracks and overhead construction already in existence at said location; and to run on the aforesaid tracks cars to be propelled by electricity supplied by overhead wires or by the storage system, or by any improved system which may be approved by the Mayor and Highways Engineer," subject to the conditions, stipulations and agreements set forth in said "Exhibit A," filed in these proceedings, be and the same is hereby permitted and approved.

2. That authority is hereby given to The Maryland Electric Railways Company to construct said railway as provided in said grant, and to The United Railways and Electric Company of Baltimore to take possession of said railway and use the same, in accordance with the terms of the lease and agreement hereinbefore referred to, the same being "Exhibit B," filed in Case No. 29 of this Commission.

ORDER No. 4626

In the Matter of

The Application of THE MARYLAND ELECTRIC RAILWAYS COMPANY and THE UNITED RAILWAYS AND ELECTRIC COMPANY OF BALTIMORE for an Order Permitting and Approving the Exercise of the Franchise Granted Them by the State Roads Commission by Order Entered December 27th, 1918, and to Begin the Construction of the Tracks and the Operation of Cars Thereon as Provided in Said Order.

Before the

Public Service Commission of Maryland.

Case No. 1620.

WHEREAS, The Maryland Electric Railways Company and The United Railways and Electric Company of Baltimore have applied to this Commission for its permission and approval of the franchises granted to said The Maryland Electric Railways Company by the State Roads Commission of Maryland, as set forth in "Exhibit A," filed in these proceedings, and for the construction by The Maryland Electric Railways Company of the railway to be constructed in pursuance of said franchise, and the possession and use thereof by The United Railways and Electric Company of Baltimore, in accordance with the terms of the lease and agreement between said corporations, under date of September 15th, 1906, a copy of which, marked "Exhibit B," is filed in Case No. 29 of this Commission; and

WHEREAS, This Commission has determined, after due hearing, that the exercise of said franchise and the construction, possession and use of said railway is convenient for the public service,

IT IS, THEREFORE, This 17th day of January, in the year Nineteen Hundred and Nineteen, by the Public Service Commission of Maryland,

𝔇𝔯𝔡𝔢𝔯𝔢𝔡, 1. That the exercise by said The Maryland Electric Railways Company of the franchise granted to it by the State Roads Commission of Maryland, on December 27th, 1918, to wit: "To construct, operate and maintain a double track line, with all necessary overhead wires and other overhead and side pole construction over the State Road No. 1 from the western boundary line of Baltimore City, where the same crosses Columbia avenue, and there connecting with tracks to be laid on Columbia avenue under a franchise from the City of Baltimore; thence extending along the center of Columbia avenue for a distance of about twenty-two hundred (2200) feet to a point approximately three hundred (300) feet west of Sixth street and curving thence southwardly into private property, and to run on the aforesaid tracks cars propelled by electricity supplied by overhead wires or by the storage system, or by any other improved motive power other than steam, which may be approved by the State Roads Commission and its Chief Engineer," subject to the conditions, stipulations and agreements set forth in said "Exhibit A," filed in these proceedings, be and the same is hereby permitted and approved.

2. That authority is hereby given to The Maryland Electric Railways Company to construct said railway as provided in said grant, and to The United Railways and Electric Company of Baltimore to take possession of said railway and use the same, in accordance with the terms of the lease and agreement hereinbefore referred to, the same being "Exhibit B," filed in Case No. 29 of this Commission.

ORDER No. 4629

In the Matter of

The Application of CONSOLIDATED GAS
ELECTRIC LIGHT AND POWER COMPANY
OF BALTIMORE for the Approval of an
Agreement Between It and BALTIMORE
DRY DOCKS AND SHIPBUILDING COM-
PANY OF BALTIMORE for the Sale by the
Former to the Latter of Ten Poles Sit-
uated Along the West Side of Ship-
building Company's Property South of
Fort Avenue in the City of Baltimore,
Maryland, Under the Terms and Pro-
visions of Order No. 2954, Entered
July 26th, 1916, in Case No. 1151.

Before the

Public Service Commission
of Maryland.

Case No. 1627.

The agreement or other written instrument evidencing the transaction in this case having been submitted to this Commission for the
purpose of securing its consent to the consummation thereof and the
Commission having determined that a hearing is unnecessary,

IT IS, THEREFORE, On this twentieth day of January, in the year
1919, by the Public Service Commission of Maryland,

Ordered, That the consent of this Commission be and the same is
hereby given to the disposition of the property described in said agreement, or other written instrument, evidencing the transaction in accordance with the terms outlined therein.

ORDER No. 4630

In the Matter of

The Application of THE CHESAPEAKE AND
POTOMAC TELEPHONE COMPANY OF BAL-
TIMORE CITY for the Approval of an
Agreement Between It and THE CON-
SOLIDATED POWER COMPANY OF BALTI-
MORE, Dated September 17th, 1918, for
the Joint Use by the Former and the
Latter of Certain Poles Located on the
Liberty Road, District No. 2, Balti-
more County, Maryland, Under the
Terms and Provisions of Order No.
2913, Entered June 20th, 1916, in Case
No. 1131.

Before the

Public Service Commission
of Maryland.

Case No. 1628.

The agreement or other written instrument evidencing the transaction in this case having been submitted to this Commission for the
purpose of securing its consent to the consummation thereof and the
Commission having determined that a hearing is unnecessary,

IT IS, THEREFORE, On this twentieth day of January, in the year
1919, by the Public Service Commission of Maryland,

Ordered, That the consent of this Commission be and the same is
hereby given to the disposition of the property described in said agreement, or other written instrument, evidencing the transaction in accordance with the terms outlined therein.

ORDER No. 4638

In the Matter of

The Carriers Not Under Federal Control
Named in the Official Classification, by
R. N. COLLYER, Their Agent, for Per-
mission Under Section 15 of the Public
Service Commission Law to File and
Publish on Less Than Statutory Notice
Supplement to Official Classification
No. 44, P. S. C. Md. O. C. No. 44.

Before the

Public Service Commission
of Maryland.

S. N. & R. Docket.

Case No. 554.

The above mentioned petition having been received and filed, upon
consideration thereof, it is this 27th day of January, 1919, by the Public Service Commission of Maryland,

Ordered, That permission be, and is hereby given, the carriers not under Federal control named in the Official Classification, by R. N. Collyer, their Agent, to file and publish on one day's notice to the Commission and the public, supplement to Official Classification No. 44, P. S. C. Md. O. C. No. 44, revising Note 1-A to household goods specifications shown in Item 6, page 6 of Supplement No. 29 to Official Classification No. 44, P. S. C. Md. O. C. No. 44, to correct typographical error in said specifications, as set forth in petition herein: and to include in same supplement, on full statutory notice, revision of the specifications for boots and shoes and for trunks containing merchandise, and providing lumber ratings on silo staves cut to dimensions or fitted and K. D., as set forth in petition and exhibit filed therewith; said supplement issued under authority hereof to depart from the provisions of this Commission's Circular No. 10A in so far as volume of supplemental matter is concerned, and including necessary additions to, changes in and eliminations from the list of participating carriers contained in said classification.

PROVIDED, Said supplement be filed with the Commission upon issuance of this Order, and published by posting as required by law, and that all copies of said supplement shall bear the following notation:

> "Issued under special permission of the Public Service Commission of Maryland, Order No. 4638 of date January 27th, 1919."

OPINION

In the Matter of

The Complaint and Protest of the MAYOR AND COUNCIL OF HAGERSTOWN

vs.

THE HAGERSTOWN LIGHT AND HEAT COMPANY.

Before the

Public Service Commission of Maryland.

Case No. 1589.

Appearances:

ALEXANDER R. HAGNER, ESQ., representing the Complainant.
GEORGE WEEMS WILLIAMS, ROBERT H. McCAULEY and THOMAS J. PERKINS, ESQUIRES, representing the respondent.

By the Commission.   Filed January 27, 1919.

This complaint involves the reasonableness of the rates now being charged by the Hagerstown Light and Heat Company of Washington

County for the supply of gas within the corporate limits of the City of Hagerstown.

On August 3rd, 1918, the Hagerstown Light and Heat Company, hereinafter referred to as the "Gas Company," filed with the Commission Supplement No 1 to its gas rate schedule P. S. C. Md. No. 7 to become effective on October 1st, 1918, after the September, 1918, meter readings. This supplemental schedule operates to bring about an increase in the rates charged by the Gas Company for gas supplied by it in Hagerstown and adjacent territory served by it, ranging from 5 cents to 35 cents per 1,000 cubic feet, varying with the amount of consumption. The rates of the Gas Company had been increased an average of 10 cents per 1,000 cubic feet on April 1st, 1918, the following tabulation showing the present rates as well as the rates which became effective April 1st, 1918, and the rates in effect immediately prior thereto:

HAGERSTOWN LIGHT AND HEAT COMPANY OF WASHINGTON COUNTY

Monthly Consumption	Effective Prior to April 1st, 1918	Effective April 1st, 1918	Effective October 1st, 1918
First 1,000 cubic feet.......	$1.25	$1.35	$1.40
Next 1.000 " "	1.15	1.25	1.40
" 1.000 " "	1.05	1.15	1.40
" 1,000 " "	.95	1.15	1.40
" 1,000 " "	.95	1.15	1.40
" 5,000 " "	.85	1.10	1.35
" 15,000 " "	.85	1.00	1.35
" 25,000 " "	.80	.95	1.25
" 50,000 " "	.80	.90	1.15
" 100,000 " "	.80	.85	1.00
" 100,000 " "	.80	.80	.90
Over 300,000 " "	.80	.75	.90
Minimum Monthly Charge....	.25	.50	.50

The gross rates of the company are and were 10 cents per 1,000 cubic feet higher than those shown in the above statement, discount of 10 cents per 1,000 cubic feet being allowed on all bills paid at the office of the company on or before the 15th day of the month following that for which the bill is rendered.

On April 1st, 1918, the company withdrew secondary rate of 70 cents per 1,000 cubic feet on all domestic consumption over 3,000 cubic feet per month in houses of 6 rooms or less, with 1,000 cubic feet for each additional room, established May 1st, 1916. In automatically applying same to the then customers of the company the primary rating was taken, subject to certain limitations, as the number of cubic feet, of consumption in corresponding month of previous year, with the right to change to room basis.

On September 26th, 1918, the Mayor and Council of Hagerstown, acting for itself and in behalf of all the consumers of gas within the corporate limits of Hagerstown, filed with the Commission a protest against the rates which had been filed with the Commission to become effective on October 1st, 1918. This protest alleges, among other things, that there had been no change in conditions which would justify the increase proposed, that the rates had been increased 10 cents per 1,000 cubic feet but a few weeks before, that the Gas Company had recently leased a large building on one of the most prominent streets in Hagerstown at a very large annual rental and that in addition it had spent large sums of money improving said building, that the accounts of the Gas Company are so intermingled with the accounts of other utilities operated by the same interests that it is impossible to determine the exact financial conditions of the respondent company, and concludes with a prayer to the Commission that the increase be denied.

Answer denying the allegations of the complaint was thereafter filed by the Gas Company, and the case was thereupon set for hearing before the Commission on December 20th, 1918, and subsequently postponed until January 6th, 1919, on which date hearing was duly had.

At the hearing the respondent filed several exhibits showing the result of its operations in the past, the increased costs of labor and supplies, and the return likely to be yielded under the rates which became effective on October 1st, last. During the year ended September 30th, 1918, the Gas Company sold 96,167,000 cubic feet of gas and had a deficit of $7,471.75 after making allowances of $3,000.00 for depreciation and $780.00 to amortize bond discount and paying $14,-550.00 interest on bonds. There are issued and outstanding bonds to the amount of $291,000.00 face value, bearing interest at the rate of 5% per annum, and capital stock of the par value of $200,000.00, no dividend being paid thereon.

The exhibits aforesaid and oral testimony offered at the hearing in support thereof show that if the consumption during the year starting October 1st, 1918, and ending September 30th, 1919, is the same as the consumption in the preceding year, 96,167,000 cubic feet, the Gas Company will, under the rate schedule which became effective October 1st, 1918, operate at a deficit of $168.00 after making the same allowances for depreciation and amortization and payment of same interest charges as in the previous year. In estimating the operating expenses for this year the Gas Company used as a basis the labor and material costs obtaining in the month of August, 1918, except in the case of oil, the cost of which was taken as 11 cents per gallon, which is the contract price for the year covered by the estimate. Should the sales

show a normal increase of about 15%, making the total sales 112,-
150,000 cubic feet, it is estimated that there would remain $9,648.00
after making provision for depreciation, amortization and interest
charges. It would seem extremely doubtful, however, that the Gas
Company's sales during the ensuing year will exceed the sales during
the preceding year by very much, if in fact there is any increase at all.
The Gas Company's largest customer during the last year or so has been
engaged largely in the manufacture of munitions of war and its use of
gas has, it is testified, averaged about 2,000,000 cubic feet per month,
but since the signing of the armistice the consumption of this customer has already fallen off 1,000,000 cubic feet per month. This
means that the normal year to year increase must first absorb this
falling off of 1,000,000 cubic feet per month, or 12,000,000 cubic feet
for the year, before the total consumption will show any increase, and
for this reason it is deemed unlikely that there will be any substantial increase in the consumption during the coming year.

The method followed by the Gas Company in determining its probable operating expenses during the year ending September 30th, 1919,
seems proper, and the allowance for depreciation certainly cannot be
attacked as being excessive. With respect to the charge that the Gas
Company had unnecessarily incurred additional expense when it recently leased a building in Hagerstown for office and salesroom purposes, the uncontradicted testimony is to the effect that the company
was compelled to vacate the building formerly occupied by it and that
the monthly rental paid for the present building is about $10.00 less
than that paid for the building formerly occupied. The Gas Company
spent about $3,000.00 in improving the property and adapting same to
its requirements, which amount is being charged to operating expenses over a period of five years at the rate of $50.00 per month. The
net effect of this is to make the total charge to the Gas Company
$40.00 per month more than formerly, for a period of five years, after
which the charge will be $10.00 per month less than the rental charge
for the old building, if the lease is continued. It further appears that
the new building better suits the purposes of the Gas Company, in
that it enables it to have its office, shop, salesroom and storeroom
under one roof. While the respondent did not in these proceedings
attempt to establish the fair value of its property used and useful in
the public service, or the proper rate of return to be allowed thereon,
the Commission is convinced that the present rates will not produce
an excessive return upon the Gas Company's investment.

The Commission therefore finds that the rates established by the
respondent on October 1st, 1918, are neither unjust nor unreasonable.
At the hearing counsel for complainant urged that should the Commission determine that the present rates are reasonable, some limit in
point of time should be placed thereupon, and suggested that the
period might properly be made the same as the time limit specified in
the Act of Congress providing for Federal operation of the railroads

of the country, which time was made twenty-one months after the ratification of the treaty of peace. The Commission feels that there is merit in this suggestion and will accordingly provide in its order that the rates shall remain in effect until December 31st, 1920, a period of slightly less than two years from the present date, unless earlier changed by further order of the Commission. At the same time the Commission will require the Gas Company to make periodic reports showing its operating results, so that the Commission will be in a position to promptly take further action in the matter should the showing made under the existing rates make such action possible or desirable.

ORDER No. 4639

In the Matter of	Before the
The Complaint and Protest of the MAYOR AND COUNCIL OF HAGERSTOWN	Public Service Commission of Maryland.
vs.	Case No. 1589.
THE HAGERSTOWN LIGHT AND HEAT COMPANY.	

This case being at issue upon complaint and answer on file and having been duly heard and submitted by the parties and full investigation of the matters and things involved having been had and the Commission, on the date hereof, having rendered and filed an opinion containing its findings of fact and conclusions therein,

IT IS, THEREFORE, This 27th day of January, in the year Nineteen Hundred and Nineteen, by the Public Service Commission of Maryland,

Ordered, (1) That the rates contained in Supplement No. 1 to gas rate schedule P. S. C. Md. No. 7 of the Hagerstown Light and Heat Company of Washington County, filed with this Commission on August 31st, 1918, to become effective October 1st, 1918, be and they are hereby approved, to remain effective until December 31st, 1920, unless earlier modified or changed by the further order of this Commission.

(2) That the said Hagerstown Light and Heat Company of Washington County shall furnish to this Commission accurate and complete statements under oath setting forth the operating and other receipts and expenditures of said company for the six months ending June 30th, 1919, as soon after said date as possible, and thereafter for each six month period and for any other period which this Commission may hereafter require.

(3) That this Commission retains jurisdiction in this matter to the end that it may enter such further order or orders as may be found necessary in view of the results shown by any statement or statements filed with the Commission in compliance with the next preceding paragraph of this order.

ORDER No. 4645

In the Matter of

The Mortgage from the WASHINGTON RAILWAY AND ELECTRIC COMPANY to the MERCANTILE TRUST AND DEPOSIT COMPANY OF BALTIMORE, Dated December 2nd, 1918, Given to Secure an Issue of Five Million Dollars of Its General Mortgage Five Year Six Per Cent. Gold Bonds, In So Far As Said Mortgage Will Be a Lien Upon the Franchises of Said Railway Company Within the State of Maryland.

Before the

Public Service Commission of Maryland.

Case No. 1629.

The application of the Washington Railway and Electric Company filed with the Public Service Commission of Maryland in the above entitled matter, praying the approval of the Commission of including in its General Mortgage dated December 2nd, 1918, its franchises in the State of Maryland, in order that the said mortgage may be a lien thereon, coming on to be heard; and it appearing to the Commission that its jurisdiction in the matter now pending before it is limited to the consideration of whether its approval should be given to the assignment and transfer by way of mortgage of the franchises of the Company to operate within the State of Maryland; and it further appearing to the Commission that its approval of said assignment and transfer by way of mortgage is proper and convenient for the public service,

It Is, Therefore, This 28th day of January, in the year Nineteen Hundred and Nineteen, by the Public Service Commission of Maryland,

Ordered, That the approval and permission of the Public Service Commission of Maryland are hereby given to the Washington Railway and Electric Company, the petitioner herein, to assign and transfer by way of mortgage at the present time its franchises to operate so far as the same applies to operation within the State of Maryland,

And It Is Further Ordered, That this order be effective as of the first day of December, 1918.

ORDER No. 4646

In the Matter of

The Application of THE UNITED RAIL-
WAYS AND ELECTRIC COMPANY OF BAL-
TIMORE for Permission to Make a Uni-
form Increase of One Cent in Cash
Fares Heretofore Charged.

Before the

Public Service Commission
of Maryland.

Case No. 1568.

In the Matter of

The Complaint of the PUBLIC SERVICE
COMMISSION OF MARYLAND

vs.

THE UNITED RAILWAYS AND ELECTRIC
COMPANY OF BALTIMORE, With Respect
to the Fairness and Reasonableness of
Its Proposed General Increase in Its
Passenger Rates.

Before the

Public Service Commission
of Maryland.

Case No. 1583.

The United Railways and Electric Company of Baltimore having
heretofore filed with the Commission a petition praying for certain
modifications of Order No. 4608 passed in this cause on January 7th,
1919, it is upon consideration thereof, this 28th day of January, in
the year Nineteen Hundred and Nineteen, by the Public Service Commission of Maryland,

Ordered, That Sections (b), (c) and (d) of the first paragraph,
and the whole of the second paragraph of Order No. 4608 entered
herein by this Commission on January 7th, 1919, be and they are
hereby modified and amended so as to read as follows:

1. (b) Full fare and half fare continuous trip tickets, good as fare
on connecting lines, to be sold on the lines and between the points, on
the Company's Gorsuch Avenue, East Monument Street (Orangeville), Third and 8th Streets, Union Avenue, South Charles Street,
Walbrook-Hillsdale, Shore Line and Ferry Bar lines, as designated in
said schedule P. S. C. Md. No. 8, otherwise the regular fare to be collected between the points so designated.

1. (c) Four and one-half cents when paid by commutation tickets
sold for use on the first county fare zone between the points so designated in the schedule P. S. C. Md. No. 8, aforesaid, and five cents when
paid by commutation tickets sold for use on second and third county
fare zones, between the points so designated in said schedule, said
commutation tickets to be sold in the manner and subject to the con-

ditions set forth in said schedule with respect thereto, the full fare in each of said cases otherwise to be paid.

1.   (d) Four and one-half cents between Sparrows Point and Dundalk and four and one-half cents between Dundalk and Highlandtown when paid by employee's tickets from 20-trip books sold in lots to the Maryland Steel Company for distribution; five cents between Dundalk and Highlandtown and five cents between Highlandtown and city points, when paid by strip tickets sold in lots to the Central Foundry Company for distribution, and two and one-half cents on the Lakeside line when paid by tickets from 200-trip books sold to the landowners along such line, all such tickets to be subject to the conditions printed thereon and to the rules of the Company governing the use thereof, the full fare in each of said cases otherwise to be paid.

2. ' That from and after the hour of midnight on the thirty-first of December, Nineteen Hundred and Nineteen, said Company's right and privilege to charge and collect the increased fares authorized hereby shall cease and determine and said company shall thereupon put in force and effect and maintain until thereafter lawfully changed, the schedule of fares operative on the thirtieth of September, Nineteen Hundred and Eighteen, unless this Commission shall, in the meantime, by its Order in writing have extended or superseded this Order; PROVIDED, however, that if this Order has not been so extended or superseded and there shall be pending on December thirty-first, Nineteen Hundred and Nineteen, an application by said company filed before November thirtieth, Nineteen Hundred and Nineteen, for a continuance in whole or in part of the relief hereby granted, then the right to collect the fares authorized by this Order shall continue until the determination by the Commission of said pending proceeding; and PROVIDED, further, that in case of any proceeding hereafter for the right to charge and collect any fares in excess of those in effect on the thirtieth of September, Nineteen Hundred and Eighteen, the burden of proving the reasonableness of any such excess fare shall be and remain on said Company.

AND IT IS FURTHER Ordered, That except as hereby modified and amended Order No. 4608 aforesaid shall be and remain in full force and effect.

AND IT IS FURTHER Ordered, That a copy of this order be forthwith served upon the proper officers of the respondent, The United Railways and Electric Company of Baltimore, and that said Company, within ten days from the date of the service of such copy, advise this Commission in writing whether or not it will accept and abide by Order No. 4608 aforesaid as modified and amended by this Order.

ORDER No. 4652

In the Matter of

The Petition of EMMITSBURG RAILROAD COMPANY and WASHINGTON, BRANDYWINE AND POINT LOOKOUT RAILROAD COMPANY, by J. E. FAIRBANKS, Their Agent, for Permission Under Section 15 of the Public Service Commission Law to File and Publish on Less Than Statutory Notice Supplement to Storage Tariff P. S. C. Md. S. No. 1 Adding Said Emmitsburg Railroad Company and Said Washington, Brandywine and Point Lookout Railroad Company As Participating Carriers to Said Tariff P. S. C. Md. S. No. 1.	Before the Public Service Commission of Maryland. S. N. & R. Docket. Case No. 555.

The above mentioned petition having been received and filed, upon consideration thereof, it is this 1st day of February, 1919, by the Public Service Commission of Maryland,

Ordered, That permission be, and is hereby given, Emmitsburg Railroad Company and Washington, Brandywine and Point Lookout Railroad Company to file and publish on five days' notice to the Commission and the public, supplement to storage tariff P. S. C. Md. S. No. 1 adding said Emmitsburg Railroad Company and said Washington, Brandywine and Point Lookout Railroad Company as participating carriers to said tariff P. S. C. Md. No. 1.

PROVIDED, Said supplement be filed with the Commission upon issuance of this Order, and published by posting as required by law, and that all copies of said supplement shall bear the following notation:

"Issued under special permission of the Public Service Commission of Maryland, Order No. 4652 of date February 1st, 1919."

ORDER No. 4655

In the Matter of

The Application of the WESTERN UNION TELEGRAPH COMPANY OF BALTIMORE CITY for an Order Permitting and Approving the Conveyance and Transfer of Its Property to the WESTERN UNION TELEGRAPH COMPANY.

Before the

Public Service Commission of Maryland.

Case No. 1630.

The petition of the Western Union Telegraph Company of Baltimore City, a corporation organized under the laws of the State of Maryland, for an order of the Commission permitting and approving the transfer and conveyance by it of all of its poles, wires and other property to the Western Union Telegraph Company, a corporation organized under the laws of the State of New York, coming on to be heard after due notice published in compliance with this Commission's Order No. 4640 passed January 27th, 1919, and it being the opinion and finding of the Commission after hearing that the transfer and conveyance for which the Commission's permission and approval are asked are necessary and convenient for the public service,

IT Is, THEREFORE, This 3rd day of February, in the year Nineteen Hundred and Nineteen, by the Public Service Commission of Maryland,

Ordered, That the permission and approval of this Commission are hereby granted to Western Union Telegraph Company of Baltimore City to transfer and convey, and to Western Union Telegraph Company to accept and acquire, all of the poles, wires and other property of the said Western Union Telegraph Company of Baltimore City.

ORDER No. 4656

In the Matter of

The Application of THE BALTIMORE AND OHIO RAILROAD COMPANY for Authority to Issue $20,000,000.00 of Refunding and General Mortgage Bonds.

Before the

Public Service Commission of Maryland.

Case No. 1543.

WHEREAS, This Commission on June 26th, 1918, entered an order approving the issue and sale or pledge of $20,000,000.00 of the Refunding and General Mortgage Bonds of The Baltimore and Ohio Railroad Company, said bonds to be issued as a part of Series A bearing interest at the rate of 5% per annum, none of which bonds have been issued, and said company desires to have said order amended so as to permit it to issue said bonds as a part of Series B bearing interest at the rate of 6% per annum, and the Commission is of opinion that, in view of the higher rates of interest generally prevailing, such application should be granted and that the issue of such bonds is reasonably required for the purposes of said corporation,

IT IS, THEREFORE, This 3rd day of February, in the year Nineteen Hundred and Nineteen, by the Public Service Commission of Maryland,

𝔒𝔯𝔡𝔢𝔯𝔢𝔡, That the issue and sale or pledge of $20,000,000.00 of said Refunding and General Mortgage Bonds as a part of Series B bearing interest at the rate of 6% per annum, in lieu of the issue of said bonds as a part of Series A bearing interest at the rate of 5% per annum; the coupon bonds of said Series B to be dated February 1st, 1919; all bonds to mature December 1st, 1995; interest to be payable semi-annually on February 1st and August 1st of each year, and to be redeemable on or after June 1st, 1925, at a premium of 5%, is hereby approved.

ORDER No. 4657

In the Matter of	Before the
The Application of THE BALTIMORE AND OHIO RAILROAD COMPANY for Authority to Issue $10,284,384.63 of Its Refunding and General Mortgage Bonds, Series A.	Public Service Commission of Maryland. Case No. 1460.

WHEREAS, This Commission on January 24th, 1918, entered an order approving the issue and sale or pledge of $10,284,384.63 of the Refunding and General Mortgage Bonds of The Baltimore and Ohio Railroad Company, said bonds to be issued as a part of Series A bearing interest at the rate of 5% per annum, and said company desires to have said bonds canceled and other bonds issued in exchange therefor bearing interest at the rate of 6% per annum, and the Commission is of opinion that, in view of the higher rates of interest generally prevailing, such application should be granted and that the issue of such bonds is reasonably required for the purposes of said corporation,

IT IS, THEREFORE, This 3rd day of February, in the year Nineteen Hundred and Nineteen, by the Public Service Commission of Maryland,

𝔒𝔯𝔡𝔢𝔯𝔢𝔡, That the application of The Baltimore and Ohio Railroad Company to have said $10,284,384.63 of its Refunding and General Mortgage Bonds, Series A, canceled, and a like or equivalent aggregate principal amount of Refunding and General Mortgage Bonds, Series B, issued in exchange therefor bearing interest at the rate of 6% per annum; the coupon bonds of said Series B to be dated February 1st, 1919; all bonds to mature December 1st, 1995; interest to be payable semi-annually on February 1st and August 1st of each year, and to be redeemable on or after June 1st, 1925, at a premium of 5%, is hereby approved.

ORDER No. 4658

In the Matter of	Before the
The Application of SALISBURY LIGHT, HEAT AND POWER COMPANY for Authority to Issue $47,000.00 Par Value of Its Refunding Mortgage Bonds.	Public Service Commission of Maryland. Case No. 1625.

WHEREAS, The Salisbury Light, Heat and Power Company, a corporation organized and existing under the laws of the State of Maryland, has applied to this Commission for authority to issue its Thirty-Six Year Six Per Centum Refunding Mortgage Gold Bonds of the aggregate principal amount of Ninety-two Thousand Five Hundred Dollars ($92,500.00), being part of a total authorized issue of Five Hundred Thousand Dollars ($500,000.00) secured by mortgage or deed of trust dated October 1st, 1918, upon the property, rights and franchises of the said Salisbury Light, Heat and Power Company to Philadelphia Trust Company, Trustee, a copy of which mortgage or deed of trust is filed in these proceedings, and of the bonds so issued to deliver to The Eastern Shore Gas and Electric Company, a corporation organized and existing under the laws of the State of Delaware, bonds of the aggregate principal amount of Forty-seven Thousand Dollars ($47,000.00), in exchange for Six Per Centum First Mortgage and Collateral Trust Bonds of said The Eastern Shore Gas and Electric Company of like principal amount, and to sell the bonds so obtained in exchange at not less than 86% of the par value thereof, the proceeds from the sale of said bonds to be used for the discharge or lawful refunding of said company's obligations incurred in making betterments, improvements and additions to its plant and distributing system and for the improvement and maintenance of its service since May 1st, 1915, as more particularly set forth and described in petition herein, and to issue the remaining bonds of the aggregate principal amount of Forty-five Thousand Five Hundred Dollars ($45,500.00) when and as needed for the purpose of refunding bonds of the applicant of like aggregate principal amount dated December 2nd, 1901, payable December 1st, 1921, bearing interest at rate of Five Per Centum per annum, now outstanding, and

WHEREAS, The application having come on to be heard on January 28th, 1919, after due notice published in accordance with this Commission's Order No. 4627 passed January 20th, 1919, and the hearing having been continued to February 3rd, 1919, upon request of the applicant, on which date the application was duly heard, and it being the opinion and finding of the Commission after investigation that the use of the capital to be secured by the issue, exchange and sale of said bonds is reasonably required for the purposes of said corparation, to wit: the discharge or lawful refunding of its obligations incurred in making expenditures for proper corporate capital purposes,

IT IS, THEREFORE, This 3rd day of February, in the year Nineteen Hundred and Nineteen, by the Public Service Commission of Maryland,

𝔒𝔯𝔡𝔢𝔯𝔢𝔡, 1. That the issue by the Salisbury Light, Heat and Power Company of its Thirty-six Year Six Per Centum Refunding Mortgage. Gold Bonds of the aggregate principal amount of Ninety-two Thousand Five Hundred Dollars ($92,500.00), and the delivery of said bonds of the aggregate principal amount of Forty-seven Thousand. Dollars ($47,000.00) to The Eastern Shore Gas and Electric Company in exchange for Six Per Centum First Mortgage and Collateral Trust Bonds of said The Eastern Shore Gas and Electric Company of like principal amount and the sale of the bonds so obtained in exchange, at not less than 86% of the par value thereof, for the purposes in said application set forth, the remaining bonds of the aggregate principal amount of Forty-five Thousand Five Hundred Dollars ($45,500.00) to be issued when and as needed for the purpose of refunding bonds of the applicant of like aggregate principal amount, dated December 2nd, 1901, payable December 1st, 1921, bearing interest at rate of Five Per Centum per annum, now outstanding, be and the same is hereby authorized and approved.

2. That the said Salisbury Light, Heat and Power Company shall. make reports to this Commission, duly verified by affidavits, upon the issue and exchange of its bonds, authorized and approved as aforesaid, or any part thereof, and the sale of the bonds so obtained in exchange, or any part thereof, the fact of such issue, exchange and sale or sales, the terms and conditions thereof, the amount realized therefrom, and the obligations of said company refunded with the bonds issued under the authority of this order or with the proceeds of the sale or sales of said bonds or with the proceeds of the sale or sales of the bonds secured in exchange for the bonds of the applicant company.

ORDER No. 4659

<table>
<tr><td>In the Matter of</td><td>Before the</td></tr>
<tr><td>The Application of THE PENINSULAR LIGHT AND POWER COMPANY for Authority to Issue $2,000.00 Par Value of Its First Mortgage Bonds.</td><td>Public Service Commission of Maryland.

Case No. 1626.</td></tr>
</table>

WHEREAS, The Peninsular Light and Power Company, a corporation organized and existing under the laws of the State of Maryland, has applied to this Commission for authority to issue its Thirty-six Year Six Per Centum First Mortgage Gold Bonds of the aggregate principal amount of Two Thousand Dollars ($2,000.00), being part of a total authorized issue of Two Hundred Thousand Dollars ($200,000.00) secured by mortgage or deed of trust dated October 1st, 1918, upon the property, rights and franchises of said The Peninsular Light and Power Company to Philadelphia Trust Company, Trustee, copy of which mortgage or deed of trust is filed in these proceedings, and to deliver said bonds to The Eastern Shore Gas and Electric Company, a corporation organized and existing under the laws of the State of Delaware, in exchange for Six Per Centum First Mortgage and Collateral Trust Bonds of said The Eastern Shore Gas and Electric Company of like principal amount, and to sell the bonds so obtained in exchange at not less than 86% of the par value thereof, the proceeds from the sale of said bonds to be used for the discharge or lawful refunding of said company's obligations incurred in making betterments, improvements and additions to its plant and distributing system, and for the improvement and maintenance of its service since July 1st, 1916, as more particularly set forth and described in petition herein, and

WHEREAS, The application having come on to be heard on January 28th, 1919, after due notice published in accordance with this Commission's Order No. 4628 passed January 20th, 1919, and the hearing having been continued to February 3rd, 1919, upon request of the applicant, on which date the application was duly heard, and it being the opinion and finding of the Commission after investigation that the use of the capital to be secured by the issue, exchange and sale of said bonds is reasonably required for the purposes of said corporation, to wit: the discharge or lawful refunding of its obligations incurred in making expenditures for proper corporate capital purposes,

IT IS, THEREFORE, This 3rd day of February, in the year Nineteen Hundred and Nineteen, by the Public Service Commission of Maryland,

Ordered, 1. That the issue by The Peninsular Light and Power Company of its Thirty-six Year Six Per Centum First Mortgage Gold Bonds of the aggregate principal amount of Two Thousand Dollars ($2,000.00), and the delivery of said bonds to The Eastern Shore Gas and Electric Company in exchange for Six Per Centum First Mortgage and Collateral Trust Bonds of said The Eastern Shore Gas and Electric Company of like principal amount, and the sale of the bonds so .obtained in exchange at not less than 86% of the par value thereof, for the purposes in said application set forth, be and the same is hereby authorized and approved.

2. That said The Peninsular Light and Power Company shall make reports to this Commission, duly verified by affidavits, upon the issue and exchange of its bonds, authorized and approved as aforesaid, or any part thereof, and the sale of the bonds so obtained in exchange, or any part thereof, the fact of such issue, exchange and sale or sales, the terms and conditions thereof, the amount realized therefrom, and the obligations of said company refunded with the proceeds of the sale or sales of the bonds secured in exchange for the bonds of the applicant company.

ORDER No. 4663

In the Matter of	Before the
The Petition of THE CAPITAL TRACTION COMPANY for Permission Under Section 15 of the Public Service Commission Law to File and Publish on Less Than Statutory Notice Supplement No. 1 to Petitioner's Passenger Rate Schedule P. S. C. Md. No. 2.	Public Service Commission of Maryland. S. N. & R. Docket. Case No 556.

The above mentioned petition having been received and filed, upon consideration thereof, it is this 8th day of February, 1919, by the Public Service Commission of Maryland,

Ordered, That permission be, and is hereby given, The Capital Traction Company to file and publish on one day's notice to the Commission and the public, Supplement No. 1 to petitioner's passenger rate schedule P. S. C. Md. No. 2,

PROVIDED, Said supplement be filed with the Commission upon issuance of this Order, and published by posting as required by law, and that all copies of said supplement shall bear the following notation:

"Issued under special permission of the Public Service Commission of Maryland, Order No. 4663 of date February 8th, 1919."

ORDER No. 4665

In the Matter of

The Application of THE DORCHESTER WATER COMPANY, a Corporation Under the Laws of Maryland, for Authority to Issue Additional Capital Stock to the Amount of $12,800.00 Par Value for the Purpose of Making Extensions and Improvements to Its Property.	Before the Public Service Commission of Maryland. Case No. 1632.

WHEREAS, The Dorchester Water Company, a corporation organized and existing under the laws of the State of Maryland, has applied to this Commission for authority to issue its capital stock in the amount of Twelve Thousand Eight Hundred Dollars ($12,800.00), including capital stock in the amount of Twenty-one Hundred and Ten Dollars ($2,110.00) heretofore authorized by this Commission but not required or issued by the applicant for the purposes heretofore authorized, the proceeds from the sale thereof to be used to reimburse said company for expenditures incurred in the acquisition of property, the construction, completion, extension and improvement of its plant and distributing system, and for the improvement and maintenance of its service since January 1st, 1915, and for the acquisition of property, the construction, completion, extension and improvement of its plant and distributing system, and for the improvement and maintenance of its service, as more particularly set forth and described in petition herein, and

WHEREAS, The application having this day come on to be heard after due notice published in accordance with this Commission's Order No. 4651 passed January 30th, 1919, and it being the opinion and finding of the Commission after investigation that the use of the capital to be secured by the issue and sale of said stock is reasonably required for the purposes of said corporation,

IT IS, THEREFORE, This 12th day of February, in the year Nineteen Hundred and Nineteen, by the Public Service Commission of Maryland,

ORDERED, 1. That the issue and sale at par for cash by said The Dorchester Water Company of its capital stock in the amount of Twelve Thousand Eight Hundred Dollars ($12,800.00) be and the same is hereby authorized and approved.

2. That said The Dorchester Water Company shall make reports to this Commission, duly verified by affidavits, as follows:

(a) Upon the sale for cash of its stock, authorized and approved as aforesaid, or any part thereof, the fact of such sale or sales, the terms and conditions thereof, and the amount realized therefrom.

(b) At the termination of each and every period of six months from the date of this order, the disposition and use made of the proceeds of said stock, and the facts and circumstances as to the property acquired and the construction, completion, extension and improvement of its facilities, and the improvement and maintenance of its service.

ORDER No. 4666

In the Matter of

The Application of the IDLEWILD ELEC-
TRIC LIGHT, HEAT AND POWER COM-
PANY OF FEDERALSBURG, MARYLAND, for
Authority to Issue Its First Mortgage
Bonds to the Amount of $6,000 Par
Value.

Before the

Public Service Commission
of Maryland.

Case No. 1633.

WHEREAS, The Idlewild Electric Light, Heat and Power Company
of Federalsburg, Maryland, a corporation organized and existing
under the laws of the State of Maryland, has applied to this Commission for authority to issue its Forty Year Six Per Centum First Mortgage Gold Bonds of the aggregate principal amount of Six Thousand
Dollars ($6,000.00), being part of a total authorized issue of One
Hundred and Fifty Thousand Dollars ($150,000.00) secured by mort-
gage or deed of trust dated April 1st, 1916, upon the property, rights
and franchises of the said Idlewild Electric Light, Heat and Power
Company of Federalsburg, Maryland, to Philadelphia Trust Company,
Trustee, copy of which mortgage or deed of trust has heretofore been
filed with this Commission in Case No. 1106, and to deliver said bonds
to The Eastern Shore Gas and Electric Company, a corporation organized and existing under the laws of the State of Delaware, in exchange
for Six Per Centum First Mortgage and Collateral Trust Bonds of
said The Eastern Shore Gas and Electric Company of like principal
amount, and to sell the bonds so obtained in exchange at not less than
Eighty-six Per Centum of the par value thereof, the proceeds from the
sale of said bonds to be used for the discharge or lawful refunding of
said company's obligations incurred in making betterments, improvements and additions to its plant and distributing system and for the
improvement and maintenance of its service since December 1st, 1915,
as more particularly set forth and described in petition herein, and

WHEREAS, The application having this day come on to be heard,
after due notice published in accordance with this Commission's Order
No. 4653 passed February 1st, 1919, and it being the opinion and
finding of the Commission after investigation that the use of the
capital to be secured by the issue, exchange and sale of said bonds is
reasonably required for the purposes of said corporation, to wit: the
discharge or lawful refunding of its obligations incurred in making
expenditures for proper corporate capital purposes,

IT IS, THEREFORE, This 12th day of February, in the year Nineteen
Hundred and Nineteen, by the Public Service Commission of Maryland,

ORDERED, 1. That the issue by Idlewild Electric Light, Heat and
Power Company of Federalsburg, Maryland, of its Forty Year Six
Per Centum First Mortgage Gold Bonds of the aggregate principal

amount of Six Thousand Dollars ($6,000.00), and the delivery of said bonds to The Eastern Shore Gas and Electric Company in exchange for Six Per Centum First Mortgage and Collateral Trust Bonds of said The Eastern Shore Gas and Electric Company of like principal amount and the sale of the bonds so obtained in exchange at not less than Eighty-six Per Centum of the par value thereof, for the purposes in said application set forth, be and the same is hereby authorized and approved.

2. That the said Idlewild Electric Light, Heat and Power Company of Federalsburg, Maryland, shall make reports to this Commission, duly verified by affidavits, upon the issue and exchange of its bonds, authorized and approved as aforesaid, or any part thereof, and the sale of the bonds so obtained in exchange, or any part thereof, the fact of such issue, exchange and sale or sales, the terms and conditions thereof, the amount realized therefrom, and the obligations of said company refunded with the proceeds of the sale or sales of the bonds secured in exchange for the bonds of the applicant company.

ORDER No. 4667

In the Matter of	Before the
The Application of CAMBRIDGE GAS, ELECTRIC LIGHT AND POWER COMPANY for Authority to Issue Its First and Refunding Mortgage Bonds to the Amount of $17,000 Par Value.	Public Service Commission of Maryland. Case No. 1634.

WHEREAS, The Cambridge Gas, Electric Light and Power Company, a corporation organized and existing under the laws of the State of Maryland, has applied to this Commission for authority to issue its Thirty-nine Year Six Per Centum First and Refunding Mortgage Gold Bonds of the aggregate principal amount of Seventeen Thousand Dollars ($17,000.00), being part of a total authorized issue of Three Hundred and Fifty Thousand Dollars ($350,000.00) secured by mortgage or deed of trust dated June 1st, 1916, upon the property, rights and franchises of the said Cambridge Gas, Electric Light and Power Company to Philadelphia Trust Company, Trustee, a copy of which mortgage or deed of trust has heretofore been filed with this Commission in Case No. 1127, and to deliver said bonds to The Eastern Shore Gas and Electric Company, a corporation organized and existing under the laws of the State of Delaware, in exchange for Six Per Centum First Mortgage and Collateral Trust Bonds of said The Eastern Shore Gas and Electric Company of like principal amount, and to sell the bonds so obtained in exchange at not less than 86 Per Centum of the par value thereof, the proceeds from the sale of said bonds to be used for the discharge or lawful refunding of said company's obligations incurred in making betterments, improvements and additions to its plant and distributing system and for the improvement and maintenance of its service since May 1st, 1915, as more particularly set forth and described in petition herein, and ·

WHEREAS, The application having this day come on to be heard, after due notice published in accordance with this Commission's Order No. 4654 passed February 1st, 1919, and it being the opinion and finding of the Commission after investigation that the use of the capital to be secured by the issue, exchange and sale of said bonds is reasonably required for the purposes of said corporation, to wit: the discharge or lawful refunding of its obligations incurred in making expenditures for proper corporate capital purposes,

IT IS, THEREFORE, This 12th day of February, in the year Nineteen Hundred and Nineteen, by the Public Service Commission of Maryland,

Ordered, 1. That the issue by Cambridge Gas, Electric Light and Power Company of its Thirty-nine Year Six Per Centum First Mortgage and Refunding Gold Bonds of the aggregate principal amount of Seventeen Thousand Dollars ($17,000.00), and the delivery of said bonds to The Eastern Shore Gas and Electric Company in exchange for Six Per Centum First Mortgage and Collateral Trust Bonds of said The Eastern Shore Gas and Electric Company of like principal amount and the sale of the bonds so obtained in exchange at not less than Eighty-six Per Centum of the par value thereof, for the purposes in said application set forth, be and the same is hereby authorized and approved.

2. That the said Cambridge Gas, Electric Light and Power Company shall make reports to this Commission, duly verified by affidavits, upon the issue and exchange of its bonds, authorized and approved as aforesaid, or any part thereof, and the sale of the bonds so obtained in exchange, or any part thereof, the fact of such issue, exchange and sale or sales, the terms and conditions thereof, the amount realized therefrom, and the obligations of said company refunded with the proceeds of the sale or sales of the bonds secured in exchange for the bonds of the applicant company.

ORDER No. 4669

In the Matter of

The Complaint of the Town of Kensington, By Its Mayor and Council,

vs.

Capital Traction Company of
Washington.

Before the

Public Service Commission
of Maryland.

Case No. 1599.

Whereas, This case involving the reasonableness of the fares established by the respondent, The Capital Traction Company, by its rate
schedule P. S. C. Md. No. 2, effective November 1st, 1918, being at
issue upon complaint and answer on file and having been duly heard
and submitted by the parties and the complainant and other protestants, by their attorneys of record, having at the hearing of this case
at Chevy Chase, Maryland, on February 6th, 1919, expressed themselves as satisfied with the modified rates of fare which the respondent
at that time offered to establish and which said modified rates of fare
were thereafter filed with the Commission on February 8th, 1919, and
made effective February 10th, 1919,

It Is, Therefore, This 13th day of February, in the year Nineteen
Hundred and Nineteen, by the Public Service Commission of Maryland,

Ordered, That the above entitled case be and it is hereby entered
as satisfied and closed.

ORDER No. 4670

In the Matter of

The Application of The Hagerstown
And Frederick Railway Company for
Authority to Issue $100,000.00, Par
Value, of Its First and Refunding
Bonds.

Before the

Public Service Commission
of Maryland.

Case No. 1635.

The above entitled matter having this day come on for hearing after
due notice published in compliance with this Commission's Order No.
4664, passed February 10th, 1919, and it being the opinion and finding
of the Commission after due hearing that the issue by the applicant,
The Hagerstown and Frederick Railway Company, of $100,000.00 face

amount of its First and Refunding Mortgage Thirty-Year Sinking
Fund Gold Bonds, Six Per Cent. Series, is reasonably required for the
purposes of said corporation,

It Is, THEREFORE, This 14th day of February, in the year Nineteen
Hundred and Nineteen, by the Public Service Commission of Maryland,

Ordered, That the applicant, The Hagerstown and Frederick Railway Company, be and it is hereby authorized to issue and deliver not
exceeding $100,000.00, face amount, of its First and Refunding Mort-
gage Thirty-Year Sinking Fund Gold Bonds, Six Per Cent. Series, and
to use the same for collateral purposes as mentioned in said petition,
and with the further right to the said Company to sell and dispose of
the said bonds, or any part thereof, at any time, at not less than 95%
of the face value of the same; the proceeds to be applied as in said
petition set forth, the Commission having determined that the use of
the capital to be secured by the issue of said bonds is reasonably required for the purposes of said company, to wit: the lawful discharge
and refunding of its obligations incurred in making expenditures for
proper corporate capital purposes.

It Is FURTHER Ordered, That The Hagerstown and Frederick
Railway Company report to this Commission the fact of the issuance
and delivery of said bonds, and if the same are sold, the amount
thereof so sold and the price obtained therefor.

OPINION

In the Matter of	Before the
The Complaint of F. G. HEATON, ET AL.,	Public Service Commission
vs.	of Maryland.
WASHINGTON AND ROCKVILLE RAILWAY COMPANY.	Case No. 1622.

Appearances:
> JOSEPH S. GOLDSMITH, ESQ., Assistant General Counsel of the
> Commission.
> MORGAN H. BEACH, ESQ., representing the complainants.
> S. R. BOWEN, ESQ., representing the respondent.

By the Commission.   Filed February 24th, 1919.

On November 6th, 1919, there was filed with the Commission a letter
signed by Mr. Heaton, advising that a meeting of residents of Mont-
gomery County, Maryland, had been held at Bethesda, Maryland, on

the night of November 4th, and that Mr. Heaton had been authorized and instructed by those present at said meeting to file a protest with the Public Service Commission of Maryland against the increase in fares proposed by the Washington and Rockville Railway Company (in error stated as the Washington Railway and Electric Company) and that the Commission be requested to withhold its approval of the increased fares until such time as the protestants had been given opportunity to appear before the Commission in support of their protests.

Under the terms of the Public Service Commission Law common carriers are not required to obtain the approval of the Commission before making changes, either increases or decreases, in existing rates and fares except where the rates or fares it is desired to change have themselves been established by the Commission. Section 15 of the Public Service Commission Law provides in part as follows:—

> "Unless the Commission otherwise orders, no change shall be made in any rate, fare or charge, or joint rate, fare or charge, which shall have been filed and published by a common carrier in compliance with the requirements of this Act, except after thirty days' notice to the Commission and publication for thirty days, as required by Section 25 of this Act, which shall plainly state the changes proposed to be made in the schedule then in force, and the time when the changed rate, fare or charge will go into effect, and all proposed changes shall be shown by printing, filing and publishing new schedules, or shall be plainly indicated upon the schedules in force at the time and kept open to public inspection. The Commission, for good cause shown, may allow changes in rates without requiring the thirty days' notice and publication herein provided for by duly filing and publishing, in such manner as it may direct, an order specifying the change so made and the time when it shall take effect; all such changes shall be immediately indicated upon its schedule by the common carrier."

Acting under authority of the above provision of the law, the Washington and Rockville Railway Company on October 30th, 1918, filed with the Commission its tariff schedule P. S. C. Md. No. 3 to become effective December 1st, 1918, canceling tariff schedule P. S. C. Md. No. 2 of that company. Both schedules were concurred in by the Georgetown and Tennalltown Railway Company, under concurrence of that company filed with the Commission as required by the Public Service Commission Act. The Commission is powerless to suspend the application of tariffs publishing increased rates, fares and charges filed with it pending the determination of complaints and investigations involving the reasonableness thereof, and to remedy the situation in this respect the Commission has endeavored to have an amendment

enacted at each session of the General Assembly since the creation
of the Commission giving it the power of suspension, but has been
unsuccessful in its efforts. Consequently the increased fares published in tariff P. S. C. Md. No. 3 became operative on December 1st,
1918.

A number of other patrons wrote to the Commission protesting
against the increased fares, some of which complaints also involve
the adequacy of the service of the respondent. One effect of the
aforesaid schedule P. S. C. Md. No. 3 was to discontinue the sale.of
monthly commutation books, containing 26 round trips, and family
commutation books containing 40 single trip tickets, theretofore sold
between certain Maryland points, and to very materially increase the
rates charged for monthly school commutation books containing 22
round trips, the rates for which tickets, as well as for single trip
tickets, had been prescribed by the General Assembly of Maryland,
sessions of 1910 and 1912. The right of the railway company to
increase the fares theretofore established by the General Assembly
was questioned by certain of the protestants and the Commission
thereupon referred the matter to its General Counsel for advice respecting this phase of the situation, and on November 7th, 1918,
General Counsel Bruce filed his Opinion No. 369, wherein he held that:

> "In my opinion, both of these enactments (1910 and 1912)
> are unconstitutional and void, so far as they attempt to
> prescribe fare zones and to fix rates for the Railway Com-
> pany, because they violate the provisions of Section 33 of
> Article 3 of the Maryland State Constitution, which declare:
> 'And the General Assembly shall pass no special law for
> any case for which provision has been made by any existing
> general law.'
> When the Act of 1910 was approved, on April 11th, 1910,
> the Public Service Commission Law, which was approved on
> April 5th, 1910, was already on the statute book. . . ."

The answers of the respondent not being satisfactory, the case was
set for hearing at Bethesda, Maryland, and the Assistant General
Counsel of the Commission was assigned to represent and assist the
complainants in the presentation and prosecution of their complaint.
Hearing was held on February 4th, 1919, and opportunity given all
persons to present such testimony and evidence as they might deem
desirable.

The line of the respondent from District Line to Rockville, Maryland, is approximately 10½ miles in length, being divided into four
zones, the cash fare for each zone having been increased from 5 cents
to 6 cents on December 1st, last. The increase on school tickets made
effective on same date was as follows:

| | Rates Per Book (22 Round Trips) | | Increase | |
	Former	Present	Amount	Per Cent.
Through one zone......$ .93		$1.85	$ .92	100
" two zones..... 1.87		2.38	.51	27
" three zones... 2.80		3.56	.76	27
" four zones.... 3.74		4.75	1.01	27

A statement just submitted by the respondent in compliance with request of the Commission shows that of a total of 56 monthly school commutation tickets sold during the past month 48 were for use in one zone, four for use in two zones, one for use in three zones and three for use in four zones. From this it will be seen that the rate charged for these books was increased almost four times as much for travel in one zone, where almost 90% of the books are used, as were the rates for travel in two, three or four zones. At the hearing a large amount of testimony was directed against the increase in the rates charged for these school tickets. In point of fact, aside from the travel of those using school tickets, there is comparatively little Maryland intrastate traffic moving over the line of the respondent, it being estimated that 95% of the total traffic is to and from Washington, D. C., and consequently interstate in character. The Interstate Commerce Commission has recently permitted the respondent to increase its rates of fare on such traffic, the increased interstate fares becoming effective on January 1st, 1919. The interstate one-way fares are based upon the Maryland zone fares, plus 5 cents to cover transportation within the District of Columbia. For example, the intrastate fare between the District Line and Rockville (through four fare zones) is 24 cents, and the interstate fare between Washington, D. C., and Rockville is 29 cents. If the Commission should attempt to reduce the zone fares in Maryland the result would be to defeat the through rate of fare permitted by the Interstate Commerce Commission, and thus create a situation similar to that in the so-called "Shreveport Case" (Houston East and West Texas Railway Company and Houston and Shreveport Railroad Company, et al., vs. United States Interstate Commerce Commission, et al., 234 U. S. 342) in which case it was held that the railroad companies were not required to observe the intrastate rates established by the state authorities where to do so would result in discrimination in favor of intrastate traffic and against interstate traffic. Practically the same situation was presented to the Commission in the complaint of F. L. Hawley vs. City and Suburban Railway of Washington, D. C., Case No. 708, (P. S. C. Md. Reports, Vol. V, p. 598) and the Commission concurred in the opinion of its General Counsel filed in that case wherein he held that:

"In my judgment, the Public Service Commission of Maryland is powerless to impose four fare zones only on an intrastate passenger between the town of Laurel and the boundary of the District of Columbia, when the Interstate Commerce Commission imposes five fare zones between these termini on a passenger bound from the town of Laurel to the city of Washington within the District of Columbia. A higher rate payable by an interstate passenger and a lower rate payable by an intrastate passenger for one and the same service rendered under substantially the same conditions cannot, in my opinion, co-exist. The case is one where, as in the Shreveport Case, the interstate and intrastate transactions of the carrier are so related that the government of one involves the control of the other and it is the Interstate Commerce Commission and not the Public Service Commission of Maryland that is entitled to prescribe the final and determining rule."

While that particular case involved the number of fare zones, rather than the rate of fare per zone, the underlying principle in the two cases is the same.

In view of the law laid down by the decisions in these cases, it is manifest that it would be a vain thing for this Commission to now undertake to establish intrastate one-way fares on a basis lower than that obtaining at the present time, and the Commission will therefore not pass upon the reasonableness of these fares in the present case. While the present interstate fares have been permitted by the Interstate Commerce Commission, their reasonableness has not been passed upon by that body, and should they subsequently be held to be unreasonable by the Interstate Commerce Commission in an appropriate proceeding before that tribunal, this Commission will then be in a position to make such revision of the Maryland intrastate fares as may seem proper in the light of such decision.

The respondent filed with the Commission a statement showing that the ratio of operating expenses and taxes to operating revenues had increased from 83.05% in 1914, 84.79% in 1915 and 93.38% in 1916, to 103.40% in 1918, the first eight months of each of these years being used in this comparison. Testimony was also introduced at the hearing tending to show the increased costs of labor and materials which have been encountered by the respondent in the operation of its line of railway.

The Commission finds that the rates established by the respondent's tariff P. S. C. Md. No. 3, effective December 1st, 1918, for monthly school commutation books are unjust, unreasonable and excessive, and will require the respondent to establish, on or before March 1st, 1919, rates for these tickets not more than 25% in excess of those in effect immediately prior to December 1st, 1918.

With respect to the service being furnished by the respondent, the main complaint was with respect to that furnished during the morning and evening rush hours, and on Sundays. Since the hearing the respondent has advised the Commission that additional cars will be operated during the periods complained of, and the Commission believes that this additional service will materially improve the conditions and to a large extent eliminate the cause of complaint.

An order will be passed in accordance with the conclusions herein contained.

ORDER No. 4686

In the Matter of	Before the
The Complaint of F. G. HEATON, ET AL.,	Public Service Commission
vs.	of Maryland.
WASHINGTON AND ROCKVILLE RAILWAY COMPANY.	Case No. 1622.

This case being at issue upon complaint and answer on file and having been duly heard and submitted by the parties and full investigation of the matters and things involved having been had and the Commission, on the date hereof, having rendered and filed an opinion containing its findings of fact and conclusions therein, which opinion is hereby referred to and made part hereof,

IT IS, THEREFORE, This 24th day of February, in the year Nineteen Hundred and Nineteen, by the Public Service Commission of Maryland,

𝔒𝔯𝔡𝔢𝔯𝔢𝔡, (1) That the rates charged under the tariff P. S. C. Md. No. 3 of the Washington and Rockville Railway Company, filed with this Commission on October 30th, 1918, and effective December 1st, 1918, for monthly school commutation books be, and they are hereby declared to be unreasonable, unjust and excessive, and the said respondent is hereby directed and required to establish and make effective on or before March 1st, 1919, rates for the said monthly school commutation books not more than 25% in excess of the rates in effect for said books immediately prior to December 1st, 1918.

(2) That with respect to the other matters and things complained of, the complaint be and it is hereby dismissed.

(3) That this order shall become effective on March 1st, 1919, and remain in effect for a period of two (2) years thereafter, unless earlier modified or abrogated by this Commission, and that a certified copy thereof be forthwith served upon the proper official of the respondent company and that said company notify the Commission in writing within five (5) days of the date of service of such copy whether it will abide by and obey the same.

ORDER No. 4698

In the Matter of	Before the
The Complaint of B. CAVALIER	Public Service Commission
vs.	of Maryland.
THE ARTESIAN WATER COMPANY.	Case No. 1638.

The above cause having been previously set for hearing and having been heard on February 27th, 1919, when both parties were represented, and it being the opinion and finding of the Commission that the amount of water registered by meter and billed the complainant by the respondent actually passed through the meter and was used by said complainant or wasted by reason of leaks in the fixtures upon the premises occupied by the complainant, but that said consumption during the two quarters ended December 31st, 1918, should be prorated equally between said quarters and the bills heretofore rendered corrected accordingly.

IT IS, THEREFORE, This 4th day of March, in the year Nineteen Hundred and Nineteen, by the Public Service Commission of Maryland,

ORDERED, (1) That bills rendered the complainant by the respondent for water consumed during the two quarters ended December 31st, 1918, shall be adjusted on the basis of equal consumption of water in each of said quarters.

(2) That with respect to the other matters and things complained of, the complaint be and it is hereby dismissed.

ORDER No. 4807

In the Matter of	Before the
The Complaint of UNITED STATES HOUSING CORPORATION	Public Service Commission of Maryland.
vs.	Case No. 1636.
HAVRE DE GRACE ELECTRIC COMPANY.	

Upon the Order of the Solicitors for the Complainant filed herein, it is this tenth day of March, 1919, by the Public Service Commission of Maryland,

𝔒𝔯𝔡𝔢𝔯𝔢𝔡, That this Complaint be and the same is hereby dismissed.

NOTE—Order No. 4807 should be Order No. 4707. This error was discovered too late for correction and all orders following Order No. 4706 are numbered 100 numbers in advance of what they should be.

ORDER No. 4809

In the Matter of	
The Application of THE CHESAPEAKE AND POTOMAC TELEPHONE COMPANY OF BALTIMORE CITY for the Approval of an Agreement Between It and the PRINCESS ANNE TELEPHONE COMPANY OF SOMERSET COUNTY for the Sale by the Latter to the Former of All Its Property, Real and Personal, and All Rights, Privileges and Franchises Situated in the Town of Princess Anne and Elsewhere in Somerset County, Maryland.	Before the. Public Service Commission of Maryland. Case No. 1639.

The application of The Chesapeake and Potomac Telephone Company of Baltimore City and of Princess Anne Telephone Company of Somerset County, both being corporations organized under the laws of the State of Maryland, filed with the Commission on February 27th, 1919, praying for an Order of the Commission approving the sale by the latter company and the purchase by the former company of all the property, real and personal, and all the rights, privileges and franchises of the said Princess Anne Telephone Company of Somerset County, for the sum of Eighteen Hundred Dollars ($1,800.00), upon the terms and conditions of the agreement between the said two companies dated February 14th, 1919, filed with said application, having this day come on to be heard after due notice published in accordance with this Commission's Order No. 4693 passed February 27th, 1919, and it being the opinion and finding of the Commission after due hearing that the things to which its permission and approval are prayed in the petition will be to the benefit and for the convenience and advantage of the general public and the public service,

IT IS, THEREFORE, This 12th day of March, in the year Nineteen Hundred and Nineteen, by the Public Service Commission of Maryland,

Ordered, That the approval, permission and authority of the Commission is hereby given to the sale by the Princess Anne Telephone Company of Somerset County and the purchase by The Chesapeake and Potomac Telephone Company of Baltimore City of all the property, real and personal, and all the rights, privileges and franchises of the said Princess Anne Telephone Company of Somerset County, at and for the sum of Eighteen Hundred Dollars ($1,800.00); and upon the other terms, conditions and stipulations set forth in the said agreement between the said two corporations, dated February 14th, 1919, copy of which agreement is filed in these proceedings.

ORDER No. 4817

In the Matter of	
The Complaint of FRANK VOGEL, GEORGE D. MYERLY, ET AL.,	Before the
	Public Service Commission of Maryland.
vs.	
THE UNITED RAILWAYS AND ELECTRIC COMPANY OF BALTIMORE.	Case No. 1641.

The above cause having been previously set for hearing and having been duly heard on the date hereof, when both parties were represented in person or by counsel, and it being the opinion and finding of the Commission that the respondent, The United Railways and Electric Company of Baltimore, should restore the stop at Nicoll Avenue and York Road on the York Road Line of respondent,

IT IS, THEREFORE, This 17th day of March, in the year Nineteen Hundred and Nineteen, by the Public Service Commission of Maryland,

Ordered, That The United Railways and Electric Company of Baltimore forthwith restore the stop at Nicoll Avenue and York Road, on its York Road Line.

AND IT IS FURTHER **Ordered,** That a copy of this Order be forthwith served upon the proper official of said The United Railways and Electric Company of Baltimore, and that said company notify this Commission within five days after the receipt of said copy whether or not it will accept and abide by this Order.

ORDER No. 4818

In the Matter of

The Application of THE CHESAPEAKE AND POTOMAC TELEPHONE COMPANY OF BALTIMORE CITY for the Approval of an Agreement Dated February 6th, 1919, Between It and EASTON UTILITIES COMMISSION for the Sale by the Former to the Latter of Three Poles Located in Easton, Talbot County, Maryland.

Before the

Public Service Commission of Maryland.

Case No. 1643.

The agreement or other written instrument evidencing the transaction in this case having been submitted to this Commission for the purpose of securing its consent to the consummation thereof and the Commission having determined that a hearing is unnecessary,

IT IS, THEREFORE, On this seventeenth day of March, in the year 1919, by the Public Service Commission of Maryland,

Ordered, That the consent of this Commission be and the same is hereby given to the disposition of the property described in said agreement, or other written instrument, evidencing the transaction in accordance with the terms outlined therein.

ORDER No. 4819

In the Matter of

The Joint Application of ARTESIAN WATER COMPANY and REALTY FINANCE CORPORATION for an Order Permitting and Approving the Purchase by the Former from the Latter and the Sale by the Latter to the Former of All of Its Property, Assets, Rights, etc., Also Permitting and Approving the Abandonment by the Latter of Any Franchises Now Owned or Exercised by It and at the Same Time Permitting The Artesian Water Company to Own Said Franchises and Exercise All Rights Thereunder.

Before the

Public Service Commission of Maryland.

Case No. 1642.

WHEREAS, The Artesian Water Company and The Realty Finance Corporation, both corporations organized under the laws of the State of Maryland, have applied to this Commission for an order permitting and approving the purchase by the former company from the latter company and the sale by the latter company to the former company of all of the property, assets, rights, etc., of The Realty Finance Corporation; and permitting and approving the abandonment by the latter company of any franchises now owned or exercised by it; and permitting said The Artesian Water Company to acquire said franchises and exercise all rights thereunder, and

WHEREAS, This case having this day come on to be heard after due notice published in accordance with this Commission's Order No. 4816 passed March 13th, 1919, and it being the opinion and finding of the Commission after due hearing that the things to which its permission and approval are asked are necessary and convenient for the public service,

IT Is, THEREFORE, This 20th day of March, in the year Nineteen Hundred and Nineteen, by the Public Service Commission of Maryland,

Ordered, That the approval, permission and authority of this Commission is hereby given to:

(1) The purchase by The Artesian Water Company and the sale by The Realty Finance Corporation of all of the property, assets, rights, etc., of said The Realty Finance Corporation, at and for the sum of Five Dollars ($5.00).

(2) The abandonment by The Realty Finance Corporation of any franchises now owned or exercised by it.

(3) The acquisition by The Artesian Water Company of any franchises now owned or exercised by The Realty Finance Corporation, and the exercise by said The Artesian Water Company of all rights thereunder.

ORDER No. 4820

In the Matter of

The Application of THE CHESAPEAKE AND POTOMAC TELEPHONE COMPANY OF BALTIMORE CITY for the Approval of an Agreement Between It and CHARLES E. STEWART and CHARLES JARRELL of the Town of Hillsboro, Caroline County, Trading as HILLSBORO ELECTRIC LIGHT COMPANY, for the Sale by the Former to the Latter of Three Poles Located on the Southwest Side of Front Street, Northwest of Lewis Road, District No. 6, Talbot County, Maryland.

Before the

Public Service Commission of Maryland.

Case No. 1644.

The agreement or other written instrument evidencing the transaction in this case having been submitted to this Commission for the

purpose of securing its consent to the consummation thereof and the Commission having determined that a hearing is unnecessary,

It Is, THEREFORE, On this 20th day of March, in the year 1919, by the Public Service Commission of Maryland,

Ordered, That the consent of this Commission be and the same is hereby given to the disposition of the property described in said agreement, or other written instrument, evidencing the transaction in accordance with the terms outlined therein.

ORDER No. 4822

In the Matter of	
The Petition of Carriers Not Under Federal Control, by F. S. DAVIS, Tariff Publishing Agent, for Permission Under Section 15 of the Public Service Commission Law to File and Publish on Less Than Statutory Notice Rates Based on 90% of Sixth Class Rates on Building and Roofing Paper, Roofing Composition, Paper Boards and Related Articles.	Before the Public Service Commission of Maryland. S. N. & R. Docket. Case No. 557.

The above mentioned petition having been received and filed, upon consideration thereof, it is this 21st day of March, 1919, by the Public Service Commission of Maryland,

Ordered, That permission be, and is hereby given, carriers not under Federal control to file and publish on five days' notice to the Commission and the public, rates based on 90% of sixth class rates on building and roofing paper, roofing composition, paper boards and related articles,

PROVIDED, Tariffs containing said rates be filed with the Commission upon issuance of this Order, and published by posting as required by law, and that all copies of said tariffs shall bear the following notation:

"Issued under special permission of the Public Service Commission of Maryland, Order No. 4822 of date March 21st, 1919."

ORDER No. 4824

In the Matter of

The Application of CONSOLIDATED GAS
ELECTRIC LIGHT AND POWER COMPANY
OF BALTIMORE for the Approval of an
Agreement Between It and THE CHES-
APEAKE AND POTOMAC TELEPHONE COM-
PANY OF BALTIMORE CITY for the Sale
by the Former to the Latter of One
Pole, No. 12005, Located on the West
Side of Beechwood Avenue, 50 Feet
South of South Building Line of Ed-
mondson Avenue Produced in District
No. 1, Baltimore County, Maryland,
Under the Terms and Provisions of
Order No. 2954, Entered July 26th,
1916, in Case No. 1151.

Before the

Public Service Commission
of Maryland.

Case No. 1646.

The agreement or other written instrument evidencing the transaction in this case having been submitted to this Commission for the
purpose of securing its consent to the consummation thereof and the
Commission having determined that a hearing is unnecessary,

IT IS, THEREFORE, On this twenty-first day of March, in the year
1919, by the Public Service Commission of Maryland,

ORDERED, That the consent of this Commission be and the same is
hereby given to the disposition of the property described in said agreement, or other written instrument, evidencing the transaction in accordance with the terms outlined therein.

OPINION

In the Matter of

The Complaint of W. A. BROOKS, Mayor of Hyattsville, SUBURBAN CITIZENS' ASSOCIATION OF PRINCE GEORGE'S COUNTY, MARYLAND, ET AL.,	Before the Public Service Commission of Maryland.
vs.	Case No. 1623.
CITY AND SUBURBAN RAILWAY OF WASHINGTON.	

Appearances:

JOSEPH S. GOLDSMITH, ESQ., Assistant General Counsel of the Commission.

JACKSON H. RALSTON, ESQ., and WILLIAM B. CLAGGETT, ESQ., representing the complainants.

S. R. BOWEN, ESQ., representing the respondent.

By the Commission.   Filed March 24th, 1919.

On October 30th, 1918, the City and Suburban Railway of Washington filed with the Commission its passenger fare schedule P. S. C. Md. No. 3, to become effective December 1st, 1918. The effect of this schedule was to increase, among other rates, the local one-way fares within the State of Maryland from five cents to six cents per zone, the line of the railway company in this State from the District of Columbia line to Laurel being divided into five fare zones. The length of these zones, in miles, is as follows:

1st zone	2.539
2nd "	2.253
3rd "	3.401
4th "	3.109
5th '	2.416
Average length of zones	2.7436

The aforesaid schedule also increased the rates charged for 22-trip monthly school tickets for travel between Maryland points 20%, the former and increased rates being as follows:

	Former	*Increased*
1 zone	$1.54	$1.85
2 zones	1.98	2.38
3 "	2.97	3.56
4 "	3.96	4.75
5	4.95	5.94

The charge for family commutation books, containing twenty single trip tickets honored for passage between College Park and Hyattsville, was at same time increased from $1.00 to $1.20 per book, or 20%.

The Public Service Commission Law does not require common carriers to seek and obtain the approval of the Commission before increasing or decreasing existing rates and fares, except in cases where the rates or fares it is proposed to change have been established by the Commission and the maintenance thereof is required by an unexpired order of the Commission. Section 15 of the Public Service Commission Law permits carriers to make effective upon not less than thirty days' notice to the Commission and the public increased or decreased rates, fares and charges, the same to be subject to investigation and correction upon complaint or upon the Commission's own motion, under the provisions of the Public Service Commission Law. The Act authorizes the Commission, for good cause shown, to waive the statutory notice either in whole or in part, but the Commission exercises this power in the case of increased rates in only the most exceptional cases. The provisions of the law respecting changes in rates are here referred to in order to remove any misapprehension concerning the Commission's authority in the matter, the Commission being without power to suspend the application of any increased rates pending termination of investigation concerning the reasonableness thereof.

On November 12th, 1918, a complaint against the proposed increased fares was filed with the Commission by the Suburban Citizens' Association of Prince George's County, Maryland, and on November 18th a similar complaint and protest was filed by the Mayor and Common Council of Hyattsville asking that a hearing be held by the Commission in Hyattsville in order to give the citizens of that town an opportunity to present to the Commission their objections against the increases. Subsequently other protests against the increased rates were filed with the Commission by various civic associations and individuals.

Practically all of the protests against the rates proposed to be charged by the company also complained of the service at that time being furnished by the respondent company. On November 27th, 1918, the respondent filed with the Commission answer to the complaints, alleging in support of the reasonableness of the increased rates the fact that the company has had to greatly increase the rates of pay of its trainmen to meet wage scale adopted by the National War Labor Board, in addition to which it has had to increase the salaries of other employes, besides encountering increased costs of materials and supplies. The answer of the respondent not being satisfactory to the complainants the matter was set for hearing at Hyattsville on January 29th, 1919. After this hearing the case was set for further hearing at the offices of the Commission on March 10th, 1919.

Much of the testimony at the earlier hearing had to do with the poor service, which was then and had for some time past been furnished by the railway company and the Commission is convinced that at the time these complaints were filed the service was far from satisfactory. However, inspections subsequently made from time to time by the Transportation Department of the Commission have demonstrated that the service has been improving and that many of the conditions complained of have been materially relieved. In the fall of last year labor was scarce and hard to obtain and when secured was not always of the highest class. The condition in this respect has changed for the better and will doubtlessly continue to improve and the company will be able to properly discipline its employes, thereby removing the necessity for complaints respecting cars running by persons waiting to board them, and similar complaints due largely to the inattention or incivility of the platform employes. Recent checks also indicate that the crowding of cars has very materially been relieved, and the Commission is of the opinion that the company is at this time doing all that it can reasonably be expected to do towards improving the service. The Commission will continue its traffic checks and will take such steps from time to time as may be necessary in order to insure the utmost in the way of service.

The Interstate Commerce Commission has recently permitted the respondent company to increase the interstate one-way fares and commutation rates, which increased rates and fares became effective January 1st, 1919. The interstate one-way fares are based upon the Maryland zone fares, plus 5 cents to cover the portion of the journey within the District of Columbia. For example, the intrastate fare between the District Line and Laurel (through five fare zones) is 30 cents, and the interstate fare between Washington, D. C., and Laurel is 35 cents. The Commission cannot change the Maryland zone fares without defeating the through interstate fare permitted by the Interstate Commerce Commission. A similar situation was recently presented to the Commission by the complaint of F. G. Heaton, et al., vs. Washington and Rockville Railway Company, Case No. 1622. The opinion of the Commission filed in that case on February 24th, 1919, sets forth the views and conclusions of the Commission upon this point and it has been thought desirable to here quote therefrom at some length:

"If the Commission should attempt to reduce the zone fares in Maryland the result would be to defeat the through rate of fare permitted by the Interstate Commerce Commission, and thus create a situation similar to that in the so-called 'Shreveport Case' (Houston East and West Texas Railway Company and Houston and Shreveport Railway Company, et al., vs. United States Interstate Commerce Commission, et al., 234, U. S. 342), in which case it was held that the railroad companies were not required to observe the intrastate rates established by the state authorities where to do so would result in discrimination in favor of intrastate traffic and against interstate traffic. Practically the same situation was presented to the Commission in the complaint of F. L. Hawley vs. City and Suburban Railway of Washington, D. C., Case No. 708 (P. S. C. Md. Reports, Vol. V, p. 598), and the Commission concurred in the opinion of its General Counsel filed in that case wherein he held that:

" 'In my judgment, the Public Service Commission of Maryland is powerless to impose four fare zones only on an intrastate passenger between the town of Laurel and the boundary of the District of Columbia, when the Interstate Commerce Commission imposes five fare zones between these termini on a passenger bound from the town of Laurel to the City of Washington within the District of Columbia. A higher rate payable by an interstate passenger and a lower rate payable by an intrastate passenger for one and the same service rendered under substantially the same conditions cannot, in my opinion, co-exist. The case is one where, as in the Shreveport Case, the interstate and intrastate transactions of the carrier are so related that the government of one involves the control of the other and it is the Interstate Commerce Commission and not the Public Service Commission of Maryland that is entitled to prescribe the final and determining rule.'

"While that particular case involved the number of fare zones, rather than the rate of fare per zone, the underlying principle in the two cases is the same.

"In view of the law laid down by the decisions in these cases, it is manifest that it would be a vain thing for this Commisison to now undertake to establish intrastate one-way fares on a basis lower than that obtaining at the present time, and the Commission will therefore not pass upon the reasonableness of these fares in the present case. While the present interstate fares have been permitted by the Interstate Commerce Commission, their reasonableness has not been passed upon by that body, and should they subsequently be held to be unreasonable by the Interstate Commerce Commission in an appropriate proceeding before that tribunal, this Commission will then be in a position to make such revision of the Maryland intrastate fares as may seem proper in the light of such decision."

Respondent introduced and filed with the Commission statements showing the results of its operations for the years 1914, 1915, 1916, 1917 and 1918. The net income for these years, after paying interest on funded debt, etc., but excluding any allowances for depreciation or dividends upon stock, has been:

1914	$99,009.05
1915	82,422.22
1916	67,829.02
1917	33,234.75
1918	5,343.20
Average	44,273.75

During the same period the revenue from transportation has increased from $578,421.14 in 1914 to $699,098.85 in 1918, the poor showing in net income in the last year being due to the increased cost of operation. Based upon the volume of traffic in 1918, it is estimated that the increased fares inaugurated by the respondent (including increase in the District of Columbia brought about by the discontinuance of sale of six tickets for twenty-five cents and charging five cents per ride instead) will produce additional revenue of $99,678.33. Trainmen's wages were increased in October, 1918, to the extent of $80,143.27 per annum, and as the increased wages were in effect during only 2⅔ months of 1918, there must be made an allowance of $62,333.60 for increased cost of labor, as it is not likely that there will be any substantial decrease in the wage scale during the current year. Deducting from the estimated increase in revenue, $99,678.33, the additional costs of operation due to labor increases not entirely reflected in 1918 figures, $62,333.60, we obtain a net increase of $37,344.73 in net income, to which must be added the actual net income in 1918 of $5,343.20, making the estimated net income for 1919 $42,687.93. It will be seen that this is considerably less than the net income during either of the first three years above given, and slightly less than the average for the past five years, which period includes the lean years of 1917 and 1918. It is not likely that the actual operations will produce results greatly different from those forecast at this time. On the one hand, it is possible that the traffic will fall off during the current year, while on the other it is not improbable that there will be a slight falling off in cost of materials and supplies.

Some years ago this Commission had occasion to consider the rates of fare charged school children traveling over the line of the respondent company upon the complaint of Rev. B. Tobias, filed April 12th, 1912. At the time this complaint was filed no school commutation rates were published by the railway company, and the Commission was urged to establish a rate of fare not in excess of one-half cent per mile. After full investigation the Commission in that case declined to establish rates upon the basis prayed, but ordered the respondent to establish school commutation fares at a rate not exceeding 2¼ cents per zone, except in single zone, where rate of 3½ cents was fixed. The rate prescribed by the Commission was the same rate as applied to the Maryland portion of interstate travel on 52-trip monthly commutation tickets between Washington, D. C., and Laurel, Maryland. That is to say, the charge for 52 trips between Washington and Laurel was found to be $8.00; deducting from this the ticket rate of 4⅙ cents in the District of Columbia and dividing the balance by the number of Maryland zones (5) produced a fare of 2.24 cents per zone. The fares prescribed by the Commission became effective on May 1st, 1918, and continued in effect until December 1st, 1918, when they were superseded by the fares published in tariff P. S. C. Md. No. 3, here in controversy. The opinion and order of the Commission in the earlier case (No. 344) are reported in P. S. C. Md. Reports, Vol. IV, p. 116

and following. After due consideration of all facts surrounding the establishment of the original school fares, the subsequent increased cost of operation and the fact that other fares, including commutation fares, have since been increased, the Commission finds that the respondent has justified the reasonableness of the increased fares for school commutation tickets.

There remains to be considered but one other form of ticket sold for travel exclusively within the State of Maryland, this being the family commutation book entitling the purchaser to twenty rides between College Park (College Avenue) and Hyattsville (Johnson Avenue). This book formerly sold for $1.00 and the rate was increased to $1.20 on December 1st, 1918. The points between which these tickets are honored are in different zones, and consequently two cash fares are collected between the points. The average length of the Maryland fare zone is 2.7436 miles and the distance between College Park and Hyattsville is given as 3.25 miles. It will thus be seen that the holders of these books, besides being permitted an "over-lap" into the next fare zone for one fare (which is in effect what the ticket accomplishes), are carried about one-half mile further than the average length of the fare zones. On the other hand, the users of these books are required to purchase same in advance, and for this, as well as for other well-known reasons applicable to all forms of commutation tickets, a rate lower than that charged the individual rider is justifiable and proper. Nevertheless, the Commission feels that the present rate for the family commutation book is neither unreasonable nor excessive.

It follows that the several complaints herein should be dismissed and it will be so ordered.

ORDER No. 4826

In the Matter of

The Complaint of W. A. BROOKS, Mayor of Hyattsville, SUBURBAN CITIZENS ASSOCIATION OF PRINCE GEORGE'S COUNTY, MARYLAND, ET AL.,

vs.

CITY AND SUBURBAN RAILWAY OF WASHINGTON.

Before the

Public Service Commission of Maryland.

Case No. 1623.

In accordance with Opinion of the Commission filed in the above case on the date hereof, it is this 24th day of March, in the year Nineteen Hundred and Nineteen, by the Public Service Commission of Maryland,

Ordered, That the complaints in the above entitled matter be and the same are hereby dismissed.

ORDER No. 4827

In the Matter of	
The Complaint of UNGER & MAHON, INC., ET AL., vs. THE UNITED RAILWAYS AND ELECTRIC COMPANY OF BALTIMORE.	Before the Public Service Commission of Maryland. Case No. 1631.

The above cause having been previously set for hearing and having been heard on February 28th, 1919, when both parties were represented in person or by counsel, and it being the opinion and finding of the Commission that the complainants are not entitled to the relief for which they have prayed,

IT IS, THEREFORE, This 24th day of March, in the year Nineteen Hundred and Nineteen, by the Public Service Commission of Maryland,

ORDERED, That the complaint in the above entitled matter be, and the same is hereby dismissed.

ORDER No. 4830

In the Matter of	
The Complaint of CHESAPEAKE REALTY COMPANY vs. CONSOLIDATED GAS ELECTRIC LIGHT AND POWER COMPANY OF BALTIMORE.	Before the Public Service Commission of Maryland. Case No. 1536.

The above entitled matter being under consideration, and it appearing that the matters and things therein complained of are substantially the same as those involved in Case No. 1476, being complaint of the Public Service Commission of Maryland vs. Consolidated Gas

Electric Light and Power Company of Baltimore, a body corporate, with respect to its latest rules in relation to gas and electric extensions and service connections,

IT IS, THEREFORE, This 24th day of March, in the year Nineteen Hundred and Nineteen, by the Public Service Commission of Maryland,

Ordered, That the Secretary of the Commission be and he is hereby directed to consolidate Case No. 1536 with Case No. 1476, and to notify interested parties of the action taken by the Commission.

ORDER No. 4831

In the Matter of	Before the
The Complaint and Petition of MAYOR AND CITY COUNCIL OF HAVRE DE GRACE	Public Service Commission of Maryland.
vs.	Case No. 1421.
HAVRE DE GRACE WATER COMPANY.	

The above entitled matter being under consideration, and it appearing that the matters and things therein complained of are substantially the same as those involved in Case No. 1586, being complaint of Mayor and City Council of Havre de Grace vs. Havre de Grace Water Company of Harford County, Maryland,

IT IS, THEREFORE, This 24th day of March, in the year Nineteen Hundred and Nineteen, by the Public Service Commission of Maryland,

Ordered, That the Secretary of the Commission be and he is hereby directed to consolidate Case No. 1421 with Case No. 1586, and to notify interested parties of the action taken by the Commission.

ORDER No. 4834

In the Matter of

The Complaint of BELMONT ASSOCIATION
OF WALBROOK

vs.

THE UNITED RAILWAYS AND ELECTRIC
COMPANY OF BALTIMORE.

Before the

Public Service Commission
of Maryland.

Case No. 1587.

Upon the order of the solicitor for the Complainant filed herein, it is this twenty-sixth day of March, 1919, by the Public Service Commission of Maryland,

Ordered, That this complaint be, and the same is hereby, dismissed.

ORDER No. 4835

In the Matter of

The Application of THE CHESAPEAKE
AND POTOMAC TELEPHONE COMPANY OF
BALTIMORE CITY for the Approval of
an Agreement, Dated November 23rd,
1918, With CONSOLIDATED POWER COM-
PANY OF BALTIMORE for the Sale by the
Former to the Latter of One Pole Lo-
cated on the Southeast Corner of Glen-
wood Avenue and York Road, District
No. 9, Baltimore County, Maryland.

Before the

Public Service Commission
of Maryland.

Case No. 1649.

The agreement or other written instrument evidencing the transaction in this case having been submitted to this Commission for the purpose of securing its consent to the consummation thereof and the Commission having determined that a hearing is unnecessary,

IT IS, THEREFORE, On this twenty-sixth day of March, in the year 1919, by the Public Service Commission of Maryland,

Ordered, That the consent of this Commission be and the same is hereby given to the disposition of the property described in said agreement, or other written instrument, evidencing the transaction in accordance with the terms outlined therein.

ORDER No. 4841

In the Matter of

The Application of THE BALTIMORE AND
OHIO RAILROAD COMPANY for Author-
ity to Issue $3,000,000.00 of Six Per
Cent. Collateral Trust Five Year Gold
Bonds.

Before. the

Public Service Commission
of Maryland.

Case No. 1648.

Application having been made to the Commission for an order permitting and approving the issue of $3,000,000 of The Baltimore and
Ohio Railroad Company's Six Per Cent. Collateral Trust Five Year
Gold Bonds to be dated April 1st, 1919; to be payable April 1st, 1924;
to bear interest at the rate of 6% per annum, and to be secured by a
pledge of $5,000,000 of Coal and Coke Railway Company First Mort-
gage Bonds; the Commission, having heard testimony, is of opinion
that such application should be granted and that the issue of such
bonds is reasonably required for the purposes of said corporation,

IT IS, THEREFORE, This 28th day of March, in the year Nineteen
Hundred and Nineteen, by the Public Service Commission of Maryland, ·

Ordered, That the issue and sale of $3,000,000 of said The Balti-
more and Ohio Railroad Company's Six Per Cent. Collateral Trust
Five Year Gold Bonds is hereby permitted and approved.

ORDER No. 4845

In the Matter of

The Complaint of MRS. J. M. HORNER and
REV. S. M. ENGLE

vs.

THE PENNSYLVANIA RAILROAD COMPANY.

Before the

Public Service Commission
of Maryland.

Case No. 1606.

The petition of Walker D. Hines, Director General of Railroads,
praying that he be made a party defendant in the above entitled matter, having been received and duly considered, it is this thirty-first day
of March, 1919, by the Public Service Commission of Maryland,

Ordered, That Walker D. Hines, Director General of Railroads, be,
and he is hereby, made a party defendant in the said matter, now
pending before the Commission.

ORDER No. 4852

In the Matter of

The Petition of the Carriers Not Under
Federal Control Named in the Official
Classification, by R. N. COLLYER, Their
Agent, for Permission Under Section
15 of the Public Service Commission
Law to File and Publish on Statutory
Notice Supplement to Official Classifi-
cation No. 44, P. S. C. Md. O. C. No.
44, Departing from the Provisions of
the Commission's Circular No. 10A In
So Far As Volume of Supplemental
Matter Is Concerned.

Before the

Public Service Commission
of Maryland.

S. N. & R. Docket.

Case No. 558.

The above mentioned petition having been received and filed, upon
consideration thereof, it is this 31st day of March, 1919, by the Public
Service Commission of Maryland,

Ordered, That permission be, and is hereby given, the carriers not
under Federal control named in the Official Classification, by R. N.
Collyer, their Agent, to file and publish on statutory notice to the
Commission and the public, supplement to Official Classification No. 44,
P. S. C. Md. O. C. No. 44, departing from the provisions of the Commission's Circular No. 10A in so far as volume of supplemental matter
is concerned, including necessary additions to, changes in and eliminations from the list of participating carriers contained in said classification, and publishing revision of the classification specifications
for anthracene; food curing or preserving compounds; burners, spray-
ers or vaporizers; phosphate rock; radiator guards or shields; and
wooden rollers, N. O. I. B. N.—and the addition of specific entries for
sheet iron hog oilers; lumbang oil and peach kernel oil, as set forth in
petition herein and accompanying exhibit.

PROVIDED, Said supplement be filed with the Commission upon
issuance of this Order, and published by posting as required by law,
and that all copies of said supplement shall bear the following notation:

"Issued under special permission of the Public Service Commission of Maryland, Order No. 4852 of date March 31st,
1919."

ORDER No. 4864

In the Matter of

The Complaint of MRS. J. M. HORNER and REV. S. M. ENGLE

vs.

THE PENNSYLVANIA RAILROAD COMPANY

Before the

Public Service Commission of Maryland.

Case No. 1606.

The above cause having been previously set for hearing and having been heard on the date hereof, when both parties were represented in person or by counsel, and it being the opinion and finding of the Commission that the complainants are not entitled to the relief for which they have prayed,

IT Is, THEREFORE, This 4th day of April, in the year Nineteen Hundred and Nineteen, by the Public Service Commission of Maryland,

Ordered, That the complaint in the above entitled matter be, and the same is hereby dismissed.

ORDER No. 4878

In the Matter of

The Application of the CLAIBORNE-ANNAPOLIS FERRY, INCORPORATED, a Maryland Corporation, for the Approval of Rates for Transportation of Automobiles, Automobile Trucks and Passengers Under Contract With the State Roads Commission of Maryland.

Before the

Public Service Commission of Maryland.

Case No. 1645.

WHEREAS, By Section 1 of Chapter 708 of the Acts of General Assembly of Maryland, Session of 1916, it is provided that:

"Be it enacted by the General Assembly of Maryland, that the State Roads Commission be and they are hereby authorized and directed in their discretion to provide a suitable steamer or steamers to connect said town of Claiborne with the City of Annapolis or some adjoining suburb, such steamer or steamers to have ample dock room for the transportation of passengers and automobiles and other vehicles, and to provide wharf facilities at each terminal, and to make such trips across the Bay as may be justified, and to charge such rates therefor as may be established by the Public Service Commission of Maryland," and

WHEREAS, On March 14th, 1919, the State Roads Commission of Mayland, acting under authority of Chapter 708 of the Acts of 1916 aforesaid, entered into an agreement with Frank A. McNamee and Hampden D. Mepham for the operation of a ferry between Claiborne, Maryland, and Annapolis, Maryland, upon the terms and conditions set forth in said agreement, copy of which is filed in these proceedings, and

WHEREAS, On same date said Frank A. McNamee and Hampden D. Mepham did assign the aforesaid agreement between them and the State Roads Commission of Maryland to Claiborne-Annapolis Ferry, Incorporated, a corporation organized under the laws of the State of Maryland, copy of certificate of incorporation of said Claiborne-Annapolis Ferry, Incorporated, being filed in these proceedings, and

WHEREAS, The Claiborne-Annapolis Ferry, Incorporated, having made application to this Commission to establish the rates, fares and charges proposed to be charged by it for the transportation of persons and vehicles between Claiborne and Annapolis via said ferry, as required by Section 1 of Chapter 708 of the Acts of 1916 aforesaid, which Act limits the jurisdiction of this Commission to the establishment of rates for said ferry; the Commission has no jurisdiction with respect to the capitalization or method of financing of said corporation, while its operations are limited to carrying out the purposes of the Act, and

WHEREAS, The application having come on to be heard on March 25th, 1919, after due notice published in accordance with this Commission's Order No. 4821 passed March 20th, 1919, and it being the opinion and finding of the Commission that as the expenditures necessary to be made by the company in order to take care of its profession of service to the public have not been completed to the point where it is possible to ascertain with any reasonable degree of accuracy the fair value of the property dedicated to the public service, and as neither the probable income nor expenses are now determinable, it should postpone the further examination necessary to the ascertainment of fair value, rate of return, operating income and expenses (which are all factors necessary to be determined and considered in connection with the establishment of just and reasonable rates) until such time as the capital expenditures have been completed and the operating revenues and expenses can be judged in the light of experience and in the interim to establish the rates set forth in the agreement between the State Roads Commission and the operators of the ferry, feeling that no injustice will thereby be done the public, consideration being given to the fact that in order to bring about the establishment of this much-desired enterprise, the State Roads Commission of Maryland has been obliged to subsidize the Claiborne-Annapolis Ferry, Incorporated, to the amount of Eighteen Thousand Dollars ($18,000.00) per annum,

IT IS, THEREFORE, This 7th day of April, in the year Nineteen Hundred and Nineteen, by the Public Service Commission of Maryland,

Ordered, That until the further order of this Commission in the premises the rates, fares and charges to be demanded and collected by the Claiborne-Annapolis Ferry, Incorporated, for the transportation of persons and vehicles between Claiborne, Maryland, and Annapolis, Maryland, shall be as follows:

> For automobiles, $2.00 each way, including the driver or chauffeur.
>
> For automobile trucks, including the driver or chauffeur, $2.00 each way for the first ton or fraction thereof, and 50c for each additional ton or fraction of a ton.
>
> For passengers each way, 50c. For passengers round trips, with the privilege of returning not later than two days following the date of issue, 75c; children under six years, free; six to twelve years, one-half fare.

FURTHER **Ordered,** That by passing this order permitting and establishing the rates, fares and charges above set forth, this Commission is not to be taken as having relinquished its control and jurisdiction over these rates, fares and charges or any other rates, fares and charges hereafter established, the Commission hereby expressly reserving unto itself full and complete jurisdiction with respect thereto, with the right at any time to enter into an investigation concerning the reasonableness thereof, either upon complaint or upon the Commission's own motion, and to pass such further order or orders respecting the same as may be found right and proper.

ORDER No. 4874

In the Matter of	
The Application of THE CHESAPEAKE AND POTOMAC TELEPHONE COMPANY OF BALTIMORE CITY for the Approval of an Agreement Dated August 30th, 1918, Between It and CONSOLIDATED GAS ELECTRIC LIGHT AND POWER COMPANY OF BALTIMORE for the Sale by the Former to the Latter of Three Poles Located Along the Southwest Side of Baltimore and Sparrows Point Railroad, Southeast of St. Helena Station, District No. 12, Baltimore County, Maryland, Under the Terms and Provisions of Order No. 2913, Entered June 20th, 1916, in Case No. 1131.	Before the Public Service Commission of Maryland. Case No. 1660.

The agreement or other written instrument evidencing the transaction in this case having been submitted to this Commission for the purpose of securing its consent to the consummation thereof and the Commission having determined that a hearing is unnecessary,

IT IS, THEREFORE, On this ninth day of April, in the year 1919, by the Public Service Commission of Maryland,

Ordered, That the consent of this Commission be and the same is hereby given to the disposition of the property described in said agreement, or other written instrument, evidencing the transaction in accordance with the terms outlined therein.

ORDER No. 4875

In the Matter of

The Application of THE CHESAPEAKE AND POTOMAC TELEPHONE COMPANY OF BALTIMORE CITY for the Approval of an Agreement Dated March 13th, 1919, Between It and BEL AIR ELECTRIC COMPANY for the Sale by the Former to the Latter of Three Poles and Two Anchor Guys Located on the West Side of Harford Road North of the County Road at Fork, District No. 11, Baltimore County, Maryland, Under the Terms and Provisions of Order No. 2913, Entered June 20th, 1916, in Case No. 1131.

Before the

Public Service Commission of Maryland.

Case No. 1661.

The agreement or other written instrument evidencing the transaction in this case having been submitted to this Commission for the purpose of securing its consent to the consummation thereof and the Commission having determined that a hearing is unnecessary,

IT IS, THEREFORE, On this ninth day of April, in the year 1919, by the Public Service Commission of Maryland,

Ordered, That the consent of this Commission be and the same is hereby given to the disposition of the property described in said agreement, or other written instrument, evidencing the transaction in accordance with the terms outlined therein.

ORDER No. 4876

In the Matter of

The Application of THE CHESAPEAKE AND POTOMAC TELEPHONE COMPANY OF BALTIMORE CITY for the Approval of an Agreement Dated March 17th, 1919, Between It and the U. S. INDUSTRIAL CHEMICAL COMPANY for the Sale by the Former to the Latter of Five Poles Located on the North Side of Old Wagner's Point Road West of Fairfield Road, Baltimore, Maryland, Under the Terms and Provisions of Order No. 2913, Entered June 20th, 1916, in Case No. 1131.

Before the

Public Service Commission of Maryland.

Case No. 1662.

The agreement or other written instrument evidencing the transaction in this case having been submitted to this Commission for the purpose of securing its consent to the consummation thereof and the Commission having determined that a hearing is unnecessary,

IT IS, THEREFORE, On this ninth day of April, in the year 1919, by the Public Service Commission of Maryland,

Ordered, That the consent of this Commission be and the same is hereby given to the disposition of the property described in said agreement, or other written instrument, evidencing the transaction in accordance with the terms outlined therein.

ORDER No. 4879

In the Matter of

The Petition of the WASHINGTON, BALTI-
MORE AND ANNAPOLIS ELECTRIC RAIL-
ROAD COMPANY, for the Approval of
the Certification and Delivery of Four
Hundred and Thirty-nine (439) of Its
First Mortgage Five Per Cent. Thirty-
Year Gold Bonds of the Par Value of
One Thousand Dollars ($1,000) Per
Bond, Being a Part of an Issue of
Bonds Secured by Its First Mortgage
Deed of Trust, to the CLEVELAND TRUST
COMPANY, as Trustee, Dated March
1st, 1911, and Being a Part of That
Portion of Said Issue of Said Bonds
Reserved to Be Certified and Delivered
and Used for the Enlargement, Better-
ment and Extension of or Additions to
Properties Covered by Said First
Mortgage Deed of Trust.

Before the

Public Service Commission
of Maryland.

Case No. 1655.

Petition of the Washington, Baltimore and Annapolis Electric Railroad Company, and exhibit filed therewith, and the testimony and evidence offered in support thereof, and all proceedings having been read
and considered, and it appearing to the Public Service Commission of
Maryland that the permission and approval asked for in said petition
are proper and the granting of the same would be convenient to the
public service, and the Commission being of the opinion that the use
of capital secured by the certification, issue and delivery of the bonds
hereinafter mentioned, and authorized to be certified, issued and delivered, is reasonably required for the purposes of said corporation:

IT IS, THEREFORE, This 15th day of April, in the year Nineteen Hundred and Nineteen, by the Public Service Commission of Maryland,

Ordered, That the Washington, Baltimore and Annapolis Electric
Railroad Company is hereby authorized to receive from the Cleveland
Trust Company, as Trustee, under the First Mortgage Deed of Trust,
from the said railroad company, dated March 1st, 1911, four hundred
and thirty-nine (439) bonds numbered from five thousand six hundred
and eighty-three (5683) to six thousand one hundred and twenty-one
(6121), both numbers inclusive, of an issue of First Mortgage Five
Per Cent. Thirty-Year Gold Bonds of the aggregate par value of Seven
Million Five Hundred Thousand Dollars ($7,500,000) secured by said
First Mortgage Deed of Trust, the said four hundred and thirty-nine
(439) bonds being a portion of the bonds of said issue reserved for

certification, issue and delivery for the purposes of the enlargement, betterment, extension of or additions to the properties covered by the said First Mortgage Deed of Trust, and the said Cleveland Trust Company, as Trustee, is hereby authorized to certify and deliver the said four hundred and thirty-nine (439) bonds to the said railroad company, the same to be received by the said railroad company as reimbursement for the enlargement, betterment, extension of or additions to the property covered by the said First Mortgage Deed of Trust, amounting to Five Hundred and Twenty-six Thousand Five Hundred and Eighty-one Dollars and Sixty Cents ($526,581.60), as set forth in an exhibit filed with said petition and marked "Exhibit of Expenditures for the enlargement, betterment, etc., from January 1st, 1918, to December 31st, 1918," and also as reimbursement for the sum of One Thousand and Five Dollars and Sixty-three Cents ($1005.63) expended in acquisition and permanent improvements made prior to January 1st, 1918, and not covered by the bonds heretofore authorized by this Commission, so that after the delivery of said bonds there will remain a credit of Seven Hundred and Eighty-seven Dollars and Twenty-three Cents ($787.23) on bonds to be certified in the future, said four hundred and thirty-nine (439) bonds, when so certified, issued and delivered to the said Washington, Baltimore and Annapolis Electric Railroad Company, to be and become, and to be treated as bonds in the treasury of said company, with full power and authority of said company, acting through its duly authorized officers or Board of Directors, from time to time to sell or pledge said bonds or any of them, provided, however, that before the said company sells said bonds or any part of them, as hereinbefore authorized, it shall report to this Commission the terms and conditions of said sale and shall secure the approval of this Commission of said sale without, however, the necessity of a hearing being had, or any publication of notice of said sale or sales.

It Is Further Ordered, That said Washington, Baltimore and Annapolis Electric Railroad Company shall make reports duly verified by affidavit as follows:

(a) Upon the issue or sale of said bonds hereby authorized and approved as aforesaid, or any part thereof, the fact of such issue or sale, the terms and conditions thereof and the amount realized therefrom.

ORDER No. 4882

———

In the Matter of	Before the
The Application of THE BALTIMORE AND OHIO RAILROAD COMPANY for Authority to Issue $20,000,000.00 of Refunding and General Mortgage Bonds.	Public Service Commission of Maryland. Case No. 1543.

WHEREAS, This Commission on June 26th, 1918, entered its Order No. 4372 approving the issue and sale or pledge of $20,000,000.00 of the Refunding and General Mortgage Bonds of The Baltimore and Ohio Railroad Company, said bonds to be issued as a part of Series A bearing interest at the rate of 5% per annum, the proceeds therefrom to be used for proper corporate capital purposes, and

WHEREAS, Upon petition of The Baltimore and Ohio Railroad Company this Commission on February 3rd, 1919, entered its Order No. 4656, authorizing said company to issue, sell or pledge its Series B bonds bearing interest at rate of 6% per annum, to the amount of $20,000,000.00, in lieu of its Series A bonds aforesaid, and

WHEREAS, The Baltimore and Ohio Railroad Company has now petitioned this Commission for the passage of a supplemental order expressly authorizing said company to apply $700,000.00 of its Refunding and General Mortgage Bonds, Series B, authorized aforesaid, for the purpose of refunding $700,000.00 of the Monongahela River Railroad Company's First Mortgage Five Per Cent. Bonds and to accomplish said refunding, to issue and deposit with the Trustee of its Refunding and General Mortgage $700,000.00 of its Pittsburg, Lake Erie and West Virginia System Refunding Mortgage Bonds, and

WHEREAS, It being the opinion and finding of the Commission, after due consideration, that said application should be granted,

IT IS, THEREFORE, This 16th day of April, in the year Nineteen Hundred and Nineteen, by the Public Service Commission of Maryland,

Ordered, That The Baltimore and Ohio Railroad Company is authorized to apply $700,000.00 of its Refunding and General Mortgage Bonds, Series B, authorized to be issued under order entered in this cause June 26th, 1918, as amended by order entered in this cause February 3rd, 1919, for the purpose of refunding $700,000.00 of the Monongahela River Railroad Company's First Mortgage Five Per Cent. Bonds, and, to accomplish said refunding, is authorized to issue $700,000.00 of its Pittsburg, Lake Erie and West Virginia System Refunding Mortgage Bonds to be deposited with the Trustee of its Refunding and General Mortgage.

ORDER No. 4894

In the Matter of

The Petition of the Carriers Not Under Federal Control Named in the Official Classification, by R. N. COLLYER, Their Agent, for Permission Under Section 15 of the Public Service Commission Law to File and Publish Supplement to Official Classification No. 44, P. S. C. Md. O. C. No. 44.

Before the

Public Service Commission of Maryland.

S. N. & R. Docket.

Case No. 559.

The above mentioned petition having been received and filed, upon consideration thereof, it is this 24th day of April, 1919, by the Public Service Commission of Maryland,

Ordered, That permission be, and is hereby given, the carriers not under Federal control named in the Official Classification, by R. N. Collyer, their Agent, to file and publish on full statutory notice to the Commission and the public, supplement to Official Classification No. 44, P. S. C. Md. O. C. No. 44, providing revision of the specifications for boots and shoes and for trunks containing merchandise, as set forth in petition and exhibit filed therewith; said supplement issued under authority hereof to depart from the provisions of this Commission's Circular No. 10A in so far as volume of supplemental matter is concerned, and including necessary additions to, changes in and eliminations from the list of participating carriers contained in said classification,

PROVIDED, Said supplement be filed with the Commission upon issuance of this Order, and published by posting as required by law, and that all copies of said supplement shall bear the following notation:

"Issued under special permission of the Public Service Commission of Maryland, Order No. 4894 of date April 24th, 1919."

ORDER No. 4899

In the Matter of

The Complaint of MRS. JAMES S. NOPHLIN

vs.

CONSOLIDATED GAS ELECTRIC LIGHT AND POWER COMPANY OF BALTIMORE.

Before the

Public Service Commission of Maryland.

Case No. 1650.

The above cause being at issue upon complaint and answer on file and having been previously set for hearing and having been heard on the date hereof, when both parties were represented in person or by counsel, and it being the opinion and finding of the Commission after due consideration of all papers filed herein and the testimony adduced at the hearing aforesaid that the original subject matter of the complaint has been satisfactorily adjusted between the parties and that the Commission is without jurisdiction to grant the further relief for which the complainant has prayed,

IT IS, THEREFORE, This 25th day of April, in the year Nineteen Hundred and Nineteen, by the Public Service Commission of Maryland,

ORDERED, That the complaint in the above entitled matter be, and the same is hereby dismissed.

ORDER No. 4901

In the Matter of

The Application of THE DIRECTOR GENERAL OF RAILROADS, Operating the Pennsylvania Railroad in Maryland, for Authority to Change Leeland Station in Prince George's County, Maryland, from an Agency Station to a Non-Agency Station.

Before the

Public Service Commission of Maryland.

Case No. 1653.

WHEREAS, The Director General of Railroads, operating the Pennsylvania Railroad in Maryland, has applied to this Commission for authority to change Leeland station, in Prince George's County, Maryland, from an agency station to a non-agency station, and

WHEREAS, The application having come on to be heard on April 17th,

1919, after due notice published in accordance with this Commission's Order No. 4846 passed March 31st, 1919, and it being the opinion and finding of the Commission after due hearing that the maintenance of Leeland station as an agency station is no longer reasonably necessary or convenient for the public service, but that a station-keeper should be provided at said station to look after the receipt and delivery of less than carload freight and to perform such other duties as ordinarily devolve upon such an employe, if the services of such station-keeper can be secured at a reasonable compensation,

It Is, Therefore, This 28th day of April, in the year Nineteen Hundred and Nineteen, by the Public Service Commission of Maryland,

Ordered, That the Director General of Railroads, operating the Pennsylvania Railroad in Maryland, be and he is hereby authorized and permitted to change Leeland station, Prince George's County, Maryland, from an agency station to a non-agency station, effective on and after May 1st, 1919.

It Is Further Ordered, That the said Director General of Railroads, operating the Pennsylvania Railroad in Maryland, shall provide a station-keeper at Leeland station not later than the day on which the agency at that point is discontinued, and thereafter employ such station-keeper so long as Leeland station is continued as a non-agency station, provided the services of such station-keeper can be secured at a salary not exceeding $25.00 per month.

ORDER No. 4902

In the Matter of

The Application of the Director General of Railroads, Operating the Pennsylvania Railroad in Maryland, for Authority to Change Port Tobacco Station, in Charles County, Maryland, from an Agency to a Non-Agency Station.

Before the

Public Service Commission of Maryland.

Case No. 1654.

Whereas, The Director General of Railroads, operating the Pennsylvania Railroad in Maryland, has applied to this Commission for authority to change Port Tobacco station, in Charles County, Maryland, from an agency station to a non-agency station, and

Whereas, The application having come on to be heard on April 17th, 1919, after due notice published in accordance with this Commission's Order No. 4847 passed March 31st, 1919, and it being the opinion and finding of the Commission after due hearing that the maintenance of

Port Tobacco station as an agency station is no longer reasonably necessary or convenient for the public service, but that a station-keeper should be provided at said station to look after the receipt and delivery of less than carload freight and to perform such other duties as ordinarily devolve upon such employe, if the services of such station-keeper can be secured at a reasonable compensation,

IT IS, THEREFORE, This 28th day of April, in the year Nineteen Hundred and Nineteen, by the Public Service Commission of Maryland,

Ordered, That the Director General of Railroads, operating the Pennsylvania Railroad in Maryland, be and he is hereby authorized and permitted to change Port Tobacco station, Charles County, Maryland, from an agency station to a non-agency station, effective on and after May 1st, 1919.

IT IS FURTHER **Ordered,** That the said Director General of Railroads, operating the Pennsylvania Railroad in Maryland, shall provide a station-keeper at Port Tobacco station not later than the day on which the agency at that point is discontinued, and thereafter employ such station-keeper so long as Port Tobacco station is continued as a non-agency station, provided the services of such station-keeper can be secured at a salary not exceeding $25.00 per month.

ORDER No. 4905

In the Matter of	Before the
The Complaint of R. E. DUVALL AND COMPANY *vs.* THE HAGERSTOWN AND FREDERICK RAILWAY COMPANY.	Public Service Commission of Maryland. Case No. 1640.

The above cause being at issue upon complaint and answer on file and having been previously set for hearing and having been heard on March 27th, 1919, when both parties were represented in person or by counsel, and it being the opinion and finding of the Commission after due consideration of all papers filed herein, especially the opinion of its General Counsel, and the testimony adduced at the hearing aforesaid that it is without jurisdiction to grant the relief for which the complainant has prayed,

IT IS, THEREFORE, This 28th day of April, in the year Nineteen Hundred and Nineteen, by the Public Service Commission of Maryland,

Ordered, That the complaint in the above entitled matter be, and the same is hereby dismissed without prejudice, for lack of jurisdiction upon the part of this Commission to pass upon the issue thereby presented.

ORDER No. 4906

In the Matter of

The Petition of the Carriers Not Under
Federal Control Named in the Official
Classification, by R. N. COLLYER, Their
Agent, for Permission Under Section
15 of the Public Service Commission
Law to File and Publish Supplement
to Official Classification No. 44, P. S.
C. Md. O C. No. 44.

Before the

Public Service Commission
of Maryland.

S. N. & R. Docket.

Case No. 560.

The above mentioned petition having been received and filed, upon
consideration thereof, it is this 29th day of April, 1919, by the Public
Service Commission of Maryland,

Ordered, That permission be, and is hereby given, the carriers not
under Federal control named in the Official Classification, by R. N.
Collyer, their Agent, to file and publish on full statutory notice to the
Commission and the public, supplement to Official Classification No. 44,
P. S. C. Md. O. C. No. 44, providing additional classification for beet
or cane residuum potash, and changing the classification for self-
propelling freight delivery wagons or trucks, as set forth in petition
herein and including necessary additions to, changes in and eliminations from the list of participating carriers contained in said classification; said supplement issued under authority hereof to depart from
the provisions of this Commission's Circular No. 10A in so far as volume of supplemental matter is concerned,

Provided, Said supplement be filed with the Commission upon
issuance of this Order, and published by posting as required by law,
and that all copies of said supplement shall bear the following notation:

"Issued under special permission of the Public Service Commission of Maryland, Order No. 4906 of date April 29th,
1919."

ORDER No. 4907

In the Matter of

The Application of WASHINGTON, BALTI-
MORE AND ANNAPOLIS ELECTRIC RAIL-
ROAD COMPANY for an Order Permit-
ting and Approving the Construction
of a Siding Connecting With Its
North-Bound Track Between Elk and
Bush Streets, Baltimore, Maryland.

Before the

Public Service Commission
of Maryland.

Case No. 1670.

WHEREAS, It appears from the petition and exhibit filed in the above
entitled matter, that the proposed construction is necessary and convenient for the public service, and

WHEREAS, The said construction is not a matter of such character
as to require the same to be set for hearing under the provisions of
Section 26 of the Public Service Commission law,

IT IS, THEREFORE, This twenty-ninth day of April, 1919, by the Public Service Commission of Maryland,

ORDERED, That the construction proposed in the above entitled application be, and the same is hereby, permitted and approved.

ORDER No. 4908

In the Matter of

The Application of THE HAGERSTOWN
AND FREDERICK RAILWAY COMPANY for
Authority to Issue $40,000.00 Par
Value of Its First and Refunding
Bonds.

Before the

Public Service Commission
of Maryland.

Case No. 1669.

The above entitled matter having this day come on for hearing after
due notice published in compliance with this Commission's Order No.
4900 passed April 25th, 1919, and it being the opinion and finding of
the Commission after due hearing that the issue by the applicant, The
Hagerstown and Frederick Railway Company, of $40,000.00 face
amount of its First and Refunding Mortgage Thirty-Year Sinking
Fund Gold Bonds, Six Per Cent. Series, is reasonably required for the
purposes of said corporation,

IT IS, THEREFORE. This 30th day of April, in the year Nineteen Hundred and Nineteen, by the Public Service Commission of Maryland,

ORDERED, That the applicant, The Hagerstown and Frederick Railway Company, be and it is hereby authorized to issue and deliver not exceeding $40,000.00, face amount, of its First and Refunding Mortgage Thirty-Year Sinking Fund Gold Bonds, Six Per Cent. Series, and to use the same for collateral purposes as mentioned in said petition, and with the further right to the said Company to sell and dispose of the said bonds, or any part thereof, at any time, at not less than 95% of the face value of the same; the proceeds to be applied as in said petition set forth, the Commission having determined that the use of the capital to be secured by the issue of said bonds is reasonably required for the purposes of said company, to wit: the lawful discharge and refunding of its obligations incurred in making expenditures for proper corporate capital purposes.

IT IS FURTHER *Ordered*, That The Hagerstown and Frederick Railway Company report to this Commission the fact of the issuance and delivery of said bonds, and if the same are sold, the amount so sold and the price obtained therefor.

ORDER No. 4910

In the Matter of

The Petition of the Carriers Not Under Federal Control Named in the Official Classification, by R. N. COLLYER, Their Agent, for Permission Under Section 15 of the Public Service Commission Law to File and Publish Supplements to Official Classification No. 44, P. S. C. Md. O. C. No. 44, Departing from the Provisions of This Commission's Circular No. 10A In So Far As Volume of Supplemental Matter Is Concerned.

Before the

Public Service Commission of Maryland.

S. N. & R. Docket.

Case No. 561.

The above mentioned petition having been received and filed, upon consideration thereof, it is this 1st day of May, 1919, by the Public Service Commission of Maryland,

Ordered, That pending the issue of the Consolidated Classification, now in course of preparation, permission be, and is hereby given, the carriers not under Federal control named in the Official Classification, by R. N. Collyer, their Agent, to file and publish on full statutory notice to the Commission and the public, supplements to Official Classification No. 44, P. S. C. Md. O. C. No. 44, departing from the provisions of this Commission's Circular No. 10A in so far as volume of supplemental matter is concerned; such supplements to include necessary additions to, changes in and eliminations from the list of participating carriers contained in said classification, as well as any other changes in, additions to or eliminations from, ratings, classification descriptions, or rules contained in said classification, as may be required; the special permission contained herein does not waive any of the requirements of the Public Service Commission Law or of the rules of the Commission except as herein provided.

PROVIDED. Said supplements be filed with the Commission upon issuance thereof, and published by posting as required by law, and that all copies of said supplements shall bear the following notation:

"Issued under special permission of the Public Service Commission of Maryland, Order No. 4910 of date May 1st, 1919."

ORDER No. 4912

In the Matter of

The Application of the DIRECTOR GENERAL OF RAILROADS, Operating the Pennsylvania Railroad in Maryland, for Authority to Change Melvale Station, Baltimore City, Maryland, from an Agency to a Non-Agency Station.

Before the

Public Service Commission of Maryland.

Case No. 1666.

WHEREAS, The Director General of Railroads, operating the Pennsylvania Railroad in Maryland, has applied to this Commisson for authority to change Melvale station, Baltimore City, Maryland, from an agency station to a non-agency station, and

WHEREAS, The application having this day come on to be heard after due notice published in accordance with this Commission's Order No. 4889 passed April 23rd, 1919, and no protests thereto having been made and it being the opinion and finding of the Commission after due hearing that the maintenance of Melvale station as an agency station is no longer reasonably necessary or convenient for the public service,

IT IS, THEREFORE, This 2nd day of May, in the year Nineteen Hundred and Nineteen, by the Public Service Commission of Maryland,

Ordered. That the Director General of Railroads, operating the Pennsylvania Railroad in Maryland, be and he is hereby authorized and permitted to change Melvale station, Baltimore City, Maryland, from an agency station to a non-agency station, effective on and after May 15th, 1919.

ORDER No. 4913

In the Matter of

The Petition of the DIRECTOR GENERAL OF RAILROADS, Operating the Pennsylvania Railroad Company, for an Order Approving the Operation of Mattawoman Station, Charles County, Maryland, as a Non-Agency Passenger, Baggage and Freight Station.

Before the

Public Service Commission of Maryland.

Case No. 1665.

WHEREAS, The Director General of Railroads, operating the Pennsylvania Railroad in Maryland, has applied to this Commission for authority to change Mattawoman station, Charles County, Maryland, from an agency freight station to a non-agency station, and

WHEREAS, The application having this day come on to be heard after due notice published in accordance with this Commission's Order No. 4887 passed April 22nd, 1919, and no protests thereto having been made and it being the opinion and finding of the Commission after due hearing that the maintenance of Mattawoman station as an agency freight station is no longer reasonably necessary or convenient for the public service,

IT IS, THEREFORE, This 2nd day of May, in the year Nineteen Hundred and Nineteen, by the Public Service Commission of Maryland,

ORDERED, That the Director General of Railroads, operating the Pennsylvania Railroad in Maryland, be and he is hereby authorized and permitted to change Mattawoman station, Charles County, Maryland, from an agency freight station to a non-agency station, effective on and after May 15th, 1919.

ORDER No. 4915

In the Matter of

The Application of the DIRECTOR GENERAL OF RAILROADS, Operating the Pennsylvania Railroad in Maryland, for Authority to Change Croom Station, Prince George's County, Maryland, from an Agency to a Non-Agency Station.

Before the

Public Service Commission of Maryland.

Case No. 1668.

WHEREAS, The Director General of Railroads, operating the Pennsylvania Railroad in Maryland, has applied to this Commission for authority to change Croom Station, Prince George's County, Maryland, from a second-class agency station to a non-agency station, and

WHEREAS, The application having this day come on to be heard after due notice published in accordance with this Commission's Order No. 4891 passed April 23rd, 1919, and it being the opinion and finding of the Commission after due hearing that public necessity and convenience reasonably require the maintenance of Croom Station as an agency station, and that an agent should be employed at that point if the services of such an agent can be secured at a reasonable compensation,

IT IS, THEREFORE, This 5th day of May, in the year Nineteen Hundred and Nineteen, by the Public Service Commission of Maryland,

Ordered, That the application of the Director General of Railroads, operating the Pennsylvania Railroad in Maryland, for authority to change Croom Station, Prince George's County, Maryland, from a second-class agency station to a non-agency station be and it is hereby denied and dismissed.

AND IT IS FURTHER Ordered, That until the further order of this Commission in the premises, the Director General of Railroads, operating the Pennsylvania Railroad in Maryland, be and he is hereby directed and required to continue Croom Station as a second-class agency station, provided the services of an agent can be secured at a salary not exceeding $50.00 per month, with the right to the Director General of Railroads to have the Commission reopen this case for further consideration in the event of his being unable to secure the services of an agent at the compensation fixed by the Commission.

ORDER No. 4916

In the Matter of

The Application of CONSOLIDATED GAS ELECTRIC LIGHT AND POWER COMPANY OF BALTIMORE for the Approval of an Agreement Between It and THE CHESAPEAKE AND POTOMAC TELEPHONE COMPANY for the Sale by the Former to the Latter of Eleven Poles on College Avenue and Three Anchor Guys, All Located in District No. 2, Howard County, Maryland, Under the Terms and Provisions of Order No. 2954, Entered July 26th, 1916, in Case No. 1151.

Before the

Public Service Commission of Maryland.

Case No. 1672.

The agreement or other written instrument evidencing the transaction in this case having been submitted to this Commission for the

purpose of securing its consent to the consummation thereof and the Commission having determined that a hearing is unnecessary,

It Is, THEREFORE, On this fifth day of May, in the year 1919, by the Public Service Commission of Maryland,

ORDERED, That the consent of this Commission be and the same is hereby given to the disposition of the property described in said agreement, or other written instrument, evidencing the transaction in accordance with the terms outlined therein.

ORDER No. 4924

In the Matter of	Before the
The Petition of THE EMMITSBURG RAILROAD and HAGERSTOWN AND FREDERICK RAILWAY COMPANY, by W. L. PRATT, Their Agent, for Permission Under Section 15 of the Public Service Commission Law to File and Publish on Less Than Statutory Notice Tariff of Summer Tourist Fares.	Public Service Commission of Maryland. S. N. & R. Docket. Case No. 562.

The above mentioned petition having been received and filed, upon consideration thereof, it is this 7th day of May, 1919, by the Public Service Commission of Maryland,

ORDERED. That permission be, and is hereby given, The Emmitsburg Railroad and Hagerstown and Frederick Railway Company, by W. L. Pratt, their Agent, to file and publish on one day's notice to the Commission and the public, tariff of summer tourist fares applying between points in Maryland on lines under Federal control and points in Maryland on or via lines of petitioning carriers,

PROVIDED, Said tariff containing said fares be filed with the Commission upon issuance of this Order, and published by posting as required by law, and that all copies of said tariff shall bear the following notation:

> "Issued under special permission of the Public Service Commission of Maryland, Order No. 4924 of date May 7th, 1919."

ORDER No. 4925

In the Matter of	Before the
The Petition of NORTHERN NATURAL GAS COMPANY for Permission to File and Publish on Less Than Statutory Notice Supplement No. 2 to Petitioner's Rate Schedule P. S. C. Md. No. 4.	Public Service Commission of Maryland. S. N. & R. Docket. Case No. 563.

The above mentioned petition having been received and filed, upon consideration thereof, it is this 7th day of May, 1919, by the Public Service Commission of Maryland,

Ordered, That permission be, and is hereby given, Northern Natural Gas Company to file, publish and make effective as of May 1st, 1919, Supplement No. 2 to petitioner's rate schedule P. S. C. Md. No. 4, which supplement does not effect any change in the rates charged for natural gas up to and including consumption of 200,000 cubic feet per month, but makes provision for the supply of consumption in excess of 200,000 cubic feet per month during the months of May, June, July, August, September and October, 1919, when available, at rates specified in said supplement, copy of which is filed herein,

PROVIDED, Said supplement be filed with the Commission upon issuance of this Order, and published by posting as required by law, and that all copies of said supplement shall bear the following notation:

> "Issued under special permission of the Public Service Commission of Maryland, Order No. 4925 of date May 7th, 1919."

PROVIDED FURTHER, That the permission hereby given shall not be taken or construed to be an approval by the Commission of the justness or reasonableness of the rates contained in said supplemental schedule, said rates remaining subject to investigation and correction upon complaint or upon the Commission's own motion, under the provisions of the Public Service Commission Law as fully as if this order had not been entered.

ORDER No. 4926

In the Matter of	Before the
The Petition of WEST VIRGINIA AND MARYLAND GAS COMPANY OF MARYLAND for Permission to File and Publish on Less Than Statutory Notice Supplement No. 5 to Petitioner's Rate Schedule P. S. C. Md. No. 4.	Public Service Commission of Maryland. S. N. & R. Docket. Case No. 564.

The above mentioned petition having been received and filed, upon consideration thereof, it is this 7th day of May, 1919, by the Public Service Commission of Maryland,

Ordered, That permission be, and is hereby given, West Virginia and Maryland Gas Company of Maryland to file, publish and make effective as of May 1st, 1919, Supplement No. 5 to petitioner's rate schedule P. S. C. Md. No. 4, which supplement does not effect any change in the rates charged for natural gas up to and including consumption of 200,000 cubic feet per month, but makes provision for the supply of consumption in excess of 200,000 cubic feet per month during the months of May, June, July, August, September and October, 1919, when available, at rates specified in said supplement, copy of which is filed herein,

PROVIDED, Said supplement be filed with the Commission upon issuance of this Order, and published by posting as required by law, and that all copies of said supplement shall bear the following notation:

> "Issued under special permission of the Public Service Commission of Maryland, Order No. 4926 of date May 7th, 1919."

PROVIDED FURTHER, That the permission hereby given shall not be taken or construed to be an approval by the Commission of the justness or reasonableness of the rates contained in said supplemental schedule, said rates remaining subject to investigation and correction upon complaint or upon the Commission's own motion, under the provisions of the Public Service Commission Law as fully as if this order had not been entered.

ORDER No. 4927

In the Matter of

The Petition of WEST VIRGINIA AND MARYLAND GAS COMPANY for Permission to File and Publish on Less Than Statutory Notice Supplement No. 5 to Petitioner's Rate Schedule P. S. C. Md. No. 7.

Before the

Public Service Commission of Maryland.

S. N. & R. Docket.

Case No. 565.

The above mentioned petition having been received and filed upon consideration thereof, it is this 7th day of May, 1919, by the Public Service Commission of Maryland,

Ordered, That permission be, and is hereby given, West Virginia and Maryland Gas Company to file, publish and make effective as of May 1st, 1919, Supplement No. 5 to petitioner's rate schedule P. S. C. Md. No. 7, which supplement does not effect any change in the rates charged for natural gas up to and including consumption of 200,000 cubic feet per month, but makes provision for the supply of consumption in excess of 200,000 cubic feet per month during the months of May, June, July, August, September and October, 1919, when available, at rates specified in said supplement, copy of which is filed herein,

PROVIDED, Said supplement be filed with the Commission upon issuance of this Order, and published by posting as required by law, and that all copies of said supplement shall bear the following notation:

"Issued under special permission of the Public Service Commission of Maryland, Order No. 4927 of date May 7th, 1919."

PROVIDED, FURTHER, That the permission hereby given shall not be taken or construed to be an approval by the Commission of the justness or reasonableness of the rates contained in said supplemental schedule, said rates remaining subject to investigation and correction upon complaint or upon the Commission's own motion, under the provisions of the Public Service Commission Law as fully as if this order had not been entered.

ORDER No. 4928

In the Matter of	Before the
The Petition of THE BERLIN AND LOVETTSVILLE BRIDGE COMPANY for Permission Under Section 15 of the Public Service Commission Law to File and Publish on Less Than Statutory Notice Rates for Tractors Crossing Toll Bridge of Petitioner.	Public Service Commission of Maryland. S. N. & R. Docket. Case No. 566.

The above mentioned petition having been received and filed, upon consideration thereof, it is this 7th day of May, 1919, by the Public Service Commission of Maryland,

𝔒𝔯𝔡𝔢𝔯𝔢𝔡, That permission be, and is hereby given, The Berlin and Lovettsville Bridge Company to file and publish on one day's notice to the Commission and the public, rates for tractors crossing toll bridge of petitioner, as follows:

```
One way, without load............................ $ .60
One way, with load and equipment (not exceeding five
  tons) .......................................... 1.00
```

PROVIDED, Tariff containing said rates be filed with the Commission upon issuance of this Order, and published by posting as required by law, and that all copies of said tariff shall bear the following notation:

"Issued under special permission of the Public Service Commission of Maryland, Order No. 4928 of date May 7th, 1919."

ORDER No. 4930

In the Matter of	Before the
The Complaint of HAROLD H. BALLARD vs. THE BALTIMORE COUNTY WATER AND ELECTRIC COMPANY.	Public Service Commission of Maryland. Case No. 1671.

WHEREAS, It appears from the papers filed in this case, and particularly from the letter of the complainant filed herein on the date hereof that the complaint has been satisfied,

IT IS, THEREFORE, This seventh day of May, 1919, by the Public Service Commission of Maryland,

𝔒𝔯𝔡𝔢𝔯𝔢𝔡, That the said complaint be entered as satisfied and the same is hereby dismissed.

ORDER No. 4932

In the Matter of

The Application of THE CHESAPEAKE
AND POTOMAC TELEPHONE COMPANY OF
BALTIMORE CITY for the Approval of
an Agreement, Dated March 12th,
1919, Between It and THE AMERICAN
TELEPHONE AND TELEGRAPH COMPANY
for the Lease by the Former to the
Latter of a Storeroom, Garage and
Storage Yard in Havre de Grace, Har-
ford County, Maryland.

Before the

Public Service Commission
of Maryland.

Case No. 1674.

The agreement or other written instrument evidencing the transaction in this case having been submitted to this Commission for the
purpose of securing its consent to the consummation thereof and the
Commission having determined that a hearing is unnecessary,

IT IS, THEREFORE, On this ninth day of May, in the year 1919, by
the Public Service Commission of Maryland,

𝔒𝔯𝔡𝔢𝔯𝔢𝔡, That the consent of this Commission be and the same is
hereby given to the disposition of the property described in said agreement, or other written instrument, evidencing the transaction in accordance with the terms outlined therein.

ORDER No. 4937

In the Matter of

Before the

The Application of the DIRECTOR GEN-
ERAL OF RAILROADS, Operating the
Pennsylvania Railroad in Maryland,
for Authority to Change Melvale Station, Baltimore City, Maryland, from
an Agency to a Non-Agency Station.

Public Service Commission
of Maryland.

Case No. 1666.

Upon petition of Columbus O'D. Lee and a number of other patrons
of the Pennsylvania Railroad using Melvale station, Baltimore, Maryland, for the suspension of Order No. 4912 entered herein by the Commission on May 2nd, 1919, by which order the Director General of
Railroads, operating the Pennsylvania Railroad in Maryland, was
authorized and permitted to change Melvale station from an agency
station to a non-agency station, effective May 15th, 1919, and further

praying that they be given opportunity to be heard with respect to the proposed discontinuance of agency at said station.

IT Is, This 12th day of May, in the year Nineteen Hundred and Nineteen, by the Public Service Commission of Maryland,

Ordered, That this Commission's Order No. 4912 entered herein on May 2nd, 1919, be and it is hereby suspended pending rehearing of this matter.

FURTHER *Ordered,* That the above entitled matter be and it is hereby set for rehearing at the office of the Commission, Baltimore, Maryland, on Monday, May 26th, 1919, at 10 o'clock A. M.

ORDER No. 4938

In the Matter of

The Complaint of ENGLISH CONSUL ESTATE IMPROVEMENT ASSOCIATION, INC., and JOHN GLASS

vs.

WASHINGTON, BALTIMORE AND ANNAPOLIS ELECTRIC RAILROAD COMPANY.

Before the

Public Service Commission of Maryland.

Case No. 1663.

The above cause having been previously set for hearing and having been heard on April 24th, 1919, when both parties were represented in person or by counsel, and it being the opinion and finding of the Commission that the complainants are not entitled to the relief for which they have prayed,

IT Is, THEREFORE, This 18th day of May, in the year Nineteen Hundred and Nineteen, by the Public Service Commission of Maryland,

Ordered, That the complaint in the above entitled matter be, and the same is hereby dismissed.

ORDER No. 4939

In the Matter of

The Petition and Application of THE
PENNSYLVANIA RAILROAD COMPANY and
THE CUMBERLAND VALLEY RAILROAD
COMPANY for an Order Permitting and
Approving the Acquisition by the For-
mer Company of the Corporate Rights,
Franchises and Privileges, and All the
Railroads and Other Corporate Prop-
erty, Rights and Credits of The Cum-
berland Valley Railroad Company.

Before the

Public Service Commission
of Maryland.

Case No. 1673.

The petition and application of The Pennsylvania Railroad Company and The Cumberland Valley Railroad Company praying for an
order of the Commission approving the acquisition by the former company of the corporate rights, franchises and privileges, and all the
railroads and other corporate property, rights and credits of the said
The Cumberland Valley Railroad Company, together with the Exhibits
A, B, C, D and E referred to therein, having been filed; and the matter having been set down for hearing, by the order of the Commission
passed on the 9th day of May, 1919, at 10 o'clock A. M., on the 14th
day of May, 1919, and now coming on to be heard; and it appearing
to the Commission that due publication of the notice of hearing in
accordance with the Commission's order has been made by the publication of the Commission's order setting this matter down for hearing; and it further appearing to the Commission from its consideration of the petition and exhibits and the evidence therein offered at
the hearing that the things of and for which the Commission's approval and permission are asked herein are necessary or convenient
for the public service,

IT IS, THEREFORE, This 14th day of May, in the year Nineteen Hundred and Nineteen, by the Public Service Commission of Maryland,

Ꝋrdered, That the permission and approval of the Public Service
Commission of Maryland are hereby given to the acquisition by The
Pennsylvania Railroad Company of the corporate rights, franchises
and privileges, and all the railroads and other corporate property,
rights and credits of The Cumberland Valley Railroad Company, said
corporations being the petitioners and applicants herein, upon the
terms, stipulations and conditions set out in the agreement dated January 22nd, 1919, between the said The Pennsylvania Railroad Company
and the said Cumberland Valley Railroad Company, a certified copy
of which has been filed in these proceedings with the petition and
application marked "Exhibit E," subject, however, in all respects, to

the rights of the United States of America, the President thereof, or the Director General of Railroads, incident to or growing out of the taking over of the railroads and property of the corporations, parties to said agreement, pursuant to the proclamation of the President of the United States dated December 26th, 1919; and

It Is Further Ordered, That, after the above agreement has been filed in the office of the Secretary of the State of Maryland in accordance with law, a copy thereof, certified by the Secretary of State, be filed in these proceedings.

ORDER No. 4940

In the Matter of	Before the
The Application of MARION CURRAN and WILLIAM JOHNSTONE for a Permit to Operate a Motor Vehicle for Public Use.	Public Service Commission of Maryland. Case No. 1441.

The applicants in the above cause having failed to take further action in connection therewith,

It Is, Therefore, This 14th day of May, in the year Nineteen Hundred and Nineteen, by the Public Service Commission of Maryland,

Ordered, That the application herein be and the same is hereby dismissed without prejudice.

ORDER No. 4941

In the Matter of	
The Complaint of ELLICOTT MACHINE CORPORATION vs. THE UNITED RAILWAYS AND ELECTRIC COMPANY OF BALTIMORE.	Before the Public Service Commission of Maryland. Case No. 1500.

The Ellicott Machine Corporation having advised the Commission in letter dated March 14th, 1919, that hearing is not desired in the above entitled matter, and the co-complainants having failed to prosecute further, after due notice,

It Is, Therefore, This 14th day of May, in the year Nineteen Hundred and Nineteen, by the Public Service Commission of Maryland,

Ordered, That the complaint herein be and the same is hereby dismissed without prejudice.

ORDER No. 4943

In the Matter of	Before the
The Application of the WASHINGTON SUBURBAN SANITARY COMMISSION for Authority to Issue $50,000.00 of Its Five Per Cent. Bonds.	Public Service Commission of Maryland. Case No. 1524.

WHEREAS, This Commission on July 19th, 1918, entered its Order No. 4416 herein permitting and approving the issue and sale for cash at not less than par of $50,000.00 face amount of bonds of the Washington Suburban Sanitary Commission, the proceeds therefrom to be applied to the purposes set forth in the application herein, including the retirement of outstanding bonds to the amount of $10,000.00 theretofore issued by authority of Chapter 313 of the Acts of the General Assembly of Maryland, Session of 1916, and

WHEREAS, Said Washington Suburban Sanitary Commission has now petitioned this Commission for the passage of an order authorizing it to expend said $10,000.00, being part of the total issue of $50,000.00 authorized by this Commission's Order No. 4416 aforesaid, for certain additional engineering purposes, in lieu of applying same to the retirement of the bonds aforesaid, it having been found impracticable at this time to retire the said bonds, and

WHEREAS, It being the opinion and finding of the Commission after due consideration that said petition is reasonable and proper and should be granted,

IT IS, THEREFORE, This 15th day of May, in the year Nineteen Hundred and Nineteen, by the Public Service Commission of Maryland,

ORDERED, That the Washington Suburban Sanitary Commission is hereby authorized and permitted to apply $10,000.00 of the proceeds from the sale of bonds of the aggregate face amount of $50,000.00 authorized to be issued by this Commission's Order No. 4416 entered July 19th, 1918, for engineering purposes, in lieu of applying said $10,000.00 to the retirement of bonds of like face amount theretofore issued.

OPINION

In the Matter of

The Complaint of the INTER-OCEAN OIL
COMPANY, the PRUDENTIAL OIL COM-
PANY, the UNITED STATES ASPHALT RE-
FINING COMPANY, the UNION SHIP-
BUILDING COMPANY, MARTIN WAGNER
COMPANY, SWIFT AND COMPANY, F. S.
ROYSTER GUANO COMPANY, RASIN MON-
UMENTAL COMPANY, STANDARD ACID
WORKS, and the BALTIMORE CAR FOUN-
DRY COMPANY

vs.

THE UNITED RAILWAYS AND ELECTRIC
COMPANY OF BALTIMORE.

Before the

Public Service Commission
of Maryland.

Case No. 1583. .

By the Commission.   Filed May 16th, 1919.

Order No. 4609 was passed in the above case January 7th, 1919, and
provided in substance as follows:

1.   That beginning January 19th, 1919, and until December 31st,
1919, the respondent company should issue on its Curtis Bay Line
transfers entitling the holder to a continuous ride thereon as such
transfers were issued on and prior to September 30th, 1919, except
that the charge for such transfers should thereafter be four cents
instead of three cents, as formerly.

2.   That within thirty days from the date of the order, or within
such further period of extension as might be granted for good cause
shown, the respondent company should render reasonably adequate
and proper service over said line, and to its patrons generally in the
Fairfield and East Brooklyn Districts, "the means by which such adequate service is to be rendered to be left for the present to the judgment and discretion of the respondent company, subject to more specific orders by this Commission in case the relief hereby ordered is not
speedily afforded."

In the opinion in the main cases, Nos. 1568 and 1583, of which this
case was a part, it was stated that three ways had been pointed out
by which the service to the Fairfield district could be materially improved without any very great expense, (1) by side-tracking some of
the Curtis Bay main line cars at Stone House Cove; (2) by completing the Fairfield extension as originally contemplated in the form
of a complete loop over one or the other of the routes suggested, and

putting additional cars thereon, or (3) by installing a series of turn-out switches on the existing jerk-water line pending the completion of such loop, and running additional cars over the same.

On January 16th, 1919, the respondent company filed a petition with the Commission praying a modification of the above opinion and order filed January 7th, 1919, so far as the same affected the question of the respondent company's service over the Fairfield extension of its Curtis Bay Line, and to its patrons generally in the Fairfield and East Brooklyn districts, more particularly during the rush hours on said line. In this connection the company suggested:

1. That the Commission should by its order, and as a condition of any additional service, require the complainants to perform and carry out the agreement made by them with the respondent for permits and rights of way, as disclosed in the testimony; and, incidentally, that the complainants should be required to refund to the respondent the sum of Five Hundred Dollars which it was compelled to pay for a permit to the State Roads Commission of Maryland. The respondent further stated in this connection that without rights of way from some of the petitioners it could not construct the switches suggested in the opinion, and that even with the right of way which it expected to obtain from the Baltimore & Ohio Railroad Company, the projected extension to Fairfield could not be completed within the thirty days' period fixed by the Commission.

2. That the petitioners should, by an order of the Commission, and as a condition of further relief, be required to co-operate with the respondent by reasonably adjusting their opening and closing hours to the conditions created by the morning and evening peaks of the rush-hour demands upon the respondent's service, the respondent stating that its investment in the building and maintenance of the Fairfield extension would be a substantial one, and involved, as contemplated at the time of the filing of the petition, no additional fare.

The petitioners referred to in the above petition for modification were the Inter-Ocean Oil Company, the United States Asphalt Refining Company, the Union Shipbuilding Company, the Martin Wagner Company, Swift & Company, the Rasin Monumental Company, the F. S. Royster Guano Company, and the Standard Acid Works, all large employers of labor, with plants located at or near Fairfield in the Curtis Bay district, said district being reached by the Curtis Bay Line of the respondent company. The above parties had filed a petition in the main cause complaining both of the proposed increases in fares effective October 1st, 1918, and also of the equipment and service of the company on the lines leading to Fairfield.

It appeared from the evidence and statements of counsel in the argument that some months prior to the docketing of these cases certain of the above petitioning corporations requested the respondent to construct the Fairfield extension of the Brooklyn Line by carrying the same through Fairfield in the form of a loop, and in this connection had agreed to give certain rights of way, acquire certain necessary permits and pay certain of the expenses in connection therewith, the specific claim of the respondent being for $500.00 which it had been compelled to pay the State Roads Commission of Maryland for a permit to run such extension over the public road leading to Fairfield.

It further appeared that a great deal of the difficulty in connection with the respondent's service to the Fairfield district was due to the fact that the above-named petitioning corporations and others employed in the aggregate many thousands of workmen who began work and were discharged at approximately uniform morning and afternoon hours, respectively, the result being great congestion at these particular periods.

It further appeared that several of the above-named petitioning corporations operated boats or barges for the transportation of their employes, and it was contended by the respondent company that if its service should be greatly improved to its Fairfield district, those operating these boats would discontinue the same, with the result that the thousands now using such boats daily would be rendered entirely dependent upon the respondent corporation for transportation to and from work, thus greatly adding to the difficulties of an already difficult situation.

Since the hearing of the above petition of the respondent for a modification of Order No. 4609 the respondent company has completed the Fairfield loop and is now engaged in operating cars over the same. The Commission is advised by its Transportation Department that service over this extension is at the present time reasonably satisfactory. These facts dispose of the respondent company's first ground for modification of the order. Any questions which may still remain open between the respondent company and any of the above-named petitioning corporations with respect to their relative pecuniary obligations growing out of this extension must be left by this Commission to the parties for adjustment among themselves or for settlement in some appropriate forum, this Commission having no jurisdiction to determine any such question.

Nor is this Commission of the opinion that it has any jurisdiction to pass an order requiring the petitioning corporations or any of them to co-operate with the respondent by reasonably adjusting their opening and closing hours to the conditions created by the morning and evening peaks of the rush-hour demands upon the respondent's service, as prayed in the second clause of the respondent's petition for a modification.

While the petition of the above corporations was nominally in their individual names, the thing they demanded was an improvement in the respondent company's service to the public using the company's lines in this particular district. The obligation of a public service corporation to render reasonably adequate service is an obligation which such corporation owes to the general public and not to individuals as such, except in so far as such individuals are members of the general public. It is a public, not a private obligation, which it, and it alone, owes to the public. Therefore an order of the Commission requiring a public service corporation to render reasonably adequate service cannot properly be conditioned upon certain individual members of the general public being required to render their co-operation toward the general improvement of such service. This Commission has full and complete jurisdiction over the respondent company so far as its obligations to render reasonably adequate service to the public is concerned; but it has no jurisdiction over the manufacturers of the community and no right to regulate the opening or closing hours of such.

The Commission has, however, the power primarily to determine what shall or shall not constitute reasonably adequate street railway service in any given case. Reasonably adequate service is a relative term, and what shall or shall not constitute reasonably adequate service in any given case depends largely upon the facts and circumstances of that particular case. This fact has been realized by this Commission in the past, as is evidenced by the rules adopted by it for the governance of street railway corporations in Baltimore City subject to its jurisdiction. In those rules it was provided in substance that reasonably adequate service during the non-rush hours required a seat for each passenger, whereas during the rush hours the requirement might be complied with even though a number of passengers were required to stand. The same principle will govern this Commission in determining whether or not the respondent company's service in the Fairfield district is or is not reasonably adequate. The company owes the obligation to render reasonably adequate service not only to those in the Fairfield district, but as well to those in every other portion of the large community which it serves. To require it to render service of a certain standard in the Fairfield district might well render the company unable to furnish reasonably adequate service in other districts, and the Commission must pass upon this question in the different districts as they arise in the light of the circumstances surrounding each. In the case of the Fairfield district it would not be reasonable to expect the respondent company to furnish a seat for each passenger during the rush-hour period if all the large manufacturers of this community open their factories at the same hours and close them at the same hours, since so to require would compel the company to keep available for this particular service a large proportion of its equipment and to run its cars at such short intervals as to make their operation extremely dangerous to those using the same, and would also greatly inconvenience other patrons using other lines of the company. Reasonably adequate service under such conditions may well mean that a large number of the patrons of the Fairfield extension and connecting Brooklyn main line may have to stand, or may even have to wait for considerable periods before even getting an opportunity to find standing-room. All that can be expected of the company under the circumstances is that it shall use reasonable effort to accommodate the traffic at this particular point under the circumstances as they may exist from time to time. The control of these circumstances lies largely with the large employers of labor in this district. With their co-operation along the lines suggested in the company's petition it may well be that the company will be able to render satisfactory service in this district. Without such co-operation it will unquestionably be difficult, if not impossible, for the company so to do.

Therefore while this Commission has no power to regulate the opening and closing hours of these manufacturers, it considers it proper to say to them through the medium of this opinion that if the question of adequate service in this district again comes before this Commission for consideration, we will be guided largely in our conclusions by the extent to which the large employers of labor in said district have or have not co-operated with the respondent company in its efforts to render better service to its patrons therein.

For the reasons stated, the petition of the respondent for a modification upon the above points will be denied, and an order will be passed to that effect.

ORDER No. 4944

In the Matter of

The Complaint of the INTER-OCEAN OIL COMPANY, the PRUDENTIAL OIL COMPANY, the UNITED STATES ASPHALT REFINING COMPANY, the UNION SHIPBUILDING COMPANY, MARTIN WAGNER COMPANY, SWIFT AND COMPANY, F. S. ROYSTER GUANO COMPANY, RASIN MONUMENTAL COMPANY, STANDARD ACID WORKS, and the BALTIMORE CAR FOUNDRY COMPANY

vs.

THE UNITED RAILWAYS AND ELECTRIC COMPANY OF BALTIMORE.

Before the

Public Service Commission of Maryland.

Case No. 1583.

For the reasons stated in the aforegoing opinion it is this 16th day of May, 1919, by the Public Service Commission of Maryland,

Ordered, That the petition of the respondent for a modification of the opinion and order passed herein January 7th, 1919, be and the same is hereby dismissed.

ORDER No. 4945

In the Matter of

The Application of THE CHESAPEAKE AND POTOMAC TELEPHONE COMPANY OF BALTIMORE CITY for the Approval of an Agreement Between It and CONSOLIDATED GAS ELECTRIC LIGHT AND POWER COMPANY OF BALTIMORE, Dated January 17th, 1919, for the Sale by the Former to the Latter of Six Poles Located on Various Streets in the City of Baltimore, Maryland.

Before the

Public Service Commission of Maryland.

Case No. 1679.

The agreement or other written instrument evidencing the transaction in this case having been submitted to this Commission for the purpose of securing its consent to the consummation thereof and the Commission having determined that a hearing is unnecessary,

IT IS, THEREFORE, On this sixteenth day of May, in the year 1919, by the Public Service Commission of Maryland,

Ordered, That the consent of this Commission be and the same is hereby given to the disposition of the property described in said agreement, or other written instrument, evidencing the transaction in accordance with the terms outlined therein.

ORDER No. 4948

In the Matter of

The Application of THE UNITED RAILWAYS AND ELECTRIC COMPANY OF BALTIMORE for an Order Permitting and Approving the Execution by It of a Contract Between THE UNITED STATES HOUSING CORPORATION and THE UNITED RAILWAYS AND ELECTRIC COMPANY OF BALTIMORE, for the Leasing by It of Ten (10) Cars Fully Equipped for Operation to Be Purchased by THE UNITED STATES HOUSING CORPORATION, Subject to the Terms and Conditions Contained in Said Agreement.

Before the

Public Service Commission of Maryland.

Case No. 1678.

WHEREAS, The United Railways and Electric Company of Baltimore has applied to the Public Service Commission of Maryland for its permission and approval to execute a contract between The United States Housing Corporation and The United Railways and Electric Company of Baltimore for the leasing of ten (10) cars fully equipped for operation, to be purchased by The United States Housing Corporation, subject to the terms and conditions contained in said contract, with Specifications dated Philadelphia, Pennsylvania, September 24, 1918, as amended by addenda sheet dated Baltimore, Maryland, May 13, 1919, copies of which have heretofore been filed with the Commission; and

WHEREAS, The Commission has examined said contract and finds that the execution of the same by The United Railways and Electric Company of Baltimore is convenient for the public service,

IT IS, THEREFORE, This nineteenth day of May, in the year nineteen hundred and nineteen, by the Public Service Commission of Maryland,

ORDERED, That the approval and permission of the Commission is hereby given to the execution by The United Railways and Electric Company of Baltimore of said contract between The United States Housing Corporation and The United Railways and Electric Company of Baltimore for the leasing by it of ten (10) cars fully equipped for operation, to be purchased by The United States Housing Corporation, subject to the terms and conditions therein contained,

PROVIDED, That when the total price to be paid for the cars in question by The United States Housing Corporation is determined upon, said amount shall be forthwith reported to this Commission by The United Railways and Electric Company of Baltimore; and should said The United Railways and Electric Company of Baltimore acquire said cars under the terms of the aforesaid contract, the amount paid by said company for said cars shall likewise be forthwith reported to this Commission.

ORDER No. 4954

In the Matter of

The Petition of CONSOLIDATED GAS ELECTRIC LIGHT AND POWER COMPANY OF BALTIMORE for Permission to File and Publish on Less Than Statutory Notice Supplement No. 33 to Petitioner's Electric Rate Schedule P. S. C. Md. No. E-4 and Supplement No. 18 to Petitioner's Gas Rate Schedule P. S. C. Md. No. G-6.

Before the

Public Service Commission of Maryland.

S. N. & R. Docket.

Case No. 567.

The above mentioned petition having been received and filed, upon consideration thereof, it is this 21st day of May, 1919, by the Public Service Commission of Maryland,

Ordered, That permission be, and is hereby given, Consolidated Gas Electric Light and Power Company of Baltimore to file and publish on one day's notice to the Commission and the public Supplement No. 33 to petitioner's electric rate schedule P. S. C. Md. No. E-4 and Supplement No. 18 to petitioner's gas rate schedule P. S. C. Md. No. G-6, revising the rules and charges of said company governing gas and electric main extensions and service connections,

PROVIDED, Said supplements be filed with the Commission upon issuance of this order, and published by posting as required by law, and that all copies of said supplements shall bear the following notation:

"Issued under special permission of the Public Service Commission of Maryland, Order No 4954 of date May 21st, 1919."

PROVIDED FURTHER, That this Commission by passing this order is not to be taken or construed as in any sense whatsoever passing upon the reasonableness of the rules and charges contained in aforesaid supplements filed hereunder, such rules and charges being left as fully subject to investigation and correction upon complaint or upon the Commission's own motion as if this order had never been passed.

ORDER No. 4957

In the Matter of	
The Application of JACOB PIMES, MAX PIMES and FREDERICK M. COBLENZER, Partners, Trading as THE MIDDLE RIVER FERRY COMPANY, for Permission to Operate a Boat for the Transportation of Passengers on Middle River and Its Tributaries.	Before the Public Service Commission of Maryland. Case No. 1680.

WHEREAS, Jacob Pimes, Max Pimes and Frederick M. Coblenzer, partners, trading as The Middle River Ferry Company, having made application to this Commission for permission to operate a boat for the transportation of passengers on Middle River and its tributaries, and

WHEREAS, The application having this day come on to be heard after due notice published in accordance with this Commission's Order No. 4946 passed May 16th, 1919, and it being the opinion and finding of the Commission after due hearing that the operation of said boat is convenient for the public service,

It Is, THEREFORE, This 23rd day of May, in the year Nineteen Hundred and Nineteen, by the Public Service Commission of Maryland,

Ordered, That the operation of a boat for the transportation of passengers on the Middle River and its tributaries by Jacob Pimes, Max Pimes and Frederick M. Coblenzer, partners, trading as The Middle River Ferry Company, be and the same is hereby permitted and approved.

ORDER No. 4963

In the Matter of	Before the
The Application of THE NEW TAXI SERVICE COMPANY for an Order Permitting and Approving the Exercise of Its Franchise and for Authority to Issue $50,000.00 Par Value of Its Capital Stock.	Public Service Commission of Maryland. Case No. 1652.

WHEREAS, The New Taxi Service Company, a corporation organized under the laws of the State of Maryland, has applied to this Commission for an order permitting and approving the exercise of its franchise granted it under its certificate of incorporation, a copy of which is filed in these proceedings, and for authority to issue Ten Thousand Dollars ($10,000.00) par value of its capital stock; and

WHEREAS, The application having this day come on to be heard in accordance with this Commission's Order No. 4956 passed May 22nd, 1919, and it being the opinion and finding of the Commission after due hearing that the exercise of said franchise is convenient for the public service, and that the issue of said capital stock is reasonably required for the purposes of said corporation,

It Is, THEREFORE, This 28th day of May, in the year Nineteen Hundred and Nineteen, by the Public Service Commission of Maryland,

Ordered, 1. That the exercise by The New Taxi Service Company of the franchise granted by the certificate of incorporation above referred to, be, and the same hereby is permitted and approved.

2. That the issue and sale at par for cash by said The New Taxi Service Company of Ten Thousand Dollars ($10,000.00) par value of its capital stock for the acquisition of property and the construction, completion, extension and improvement of its facilities is hereby authorized and approved.

3. That said The New Taxi Service Company shall make reports to the Commission duly verified by affidavits as follows:

(a) Upon the issue and sale for cash of its stock, authorized and approved as aforesaid, or any part thereof, the fact of such issue and sale, the terms and conditions thereof, and the amount realized therefrom.

(b) At the termination of each and every period of six months from the date of this order, the disposition and use made of the proceeds of said stock, and the facts and circumstances as to the property acquired and the construction, completion, extension and improvement of its facilities.

ORDER No. 4965

In the Matter of	Before the
The Application of THE UNION BRIDGE ELECTRIC MANUFACTURING COMPANY for Authority to Issue $30,000.00 Par Value of Its 6% Twenty-Year Bonds.	Public Service Commission of Maryland. Case No. 1657.

WHEREAS, The Union Bridge Electric Manufacturing Company, a corporation organized and existing under the laws of the State of Maryland, has applied to this Commision for an order permitting and approving the exercise of the franchise granted to it by Ordinance No. 94 of The Burgess and Commissioners of Taneytown, Maryland, certified copy of which ordinance is filed in these proceedings, and for authority to issue its Twenty-Year Six Per Centum Mortgage Gold Bonds of the aggregate principal amount of Thirty Thousand Dollars ($30,000.00), being the total authorized issue secured by mortgage or deed of trust to be dated May 31st, 1919, upon the property, rights and franchises of said The Union Bridge Electric Manufacturing Company, to Maryland Surety and Trust Company, Trustee, copy of which mortgage or deed of trust is filed in these proceedings, and

WHEREAS, The application having come on to be heard on April 14th, 1919, after due notice published in accordance with this Commission's Order No. 4865 passed April 4th, 1919, and it being the opinion and finding of the Commission after due hearing that the exercise of said franchise is convenient for the public service, and that the issue of said bonds is reasonably acquired for the purposes of said corporation, to wit: the discharge or lawful refunding of its obligations incurred for lawful corporate capital purposes and for the acquisition of property, the construction, completion, extension and improvement of its plant and distributing system, and for the improvement and maintenance of its service, as more particularly set forth and described in the petition herein,

IT IS, THEREFORE, This 28th day of May, in the year Nineteen Hundred and Nineteen, by the Public Service Commission of Maryland,

Ordered, (1) That the exercise by The Union Bridge Electric Manufacturing Company of the franchise granted it by Ordinance No. 94 of The Burgess and Commissioners of Taneytown, Maryland, be, and the same hereby is, permitted and approved.

(2) That the issue and sale at par for cash by said The Union Bridge Electric Manufacturing Company of its Twenty-Year Six Per Centum Mortgage Gold Bonds in the amount of Thirty Thousand Dollars ($30,000.00) be and the same is hereby authorized and approved.

(3) That the said The Union Bridge Electric Manufacturing Company shall make reports to this Commission, duly verified by affidavits, as follows:

(a) Upon the sale for cash of its bonds, authorized and approved as aforesaid, or any part thereof, the fact of such sale or sales, the terms and conditions thereof, and the amount realized therefrom.

(b) At the termination of each and every period of six months from the date of this order, the disposition and use made of the proceeds of said bonds, and the facts and circumstances as to the property acquired and the construction, completion, extension and improvement of its facilities, and the improvement and maintenance of its service.

ORDER No. 4967

In the Matter of

The Application of CONSOLIDATED GAS ELECTRIC LIGHT AND POWER COMPANY OF BALTIMORE and THE CONSOLIDATED POWER COMPANY OF BALTIMORE for Permission and Authority to Issue $5,000,000 of 3½-Year 7% Secured Convertible Notes of the Former Corporation and, as Collateral Therefor, $2,500,000 of First Mortgage 5% Bonds of the Latter Corporation and $3,500,000 of First Refunding Mortgage 6% Bonds Out of a Total Authorized Issue of $100,000,000 of Bonds of the Former Corporation, and Also to Issue, When and As Needed for Conversion of Said Notes, $1,500,000 of First Refunding Mortgage 6% Bonds (in Addition to the $3,500,000 of Such Bonds to Be Issued as Collateral).

Before the

Public Service Commission of Maryland.

Case No. 1656.

WHEREAS, The Consolidated Gas Electric Light and Power Company of Baltimore has applied to this Commission for an order authorizing and approving the issue by said corporation of five million dollars ($5,000,000) of 3½-Year Seven Per Cent. Secured Convertible Gold Notes, to be issued under an indenture between said corporation and the Maryland Trust Company, as Trustee, and also authorizing and approving the issue by said corporation of three million five hundred thousand dollars ($3,500,000) of Thirty-Year Six Per Cent. First Refunding Mortgage Sinking Fund Gold Bonds, to be issued under an indenture between said corporation and the Bankers Trust Company (of New York), as Trustee, (upon deposit with said Trustee of three million seventy-seven thousand dollars ($3,077,000) in cash, to be applied to certain capital expenditures on or after February 1, 1919, which, together with similar expenditures of four hundred and twenty-three thousand dollars ($423,000) prior to February 1, 1919, aggregate three million five hundred thousand dollars, the principal amount of said bonds), and to be deposited as collateral to secure said issue of notes, and also authorizing and approving the issue by said corporation (if, when and as needed for the conversion of the aforesaid notes) of one million five hundred thousand dollars ($1,500,000) par value of Thirty-Year Six Per Cent. First Refunding Mortgage Sinking Fund Gold Bonds (in addition to the $3,500,000 of such bonds to be issued as collateral for such notes and also to be used if, when and as needed for such conversion); and   •

WHEREAS, The Consolidated Power Company of Baltimore has applied to this Commission for an order authorizing and approving the issue by said corporation of two million five hundred thousand dollars ($2,500,000) of First Mortgage Five Per Cent. Twenty-Year Bonds, to be issued under the existing indenture between said corporation and the Maryland Trust Company, as Trustee, (upon deposit with said Trustee of two million five hundred thousand dollars ($2,500,000) in cash, and to be deposited as collateral to secure said issue of notes, the property to be acquired by said corporation with the proceeds of such pledge of said bonds to be leased to the Consolidated Gas Electric Light and Power Company of Baltimore, subject to, for the term and upon the terms and conditions of, the existing twenty-five-year lease from The Consolidated Power Company of Baltimore to the Consolidated Gas Electric Light and Power Company of Baltimore; and

WHEREAS, After consideration of the said application of the Consolidated Gas Electric Light and Power Company of Baltimore and The Consolidated Power Company of Baltimore and the exhibits filed therewith and thereafter, and after due hearing, the Commission is of the opinion that the use of the capital to be secured by said issue of $5,000,000 of notes, and of $3,500,000 of bonds of the Consolidated Gas Electric Light and Power Company of Baltimore and $2,500,000 of bonds of The Consolidated Power Company of Baltimore as collateral for said notes (the excess of one million dollars ($1,000,000) cash to be deposited, over and above the principal amount of said notes, upon the issuance of said bonds, to be temporarily financed by the Consolidated Company through call or short time loans), and of $1,500,000 of bonds of the Consolidated Gas Electric Light and Power Company of Baltimore (in addition to said $3,500,000 thereof) if, when and as needed for the conversion of said notes, is reasonably required for the purposes of the Consolidated Gas Electric Light and Power Company of Baltimore and The Consolidated Power Company of Baltimore, respectively, as in said application set forth, to wit, for the acquisition of property and for the construction, completion, extension and improvement of the plants and distributing systems and for the discharge of the obligations. of said corporations.

IT IS, THEREFORE, This 29th day of May, 1919, by the Public Service Commission of Maryland,

Ordered, That the Consolidated Gas Electric Light and Power Company of Baltimore be and it is hereby authorized:

To issue its 3½-Year Seven Per Cent. Secured Convertible Gold Notes, as aforesaid, in the amount of $5,000,000 for the purposes aforesaid, and to issue and deposit as collateral to secure said notes its Thirty-Year Six Per Cent. First Refunding Mortgage Sinking Fund Gold Bonds in the amount of $3,500,000, and to issue (if, when and as needed for the conversion of said notes) its Thirty-Year Six Per Cent. First Refunding Mortgage Sinking Fund Gold Bonds in the amount of $1,500,000 (in addition to the $3,500,000 of such bonds to be issued as collateral and also to be used if, when and as needed for such conversion).

AND IT IS FURTHER Ordered, That The Consolidated Power Company of Baltimore be and it is hereby authorized:

To issue its First Mortgage Five Per Cent. Twenty-Year Bonds in the amount of $2,500,000 for the purposes aforesaid and to deposit the same as collateral to secure said notes of the Consolidated Gas Electric Light and Power Company of Baltimore (with like authority to the Consolidated Gas Electric Light and Power Company of Baltimore and The Consolidated Power Company of Baltimore to re-deposit, as collateral to secure the First Refunding Mortgage Sinking Fund Gold Bonds of the Consolidated Gas Electric Light and Power Company of Baltimore, $1,500,000 of said bonds of The Consolidated Power Company of Baltimore if, when and as needed to effect the conversion of a like amount of the aforesaid notes of the Consolidated Gas Electric Light and Power Company of Baltimore into a like amount of Thirty-Year Six Per cent. First Refunding Mortgage Sinking Fund Gold Bonds of the Consolidated Gas Electric Light and Power Company of Baltimore).

AND IT IS FURTHER Ordered, That the Consolidated Power Company of Baltimore and the Consolidated Gas Electric Light and Power Company of Baltimore be and they are hereby authorized to execute, make and carry out a lease by The Consolidated Power Company of Baltimore to the Consolidated Gas Electric Light and Power Company of Baltimore of the property acquired, or to be acquired, with the proceeds of the pledge of any of said bonds of The Consolidated Power Company of Baltimore, subject to, for the term and upon the terms and conditions of, the existing twenty-five-year lease from The Consolidated Power Company of Baltimore to the Consolidated Gas Electric Light and Power Company of Baltimore heretofore authorized and approved by this Commission.

AND IT IS FURTHER Ordered, That the said Consolidated Gas Electric Light and Power Company of Baltimore shall make reports, verified by affidavits, to this Commission as follows:

(a) Upon the sale for cash of said notes authorized and approved as aforesaid, or any part thereof, the fact of such sale or sales, the terms and conditions thereof, and the amount realized therefrom,

(b) Upon the issuance, and the deposit thereof as collateral, of said bonds of said corporation authorized and approved as aforesaid, or any part thereof, the fact of such issuance and deposit, the terms and conditions thereof, and the amount realized therefrom,

(c) All conversions of such notes into bonds, or exchanges of such notes for bonds, as aforesaid,

(d) At the termination of every period of six months from the date of this order, the disposition or the use made of the proceeds of said notes.

AND IT IS FURTHER Ordered, That the said The Consolidated Power Company of Baltimore shall make reports, verified by affidavits, to this Commission as follows:

(a) Upon the issuance, and the deposit thereof as collateral, of said bonds of said corporation authorized and approved as aforesaid, or any part thereof, the fact of such issuance and deposit, the terms and conditions thereof, and the amount realized therefrom.

(b) All re-deposits of bonds of said corporation upon conversion of notes of the Consolidated Gas Electric Light and Power Company of Baltimore into bonds of The Consolidated Gas Electric Light and Power Company of Baltimore.

(c) Upon the consummation of such lease to the Consolidated Gas Electric Light and Power Company of Baltimore (if any additional or supplemental lease or leases be deemed necessary and be executed pursuant hereto) the fact of such lease and the terms and conditions thereof, including a complete copy thereof.

ORDER No. 4968

In the Matter of

The Petition of the Carriers Not Under
Federal Control Named in the Official
Classification, by R. N. COLLYER, Their
Agent, for Permission Under Section
15 of the Public Service Commission
Law to File and Publish on Less Than
Statutory Notice Supplement to Offi-
cial Classification No. 44, P. S. C. Md.
O. C. No. 44.

Before the

Public Service Commission
of Maryland.

S. N. & R. Docket.

Case No. 568.

The above mentioned petition having been received and filed, upon
consideration thereof, it is this 29th day of May, 1919, by the Public
Service Commission of Maryland,

Ordered, That permission be, and is hereby given, the carriers not
under Federal control named in the Official Classification, by R. N.
Collyer, their Agent, to file and publish on one day's notice to the
Commission and the public, supplement to Official Classification No. 44,
P. S. C. Md. O. C. No. 44, revising rules 15B and 15C of said Official
Classification as set forth in petition herein and including on full statutory notice necessary additions to, changes in and eliminations from
the list of participating carriers contained in said classification; said
supplement issued under authority hereof to depart from the provisions of this Commission's Circular No. 10A in so far as volume of
supplemental matter is concerned,

PROVIDED, Said supplement be filed with the Commission upon
issuance of this Order, and published by posting as required by law,
and that all copies of said supplement shall bear the following notation :

"Issued under special permission of the Public Service Commission of Maryland, Order No. 4968, of date May 29th,
1919."

ORDER No. 4973

In the Matter of

The Application of THE UNITED RAIL-
WAYS AND ELECTRIC COMPANY OF BAL-
TIMORE for an Order Permitting and
Approving the Removal of Its Tracks
from McCulloh Street Between North
Avenue and Madison Avenue Car Barn
and the Curve Connections at the In-
tersection of North Avenue and Mc-
Culloh Street.

Before the

Public Service Commission
of Maryland.

Case No. 1683.

This case coming on to be heard, after due notice published in compliance with Order No. 4959 of this Commission, passed May 26th,
1919, and no protest thereto having been made, and the Commission
having determined after hearing that the tracks of The United Railways and Electric Company of Baltimore from McCulloh street between North avenue and Madison avenue Car House, an approximate distance of 3,270 feet; and the curve connections at North avenue and McCulloh street, an approximate distance of 450 feet, as mentioned in the petition of The United Railways and Electric Company
of Baltimore and as shown in red on blue print attached to said petition, are no longer necessary or convenient for the public service,

IT IS, THEREFORE, This 3rd day of June, in the year Nineteen Hundred and Nineteen, by the Public Service Commission of Maryland,

Ordered, That the approval and permission of the Commission is
hereby given to the removal of the tracks of The United Railways and
Electric Company of Baltimore from McCulloh street between North
avenue and Madison avenue Car House, an approximate distance of
3,270 feet; and the curve connections at North avenue and McCulloh
street, an approximate distance of 450 feet, as mentioned in the petition of The United Railways and Electric Company of Baltimore, and
as shown in red on the blue print attached to said petition.

ORDER No. 4974

In the Matter of

Rate Schedule P. S. C. Md. No. 2 of
MARYLAND WATER COMPANY OF CECIL
COUNTY and THE ELKTON WATER
WORKS, INCORPORATED.

Before the

Public Service Commission
of Maryland.

WHEREAS, Rate schedule P. S. C. Md. No. 2 of Maryland Water
Company of Cecil County and The Elkton Water Works, Incorporated,

was filed with the Commission on May 1st, 1919, to become effective June 1st, 1919, the effect of which schedule is to considerably increase the rates charged for water furnished in the town of Elkton, Maryland, and

WHEREAS, Application has been made to this Commission by Omar D. Crothers and Frank E. Welsh, Jr., receivers of said Maryland Water Company of Cecil County and of said The Elkton Water Works, Incorporated, for permission to withdraw the aforesaid schedule P. S. C. Md. No. 2, and to continue in effect the rates lawfully effective prior to June 1st, 1919, until such time as said rates are changed in the manner provided by the Public Service Commission Law and the rules of the Commission, and

WHEREAS, After due consideration it appears to the Commission that said request is reasonable and proper, and should be granted,

IT IS, THEREFORE, This 3rd day of June, in the year Nineteen Hundred and Nineteen, by the Public Service Commission of Maryland,

ORDERED, That Omar D. Crothers and Frank E. Welsh, Jr., receivers of Maryland Water Company of Cecil County and of The Elkton Water Works, Incorporated, be and they are hereby permitted to withdraw the increased water rates contained in their schedule P. S. C. Md. No. 2, heretofore filed with the Commission to become effective on June 1st, 1919, and to continue in force the rates and charges theretofore effective until such time as said rates and charges are lawfully changed.

OPINION

In the Matter of

The Complaint of JOHN R. WARFIELD, J. M. PATTERSON, ET AL.,

vs.

CUMBERLAND AND WESTERNPORT ELECTRIC RAILWAY COMPANY.

Before the

Public Service Commission of Maryland.

Case No. 1603.

Appearances:
   W. CARL RICHARDS, ESQ., for Complainants.
   BENJAMIN A. RICHMOND, ESQ., for Respondent.

LEGG, Commissioner.   Filed June 5th, 1919.

On October 21st, 1918, the Cumberland and Westernport Electric Railway Company filed with the Commission its rate schedule P. S. C. Md. No. 4, to become effective November 21st, 1918. The effect of this schedule was to increase the one-way fares charged by said company from 6 cents to 7 cents per zone, except in the case of the zone between Cumberland and Narrows Park, in which zone the fare was increased from 5 cents to 6 cents; fares charged miners riding in miner's car were increased from 5 cents to 6 cents per zone, books containing 100 zone tickets sold to clergymen were increased from $3.00 to $4.00 per book, and books containing 50 zone tickets sold to school children were increased from $1.50 to $2.00 per book.

The Cumberland and Westernport Electric Railway extends from Narrows Park to Westernport, entry into the City of Cumberland from Narrows Park being made over the line of the Cumberland Electric Railway Company, under an operating agreement between the two companies. There are ten fare zones between Cumberland and Westernport, the one-way fares and mileage between Cumberland and Westernport and intermediate points being as follows:

	Fare to or from Cumberland (Cents)	Mileage to Cumberland	Mileage of Fare Zone
Narrows Park............	6	2.25	2.25
Six-Mile House..........	13	5.754	3.504
Clarysville	20	8.178	2.424
Frostburg ....`..........	27	10.829	2.651
Emericks	34	14.705	3.876
Midland	41	16.524	1.819
Lonaconing	48	19.498	2.974
Moscow	55	22.018	2.520
Franklin	62	26.374	4.356
Westernport	69	29.651	3.277

There are over-laps in several of the fare zones.

On November 14th, 1918, there was filed with the Commission a complaint, signed by John R. Warfield and J. M. Patterson, as follows:

"We, the undersigned, herewith submit to your Honorable Body, the enclosed petition, protesting against the increased fares, as published by the Cumberland and Westernport Electric Railway Company, and respectfully ask that your Commission set a date for a hearing, in the City of Cumberland, as early as possible.

"We further request that your Commission issue an order compelling the Cumberland and Westernport Electric Railway Company to issue rebate slips, covering the increased fares, on and after November 21, 1918, these rebate slips to be issued for each fare paid, until such time as the case is decided."

On same date a supplemental petition was filed with the Commission, signed by Mr. Warfield and 128 others, reading:

"We, the undersigned, who live along the line of the Cumberland and Westernport Electric Railway Company, hereby respectfully petition your Honourable Commission that the said Railway Company be refused the right to increase the fare on said road one cent per zone as per their advertisement, which will go into effect November 21, 1918.

"In support of this petition, we respectfully submit that last summer a similar increase was allowed, raising the rate from five to six cents per zone, which said six cents per zone is now the rate.

"We further submit that the franchise contract entered into between the said Railway Company and the County Commissioners of Allegany County provides the following condition: 'This franchise is granted upon the express condition that the party of the second part in fixing its rates of fare shall not charge travellers more than five cents for any distance of not more than three miles and less, and not more than fifteen cents for the whole distance between its termini.' "

Case as numbered above was thereupon docketed and order entered directing the respondent to satisfy the matters complained of, or to answer the complaint within ten days. Answer was duly filed, showing that the respondent has been compelled to greatly increase the rates of pay of its platform labor, as well as of its other employes, in order to retain such employes in its service, as otherwise they would have sought more profitable employment in other fields, and that the costs of all materials and supplies used by it had greatly advanced in price. With its answer respondent submitted several statements intended to demonstrate its need for additional revenue in order to meet its requirements for operating expenses, taxes, depreciation, fixed charges, etc. It appears that during its seventeen years of operation the respondent has paid but one dividend, that being 12%, or at the rate of 1% per annum during the first twelve years of operation.

The right of the Commission to require a common carrier to issue receipt slips for amount of fare paid in excess of the former fare pending determination of the reasonableness of the increased fare was presented to the Commission in connection with increase in fare by The United Railways and Electric Company of Baltimore and the Commission's General Counsel held in his Opinion No. 367 filed on October 2nd, 1918 (P. S. C. Md. Reports, Vol. 9, p. 467) that the Commission is without power to require this. The question of the right of the respondent to file with the Commission and make effective tariff schedules establishing rates of fare in excess of those prescribed by the franchise agreement referred to by complainants was referred by the Commission to its General Counsel, and Opinion No. 370, filed November 22nd, 1918, and concurred in by the Commission, (P. S. C. Md. Reports, Vol. 9, p. 473), holds that the respondent company has the legal power to do so.

On December 12th, 1918, a committee of Local Union No. 2523, United Mine Workers of America, filed a petition asking that the fares of the respondent "be reduced to a more reasonable rate." Answer thereto was filed by the respondent, which answer has to do largely with the rates of fare charged miners, and details the history of these rates and the reasons leading up to the establishment of such special rates.

On February 24th, 1919, an amended complaint was filed with the Commission by Mr. Patterson, which complaint, besides attacking the legality of the zone fares being collected by the respondent, involves the question of service as well, which amended complaint was duly answered by the respondent, and same not being satisfactory to the complainants, the case was set for hearing at the Council Chambers, City Hall, Cumberland, Maryland, on March 6th, 1919.

At this hearing a number of witnesses appeared and testified. The complaints respecting service were practically presented and divided into two parts, that is, between Cumberland and Frostburg and between Frostburg and Westernport. After various witnesses had testified, counsel for complainants stated (p. 144 of stenographic record) that he was willing to waive all of the minor points, thus narrowing the issue down to three points:

1. The necessity for the respondent to furnish two cars leaving Cumberland for Westernport at 5 P. M. in order to provide reasonably adequate service.

2. The reasonableness of requiring the 5 P. M. car to wait at Narrows Park until the arrival of the car of the Cumberland Electric Railway Company scheduled to leave Cumberland at 5 P. M. and to immediately follow the cars of the respondent to Narrows Park.

3. The length of time the increased fares shall be permitted to remain in effect.

The Commission realizes that some of the conditions with respect to service complained of existed at the time the complaints were filed, and that they caused annoyance, inconvenience and sometimes hardship, to the patrons of the Railway Company, but the Commission recognizes that at that time the company was confronted with the unsatisfactory conditions of labor and difficulty of obtaining materials and supplies then being so generally encountered by utilities throughout the country, due to the war. From the testimony it is apparent that many of the conditions originally complained of have now been remedied, and the respondent evidences a desire to render the best possible service.

With respect to the first point at issue, the evidence shows that the respondent has recently been using two cars on the 5 P. M. run from Cumberland; one large type car seating 58 passengers, operated through to Westernport, and a second car of smaller type, seating 42 passengers, which car does not go beyond Frostburg. Respondent's Exhibit No. 1, showing passengers carried on each of said cars from February 16th to 28th, both inclusive, and the testimony offered at the hearing, justify the continuance of the second 5 P. M. car, and the Commission will enter an order requiring the company to continue the second car. Should traffic conditions hereafter change so as to render it unnecessary to longer operate this car, the Commission will relieve the company of the requirement to so do.

Concerning the second point at issue, the testimony shows that passengers for points on the line of respondent beyond Narrows Park, traveling on cars of the Cumberland Electric Railway to that point, are frequently left at Narrows Park, due to the failure of car of Cumberland and Westernport Electric Railway to await the arrival of car of the Cumberland Electric Railway Company. Complainants expressed themselves as fully satisfied if the car of respondent would be held at Narrows Park at least five minutes, so as to enable passengers arriving on car of Cumberland Electric Railway to connect therewith, and the testimony is to the effect that such action would not interrupt the traffic over the line of the respondent. In view of the facts presented the Commission deems the request to be reasonable and will require in its order that cars of the respondent be held at Narrows Park for a period of not exceeding five minutes, awaiting the arrival of cars of Cumberland Electric Railway Company.

This brings us to a consideration of the third point at issue, which is the length of time the increased fares shall be permitted to remain in effect. Statements and exhibits filed by the respondent show that the increased fares are necessary for the proper conduct of its business, and the need for this additional revenue was conceded by counsel for complainants, the only question to be determined in this connection being length of time the increased fares shall remain effective. The Commission is of the opinion that so long as the present scale of wages and the present standard of costs of materials, etc., continue, it will probably be impossible to accomplish any reduction in these fares, and when a readjustment of prices will occur it is, of course, impossible for the Commission to prognosticate. In other cases in which the Commission has approved increased rates, fares and charges found to be necessary in order to meet increased costs of operation resulting from the inflation in prices during the war, the Commission has in its orders granting such relief provided that the rates shall remain in effect for periods ranging from one to two years. In the instant case the Commission will stipulate in its order that the present fares shall remain in effect for a period of two years from November 21st, 1918, subject to the further order of the Commission, and will further require the respondent to furnish the Commission quarterly reports of its financial condition. Should these statements disclose earnings sufficient to justify a reduction in the rates of fare, the Commission will prescribe lower fares.

Complaints respecting the service and rates of the respondent, particularly from Frostburg to Westernport, were made at the hearing by Local Union to 4414, United Mine Workers of America, represented by its president, James J. Watson, who testified at length. The complaints respecting service grew largely out of the undoubtedly inferior service furnished during the past fall and winter, but the Commission is convinced that the difficulty in this respect was the result of the unsettled labor conditions, etc., at that time obtaining generally throughout the country, and that the situation has since been remedied. The Commission has hereinbefore found that the additional revenue accruing from the increased fares is necessary in order to provide for the requirements of the respondent. This narrows the question of fares down to the zone system as applied to Lonaconing, which was the chief source of complaint of Local Union No. 4414. The testimony shows that a passenger from Frostburg to Lonaconing pays 21 cents (3 zones), being thereby enabled to ride to the westerly outskirts of Lonaconing, whereas a passenger from Westernport traveling to the extreme easterly end of Lonaconing is required to pay 28 cents (4 zones), though the published fare between Westernport and Lonaconing is 21 cents. This is no doubt caused by the manner in which the zones are divided in Lonaconing, and naturally provokes much dissatisfaction. A lap-over in each direction would easily adjust the situation, and the Commission is of the opinion that the respondent should make some change in its present system of fare collections at this point, and unless this change is voluntarily effected within a reasonable time the Commission will make a further investigation of the matter and pass such order as may be necessary in order to remove the cause of complaint in this respect.

An order will be passed by the Commission in accordance with the findings herein contained.

ORDER No. 4977

In the Matter of

The Complaint of JOHN R. WARFIELD,
J. M. PATTERSON, ET AL.,

vs.

CUMBERLAND AND WESTERNPORT ELEC-
TRIC RAILWAY COMPANY.

Before the

Public Service Commission
of Maryland.

Case No. 1603.

This case being at issue upon complaints and answers on file and
having been duly heard and submitted by the parties and full investigation of the matters and things involved having been had and the
Commission, on the date hereof, having rendered and filed an opinion
containing its findings of fact and conclusions therein, which said
opinion is hereby referred to and made part hereof,

IT IS, THEREFORE, This 5th day of June, in the year Nineteen Hundred and Nineteen, by the Public Service Commission of Maryland,

ORDERED, (1) That the rates, fares and charges contained in rate
schedule P. S. C. Md. No. 4 of Cumberland and Westernport Electric
Railway Company, filed with this Commission on October 21st, 1918,
to become effective November 21st, 1918, be and they are hereby approved, to remain effective until November 21st, 1920, unless earlier
modified or changed by the further order of this Commission.

(2) That the said Cumberland and Westernport Electric Railway
Company shall furnish to this Commission accurate and complete
statements under oath setting forth the operating and other receipts
and expenditures of said company for the three months ending March
31st, 1919, as soon as possible after receipt of copy of this order, and
thereafter for each three-month period and for any other period which
this Commission may hereafter require.

(3) That this Commission retains jurisdiction in this matter to the
end that it may enter such further order or orders as may be found
necessary in view of the results shown by any statement or statements
filed with the Commission in compliance with the next preceding paragraph of this order.

(4) That until otherwise ordered by this Commission, the said Cumberland and Westernport Electric Railway Company shall continue to
operate two cars leaving Cumberland daily, except Sunday, at 5.00
P. M., one car to be run to Frostburg and the other car to be operated through to Westernport.

(5) That until otherwise ordered by this Commission, the said Cumberland and Westernport Electric Railway Company shall hold its

cars leaving Cumberland at 5.00 P. M. at Narrows Park for a period not less than five (5) minutes, awaiting the arrival of cars of Cumberland Electric Railway Company at that point.

(6) That with respect to the other matters and things complained of, the complaints in the above entitled matter be and the same are hereby dismissed.

ORDER No. 4978

In the Matter of

The Application of the DIRECTOR GENERAL OF RAILROADS, Operating the Pennsylvania Railroad in Maryland, for Authority to Change Rogers Station, Baltimore County, Maryland, from an Agency to a Non-Agency Station.

Before the

Public Service Commission of Maryland.

Case No. 1667.

WHEREAS, The Director General of Railroads, operating the Pennsylvania Railroad in Maryland, has applied to this Commission for authority to change Rogers Station, Baltimore County, Maryland, from an agency station to a non-agency station, and

WHEREAS, The application having come on to be heard on May 5th, 1919, after due notice published in accordance with this Commission's Order No. 4890 passed April 23rd, 1919, and it being the opinion and finding of the Commission after due hearing that public necessity and convenience reasonably require the maintenance of Rogers Station as an agency station, and that an agent should be employed at that point if the service of such an agent can be secured at a reasonable compensation,

IT IS, THEREFORE, This 5th day of June, in the year Nineteen Hundred and Nineteen, by the Public Service Commission of Maryland,

Ordered, That the application of the Director General of Railroads, operating the Pennsylvania Railroad in Maryland, for authority to change Rogers Station, Baltimore County, Maryland, from an agency station to a non-agency station be and it is hereby denied and dismissed.

AND IT IS FURTHER Ordered, That until the further order of this Commission in the premises, the Director General of Railroads, operating the Pennsylvania Railroad in Maryland, be and he is hereby directed and required to continue Rogers Station as an agency station, provided the services of an agent can be secured at a salary not exceeding $25.00 per month, with the right to the Director General of Railroads to have the Commission reopen this case for further consideration in the event of his being unable to secure the services of an agent at the compensation fixed by the Commission.

ORDER No. 4979

In the Matter of	Before the
The Application of JOHN SCHENNING for a Permit for the Operation of a Motor Vehicle for Public Use Between Baltimore and Poplar, Maryland.	Public Service Commission of Maryland. Case No. 1659.

WHEREAS, John Schenning, having made application to this Commission for a permit for the operation of a motor vehicle for public use between Baltimore, Maryland, and Poplar, Maryland, and

WHEREAS, The application having come on to be heard on April 11th, 1919, in accordance with this Commission's Order No. 4867 passed April 4th, 1919, and it being the opinion and finding of the Commission after due hearing that the public welfare and convenience do not require the granting of said permit, but that, on the contrary, the granting of such permit would be prejudicial to the welfare and convenience of the public,

IT IS, THEREFORE, This 5th day of June, in the year Nineteen Hundred and Nineteen, by the Public Service Commission of Maryland,

Ordered, That the application of John Schenning, in this case exhibited, be and the same is hereby refused and dismissed.

ORDER No. 4980

In the Matter of	
The Complaint of Citizens of Berwyn Heights, by ADENE WILLIAMS, Secretary, et Al.,	Before the
vs.	Public Service Commission of Maryland.
THE WASHINGTON INTERURBAN RAILROAD COMPANY.	Case No. 1624.

WHEREAS, This case involving the reasonableness of the rates of fare charged and collected by The Washington Interurban Railroad Company under its rate schedule P. S. C. Md. No. 2, effective December 1st, 1918, and the adequacy of the service furnished by said company, being at issue upon complaints and answers on file, and having been duly heard and submitted by the parties and full investigation of the matters and things involved having been made by the Commission, and

WHEREAS, It being the opinion and finding of the Commission that the rates of fare charged and collected by the respondent under its rate schedule P. S. C. Md. No. 2 aforesaid are just and reasonable, and it appearing to the Commission that subsequent to hearing in this case a new time schedule has been inaugurated by the respondent, which new time schedule provides better service to the complainants and tends to greatly reduce the cause of complaint, as shown by letters from complainants filed herein, and it being the further opinion and finding of the Commission that the service furnished at the present time by the respondent is reasonably adequate,

IT IS, THEREFORE, This 5th day of June, in the year Nineteen Hundred and Nineteen, by the Public Service Commission of Maryland,

Ordered, That the complaints in the above entitled matter be, and the same are hereby dismissed.

OPINION

In the Matter of

The Complaint of EVERETT DUFOUR and Thirty-five Other Citizens of Southern Maryland

vs.

THE CHESAPEAKE BEACH RAILWAY COMPANY.

Before the

Public Service Commission of Maryland.

Case No. 1658.

Appearances:
EVERETT DUFOUR, ESQ., for Complainants.
MESSRS. H. HERSCHBERGER and WALTER J. HEYWOOD, for Respondent.

LEGG, Commissioner.   Filed June 6th, 1919.

On April 4th, 1919, there was filed with the Commission a complaint signed by Everett Dufour and thirty-five other citizens of Southern Maryland, directed against the Chesapeake Beach Railway Company, hereinafter called the Railway Company. This complaint covers nineteen specific points respecting the freight rates and passenger fares charged and collected and the service furnished by the Railway Company.

Copy of the complaint was served upon the Railway Company, and order entered requiring it to satisfy the things complained of or to answer the charges therein made. Answer was duly filed with the Commission, which answer constitutes a general denial of the things complained of, and same not being satisfactory to the complainants, the case was set for hearing.

Hearing was had at the offices of the Commission in Baltimore on April 30, 1919, at which hearing a number of witnesses appeared and testified. At the hearing the Railway Company filed with the Commission statements signed by twelve of the persons whose names appear on the complaint, showing that the complaint had not been read by them before signing and disclaiming any knowledge of the contents thereof or the purpose of the complaint, other than that same was intended to secure lower rates.

A number of the items of the complaint respect minor questions of service and facilities, and with the assurance of the Railway Company that these matters will be promptly remedied, the Commission will not deal with them in this opinion. There is one minor matter, however, which seems to deserve the attention of the Commission, and that is the complaint as to dirty windows in passenger coaches of the Railway Company. The testimony on this subject developed that the coaches are equipped with stationary window screens, making it impossible to wash the windows without removing the screens, a laborious and expensive process, and the result being that windows remain unwashed for months. The Commission believes that if the screens are kept in the cars only during the summer months, when windows are usually raised, and removed during the remainder of the year, the cause of complaint in this respect will be largely removed, and it will so order.

The Railway Company operates a local train from District Line to Chesapeake Beach and intermediate stations, leaving District Line at 5:40 P. M. Passengers from Washington, D. C., use cars of the Washington Railway and Electric Company to District Line, and as these street cars are sometimes delayed, due to the evening rush-hour traffic, it not infrequently happens that persons on the car leaving 15th Street and New York Avenue at 4:50 P. M. (which is the last car scheduled to connect with the 5:40 P. M. train from District Line) arrive at the District Line only to find that the 5:40 P. M. train has departed. During the excursion season, from June to September, the Railway Company operates a through excursion train to Chesapeake Beach, leaving District Line at 6:30 P. M. It appears that it is the practice of the Railway Company to stop this train for local passengers who miss the 5:40 P. M. train, when their failure to catch the earlier train is due to a tie-up of the street cars in the District of Columbia. The Commission is of the opinion that the 5:40 P. M. train should be held at the District Line for not less than ten minutes to await the arrival of the car of the Washington Railway and Electric

Company which leaves 15th Street and New York Avenue at 4:50 P. M., when such car is delayed, and will require this to be done.

The Commission is asked to require the Railway Company to install railroad track scales. The record shows that the local freight business of the Railway Company is not sufficient to justify the Commission in requiring it to incur the expenses incident to the installation and maintenance of such scales.

Nor does the Commission find that the traffic warrants the installation of sidings at Mt. Calvert and Pennsylvania Junction. An investigation by the Engineering Department of the Commission shows the approximate cost of installing switch, exclusive of grading at Mt. Calvert, to be over $500.00.

The complaint alleges that the draw-bridge of the Railway Company over the Patuxent River is in an unsafe condition, and that all trains should be required to stop before crossing the draw. The Commission's Engineering Department made an examination of this bridge and reports that all rotten timbers upon the bridge are being replaced, and that after this work, as well as some additional reconstruction suggested by the Engineering Department and acquiesced in by the Railway Company, is completed, the bridge will be in a safer condition than when first constructed. The Engineering Department further advises against requiring the stopping of trains before crossing the draw, and in this recommendation the Commission concurs.

The complaint, so far as the same respects rates and fares, has to do largely with the practice of the Railway Company of selling commutation tickets only between District Line and Chesapeake Beach, persons residing at intermediate points who desire to purchase commutation tickets being required to purchase tickets good for travel between the termini. These commutation tickets permit passengers to travel at rates of fare considerably lower than the straight fare rates between local stations, and in view of the small number of persons traveling daily between intermediate stations the Commission considers the practice in this respect reasonable and does not feel that it would be justified in requiring the sale of commutation tickets between intermediate stations at proportionate rates. Nor does it appear that the revenues of the Railway Company can well be reduced, particularly when consideration is given to the fact that such revenues are hardly more than sufficient to meet operating expenses, and not sufficient to pay interest on its bonds or dividends upon its outstanding stock.

An order will be entered in accordance with the findings herein contained.

ORDER No. 4983

In the Matter of

The Complaint of EVERETT DUFOUR and
Thirty-five Other Citizens of Southern
Maryland

vs.

THE CHESAPEAKE BEACH RAILWAY
COMPANY.

Before the

Public Service Commission
of Maryland.

Case No. 1658.

This case being at issue upon complaint and answer on file and having been duly heard and submitted by the parties and full investigation of the matters and things involved having been had and the Commission, on the date hereof, having rendered and filed an opinion containing its finding of fact and conclusions therein, which said opinion is hereby referred to and made part hereof,

IT IS, THEREFORE, This 6th day of June, in the year Nineteen Hundred and Nineteen, by the Public Service Commission of Maryland,

Ordered, (1) That the Chesapeake Beach Railway Company be and it is hereby directed and required to hereafter and until the further order of this Commission in the premises keep the stationary window screens in its passenger coaches during only the summer months, and to remove such screens during the remainder of the year.

(2) That the said Chesapeake Beach Railway Company be and it is hereby directed and required to hereafter, and until the further order of this Commission in the premises, to hold its train scheduled to leave District Line at 5:40 P. M. for a period of not less than ten (10) minutes, to await the arrival of car of the Washington Railway and Electric Company which leaves 15th Street and New York Avenue, Washington, D. C., at 4:50 P. M., when such car is delayed.

(3) That with respect to the other matters and things complained of, the complaint in the above entitled matter be and the same is hereby dismissed.

ORDER No. 4984

In the Matter of	
The Complaint of L. D. CRAWFORD, ET AL.,	Before the
	Public Service Commission of Maryland.
vs.	
THE WESTERN MARYLAND RAILWAY COMPANY.	Case No. 1681.

The above cause being at issue upon complaint and answer on file and having been duly heard and submitted by the parties and it appearing that subsequent to the hearing of the complaint arrangements have been made by the respondent to resume its freight and passenger agency at Deerfield, Maryland, thereby satisfying the complaint, as shown by letter from the General Attorney of the respondent company filed herein on the date hereof,

It Is, THEREFORE, This 6th day of June, in the year Nineteen Hundred and Nineteen, by the Public Service Commission of Maryland,

Ordered, That the above entitled case be and it is hereby entered as satisfied and closed.

ORDER No. 4986

In the Matter of	
The Petitions of the Carriers Not Under Federal Control Named in the Official Classification, by R. N. COLLYER, Their Agent, for Permission Under Section 15 of the Public Service Commission Law to File and Publish on Less Than Statutory Notice Supplements to Official Classification No. 44, P. S. C. Md. O. C. No. 44.	Before the
	Public Service Commission of Maryland.
	S. N. & R. Docket.
	Case No. 569.

The above mentioned petitions having been received and filed, upon consideration thereof, it is this 9th day of June, 1919, by the Public Service Commission of Maryland,

Ordered, That permission be, and is hereby given, carriers not under Federal control named in the Official Classification, by R. N. Collyer, their Agent, to file and publish on not less than five days'

notice to the Commission and the public, supplement or supplements to Official Classification No. 44, P. S. C. Md. O. C. No. 44, revising the classification specifications for lamps, and establishing special regulations governing descriptions, marks, inspection and delivery of eggs, and the handling of claims thereunder, as set forth in petitions herein and exhibits filed therewith,

PROVIDED, Said supplement or supplements be filed with the Commission upon issuance of this Order, and published by posting as required by law, and that all copies of said supplement or supplements shall bear the following notation:

"Issued under special permission of the Public Service Commission of Maryland, Order No. 4986 of date June 9th, 1919."

ORDER No. 4987

In the Matter of	
The Complaint of SAMUEL W. PFOUTZ, ET AL., Patrons of The Western Maryland Railway Company at Linwood, New Windsor, Wakefield, Medford, Avondale and Westminster Stations,	Before the Public Service Commission of Maryland. Case No. 618.
vs.	
WESTERN MARYLAND RAILWAY COMPANY.	

The respondent in the above entitled matter having notified this Commission of its intention to put into effect on June 22nd, 1919, its summer time-table, under which the leaving time of train No. 22 at Union Bridge, Maryland, would be 6:20 A. M., and the shippers of milk located along the line of respondent and using said train No. 22 for the shipment of milk to Baltimore having filed protests with the Commission against the proposed schedule, and the matter having been duly heard by the Commission on June 9th, 1919, in accordance with the Commission's Order No. 4975 passed June 3rd, 1919, and it being the opinion and finding of the Commission that the leaving time of said train No. 22 at Union Bridge should be 6:35 A. M., and that said train should arrive at Hillen Station, Baltimore, Maryland, at 9:20 A. M., the necessary reduction in running time of said train to be made east of Westminster, Maryland,

IT IS, THEREFORE, This 10th day of June, in the year Nineteen Hundred and Nineteen, by the Public Service Commission of Maryland,

Ordered, That The Western Maryland Railway Company be and it hereby is directed and required to make the leaving time of its train No. 22 at Union Bridge 6:35 A. M., and the scheduled time of said train's arrival at Hillen Station, Baltimore, 9:20 A. M., the necessary reduction in running time of said train to be made east of Westminster.

IT IS FURTHER *Ordered,* That this order shall become effective on June 22nd, 1919, and remain in effect until the adoption of the respondent's winter time-table.

ORDER No. 4988

In the Matter of	
The Application of WASHINGTON, BALTIMORE AND ANNAPOLIS ELECTRIC RAILROAD COMPANY for an Order Permitting and Approving the Construction of a Side Track Connecting With Its North-bound Track at High Bridge, Maryland, Also a Freight Shed Adjacent Thereto.	Before the Public Service Commission of Maryland. Case No. 1685.

WHEREAS, It appears from the petition and exhibit filed in the above entitled matter that the proposed construction of a side track and freight shed at High Bridge, Maryland, are necessary and convenient for the public service, and

WHEREAS, The Commission being of the opinion that a formal hearing in the matter is not necessary,

IT IS, THEREFORE, This tenth day of June, 1919, by the Public Service Commission of Maryland,

Ordered, That the proposed construction of a side track and freight shed at High Bridge, Maryland, on the Washington, Baltimore and Annapolis Electric Railroad, as set forth and shown in said petition and exhibit filed herein, be, and the same is hereby, permitted and approved.

ORDER No. 4991

In the Matter of

The Petition of THE MARYLAND ELECTRIC RAILWAYS COMPANY for Permission Under Section 15 of the Public Service Commission Law to File and Publish on Less Than Statutory Notice Rate of $15.00 Per Car on Sand and Gravel, Carloads, from Annapolis, Maryland, to Stations to and Including Glenburnie, Maryland.

Before the

Public Service Commission of Maryland.

S. N. & R. Docket.

Case No. 570.

The above mentioned petition having been received and filed, upon consideration thereof, it is this 12th day of June, 1919, by the Public Service Commission of Maryland,

Ordered, That permission be, and is hereby given, The Maryland Electric Railways Company to file and publish on one day's notice to the Commission and the public, rate of $15.00 per car on sand and gravel, carloads, from Annapolis, Maryland, to stations to and including Glenburnie, Maryland,

PROVIDED, Tariff containing said rate be filed with the Commission upon issuance of this Order, and published by posting as required by law, and that all copies of said tariff shall bear the following notation:

"Issued under special permission of the Public Service Commission of Maryland, Order No. 4991 of date June 12th, 1919."

ORDER No. 4997

In the Matter of

The Application of the DIRECTOR GENERAL OF RAILROADS, Operating the Pennsylvania Railroad in Maryland, to Change Catonsville Station, Maryland, from an Agency Station to a Non-Agency Station.

Before the

Public Service Commission of Maryland.

Case No. 1684.

WHEREAS, The Director General of Railroads, operating the Pennsylvania Railroad in Maryland, has applied to this Commission for authority to change Catonsville Station, Maryland, from an agency freight station to a non-agency station, and

WHEREAS, The application having this day come on to be heard after due notice published in accordance with this Commission's Order No. 4985 passed June 6th, 1919, and it being the opinion and finding of the Commission after due hearing that the maintenance of Catonsville Station as an agency freight station is no longer reasonably necessary or convenient for the public service,

IT IS, THEREFORE, This 17th day of June, in the year Nineteen Hundred and Nineteen, by the Public Service Commission of Maryland,

Ordered, That the Director General of Railroads, operating the Pennsylvania Railroad in Maryland, be and he is hereby authorized and permitted to change Catonsville Station, Maryland, from an agency freight station to a non-agency station, effective on and after July 1st, 1919.

ORDER No. 4999

In the Matter of

The Application of the DIRECTOR GENERAL OF RAILROADS, Operating the Pennsylvania Railroad in Maryland, for Authority to Change Rogers Station, Baltimore County, Maryland, from an Agency to a Non-Agency Station.

Before the

Public Service Commission of Maryland.

Case No. 1667.

WHEREAS, The Director General of Railroads, operating the Pennsylvania Railroad in Maryland, having notified this Commission that he is unable to secure the services of an agent at Rogers Station, Baltimore County, Maryland, at the compensation prescribed by the Commission's Order No. 4978 entered herein on June 5th, 1919, and praying that said Order No. 4978 be modified so as to permit the employment of a station-keeper at Rogers Station instead of continuing that point as an agency station, it is, upon consideration, this 17th day of June, in the year Nineteen Hundred and Nineteen, by the Public Service Commisson of Maryland,

Ordered, (1) That Order No. 4978 entered herein on June 5th, 1919, be and the same is hereby annulled and rescinded.

(2) That the Director General of Railroads, operating the Pennsylvania Railroad in Maryland, be and he is hereby authorized and permitted to change Rogers Station, Baltimore County, Maryland, from an agency station to a non-agency station, effective on and after July 1st, 1919.

IT IS FURTHER **Ordered,** That the said Director General of Railroads, operating the Pennsylvania Railroad in Maryland, shall provide a station-keeper at Rogers Station not later than the day on which the agency at that point is discontinued, and thereafter employ such station-keeper so long as Rogers Station is continued as a non-agency station, provided the services of such station-keeper can be secured at a salary not exceeding $25.00 per month.

ORDER No. 5000

In the Matter of

The Application of THE CHESAPEAKE
AND POTOMAC TELEPHONE COMPANY for
the Approval of an Agreement, Dated
May 20th, 1919, Between It and
MAYOR AND COUNCIL OF BERLIN for the
Sale by the Latter to the Former of
Two Poles Located on the South Side
of Pitts Street, West of Church Street
and East of Williams Street, Berlin,
Worcester County, Maryland.

Before the

Public Service Commission
of Maryland.

Case No. 1688.

The agreement or other written instrument evidencing the transaction in this case having been submitted to this Commission for the purpose of securing its consent to the consummation thereof and the Commission having determined that a hearing is unnecessary,

IT IS, THEREFORE, On this eighteenth day of June, in the year 1919, by the Public Service Commission of Maryland,

Ordered, That the consent of this Commission be and the same is hereby given to the disposition of the property described in said agreement, or other written instrument, evidencing the transaction in accordance with the terms outlined therein.

OPINION

In the Matter of

The Complaint of the MAYOR AND COUN-
CILMEN OF LONACONING

vs.

THE LONACONING WATER COMPANY.

Before the

Public Service Commission
of Maryland.

Case No. 1616.

Appearances:
  GEORGE L. EPPLER, ESQ., for Complainants.
  D. L. SLOAN, ESQ., for Respondent.

LEGG, Commissioner.   Filed June 19th, 1919.

On November 21st, 1918, the Lonaconing Water Company filed with
the Commission its rate schedule P. S. C. Md. No. 4 to become effective
January 1st, 1919. The effect of this schedule was to increase the rate
for dwellings with one spigot or hydrant from $9.00 to $12.00 per
year. The minimum charge for metered service was increased to the
same amount, and changes were made in certain other flat rate fixture
charges.

On December 28th, 1918, the Mayor and Councilmen of Lonaconing
filed with the Commission a protest against the increased rates, alleging same to be excessive, unfair and unreasonable, and further protesting against an inventory of the assets of the company previously
made and used by it as a basis for a former increase in rates, alleging
that said inventory is not a true statement of its assets and does not
show the true amount invested in the plant of said company.

The complaint was duly answered by respondent, and same not being
satisfactory to the complainants, the case was set for hearing at the
Hotel Gladstone, Frostburg, Maryland, on March 7th, 1919.

Prior to the hearing, the Auditor of the Commission made an examination of the books of the company, filing two complete reports showing a comparative statement of income and operating expenses for a
series of years, and bringing the books of the company down to December 31st, 1918.

To conform to the date of the book value in the Auditor's report, the
Engineering Department supplemented its previous valuation reports,
Nos. 981 and 1066, by filing Report 1259, bringing the valuation of the
company's property down to December 31st, 1918. The earlier reports
above referred to were filed by the Commission's Engineering Department in Case No. 1263, which case involved the reasonableness of the
rates of the respondent published in its schedule P. S. C. Md. No. 3,
effective January 1st, 1917, the chief effect of which schedule was to

increase the single spigot charge for dwellings from $6.00 to $9.00 per annum, the $6.00 charge having been maintained since the formation of the company. An exhaustive inquiry into the affairs of the respondent company was made in that case, but complainants having failed to indicate that hearing was desired, same has never been heard and accordingly remains open on the Commission's dockets.

Copies of the Auditor's and Engineer's reports were furnished the complainants and respondent.

From a copy of the original charter filed herein and testimony of witnesses at the hearing, a historical review of the respondent can be briefly summarized.

In 1895, by ordinance, the Mayor and Councilmen of Lonaconing granted Malcolm Sinclair, his assigns, etc., the right to supply water to the town of Lonaconing. In the same year the Lonaconing Water Company was incorporated under the General Laws of Maryland for the purpose of supplying the town of Lonaconing and vicinity with water, with an authorized issue of common stock of $70,000.00.

Malcolm Sinclair and two associates, John J. Bell and Jacob Schimiller, assigned the franchise to the respondent company. First Mortgage Bonds to the amount of $33,000.00 were issued and construction work begun, which included the building of a reservoir known now as the Charlestown reservoir on a tract of 13 acres of land purchased from David M. Evans, being the outlet of about an 800-acre watershed.

To each of the original promoters was given a thousand-dollar bond, or $3,000.00, and among them was divided the $70,000.00 common stock, 1400 shares of a par value of $50.00 as compensation for promotion, surveys, engineering, financing and other services. It appears that $30,000.00 went into the property.

David M. Evans purchased some of the bonds and later bought a sufficient number of shares of the outstanding common stock to give him control of the company, and it is shown at this time that the entire 1,400 shares of stock are owned by the three officers of the company, sons of the David M. Evans, and were acquired, according to the testimony, at from $10.00 to $25.00 per share and now assessed by the State Tax Commission at $40.00 per share.

With an increase in population and a more general use of water, it became necessary for the respondent to increase the supply, and to this end additional water rights were obtained and what is known as the Koontz reservoir was built. The company is now contemplating constructing an additional reservoir on Orr's Run, and to enlarge the Charlestown reservoir.

At the hearing, many witnesses appeared and the testimony covered a wide range of complaints, which may be summarized under the following heads:

Inadequacy of supply.
Quality of water.
Contamination of water-sheds.
Inefficient operating conditions.
Unsatisfactory fire plugs.
Unsatisfactory rules for metered service.
Capitalization of the Company.
Engineering Dept. Appraisal.
Excessive rates.

The testimony of witnesses on the inadequacy of supply recited conditions existing three or more years ago, and after a full investigation the Commission is of the opinion that the supply is fully adequate for all present requirements and the future is being considered by the company in its plans for an enlargement of the Charlestown reservoir and development at Orr's Run.

The complaints respecting the quality of water and contamination of the water-sheds can be considered as one factor under the present operating system of the company. Water is supplied by what is known as the gravity system, mountain streams being impounded and water furnished direct to consumers by mains in its raw state, no filtration or chemical treatment being afforded.

The Commission is convinced by the testimony that the company has not given proper supervision to the water-shed, having permitted cattle to graze adjacent to the reservoir on land owned by it and dedicated to public use.

While the quality of water furnished and the protection of the sources of supply are without the jurisdiction of the Commission, being regulated by the State Board of Health, they are, however, matters to be given serious consideration by the Commission when it comes to determine the worth of the service.

At the instance of the Commission, the State Board of Health, on April 17th, 1919, reported its knowledge of these alleged conditions, advising that the quality of the water was only fair; that cattle had been permitted to graze near the reservoir; that other matters of complaint arising from lumbering operations, sulphured water from abandoned mines, etc., had been remedied by the company when found existing.

The complaint of inefficient operating conditions arises mainly from muddy water furnished some consumers after a heavy rainfall.

The Charlestown reservoir on Jackson's Run has an elevation of about 200 feet, and the Koontz reservoir about 400 feet. These reservoirs are on opposite sides of the town and about four miles apart.

The water-shed of Jackson Run affords such protection that the water in the Charlestown reservoir rarely becomes muddy, but the elevation of this reservoir is insufficient to supply the entire system, and it is now used as a reserve supply. The Koontz reservoir has sufficient elevation to supply all users, but its water-shed is not so protected, and heavy rains cause the water to become very muddy. By a system of valves, it is possible to shut off this reservoir and cut in the Charlestown reservoir, and thereby all but about 85 services can be furnished a continuous supply of clear water. It is evident from the testimony that the company has not exercised proper dispatch and care in this matter, and while no order will be passed relative to the complaint, the Commission admonishes the officials of the company to give closer supervision to this simple but necessary operating detail. It will be necessary to provide some relief for the 85 or thereabout services which cannot be supplied from the Charlestown reservoir, and in considering the steps to be taken to afford the desired relief the Commission suggests the possibility of a settling basin, and will be glad to have its Engineering Department co-operate with the water company in reaching a solution of the problem.

The complaints as to the unsatisfactory fire plugs were that the plugs are so rarely flushed that deposits of mud and gravel accumulate and require undue flushing to prevent the bursting of the fire hose; that the type of plug was not satisfactory, and, through ignorance of mechanism, they were frequently broken. Testimony on this subject was most conflicting.

There were 33 fire plugs in service, for which the town authorities pay $1,100 annually, or $33.83⅓ per plug. The Commission deems this sum a very fair compensation and is of the opinion that desirable experience in the operation of these fire plugs can be obtained for the volunteer fire company through drills, and recommends that the company and town authorities devise some plan which will accomplish this result.

The testimony is that if a consumer desires a meter installed he is required to pay the cost thereof, and as a minimum charge equal to the single spigot flat rate charge is exacted of the metered consumers, the practice of the respondent is complained of as being unreasonable. The schedule of the respondent here under discussion contains no provisions requiring the consumer to pay for meter, and as the cost of meter is properly borne by the utility and charged to its capital account, the Commission will expect the respondent to change its practice in this respect and cease requiring consumers to pay for meters installed. Reasonable rules under which meters will be installed should be promulgated by the respondent and filed with the Commission. The practice of water utilities of making either a minimum charge or a readiness to serve charge is so universal and founded upon such sound principles, and is so generally recognized as being justifiable, that the Commission will not here attempt to detail the reasons why such minimum charge should be allowed in the instant case.

The main complaint as to the capitalization of the respondent is that the capital account as shown on the books of the company is excessive and does not represent the true value of the plant. Fixed capital shown on books of the company as of December 31st, 1918, is $130,-

219.41. The Superintendent or General Manager testified that when control was obtained by his father January 1st, 1898, the company then having been in existence three years, the fixed capital shown on the books was $100,658.00, but that he had no knowledge what this amount represented; the book entries showing the first item—

Organization and financing.............................	$69,850.00
That in 1896 was added...............................	29,041.00
And in 1898..	1,767.00
Or a total of......................................	$100,658.00

Testimony of the Auditor of the Commission shows that on January 1st, 1914, when the books of the company were opened to conform to the uniform system of accounts adopted by the Commission, the plant valuation as shown by the system of accounts then used was $126,-698.24. No records were available, however, to verify this amount, though it was possible to verify additions to capital account made from January 1st, 1914, to December 31st, 1918, of $3,521.17. Counsel for the complainants, through exhibits filed and testimony of witnesses, endeavored to show the original cost of the plant. Prior to the creation of the Public Service Commission in 1910 there was no uniform system of accounts used, and therefore it has been rarely possible to determine actual expenditures by any of the public utilities which the Commission has heretofore had occasion to investigate. However, the Commission does not deem this information absolutely essential to a proper determination of the present case, though very desirable in any case when same can be had.

The principles governing the determination of the fair value of the property of public utilities for rate-making purposes, particularly as applied to water companies, adopted by this Commission are set forth at length in its opinion filed July 25th, 1918, Case No. 375, Baltimore County Water Company, and without herein fully stating the reasoning to be followed in reaching such conclusion, it will determine the fair value of the property of the respondent by the same methods therein used.

The Engineering Department's estimate of value of the Company's property as of December 31st, 1918, is

	Cost New	Depreciation	Present Value
Original Property........	$90,699.67	$4,485.50	$86,214.17
Working Capital...			1,270.00
			$87,484.17

the basis of such valuation being shown in its Reports Nos. 961 of April 9th, 1917, and 1066 of October 17th, 1917, filed in Case 1263, and 1259 filed March 5th, 1919, in the present case.

The value placed on the 13 acres of land purchased from the late David M. Evans, and on a portion of which was constructed the Charlestown reservoir, shown in Report No. 961, is $1,625.00. Conclusive evidence at the hearing showed that $3,500.00 was paid for this tract of land. Therefore, there should be added to the Engineer's valuation this difference—$1,875.00.

In considering the value of the property, an allowance for going value should be added to the Engineer's appraisal. Authorities are so unanimous in holding going value to be an element of actual value which must be duly considered in rate-making, and this Commission having made due allowance for it in most of its recent valuation cases, it will be allowed here.

There is no fixed standard which may be followed in determining the going value of any particular utility. In the Baltimore County Case (above referred to) the Commission's allowance for going value was 2.7% of the estimated cost new of the physical property, while the water company in that case contended for an allowance of about 20%. The Baltimore County Water Company serves a large territory, composed of city, urban and rural sections, and from its source of supply to one large town the mains extend over twenty miles. With such a widely scattered business, the cost of securing the patronage was naturally greater than would seem possible in the case of the respondent, and in determining an allowance in the case the Commission gives due consideration to this element. We feel that a conservative allowance would be 2% of the appraised value of the property, or $1,787.18, which is approximately $2.00 per connection.

Giving consideration to the value of the stocks and bonds of the company, and it being impossible to determine the present market prices, it is interesting to note that if the value of the present outstanding bonds of $31,500.00 is taken at par, and the 1,400 shares of stock at the assessed value of $40.00 per share, or a total of $87,500.00, compares with $87,484.17 appraised value by the Engineering Department.

After fully considering the present compared with the original cost of construction, the value of outstanding stocks and bonds, the capitalization of the company, the probable earning capacity under prescribed rates and amount necessary to meet operating expenses, with such other matters pertinent in this case, the Commission finds the value of the property of the respondent as of December 31, 1918, to be $91,146.17, which is made up as follows:

Appraisal of Engineering Department	$86,214.17
Additional allowance for land	1,875.00
Working capital	1,270.00
Going value	1,787.18
	$91,146.35

It now becomes necessary for the Commission to prescribe a fair rate of return on the value of the respondent's property as determined by the Commission, and in the determination of a maximum rate of return many things are to be considered, which are treated at length by this Commission in its various opinions, particularly in Case No. 690, filed March 8th, 1916, known as the Telephone Case.

Having in mind the legal rate of interest in this State; the fact that this Commission has recently approved issues of notes for more than $5,000,000 bearing 7% interest, the class of securities yielding high returns now available to the investing public; the character of the business of the respondent, with the hazard of the enterprise; and, further, the general effect of the rate of return upon the public at large, we deem a maximum permissible rate of return of 7% for this company to be proper rate, though such a maximum rate of return will not be permitted unless it can be earned through charges otherwise reasonable to the public.

The answer of the respondent to the complaint against the present schedule of rates denies they are excessive, unjust or unreasonable, claiming the increase is necessary to pay operating expenses, a proper allowance for depreciation and to provide a balance for surplus or dividends; showing that the gross income for the year ending June 30th, 1918, was approximately $10,465.00, with operating expenses and depreciation of $6,900.00, and that after paying fixed charges about $2,000.00 was left for surplus or dividends on the $70,000.00 common stock; estimating that the new rates would increase the revenue a little over $2,000.00 per year, which would yield a net return for surplus of about 5% on the book value of the plant, $130,219.41, or about 6%, based on the Engineer's valuation, $87,484.17, shown in Report No. 1263.

On December 31st, 1918, there were 730 unmetered and 43 metered consumers. The company claims, however, that this number was greater than usual and due to abnormal labor conditions, and that recently the number of consumers has been reduced by families moving from the town.

The Auditor's report gives gross earnings for the year ending December 31st, 1918, as $9,875.88. The new rates increase unmetered service $3.00 per annum, and with 730 such customers on December 31st, 1918, this increase would mean about $2,200.00.

The Commission could probably show here the effect of the new rates with reasonable correctness, but believes the company's estimate of its revenue to be approximately correct, and therefore for consideration of the reasonableness of the present schedule will base its conclusions on the estimated amount of revenue for the ensuing year, $12,500.00.

Analysis of the Auditor's Report showing operating expenses develops that the ratio of operating expenses to operating revenue has materially increased, being

37.77% in 1915
51.63% in 1916
36.24% in 1917
79.39% in 1918

It is a matter of common knowledge that costs in practically every industry have materially increased during the war period, resulting largely from the increase in cost of labor and coal, and the apparently heavy operating expenses of public utilities have been justified where a large number of employes and use of coal were required.

This condition, however, does not exist with the respondent to the extent that would justify the tremendous increase in operating expenses. Its operation requires no pumping and no increased cost of power is involved. The testimony showed that other than its three executive officers, only two regular employes were on the pay roll, a clerk in the office and an outside man. Additional labor is employed on a per diem basis when required.

Therefore, in seeking the reason for the increase in operating expenses, testimony at the hearing was largely centered on this condition and examination was complete on the various items involved.

It was shown that, occasioned by the unusual severity of the weather in the winter months of 1918, service pipes and mains to an unusual extent were frozen and broken, many customers being without water for months. A heavy cost was involved in remedying the damage, and to this unparalleled weather is due, in part, the increased costs shown for the year ending in December 31st, 1918.

Three other items of expense, i. e., administration, taxes and depreciation, claim attention of the Commission.

The administration cost for the past year was $2,805.34, or over 28% of the gross income. The Commission considers this excessive when account is taken of the volume of business and character of the plant. Testimony showed there were three executives—a president, secretary and treasurer and general manager—drawing salaries of $600.00, $900.00 and $900.00, respectively; that the entire time of none was devoted to its business, nor does it clearly appear just what services rendered by the president are necessary for the conduct of the business.

The Commission does not feel that the public should be charged with high salaries of officers who render little or no service to the company.

It is noted that the taxes showed a material increase during the past year. This is due in part to an increased valuation by the authorities.

Prior to 1917 no reserve for depreciation was set aside. The Auditor's report shows that, in both 1917 and 1918, $1,500 was set aside for depreciation, this amount having been based on a weighted average of the value of the plant, and recommended by the former Auditor of the Commission.

In the Engineering Department's appraisal, depreciation was computed on a 4 per cent. sinking fund basis, with no allowance for depreciation of land.

The average age of the depreciable property of the Company is about thirteen years and its average life about eighty-seven years; consequently, there is a remaining life of about seventy-four years.

The Company accumulated $3,000 depreciation reserve in the past two years. The value found by the Commission of the depreciable property is $83,989.17.

Therefore, $80,989.17 remains to be accumulated.

On a sinking fund basis the following accumulations are shown:

$400 per annum at 5% amounts to $83,740 in 50 years
400 " " " 4½% " " 82,720 " 53 "
400 " " " 4% " " 83,516 " 57 "
400 " " " 3½% " " 81,756 " 60 "
300 " " " 5% " " 81,810 " 55 "
300 " " " 4½% " " 82,800 " 59 "
300 " " " 4% " " 81,240 " 63 "
300 " " " 3½% " " 80,340 " 68 "

The present depreciation reserve of $3,000 set aside at 4% interest will in 55 years amount to $25,950.00.

Deducting the $25,950 from the depreciable property, $83,989.17, leaves $58,039 to be provided by annual installments to a sinking fund depreciation reserve.

In 55 years, $300 annual installments at 4% will amount to $57,347.00.

An annual depreciation of $1,500.00 at 4% will in 28 years amount to $74,952.00, and the present reserve of $3,000 for a like period at 4% to $8,996.00, or a total of $83,948.00, as compared with the value of the property to be retired, $83,989.00, the value being recovered in about one-third of its probable life.

These simple computations show conclusively that an allowance of $1,500.00 annually for depreciation is without reason, and in determining the proper schedule of rates an annual depreciation reserve of $300 will be allowed.

The Commission recognizes that the abnormal weather conditions occasioned material damage in the past, requiring heavy expenditures for replacements. Such contingencies should be provided for out of a special fund rather than being considered in the nature of a normal operating expense and a basis upon which the need of increased rates is reflected. As before stated, much of the heavy operating cost of last year was due to unusual weather conditions.

The Commission therefore will permit the Company to establish a contingency reserve fund and allow an annual reserve of $100.00 to be set aside until the fund accumulates an amount not in excess of $1,000.00.

It was on basis of the abnormal expenditures in 1918 that the company felt the need for increased revenue and filed its new schedule of rates effective January 1st, 1919.

The Commission does not feel these operating costs can justly be used as a basis of calculation in estimating the probable expenditures for the future. It has in mind that with the replacements made in

1918 the plant is now in such a good condition that probably less than
normal repairs will be required in the near future. It has considered
the costs for a series of years, adding thereto a reasonable allowance
for increased costs of labor and material, and considers the following
set up to be a reasonable assumption of operating costs per year:

Collecting System......	$150.00
Distribution Maintenance....	150.00
Service Pipes and Stops...	100.00
Meters, Boxes and Vaults...	75.00
Fire Hydrants and Cisterns...	75.00
Repairs Col. System...	200.00
" Dis. "	150.00
" Buildings and Equipment...	100.00
Administration Expenses...	2,200.00
Insurance	60.00
Stable and Shop Expenses...	100.00
Miscellaneous	150.00
Uncollected Bills...	100.00
	$3,610.00

The estimated income based on present schedule of rates is $12,500.00.

A fair return of 7% on $91,146.35...	$6,380.25
Operating expenses estimated...	3,610.00
Taxes	740.00
Depreciation	300.00
Contingency reserve...	100.00
	$11,130.25

It is thus shown on these assumptions that the present schedule will
produce a revenue of approximately $1,350.00 in excess of the com-
pany's requirements, and it is obvious that the said rates are excessive,
unjust and unreasonable.

Should the rates be reduced to the previous basis on a minimum
monthly charge, this would result in a $3.00 less revenue on each of
the metered and unmetered services, which totaled 773 on December
31st, 1918.

Estimating this number as 750, the reduction would approximate
$2,250.00 per annum, or yield about $900.00 less than required by the
above estimates.

If the rate of return was established on a 6% basis, then the previous schedule would provide in full for all needs.

The present schedule having been in effect six months, it is readily
determined that on our estimates the company will have earned over

$1,100.00 in excess of the amount produced by the previous rate calculated for a full year.

While this added revenue could not be projected into other years, the Commission feels economies may be effected, and considering the probable rate of return with the worth of the service, no higher rates are warranted than those in effect January 1st, 1917, and in its order will prescribe such rates as just and reasonable.

•

ORDER No. 5003

In the Matter of	
The Complaint of the MAYOR AND COUN-CILMEN OF LONACONING	**Before the** Public Service Commission of Maryland.
vs.	Case No. 1616.
THE LONACONING WATER COMPANY.	

This case being at issue upon complaint and answer on file and having been duly heard and submitted by the parties and full investigation of the matters and things involved having been had and the Commission, on the date hereof, having rendered and filed an opinion containing its findings of fact and conclusions therein, which said opinion is hereby referred to and made part hereof,

IT IS, THEREFORE, This 19th day of June, in the year Nineteen Hundred and Nineteen, by the Public Service Commission of Maryland,

𝕺𝖗𝖉𝖊𝖗𝖊𝖉, (1) That the fair value for rate-making purposes of the property of The Lonaconing Water Company on December 31st, 1918, was Ninety-one Thousand One Hundred and Forty-six Dollars and Thirty-five Cents ($91,146.35), and such valuation shall be and become final, unless protest against the same shall be filed with the Commission within ten (10) days from the date of this order, as provided by Section 30 of the Public Service Commission Law.

(2) That the maximum return which said The Lonaconing Water Company should be permitted to earn upon its property used in the public service is seven per centum (7%).

(3) That the rates and charges prescribed by schedule P. S. C. Md. No. 3 of said The Lonaconing Water Company be and they are hereby declared to be unjust and unreasonable, and said The Lonaconing Water Company is hereby directed and required to file with the Commission and make effective not later than July 1st, 1919, a schedule prescribing rates and charges not in excess of those charged and col-

lected by said company immediately prior to January 1st, 1919, which rates and charges are hereby found to be just and reasonable, and thereafter charge and collect such rates and charges until January 1st, 1921, unless earlier modified or changed by this Commission and thereafter until the further order of this Commission in the premises.

(4) That a copy of this order be served forthwith upon said The Lonaconing Water Company, and that said company within ten days from the date of the service of such copy shall advise this Commission in writing whether or not it will accept and abide by the same.

ORDER No. 5007

In the Matter of

The Application of THE CHESAPEAKE AND POTOMAC TELEPHONE COMPANY OF BALTIMORE CITY for the Approval of an Agreement Between It and THE UNITED STATES HOUSING CORPORATION, Dated June 2nd, 1919, for the Construction of Certain Pole Lines by the Former for the Latter and for the Joint Use of Said Pole Lines.

Before the

Public Service Commission of Maryland.

Case No. 1690.

The agreement or other written instrument evidencing the transaction in this case having been submitted to this Commission for the purpose of securing its consent to the consummation thereof and the Commission having determined that a hearing is unnecessary,

IT IS, THEREFORE, On this twenty-third day of June, in the year 1919, by the Public Service Commission of Maryland,

Ordered, That the consent of this Commission be and the same is hereby given to the disposition of the property described in said agreement, or other written instrument, evidencing the transaction in accordance with the terms outlined therein.

ORDER No. 5013

In the Matter of

The Application of the DIRECTOR GEN-
ERAL OF RAILROADS Operating the
Pennsylvania Railroad in Maryland for
Authority to Operate Bay View Sta-
tion, Baltimore, Maryland, As a Non-
Agency Station.

Before the

Public Service Commission
of Maryland.

Case No. 1687.

WHEREAS, The Director General of Railroads, operating the Pennsylvania Railroad in Maryland, has applied to this Commission for
authority to change Bay View Station, Baltimore, Maryland, from an
agency freight station to a non-agency station, and

WHEREAS, The application having this day come to be heard after
due notice published in accordance with this Commission's Order No.
4994 passed June 16th, 1919, and no protests thereto having been
made and it being the opinion and finding of the Commission after due
hearing that the maintenance of Bay View Station as an agency
freight station is no longer reasonably necessary or convenient for the
public service,

IT IS, THEREFORE, This 24th day of June, in the year Nineteen Hundred and Nineteen, by the Public Service Commission of Maryland,

Ordered, That the Director General of Railroads, operating the
Pennsylvania Railroad in Maryland, be and he is hereby authorized
and permitted to change Bay View Station, Baltimore, Maryland, from
an agency freight station to a non-agency station, effective on and
after July 1st, 1919.

ORDER No. 5014

In the Matter of

The Petition of the Carriers Not Under
Federal Control Named in the Official
Classification, by R. N. COLLYER, Their
Agent, for Permission Under Section
15 of the Public Service Commission
Law to File and Publish Supplement
to Official Classification No. 44, P. S.
C. Md. O. C. No. 44.

Before the

Public Service Commission
of Maryland.

S. N. & R. Docket.

Case No. 571.

The above mentioned petition having been received and filed, upon
consideration thereof, it is this 25th day of June, 1919, by the Public
Service Commission of Maryland,

𝔒𝔯𝔡𝔢𝔯𝔢𝔡, That permission be, and is hereby given, the carriers not under Federal control named in the Official Classification, by R. N. Collyer, their Agent, to file and publish on full statutory notice to the Commission and the public, supplement to Official Classification No. 44, P. S. C. Md. O. C. No. 44, containing the new forms of bills of lading prescribed by the Interstate Commerce Commission in order entered on April 14th, 1919, I. C. C. Docket No. 4844; said supplement issued under authority hereof to depart from the provisions of this Commission's Circular No. 10A in so far as number of supplements is concerned,

PROVIDED, Said supplement be filed with the Commission upon issuance of this Order, and published by posting as required by law, and that all copies of said supplement shall bear the following notation:

"Issued under special permission of the Public Service Commission of Maryland, Order No. 5014 of date June 25th, 1919."

ORDER No. 5018

In the Matter of

The Application of WESTERN MARYLAND RAILWAY COMPANY for Authority to Issue and Deliver $2,857,000.00 of Its First and Refunding Mortgage Five Per Cent. Bonds, Said Bonds to Be Pledged As Security for a Note in the Sum of $2,000,000.00, Drawn Payable on Demand to the DIRECTOR GENERAL OF RAILROADS, Bearing Interest at Six Per Cent. Per Annum, Payable Quarterly.

Before the

Public Service Commission of Maryland.

Case No. 1689.

WHEREAS, Western Maryland Railway Company has applied to this Commission for authority to issue and pledge $2,857,000 face value of its First and Refunding Mortgage Bonds, as collateral security for the six per cent. promissory demand note of the Railway Company in the face amount of $2,000,000 in favor of the Director General of Railroads, bearing interest at six per cent. per annum, payable quarterly; and

WHEREAS, This application coming on to be heard after due notice published in compliance with Order No. 5006 of this Commission passed June 23rd, 1919, and the Commission being of opinion and finding after hearing that the issue and pledge of said First and

Refunding Mortgage Bonds, as collateral security for said demand note of $2,000,000 payable to the Director General of Railroads, is reasonably required for the purposes of said corporation, to wit: the acquisition of property, the construction, completion, extension or improvement of its facilities or for the improvement or maintenance of its service, or the discharge or lawful refunding of its obligations:

IT IS, THEREFORE, This 27th day of June, in the year Nineteen Hundred and Nineteen, by the Public Service Commission of Maryland,

ORDERED, That the issue and pledge by the applicant, Western Maryland Railway Company, of $2,857,000 face value of First and Refunding Mortgage Bonds of the Railway Company, as collateral security for the six per cent. promissory demand note of the Railway Company in the face amount of $2,000.000 in favor of the Director General of Railroads, in the manner and upon the terms set forth in said application, be and the same is hereby authorized and approved for any one or more of the specific purposes hereinbefore recited, but for no other purposes.

ORDER No. 5019

In the Matter of	Before the
The Application of THE BALTIMORE AND OHIO RAILROAD COMPANY for Authority to Issue $35,000,000 of Ten-Year Six Per Cent. Secured Gold Bonds.	Public Service Commission of Maryland. Case No. 1691.

WHEREAS, The Baltimore and Ohio Railroad Company has filed with this Commission an application from which it appears that said company has not sold any of the $20,911,445.01 of its Refunding and General Mortgage Bonds, Series B, the issue and sale or pledge of which had been approved by the previous orders of the Commission, Numbers 4095, 4372, 4656 and 4657, and, with the approval of the Commission, on July 1st, 1917, the company has issued its Five Per Cent. Secured Gold Notes to the amount of $15,000,000, of which $7,500,000, Series A, were paid on July 1st, 1918, and $7,500,000, Series B, mature July 1st, 1919, and said company has from time to time borrowed other moneys for expenditures made upon its railroads and property, and proposes, for the purpose of refunding its outstanding obligations and for its other corporate purposes, to issue not exceeding $35,000,000 of its Ten-Year Six Per Cent. Secured Gold Bonds; to be dated July 1st, 1919; to be payable July 1st, 1929; to be redeemable on any interest date at a premium of 2½ per cent., and to be secured by the pledge of $15,000,000 of its Refunding and General Mortgage Bonds, Series B, and certain stock of the Reading Company; and the Commission, after due hearing, being of opinion that the use of the capital to be secured by the issue of such bonds is reasonably required for the purposes of said corporation;

IT IS, THEREFORE, This 30th day of June, in the year Nineteen Hundred and Nineteen, by the Public Service Commission of Maryland,

Ordered, That the issue and sale by The Baltimore and Ohio Railroad Company of not exceeding $35,000,000 of its Ten-Year Six Per Cent. Secured Gold Bonds, to be dated July 1st, 1919, to be payable July 1st, 1929, to bear interest at 6% per annum, and to be redeemable at a premium of 2½%, and to be secured by the pledge of $15,-000,000 of its Refunding and General Mortgage Bonds, Series B, and 120,000 Shares Reading Company First Preferred Stock, and 280,000 Shares Reading Company Second Preferred Stock, and 184,000 Shares Reading Company Common Stock, or such other amounts of the several classes of said stock as may be necessary to make up the additional collateral security required, be and the same is hereby approved.

ORDER No. 5031

In the Matter of	
The Application of WESTERN MARYLAND RAILWAY COMPANY for Authority to Execute a Mortgage of $60,000.00 to THE EVANS MARBLE COMPANY OF BALTIMORE CITY and Issue Four Mortgage Notes for the Sum of $15,000.00 Each, Bearing Interest at Six Per Cent. and Payable, Respectively, in One, Two, Three and Four Years.	Before the Public Service Commission of Maryland. Case No. 1692.

WHEREAS, Western Maryland Railway Company has applied to this Commission for authority to execute a mortgage for $60,000.00 to The Evans Marble Company of Baltimore City on certain water-front property running back (in part) to York street, in the City of Baltimore, recently purchased from the said Evans Marble Company by the Railway Company, for the sum of Seventy-five Thousand Dollars ($75,000.00), and also to issue the Railway Company's four mortgage promissory notes for Fifteen Thousand Dollars ($15,000.00) each, bearing interest at six per cent. and payable to The Evans Marble Company of Baltimore City at one, two, three and four years after date; and

WHEREAS, This application coming on to be heard after due notice published in compliance with Order No. 5020 of this Commission, passed June 30th, 1919, and the Commission being of opinion and finding after hearing that the execution of said mortgage and mortgage notes is reasonably required for the purposes of said corporation, to wit: for the acquisition of property and for the extension, maintenance or improvement of the Railway Company's facilities and service, and for the discharge or lawful refunding of its obligations;

It Is, THEREFORE, This 3rd day of July, in the year Nineteen Hundred and Nineteen, by the Public Service Commission of Maryland,

Ordered, That the execution by Western Maryland Railway Company of a mortgage for $60,000.00 to The Evans Marble Company of Baltimore City, on certain water-front property running back (in part) to York street, in the City of Baltimore, recently purchased by the Railway Company from The Evans Marble Company, and the execution by the Railway Company of four mortgage notes of $15,000.00 each, bearing interest at six per cent., payable to The Evans Marble Company of Baltimore City and falling due, respectively, one, two, three and four years after date, be and the same is hereby authorized and approved for any one or more of the specific purposes hereinbefore recited, but for no other purpose.

ORDER No. 5033

In the Matter of

The Application of THE CHESAPEAKE AND POTOMAC TELEPHONE COMPANY OF BALTIMORE CITY and THE AMERICAN TELEPHONE AND TELEGRAPH COMPANY for the Approval of Agreement, Dated April 17th, 1919, for the Lease by the Former to the Latter of a Portion of a Lot Located on the East Side of North Street About 200 Feet South of the South Building Line of High Street, Elkton, Cecil County, Maryland.

Before the

Public Service Commission of Maryland.

Case No. 1693.

The agreement or other written instrument evidencing the transaction in this case having been submitted to this Commission for the purpose of securing its consent to the consummation thereof and the Commission having determined that a hearing is unnecessary,

It Is, THEREFORE, On this third day of July, in the year 1919, by the Public Service Commission of Maryland,

Ordered, That the consent of this Commission be and the same is hereby given to the disposition of the property described in said agreement, or other written instrument, evidencing the transaction in accordance with the terms outlined therein.

ORDER No. 5035

In the Matter of	Before the
The Application of J. O. LARRIMORE and DANIEL H. HARRISON for a Permit for the Operation of a Motor Vehicle for Public Use.	Public Service Commission of Maryland.
	Case No. 1675.

WHEREAS, J. O. Larrimore and Daniel H. Harrison having made application for a permit for the operation of a motor vehicle for public use in the transportation of freight between Baltimore, Maryland, and Easton, Maryland, and Tilghman's Island, Maryland, via Annapolis, Maryland, and Claiborne-Annapolis Ferry, Inc., and

WHEREAS, The application having come on to be heard on May 20th, 1919, in accordance with this Commission's Order No. 4935 passed May 12th, 1919, and it being the opinion and finding of the Commission after due hearing that the public welfare and convenience require the granting of said permit,

IT IS, THEREFORE, This 7th day of July, in the year Nineteen Hundred and Nineteen, by the Public Service Commission of Maryland,

ORDERED, That the application of J. O. Larrimore and Daniel H. Harrison in this case exhibited be, and the same is hereby granted and that the permit applied for be issued between Baltimore, Maryland, and Easton, Maryland, and Tilghman's Island, Maryland, via Annapolis, Maryland, and Claiborne-Annapolis Ferry, Inc.,

PROVIDED, That said J. O. Larrimore and said Daniel H. Harrison shall not transport freight locally between Baltimore, Maryland, and Annapolis, Maryland, and intermediate points.

ORDER No. 5036

In the Matter of	Before the
The Petition of THE MARYLAND ELECTRIC RAILWAYS COMPANY for Permission Under Section 15 of the Public Service Commission Law to File and Publish on Less Than Statutory Notice Supplement No. 2 to Petitioner's Freight Tariff P. S. C. Md. No. 77.	Public Service Commission of Maryland.
	S. N. & R. Docket.
	Case No. 572.

The above mentioned petition having been received and filed, upon consideration thereof, it is this 9th day of July, 1919, by the Public Service Commission of Maryland,

𝔒𝔯𝔡𝔢𝔯𝔢𝔡, That permission be, and is hereby given, The Maryland Electric Railways Company to file and publish on one day's notice to the Commission and the public, Supplement No. 2 to petitioner's freight tariff P. S. C. Md. No. 77, reducing the demurrage charge after expiration of free time to $2.00 per car per day for first four days and $5.00 per car per day thereafter,

PROVIDED, Said supplement be filed with the Commission upon issuance of this order, and published by posting as required by law, and that all copies of said supplement shall bear the following notation:

"Issued under special permission of the Public Service Commission of Maryland, Order No. 5036 of date July 9th, 1919."

ORDER No. 5037

In the Matter of

The Petition of the Maryland Carriers Not Under Federal Control for Permission Under Section 15 of the Public Service Commission Law to File and Publish on Less Than Statutory Notice Tariffs Reducing Demurrage Charges.

Before the

Public Service Commission of Maryland.

S. N. & R. Docket.

Case No. 573.

The above mentioned petition having been received and filed, upon consideration thereof, it is this 10th day of July, 1919, by the Public Service Commission of Maryland,

𝔒𝔯𝔡𝔢𝔯𝔢𝔡, That permission be, and is hereby given, the Maryland carriers not under Federal control to file and publish on one day's notice to the Commission and the public tariffs reducing the demurrage charge after expiration of free time to $2.00 per car per day for first four days and $5.00 per car per day thereafter, and extending the application of average agreement to cars held for loading,

PROVIDED, Said tariffs be filed with the Commission upon issuance of this order, and published by posting as required by law, and that all copies of said tariffs shall bear the following notation:

"Issued under special permission of the Public Service Commission of Maryland, Order No. 5037 of date July 10th, 1919."

ORDER No. 5038

In the Matter of	Before the
The Complaint of MAYOR AND CITY COUN-CIL OF HAVRE DE GRACE	Public Service Commission of Maryland.
vs.	
HAVRE DE GRACE GAS COMPANY.	Case No. 1585.

The Complainant in the above entitled matter by letter filed October 23rd, 1918, having admitted satisfaction of the same and stated that hearing therein was not desired, this Commission on said date entered its Order No. 4515 dismissing the case, and

WHEREAS, Upon petition of the Complainant the case was subsequently reinstated upon the docket of the Commission and set for hearing at the office of the Commission on July 11th, 1919, and

WHEREAS, The Complainant, by William A. Leffler, Mayor, has this day filed with the Commission a letter asking that the complaint be withdrawn,

IT IS, THEREFORE, This 10th day of July, in the year Nineteen Hundred and Nineteen, by the Public Service Commission of Maryland,

ORDERED, That the complaint in the above entitled matter be, and the same is hereby, dismissed without prejudice.

ORDER No. 5039

In the Matter of	
The Application of THE CHESAPEAKE AND POTOMAC TELEPHONE COMPANY OF BALTIMORE CITY and THE BALTIMORE AND OHIO RAILROAD COMPANY for the Approval of an Agreement, Dated April 22nd, 1919, for the Sale by the Former to the Latter of One Pole Located on the East Side of Calhoun Street About 150 Feet from South of the South Curb Line of Ramsay Street, Baltimore, Maryland.	Before the Public Service Commission of Maryland. Case No. 1694.

The agreement or other written instrument evidencing the transaction in this case having been submitted to this Commission for the purpose of securing its consent to the consummation thereof and the Commission having determined that a hearing is unnecessary,

IT IS, THEREFORE, On this tenth day of July, in the year 1919, by the Public Service Commission of Maryland,

Ordered, That the consent of this Commission be and the same is hereby given to the disposition of the property described in said agreement, or other written instrument, evidencing the transaction in accordance with the terms outlined therein.

ORDER No. 5040

In the Matter of	
The Application of WASHINGTON SUBURBAN SANITARY COMMISSION for Authority to Issue $750,000.00 Par Value of Its Fifty-Year Five Per Cent. Bonds.	Before the Public Service Commission of Maryland. Case No. 1686.

WHEREAS, Washington Suburban Sanitary Commission, a body corporate created by Chapter 122 of the Acts of the General Assembly of Maryland, Session of 1918, for the purpose of supplying water and sewerage facilities for the territory in the State of Maryland immediately adjacent to the District of Columbia, and for the regulation of matters relating to the public health in said territory, has applied to this Commission for authority to issue $750,000.00 face amount of bonds of the said Washington Suburban Sanitary Commission, said bonds to bear interest at rate of Five Per Cent. (5%) per annum, payable semi-annually and to mature in not less than thirty nor more than fifty years from date of issuance, and

WHEREAS, The application having come on to be heard on June 24th, 1919, after due notice published in accordance with this Commission's Order No. 4992 passed June 12th, 1919, and it being the opinion and finding of the Commission after due hearing that the issue of said bonds is reasonably required for the purposes of said corporation as set forth in the application herein,

IT IS, THEREFORE, This 10th day of July, in the year Nineteen Hundred and Nineteen, by the Public Service Commission of Maryland,

Ordered, 1. That the issue and sale for cash at not less than par by the Washington Suburban Sanitary Commission of its Five Per Cent. (5%) 30-50-year bonds to the face amount of $750,000.00 is hereby authorized and approved.

2. That the said Washington Suburban Sanitary Commission shall make reports to this Commission, duly verified by affidavits, as follows:

(a) Upon the sale for cash of its bonds, authorized and approved as aforesaid, or any part thereof, the fact of such sale or sales, the terms and conditions thereof, and the amount realized therefrom.

(b) At the termination of each and every period of six months from the date of this order, the disposition and use made of the proceeds of said bonds.

ORDER No. 5043

In the Matter of

The Application of THE CHESAPEAKE AND POTOMAC TELEPHONE COMPANY OF BALTIMORE CITY and CONSOLIDATED GAS ELECTRIC LIGHT AND POWER COMPANY OF BALTIMORE for the Approval of an Agreement Dated May 23rd, 1919, for the Sale by the Former to the Latter of Nine Poles Located on the East Side of 16th Street, Between Foster Avenue and O'Donnell Street, Baltimore, Maryland.

Before the

Public Service Commission of Maryland.

Case No. 1695.

The agreement or other written instrument evidencing the transaction in this case having been submitted to this Commission for the purpose of securing its consent to the consummation thereof and the Commission having determined that a hearing is unnecessary,

IT IS, THEREFORE, On this fourteenth day of July, in the year 1919, by the Public Service Commission of Maryland,

Ordered, That the consent of this Commission be and the same is hereby given to the disposition of the property described in said agreement, or other written instrument, evidencing the transaction in accordance with the terms outlined therein.

ORDER No. 5044

In the Matter of

The Application of CONSOLIDATED GAS ELECTRIC LIGHT AND POWER COMPANY OF BALTIMORE and THE CHESAPEAKE AND POTOMAC TELEPHONE COMPANY OF BALTIMORE CITY for the Approval of an Agreement Dated June 10th, 1919, for the Sale by the Former to the Latter of Two Poles on South Side of Hafer Street, West of Garrison Lane, in Baltimore, Maryland, Under the Terms and Provisions of Order No. 2954, Entered July 26th, 1916, in Case No. 1151.

Before the

Public Service Commission of Maryland.

Case No. 1696.

The agreement or other written instrument evidencing the transaction in this case having been submitted to this Commission for the purpose of securing its consent to the consummation thereof and the Commission having determined that a hearing is unnecessary,

IT IS, THEREFORE, On this fourteenth day of July, in the year 1919, by the Public Service Commission of Maryland,

ORDERED, That the consent of this Commission be and the same is hereby given to the disposition of the property described in said agreement, or other written instrument, evidencing the transaction in accordance with the terms outlined therein.

ORDER No. 5045

In the Matter of

The Application of CONSOLIDATED GAS ELECTRIC LIGHT AND POWER COMPANY OF BALTIMORE and THE CHESAPEAKE AND POTOMAC TELEPHONE COMPANY OF BALTIMORE CITY for the Approval of an Agreement for the Sale by the Former to the Latter of One Pole Located on the East Side of Whiteford Avenue, 129 Feet North of the Center Line of Frederick Avenue in the City of Baltimore, Maryland, Under the Terms and Provisions of Order No. 2954, Entered July 26th, 1916, in Case No. 1151.

Before the

Public Service Commission of Maryland.

Case No. 1697.

The agreement or other written instrument evidencing the transaction in this case having been submitted to this Commission for the purpose of securing its consent to the consummation thereof and the Commission having determined that a hearing is unnecessary,

IT IS, THEREFORE, On this fourteenth day of July, in the year 1919, by the Public Service Commission of Maryland,

ORDERED, That the consent of this Commission be and the same is hereby given to the disposition of the property described in said agreement, or other written instrument, evidencing the transaction in accordance with the terms outlined therein.

ORDER No. 5046

In the Matter of

The Notice from C. FRANK CRANE That He Will Discontinue the Motor Car Freight Line Operated by Him Between Baltimore and Prince Frederick, Maryland.

Before the

Public Service Commission of Maryland.

Case No. 1677.

WHEREAS, By Order No. 4942 of this Commission entered on May 15th, 1919, the above entitled matter was set for hearing on May 27th, 1919, provided the applicant cause a copy of said order to be published in some newspaper published in Calvert County, Maryland, at least one time before the twenty-sixth day of May, 1919, and

WHEREAS, Said C. Frank Crane having failed to appear at the hearing aforesaid, and it now appearing that the applicant has discontinued the operation of the motor vehicle freight line between Baltimore, Maryland, and Prince Frederick, Maryland, no objection to or complaint concerning which discontinuance has been made to the Commission, and it further appearing that application has since been made to this Commission by another party for a permit to operate motor vehicle for public use in the conveyance of freight between the same points formerly served by said C. Frank Crane,

IT IS, THEREFORE, This 15th day of July, in the year Nineteen Hundred and Nineteen, by the Public Service Commission of Maryland,

ⓞⓡⓓⓔⓡⓔⓓ, That the applicant, the said C. Frank Crane, be and he is hereby authorized to abandon and discontinue the motor vehicle transportation service between Baltimore, Maryland, and Prince Frederick, Maryland, the Commission having determined that said service by the applicant is no longer reasonably necessary or convenient for the public service.

ORDER No. 5050

In the Matter of	
The Application of THE CHESAPEAKE AND POTOMAC TELEPHONE COMPANY OF BALTIMORE CITY and CONSOLIDATED GAS ELECTRIC LIGHT AND POWER COMPANY for the Approval of an Agreement, Dated April 28th, 1919, for the Purchase by the Former and the Sale by the Latter of a 50% Interest in Twelve Poles Located on the East Side of Maple Avenue South of Frederick Road, District No. 1, Baltimore County, Maryland, Under the Terms and Provisions of Order No. 2954, Entered July 26th, 1916, in Case No. 1151 Before This Commission.	Before the Public Service Commission of Maryland. Case No 1698.

The agreement or other written instrument evidencing the transaction in this case having been submitted to this Commission for the purpose of securing its consent to the consummation thereof and the

Commission having determined that a hearing is unnecessary,

IT IS, THEREFORE, On this twenty-first day of July, in the year 1919, by the Public Service Commission of Maryland,

Ordered, That the consent of this Commission be and the same is hereby given to the disposition of the property described in said agreement, or other written instrument, evidencing the transaction in accordance with the terms outlined therein.

ORDER No. 5061

In the Matter of	Before the
The Application of THE DUNDALK WATER COMPANY for an Order Permitting and Approving the Exercise of Its Franchises Under the Terms and Provisions of Its Certificate of Incorporation.	Public Service Commission of Maryland. Case No. 1700.

WHEREAS, The Dundalk Water Company, a corporation organized under the laws of the State of Maryland, has applied to this Commission for an order permitting and approving the exercise of the franchises granted it under its certificate of incorporation, certified copy of which certificate of incorporation is filed in these proceedings, and

WHEREAS, The application having this day come on to be heard after due notice published in accordance with this Commission's Order No. 5059 passed July 28th, 1919, and it being the opinion and finding of the Commission after due hearing that the exercise of said franchises is necessary and convenient for the public service,

IT IS, THEREFORE, This 30th day of July, in the year Nineteen Hundred and Nineteen, by the Public Service Commission of Maryland,

Ordered, That the exercise by The Dundalk Water Company of the franchises granted it under its certificate of incorporation be and the same hereby is permitted and approved.

OPINION

In the Matter of

The Complaint of the MAYOR AND COM-
MON COUNCIL OF WESTMINSTER

vs.

THE CONSOLIDATED PUBLIC UTILITIES
COMPANY OF WESTMINSTER.

Before the

Public Service Commission
of Maryland.

Cases Nos. 1525 and 1590.

APPEARANCES:

JOSEPH S. GOLDSMITH, ESQ., Assistant General Counsel of the
Public Service Commission of Maryland.

GUY W. STEELE, ESQ., Counsel for the Complainant.

F. NEAL PARKE, ESQ., of Bond & Parke, Counsel for Respondent.

By the Commission.   Filed July 31, 1919.

On September 1, 1917, The Consolidated Public Utilities Company
of Westminster filed with this Commission its rate schedule P. S. C.
Md. No. 2, canceling schedule P. S. C. Md. No. 1 of that company, to
become effective October 1, 1917. The effect of this schedule was to
increase substantially the rates, both flat and metered, charged by said
company for the supply of water in the town of Westminster and
environs.

On September 29, 1917, the Mayor and Common Council of Westminster filed a complaint with this Commission against The Consolidated Public Utilities Company of Westminster, Case No. 1410, in
which the Commission was asked to institute proceedings in the Circuit
Court for Carroll County (in which county Westminster is situated),
to have enjoined the said The Consolidated Public Utilities Company
of Westminster (hereinafter referred to as the Consolidated Company), from enforcing the rates and regulations prescribed by said
company's schedule P. S. C. Md. No. 2, aforesaid, on the ground that
these rates had not been established in conformity with the requirements of the provisions of Chapter 341 of the Acts of the General
Assembly of Maryland, Session of 1910. On same day, after full
presentation to the Commission of the views of the complainant, by its
attorney, the Commission entered its Order No. 3665 refusing to direct
its General Counsel to institute proceedings as prayed for, without
prejudice, however, to the right of the complainant to institute and
prosecute any other action or proceeding designed to bring about a
redress of the violation of its alleged rights in the premises. Thereafter the Mayor and Common Council of Westminster filed bill of complaint in the Circuit Court for Carroll County, in which case the Commission intervened, praying for an injunction restraining the enforce-

ment of the increased rates. The controversy has since been decided by the Court of Appeals of Maryland (132 Md. 374), the court holding that this Commission has complete and exclusive jurisdiction over the matter of the rates to be charged by the Consolidated Company for water.

On June 4, 1918, complaint was filed by the Mayor and Common Council of Westminster against the Consolidated Company, which, after setting forth the fact of the filing with the Commission of the increased rates which became effective October 1, 1917, and subsequent litigation with respect thereto, alleges that said rates are unjust and unreasonable, and that if same are allowed to continue in effect will yield a net revenue far in excess of a reasonable return on the fair value of the property of the Consolidated Company required to supply the municipality of Westminster and the inhabitants of that town with water. The complainant further recites that there is a duplication of water plants in the town of Westminster and that either of the two systems is of sufficient capacity to meet adequately the requirements of the town. The complainant concludes with a prayer that the Commission investigate the matter and fix fair and reasonable rates to be paid for water for fire protection and other municipal purposes and by the inhabitants of the town for domestic and industrial uses, such rates to be based upon the value of the plant reasonably required to supply the needs of the town and its inhabitants with pure water, and that the Commission prescribe just and reasonable rules and regulations to govern the furnishing of water by the Consolidated Company. On June 13, 1918, the Consolidated Company filed its answer to the complaint, aforesaid, denying the material allegations of the complaint.

While Case No. 1525, involving the reasonableness of the rates which became effective on October 1, 1917, was still pending upon the docket of the Commission and before hearings had been had in that case, the Consolidated Company on August 31, 1918, filed with the Commission its rate schedule P. S. C. Md. No. 3, canceling schedule P. S. C. Md. 2, to become effective October 1, 1918, the effect of which schedule was to increase further the flat rates and the quarterly minimum charges for metered service exacted by the Consolidated Company. On September 30, 1918, the Mayor and Common Council of Westminster, a municipal corporation, and Howard Koontz, its mayor, filed a complaint against the second increase in rates, in which it asks the Commission to hear and dispose of the entire question regarding the rates to be charged and rules to be enforced by the Consolidated Company in one proceeding. In due course the Consolidated Company filed with the Commission its answer to the second complaint denying that the rates complained of are unreasonable, unfair and unjust and alleging that the changes which became effective October 1, 1918, were necessary in order to enable it to have sufficient revenue with which to meet the current operating expenses of the company.

At the time complaint in Case No. 1525 was filed, Osborne I. Yellott, Esq., then Assistant General Counsel to the Commission, was, upon petition of the complainant, assigned by the Commission to represent and assist the complainant in the presentation and prosecution of its complaint. Thereafter Mr. Yellott resigned and Joseph S. Goldsmith. Esq., was appointed to fill the vacancy caused by Mr. Yellott's resignation, Mr. Goldsmith taking up the work in connection with this proceeding. The matter was several times set for hearing, but was postponed from time to time to meet the other engagements of the interested parties and finally came on for hearing on January 21, 1919. Hearings were concluded on March 26, 1919, having occupied in all six full days. April 9, 1919, and the following day were devoted to arguments of the several counsel, who also filed briefs with the Commission in support of their respective contentions. The stenographic record in all embraces over 1,300 pages.

CORPORATE HISTORY

The Consolidated Company is engaged in the furnishing of water, electricity and gas in the town of Westminster and the adjacent portions of Carroll County. Westminster is an incorporated town and its population is shown by the 1910 census as 3,295 persons, but the evidence is to the effect that the present population of the territory served by the respondent company is approximately 4,000. Water is supplied by the Consolidated Company at both flat and metered rates, there being 511 consumers still charged at flat rates while there are 543 metered supplies, or a total of 1,054 services.

As its name indicates, the Consolidated Company is a consolidation of the various public service utilities of Westminster. Westminster Gas Light Company was incorporated by Chapter 42 of the Acts of the General Assembly of Maryland, Session of 1867. The Westminster Water Company was incorporated under an Act of the General Assembly of Maryland on May 18, 1883. Carroll County Electric Light and Power Company was formed under the general incorporation laws of the State of Maryland on May 29, 1894. The Citizens' Water and Power Company of Westminster, Carroll County, Maryland, was incorporated under the general incorporation laws of the State of Maryland on June 15, 1900.

After the Citizens' Company started operations competition between it and the Westminster Water Company became very keen. A reduction in rates made by one company was met by still further reductions by the other company, which system of counter-reductions continued until aggregate reductions in rates amounted to 40 per cent. The Westminster Water Company had entered into a contract with the City of Westminster to supply it with water for fire protection and other municipal purposes and was paid by the municipality from the proceeds of an annual levy of 5 cents on the $100.00 of the taxable property within the corporate limits of Westminster. After the forma-

tion of the second water company the Mayor and Common Council of
Westminster endeavored to have this contract rescinded and the rights
of the municipality to terminate the contract was upheld by the Court
of Appeals of Maryland (98 Md. 551). Thereafter the municipality
entered into a contract with the Citizens' Company to supply Westminster with water for all municipal purposes, including fire protection, at the rate of $800.00 per annum, which contract started on
October 2, 1902, and terminated October 2, 1917. This last contract
also stipulated the rates to be charged private consumers by the
Citizens' Company during the period of the contract, the rates being
fixed as those which were established as a result of the active competition between that company and the Westminster Water Company.

After the competition between the rival water companies had continued for some years their owners determined that the logical solution
of the problem lay in a consolidation of the two companies, and it was
thought advisable to include also the gas and electric companies in
the same combination. To this end The Public Utilities Company of
Westminster was in corporated on September 28, 1908, under the general incorporation laws of the State of Maryland, with broad corporate
powers. The five corporations were then united into The Consolidated
Public Utilities Company of Westminster by agreement of consolidation dated October 1, 1908, with an authorized capital stock of
$150,000.00, consisting of 15,000 shares of the par value of $10.00 each.
The capitalization of the five constituent companies, the basis for
stock exchange and the bonded indebtedness of these companies are
shown in the following table:

	Par Value Stock of		Outstanding Funded Debt.		
	Constituent Company	*Consolidated Company. Given in Exchange.*	*Amount.*	*Rate.*	*Maturity.*
Westminster Gas Lt. Co.....	$24,000	$24,000	....	...	....
Westminster Water Co......	60,000	60,000	$45,000	4%	1932
Carroll County Elec. Lt. and Power Co...............	5,000	10,000	20,000	5%	1924
Citizens' Water & Power Co.	40,000	42,000	40,000	4%	1940
Public Utilities Co. of West-minster	50	50	....	...	....
Total.................	$129,050	$136,050	$105,000	...	....

In addition to the stock of $24,000 of the Consolidated Company the
shareholders of the Westminster Gas Light Company (which had been
the only company paying dividends) were paid $30,000.00 in cash,
obtained by the sale of $30,000.00 of 5 per cent. bonds of the Consoli-

dated Company.   These bonds mature in 1988 and are a first lien upon
the property acquired from the Westminster Gas Light Company, and
a second lien upon the properties of the other constituent companies.
Thereafter the Consolidated Company issued and sold for cash at par
149 shares of its stock, obtaining therefor $1,490, which was used for
the purchase of electric meters, and charged to the capital investment
of the electric plant.   No securities have since been issued or sold by
the Consolidated Company, so that the total amount of outstanding
stock is $137,540.00 and of bonds $135,000.00, or a total capitalization
of $272,540.00.

By the terms of the agreement of consolidation the accounts receiv-
able and payable did not pass to the Consolidated Company, but were
received and discharged by the several constituent companies.   It has
not been possible to ascertain the actual investment of the constituent
companies in the property acquired by the Consolidated Company, as
the books of the several companies were not turned over to the officers
of the Consolidated Company, but apparently were destroyed some
time after the consolidation was effected.   However, when the books
of the Consolidated Company were opened on October 1, 1908, the same
showed the value of the assets acquired by it from the two water companies to exceed the par value of the stock issued and the funded debt
assumed by it upon these properties.

THE ISSUES PRESENTED.

The complaints and pleadings in these proceedings present to the
Commission for adjudication several issues, which are all more or less
directly related to the primary point in issue, and may be briefly summarized under the following heads:

(a) The corporate right of the Consolidated Company to
engage in the business of supplying water beyond the limits
of the town of Westminster.

(b) The fair value of the property used and useful in the
public service.

(c) The rate of return which the Consolidated Company is
to be permitted to earn upon the property dedicated to the
public service and included in the Commission's valuation.

(d) The reasonableness of the rate charged by the Consolidated Company for electrical energy generated by its electric
plant and furnished the water plant, which uses it for pumping and purification purposes.

(e) The reasonableness of the rates charged by the Consolidated Company for water service.

The complainant has urged upon the Commission that there is an unnecessary duplication of plant, in both the production and distribution systems, which contention must be considered in connection with the valuation proceedings.

The question of the reasonableness of the rates embraces all flat and metered rates charged for water for municipal and private uses, together with the rules and regulations of the Consolidated Company governing the supply of water.

RIGHT TO SUPPLY WATER OUTSIDE OF WESTMINSTER.

An examination of the record in the case leads to the inevitable conclusion that there is no merit in the contention that the action of the Consolidated Company in supplying water beyond the corporate limits of Westminster is *ultra vires*, or that the water system should be divided into two separate parts, one lying inside the town and the other beyond the town limits, and the value of the property and earnings and expenses segregated accordingly. The Commission finds nothing in the charters of any of the companies which would seem to limit the activities of the Consolidated Company to the town of Westminster proper, but on the contrary finds that said company is clearly within its corporate rights in supplying water in the vicinity of Westminster. The proposition to divide arbitrarily the water system into two distinct plants appears equally untenable. The evidence is to the effect that Westminster has grown beyond its corporate limits, and that service is supplied outside of the town limits under conditions substantially similar to those obtaining within the town. So far as the Commission is advised it is the almost universal practice and custom of privately owned utilities, including water companies, to extend their mains and services beyond the actual boundaries of the particular city, town or village primarily intended to be served, and with few, if any, exceptions such systems have been and are treated in their entirety.

It follows that in considering the proper valuation to be placed upon the property of the Consolidated Company, and in determining just and reasonable rates to be charged for the supply of water, the Commission will treat the water property of said company as a whole, and will not undertake to divide same into two separate and distinct units, one within and the other without the corporate limits.

THE VALUATION.

The Commission in this case is concerned with establishing rates which shall be just and reasonable to the public and to the utility. This Commission had occasion to fully consider the underlying principles involved in a case of this kind in the investigation and charges, property and affairs of The Chesapeake and Potomac Telephone Company of Baltimore City, and its opinion filed therein on March 8, 1916, and reported in P. S. C. Md. Reports, Vol. VII, starting at page 143, goes into the whole question at considerable length. As set forth in that opinion and in the authorities therein quoted from, the object of the Commission should be to secure adequate service to the public at rates which will be fair to both the public and the utility. Also, that the basis of all calculations as to the reasonableness of rates to be charged by the utility must be the fair value of the property used by it for the public convenience, as the utility is lawfully entitled to a fair return upon its property so dedicated to the public service, provided that such fair return can be secured by charging the public no more than what the services rendered are reasonably worth. Counsel for respondent in his argument attempted to show that the courts, including the Supreme Court of the United States, had recently departed from their earlier decisions in which the aforesaid limitation was put upon the absolute right of the utility at all times and under all conditions to earn a fair return upon the property so employed, it being contended that under such later decisions there is no such limitation upon the right of the utility to earn a fair return upon its property, but without here reviewing at length the authorities cited by counsel, the Commission does not feel that they should be construed as in conflict with the proposition above set forth.

The Supreme Court of the United States in the case of Smyth vs. Ames, 169 U. S. 466, has also laid down the rule that in ascertaining the fair value of the property used in the public service it is proper to consider the amount actually expended in original construction and permanent improvements, the amount and market value of its outstanding stocks and bonds, the present as compared with the original cost of construction, the probable earning capacity under the particular rates "prescribed by statute," and the sum required to meet operating expenses. That is to say, all of these matters, as well as any others which may be pertinent in the particular case, must be considered in determining the value of the property, and each given such weight as may be just and right in that case.

The Commission instructed its Chief Engineer to make appraisals covering the properties of the Consolidated Company, and on September 25, 1918, the Chief Engineer submitted a report containing summaries of the separate appraisals of:

> Westminster Water Company.
> Citizens' Water and Power Company.
> New water supply construction, 1918.
> Electrical property.
> Gas property.

All of the appraisals were made as of August 31, 1918, and a detailed inventory with unit prices used was furnished on October 5, 1918.

The following shows the appraised value as of August 31, not including land, rights of way and working capital:

PRESENT VALUE, AUGUST 31, 1918, EXCLUSIVE OF LAND, RIGHTS OF WAY AND WORKING CAPITAL.

	Contract Cost.	Purchaser's Overhead Expenses.	Reproduction Cost New.	Depreciation.	Present Value.
Westminster Water Co..	$77,974	$10,104	$88,078	$29,997	$58,081
Citizens' Water & Power Company	63,185	8,138	71,323	14,432	56,891
Consolidated Public Utilities Company........	41,088	5,347	46,435	157	46,278
Totals, water properties.	$182,247	$23,589	$205,836	$44,586	$161,250
Electric ....·....	65,700	8,736	74,436	19,991	54,445
Gas	43,816	5,827	49,643	18,340	31,303
Totals, all properties....	$291,763	$38,152	$329,915	$82,917	$246,998

The Chief Engineer of the Commission used the normal pre-war prices obtained over an average of five years for all construction prices to 1916. The normal unit prices were increased by 20 per cent. in determining the cost of certain electrical construction in 1916, and 70 per cent. in appraising the work done in 1918 in connection with the new water supply at Cranberry. The practice of using normal prices in an appraisal of properties such as the one here under consideration has ample support in precedents and is founded in justice. It is true that construction at the present time can be accomplished only at the abnormal prices now obtaining, but the major portion of the plants of the Consolidated Company was built under normal conditions and at normal prices. The contract prices allowed on the more recent construction have been increased, as before stated, so as to reflect reasonably the actual costs experienced in such construction. Just when, if ever, prices will reach their pre-war levels it is, of course, impossible to foretell, though we see some indications from time to time of tendencies, feeble though they may now be, in this direction. If a valuation was being made at a time when, due to a panic or some other financial disaster, prices had fallen to a point far below normal and lower than the intrinsic value of the particular materials or services, we do not feel that anyone could seriously contend that the valuation should be predicated upon the depressed prices then prevailing.

To the contract cost there has been added overhead expenses of slightly more than 13 per cent. This is to cover organization, general expenses, engineering and interest. It was assumed by the engineer in figuring upon the cost of reconstruction that the plants of the Consolidated Company were to be constructed in the period of one year, and these overhead expenses, or construction overheads, are the expenses that are encountered in such work of construction, based upon the work being completed in that period. These items are just as real an expense and are as much a part of the actual cost of constructing the physical property as are the labor and material which go to make up the contract cost. The item of "organization" included under construction overheads embraces only the organization necessary for and incident to the construction of the plant, and is not intended to include any cost encountered in the organization of the business as such. The aggregate of the percentage allowances in this case for construction overheads is fair and compares favorably with similar allowances made by the Commission in other cases. In the Chesapeake and Potomac Telephone case, supra, the allowance was 17.67 per cent. Mr. John H. Gregory, a consulting engineer and sanitary expert who has been engaged in the practice of his profession a number of years, and who has recently accepted the chair of Sanitary Engineering at Johns Hopkins University, was employed by the Commission as consulting engineer in the instant case. Professor Gregory, in his report upon the valuation of the water plant of the Consolidated Company, comments upon the failure of the Commission's engineer to make any allowance in construction overheads for omissions, which allowance, he states, might properly be made 2 per cent., and criticises the allowance of 5 per cent. included in construction overheads for engineering as unduly low, suggesting that in his opinion an allowance of 7 per cent. would be proper for a plant of the size of this one. Bearing in mind the conditions under which this plant was constructed and the character of the records available, and in further consideration of allowances hereinafter made for certain specific omissions, the Commission concludes that the aggregate allowance made by its Chief Engineer for construction overheads is reasonable, and will not further increase the same to the extent recommended by Professor Gregory.

The allowances made by the Chief Engineer for land, rights of way and working capital, and the total valuation including these items are as follows:

	Westminster Water Co.	Citizens' Water and Power Co.	Consolidated Public Utilities Company.	Total Water Properties.	Electric.	Gas.	Total All Properties.
Present value...	$58,081	$56,891	$46,278	$161,250	$54,445	$31,303	$246,998
Land and rights of way.......	1,438	1,897	8,500	11,835	1,382	613	13,830
	$59,519	$58,788	$54,778	$173,085	$55,827	$31,916	$260,828
Working capital.	....	....	....	2.900	1,470	1,140	5,510
	....	....	....	$175,985	$57,297	$33,056	$266,338

Up to this point the valuations of the electric and gas plants have been included, but as the Commission is not in these proceedings directly concerned with establishing a valuation upon the properties of the Consolidated Company utilized in generating and distributing gas and electricity, it will hereinafter confine itself to the water plants. Even if it should desire at this time and in these proceedings to determine the final valuation to be placed upon the gas and electric plants and distributing systems, the Commission does not feel that the record now before it is sufficient for such purpose, as there was little direct testimony or evidence, other than the Chief Engineer's reports, which furnishes any basis for such valuation.

Working capital has been defined by the Commission as follows:

> "Working capital is the amount of cash and supplies, or other available assets readily convertible into cash without pecuniary sacrifice, reasonably necessary to be kept on hand by the company for the purpose of meeting its current obligations as they arise, and enabling it to operate economically and efficiently. It should be taken to embrace such a stock of materials and supplies as is reasonably necessary to enable the company to make repairs and minor replacements chargeable to operation without unreasonable delay or expense, and to meet operating contingencies and emergencies not taken care of by other reserves or allowances, and generally should be a sum reasonably sufficient to bridge the gap between outlay and reimbursement. It should be determined with due regard to the company's ordinary outstandings, both payable and receivable, the ordinary condition of its stock or supplies in hand, the natural and ordinary risks of its business, the condition of its credit, its custom in the purchase of supplies, and as to carrying its account with banks and others, whether at interest or otherwise, its method of rendering bills for service and time required for the payment thereof, the character and nature of its obligations funded and unfunded, and all other circumstances bearing upon the economical and efficient operation of the business."

The allowance of $2,900.00 as working capital for the water business was arrived at by taking four months' estimated payroll, materials and supplies costing $1,500.00 and $250.00 cash. Considering the basis upon which the business of the respondent is conducted, the Commission finds that the allowance for working capital is reasonable and in keeping with allowances ordinarily made by the Commission for this purpose.

Professor Gregory reported to the Commission that the unit prices applied by the Commission's engineer to the quantities given in the inventory were in the main fair and reasonable, but he points out certain specific items where in his judgment the unit prices used were unduly low. The particular items respecting which his criticism was directed are as follows:

Description.	Quantity Cubic Yds.	Unit Price Used.	Gregory Unit Price.	Difference Per Cubic Yard.	Total Difference
Clay puddle...............	1,760	$1.00	$2.00	$1.00	$1,760.00
Rip rap...................	370	1.00	2.00	1.00	370.00
Rock excavation...........	850	1.25	2.75	1.50	1,275.00
Reinforced concrete filter work	97	20x1.7	25x1.7	8.50	825.00
Sand and gravel for filters.	36	4.00	8.00	4.00	144.00
Total difference in contract cost....................					$4,374.00

To this is to be added the construction overheads of 13.3 per cent., or $582.00, making the total addition to reproduction cost new $4,956.00. The accrued depreciation to be deducted, based on the age of the several items and the annual rate of depreciation thereof, is $639.00, making the net addition to the Chief Engineer's appraisal recommended by Professor Gregory on account of the correction in unit prices $4,317.00. Professor Gregory also recommended that two wells under the clear water basin at Cranberry Station be included, and gives the contract cost as $800.00, based upon an average depth of 100 feet and the contract cost thereof $4.00 per foot. It was first assumed that these wells were covered up by the floor of the clear water basin, but it subsequently developed that the wells have been carried up through the floor and capped and that same are still available for use. He further found that two additional wells near Cranberry Station should be added to the inventory, and assuming the same average depth and contract cost, as found for the two wells above mentioned, suggests that $800.00 might properly be added to the contract cost, in addition to which should be added $50.00 per well for the piping for the same, or a total addition to the contract cost on account of these wells of $900.00. Adding 13.3 per cent. construction overheads on account of the four wells, or $226.00, makes the total addition on this account to reproduction cost new $1,926.00. The accrued depreciation is found to be 28 per cent., or $539.00, which makes the net addition to the appraisal $1,387.00.

It has also been recommended by Professor Gregory that 23 acres of land owned by the Consolidated Company at Routzahn's Mill be included in the inventory, in addition to 5 acres included by the Commission's engineer, and gives the value thereof as $100.00 per acre, or a total increase of $2,300.00. The Consolidated Company owns 28 acres at this point, on part of which is located the wells and pumping station, the remaining acreage being used to protect the source of supply.

The Commission's engineer agrees that the unit prices used by him might properly be increased to the extent indicated by Prof. Gregory, and the additional wells at Cranberry Station and the additional land at Routzahn's Mill included in the appraisal.

Subsequent to Professor Gregory's report, and after the case was submitted, two members of the Commission made a personal inspection of the plant of the Consolidated Company, and after giving due consideration to the entire matter the Commission concluded that the 23 acres of land are not essential to protect the water supply of the Consolidated Company, and should not be included in the valuation. Nor does the Commission believe that the unit prices for the clay puddle and rip rap used in the construction of the high service reservoir should be increased to the amount suggested by Professor Gregory, and in reaching this conclusion the Commission has been largely influenced by the lack of effectiveness of this work, it being shown of record that the seepage from the reservoir is abnormally high.

The Commission is convinced that the unit prices recommended by Professor Gregory for the rock excavation, reinforced concrete filter work and sand and gravel for filters should properly be used, and applying these unit prices has the effect of increasing the Chief Engineer's appraisal $2,543.00, including construction overheads; there is no depreciation to be deducted, as these items were all used in the 1918 construction. The Commission likewise agrees that the allowance recommended by Professor Gregory for additional wells should be included.

The Chief Engineer's appraisal of the depreciated value as of August 31, 1918, of the water property of the Consolidated Company, including land, rights of way and working capital, was $175,985.00, which figure is subject to the additions hereinbefore noted. We therefore obtain:

Chief Engineer's appraisal	$175,985.00
Correction in unit prices	2,543.00
Additional wells	1,387.00
Corrected total value as of August 31, 1918	$179,915.00

That is to say, it would cost $210,305.00 to reproduce new the water plants and systems of the Consolidated Company on the basis of prewar prices (except for such portion thereof as was constructed in 1918, upon which portion the construction cost was based upon 70 per cent. above normal cost), and the property has depreciated by reason of age, obsolescence and other elements of depreciation to the extent of $45,125.00, or an average depreciation of 21.5 per cent., making the net value as of August 31, 1918, $165,180.00, to which must be added $14,735.00, being the value of land and rights of way $11,835.00, and $2,900.00 working capital.

The respondent introduced in evidence a number of deeds covering water diversion rights, rights of way, etc., which were not considered by the Chief Engineer in his appraisal. No attempt was made to establish either the original cost or the present value thereof, and as the rights conveyed by these deeds appear to be of a very indefinite nature and as the value of such rights at the present time is a matter of conjecture, the Commission will exclude the same from its valuation of the property of the Consolidated Company.

During the trial of this case it was urged upon the Commission by the complainant that either the plant of the Westminster Water Company or the plant of the Citizens' Water and Power Company would be sufficient in itself to furnish Westminster with a safe and adequate supply of water. The Commission's engineer reported that one of either sets of mains would not be adequate for the purpose and that there is no excess of capacity beyond what reasonable prudence demands. The supply of water for Westminster was originally obtained from wells and springs, but with the increasing demands upon the company these sources of supply were found to be inadequate, and the company was compelled to seek a further source of supply. This additional source of supply has been obtained by utilizing the flow of the Luckabaugh Stream, and during the past year a purification plant and pumping station have been erected at Cranberry Station to render the surface water so obtained potable for human consumption and to pump the same to the company's storage reservoirs, from which the water is supplied by gravity. The capacities of the Beaver Run and Routzahn's Mill sources of supply in dry weather were 240,000 gallons per day and 180,000 gallons per day, respectively, or a total of 420,000 gallons per day, though the company has not always been able to obtain the necessary amount of water from the stream, due to the fact that sometimes water is held back at the mill above, and to correct this condition the company contemplates the construction of an impounding reservoir above the pumping plant. The average daily output of the filtration plant is about 415,000 gallons, of which approximately 300,000 gallons are consumed by the water takers. The company also contemplates installing reserve pumping equipment at its Cranberry plant and reserve electrical equipment at its electrical plant adjoining the water plant at Cranberry Station, which will naturally necessitate a considerable expenditure of additional capital, the exact amount of which does not appear of record. When the additions and the improvements at Cranberry Station are completed, it is the purpose of the company to abandon the Beaver Run and Routzahn's Mill sources of supply, but until the improvements at Cranberry Station are completed it is the intention of the Consolidated Company to hold these supplies in reserve, and the policy of so doing has been approved and recommended by both the Commission's engineer and Professor Gregory.

The complainant expressed itself as dissatisfied with the appraisal of the Chief Engineer, and with his conclusion that there was no unnecessary duplication in the sources of water supply, pumping facilities and distribution system of the Consolidated Company, and asked the Commission to employ an engineer to make an independent investigation and report his findings to the Commission. The Commission was at first reluctant to acquiesce in this request, due to both the additional expense involved by such employment and its faith in the ability of its own engineering department to make the appraisal intelligently, conscientiously and impartially and pass upon the question of duplication of facilities, but finally concluded that the better course would be to employ a special engineer to review the situation, if a competent man could be secured at a reasonable compensation, and was fortunate in securing the services of Prof. John H. Gregory. Professor Gregory made a personal inspection of the water works properties of the Consolidated Company and a study of the papers in the case, and reported to the Commission under date of March 8, 1919, after which he was called to the witness stand and questioned at some length by counsel. The findings and recommendations of Professor Gregory have hereinbefore been referred to, and might be recapitulated as follows:

1. The prices used by the Commission's engineer are in the main fair and reasonable, but the same should properly be increased in the case of several items.

2. Certain additional land, wells and water rights should be added to the inventory.

3. An allowance of 2 per cent. for omissions should be added to contract cost.

4. The allowance for engineering should be increased from 5 per cent. to 7 per cent.

5. That the two sets of distribution mains and the two storage reservoirs should be included.

6. That the Beaver Run and Routzahn's Mill sources of supply should be included until such time as the contemplated additions and improvements at Cranberry Station are completed, when they should be retired and due allowance made for the additional investment at Cranberry Station.

The Commission concludes that there is no unnecessary duplication of water facilities at Westminster and will therefore make no deduction from the appraisal on this account. On the other hand, the Commission finds little merit in the contention of counsel for respondent that something over $100,000.00 might properly be added to the cost of plant for going value, which amount he obtains by assuming a fair return to the stockholders of the water companies of 6 per cent. and applying this percentage to the amount of outstanding stock each year from 1900 to 1918, inclusive, during none of which years the stockholders received any dividend. While there may be no duplication at the present time, the Commission cannot be unmindful of the conditions and circumstances surrounding the formation of the second water company, as testified to at the hearings, and the almost ruinous competition which developed after the second water works was built. During this period the rates were forced down to a point at which the service was probably furnished at less than the actual cost of furnishing the same and these rates were inherited by the Consolidated Company. Nevertheless, the Commission cannot entirely disregard the question of going value even though it does not agree with the method proposed by the respondent for determining such going value. As has been pointed out in other valuation cases heretofore decided by the Commission, there is no fixed standard or mathematical formula which can be followed in determining the going value of a utility, and each case must be considered in the light of the facts that are developed in the particular case. The evidence in this case shows that the organization of the Citizens' Company and the resulting competition between the two companies had the effect of increasing the number of water consumers in Westminster. The cost of attaching business is one of the elements which must be considered in arriving at going value, and the Commission has given due consideration to the effect of the competition between the rival water companies in Westminster with respect to the increase in the number of water users. After mature deliberation the Commission finds that an allowance of 3 per cent. upon the depreciated value of the property of the respondent $177,015.00, or $5,310.00, for going value is reasonable, and proper. This added to the valuation of $179,915.00 (which figure includes $2,900.00 working capital) brings the value up to $185,225.00. It might be noted that the percentage allowance for going value in the present case is the same as that made by the Commission in valuation of the property of the Baltimore County Water and Electric Company, the Commission's opinion in which case appears in P. S. C. Md. Reports, Vol. VIII, p. 182.

It has been found impossible to ascertain the exact actual original cost of the water property of the Consolidated Company, and our experience in this case is not an exception to what has been generally found in connection with the valuation of other utilities, as the books and records of such companies are almost universally shown to be sadly lacking with respect to such information, particularly where the utility has been in service a long period of time. There is evidence before the Commission, however, that the stocks and bonds of both the Westminster Water Company and the Citizens' Company were sold by the respective companies for cash at par, and that the stocks of the Consolidated Company given in exchange at the time of the consolidation were not in excess of the stockholders' equity in the plants after making allowance for the outstanding funded debt. The amount of stock so given in exchange was $102,000.00, and there was then and is now an aggregate of $85,000.00 of bonds which are a first lien upon the water properties, making the total capitalization $187,000.00.

The market value of the securities of the respondent company in this case also furnishes little, if any, basis for a determination of the fair value of the property used and useful in the public service. There is no clear evidence before the Commission respecting such market value, and it is natural that the company's securities should reflect in their market value the lack of ability upon the part of the utility to earn a sufficient return upon its investment. The same might be said with respect to the earning value of the property as an element to be considered in connection with the establishment of a fair valuation. If the former rates were unduly low and inadequate for its requirements, the company could not be said to have much earning value under such rates, though this should not be taken as conclusive evidence that the company would not have an earning capacity under adequate rates which would be just and reasonable to the company and its patrons. The question of the amount required to meet the respondent's operating expenses will be dealt with hereinafter.

After giving due consideration to all of the elements which properly entered into a consideration of the fair value of the water properties of The Consolidated Public Utilities Company of Westminster, and giving such weight to each of these elements as seems justified under the particular circumstances and conditions here presented, the Commission concludes that such value as of August 31, 1918, is $185,000.00.

THE RATE OF RETURN.

The Commission has heretofore given much consideration to the general principles which are to govern in the establishment of the rate of return which a public utility is to be permitted to earn upon its property employed in the public service, and its opinion in the Telephone Case, supra, contains a discussion upon this subject at some length.

In some cases this Commission has permitted a maximum rate of return of as much as 8 per cent., while in others the permissible rate of return has been made 7 per cent. and in still others 6 per cent. In fixing the rate of return in a particular case the Commission must take into account all of the facts and circumstances surrounding such case. For example, in the Telephone Case the Commission fixed 8 per cent. as the maximum rate of return, and in arriving at this figure the Commission took into account the character of the business conducted by that particular utility and the changing conditions under which the business had been conducted. Due to the perfection of the industry, new methods and equipment were frequently being demanded, and equipment which was considered the last word today might, on account of some revolutionary invention, be obsolete tomorrow, and such possibilities naturally add to the hazards of the business and increase the risk attending investment in the securities of such an enterprise. This element probably exists to a more or less degree in all public utility undertakings, but it is probably safe to say that the hazard of water companies is less than that of most classes of utilities. It is true that improvements are constantly occurring in the water business, as in other businesses, but such changes have heretofore been gradual and not of such a revolutionary nature as to require the scrapping of property which had theretofore been found adequate for the purpose. This company has recently been called upon to make a considerable capital outlay in connection with its supply at Cranberry Station, but this was caused, not by any startling change in the industry, but rather by the necessity for securing further sources of water supply, in order to keep pace with the increasing demands upon the utility. If it had been found necessary as late as ten years ago to add to the company's water supply, in all probability additional wells would have been sunk, or more running springs sought. The evolution of the industry has made it possible to utilize surface water, no matter how contaminated, and render same sterile and fit for human consumption, and the company therefore, instead of attempting to augment its water supply by means of additional wells and springs, has sought and obtained a source of supply which, after the further capital outlay hereinbefore referred to, bids fair to prove adequate for many years to come.

It is interesting to compare the investment per consumer of the Consolidated Company with that of other water companies in Maryland, and the following table makes this possible. The information therein contained was prepared by the Commission's Chief Engineer several years ago for use in connection with a matter then pending before the Commission, and the investment of the several companies shown in the table was arrived at by taking the total capitalization of each company, which is divided by the number of customers at that time in order to determine the investment per customer.

	Number of Consumers.	Investment per Consumer.
Cambridge Water Company	1,439	$30.54
Annapolis Water Company	2,000	64.11
Easton Water Company	630	87.14
Frostburg Water Company	145	103.45
Midland Elk-Lick Water Company	340	132.13
Baltimore County Water and Electric Co.	8,808	175.83
Suburban Water Company	1,040	179.24
Washington County Water Company	4,120	206.54
Lonaconing Water Company	600	209.92
Bel Air Water and Light Company	399	212.80
Havre de Grace Water Company	580	215.52
Roland Park Water Company	866	227.55
Consolidated Public Utilities Company	1,054	*177.42
Consolidated Public Utilities Company	1,054	†166.03

* On basis of capitalization.
† On basis of Commission's valuation.

It will be seen that the investment of the Consolidated Company per consumer is not unduly high, though there are a number of companies which have a lower per consumer investment. The investment per consumer is naturally a matter of importance to the individual water taker, as the return upon such investment becomes a fixed charge which he is compelled to meet, and which return represents a considerable portion of the total charge which he is required to pay for water. At the same time, the investment per consumer cannot be taken as absolutely and entirely controlling the aggregate charge to the consumer, as it not infrequently happens that by increasing the capital investment the operating expenses may be greatly reduced. Thus a company supply water by gravity may have a comparatively high investment per consumer, which will be more than offset by lower operating costs.

The Commission finds nothing in this case which would indicate that, due to the hazard of the business, the particular efficiency of the plant and its management, or any other consideration, a rate of return in excess of that allowed by the Commission in other water utility cases, i. e., the Baltimore County Water Company case. supra, and the Lonaconing Water Company, Case No. 1616, decided by the Commission on June 19, 1919, and the Commission accordingly fixes 7 per cent. per annum as the maximum rate of return which The Consolidated Public Utilities Company of Westminster will be permitted to earn upon the fair value of its water property as hereinbefore determined by the Commission.

The Commission's opinion in the Telephone Case, supra, contains the following:

"But by this conclusion we are not to be taken as determining that the respondent company is to be permitted to raise its existing rates to the point at which they will yield an 8 per cent. return upon its investment. We simply determine that as long as the company's earnings under its published schedules, taken as a whole, do not yield a return upon the fair value of its entire property in this State in excess of 8 per cent., said schedules as a whole will not be reduced. As hereinbefore stated, under the Public Service Commission Law of this State by which our powers are governed, we must reserve, and could not surrender if we would, the power at any time to reduce any specific charges for service which subject any particular person or locality to any unfair prejudice or disadvantage, or which are in any other respect unfair, unreasonable or discriminatory."

Except in so far as the amount of the rate of return is concerned, this statement is equally applicable to the company here under investigation, subject to the qualifications hereinafter contained respecting specific rates.

RATE PAID FOR ELECTRICAL ENERGY

Under date of February 13, 1919, the Assistant General Counsel of the Commission requested that Professor Gregory be further employed to report to the Commission upon the following points:

1. As to the lowest rate at which water can be furnished a large consumer without loss to the Consolidated Company.

2. As to whether or not a charge of two and three-quarters cents (2¾) per k.w.h. for electrical energy made by the electric plant of the Consolidated Company to the water plant yields a profit to the electric plant, and if so, the amount thereof.

The proposition was submitted to Professor Gregory, who advised the Commission that he would be unable to accept the employment, and the query was thereupon referred to the Chief Engineer of the Commission with instructions to investigate and report his findings to the Commission. Report upon both points presented by Mr. Goldsmith was rendered on March 3, 1919, but we will at this point consider only the question of the reasonableness of the rate charged for electrical energy.

In the quarter ended December 31, 1918, the electric plant of the Consolidated Company generated 178,453 kilowatt hours of electrical energy, of which amount 166,472 k.w.h. were sold, 104,720 k.w.h. going to the water plant and used by it for pumping and for the operation of its ultra violet rays water purification system. The water plant at Cranberry Station adjoins the electric plant, and as the current is delivered to the water company at the tension at which it is generated and is measured through meter located on the electric switchboard there is no loss to the electrical company through distribution or transforming. Of the remaining 73,733 k.w.h. generated during the quarter above referred to, 11,981 k.w.h. were so lost through distribution, transforming, meters, etc. Reduced to tabular form, this is:

	k.w.h.
Sold to water plant	104,720
Sold to other users	61,752
Total sold	166,472
Lost in transforming, etc	11,981
Total generated	178,453

The Commission's engineer found that under the conditions existing at the time of his report the cost of the electrical energy supplied the water plant was 2 cents per k.w.h., and that consequently the rate of 2¾ cents at which the water plant is billed represents a profit of ¾ of a cent per k.w.h., but points out that further additions to the capital investment will be required, which will increase the cost of the service, and that as this report covers the operation of new plant in a single quarter, in which the maintenance charges were very low, a substantial increase in maintenance charges may be expected as the plant grows older.

Undoubtedly the water plant is a valuable customer of the electric plant, and should be accorded as low a rate as possible, due regard. being had to the respective interests of the patrons of the water and electric plants. That the service should be furnished at not less than the actual cost goes without saying, and it may be said to be equally true that the water plant should pay a rate sufficient to pay not only the bare costs of operation, but including a reasonable return upon the investment of the electric plant as well.

The profit obtained from the rate of 2¾ cents per k.w.h. does not appear excessive, and bearing in mind the admonition of the Chief Engineer regarding probable further increases in both the capital investment of the electric plant and operating expense thereof, the Commission will not order a reduction in the rate charged for electrical energy.

Any substantial diminution of the revenues of the electric plant by reason of a reduction of the rate charged the water plant would likely result in an effort upon the part of the electric plant to recoup such loss in revenue from its other customers, and while such a possibility should not in itself deter the Commission from requiring the electric plant to reduce the rate at which it furnishes current to the water works, the Commission is convinced that no injustice will be done by permitting the rate to remain as at present.

RATES CHARGED WATER CONSUMERS

This brings us to a consideration of the final point, which is the reasonableness of the rates charged by the Consolidated Company for water service, and all that has gone before has direct bearing upon this final point, which is the real issue in controversy in the present proceedings.

The following compilations show the metered and flat rates in effect prior to October 1, 1917, the rates charged at the present time, and the increases effected by the several schedules. The only change in. connection with metered rates made by the schedule which became effective October 1, 1918, was to further increase the quarterly minimum charges as shown.

CONSOLIDATED PUBLIC UTILITIES COMPANY OF WESTMINSTER

METERED RATES

Prior to October 1, 1917

	Less than 100 gallons per day					...... 36c.	per 1,000 gallons			
Between	100 and 300	"	"	"	...... 28c.	"	"	"
"	300 " 500	"	"	"	... .. 20c.	"	"	"
"	500 " 1,000	"	"	"	.. 16c.	"	"	"
"	1,000 " 2,000	"	"	"	...... 14½c.	"	"	"
"	2,000 " 3,000	"	"	"	.. 13c.	"	"	"
"	3,000 " 5,000	"	"	"	.. 12c.	"	"	"
"	5,000 " over	"	"	"	...... 9½c.	"	"	"

Minimum not less than $2.00 per quarter.

Effective October 1, 1917

1st	15,000 gallons or less (per quarter)				...... 40c.	per 1,000 gallons			
2nd	15,000	"	"	"	"	...... 30c.	"	"	"
3rd	15,000	"	"	"	"	.. 25c.	"	"	"
4th	15,000	"	"	"	"	.. 20c.	"	"	"
5th	15,000	"	"	"	"	.. 18c.	"	"	"
2nd	75,000	"	"	"	"	.. 16c.	"	"	"
2nd	150,000	"	"	"	"	.. 15c.	"	"	"
2nd	300,000	"	"	"	"	.. 14c.	"	"	"
3rd	300.000	"	"	"	"	.. 13c.	"	"	"
4th	300,000	"	"	"	"	.. 12c.	"	"	"
5th	300,000	"	"	"	"	.. 11c.	"	"	"
2nd	1,500,000	"	"	"	"	.. 10c.	"	"	"

MINIMUM CHARGE PER QUARTER

	Effective	
	10/1/17	10/1/18
⅝" meter...................................	$2.00	$3.50
¾" "	3.25	4.50
1 " "	5.00	7.50
1¼"	8.50	12.00
2 "	12.50	15.00
3 "	25.00	30.00

COMPARISON OF CHARGES UNDER METERED RATES, OLD AND PRESENT, FOR SPECIFIED QUARTERLY CONSUMPTION

Consumption (Gallons)	Charge Old	Present	Increases Amount	Per Cent.
5,000.............	$2.00 Min.	$3.50 Min.	$1.50	75
6,000.............	2.16	3.50	1.34	62
8,000.............	2.88	3.50	.62	22
10,000.............	3.52	4.00	.48	14
15,000.............	4.92	6.00	1.08	22
20,000.............	6.32	7.50	1.18	19
25,000.............	7.72	9.00	1.28	17
30,000.............	8.88	10.50	1.62	18
35,000.............	9.88	12.00	2.12	21
40,000.............	10.88	13.50	2.62	24
50,000.............	12.68	15.25	2.57	20
60,000.............	14.28	17.25	2.97	21
75,000.............	16.68	19.95	3.27	20
100,000.............	20.53	23.95	3.42	17
150,000.............	27.78	31.95	4.17	15
200,000.............	34.73	39.45	4.72	14
250,000.............	41.23	46.95	5.72	14
300,000.............	47.43	54.45	7.02	15
400,000.............	59.43	68.45	9.02	15
500,000.............	70.18	82.45	12.27	17
600,000.............	79.68	96.45	16.77	21
700,000.............	89.18	109.45	20.27	23
800,000.............	98.68	122.45	23.77	24
900,000.............	108.18	135.45	27.27	25
1,000,000.............	117.68	147.45	29.77	25
1,200,000.............	136.68	171.45	34.77	25
1,500,000.............	165.18	204.45	39.27	24
3,000,000.............	307.68	354.45	46.77	15

CONSOLIDATED PUBLIC UTILITIES COMPANY OF WESTMINSTER

	Flat Rates — Rate Prior to 10/1/17			Present	Increase	
	Per Month	Per Quarter	Per Annum	Rate per Annum	Amount per Annum	Per Cent.
Dwellings of 5 rooms	$ .40	$1.00	$4.00	$14.00	$10.00	250
" 8 to 10 rooms	.48	1.20	4.80	14.00 to 16.00	9.20 to 11.20	192 to 233
" 12 " "	.60	1.60	6.40	18.00	11.60	181
" over 12 "	.80	2.10	8.40	19.00 & up	10.60 & up	126 & up
" of 8 " or less (one spigot for hot or cold water in kitchen)				14.00		
" each room over 8				1.00		
Bath tub, each				4.00		
" residence	.24	.60	2.40			
" barber shop	.40	1.00	4.00			
" hotel	.60	1.60	6.40			
Washstand in bathroom				3.00		
" hotel	.40	1.00	4.00			
Toilet:						
" residence	.24	.60	2.40	4.00	1.60	67
" hotel		1.00 to 1.80	4.00 to 6.40			
Pave wash or hose attachment for 30 ft. front				12.00		
Additional front foot				.80		

Pave wash and steet sprinkler	.25	.50	2.00	12.00	10.00	500
Drug store, each faucet	.40	1.00	4.00	10.00	6.00	150
Other stores and Gas, each faucet	.40	1.00	4.00	10.00	6.00	150
Saloons	.80	1.60	6.40	....	....	....
Barber shop, per chair	.20	.50	2.00	8.00	6.00	300
Smith shop, each fire	....	....	....	8.00	....	....
Private stable, each animal or vehicle	.08	.20	.80	2.00	1.20	150
Livery stable, each animal or vehicle	.12	.30	1.20	....	....	....
Garage, each automobile	....	....	....	4.00	....	....
Hotel, up to 20 rooms	1.00	2.37½	9.50	....	....	....
" " 50 "	2.00	5.40	21.60	....	....	....
" more than 50 rooms	3.20	9.00	36.00	....	....	....
Slaughter house	4.00	1.00	4.00	....	....	....
Bakery	.40	1.00	4.00	....	....	....
Church	.40	1.00	4.00	....	....	....
Steam engine, per h.p.	.40	1.00	4.00	....	....	....
Restaurant	.40 to .60	1.20 to 1.60	4.80 to 6.40	....	....	....
Fire protection service—4" connection or less	....	....	....	....	....	....
" " 6" " "	....	....	....	....	....	....
Building purposes:						
Concrete work, per cubic yard	....	....	....	.25	....	....
Brick, per 1,000	....	....	....	.15	....	....
Stone, per perch	....	....	....	.15	....	....
Plastering, per 100 square yards	....	....	....	.75	....	....

NOTE.—Schedule P. S. C. Md. No. 2, which became effective on October 1, 1917, and remained in effect until October 1, 1918, when same was superseded by schedule P. S. C. Md. No. 3 (which schedule remains in effect at the present time) published rate of $2.00 per quarter for houses of eight rooms or less with one spigot.

The Commission's Auditor has prepared a statement showing the operating revenue and expenses of the combined water companies for the years ended June 30, 1916, 1917 and 1918, and for the year ended September 30, 1918, as follows:

	1916	1917	1918	Sept. 30, 1918
*Operating revenue.............	$12,390	$12,051	$15,580	$17,049
Operating expenses, etc.........	10,713	11,144	15,417	17,550
Net revenue..................	$1,677	$907	$163	†501

*Does not include any revenue for fire protection service from October 1, 1917, to September 30, 1918.

†Denotes deficit.

The year ended June 30, 1918, includes three-quarters during which the first increased rates were in effect, and such rates were in effect throughout the year ended September 30, 1918, during which period there was also non-operating revenue of $310.00.

There are 467 water users charged at flat rates, the single fixture rate for which service was increased from $2.00 per quarter to $3.50 per quarter on October 1, 1918, an increase of $6.00 per annum, and applying this increase to the number of flat rate services, 467, it is found that the probable revenue from such services during the year ending September 30, 1919, will exceed the revenue from such services during the preceding year by $2,802.00. Estimate has also been prepared by the Auditor showing an increase of $2,691.00 in gross revenue from metered consumers under present rates during the calendar year 1919. Applying this same increase to the year ending September 30, 1919, we obtain:

1918 operating revenue.....................	$17,049.00
Estimated increase, flat rates...............	2,802.00
Estimated increase, metered rates...........	2,691.00
Total	$22,542.00
Non-operating revenue.....................	310.00
Total	$22,852.00

That is to say, under the present effective rates of the Consolidated Company the revenue which it will receive from its private water consumers during the year which ends on September 30 next is estimated to be $22,542.00, in addition to which it will receive non-operating revenue of $310.00 (assuming the same non-operating revenue as in the previous year), making a total of $22,852.00 exclusive of the revenue which it will receive from the town for fire protection service.

The total operating expenses in the quarter ended September 30, 1918, were $3,805.69, as against $2,653.73 in the corresponding period of the preceding year, an increase of $1,151.96. The major portion of this increase is due to increases in pumping expense, which item increased from $1,862.88 to $2,802.09, or an increase of $939.21. The operating expenses in quarter ended December 31, 1918, were $5,351.03, as against $3,691.16 in same quarter of previous year, an increase of $1,659.87. A large portion of this increase is likewise attributable to greater cost of pumping, which increased from $2,646.22 to $3,492.98, an increase of $846.76. There is also an item of expense, i. e., purification expenses, which was not encountered in 1917, and which was $608.36 in the last quarter of the calendar year 1918.

As before stated, prior to August 25, 1918, the Consolidated Company obtained its water from wells and running springs, and pumped it to storage reservoirs by steam power. Finding that these sources of supply were not adequate to meet the increasing demands for water it took the question up with the State Board of Health, and after investigation it was decided to utilize the water in the Luckabaugh stream. The State Board of Health very properly insisted that this water be purified before being supplied to the town, inasmuch as same is not fit for human consumption in its raw state, and recommended that the water be first given a treatment of chlorine and then subjected to ultra violet rays, and this suggestion was adopted by the Consolidated Company and a modern filtration and pumping plant established at Cranberry Station, the plant being put into operation on August 25th last. In addition to the item of $608.36 purification expenses before referred to, which includes the cost of chemicals and supplies, a considerable amount of electrical energy is used in the operation of the ultra violet rays, but as the current so used is not separately metered, and as it has not been possible to estimate with any degree of accuracy the amount of energy so consumed, it is included with the energy used for pumping, and so charged.

It is unfortunate that the Commission has before it the operating expenses under the new conditions for but one full quarter. The expenses of operating the old steam plants cannot be taken as indicating the probable cost of operation under the present conditions. Nevertheless, the Commission believes that it would not be justified in taking the full operating expenses during the single quarter as the basis for future operating expenses. The operating expenses in the quarter ended September 30, 1918, during a considerable portion of which period the new plant was in operation, were $3,805.69, and in quarter ended December 31, 1918, were $5,351.03. An allowance of $5,000.00 per quarter for operating expenses appears to be reasonable, and on this basis the requirements for the company would be, per annum:

```
Operating expenses, $5,000 per quarter.............  $20,000
Taxes (based on year ended 6/30/1918)............   1,000
Depreciation (Chief Engineer's calculation)........   2,162
7 per cent. return on fair value of $185,000.00.......  12,950
                                                      ─────────
    Total  .........................................  $36,112
```

This opinion has already reached such length that the Commission will not attempt here to enter into a discussion of the theory of depreciation, particularly as its earlier opinions, including that in the Telephone Case, go into this subject at some length. Suffice it to say that an ample reserve for depreciation is an actual necessity in the case of every public utility and the rates should be such as to permit the creation and maintenance of such depreciation reserve, and that the allowance for depreciation above given is reasonable from the point of view of the public and is somewhat low as compared with similar allowance heretofore made by the Commission for other companies.

It will be seen that the estimated revenues which the Consolidated Company will receive from its private water takers will fall short of its requirements for paying operating expenses, taxes, a proper depreciation reserve allowance, and a fair return upon the fair value of its property, by something over $13,000.00.

The rate schedules of the Consolidated Company which became effective October 1, 1917, and October 1, 1918, both provide a charge of $25.00 per hydrant per annum for fire plugs used for public fire protection service. Prior to October 1, 1918, the municipality paid a flat rate of $800.00 per annum for fire protection service under contract. There are at present approximately 92 fire plugs installed, and if the charge of $25.00 per plug was assessed on each of these it would make the yearly charge to the municipality $2,300.00. The record is not entirely clear as to the number of fire plugs which the town officials desire to continue in use, though it would appear from discussion at the close of the case that about 60 plugs is what the town authorities desire. The Commission believes that there is merit in the suggestion of counsel for the complainant that the rate per plug should be materially reduced for all plugs in excess of a certain number, though it finds the suggested secondary charge unduly low, and will therefore make the rate for public fire protection service $25.00 per plug for the first 60 plugs and $10.00 per plug for each plug in excess of this amount. According to the report of the Chief Engineer the number of plugs installed falls far short of meeting the requirements of the fire underwriters, so the rate established by the Commission will permit the municipality in its discretion to increase the number of plugs in service without greatly adding to the cost of fire protection service. Under this arrangement it will be incumbent upon the municipal authorities to designate which and what number of the existing plugs it desires to continue in service, as the responsibility for determining the number of fire plugs necessary in order to furnish adequate fire protecting service rests entirely with the Mayor and Common Council of Westminster.

Assuming an aggregate annual payment of somewhere between $1,500.00 and $1,800.00 for public fire protection service, it is found that the revenues of the company will still be insufficient to meet its proper corporate requirements.

As before stated, the Chief Engineer reported to the Commission on March 3, 1919, in answer to inquiry of the Assistant General Counsel as to the lowest rate at which water can be furnished to a large consumer without loss to the Consolidated Company. The Western Maryland Railroad takes water from the Consolidated Company at its coal chute at Cranberry Station, using 23,260,950 gallons in the calendar year 1917, 17,786,475 gallons in 1918, its use during the last quarter of that year being 5.348,775 gallons (or 41.95 per cent. of the total metered consumption of the Consolidated Company during that quarter), for which it paid $698.24, or at an average of 11.1 cents per 1,000 gallons.

The report of the Commission's engineer, after a most thorough presentation and analysis of the various factors which must be considered in connection with the inquiry presented, concludes as follows:

"It is obvious from the foregoing that in the schedule of rates here considered that the lowest rate in the sliding scale should not be below 20 cents. It is to be noted that this conforms with the general experience; namely that the slide in such schedules should not exceed the ratio of 2 to 1.

"The application of this rate will, if the railway company continues to use water in the same manner as in the last quarter, have the effect of increasing their water bill 54 per cent., or about $1,500 per annum. That is from the present amount $2,792 to $4,300 per annum.

"On the other hand, it is worthy of note that in case the railway ceases altogether to take water the probable saving to the water company will be about $2,000 per annum. That is, the company will lose $2,792 and save $2,000, a net loss uf $792 by reason of losing a losing customer. This apparent paradox is explained by the fact that the one saving effected by ceasing the service is power charges for pumping, sterilization and materials used in filtration. The fixed charges and operating labor expense is in no way affected by the diminished demand.

"It might be suggested parenthetically that by a small additional investment the cost of operating the Western Maryland chute supply might be substantially reduced."

It is evident to the Commission that the present rate at which water is being furnished the Western Maryland Railway is not compensatory to the Consolidated Company, but it will not here undertake to say just what rates should properly be charged this customer, believing that this is a matter which should originate with the respondent, subject to review by the Commission.. It is also possible that the water company may, by adopting the suggestion of the Commission's engineer and the expenditures of additional capital, materially reduce the cost of supplying water to the Western Maryland Railroad.

The Commission concludes that the rates at present being charged by the Consolidated Company for water furnished by it are neither unjust nor unreasonable, except in the case of fire protection service, and in reaching this conclusion the Commission has given due consideration not only to the cost of furnishing such service but to the worth of the service to the customer as well, some evidence of which value is gathered from the rates charged by other utilities in the State furnishing similar service. While these rates will not furnish a revenue sufficient to provide for the corporate requirements of the respondent company, as determined by the Commission, including a fair return upon the property employed in the public service, the Commission believes that the water company should seek to augment its net income by obtaining a more adequate compensation from its largest user, and by increasing the efficiency of its plant, with particular reference to its high service reservoir, the leakage through which appears to be unduly high.

At the direction of the Commission, its rate clerk reported upon the rules contained in respondent's rate schedule P. S. C. Md. No. 2, which rules were subsequently reissued in rate schedule P. S. C. Md. No. 3. At the hearing the rules were taken up seriatim, and full discussion had respecting the same. Subsequently counsel for the respondent filed an amended series of rules designed to meet some of the objections which had developed to the rules originally filed. Such proposed amended rules will be referred to as the "modified rules." Rules 2, 8, 12, 17, 23, 24, 25, 26 and 27 appear to be reasonable and proper. Under the Public Service Commission Law water companies are required to furnish service which is "reasonably safe and adequate," and no rules which the utility may adopt can relieve it of the obligation thus imposed upon it. Consequently, second paragraph of Rule 11, and Rules 16, 18, 19, 20 and 21, all of which attempt to limit the responsibility of the respondent, should be eliminated. Modified Rules 1, 4, 6, 10, 13 and 15 are reasonable. The first paragraph of modified Rule 3 is unobjectionable; the second paragraph of this modified rule is in the nature of an additional rule and appears to be in conformity with present practice of the Consolidated Company, but the Commission will not now pass upon the propriety thereof and if same is included in new schedule it will remain subject to review by the Commission. Rules 5 and 7 will be eliminated by modified Rule 6. Rule 9 should be amended so as to provide that the Consolidated Company will, at its own expense, bring service pipe to the curb; the present practice is to require the prospective customer to pay for the digging and filling of trench, the Consolidated Company furnishing and installing the pipe. The first paragraph of Rule 11 is unobjectionable. Rule 14 should be changed to read:

"In every instance of metered water supply service the owner shall provide and maintain a location for the meter which is acceptable to the company. When any meter has once been placed, its position shall not be changed except by the company, and in the event any owner makes any changes in his premises which requires any change in the location of or position of the meter or meter box or vault, such change in location or position shall be made by the company, at the cost and expense of the owner."

Rule 22 as modified appears to be proper, except that the maximum distance beyond street main which the Consolidated Company extends pipe at its own expense should be made not less than 30 feet, instead of 15 feet as proposed, and the total distance pipe will be run to supply fire plug should remain 100 feet.

Rule 28 should be made to read:

"Each and every change or modification, alteration or amendment to and of any of the rates and rules of the company shall be made only in the manner prescribed by the Public Service Commission Law of Maryland."

Rule 29 apparently serves no useful purpose and should accordingly be omitted.

An order will be entered by the Commission in accordance with its findings herein.

ORDER No. 5063.

In the Matter of

The Complaint of the MAYOR AND COMMON COUNCIL OF WESTMINSTER

vs.

THE CONSOLIDATED PUBLIC UTILITIES COMPANY OF WESTMINSTER.

Before the

Public Service Commission of Maryland.

Cases Nos. 1525 and 1590.

These cases being at issue upon complaints and answers on file and having been duly heard and submitted by the parties and full investigation of the matters and things involved having been had and the Commission, on the date hereof, having rendered and filed an opinion containing its findings of fact and conclusions therein, which said opinion is hereby referred to and made part hereof,

IT IS, THEREFORE, This 31st day of July, in the year Nineteen Hundred and Nineteen, by the Public Service Commission of Maryland,

Ordered, (1) That the fair value for rate-making purposes of the water property of The Consolidated Public Utilities Company of Westminster on August 31, 1918, was One Hundred and Eighty-five Thousand Dollars ($185,000), and such valuation shall be and become final unless protest against the same shall be filed with the Commission within ten (10) days from the date of this order, as provided by Section 30 of the Public Service Commission Law.

(2) That the maximum return which said The Consolidated Public Utilities Company of Westminster should be permitted to earn upon its water property used in the public service is seven per centum (7%).

(3) That the rates and charges for fire protection service prescribed by Schedule P. S. C. Md. No. 3 of said The Consolidated Public Utilities Company of Westminster be and they are hereby declared to be unjust and unreasonable, to the extent that the rate or charge for fire plugs in excess of sixty (60) in number exceeds Ten Dollars ($10.00) per plug per annum, and said The Consolidated Public Utilities Company of Westminster is hereby directed and required to file with the Commission and make effective not later than August 15, 1919, a schedule providing a rate or charge of Ten Dollars ($10.00) per plug per annum for all fire plugs in excess of sixty (60) in number, and thereafter charge and collect such rate or charge until July 1, 1921, unless earlier modified or changed by this Commission, and thereafter until the further order of this Commission in the premises.

(4) That the rates and charges for other than fire protection service prescribed by Schedule P. S. C. Md. No. 3 of said The Consolidated Public Utilities Company of Westminster be and they are hereby found to be just and reasonable.

(5) That the rules and regulations prescribed by Schedule P. S. C. Md. No. 3 of said The Consolidated Public Utilities Company of Westminster be and they are hereby declared to be unjust and unreasonable and said The Consolidated Public Utilities Company of Westminster is hereby directed and required to file with the Commission and make effective not later than August 15, 1919, a schedule containing rules and regulations in accordance with the findings of the Commission contained in its opinion filed herewith, and thereafter continue such rules and regulations until the further order of this Commission in the premises.

(6) That a copy of this order be forthwith served upon said The Consolidated Public Utilities Company of Westminster, and that said company within ten (10) days from the date of the service of such copy shall advise the Commission in writing whether or not it will accept and abide by the same.

ORDER No. 5065

In the Matter of

The Petition of the Carriers Not Under Federal Control Named in the Official Classification, by R. N. COLLYER, Their Agent, for Permission Under Section 15 of the Public Service Commission Law to File and Publish on Less Than Statutory Notice Supplement to Official Classification No. 44, P. S. C. Md. O. C. No. 44.

Before the

Public Service Commission of Maryland.

S. N. & R. Docket.

Case No. 574.

The above mentioned petition having been received and filed, upon consideration thereof, it is this 1st day of August, 1919, by the Public Service Commission of Maryland,

Ordered, That permission be, and is hereby given, the carriers not under Federal control named in the Official Classification, by R. N. Collyer, their Agent, to file and publish on one day's notice to the Commission and the public, supplement to Official Classification No. 44, P. S. C. Md. O. C. No. 44, containing additions to the specifications for wooden standard railroad containers for the shipment of boots and shoes, as shown by petitioners' exhibit filed herein,

PROVIDED, Said supplement be filed with the Commission upon issuance of this order, and published by posting as required by law, and that all copies of said supplement shall bear the following notation:

"Issued under special permission of the Public Service Commission of Maryland, Order No. 5065 of date August 1st, 1919."

ORDER No. 5066

In the Matter of

The Application of THE CHESAPEAKE AND POTOMAC TELEPHONE COMPANY OF BALTIMORE CITY for the Approval of an Agreement, Dated July 2nd, 1919, for the Lease of Space in the Premises Located at No. 6 Court Street, Easton, Talbot County, Maryland, to FRED. S. LEWIS, Under the Terms and Provisions of Order No. 2913, Entered June 20th, 1916, in Case No. 1131.

Before the

Public Service Commission of Maryland.

Case No. 1702.

The agreement or other written instrument evidencing the transaction in this case having been submitted to this Commission for the purpose of securing its consent to the consummation thereof and the Commission having determined that a hearing is unnecessary,

It Is, Therefore, On this first day of August, in the year 1919, by the Public Service Commission of Maryland,

Ordered, That the consent of this Commission be and the same is hereby given to the disposition of the property described in said agreement, or other written instrument, evidencing the transaction in accordance with the terms outlined therein.

ORDER No. 5067

In the Matter of

The Application of CONSOLIDATED GAS ELECTRIC LIGHT AND POWER COMPANY OF BALTIMORE for the Approval of an Agreement Between It and THE CHESAPEAKE AND POTOMAC TELEPHONE COMPANY OF BALTIMORE CITY for the Sale by the Former to the Latter of One Pole on the North Side of a Private Alley in the Rear of 313 Elliott Street in the City of Baltimore, Maryland, Under the Terms and Provisions of Order No. 2954, Entered July 26th, 1919, in Case No. 1151.

Before the

Public Service Commission of Maryland.

Case No. 1703.

The agreement or other written instrument evidencing the transaction in this case having been submitted to this Commission for the purpose of securing its consent to the consummation thereof and the Commission having determined that a hearing is unnecessary,

IT IS, THEREFORE, On this first day of August, in the year 1919, by the Public Service Commission of Maryland,

Ordered, That the consent of this Commission be and the same is hereby given to the disposition of the property described in said agreement, or other written instrument, evidencing the transaction in accordance with the terms outlined therein.

ORDER No. 5071

In the Matter of

| The Petition of the Carriers Not Under Federal Control Named in the Official Classification, by R. N. COLLYER, Their Agent, for Permission Under Section 15 of the Public Service Commission Law to File and Publish on Less Than Statutory Notice Supplement to Official Classification No. 44, P. S. C. Md. O. C. No. 44. | Before the Public Service Commission of Maryland. S. N. & R. Docket. Case No. 575. |

The above mentioned petition having been received and filed, upon consideration thereof, it is this 15th day of August, 1919, by the Public Service Commission of Maryland,

Ordered, That permission be, and is hereby given, the carriers not under Federal control named in the Official Classification, by R. N. Collyer, their Agent, to file and publish on one day's notice to the Commission and the public, supplement to Official Classification No. 44, P. S. C. Md. O. C. No. 44, containing additions to the specifications for wooden standard railroad containers for the shipment of boots and shoes, as shown by petitioners' exhibit filed herein,

PROVIDED, Said supplement be filed with the Commission upon issuance of this order, and published by posting as required by law, and that all copies of said supplement shall bear the following notation:

"Issued under special permission of the Public Service Commission of Maryland, Order No. 5071 of date August 15th, 1919."

ORDER No. 5073

In the Matter of

The Application of THE CHESAPEAKE AND POTOMAC TELEPHONE COMPANY OF BALTIMORE CITY and the MAYOR AND CITY COUNCIL OF BALTIMORE for the Approval of an Agreement, Dated July 15th, 1919, for the Sale by the Former to the Latter of One Pole on the North Side of the Philadelphia Road, Fifteen Feet West of the West Side of Robinson Street, in the City of Baltimore, Maryland, Under the Terms and Provisions of Order No. 2913, Entered June 20th, 1916, in Case No. 1131 Before This Commission.

Before the

Public Service Commission
of Maryland.

Case No. 1705.

The agreement or other written instrument evidencing the transaction in this case having been submitted to this Commission for the purpose of securing its consent to the consummation thereof and the Commission having determined that a hearing is unnecessary,

IT IS, THEREFORE, On this twenty-first day of August, in the year 1919, by the Public Service Commission of Maryland,

Ordered, That the consent of this Commission be and the same is hereby given to the disposition of the property described in said agreement, or other written instrument, evidencing the transaction in accordance with the terms outlined therein.

ORDER No. 5074

In the Matter of

The Application of EDWARD C. YINGLING for an Order Permitting and Approving the Exercise of a Franchise Granted Him by the Board of County Commissioners of Carroll County, Maryland.

Before the

Public Service Commission
of Maryland.

Case No. 1699.

WHEREAS, Edward C. Yingling having applied to this Commission for an order permitting and approving the exercise by him of a franchise granted him by the Board of County Commissioners of Carroll

County, Maryland, by resolution dated May 5th, 1919, copy of which franchise is filed in these proceedings, and for permission to begin the construction of an electric plant and distributing system under said franchise in Pleasant Valley, Carroll County, Maryland, and

WHEREAS, The case having come on for hearing on July 31st, 1919, in accordance with this Commission's Order No. 5058 passed July 25th, 1919, and no protests against the granting of the permission and approval prayed for having been received, and it being the opinion and finding of the Commission that the exercise of such franchise and the construction of such electric plant and distributing system under said franchise are necessary and convenient for the public service,

IT IS, THEREFORE, This 21st day of August, in the year Nineteen Hundred and Nineteen, by the Public Service Commission of Maryland,

𝔒𝔯𝔡𝔢𝔯𝔢𝔡, That the exercise by Edward C. Yingling of the franchise granted him by the Board of County Commissioners of Carroll County, Maryland, by resolution dated May 5th, 1919, and the construction of an electric plant and distributing system under said franchise be, and the same are hereby, permitted and approved.

ORDER No. 5078

In the Matter of	Before the
The Petition of THE TOLCHESTER BEACH IMPROVEMENT COMPANY for Permission Under Section 15 of the Public Service Commission Law to File and Publish on Less Than Statutory Notice Supplement No. 1 to Petitioner's Local Passenger Tariff P. S. C. Md. No. 9.	Public Service Commission of Maryland. S. N. & R. Docket. Case No. 576.

The above mentioned petition having been received and filed, upon consideration thereof, it is this 27th day of August, 1919, by the Public Service Commission of Maryland,

𝔒𝔯𝔡𝔢𝔯𝔢𝔡, That permission be, and is hereby given, The Tolchester Beach Improvement Company to file and publish on three days' notice to the Commission and the public, Supplement No. 1 to Petitioner's Local Passenger Tariff P. S. C. Md. No. 9, containing fares effective other than during the summer excursion season between various points served by the petitioner, as per copy of said supplement filed herein as exhibit,

PROVIDED, Said supplement be filed with the Commission upon issuance of this order, and published by posting as required by law, and that all copies of said supplement shall bear the following notation:

"Issued under special permission of the Public Service Commission of Maryland, Order No. 5078 of date August 27th, 1919."

ORDER No. 5083

———

In the Matter of

The Application of CONSOLIDATED GAS
ELECTRIC LIGHT AND POWER COMPANY
OF BALTIMORE for the Approval of an
Agreement Between It and THE
CHESAPEAKE AND POTOMAC TELEPHONE
COMPANY OF BALTIMORE CITY for the
Sale by the Former to the Latter of
One Pole Located on the Northeast
Corner of Pulaski Street and Alley
South of Lafayette Avenue Under the
Terms and Provisions of Order No.
2954, Entered July 26th, by This Com-
mission in Case No. 1151.

Before the

Public Service Commission
of Maryland.

Case No. 1707.

The agreement or other written instrument evidencing the transaction in this case having been submitted to this Commission for the
purpose of securing its consent to the consummation thereof and the
Commission having determined that a hearing is unnecessary,

IT IS, THEREFORE, On this third day of September, in the year 1919,
by the Public Service Commission of Maryland,

Ordered, That the consent of this Commission be and the same is
hereby given to the disposition of the property described in said agreement, or other written instrument, evidencing the transaction in accordance with the terms outlined therein.

ORDER No. 5103

In the Matter of

The Petition of W. Edwin Manifold, Henry S. Merryman, A. H. Morris and James T. Smith, Parties of the First Part, and Fawn Light and Power Company, Party of the Second Part, for an Order Permitting and Approving the Transfer by the Parties of the First Part to the Party of the Second Part All of the Franchises, Rights and Privileges Granted Them by the County Commissioners of Harford County, Maryland, by Resolution Dated June 3rd, 1918.

Before the

Public Service Commission of Maryland.

Case No. 1712.

Whereas, This Commission by its Order No. 4509 entered in Case No. 1527 on October 15th, 1918, permitted and approved the exercise by W. Edwin Manifold, Henry S. Merryman, A. H. Morris and James T. Smith of the franchise granted them by the County Commissioners of Harford County, Maryland, by resolution dated June 3rd, 1918, and the construction of an electric plant and distributing system under said franchise, and

Whereas, The said W. Edwin Manifold, Henry S. Merryman, A. H. Morris and James T. Smith and the Fawn Light and Power Company, a corporation organized under the laws of the Commonwealth of Pennsylvania by the merger and consolidation of the Fawn Grove Light and Power Company and the Fawn Township Light and Power Company, both being corporations organized under the laws of the Commonwealth of Pennsylvania, certified copies of the certificates of incorporation of the two constituent corporations and certified copy of the agreement of merger and consolidation, together with letters patent issued thereon, being filed herein, have applied for the written consent of this Commission to the conveyance by the former and the acceptance by the latter of the franchise hereinbefore referred to and the electric plant and distributing system constructed under authority of said franchise, and

Whereas, It being the opinion and finding of the Commission after due consideration that the conveyance by the said W. Edwin Manifold, Henry S. Merryman, A. H. Morris and James T. Smith, and the acceptance by the said Fawn Light and Power Company of the franchise and electric plant and distributing system aforesaid, and the exercise by the said Fawn Light and Power Company of all of the rights and privileges under the franchise granted the said W. Edwin

Manifold, Henry S. Merryman, A. H. Morris and James T. Smith by the County Commissioners of Harford County, Maryland, by resolution dated June 3rd, 1918, are necessary and convenient for the public service,

IT IS, THEREFORE, This 17th day of September, in the year Nineteen Hundred and Nineteen, by the Public Service Commission of Maryland,

𝔒𝔯𝔡𝔢𝔯𝔢𝔡, That the permission and approval of the Commission are hereby given to the conveyance by W. Edwin Manifold, Henry S. Merryman, A. H. Morris and James T. Smith and the acceptance by the Fawn Light and Power Company of the franchise granted the said W. Edwin Manifold, Henry S. Merryman, A. H. Morris and James T. Smith, by the County Commissioners of Harford County, Maryland, by resolution dated June 3rd, 1918, and the electric plant and distributing system constructed under authority of said franchise, and to the exercise by the said Fawn Light and Power Company of all of the rights and privileges under said franchise.

ORDER No. 5101.

In the Matter of

The Application of THE CHESAPEAKE AND POTOMAC TELEPHONE COMPANY OF BALTIMORE CITY and THE CONSOLIDATED POWER COMPANY OF BALTIMORE for the Approval of an Agreement, Dated July 10th, 1919, for the Sale by the Former to the Latter of Nine Poles Located Along the West Side of Rolling Road South of the South Side of Liberty Road in District No. 2, Baltimore County, Maryland, Under the Terms and Provisions of Order No. 2913, Entered June 20th, 1919, in Case No. 1131.

Before the

Public Service Commission of Maryland.

Case No. 1710.

The agreement or other written instrument evidencing the transaction in this case having been submitted to this Commission for the purpose of securing its consent to the consummation thereof and the Commission having determined that a hearing is unnecessary,

IT IS, THEREFORE, On this sixteenth day of September, in the year 1919, by the Public Service Commission of Maryland,

𝔒𝔯𝔡𝔢𝔯𝔢𝔡, That the consent of this Commission be and the same is hereby given to the disposition of the property described in said agreement, or other written instrument, evidencing the transaction in accordance with the terms outlined therein.

QRDER No. 5102.

In the Matter of

The Application of THE CHESAPEAKE AND POTOMAC TELEPHONE COMPANY OF BALTIMORE CITY and THE CONSOLIDATION POWER COMPANY OF BALTIMORE for the Approval of an Agreement, Dated March 26th, 1919, for the Sale by the Former to the Latter of Two Poles Situated on the South Side of Baltimore Avenue in St. Helena, District No. 12, Baltimore County, Maryland, Under the Terms and Provisions of Order No. 2913, Entered June 20th, 1916, in Case No. 1131.

Before the

Public Service Commission of Maryland.

Case No. 1711.

The agreement or other written instrument evidencing the transaction in this case having been submitted to this Commission for the purpose of securing its consent to the consummation thereof and the Commission having determined that a hearing is unnecessary,

IT IS, THEREFORE, On this sixteenth day of September, in the year 1919, by the Public Service Commission of Maryland,

Ordered, That the consent of this Commission be and the same is hereby given to the disposition of the property described in said agreement, or other written instrument, evidencing the transaction in accordance with the terms outlined therein.

ORDER No. 5111.

In the Matter of

The Application of MARYLAND TELEPHONE COMPANY OF BALTIMORE CITY and CONSOLIDATED GAS ELECTRIC LIGHT AND POWER COMPANY OF BALTIMORE for the Approval of an Agreement, Dated June 18th, 1919, for the Sale by the Former to the Latter of One Pole Located on Wagners Point. East of Fairfield Road, Baltimore, Maryland, Under the Terms and Provisions of Order No. 2913, Entered June 20th, 1916, in Case No. 1131.

Before the

Public Service Commission of Maryland.

Case No. 1715.

The agreement or other written instrument evidencing the transaction in this case having been submitted to this Commission for the

purpose of securing its consent to the consummation thereof and the Commission having determined that a hearing is unncessary,

IT IS, THEREFORE, On this twenty-fourth day of September, in the year 1919, by the Public Service Commission of Maryland,

Ordered, That the consent of this Commission be and the same is hereby given to the disposition of the property described in said agreement, or other written instrument, evidencing the transaction in accordance with the terms outlined therein.

ORDER No. 5112.

In the Matter of	
The Application of THE CHESAPEAKE AND POTOMAC TELEPHONE COMPANY OF BALTIMORE CITY for Permission to Use INTERSTATE COMMERCE COMMISSION Form for Its Annual Report to This Commission for the Year Ending December 31st, 1919, and to Use This Form Thereafter Until Required by Order of This Commission to Do Otherwise.	Before the Public Service Commission of Maryland. Case No. 1716.

WHEREAS, Application has been made by The Chesapeake and Potomac Telephone Company of Baltimore City for permission to use the form of annual report prescribed by the Interstate Commerce Commission in rendering its annual report to the Public Service Commission of Maryland for the year ending December 31st, 1919, and to use said form thereafter unless and until required by order of this Commission to do otherwise, instead of the form of annual report prescribed by this Commission, and

WHEREAS, The Auditor of this Commission has reported that such changes as will be occasioned thereby relate to subordinate matters, and it appearing to the Commisson that the public interest will not be affected thereby,

IT IS, THEREFORE, This 24th day of September, in the year Nineteen Hundred and Nineteen, by the Public Service Commission of Maryland,

Ordered, That The Chesapeake and Potomac Telephone Company of Baltimore City be and it is hereby permitted to use the form of annual report prescribed by the Interstate Commerce Commission in rendering its annual report to the Public Service Commission of Maryland for the year ending December 31st, 1919, and to use said form thereafter unless and until required by order of this Commission to do otherwise, instead of the form of annual report prescribed by this Commission.

ORDER No. 5115.

In the Matter of	Before the
The Petition of the Carriers Not Under Federal Control Named in the Official Classification by R. N. COLLYER, Their Agent, for Permission Under Section 15 of the PUBLIC SERVICE COMMISSION Law to File and Publish on Less Than Statutory Notice Supplement to Official Classification No. 44, P. S. C. Md. O. C. No. 44.	Public Service Commission of Maryland.
	S. N. & R. Docket.
	Case No. 577.

The above mentioned petition having been received and filed, upon consideration thereof, it is this 29th day of September, 1919, by the Public Service Commission of Maryland,

Ordered, That permission be and is hereby given the carriers not under Federal control named in the Official Classification, by R. N. Collyer, their Agent, to file and publish supplement to Official Classification No. 44, P. S. C. Md.—O. C. No. 44, departing from the provisions of this Commission's Circular No. 10A in so far as number of effective supplements is concerned; said supplement to contain the revised specifications set forth in petition filed herein and to become effective on not less than thirty days' notice to the Commission and the public, except that the first item contained in said petition shall become effective on not less than one day's notice to the Commission and the public,

PROVIDED, Said supplement be filed with the Commission upon issuance of this Order, and published by posting as required by law, and that all copies of said supplement shall bear the following notation:

"Issued under special permission of the Public Service Commission of Maryland, Order No. 5115 of date September 29th, 1919."

OPINION

In the Matter of
·The Petition of THE UNITED RAILWAYS
AND ELECTRIC COMPANY OF BALTIMORE
for a Modification of Certain Orders,
Now in Force, Fixing the Rates of
Fare to Be Charged by Said Company
and for Permission to File, Publish and
Put in Effect a New Schedule of Rates
of Fare, Increasing Existing Rates, as
Set Forth in This Petition.

Before the
Public Service Commission
of Maryland.

Case No. 1682.

Appearances:

JOSEPH C. FRANCE, ESQ., and WILLIAM H. MALTBIE, ESQ., representing the United Railways and Electric Company of Baltimore;

JOSEPH S. GOLDSMITH, ESQ., People's Counsel, and OSBORNE I. YELLOTT, Special Counsel, both representing the general public;

JAMES J. MCNAMARA, ESQ., Counsel for the Federation of Labor;

S. S. FIELD, ESQ., City Solicitor (by printed brief only), representing the Board of Estimates of Baltimore City.

By the Commission.   Filed September 30th, 1919.

STATEMENT OF PROCEEDINGS.

On July 19th, 1918, The United Railways and Electric Company of Baltimore filed its application for an increased rate of fare from five to six cents and a uniform increase of one cent in the case of children between the ages of four and twelve years and the users of commutation books. In its petition the Company alleged in substance that by reason of war conditions it was no longer possible to render adequate service to the public at the existing rates of fare. It also expressly disclaimed any intention to establish by the proceeding any permanent rate of fare, stating that it asked for relief purely as a war emergency measure and during the period of war conditions, solely for the purpose of preserving its pre-war efficiency and to prevent, as far as possible, injury to its credit and to its organization and the deterioration of its plant, which would otherwise result. It further stated that "it is not intended that any part of the increased revenue hereby sought should increase the margin of profit which the Company had heretofore earned."

Subsequently, without waiting for the Commission to act upon this application, the Company, acting under Section 15 of the Public Service Commission Law filed its Schedule "P. S. C. Md. No. 8" effective October 1st, 1918, in which it provided for a flat increase of one cent in each of its existing adult, children and commutation fares.

On September 18th, 1918, the Commission, of its own motion, filed a complaint alleging that the proposed increases in fares as set forth in the above revised schedule were "excessive, unjust, unfair and unreasonable."

The Company's application of July 19th, 1918 (Case No. 1568), and the Commission's complaint (Case No. 1583) were subsequently consolidated and came to hearing November 18th, 1918. The hearing adjourned on that date until December 2nd, on which date the hearings were resumed and continued until December 19th.

On January 7th, 1919, the Commission filed its opinion in these two cases, the same being accompanied by its Order No. 4608 of that date prescribing a six-cent fare for the conveyance of each passenger over twelve years of age and four cents for each child between the ages of four and twelve years, with substantially equivalent increases in the case of other special and commutation rates.

By the express terms of Order No. 4608 the rates therein prescribed were to become effective from and after January 7th, 1919, and continue "until December 31st, 1919, and for no longer, unless such period be extended for a further period as hereinafter provided, or this order be earlier modified or abrogated by further order of this Commission." The order further provided in this connection, as follows:

"2. That from and after the hour of midnight on the 31st day of December, 1919, said Company's right and privilege to charge and collect the increased fares herein authorized to be charged and collected shall cease and determine, and said Company shall thereafter be permitted to charge no fares in excess of those charged by it on September 30th, 1918, unless this Commission shall in the meantime, by its order in writing, for such cause as may then seem to it, and be in law, good and sufficient, authorize said Company to charge fares in excess of those which were in effect September 30th, 1918;

"3. That so soon after the date of this order as may be reasonably practicable and convenient, and in no event later than January 31st, 1919, said Company shall furnish to this Commission accurate and complete statements under oath, and in convenient form, setting forth the number of revenue and transfer passengers carried, and the number of car-miles operated, the cash receipts from operation and other sources, and the operating and other expenditures of the Company, all set forth in the manner prescribed by the rules of this Commission for accounting by street railway companies, for the calendar months of October, November and December, 1918, respectively; and thereafter, so soon as may be reasonably practicable and convenient after the end of such calendar month during the year 1919, and in no event later than the last day of the next succeeding calendar month, said Company shall furnish this Commission a complete statement as aforesaid covering the operations of the Company during the next preceding month;

"4· That the right of the respondent Company to charge and collect the fares in this order prescribed shall be held subject at all times during the period covered by such order, or any extension thereof which may hereafter be granted as aforesaid, to the right and power of this Commission to reopen this case in the light of the facts disclosed by the monthly reports, aforesaid, or of other facts otherwise coming to the attention of this Commission and modify the rates of fare by this order authorized to be charged and collected by the respondent Company."

Meanwhile the rates of fare prescribed in the Company's revised schedule "P. S. C. Md. No. 8" had become effective October 1st, 1918, as provided in such schedule.

On May 23rd, 1919, seven months and twenty-three days after the rates so prescribed became effective, and a little over seven months before the date set for their termination unless further extended by the Commission as provided in said Order No. 4608, the Company filed its petition alleging that while its passenger traffic had continued with no diminution since the cessation of hostilities in the early part of November, 1918, and its gross revenues had increased, nevertheless, by reason of its increased service at war wages and costs, and increased cost in operating expenses and maintenance, the Company since the first of October, 1918, when the additional fare became effective, to April 1st, 1919, had accumulated a deficit of $167,088.90 as to its interest charges and a deficit of $619,894.90 as to its pre-war surplus and interest, and asked that the Commission's Order No. 4608 of January 7th, 1919, be modified to increase the base rate from six cents to six and one-fourth cents adult fare (four tickets for twenty-five cents or multiple thereof, when paid for in tickets), or seven cents for a single cash fare, with proportionate increases in all other rates except children's fares, which the Company suggested should remain unchanged.

This application came to be heard August 7th, 1919, the hearings and arguments consuming eighteen days and being concluded September 5th, 1919.

Meanwhile the Company had voluntarily entered into an agreement with its employees, under which agreement wages and salaries were materially increased, the Company's estimate of the aggregate of these increases being $805,524 per year. Inasmuch as the estimates both of the Company and of counsel representing the public had been prepared before this wage increase was made, and it was not practicable to redraft them at that late date, there was no official mention of such increase until near the conclusion of the hearings, when it was suggested that proper allowances be made therefor in the exhibits as originally prepared. The Company also filed additional exhibits based on the inclusion of such wage increases, and contended that an increase of fares from six to seven cents, with four tickets for twenty-five cents, would not suffice to enable it to render adequate service and meet its corporate requirements, including such wage increase, and that for these purposes a fare of ten cents would be required, with two tickets for fifteen cents. It was estimated by the Company's witness, Mr. John E. Zimmermann, of the firm of Day & Zimmermann of Philadelphia, that with the base rate at ten cents, from ninety to ninety-nine per cent. of the Company's patrons would use tickets at the reduced rate of seven and one-half cents each. Subsequently it was suggested that a base rate of eight cents, with tickets at the rate of seven and one-half cents, would produce substantially the same result and would be satisfactory to the Company.

On behalf of the public it was contended that with the introduction of proper and possible economies a base rate of seven cents, with four tickets for twenty-five cents, or six and a quarter cents each, would yield the Company a sufficient net operating income to enable it to render adequate service and at the same time meet all its corporate requirements. Representatives of the Federation of Labor contended that there should be no further increases over the existing base rate of six cents; and there were petitions filed in the case asking the Commission to reduce the base rate to the former rate of five cents.

At the date of the conclusion of the argument the Company's operating figures for the month of August, 1919, were not available, but have since been furnished the Commission. Inasmuch as they were furnished in compliance with Order No. 4608 above referred to, the figures for August will be used in this opinion along with the other figures and data which were given in evidence at the hearings. It is important to note in connection with these August figures that the wage increase above referred to became effective August 17th, 1919, and that the effect of such wage increase is therefore reflected in part in the figures for that month.

EFFECT OF FORMER INCREASE.

In its opinion in the Six-Cent Fare Case this Commission estimated that the one-cent increase provided for in its Order No. 4608 would yield the Company approximately $2,240,000 additional gross revenue.

It was shown in that case that the Company's average net earnings from 1912 to 1917, inclusive, after the payment of operating and maintenance expenses, depreciation allowances, taxes and fixed charges, had been $848,802, this sum having been available for dividends and surplus during that period.

It was also shown that in view solely of the higher wage scales prevailing at the date of our order, and without any regard whatever to the higher prices of materials and supplies, the operations of the Company under the existing five-cent fare would result in a deficit of

$2,163,057 for the ensuing year as compared with the above pre-war period.

The Commission concluded in that case that "if the respondent Company is to be put in a position to render adequate service to the people of this community, it must have a substantial increase in its revenues, and that the amount of such increase required in the immediate future is approximately the amount which may reasonably be anticipated to be yielded by the increase of one cent in practically all the Company's fares."

It will be noted that the Commission did not, in this opinion, commit itself absolutely to the proposition that the Company should be permitted, at all hazards, to increases in fares sufficient to yield its full and exact pre-war surplus. It is true, the computations were made upon that basis, but these computations took account only of increased labor costs, and ignored entirely increased costs of materials, the Company itself having elected this method of presenting its case, and having asked only for an increase of one cent in its fares to meet this additional expense of labor.

Notwithstanding the fact that for these reasons the six-cent fare was not designed to yield the Company its full pre-war surplus, it will nevertheless prove interesting and helpful to see how far this one-cent increase has fallen short of yielding such pre-war surplus during the eleven months from October 1st, 1918, to August 31st, 1919, the latest date for which operating figures are available.

The Commission's estimate in the former case that the increase in fare from five to six cents would yield the Company increased gross revenues of $2,240,000 during the year was upon the assumption that the Company would transport during that year 224,000,000 revenue passengers, this figure having been the estimate of the Commission's Special Counsel, and the Company's representatives having contended that such estimate was excessive.

The following table shows actual results as compared with such estimate:

TABLE I

REVENUE PASSENGERS

(Actual and Estimated)

1918	Estimated	Actual
November	19,250,000	18,642,833
December	18,750,000	19,402,443
Total Bal. 1918	38,000,000	38,045,276

1919

January	17,500,000	18,771,764
February	16,500,000	17,540,547
March	18,000,000	19,613,464
April	18,000,000	19,711,271
May	19,000,000	21,260,540
June	19,500,000	21,021,534
July	19,700,000	20,966,521
August	19,500,000	21,557,818
September	19,000,000	....
October	19,500,000	....
Total 10 mos. 1919	186,200,000	
" 12 "	224,200,000	

It will be noted that the actual number of revenue passengers carried by the Company since December 1st, 1918, have far exceeded the estimates adopted by the Commission in its opinion in the former case. This fact is unquestionably due to the more pronounced prosperity and business activity of the community following the cessation of hostilities than was anticipated by the Commission at the date of its opinion, a demonstrated fact which should not be lost sight of when we come later in this opinion to estimate upon the number of revenue passengers to be carried in the future.

The excess revenue passengers over the Commission's estimate resulted in a corresponding excess in the Company's gross receipts over the Commission's estimates.

But on the other hand the transportation of this greater number of passengers required the Company to operate its cars a greater number of car miles, this fact being directly reflected in the Company's operating expenses during the period.

The books of the Company show that since October 1st, 1918, the date when the existing rate became effective, the earnings of the Company, after the payment of operating expenses, taxes, depreciation allowances and fixed charges, have been materially less than they were during corresponding periods in the past. The balance remaining after the payment of the above items, including fixed charges, has been referred to in the exhibits and by the witnesses and counsel throughout the hearings as the "balance to surplus," and that phrase will be used with such meaning throughout this opinion.

The following table shows this "balance to surplus" by months since October 1st, 1918, and until August 31st, 1919, with figures showing revenue passengers and car-miles during this period, and the corresponding figures for each month during the preceding year for comparison:

TABLE II

OPERATING RESULTS BY MONTHS UNDER NEW RATES
(Compared with same months in preceding year)

	Revenue Passengers		Car-Miles		Bal. to Surplus	
	1917	1918	1917	1918	1917	1918
Oct.....	18,499,163	16,649,510	2,874,178	2,578,092	$64,688	*$60,731
Nov....	17,517,946	18,642,833	2,748,368	2,738,459	20,347	*10,425
Dec....	17,848,006	19,402,443	2,624,763	2,927,161	47,076	*16,688
	1918	1919	1918	1919	1918	1919
Jan....	16,486,891	18,771,764	2,498,672	2,910,073	*18,665	*54,190
Feb....	15,586,460	17,540,547	2,296,109	2,686,216	*20,160	*50,077
March..	18,462,512	19,613,464	2,681,786	2,928,263	63,603	25,023
April..	18,772,227	19,711,271	2,638,216	2,871,591	40,547	30,175
May....	20,472,092	21,260,540	2,842,175	3,051,285	111,654	83,720
June...	20,243,356	21,021,534	2,780,732	2,987,337	99,731	63,575
July....	20,830,858	20,966,521	2,917,713	3,092,077	48,465	44,392
Aug....	20,929,425	21,557,818	2,922,891	3,124,480	30,169	*13,043
Sept....	20,355,921	....	2,747,900	....	*72,205	......

*Deficit in Balance to Surplus.

NOTE.—October, 1918, influenza epidemic.

The above table shows that during the eleven months the six-cent fare has been in force the Company has earned a net balance to surplus of but $41,731, as against $488,485 earned during the corresponding eleven months beginning October 1, 1917, and as against the average of $848,802 during the entire years 1912 to 1917, inclusive.

During these eleven months the Company transported 215,138,245 revenue passengers, the additional revenue from whom, through the one-cent increase in fare, may roughly be estimated at $2,150,000. Without this additional revenue during these eleven months the Company would have sustained a deficit in operating and fixed charges of $2,108,269, on the basis of the above figures.

Its fixed charges during these eleven months were $2,916,411, so that it is clearly demonstrated that, without such increased fares granted by our Order No. 4608, the Company would have fallen $808,142 short of being able to pay the interest on its bonds and other interest-bearing obligations.

These facts do at least two things:

First, they demonstrate conclusively both the wisdom and reasonableness of the increase in fares granted by our Order No. 4608 of January 7th, 1919; and

Second, they demonstrate just as conclusively the utter unreasonableness, certainly at the present time, of the applications which we have received for an order requiring the restitution of the former five-cent base rate of fare.

THE COMPANY'S PRESENT NECESSITIES

The above figures do not, however, necessarily in themselves, justify the present application for an increase in the fares of the Company beyond the six-cent base rate established by our former order.

In the case now before us the Commission has had the benefit of much more elaborate and exhaustive studies of the operating results of the Company in the past and other relevant data than we had before us in the former case.

The exhibits containing this data included detailed studies of the Company's primary and sub-accounts, respectively, by years from 1912 to 1918, inclusive; of the same by months from January 1st, 1916, to June 30th, 1919, supplemented by further more general statements of operating results for July and August, 1919, furnished as those figures became available; tables and charts showing the nature, extent and effect of increases in the cost of labor and materials; comparisons with the operating results of similar companies in other cities; elaborate estimates of probable future operating results, accompanied by voluminous supporting sheets and data; and much other information and data not within the above general classifications.

In addition to the above data, which was furnished principally by the Company, the Commission has had the benefit of independent estimates and supporting data prepared by People's Counsel Joseph S. Goldsmith, and of an elaborate typewritten analysis of the Company's books, and estimate of probable future operating results, prepared by Osborne I. Yellott, who was for five and a half years the Assistant General Counsel of this Commission, subsequently participated in the Six-Cent Fare Case, and was again employed by the State as Special Counsel to assist in the presentation of this case.

The Company's only witness was John E. Zimmermann of Day & Zimmermann. Mr. Zimmermann was on the stand under direct examination for six days, and under cross-examination for eight days.

While under direct examination, he filed a large number of exhibits dealing almost exclusively with the past earnings of the Company and its prospective earnings under existing and proposed rates up to December 31st, 1919, all these estimates ignoring the wage increase of $805,524 above referred to. Mr. Zimmermann's general plan in these estimates was to take the actual figures for the first six months of the calendar year 1919 and add to them his estimates for the remaining six months of that year, thus showing the balance to surplus as it would be during that calendar year if his estimates were correct, and also showing how far this balance to surplus would fall short of the balance to surplus earned by the Company during the year 1916. His estimates for the remaining six months in 1919 were based mainly upon actual car-mile costs during the first six months of 1919 applied to his estimates of the car-miles which it would be necessary to operate in order to carry the number of passengers which he estimated would be carried during such six months.

The original estimates of Mr. Zimmermann, Mr. Goldsmith and Mr. Yellott were all predicated upon the assumption that the six-cent fare would continue in force to the end of the year, that the amount of maintenance work would be proportionately the same as that done during the first six months of the year, that the proportion of car-miles operated to revenue passengers carried would remain substantially the same, and that there would be no increase in wages.

The estimates of Mr. Zimmermann, Mr. Goldsmith and Mr. Yellott, respectively, are shown in comparative form in the following table:

TABLE III

COMPARATIVE ESTIMATES FOR 1919

	Estimate for Year of 1919		
	Yellott	*Zimmermann*	*Goldsmith*
Revenue Passengers..........	240,000,000	240,777,100	244,620,000
Car-Miles	35,520,821	35,721,405	....
Average Fare...............	5.897c	5.887c	5.887c
Passenger Revenue.........	$14,140,819	$14,174,548	$14,400,786
Other Operating Revenue.....	122,360	125,000	122,055
Total Operating Revenue....	$14,263,179	$14,299,548	$14,522,841
Maintenance Ways and Structures	$885,559	$689,429	$682,356
Equipment	856,033	860,867	825,207
Power Plants, etc.	58,450	58,229	57,984
Total	$1,600,042	$1,608,525	$1,565,547
Operating Power............	$985,392	$985,392	$989,445
Platform Labor-Pass. Service..	3,735,211	3,736,297	3,738,354
Other Transpor. Expense......	948,420	975,599	927,246
Traffic	17,896	21,701	25,152
Accidents and Damages.......	......	644,324	544,278
General and Miscellaneous....	1,212,243	700,474	706,584
Total	$6,899,162	$7,063,737	$6,931,059
Taxes	$1,410,839	$1,420,142	$1,510,823
Total Maint. Oper. and Taxes..	$9,910,043	$10,092,454	$10,006,929

Balance	$4,353,136	$4,207,094	$4,515,912
Depreciation	713,598	717,609	514,248
Balance	$3,639,538	$3,489,485	$4,001,664
Non-operating Income	40,000	24,250	20,562
Total	$3,679,538	$3,513,735	$4,022,226
Fixed Charges	3,178,949	3,178,950	3,202,854
Balance to Surplus Before Income Tax	$500,589	$334,785	$819,372
1918 Federal Income Tax Paid in 1919	....	86,221	....
Balance	....	$248,564	....

Subsequently Mr. Zimmermann introduced a number of additional exhibits through which he undertook to demonstrate the Company's necessity for greater allowances on account of maintenance, depreciation and accidents and damages than he had made in his original estimates, which were based mainly, as we have stated, upon actual expenditures during the first six months of 1919. Still later in the hearings he presented other exhibits designed to show the effect of the wage increases above referred to, his final exhibit (Company's Exhibit B) indicating the necessity for a ten-cent straight fare, with two tickets for fifteen cents, in order to yield a balance to surplus of $1,017,476 (a little less than the 1916 balance) after the allowance of the sums which he claimed would be necessary for the proper operation of the Company's system.

The cross-examination of Mr. Zimmermann developed the fact that the main differences between his estimates and those of counsel for the public were in respect to the following items:

1. Passenger Revenue;
2. Maintenance;
3. Depreciation allowance;
4. Accidents and Damages;
5. Federal Income Tax;
6. Proper balance to Surplus.

Both People's Counsel Goldsmith and Special Counsel Yellott, at the time of making up their respective original estimates, had before them the complete figures only up to the end of May, 1919, although they subsequently received from the Company a few days prior to the first day of the hearings the complete figures for the month of June. The operating figures for the month of July were not furnished them until the hearings were well under way. Under the Company's methods of accounting it is possible to furnish the traffic figures a day or two after the close of each month, but the revenue and expense figures cannot be shown until the books for the month have been closed, which usually takes from two to three weeks.

It goes almost without saying that in a case of this kind, where a new rate of fare has been in force for only a comparatively short time, more satisfying estimates can be made as to probable future results from the figures covering a period of nine, ten or eleven months, respectively, than from the figures for shorter periods.

The Commission now has before it the full figures for the period from January 1st, 1912, to September 30th, 1918, while the old fare of five cents was in force, and for the further period of October 1st, 1918, to August 31st, 1919, covering the period the new six-cent rate has been in force.

In view of the fact that the estimates of counsel for the public were prepared before the figures after May 30th, 1919, were available, that Mr. Zimmermann's original estimates were prepared with only one more month's data at hand, and that many of the differences between the respective estimates are due to the fact that they were made upon the basis of incomplete and different data, the Commission has concluded that it is incumbent upon it to go through the painfully laborious task of making its own estimate of what would have been the probable operating results for the entire calendar year of 1919 upon the assumption that the six-cent fare had remained in effect throughout the entire year.

In making this analysis the Commission adopted the methods about to be stated, using the order in which the items are set up in Table III:

Revenue Passengers

The first step in estimating probable operating receipts and expenses is to determine the number of revenue passengers likely to be carried during the period under consideration. In this case the period under consideration is the calendar year 1919.

Mr. Yellott's estimate of the number of passengers likely to be carried during the year was 240,000,000. At the time of making this estimate he had before him the number of revenue passengers carried each year during the years 1912 to 1918, inclusive, and the number carried each month during the years 1916 to 1918, inclusive. He also had before him the figures showing the actual number of passengers carried during the first six months of 1919. Analyzing the above figures, he found that the average number of passengers carried during the first six months of 1916, 1917 and 1918 was 48.4 per cent. of the average for the entire year. Applying this percentage to the total for the first six months of 1919, he found that the number to be carried during the entire year upon this basis would be 243,634,535. He then applied the average percentage which each month bore to the entire year during the years 1916 to 1918, inclusive, and found that these figures ranged between 239,000,000 and 249,000,000, the average being 243,330,500 for the entire year. He also found that the January and February figures were abnormal, and, in order to be conservative, took the average indicated by the remaining four months in the first half of 1919, which was approximately 240,000,000 for the entire year.

Mr. Goldsmith took the number of revenue passengers actually carried during the months of March, April and May, 1919, and multiplied this by four, thus arriving at his estimate of 244,620,000.

Mr. Zimmermann had available the monthly figures for the entire period, 1912 to 1918, inclusive, but excluded the year 1918 for the reason that it was in some respects abnormal, especially with respect to the severe weather in January and February and the epidemic of influenza in October. He then ascertained the average percentage which the revenue passengers carried each month bore to the number carried during the whole year throughout the period 1912 to 1917, inclusive, and applied these percentages to the last six months of 1919, adding the result so obtained to the actual number carried during the first six months. This method resulted in his estimate of 240,777,100 for the year. Incidentally, Mr. Zimmermann's table of these percentages showed that from 1912 to 1917, inclusive, the Company had carried during the first eight months of each year an average of 65.991 per cent. of the number carried for the entire twelve months.

It will be noted that the methods adopted by Mr. Yellott and Mr. Zimmermann were strikingly similar, but inasmuch as the latter had available more data than the former, the Commission in making its estimate has adopted the method and figures used by Mr. Zimmermann. In short, we have accepted Mr. Zimmermann's calculations that 65.991 per cent. of the passengers carried during the year, from 1912 to 1917, inclusive, were carried during the first eight months of the year, and have applied this percentage to the known figures for the first eight months of 1919, the result being an estimate of 243,-129,230 revenue passengers for the entire year 1919. In our estimate we have used the round figure 243,000,000.

Car-Miles

In estimating the number of car-miles necessary to be run in order to carry the number of revenue passengers which he had estimated would be carried during the last six months, Mr. Yellott first found that the number of revenue passengers carried per car-mile had increased gradually from 5.84 in 1912 to 6.96 in 1918, the average for the seven years being 6.25. He attributed this increase from year to year to growth in population, greater business activity, increase in riding habit, larger cars and improvements in distribution of cars. He then found that the average for the first six months of 1919 had been 6.75, as against 6.98 during the first six months of 1918, 6.29 during the first six months of 1917, and 6.33 during the first six months of 1916. Under these circumstances he took the figure for the first six months of 1919, to wit, 6.75, rather than the higher figure of 1918. He

then applied this figure to the number of revenue passengers estimated by him to be carried during the remainder of the year and
finally reached his estimate of 35,520,821 car-miles to be operated
during the entire year.

Mr. Zimmermann's estimate of the number of revenue passengers to
be carried per car-mile during the last six months of 1919 was 6.74, as
against Mr. Yellott's estimate of 6.75.

Mr. Goldsmith made no independent estimate as to the number of
passengers per car-mile or number of car-miles to be operated.

The Commission found that the number of revenue passengers carried per car-mile during the first eight months of 1919 was 6.7837.
They then found that the number of car-miles operated during the
first eight months of each year from 1912 to 1917, inclusive, averaged
66.954 per cent. of the number operated during the entire year. This
percentage was applied to the 23,651,322 car-miles operated during the
first eight months of 1919 and it was found that the total for the year
would be 35,324,733, this figure being used in its subsequent estimate
of operating costs. The use of this figure in our estimates results in
the assumption that the Company will be able to carry an average of
6.879 revenue passengers per car-mile during the entire calendar year
1919, as against the average of 6.7837 carried during the first eight
months of the year. This will require a somewhat better distribution
of service than the Company has maintained in the past, but this is
one of the efficiencies which this Commission has in mind the Company
should adopt in the future. The exhibits show that the number of
revenue passengers carried per car-mile during the last four months
of the year is normally greater than the average for the first eight
months.

Passenger Revenue

An estimate of the probable revenue to be derived from a given
number of revenue passengers at a given rate of fare involves necessarily the ascertainment of the amount of revenue produced per revenue passenger by that rate of fare. Owing to the use of half fare,
commutation books and special tickets, this average revenue per revenue passenger is never as great as the nominal fare itself.

Mr. Yellott found that the average rate of fare received by the Company while the five-cent base fare was in force was 4.865 cents. He
estimated that since the six-cent fare had been in effect the average
fare collected had been 5.897 cents, but at the time of making this estimate the figures for May and June were not available. Applying the
above figures to his estimate of revenue passengers, he found that the
passenger revenue would be $14,140,819.

At the time of testifying, Mr. Zimmermann had the figures for the
entire period October 1st, 1918, to July 31st, 1919, and found that during this period the average fare had been only 5.887 cents.

Applying the figure 5.887 cents to his total estimated revenue passengers, Mr. Zimmermann got the figure $14,174,548 as the probable passenger revenue during the year.

Mr. Goldsmith in his estimate took the actual passenger revenue for the months March, April and May, 1919, multiplied this by four and reached the figure $14,400,786 for the entire year.

Under these circumstances the Commission has used the Zimmermann figure of 5.887 cents, and applying the same to its estimate of revenue passengers for the year has reached the conclusion that the passenger revenue during the year will be $14,305,410.

Other Operating Revenue

There being less than $3,000 difference between the estimates of Mr. Zimmermann and either of the representatives of the public in the case of this item, the Commission has accepted the Zimmermann estimate of $125,000.

Maintenance and Depreciation

Reference to Table III will show that there was relatively little difference between the several estimates on account of maintenance in the original exhibits filed by Mr. Yellott, Mr Zimmermann and Mr. Goldsmith, respectively, these exhibits having been as follows:

	Yellott	Zim- mermann	Goldsmith
Maintenance Ways and Structures...	$685,559	$689,429	$682,356
Equipment	856,033	860,867	825,207
Power Plants, etc.....	58,450	58,229	57,984
	$1,600,042	$1,608,525	$1,565,547

In the case of the depreciation allowance, Mr. Yellott estimated $713,598 and Mr. Zimmermann $717,609. Mr. Goldsmith's estimate was not an estimate of depreciation at all, but was accepted as the balance left over after the allowance of $819,372 balance to surplus, representing dividend payments made by the Company during the years 1913 to 1918, inclusive, although he pointed out that the resulting depreciation allowance of $514,248 was substantially equivalent to the average amount set aside on this account during those years.

Both Mr. Yellott and Mr. Zimmermann arrived at their maintenance figures by using the car-mile costs during the first six months of 1919, the difference between them being due to the fact that they used different car-mile totals. This meant that both of them assumed in these estimates that no more maintenance would be done per car-mile during the latter half of 1919 than had been done during the first half.

During the course of his testimony, Mr. Zimmermann contended most earnestly that his estimate of $1,608,525 as the cost of maintenance during the year 1919 was much less than the Commission should allow in its final estimate on this account, and also that his estimate of $717,609 (5 per cent. of estimated gross) in the case of depreciation was inadequate.

Mr. Zimmermann filed a number of special exhibits covering these points. In one series of these special exhibits he assumed that the actual maintenance work done during the year 1916 would furnish a fair criterion for the amount which should be done during the year 1919, and estimated that the cost of such amount of maintenance work at 1919 prices would be $1,919,496, as against his estimate of $1,608,-525 based upon the actual amount of maintenance done during the first half of the year 1919. He contended in this connection that there should be a corresponding increase in the depreciation allowance from $717,609 to $1,140,717—in other words, a total allowance of $3,050,213 for maintenance and depreciation on the basis of 1916 quantities and 1919 prices, as against $2,326,134 on the basis of 1919 quantities and 1919 prices, a difference of $726,079, which would amount to about one-third of a cent additional in the way of fare.

In another series of exhibits—and, in fact, this was his final recommendation and conclusion—Mr. Zimmermann contended that the Company should be given an allowance of nine cents per car-mile for maintenance and three cents per car-mile for depreciation, an estimated total of $4,286,568, against his other total of $2,326,134 based on 1919 quantities and 1919 prices, an increased allowance on this account of $1,960,434, or almost a full cent additional fare.

It is a universally accepted principle of rate-making that the proprietors of a public utility are entitled to receive from the public through the rates a sum not only sufficient to pay operating expenses, taxes and fair return upon the fair value of the property used in the public service, but in addition thereto a sum sufficient to maintain such property in repair, and replace such portions of the same as may be worn out in the public service or have to be replaced from time to time for other reasons incident to their use in such service.

There is probably no one subject in connection with rate-making that has been more discussed than this general subject of maintenance and depreciation, and the difficulties of the subject to those who attempt to approach it along technical or theoretical lines are innumerable. The Supreme Court of the United States has never attempted any full discussion of the subject which could safely be taken as a guide to rate-making bodies.

For these and other reasons, this Commission has always endeavored to approach the question in a practical as distinguished from a theoretical way, and in all the cases which have come before it has attempted to provide in the rate a sum in dollars which will be adequate to maintain the property in reasonably good operating condition, and to provide in addition a fund out of which current replacements can be made promptly as required from time to time, without any undue or abnormal enhancement in the cost of current maintenance.

The Commission sees little, if any, ground for any substantial distinction, so far as the public is concerned, between the cost of maintaining in good repair individual articles used in the public service, and replacing such articles when they are actually worn out and have to be retired from service. In either event the public should in fairness pay the bill, and it is a matter of no real concern to the public whether the bill is made out for maintenance or for replacements.

The public is, however, interested in replacements being promptly made, when and as required. It is also interested in the proper and equitable apportionment of the cost of the article replaced among those who have had the benefit of its service during its useful life. The public is also interested to a considerable extent, and the utilities and regulatory bodies to an even greater extent, in the continued maintenance of an existing charge for service, as distinguished from charges which are constantly fluctuating up or down. And it is to accomplish the first two of these ends, to wit, prompt replacement as required and equitable apportionment of the cost of the article replaced among those who have enjoyed its service—and to prevent the second, to wit, frequently fluctuating rates for service—that depreciation and kindred reserves are created. It therefore follows that it is just as much incumbent upon the general public to pay through the rates sums sufficient for adequate depreciation reserves as it is to pay the cost of actual current maintenance.

But, on the other hand, there is a correlative duty and obligation on the part of those who have dedicated their property to the public service to keep such property always in such a condition of repair as to render adequate service to the public. One who has devoted his property to the public service cannot, certainly under the law of this State, withdraw the entire property or any considerable portion of the same from the public service without the express consent of the State. And what he cannot do in gross, he cannot lawfully do by piecemeal.

In short, no public service corporation, or individual engaged in the public service, has the right, without the consent of the State, to dispose of the property dedicated to the public service and divert the proceeds thereof to the payment of dividends. And the same principle forbids the public service corporation neglecting properly to maintain its property out of the fund contributed by the public through the rates paid for the service, and use those funds for the payment of dividends. So to do is in effect to consume in the payment of dividends property which has been dedicated to the public service and in which the public has acquired a material interest by virtue of such dedication.

That the petitioning company has not kept up the maintenance of its property during the past several years to the extent to which it should properly have been kept up is a matter of common knowledge, and was frankly admitted by the Company's principal witness at the hearing. Some justification for this state of affairs was sought in the fact that owing to war conditions during this period it was not possible to keep up the maintenance of the property as well as it should have been kept up. This fact, coupled with the further fact that the operating officials of the Company no doubt felt that the prices of labor and materials were abnormally high during this period, and that true economy demanded that this maintenance be deferred, may be some justification for the Company's conduct in deferring the same to the extent that it did.

But these facts, while possibly justifying the deferring of maintenance itself, cannot be taken to justify the Company's action in neglecting to provide for such deferred maintenance during the period it was so accruing. As was pointed out so frequently at the hearings by all the counsel representing the public in this case, the Company continued throughout the entire war period to pay dividends upon its common stock at the accustomed rate of four per cent. per annum, and not only made absolutely no provision for taking care of the deferred maintenance accruing during this period, but almost entirely exhausted the depreciation reserves which it had so slowly set up in the past.

Under these circumstances this Commission feels that it would be grossly unfair to the public of today and of the immediate future to provide in the rates about to be established the large sums necessary either to pay for the deferred maintenance accruing during the period of the war, or to set up depreciation reserves which could have been so easily set up had dividends upon the common stock not been paid during the period of the war.

It is questionable under the law of this State, as declared by the Court of Appeals in the *Havre de Grace and Perryville Bridge Company* case, 132 Md., 16, whether this Commission has the power under the Public Service Commission Law to require a public service corporation, against the judgment of its directors, to set up any specific depreciation reserves, or has the power and authority to control the disposition of that reserve. But, regardless of the extent of its power in this connection, this Commission has considerable latitude in the first instance, at least, in establishing rates to be charged by public service corporations subject to its jurisdiction, and in respect to this matter can properly be guided to a considerable extent by the provisions which it finds such corporations have made both for the current maintenance of their properties and for the prompt replacement of those portions of the same which may require to be replaced from time to time for any reason. More liberal allowances for maintenance and replacement will naturally be made by this Commission in cases where it finds proper and adequate provisions are made by the owners of the property for the maintenance and replacement thereof than in cases where it finds a tendency to consume their property in the payment of unwarranted dividends.

Mr. Zimmermann contended in effect that the actual amount of maintenance done by the Company during the first half of the year 1919 was materially less than the actual amount done during the first half of the year 1916, although the aggregate cost of such maintenance in the first half of the year 1919 was greater than its aggregate cost in the first half of 1916 by reason of the much higher cost of labor and material at the present time. As we have stated, in a number of his exhibits he sets up these 1916 quantities of mainteance and 1919 prices, and his other estimates based upon nine cents per car-mile for maintenance and three cents per car-mile for depreciation allowances were only finally adopted by him at the very conclusion of his testimony on cross-examination.

The exhibits in the case show that during the years 1912 to 1918, inclusive, expenditures were made as follows on account of total maintenance and the depreciation reserve:

Year	Total Maintenance	Depreciation Allowances	Total
1912	$847,075	$428,574	$1,275,649
1913	877,309	530,226	1,407,535
1914	811,724	469,395	1,281,119
1915	719,279	410,548	1,129,827
1916	834,116	495,702	1,329,818
1917	923,641	528,042	1,451,683
1918	1,300,879	596,485	1,897,364

It will be seen from these figures that the amount expended for maintenance during the year 1916 was considerably above the average spent during the preceding years, also that the appropriation to depreciation was larger in 1916 than it had been during any of the preceding four years, with the exception of 1913, and was considerably above the average for the four years.

Under these circumstances we are constrained to adopt Mr. Zimmermann's view that the appropriations on account of maintenance and depreciation in 1916 fairly represented the Company's conception of the amounts proper to be devoted to these purposes, especially in view of the fact that the year 1916 ended with a balance to surplus of approximately $300,000 more than the Company had earned during any of the four preceding years, and that year was regarded as the most prosperous in its history. It is fair to assume under these circumstances that if the managing officers of the Company had conceived that more money was required for maintenance or depreciation during the year 1916 it would have been expended.

The actual amount of the Company's property subject to depreciation is not materially greater at the present time than it was in 1916. Therefore the only factor to be reckoned with is the increased cost of labor and materials at the present time over their cost during the year 1916.

Mr. Zimmermann filed a number of exhibits dealing with the increased cost of labor and material at the present time, some of these exhibits going as far back as 1893. In these exhibits it appeared that the 1919 costs of maintenance, labor and material included, were approximately 101 per cent. in excess of the 1916 costs.

Resorting to the exhibits showing the monthly expenditures on various accounts during the year 1916, we find that the average maintenance expenditures per month for the first seven months of that year were $66,039. During the first seven months in 1919 we find the average maintenance expenditures per month were $133,558, an increase of a trifle over 102 per cent., this fact indicating that practically as much maintenance, in quantity, was done during the first seven months of 1919 as during the first seven months of 1916.

Going further, we find that the amount spent for maintenance in August, 1916, was $75,509, whereas the amount spent for maintenance in August, 1919, was $196,826, an increase of 160.6 per cent., this larger increase in the percentage being no doubt due in part to the wage increase of August 16th, 1919.

It is somewhat difficult to reconcile Mr. Zimmermann's contention that the proper allowance for maintenance at the present time would be nine cents per car-mile with the fact that during the year 1916, when the Company did all the maintenance work which it evidently thought necessary, such cost was at the rate of but 2.66 cents per car-mile.

It is evident from the above figures as to the actual expenditures for maintenance during the first seven months of the years 1916 and 1919, respectively, if we accept Mr. Zimmermann's assumption that the costs of maintenance, labor and material have advanced approximately 101 per cent., that the Company has done substantially as much maintenance work during the first seven months of 1919 as it did during the first seven months of 1916.

The car-mile cost of maintenance during the first seven months of 1919 was 4.55 cents. Applying this figure to the 14,797,891 car-miles estimated by us to be operated during the last five months of the year, we get the sum $674,043 to be added to $934,910, the actual cost of maintenance during the first seven months, this addition resulting in a total of $1,608,953 as the estimate of the probable cost of maintenance during the entire calendar year 1919.

Or, if we take the actual maintenance cost in 1916 and increase it by 101 per cent., we get the sum of $1,676,573 as the probable cost of maintenance during the entire year 1919.

Under all the circumstances we have concluded to adopt this latter figure as our estimate.

In the case of depreciation allowances to maintain the Company's depreciation reserve, the same being referred to in the exhibits as "depreciation," the Company during the past few years has been accustomed to make these allowances in per cent. of gross, the usual allowance being five per cent. of gross. While this may be a convenient method of computing proper allowances for depreciation in cases where charges for service run along regularly the same from year to year, it must be very evident that there is little or no logic in its use where such charges fluctuate from time to time. Certain it is that this Company's depreciable property did not begin to depreciate twenty per cent. more rapidly overnight between September 30th, 1918, and October 1st, 1918, when the five-cent fare was increased to six cents, and the Company's gross revenues increased overnight proportionately.

As we have said in an earlier portion of our discussion of the subject of maintenance and depreciation, this Commission's aim is always to meet this subject in a practical way. Ordinarily depreciation allowances are expressed in percentages of the value of the depreciable property, or equated over the Commission's valuation of the whole. But in this case the valuation of the Company's property has never been completed, and we are therefore without that guide. Common sense and a knowledge of the purposes and objects of a depreciation reserve seem to dictate that by reason of the enhanced costs at the present time, depreciation allowances, when expressed in dollars, and even where there has been no material increase in quantities, should be materially larger than in the past. There would also seem to be some relation between the car-miles operated and the amount set aside from year to year to provide for replacements.

Under the circumstances we have determined, not for the purpose or with the object of establishing a precedent, but with the idea of reaching an amount which will be reasonable under the circumstances of this particular case, to base our estimate of depreciation allowances for the last four months of the year 1919 upon the car-mile ratio to such actual allowances during the first eight months of 1919. These allowances during the first eight months of 1919 amounted to $475,734, or 2.01 cents per car-mile. Upon this basis our estimate for the depreciation allowances for the last four months of the year is $234,636, which, added to the above $475,734, makes $710,370.

The allowances in the past have been as follows:

1912	$428,574
1913	530,226
1914	469,895
1915	410,548
1916	495,702
1917	528,042
1918	596,485

Operating Power Plant

Mr. Zimmermann in his estimate accepted June, 1919, as fairly representing the car-mile cost of power plant operation at the present time. We have taken the actual cost for the first six months of 1919 and estimated the cost for the remaining six months by multiplying the June cost per car-mile, 2.49 cents, by the car-miles estimated to be run during the last six months, our total being $975,516, as against Mr. Zimmermann's and Mr. Yellott's estimates of $985,392 and Mr. Goldsmith's estimate of $989,445.

Platform Labor

Mr. Zimmermann in this case took the car-mile cost of platform labor for the first six months of 1919 and multiplied it by his estimate of car-miles to be run during the remainder of the year, adding the actual and estimated, and getting $3,736,297. Mr. Yellott took the car-mile cost for the ten months, September, 1918, to June, 1919, inclusive, and in other respects following the same course as Mr. Zimmermann, estimated the cost for the year at $3,735,211. Mr. Goldsmith took the actual amount paid for platform labor during March, April and May, 1919, multiplied this sum by four, and got the figure $3,738,354.

The Commission has taken the average car-mile cost for the first seven months of 1919 and multiplied this by its estimated car-miles for the last five months, the total of actual and estimated being $3,701,102.

Other Conducting Transportation

The same methods were followed by the several parties in estimating the cost of this item as they followed respectively in estimating the cost of platform labor, with the result that the Commission's estimate is $959,391, as against Mr. Yellott's estimate of $948,-420, Mr. Zimmermann's estimate of $975,599 and Mr. Goldsmith's estimate of $927,246.

Traffic

Owing to the particular nature of the items embraced in this account, Mr. Yellott concluded that it was not properly susceptible of computation on a car-mile basis, the same embracing advertising, net cost of parks, etc., and estimated that the cost for the year would be $17,896. Mr. Zimmermann's estimate was based on the car-mile cost for the first six months and amounted to $21,701. Mr. Goldsmith's estimate was based on actual results for March, April and May, 1919, multiplied by four, and amounted to $25,152.

The Commission had the benefit of the July and August figures and found that there was a net profit from the parks during these two months which resulted in a credit item overbalancing the debits for the year. It was nevertheless necessary to estimate the probable cost during the remainder of the year, and this was done by taking the actual cost for the first six months, reducing the same to a car-mile basis, multiplying this by the estimated car-miles for the last four months, adding actual and estimated, and deducting the July and August credit items, leaving a net expense for the year of $1,086.

Accidents and Damages

In this case both Mr. Yellott and Mr. Goldsmith based their estimates upon the figures in the exhibits furnished them, which showed actual appropriations to the accident reserves instead of actual expenditures during the first six months. This error was corrected by Mr. Zimmermann in his exhibits and testimony, and he also contended that there should properly be an addition of $110,000 to the accident reserves for the current year. The Commission has accepted the Zimmermann estimate of $644,324.

General and Miscellaneous

In this case Mr. Yellott adopted the car-mile basis from October 1st, 1918, to June 30th, 1919; Mr. Zimmermann the car-mile basis for the first six months of 1919, and Mr. Goldsmith the actual payments during March, April and May, 1919, multiplied by four.

The Commission has adopted the car-mile costs for the first seven months of 1919 as the basis for the remaining five months and has combined actual and estimated, with the result that its estimate for the year is $705,077.

Taxes (Except Federal Income Tax)

In this case Mr. Yellott estimated each class of tax separately, Mr. Zimmermann applied the car-mile basis for the first six months of 1919, and Mr. Goldsmith used the actual payments for March, April and May, 1919, multiplied by four.

The Commission took the first six months of actual cost of all items except park tax and Federal income tax, multiplied such actual by two for the year, estimated the park tax on the basis of 6.91 per cent. of its total actual and estimated passenger revenue for the year, getting a total of $1,394,370, exclusive of Federal income tax.

Non-Operating Income

Mr. Zimmermann estimated this on the basis of car-mile receipts for the first six months, applying this basis to estimated car-miles during the remaining six months and adding the totals of actual and estimated. The Commission followed the same course, except that it took the car-mile basis for the first eight months, and arrived at the result $22,475, which is almost the exact result which would have been obtained by considering the actual for the first eight months as two-thirds of the year and computing the entire year upon that basis.

Fixed Charges

In this case both Mr. Yellott and Mr. Zimmermann took the actual fixed charges for the first six months of 1919 and multiplied this sum by two to get the fixed charges for the year. Mr. Goldsmith took the fixed charges for March, April and May, 1919, multiplied this amount by four and got a somewhat higher sum. The Commission adopted the method pursued by Mr. Yellott and Mr. Zimmermann, and its estimate of this item for the year is $3,178,950.

1918 Federal Income Tax

The amount of this tax was $86,221. Mr. Zimmermann originally included it in his estimate, but subsequently deducted it to make his estimate comparable with the others, reserving the question for further consideration. The Commission approved this course, thinking it better to reserve the question until the 1919 estimated net income and consequent Federal income tax on that year's receipts have been determined.

The results of the aforegoing computations of the Commission are shown in the following table:

TABLE IV
COMMISSION'S ESTIMATED INCOME STATEMENT
For Calendar Year 1919

	Amount	Per Cent. of Gross	Per Car-Mile
Car-Miles	35,324,733		
Revenue Passengers	243,000,000		
Average Fare	5.887c		
Passenger Revenue	$14,305,410	99.1338	40.4969c
Other Operating Rev	125,000	.8662	.3538
Total	$14,430,410	100.0000	40.8507
Maint. Way and Structure			
Maint. Equipment			
Maint. Power Plant			
Total Maintenance	$1,676,573	11.6183	4.7462
Oper. Power Plants, Etc	$975,515	6.7602	.2.7616
Platform Labor	3,701,102	25.6477	10.4773
Other Trans. Expense	959,391	6.6485	2.7159
Traffic	1,086	.0075	.0031
Accidents and Damages	644,324	4.4651	1.8240
General and Misc	705,077	4.8861	1.9960
Total Operating	$6,986,495	48.4151	19.7779
Taxes (except Fed. Inc. Tax)	$1,394,370	9.6627	3.9473
Total Oper. Main. and Taxes	$10,057,438	69.6961	28.4714
Balance	$4,372,972	30.3039	12.3793
Depreciation	710,370	4.9227	2.0109
Balance	$3,662,602	25.3812	10.3684
Non-Operating Income	22,475	.1557	.0636
Total	$3,685,077	25.5369	10.4320
Fixed Charges	3,178,950	22.0295	8.9992
Balance to Surplus	$506,127	3.5074	1.4328

The Wage Increase of August 17th, 1919

Company's Exhibit No. 13 F-1 shows the effect of the principal wage increases of August 17th, 1919, as follows:

TABLE V

PRINCIPAL WAGE INCREASES AUGUST 17, 1919.

	Old Rate	New Rate
Platform Employees—First 8 mos......	.41 hour	.45 hour
Next 9 mos.......	.43 "	.48 "
Thereafter	.45 "	.50 "
Line Superintendence.................	$180.00 mo.	$200.00 mo.
Dispatcher	5.50 day	6.00 day
Car Cleaners (Male).................	3.00 "	3.30 "
Street Inspectors	170.00 mo.	185.00 mo.
First-class Mechanics	5.00 day	6.00 day
Shop Foremen	200.00 mo.	230.00 mo.
Fireman	5.30 day	5.80 day
Watch Engineers	5.30 "	6.00 "
Electrical Operators	5.60 "	6.15 "
Sub-station Operators	5.50 "	6.00 "
Linemen	5.00 "	5.50 "
Asst. Engineers	200.00 mo.	225.00 mo.
Pavers	5.00 day	5.50 day
Rammers	3.75 "	4.15 "
Laborers	3.50 "	4.00 "
Construction Supervisors	150.00 mo.	165.00 mo.
General Office and Mis. Employees......		Approx. 10% inc.

Company Exhibit No. 13 F purports to show the estimated cost of the above wage increase based on hours of labor for the preceding twelve months, as follows:

TABLE VI

ESTIMATED COST OF WAGE INCREASE OF AUGUST 17, 1919

Class of Employee	Total Days	Amount
Conductors and Motormen................	834,694	$399,748
Other Transportation Employees..........	110,511	45,977
Car House Employees....................	68,447	54,305
Shop Employees........................	155,748	121,518
Power Employees.......................	102,727	46,696
Roadway Employees.....................	183,892	98,357
General Office and Miscellaneous Employees	84,658	38,923
Total.............................	1,540,677	$805,524

There was no effort upon the part of counsel for the public to attack or impeach the above estimates, and as the Commission has no reason to believe the same are not accurate, it will adopt the amount of $805,524 as the cost of such increase.

In doing so, however, we are not unmindful of the evidence in the case to the effect that certain of the above classes of labor were notoriously inefficient during a large portion of the period used as the basis of such estimate, and that there is good reason to hope that greater efficiency in the case of such classes of labor will be brought about in the near future.

While we use the above figure, therefore, for the purpose of our final calculations, it is so used with this reservation.

Balance to Surplus

Table IV shows that the Commission's estimated balance to surplus on the basis of the wage scales in effect prior to August 17th, 1919, was $506,127. From this balance to surplus the cost of the wage increase for the remainder of the year should properly be deducted in order to determine the true 1919 balance to surplus.

We will assume for our present purposes that the effect of the continuance of this wage increase for the four and a half months from August 17th to December 31st would be to increase the expenses of the Company four and one-half·twelfths the total increase, $805,524, or $302,071.

This amount deducted from our balance to surplus of $506,127, per Table V, would leave a true balance of $204,056 for the current year.

The following table shows the balance to surplus by years from 1912 to 1918, inclusive:

TABLE VII

BALANCE TO SURPLUS BY YEARS

Year	Balance to Surplus	Cumulative Average
1912	$678,042	
1913	792,322	$735,182
1914	819,368	763,244
1915	819,368	777,275
1916	1,108,124	843,445
1917	875,587	848,802
1918	332,652	775,066

Reference to an early portion of this opinion, or to our opinion in the Six-Cent Fare Case, will show that in that case we established the period 1912 to 1917, inclusive, as the pre-war period, and the pre-war surplus as $848,802.

Deducting the above $204,056 from such pre-war surplus of $848,-802, we find that by following this method of computation there would be at the end of the year a deficit of $644,746 under the pre-war surplus.

To have required all the revenue passengers since August 17th, 1919, up to December 31st, 1919, to make up this deficit would have required an increase in the fare of approximately seven-tenths of one cent, or to require those using the cars after October 1st and until December 31st to make up the same would require an increase in the fare of over one cent.

It is not possible, of course, at this date for the Commission to pass an order which would require patrons who have used the cars in the past to pay the Company the balance of the fares which they should have paid in order to render the Company adequate compensation for the service rendered, and whatever may be the justice of the Company's contention that our order now should provide compensation for the losses sustained since the date of the filing of the petition for an increase in fares, the Commission feels that the ends of justice can best be subserved by projecting the estimates for 1919 into the year 1920 and assuming that the estimates for the year January 1st, 1919, to December 31st, 1919, would apply equally well to the year October 1st, 1919, to September 30th, 1920.

There are no such evidences at the present time of prospective reductions in the cost of labor or materials as to justify this Commission in predicating the relief to be granted the Company upon the assumption that there will be such reductions. We will therefore assume that our estimated balance to surplus of $506,127 is the balance to surplus which the Company would have earned during the year October 1st, 1919, to September 30th, 1920, had there not been the wage increase of August 17th, 1919.

Special Counsel Yellott in his argument at the conclusion of the case laid particular stress upon the fact that both his and Mr. Zimmermann's estimates were based upon actual figures for the first six months of 1919, the estimated figures for the last six months having been predicated largely upon unit costs during that period, and that consequently any projection of these estimates beyond December 31st, 1919, would have to be upon the assumption that operating results would be no more efficient and conditions generally no better from the standpoint of the Company than they had been during the first six months of 1919.

The Commission thinks this point is well taken, and feels that it is but reasonable to assume that many of the unfavorable operating conditions which existed during the latter part of 1918 and the first half of 1919 will not continue on in full force and effect into any considerable period in the future. It is, however, impossible for this Commission to estimate in terms of dollars and cents the effect of this anticipated improvement in operating conditions, just as it is impossible for the Commission to foretell with any degree of accuracy whether or not there may arise other conditions in the future which will affect the Company adversely. About all we can do under the circumstances is to assume, and we think we are justified in so assuming, that operating conditions in many of the respects referred to by both the People's Counsel and Special Counsel in their arguments, and during their cross-examination of Mr. Zimmermann, will not be as unfavorable to the Company as they were during the latter part of 1918 and first half of 1919. This assumption has had some weight with this Commission in reaching its conclusions in this case, but, as we have said, is not one which can be reduced even approximately to figures.

We are therefore deducting our estimated balance to surplus of $506,127 from the $805,524 wage increase, and conclude that with such wage increase in effect the Company will earn during the year October 1st, 1919, to September 30th, 1920, $299,397 less than the amount necessary to pay its interest charges in full unless greater revenues are given it through an immediate increase in fares.

In the former case, as we have hereinbefore stated, this Commission did not commit itself absolutely to the proposition that the Company should be permitted at all hazards to charge fares which would enable it to earn its pre-war surplus, although we permitted an increase in fares designed to accomplish substantially that result.

Our hesitancy to commit ourselves absolutely upon this point in our previous opinion and order was due largely to the fact that we hoped and rather expected that with the resumption of peace there would come about a general and fairly rapid reduction in the prices of labor and commodities which would prove the continuance of the increased fare authorized in that case to be unnecessary.

At the present time we see no evidences of any such general reduction in the prices of either labor or commodities, although it is true that there are some few commodities which have recently fallen in price. These are, however, the exceptions rather than the rule.

For these and other reasons the Commission feels that it would be unwise, misleading and inexpedient to continue the fixing of rates for our public utilities upon the basis of a war emergency.

At the same time we feel that conditions today are so far from normal that it would be unwise for the present for us to revert to the former method of fixing rates solely upon the basis of valuation.

Rates for service in the case of public utilities are ordinarily fixed in the hope that they will continue in force without change for long periods of time. Realizing as we do that present costs are abnormal, that they are not likely for many years, if at all, to return to their former or pre-war level, and that they will ultimately find their new post-war level, which will probably be higher than the pre-war level but lower than the present day abnormal cost, the Commission is of the opinion that in this interim of social unrest and business uncertainty some better and more satisfactory basis of fixing rates for the period of such unrest should be found than either war emergency or valuation.

Heretofore, in this Commission's decisions and orders in the two recent cases of the Consolidated Gas Electric Light and Power Company, to wit, the Electric Rate case and the Gas Rate case, and to a very considerable extent in our former order in the United Railways & Electric Company Six-Cent Fare case, we have been largely governed in reaching our conclusion by the existing corporate requirements of the several companies under the peculiar circumstances existing at the time of our order.

In short, we have felt in all these cases that the best interests of the public of this city and State peremptorily demanded that these corporations be permitted to charge rates for their services which would yield them revenues sufficient both to enable them to render the public adequate service for the present and to maintain their properties and affairs in a condition to continue to render the public such adequate service until such time in the future as conditions can fairly be considered to have become normal. When that time comes, it will be time enough to adopt methods which will result in greater permanency of rates.

It is true that this principle furnishes no standard by which relief can be given to other public utilities operating under somewhat similar conditions, but whose corporate requirements are materially different from those of the corporation in the case of which such principle may have been applied. For illustration, the corporate requirements of a public utility having a large bonded indebtedness at a high rate of interest might well be materially greater than the corporate requirements of another utility having a relatively small funded debt in comparison with the actual value of its property and paying a correspondingly low rate of interest.

And this Commission would not for a moment contend, nor does it admit, that a proper application of the above principle would necessarily require the allowance of a larger relative balance to surplus in the case of the former company than in the case of the latter, regardless of all other circumstances.

The fixing of rates of charge for the service of public utilities is essentially a business problem, and, as was so tersely said by Mr. Justice Hughes of the Supreme Court of the United States in the Minnesota Rate Cases, is not a matter of formulas. This same proposition has repeatedly been stated by the Supreme Court in other ways.

For instance, it has been held that regulatory bodies in making their valuations of property used in the public service for the purpose of fixing rates must use their best judgment in the endeavor to arrive at a valuation which will be just and fair as between the public and the owners of the property under all the facts and circumstances of the particular case.

Again it has been held that there is no standard rate of return upon investment which should be allowed by regulatory bodies under any and all conditions, but that the proper rate of return to be allowed in any given case is the rate which would be fair and just as between the public and the owners under the circumstances of that particular case.

Likewise it has been held that in prescribing the charges to be made by the utility for its services, those charges shall not follow any set standard, but shall be such as are just and fair as between the public and the owners of the property under all the facts and circumstances of the particular case.

Thus we see that at every stage of rate-making the regulatory body is expected to use its best judgment and discretion in the premises and render judgments which will be based in large part at least upon the facts and circumstances of the particular cases before them.

In short, we must take each case as we find it, and endeavor to adopt that form and measure of relief which we think best adapted to the circumstances of that particular case.

In the course of our opinion in the Six-Cent Fare case this Commission said as to the United Railways & Electric Company of Baltimore:

"In the course of a relatively few years the street railway has become one of the most important adjuncts to life in all thickly populated communities. With water, gas and electricity, it has become one of the prime necessities of life. Without it, business would come almost to a standstill, and social life in our cities and suburban communities would be most radically changed. So dependent have the people of our cities become upon the street railway that an interruption of only an hour or so in the service is almost instantly felt throughout the length and breadth of the community, and continuous bad or inadequate service is a thing which no community will long tolerate if redress of any kind can be found.

"From the above reasons it follows that the prime obligation which any State regulatory body, such as a public service commission, owes to the public in connection with the property and affairs of a street railway corporation is, first, to see that the property of such corporation is at all times so constructed, equipped and maintained as to enable those in charge of the same to render at all times adequate service to the public, and, second, to see that such character of service is at all times rendered.

"The former proposition required that the Company shall at all times be kept in such a condition, financially, that it can command investments in its property by the investing public, in order that necessary extensions to meet the demands of a rapidly growing community may be made promptly when and as required, and that its road-bed, power-houses and equipment may always be of a type and capacity to render adequate service economically and efficiently. There is no statutory law which can be resorted to in order to compel the investing public to invest its money in a public utility rather than in any other class of enterprise, and the only laws which can be appealed to are the natural laws of trade and commerce which lead men to invest their money where it may reasonably be expected to yield them a fair return for its use, and forbid the investment of money where there is no reasonable hope or expectation of such a return.

*   *   *   *   *   *   *

"Consequently it follows that a State regulatory body could do no greater harm to a community so entirely dependent upon the service of a street railway company as the public of Baltimore is dependent upon the service of the respondent Company than to refuse to permit it to charge such rates for its service as will enable it at all times both to command the investment of money necessary for the making of required extensions and continued maintenance of its property in efficient condition, and also to render such character of service as the needs of the community reasonably require. So to refuse would not only be to render it physically impossible for the Company to render adequate service, but would also be to drive the Company itself into a position of pecuniary decrepitude which would in the end result in bankruptcy and dissolution, after a long-drawn-out period of such inadequate service, during which the property and equipment would fall into a condition of disrepair which could only be corrected after the lapse of many years and the expenditure of many millions of dollars."

The exhibits in this case show that the petitioning Company had outstanding June 30th, 1919, net funded securities amounting to $64,762,000, and our estimates show that the Company's fixed charges amount at the present time to $3,178,950, the great bulk of this amount being made up of interest charges on the above funded securities.

The exhibits also show that on June 1st, 1922, there will be due $3,000,000 of the City & Suburban Railway First Mortgage Five per Cent. underlying bonds; that on November 1st, 1929, there will be due $1,500,000 of the Baltimore Traction Company First Mortgage Five per Cent. bonds; that on October 1st, 1931, there will be due $4,946,000 Maryland Electric Railways First Mortgage Five per Cent. bonds, guaranteed by the petitioning Company, $823,000 of these bonds now being in the treasury of said Company; that on March 1st, 1932, there will be due $600,000 of the Central Railway Extension and Improvement Five per Cent. mortgage bonds, and on May 1st, 1932, $700,000 of said Central Railway Company Consolidated Five per Cent. mortgage bonds, both underlying issues.

Meanwhile, on February 1st, 1922, there will be due $1,222,000 of

the petitioning Company's five-year five per cent. gold notes; on
August 15th, 1922, $1,528,000 of the Company's five-year convertible
five per cent. gold notes, and on the same day $3,000,000 of the Com-
pany's five-year convertible six per cent. gold notes.

In addition to the above the Company has at the present time a
number of outstanding bills payable, for the funding of which arrangements must be made in the near future.

From the above it will be seen that between the present time and
August 15th, 1922, the Company must refinance over $8,000,000 of
existing interest-bearing obligations, in addition to which it must provide by some form of financing for additional large sums covering necessary additions, betterments and extensions.

In our opinion in the Six-Cent Fare case we commented upon the
fact that during the period 1912 to 1917, inclusive, the average fixed
charges of the petitioning Company had amounted to $2,810,807 and
its average balance to surplus $848,802, saying in this connection:

> "It will be noted that the above net earnings amounted to
> approximately one and one-third times the amount of the
> Company's fixed charges, a ratio by no means excessive in
> view of the desirability of upholding the credit of the Com-
> pany, and, in fact, considerably less than that demanded by
> reasonably conservative investors."

In the case now before us there was adduced a considerable amount
of testimony relative to the unmarketability under existing conditions
of street railway securities upon anything like favorable terms where
such corporations had earnings available for interest, dividends and
surplus less than one and two-thirds times or double their fixed
charges. Numerous instances were given of the high cost of money in
the case of the sale of street railway securities in the recent past.

This opinion has already been so far prolonged that we will not stop
to discuss this subject further than to say that the high cost of financing in the case of public utilities is one which ordinarily falls directly
upon the consumer and must be paid by him through the rates charged
for the service, and to refer to the latest decision of the Supreme
Court of the United States touching upon this subject and recognizing
the difficulties of financing under existing conditions in the case of
public service corporations.

In the case of the *Lincoln Gas & Electric Light Company* v. City
of Lincoln, decided June 2nd, 1919, Mr. Justice Pitney, delivering the
opinion of the Court, said:

> "It is a matter of common knowledge that, owing princi-
> pally to the World War, the costs of labor and supplies of
> every kind have greatly advanced since the ordinance was
> adopted, and largely since this cause was last heard in the
> court below And it is equally well known that annual re-

> turns upon capital and enterprise the world over have materially increased, so that what would have been a proper rate of return for capital invested in gas plants and similar public utilities a few years ago furnishes no safe criterion for the present or for the future."

Under the circumstances, this Commission has no hesitancy in saying that the best interests of the public with respect to the petitioning Company require that it should earn a balance of not materially less than one and a half times its fixed charges after the payment of operating expenses, taxes and the making of reasonable allowances for its accident and depreciation reserves.

Our calculations show that the amount of additional earnings required to produce this sum is approximately $1,000,000.

Reference to Table IV, our estimated income statement, will show that we estimate the Company's total net receipts for the year, before deducting fixed charges, to be $3,685,077. If this amount be increased by $1,000,000 it will be found to be something less than one and one-half times the Company's interest charges.

Testing the above conclusion in another way, we find that on August 31st, 1919, the Company's funded and floating debt amounted to $65,-996,000. If, now, we were to accept as correct the contention so frequently made that the Company's outstanding stock to the amount of $20,484,200 represents no actual value, and assume that the outstanding funded and floating debt represents the full fair value of the Company's property, we will find that the above return of $4,685,000, which we have stated to be a reasonable return, amounts to a return of barely seven per cent. upon the fair value of the Company's property as indicated by its outstanding funded and floating debt.

This Commission, in all its history, which includes a long pre-war period, during which the cost of money was very much lower than at present and operating risks not nearly so great as now, has never held that a return of seven per cent. was unreasonably high when rates were based upon valuation.

In the two Telephone Company cases we held that the Company should be permitted to earn a return not exceeding eight per cent.; in the case of the Baltimore County Water & Electric Company we established rates estimated to yield between seven and eight per cent. upon the fair value of the property as determined by this Commission. In the cases of the Consolidated Gas Electric Light and Power Company of Baltimore the charges authorized by us were estimated to yield the Company a return of approximately 8 per cent. upon the assumed fair value of the property. In a number of other cases we have held that, in view of the nature of the risks surrounding the operation of the properties of public utilities, the rate of return should materially exceed the current legal rate of interest, six per cent.

We are not to be understood by anything we have said with respect to the fair value of the property here in question that such fair value is to be measured by the outstanding funded debt of the Company. We have not so decided, and use that assumption only for purposes of illustration and to show that these returns in money which we have concluded the Company should have would be no more than a reasonable return if measured upon the basis of such assumption.

Our conclusion is, therefore, that the petitioning Company is entitled to charge rates which will yield it a balance to surplus of approximately $1,000,000 after the payment of its operating expenses, taxes, fixed charges, and the making of reasonable allowances for the maintenance of its accident and depreciation reserves.

It remains now to be seen what rate of fare will be necessary to yield such balance to surplus of approximately $1,000,000.

RATE OF FARE NECESSARY

Having reached the aforegoing conclusion, it now becomes necessary for the Commission to establish for the Company rates of fare which may reasonably be anticipated to yield the petitioning Company a net balance to surplus of approximately $1,000,000, after the payment of operating expenses, taxes, fixed charges and the setting aside of the amounts hereinbefore declared by us to be reasonable for the creation and maintenance of proper depreciation and accident reserves.

Reference to the Company's revised schedule P. S. C. Md. No. 8 will show that, in addition to the regular base rate of six cents for adults, there were prescribed in such schedule and are now in force under our Order No. 4608 and supplementary orders Nos. 4609, 4646 and 4944 a number of special fares, to wit: half fares, commutation tickets for first, second and third zones, cash transfers on the Curtis Bay Line and tickets in bulk for the use of the employees of the Bethlehem Steel Company and the Central Foundry Company.

The Company has proposed flat increases of from one-fourth cent to one and one-half cents in each of the above special rates with the exception of the half fares for children, as to which it has proposed no increase.

The Company has also furnished the Commission an estimate of the number of such special fares which will probably be paid during the year 1919, together with an estimate of the yield of the same in the event of such proposed increases. These figures were based on increases in the base rate of from one-fourth of a cent to one and one-half cents, respectively.

For our present purposes it will suffice to take the Company's estimate based on the supposition of a one-cent increase in both base and special fares. This estimate is shown in the following table:

TABLE VIII

YIELD OF INCREASES IN SPECIAL FARES

Increase on One-Cent Basis

7,918,283	Half Fares	4	cts.		
1,512,622	Curtis Bay Cash Transfers......	4	"	1 ct.	$15,126.22
1,437,730	1st Co. Com. Tickets...........	4½	"	1 "	14,377.30
407,740	2nd " " "	5	"	1 "	4,077.40
54,530	3rd " " "	5	"	1 "	545.30
1,947,508	Bethlehem Steel	4½	"	1 "	19,475.08
128,250	Central Foundry	5	"	1 "	1,282.50
13,406,663					$54,883.80

It will be seen from this table that the Company estimates that out of a total of 240,777,100 revenue passengers during the year there will be but 13,406,663 of the same using half fares and the above classes of special tickets, and that a flat increase of one cent in the case of each such special fares, with the exception of half fares, would yield the Company an additional revenue of but $54,883.80. It follows that an increase of one-half cent in these special fares would yield the Company but $27,441.90 additional revenue.

In case of half fares for children the former rate of three cents was sixty per cent. of the adult rate of five cents. With the increase in the adult rate from five to six cents, it seemed desirable at the time of our former order to increase the half fares to four cents, or sixty-six and two-thirds per cent. of the adult rate. Under the circumstances, the Commission would not feel justified in making any further increase in this particular fare unless it should happen that by reason of a considerable increase in the adult rate the half-fare rate would be disproportionately low as compared with the rates in force for many years before the increase in the adult fare from five to six cents.

In our previous opinion and orders in the Six-Cent Fare case the charge for Curtis Bay cash transfers was increased from three to four cents in order to be more nearly proportionate to the increase in the base rate from five to six cents. Under the circumstances, the Commission does not feel that there should now be a further increase in the charge for this cash transfer, since the effect of the increase in the base rate which we are about to authorize will be only to bring the four-cent cash transfer on the Curtis Bay Line, if permitted to remain at four cents, more nearly proportionate to the new base fare as compared with the original transfer charge of three cents and base fare of five cents.

For the same reason the Commission is not inclined to make any further increases at the present time in the case of the commutation tickets or special tickets for employees of the Bethlehem Steel Company and Central Foundry, as such increases were in our former order somewhat disproportionate to the amount of the increase in the base fare, this having been necessary at the time in order that such increases might be in convenient fractions of the cent.

The Company's estimate of 13,460,663 special fares was based upon its estimate of 240,777,100 revenue passengers for the entire year. Consequently the Commission's estimate of 243,000,000 passengers for the year, coupled with the fact that there will probably be a greater use of commutation books with the proposed readjustment of fares, would seem to justify the assumption that there will be a somewhat larger number of patrons paying these special fares in future than in the past. Without attempting to make a minute calculation based upon these factors, we have assumed that there will be approximately 14,000,000 users of these special fares during the year which will be covered by our order.

Deducting this figure from the 243,000,000 revenue passengers estimated by us leaves a balance of 229,000,000 revenue passengers who will have to make up the increase revenues required by the Company.

Any additional sums raised through increases in the fares will be subject to the park tax, which we find is 6.91 per cent. of the Company's total passenger revenues.

Since we know that one cent additional fare charged 229,000,000 passengers would yield $2,290,000, and that sum is far in excess of the amount which we conclude the Company properly requires under existing conditions, it is evident that whatever increase in the base rate of fare is made must be an increase of a fractional part of a cent, and will consequently involve the use of tickets or fare checks.

It is equally obvious that not all of the adult passengers of the Company will make use of these checks, and it therefore remains to determine what percentage of such passengers paying the full fare will probably use the same.

Mr. Zimmermann based his estimates of the probable yield of a seven-cent fare, with four tickets for twenty-five cents, upon the assumption that not less than eighty per cent. nor more than ninety per cent. would avail themselves of the privilege of purchasing checks at the reduced rate. In the case of his estimates based on a seven-cent fare, with three tickets for twenty cents, he assumed that not less than seventy per cent. nor more than eighty per cent. of the passengers paying the full fare would use such tickets, the differences in these assumptions being due to the fact that in the case of four tickets for twenty-five cents there would be a saving of three-fourths of a cent on each individual ticket, whereas in the case of three tickets for twenty cents there would be a saving of but one-third of a cent on each ticket. In the case of Mr. Zimmermann's estimates as to the effect of a ten-cent base rate, with two tickets for fifteen cents, he estimated that between ninety and ninety-nine per cent. of the passengers would avail themselves of the reduced rate through the purchase of the two tickets for fifteen cents, in view of the saving of two and one-half cents on each fare through such purchases of tickets.

The Commission is inclined to think that Mr. Zimmermann's estimates of ticket purchasers in the case of four tickets for twenty-five cents or three tickets for twenty cents are rather high, and is confirmed in this belief by its studies of the experience of the Washington Railway and Electric Company and the Capital Traction Company, both of Washington, D. C., where the use of the five-cent cash fare or six tickets for twenty-five cents has continued from 1894 until about a year ago. In this case there was a saving of five-sixths of a cent with the purchase of each ticket. In addition, as we have seen, the ticket system has been in vogue in Washington for nearly twenty-five years, during which time the public has grown accustomed to the use of the tickets and thoroughly familiar with the advantages of their purchase.

The following table shows the comparatively recent experience of the Washington companies in this respect, these being the only figures available at the date of this opinion:

TABLE IX

PER CENT. OF PASSENGERS USING TICKETS, WASHINGTON, D. C.

5c Cash or 6 Tickets for 25c

W. R. & E. Co.	*Year*	*Capital Traction Co.*
	1900	77.0
	1908	80.9
83.62	1909	80.7
84.10	1910	80.9
84.44	1911	80.9
84.71	1912	80.8
84.88	1913	80.7
85.36	1914	81.2
84.95	1915	81.1
85.37	1916	80.9
85.05	1917	80.5

In view of the experience of the Washington companies as set forth in the above table, the Commission has concluded that it would be reasonable to assume that for the present at least the people of Baltimore may be expected to purchase tickets at reduced rates between the limits of fifty per cent. as a minimum and eighty per cent. as the maximum.

The following table shows the estimated yield of additional fares at different rates upon the respective assumptions that fifty per cent., sixty-six and two-thirds per cent., seventy-five per cent. or eighty per cent. of patrons paying the full fare will use fare checks or tickets:

TABLE X

ESTIMATED YIELD OF ADDITIONAL FARES AT DIFFERENT RATES

Estimated additional revenue from
increased fare base............. 243,000,000 passengers per annum
Less passengers paying other than
full fare 14,000,000

Number of passengers paying increased fare 229,000,000

Additional Yield

	7c Cash Fare, 4 Tickets for 26c			
	50%	66⅔%	75%	80%
Full base fare increase...	$1,145,000	$763,333	$572,500	$458,000
Fractional fare increase..	572,500	763,333	858,750	916,000
Total additional revenue	$1,717,500	$1,526,666	$1,431,250	$1,374,000
Less Park Tax..........	118,679	105,492	98,899	94,943
Net additional revenue.	$1,598,821	$1,421,174	$1,332,351	$1,279,057

	7c Cash Fare, 4 Tickets for 25c			
Full base fare increase...	$1,145,000	$763,333	$572,500	$458,000
Fractional fare increase..	286,250	381,667	429,375	458,000
Total additional revenue	$1,431,250	$1,145,000	$1,001,875	$916,000
Less Park Tax..........	98,899	79,120	69,230	63,295
Net additional revenue.	$1,332,351	$1,065,880	$932,645	$852,705

	7c Cash Fare, 3 Tickets for 20c			
Full base fare increase...	$1,145,000	$763,333	$572,500	$458,000
Fractional fare increase..	763,333	1,017,777	1,145,000	1,221,333
Total additional revenue	$1,908,333	$1,781,110	$1,717,500	$1,679,333
Less Park Tax.....:....	131,865	123,074	118,679	116,042
Net additional revenue.	$1,776,468	$1,658,036	$1,598,821	$1,563,291

Mr. Zimmermann, in his testimony, gave virtually no explanation of
or reason for his assumptions as to the minimum number of passengers who would purchase tickets, and there was no other evidence
adduced at the hearings upon this point.

Under all the circumstances and after a careful study of this most important phase of the situation, the Commission has concluded that in the case of the sale of four tickets for twenty-six cents not less than sixty-six and two-thirds nor more than seventy-five per cent. of the patrons of the Company will use tickets, and that the proper estimate lies about midway between the two, or 70.833 per cent.

Applying these conclusions to the above figures in the case of four tickets for twenty-six cents, we find that the net increase in revenues, after the payment of the park tax, would be $1,376,762.

From this sum should be deducted the $805,524 wage increase less our estimated $506,127 balance to surplus under the six-cent fare without such wage increase, or $299,397, leaving a net balance to surplus of $1,077,365.

From this sum should be deducted the ten per cent. Federal income tax which the Company is required by law to pay upon its net income. Upon our estimate this would amount to $107,736, leaving a final net balance to surplus of $969,629.

A summary of the above calculations will be found in the following table: .

TABLE XI

COMMISSION'S FINAL ESTIMATE OF EFFECT OF INCREASED FARE

Net increase from additional full fare after deduction of
park tax @ 6.91%.................................... $1,376,762
Deduct wage increase......................... $805,524
Less estimated balance to surplus subject to wage
increase 506,127
                                          ———————   299,397

Balance to surplus, 7c fare, 4 tickets for 26c........... $1,077,365
Less Federal income tax............................... 107,736

Final net balance to surplus......................... $969,629

For the reasons hereinbefore stated, this Commission concludes that the above final net balance to surplus is reasonably required by the Company at the present time in order to enable it to meet its corporate requirements.

We therefore conclude that the Company should be permitted by our order about to be passed to increase its existing six-cent adult or base charge to seven cents, and required to sell four tickets or checks representing this charge for twenty-six cents.

' FUTURE MODIFICATIONS OF FARES

The Commission's order passed pursuant to this opinion will provide that the fares established therein shall remain in force and effect for one year from October 1, 1919, to September 30, 1920, unless earlier modified or abrogated by the further order of the Commission. Such order is not to be taken either by the Company or by the public as a guarantee that such fares will continue in force during the whole of that period.

In the course of our opinion we have pointed out that we are dealing at the present time with abnormal conditions, and this means that existing conditions may either remain fairly constant for some time into the future or may at any time grow materially better or materially worse so far as the Company is concerned. Our conclusions have been reached upon the assumption that they will remain practically constant during the coming twelve months.

Our order will further provide that the Company shall continue to furnish the Commission as heretofore accurate and complete monthly statements setting forth the number of revenue and transfer passengers carried, the number of car-miles operated, the cash receipts from operation and other sources, and the operating and other expenditures of the Company, all set forth in the manner prescribed by the rules of this Commission for accounting by street railway companies.

These reports will be scrutinized closely by the Commission and its staff as they are received from month to month, and if it appears at any time that our estimates of receipts and expenditures are so far wrong as to make it unjust either to the Company or to the public that the rates prescribed in our order be continued until the end of the year therein prescribed, steps will be taken at once to modify the same.

It is to be understood by all concerned that our order passed pursuant to this opinion is so far tentative that it can be reopened at any time within such twelve months upon the evidence adduced in this and the previous case and the monthly reports which will be furnished under oath by the Company as above stated.

In other words, there will be no necessity, during the coming year at least, for any lengthy, formal hearing upon applications for either the increase or decrease of the fares established by our order.

The Commission now has before it the complete operating figures of this Company for a period of approximately seven years, and there is now no necessity for further details as to such operations in the past or for further estimates of probable future operating results, except in so far as the estimates contained in this opinion may require modification from time to time by reason of actual results.

If it should happen that the experience of several months under the new rates should demonstrate that the Company is earning a larger net revenue than is anticipated by this order, and that there is a reasonable probability that such excess earnings during the course of the year would be such as to justify some reduction in the base rate of fare, the Commission will, of its own motion, require the Company to show cause why such decrease should not be made.

If, on the other hand, such reports, upon thorough investigation by the Accounting Department of the Commission and by the members of the Commission itself, should demonstrate that the Company is earning materially less than we now anticipate it will earn under such rates, the Company will be permitted to make an application for their increase, with the understanding that the Commission will confine the hearings upon such application, as far as it can reasonably do so under the law, to the precise issue of the rate necessary to yield approximately the net balance to surplus which we have declared a reasonable one for the Company to earn during the period of the next twelve months.

The order will further provide in substance that at the end of such period of twelve months the base rate shall revert to the present fare of six cents, unless it shall then be made to appear that some other rate than six cents is a proper rate thereafter to be charged by the Company.

Meanwhile the Commission expects to give much thought to the "Cost of Service" plan which has been adopted in the comparatively recent past by a number of cities in the United States and elsewhere for the better and more satisfactory regulation of fares to be charged by street railway companies.

The theory of these plans is in brief that the owners of street railway properties are entitled to receive from the public the actual cost of the service rendered, including in that cost the reasonable expenses of operation, maintenance, taxes, fixed charges and a fair return upon the fair value of the investment, with the proviso that as the cost of service increases the fares go up, and as the cost of service decreases the fares come down, such plans providing for the ready ascertainment of the pertinent facts without the necessity of prolonged hearings and investigations.

These cost of service plans are usually predicated upon the fair value of the property used in the service, that value either being fixed by the Commission or agreed upon by the public and the owners of the property.

Such plans have been adopted in Cleveland and Montreal, in both of which cities they have been reported to work with considerable satisfaction to the public as well as to the owners of the property. Somewhat similar plans have been authorized by the Massachusetts Legislature, and a modified form of the plant provided by the statutes of that State has been in use for some time in the city of Boston, where its result has been anything but satisfactory to the public at large. Such plans have also been tried in one form or another in many other cities with varying degrees of success or failure, as the case may be.

This Commission hopes within the course of the next few months to be able to formulate and present to the public a complete study of these plans with the results achieved thereunder in the various cities where they have been tried, and our conclusions in the premises. It may well be that the Commission's conclusions will be that legislation should be enacted to make provision for the adoption of plans of this general character in this State, in which event our recommendations will be made to the coming session of the General Assembly.

THE PARK TAX AND PAVING CHARGES

Under certain ordinances of comparatively long standing, ratified by the General Assembly of Maryland in some instances, the United Railways and Electric Company of Baltimore is required at the present time to pay a tax amounting to nine per cent. of its gross receipts on certain lines, this sum going into the fund for the maintenance of the public parks of the city. This tax equates at the present time 6.91 per cent. of the total passenger revenues of the Company. Upon this basis, and upon the assumption that the Company's passenger revenues during the next twelve months will be $14,305,410, as estimated by the Commission, this tax will amount to the sum of $988,504.

This sum is very much greater than the amounts paid in previous years, this fact being due to the increased amount of patronage, in the recent annexation of parts of Baltimore and Anne Arundel Counties to Baltimore City, and to the recent fare increase from five to six cents and the present increase from six to six and one-half cents.

In addition to this large percentage of its gross receipts paid directly into the park fund, the Company also pays taxes to the city, counties and State on its real estate, and is also required by law to pave between its tracks and for two feet on either side thereof, and keep such paving in repair.

These forms of taxation were all adopted in the case of the Railways Company before the days of regulation, and at a time when it was assumed that what the public got through these forms of taxation came out of profits which the stockholders would otherwise have received.

Under regulation, where the effort is to regulate the charges made by a public utility for the service rendered in almost exact proportion to the actual cost of such service, all these taxes go into and form a part of such cost, with the result that it is no longer a question whether the public at large or the stockholders will pay these taxes, but the question is whether the general public or the portion of the public getting the service of the utility shall pay the same.

In the case now before us, for instance, the sum of the park tax, general taxes and the paving charges to which this Company is subject amount to something more than the one-half cent which has been added to the fare. Without those charges the fare could have remained at six cents.

It is the purpose of the Commission to make a complete study of this subject in the immediate future, and determine what, if any, recommendation it should make to the Legislature.

In many other cities where the public has been confronted with much the same difficulties with respect to their street railway service as confronts the public of Baltimore, one of the first steps taken by the public to relieve the situation and lessen the burden upon the users of the street railways has been to abolish all or some of these forms of taxation.

The Commission is not prepared at the present time to make any recommendation in connection with any of these forms of taxes, and, in fact, has reached no definite conclusion itself as to what should be done in the premises.

ZONE EXTENSIONS TO NEW CITY LIMITS

In the Six-Cent Fare case it was contended that the legal effect of that portion of Section 2 of Chapter 82 of the Acts of 1918, providing that all existing provisions of the Baltimore City Charter should be applicable to such portions of Baltimore and Anne Arundel Counties as were annexed to Baltimore City by that act, was to extend the provisions of Section 796 of the City Charter prescribing certain fares within the old limits of the city to such annexed portions of Baltimore and Anne Arundel Counties and thereby make uniform the fares within the limits of Baltimore City as enlarged by such act.

As was stated in our opinion in the former case, this question was submitted to the Commission's General Counsel, who advised the Commission that by the Public Service Commission Law the whole matter of the rates of fare proper to be charged by the Company had been committed by the Legislature in the first instance to determinations by the Commission, subject to review by the courts as in said law provided.

In the former case the Commission said the general question of fare zones should be made the subject of an independent study, and that this could not be done until the effect of the increased fares, on the basis of the existing zones, had been demonstrated by experience over a reasonable period.

That experience has now been had, with the results set forth in an earlier portion of this opinion. Those results demonstrated conclusively that it would not have been possible to make such extensions to the city limits under the six-cent rate of fare prescribed by our order in that case.

During the hearings in the case now before us numerous applications were filed asking the Commission to require the Company to extend its first fare zone to the new city limits in various directions, and the Commission caused a study to be made of the effect of extending the first fare zone to the new city limits on each of the lines of the Company.

A study of the situation confronting the Company through the extension of the first fare zone to the new city limits involves an understanding of the mileage of the present second fare zone, which remains outside the new city limits, and determination whether it would be expedient to create a new zone out of the remaining portion of the present second fare zone or include such portion in the present third zone (which would then become the second zone). An alternative of this would be the entire elimination of the present second zone, which would mean carrying passengers a short distance beyond the new city limits for one fare. The Company's officials were of the opinion that where the portion of the present second zone extending beyond the city limits is less than two miles in length it should be added to the next zone or else be considered within the first fare zone, since it was obvious that great objection would be made to paying the full fare in a zone where the maximum ride permitted was less than two miles.

The following table shows the mileage remaining outside the new city limits:

TABLE XII

MILEAGE OUTSIDE NEW CITY LIMITS

	1st County Zone				
Line	In New City Limits	Outside New City Limits	Total	2nd County Zone	3rd County Zone
Pimlico-Pikesville	2.51	1.67	4.18	3.61	5.91
West Arlington-Gwynn Oak..	5.94	.55	6.49		
Walbrook-Gwynn Oak	2.85	.55	3.40		
Woodlawn	.89	1.02	1.91		
Curtis Bay	4.12		4.12		
Towson	.83	2.12	2.95		
Catonsville	1.52	2.11	3.63		
Lakeside	1.59	.56	2.15		
Riverview	3.47	.78	4.25		
Ellicott City	.43	2.85	3.28	2.76	
Mount Washington-Pikesville..	2.42	2.00	4.42		
Back River	2.10	2.61	4.71	2.87	
Sparrows Point-Dundalk	2.80	1.60	4.40	3.48	4.42

The following lines show a remaining mileage of less than two miles, and the portion of the zone remaining in the county would therefore have to be considered either as having been combined with the city zone or added to the next county zone:

> West Arlington-Gwynn Oak
> Walbrook-Gwynn Oak
> Woodlawn
> Lakeside
> Riverview
> Sparrows Point-Dundalk

The entire Curtis Bay line is in the new city limits and would have to be considered as eliminated under the proposed plan. Of the Pimlico-Pikesville line 1.67 miles of the second fare zone remains outside the new city limits. If this be added to the present third fare zone, this zone would have a mileage of 5.28 as compared with 5.91 miles on the present fourth fare zone of this line.

2.12 miles of the present second fare zone of the Towson line remain outside the new city limits; 2.11 miles of the present second fare zone of the Catonsville line remain outside the new city limits; 2.85 miles of the present second fare zone of the Ellicott City line remain outside the new city limits, and 2 miles of the Mount Washington-Pikesville line remain outside the new city limits. Separate zones would have to be created in each of these cases.

The Traffic Department of the Company stated that eventually all of the Back River lines would be in the first fare zone, and it was accordingly considered as being eliminated.

The following table shows the number of passengers carried on each of the present second fare zones, together with the percentages such passengers bore to the total passengers carried during the entire year 1918 and first six months of the year 1919:

TABLE XIII

NUMBER OF PASSENGERS CARRIED IN SECOND FARE ZONES

Line	Year 1918	% of Total	Six Months 1919	% of Total	Total Eighteen Months	% of Total
Pimlico-Pikesville	1,400,171	.617	700,242	.594	2 0 4?8	.609
West Arlington-Gwynn Oak	155,318	.068	61,505	.052	216,828	.068
Walbrook-Gwynn Oak	1?3	.056	52,746	.045	179,919	.052
Woodlawn	2,668	.084	68,504	.058	261,172	.076
Curtis Bay	3,252,785	1.434	1,869,813	1.162	4,622,598	1.841
Towson	3?58	.579	667,191	.566	9?49	.575
Catonsville	1,118,288	.494	6?4	.483	1,687,422	.489
Lakeside	1,?93	.076	96,507	.082	268,000	.078
Riverview	2,276,662	1.004	927,512	.787	3,204,174	.929
Ellicott City	4?94	.505	588,899	.499	1,733,893	.503
Mount Washington-Pikesville	64,014	.028	29,754	.025	98,768	.027
Back River	2,499,795	1.102	1,167,892	.990	3,667,687	1.064
Sparrows Point-Dundalk	7,211,094	3.179	3,453,795	2.928	10,664,889	3.098
Total	20,927,913	9.226	9,753,494	8.271	30,681,407	8.899
Total revenue passengers entire system	226,834,528		117,919,120		344,753,648	

The above table shows that for the year 1918, 9.226 per cent. of the total revenue passengers were carried in the second fare zones, and that during the first six months of 1919, 8.271 per cent. were so carried. As the summer months have a distinct influence on the county lines, the former percentage, 9.226, has been used hereinafter in preference to either the six months or eighteen months figures shown in the above table.

The following table shows the estimated loss in revenues from the extension of city zones in all cases upon the suppositions above set forth, the chief of such suppositions being that where the extension of an existing city zone to the new city limits would leave less than two miles of the first county fare zone, the first county fare zone will either be taken into the city zone or into the next county fare zone:

TABLE XIV

ESTIMATED LOSS IN REVENUES FROM EXTENSION OF CITY ZONES

Line	Per Cent. of Loss		
Pimlico-Pikesville	100% of	.617% or	.617%
West Arlington-Gwynn Oak	100% of	.068% or	.068%
Walbrook-Gwynn Oak	100% of	.056% or	.056%
Woodlawn	100% of	.084% or	.084%
Curtis Bay	100% of	1.434% or	1.434%
Towson	10% of	.579% or	.058%
Catonsville	10% of	.494% or	.049%
Lakeside	100% of	.076% or	.076%
Riverview	100% of	1.004% or	1.004%
Ellicott City	10% of	.505% or	.050%
Mount Washington	100% of	.028% or	.028%
Back River	100% of	1.102% or	1.102%
Dundalk	100% of	3.179% or	3.179%

Total per cent. of revenue passengers eliminated........ 7.805%

(a) Estimated revenue passengers..................... 243,000,000
    Estimated Passenger Revenue
(b)   Under existing fares................ $14,305,410
(c)   From fare increase.................   1,376,762
                                            ————— $15,682,172
(d) Average fare, entire system, new rate.............   6.453c
(e)   "   "   "   "   old " 5.887c
(f)   "   fare in second fare zone during first six months of 1919.......................   5.68c
(g) Assumed average fare in second fare zone, new rate.   6.20c
(h) 7.805% of 243,000,000.......................... 18,966,150
(g) x (h) represents total loss from eliminating above second zones $1,175,901

It will be noted that the above table assumes that but ten per cent. of the traffic originating in the second fare zones on the Towson, Catonsville and Ellicott City lines will be lost through the extension of the city zone to the new city limits the short distance required in each of these cases.

The above table shows that the effect of extending the city zone to the new city limits would be that the Company would sustain a loss in revenues of approximately $1,176,000 per annum, which is within $200,000 of the amount estimated by the Commission to be yielded by the new increase in fare. This would require the addition of approximately one-half a cent to the new six and a half cent base rate, and bring the base rate up to at least seven cents flat.

Under these circumstances, the Commission cannot see its way clear at the present time to require these extensions to be made, and thinks it would be unwise to select any of these zones for such extensions until the new rate has been given a fair trial and it is seen what the yield thereof will be.

It may well be that experience with the new rates will demonstrate earnings in excess of those estimated by the Commission.

In such event, the Commission will have to consider the relative merits of what will no doubt be a general demand on the part of all the public for a reduction in the ticket rate from six and one-half cents to six and one-quarter cents each, and the demand of those residing in these second zones for extensions of the first zone. Or it may be that the rates will yield so much in excess of our estimates that the Commission will find its way clear to grant relief in all these cases.

But, on the other hand, it may happen that our estimates of earnings will be in excess of actual earnings, and that such actual earnings, even without any of such extensions, will be inadequate to meet the requirements of the Company and yield it the return to which we have declared it properly entitled.

This Commission has no more right to assume that its estimates will be excessive than it has to assume that they will be inadequate, and until they have been given an actual trial over a reasonable period of time we must decline to direct the extension of any of these zones.

An order will be passed embodying the principal conclusions in the aforegoing opinion.

ORDER No. 5120.

In the Matter of

The Petition of THE UNITED RAILWAYS AND ELECTRIC COMPANY OF BALTIMORE for a Modification of Certain Orders, Now in Force, Fixing the Rates of Fare to Be Charged by Said Company and for Permission to File, Publish and Put in Effect a New Schedule of Rates of Fare, Increasing Existing Rates, as Set Forth in This Petition.

Before the
Public Service Commission
of Maryland.

Case No. 1682.

Pursuant to the conclusions reached in the aforegoing opinion, it is, this 30th day of September, in the year Nineteen Hundred and Nineteen, by the Public Service Commission of Maryland,

Ordered, (1) That Order No. 4608 entered by this Commission on January 7th, 1919, as modified and amended by Order No. 4646 entered on January 28th, 1919, and the first paragraph of Order No. 4609 entered on January 7th, 1919, be and they are hereby annulled and rescinded.

(2) That from and after this date and until September 30th, 1920, and for no longer, unless such period be extended for a further period as hereinafter provided, or this order be earlier modified or abrogated by further order of this Commission, The United Railways and Electric Company of Baltimore shall be permitted to charge and collect for the transportation of persons over its several street railway lines, in Baltimore City and vicinity, the following rates, fares and charges, to wit:

(a) Six and one-half cent fare when tickets or fare checks are purchased, or seven cents cash, for the conveyance of each passenger over twelve years of age, and four cents for each child between the ages of four and twelve years, on any of its lines between the points designated under the first general caption in its schedule P. S. C. Md. No. 8, filed with this Commission August 28th, 1918, effective October 1st, 1918, or between intermediate points, in either direction, on any of such lines, except in the case of its Curtis Bay line, on which line The United Railways and Electric Company of Baltimore shall issue transfers entitling the holder to a continuous ride on such line as such transfers were issued on and prior to September 30th, 1918, except that the charge for such transfers shall be four cents instead of three cents, as theretofore.

(b) Full fare and half fare continuous trip tickets, good as fare on connecting lines, to be sold on the lines and between the points, on the Company's Gorsuch Avenue, East Monument Street (Orangeville)', Third and Eighth Streets, Union Avenue, South Charles Street, Walbrook-Hillsdale, Shore line and Ferry Bar lines, as designated in said schedule P. S. C. Md. No. 8, otherwise the regular fare to be collected between the points so designated.

(c) Four and one-half cents when paid by commutation tickets sold for use on the first county fare zone between the points so designated in the schedule P. S. C. Md. No. 8, aforesaid, and five cents when paid by commutation tickets sold for use on second and third county fare zones, between the points so designated in said schedule, said commutation tickets to be sold in the manner and subject to the conditions set forth in said schedule with respect thereto, the full fare in each of said cases otherwise to be paid.

(d) Four and one-half cents between Sparrows Point and Dundalk and four and one-half cents between Dundalk and Highlandtown when paid by employee's tickets from 20-trip books sold in lots to the Maryland Steel Company for distribution; five cents between Dundalk and Highlandtown and five cents between Highlandtown and city points, when paid by strip tickets sold in lots to the Central Foundry Company for distribution; and two and one-half cents on the Lakeside line when paid by tickets from 200-trip books sold to the landowners along such line, all such tickets to be subject to the conditions printed thereon and to the rules of the Company governing the use thereof, the full fare in each of said cases otherwise to be paid.

3. That during the period this order is in effect The United Railways and Electric Company of Baltimore shall sell on its cars and at its offices and waiting rooms tickets or fare checks which shall be honored for passage on its cars, at the rate of six and one-half cents each, which said tickets or fare checks shall be sold on the cars in quantities of four (or more, in the option of the Company), and should the conductor of a car at any time be unable for any reason to sell a passenger desiring to purchase them at least four tickets or fare checks, then such passenger shall be required to pay but six cents fare.

4. That from and after the hour of midnight on the thirtieth of September, Nineteen Hundred and Twenty, said Company's right and privilege to charge and collect the increased fares authorized hereby shall cease and determine and said Company shall thereupon put in force and effect, and maintain until thereafter lawfully changed, the schedule of fares operative on the thirtieth of September, Nineteen Hundred and Nineteen, unless this Commission shall, in the meantime, by its order in writing, have modified, extended or superseded this order; provided, however, that if this order has not been so extended or superseded and there shall be pending on September thirtieth, Nineteen Hundred and Twenty, an application by said Company filed before August thirty-first, Nineteen Hundred and Twenty, for a continuance in whole or in part of the relief hereby granted, then the right to collect the fares authorized by this order shall continue until the determination by the Commission of said pending proceedings; and provided, further, that in case of any proceeding hereafter for the right to charge and collect fares in excess of those in effect on the thirtieth

of September, Nineteen Hundred and Nineteen, the burden of proving the reasonableness of any such excess fare shall be and remain on said Company.

5. That The United Railways and Electric Company of Baltimore shall furnish to this Commission accurate and complete statements under oath, and in convenient form, setting forth the number of revenue and transfer passengers carried, and the number of car-miles operated, the cash receipts from operation and other sources, and the operating and other expenditures of the Company, all set forth in the manner prescribed by the rules of this Commission for accounting by street railway companies, so soon as may be reasonably practicable and convenient after the end of each calendar month during the period this Order remains effective, and in no event later than the last day of the next succeeding calendar month, covering the operations of the Company during the next preceding month.

6. That the right of the respondent Company to charge and collect the fares in this order prescribed shall be held subject at all times during the period covered by such order, or any extension thereof which may hereafter be granted as aforesaid, to the right and power of this Commission to reopen this case in the light of the facts disclosed by the monthly reports aforesaid, or of other facts otherwise coming to the attention of this Commission, and modify the rates of fare by this order authorized to be charged and collected by the respondent Company.

AND IT IS FURTHER Ordered, That a copy of this order be forthwith served upon the proper officers of the respondent, The United Railways and Electric Company of Baltimore, and that said Company, within ten days from the date of the service of such copy, advise this Commission in writing whether or not it will accept and abide by the same.

ORDER No. 5121.

In the Matter of

The Petition of THE BALTIMORE TRANSIT COMPANY for Permission Under Section 15 of the PUBLIC SERVICE COMMISSION LAW to File and Publish on Less Than Statutory Notice a Schedule of Rates Changing Its Rate of Fare from Six Cents to Six and One-Half Cents When Tickets or Fare Checks are Purchased in Lots of Four, or Seven Cents Cash Fare.

Before the

Public Service Commission of Maryland.

S. N. & R. Docket.

Case No. 578.

WHEREAS, The Baltimore Transit Company, a corporation organized under the laws of the State of Maryland and operating a line of passenger motor buses for the public use in the City of Baltimore, having petitioned this Commission for permission under Section 15 of the Public Service Commission Law to file and publish on less than statutory notice of thirty days a schedule of rates changing its rate of fare from six cents to six and one-half cents when tickets or fare checks are purchased in lots of four, or seven cents cash fare; and

WHEREAS, It appears from statement filed with said petition that during the year from September 1st, 1918, to August 31st, 1919, both dates inclusive, the total operating revenues of petitioner were $127,251.59 and the total operating expenses, exclusive of fixed charges and taxes, but inclusive of an allowance for depreciation reserve, were $128,488.19, leaving an operating deficit of $1,236.60, to which deficit must be added interest and discount of $14,695.10 and taxes of $5,764.24 during said period, making the total deficit for the year in question $21,677.94; and

WHEREAS, This Commission by its Order No. 5120 this day entered in Case No. 1682 having permitted The United Railways and Electric Company of Baltimore, which company owns practically all of the capital stock of the petitioner, to increase its base adult fare from six cents to six and one-half cents when tickets or fare checks are purchased in lots of four, or seven cents cash fare, which increased fare becomes effective on October 1st, 1919; and

WHEREAS, It is not desirable to have a rate of fare on the line of the petitioner lower than the rate of fare contemporaneously in effect on the lines of The United Railways and Electric Company of Baltimore, the car lines of which company parallel the route of the petitioner's motor bus line, in that such lower fare would tend unduly to divert traffic to the bus line and result in severe overcrowding of said company's buses; and

WHEREAS, It being the opinion and finding of the Commission, in view of the aforegoing, that the petitioner should be permitted to file and publish on less than the statutory notice of thirty days a schedule changing its rate of fare to the extent prayed,

IT IS, THEREFORE, This 30th day of September, in the year Nineteen Hundred and Nineteen, by the Public Service Commission of Maryland,

ORDERED, That permission be and is hereby given to The Baltimore Transit Company to file and publish a schedule changing its rate of fare from six cents to six and one-half cents, when tickets or fare checks are purchased, which said tickets or fare checks shall be sold by said The Baltimore Transit Company on its buses in quantities of four (or more at the option of the company), or seven cents cash fare, except that should the conductor of a bus at any time be unable for any reason to sell a passenger desiring to purchase them at least four tickets or four checks, then such passenger shall be required to pay but six cents cash fare; such increased fare to become effective October 1st, 1919,

PROVIDED, Said schedule be filed with the Commission as required upon issuance of this Order and published by posting as required by law, and that all copies of said schedule should bear the following notation:

"Issued under special permission of the Public Service Commission of Maryland, Order No. 5121 of date September 30th, 1919."

PROVIDED FURTHER, That this Commission by passing this Order is not to be taken or construed as in any sense whatsoever passing upon the reasonableness of the rate of fare contained in schedule filed hereunder, such rate of fare being left as fully subject to investigation and correction upon complaint or upon the Commission's own motion as if this order had never been passed.

ORDER No. 5130.

In the Matter of	Before the
	Public Service Commission
The Complaint of FRANK RUCK vs. ARTE-SIAN WATER COMPANY.	of Maryland.
	Case No. 1714.

The above cause being at issue upon complaint and answer on file and having been duly heard and submitted by the parties and the Commission, through its Chairman, having rendered an oral opinion setting forth the conclusions of the Commission with respect to the rights and obligations of both parties, which satisfactorily disposes of the matter in controversy,

IT IS, THEREFORE, This 9th day of October, in the year Nineteen Hundred and Nineteen, by the Public Service Commission of Maryland,

ORDERED, That the above entitled case be and it is hereby entered as satisfied and closed.

ORDER No. 5131.

In the Matter of

The Petition of THE UNITED RAILWAYS AND ELECTRIC COMPANY OF BALTIMORE for a Modification of Certain Orders, Now in Force, Fixing the Rates of Fare to be Charged by said Company and for Permission to File, Publish and Put in Effect a New Schedule of Rates of Fare, Increasing Existing Rates, as Set Forth in This Petition.

Before the

Public Service Commission of Maryland.

Case No. 1682.

Upon the petition of The United Railways and Electric Company of Baltimore, filed herein, it is this 9th day of October, 1919, by the Public Service Commission of Maryland,

Ordered, That the time within which said Company shall advise this Commission whether or not it will accept and abide by the Order of this Commission, dated September 30th, 1919, be and the same is hereby extended for a period of ten (10) days from October 10th, 1919.

ORDER No. 5139.

In the Matter of

The Application of WASHINGTON, BALTIMORE AND ANNAPOLIS ELECTRIC RAILROAD COMPANY for Authority to Issue Twenty Thousand, Eight Hundred and Eighty-Five Shares of the Six Per Cent. Non-Cumulative Preferred Stock, and Sell the Same at a Price, and Upon the Terms and Conditions to be Fixed by the PUBLIC SERVICE COMMISSION OF MARYLAND.

Before the

Public Service Commission of Maryland.

Case No. 1719.

The above entitled matter having this day come on for hearing after due notice published in compliance with this Commission's Order No. 5116, passed September 13th, 1919, and it being the opinion and finding of the Commission after due hearing that the issue and sale by the applicant, the Washington, Baltimore and Annapolis Electric Railroad Company, of 20,885 shares of its Six Per Cent. Non-cumulative Preferred Stock, of the par value of Fifty Dollars ($50.00) per share, is reasonably required for the purposes of said corporation,

IT IS, THEREFORE, This 16th day of October, in the year Nineteen Hundred and Nineteen, by the Public Service Commission of Maryland, Ordered, That the Washington, Baltimore and Annapolis Electric Railroad Company is hereby authorized to issue and sell 20,885 shares of its Six Per Cent. Non-cumulative Preferred Stock, of the par value of Fifty Dollars ($50.00) per share, or any portion thereof, at the price of Thirty-seven Dollars and Fifty Cents ($37.50) per share, with accrued dividends from October 1st, 1919, and to enter into agreements with the bankers for the sale and issue of any portion of the said stock, at the price above named, paying to the said bankers such compensation for underwriting said stock as to the Board of Directors of the said Washington, Baltimore and Annapolis Electric Railroad Company may seem fair and just, but not exceeding the compensation per share mentioned in the evidence; the Commission having determined that the use of the capital to be secured by the issue and sale of said stock is reasonably required for the purposes of said company, sion, maintenance or improvement of its facilities, the improvement or maintenance of its service and the discharge or lawful refunding of its obligations.

2. That the said Washington, Baltimore and Annapolis Electric Railroad Company shall make reports to this Commission duly verified by affidavits, as follows:

(a) Upon the issue and sale for cash of its stock, authorized and to wit: the acquisition of property, the construction, completion extenapproved as aforesaid, or any part thereof, the fact of such issue and sale, the terms and conditions thereof, and the amount realized therefrom.

(b) At the termination of each and every period of six months from the date of this order, the disposition and use made of the proceeds of said stock, and the facts and the circumstances as to the property acquired, the construction, completion, extension, maintenance or improvement of its facilities, the improvement or maintenance of its service, and the discharge or lawful refunding of its obligations.

ORDER No. 5150.

In the Matter of

The Petition of THE UNITED RAILWAYS AND ELECTRIC COMPANY OF BALTIMORE for a Modification of Certain Orders, Now in Force, Fixing the Rates of Fare to be Charged by Said Company and for Permission to File, Publish and Put in Effect a New Schedule of Rates of Fare, Increasing Existing Rates, as Set Forth in This Petition.

Before the

Public Service Commission of Maryland.

Case No. 1682.

The United Railways and Electric Company of Baltimore having on this day filed its petition praying certain modifications of the Commission's opinion and Order No. 5120 accompanying said opinion filed in this cause on September 30th, 1919, and it not being convenient for the Commission to pass upon said petition at this time,

IT IS, THEREFORE, This 20th day of October, in the year Nineteen Hundred and Nineteen, by the Public Service Commission of Maryland,

ORDERED, That the time within which said company shall advise this Commission whether or not it will accept and abide by said order be, and the same is hereby further extended for a period of fifteen days from October 20th, 1919.

ORDER No. 5156.

In the Matter of

The Report and Petition of THE TERMINAL FREEZING AND HEATING COMPANY with Regard to Discontinuance of Service East of South Street.

Before the

Public Service Commission of Maryland.

Case No. 1725.

WHEREAS, The Terminal Freezing and Heating Company has applied to this Commission for permission to suspend the furnishing of steam heating service in the territory east of South Street, in the City of Baltimore, now served by said company; and

WHEREAS, Protests having been received from the patrons of said company who would be affected by said proposed suspension of steam heating service in the territory aforesaid; and

WHEREAS, The case having this day come on for hearing in accordance with this Commission's Order No. 5140 passed October 16th,

1919, and the Commission, through its Chairman, having rendered an oral opinion wherein it held that for the reasons in said opinion assigned it would be unjust and unreasonable to permit the suspension of steam heating service at this time,

IT IS, THEREFORE, This 21st day of October, in the year Nineteen Hundred and Nineteen, by the Public Service Commission of Maryland,

Ordered, That the petition of the Terminal Freezing and Heating Company for permission to suspend the furnishing of steam heating service in the territory east of South Street in the City of Baltimore, now served by said company, be and the same is hereby denied and dismissed.

ORDER No. 5157.

In the Matter of	Before the
The Complaint of PUBLIC SERVICE COMMISSION OF MARYLAND vs. WILLIAM E. CONAWAY.	Public Service Commission of Maryland.
	Case No. 1717.

WHEREAS, The Commission having required William E. Conaway to appear before the Commission to answer certain charges preferred against said William E. Conaway by the Transportation Expert of the Commission with respect to sundry violations of the orders, rules and regulations of the Commission by said William E. Conaway in the operation of a motor vehicle for public use in the transportation of passengers between Westminster and Gwynn Oak Junction; and

WHEREAS, Said William E. Conaway having duly appeared before the Commission on the date hereof and having answered the charges aforesaid, and the Commission, through its Chairman, having rendered an oral opinion wherein it held that for the reasons in said opinion assigned it would not at this time revoke the permit issued by it under which said William E. Conaway operates,

IT IS, THEREFORE, This 22nd day of October, in the year Nineteen Hundred and Nineteen, by the Public Service Commission of Maryland,

Ordered, That the complaint in the above entitled matter be and the same is hereby dismissed.

ORDER No. 5160.

In the Matter of

The Investigation by THE COMMISSION on
Its Own Motion of the Heating of Cars
of THE UNITED RAILWAYS AND ELEC-
TRIC COMPANY OF BALTIMORE, the Enclosing of the Vestibules of Said Cars,
and of the Equipment of Said Cars,
with Safety Appliances for the Protection of the Public on the Streets of
Baltimore City.

Before the

Public Service Commission
of Maryland.

Case No. 676.

WHEREAS, This Commission by its Order No. 2545 entered herein on
December 4th, 1915, directed and required The United Railways and
Electric Company of Baltimore, among other things, to proceed with
the work of vestibuling all of its semi-convertible open-platform cars
by installing suitable doors with simultaneously operated steps, fold-
ing up when doors are closed and vice versa, said work of vestibuling
to be prosecuted at the rate of twelve (12) cars per month until completed; and

WHEREAS, The work aforesaid proceeded up to January 1st, 1918, at
the rate required by the Commission's Order, after which the railway
company was unable to secure a sufficient number of mechanics to
enable it to continue the work at the rate required by the Commission's Order; and

WHEREAS, This Commission by its Order No. 4385 entered herein on
July 2nd, 1918, relieved the railway company from the requirements
of the Commission's Order No. 2545 aforesaid, so far as said order
required the railway company to vestibule twelve (12) cars per month;
until the further order of the Commission, or until the railway company was able to secure a sufficient number of men to enable it to
proceed again with the work of vestibuling its cars; and

WHEREAS, On April 1st, 1919, the railway company resumed the
work of vestibuling its cars at the rate required by the Commission's
Order No. 2545 aforesaid; and

WHEREAS, The railway company has now petitioned the Commission
to reduce the number of cars it is required to vestibule per month from
twelve (12) to six (6); and

WHEREAS, It appears that the petition of the railway company is
reasonable and proper, and should be granted, due regard being had
to the greatly increased cost of such vestibuling, it appearing that the
cost per car has increased approximately 100 per cent. in the last
three years, and to the further fact that the probable future life of
a number of the cars originally ordered vestibuled is of such limited

length and the physical condition of said cars such as to probably
make it unwise and uneconomical to vestibule said cars;

IT IS, THEREFORE, This 22nd day of October, in the year Nineteen
Hundred and Nineteen, by the Public Service Commission of Maryland,

𝔒𝔯𝔡𝔢𝔯𝔢𝔡, That from and after January 1st, 1920, and continuing
until the further order of this Commission in the premises, the requirements of this Commission's Order No. 2545 entered on December 4th,
1915, with respect to the vestibuling of cars, is changed so that The
United Railways and Electric Company of Baltimore shall thereafter
proceed with said work of vestibuling its cars at the rate of six (6)
cars per month, instead of twelve (12) cars per month as originally
required by said Order No. 2545, subject to the right of the Commission at any time for good cause shown to withdraw this order and to
require the work thereafter to proceed at the rate originally prescribed, or at such other rate as may be determined by the Commission.

ORDER No. 5162.

In the Matter of	Before the
The Application of THE HAGERSTOWN AND FREDERICK RAILWAY COMPANY for Authority to Issue Eighty-Five Thousand Dollars, Par Value, of Its First and Refunding Bonds.	Public Service Commission of Maryland.
	Case No. 1726.

The above entitled matter having this day come on for hearing after
due notice published in compliance with this Commission's Order No.
5144, passed October 16th, 1919, and it being the opinion and finding
of the Commission after due hearing that the issue by the applicant,
The Hagerstown and Frederick Railway Company, of $85,000.00, face
amount, of its First and Refunding Mortgage Thirty-Year Sinking
Fund Gold Bonds, Six Per Cent. Series, is reasonably required for the
purposes of said corporation,

IT IS, THEREFORE, This 28th day of October, in the year Nineteen
Hundred and Nineteen, by the Public Service Commission of Maryland,

𝔒𝔯𝔡𝔢𝔯𝔢𝔡, That the applicant, The Hagerstown and Frederick Railway Company, be and it is hereby authorized to issue and deliver not
exceeding $85,000.00, face amount, of its First and Refunding Mort-
gage Thirty-Year Sinking Fund Gold Bonds, Six Per Cent. Series, and
to use the same for collateral purposes as mentioned in said petition,
and with the further right to the said company to sell and dispose
of the said bonds, or any part thereof, at any time, at not less than
95 per cent. of the face value of the same; the proceeds to be applied
as in said petition set forth, the Commission having determined that

the use of the capital to be secured by the issue of said bonds is reasonably required for the purposes of said company, to wit: the lawful discharge and refunding of its obligations incurred in making expenditures for proper corporate capital purposes.

IT IS FURTHER Ordered, That The Hagerstown and Frederick Railway Company report to this Commission the fact of the issuance and delivery of said bonds, and if the same are sold, the amount thereof so sold and the price obtained therefor.

ORDER No. 5165.

In the Matter of

The Application of MARYLAND, DELAWARE AND VIRGINIA RAILWAY COMPANY for an Order Permitting and Approving the Construction of an Industrial Siding on Its Centreville Branch, at Perlee, Maryland, for Use of MURPHY AND HAYES COMPANY.

Before the

Public Service Commission of Maryland.

Case No. 1728.

WHEREAS, It appears from the petition and exhibit filed in the above entitled matter that the proposed construction of a siding at Perlee, Maryland, is necessary and convenient for the public service, and

WHEREAS, The Commission being of the opinion that the said construction is not a matter of such nature as to require the same to be set for hearing under the terms and provisions of Section 26 of the Public Service Commission Law,

IT IS, THEREFORE, This 29th day of October, 1919, by the Public Service Commission of Maryland,

Ordered, That the proposed construction of a siding at Perlee as set forth in the above entitled application be, and the same is hereby, permitted and approved.

ORDER No. 5166.

In the Matter of

The Application of THE BALTIMORE, CHESAPEAKE AND ATLANTIC RAILROAD COMPANY for an Order Permitting and Approving the Construction of an Extension of Three Hundred and Fifty Feet in Length to Neale's Siding, Located at Hurlock, Maryland.

Before the

Public Service Commission of Maryland.

Case No. 1729.

WHEREAS, It appears from the petition and exhibit, filed in the above entitled matter, that the proposed extension of Neale's Siding at Hurlock, Maryland, is necessary and convenient for the public service, and

WHEREAS, The Commission being of the opinion that the said construction is not a matter of such nature as to require the same to be set for hearing under the terms and provisions of Section 26 of the Public Service Commission Law,

IT IS, THEREFORE, This 29th day of October, 1919, by the Public Service Commission of Maryland,

Ordered, That the proposed extension of Neale's siding at Hurlock, Maryland, as set forth in the above entitled application be, and it is hereby, permitted and approved.

ORDER No. 5167.

In the Matter of

The Complaint of THE HAGERSTOWN AND FREDERICK RAILWAY COMPANY vs. E. V. HULL.

Before the

Public Service Commission of Maryland.

Case No. 1664.

WHEREAS, The Hagerstown and Frederick Railway Company having complained to this Commission that E. V. Hull, operating motor vehicles for public use in the transportation of passengers in the State of Maryland, has not observed the time schedule of said E. V. Hull filed with the Public Service Commission of Maryland, resulting in alleged loss of revenue to said The Hagerstown and Frederick Railway Company, by reason of the fact that E. V. Hull was operating his motor vehicles so as to attract unduly traffic which would otherwise be handled by the complainant, and

WHEREAS, The matter having come on to be heard before the Commission on May 15th, 1919, and it appearing at said hearing that while the defendant was not operating in accordance with time schedule filed with the Commission, the Commission had issued permits to said defendant authorizing more trips than the schedule filed with it provided, and that therefore the Commission necessarily must allow the filing of and approve a subsequent schedule designed to conform to the authorized permits issued to said defendant, and it being the finding and conclusion of the Commission that the complainant should have protested the application of the defendant for permits to operate motor vehicles for public use in the transportation of passengers at or about the time such applications were filed with the Commission, or at or about the time when application is made for the renewal of said permits, and that for the reasons assigned the complaint should be dismissed,

IT IS, THEREFORE, This 6th day of November, in the year Nineteen Hundred and Nineteen, by the Public Service Commission of Maryland,

Ordered, That the complaint in the above entitled matter be, and the same is hereby dismissed.

ORDER No. 5170.

In the Matter of	
The Application of IDLEWILD ELECTRIC LIGHT, HEAT AND POWER COMPANY OF FEDERALSBURG, MARYLAND, for Authority to Issue Two Thousand Dollars, Par Value, of Its First Mortgage Bonds.	Before the Public Service Commission of Maryland. Case No. 1721.

WHEREAS, The Idlewild Electric Light, Heat and Power Company of Federalsburg, Maryland, a corporation organized and existing under the laws of the State of Maryland, has applied to this Commission for authority to issue its Forty-Year Six Per Centum First Mortgage Gold Bonds of the aggregate principal amount of Two Thousand Dollars ($2,000.00), being part of a total authorized issue of One Hundred and Fifty Thousand Dollars ($150,000.00) secured by mortgage or deed of trust dated April 1st, 1916, upon the property, rights and franchises of the said Idlewild Electric Light, Heat and Power Company of Federalsburg, Maryland, to Philadelphia Trust Company, Trustee, a copy of which mortgage or deed of trust has heretofore been filed with the Commission in Case No. 1106, and to sell said bonds at not less than 89% of the par value thereof, the proceeds from the sale of said bonds to be used for the discharge or lawful refunding of said company's obligations incurred in making betterments, improvements and additions to its plant and distributing system and for the improvement and maintenance of its service since November 1st, 1918, as more particularly set forth and described in petition herein; and

WHEREAS, The application having come on to be heard on October 28th, 1919, after due notice published in accordance with this Commission's Order No. 5184 passed October 15th, 1919, and the hearing having been continued to November 7th, 1919, upon request of the applicant, on which date the application was duly heard, and it being the opinion and finding of the Commission after investigation that the use of the capital to be secured by the issue and sale of said bonds is reasonably required for the purposes of said corporation, to wit: the discharge or lawful refunding of its obligations incurred in making expenditures for proper corporate capital purposes,

IT IS, THEREFORE, This 7th day of November, in the year Nineteen Hundred and Nineteen, by the Public Service Commission of Maryland,

𝔒𝔯𝔡𝔢𝔯𝔢𝔡, 1.   That the issue by the Idlewild Electric Light, Heat and Power Company of Federalsburg, Maryland, of its Forty-Year Six Per Centum First Mortgage Gold Bonds of the aggregate principal amount of Two Thousand Dollars ($2,000.00), and the sale of said bonds at not less than 89 per cent. of the par value thereof, plus accrued interest, be and the same are hereby authorized and approved.

2.   That the said Idlewild Electric Light, Heat and Power Company of Federalsburg, Maryland, shall make reports to this Commission, duly verified by affidavits, upon the issue and sale of its bonds, authorized and approved as aforesaid, or any part thereof, the fact of such issue and sale, the terms and conditions thereof, and the amount realized therefrom.

ORDER No. 5171.

In the Matter of	Before the
The Application of THE PENINSULAR LIGHT AND POWER COMPANY for Authority to Issue Four Thousand Dollars, Par Value, of Its First Mortgage Bonds.	Public Service Commission of Maryland. Case No. 1722.

WHEREAS, The Peninsular Light and Power Company, a corporation organized and existing under the laws of the State of Maryland, has applied to this Commission for authority to issue its Thirty-six-Year Six Per Centum First Mortgage Gold Bonds of the aggregate principal amount of Four Thousand Dollars ($4,000.00), being part of a total authorized issue of Two Hundred Thousand Dollars ($200,000.00) secured by mortgage or deed of trust dated October 1st, 1918, upon the property, rights and franchises of said The Peninsular Light and Power Company to Philadelphia Trust Company, Trustee, a copy of which mortgage or deed of trust has heretofore been filed with the Commission in Case No. 1626, and to sell said bonds at not less than 89 per cent. of the par value thereof, the proceeds from the sale of said bonds to be used for the discharge or lawful refunding of said company's obligations incurred in making betterments, improvements and additions to its plant and distributing system and for the improvement and maintenance of its service since November 1st, 1918, as more particularly set forth and described in petition herein; and

WHEREAS, The application having come on to be heard on October 28th, 1919, after due notice published in accordance with this Commission's Order No. 5135 passed October 15th, 1919, and the hearing having been continued to November 7th, 1919, upon request of the applicant, on which date the application was duly heard, and it being the opinion and finding of the Commission after investigation that the use of the capital to be secured by the issue and sale of said bonds is reasonably required for the purposes of said corporation, to wit: the discharge or lawful refunding of its obligations incurred in making expenditures for proper corporate capital purposes.

IT IS THEREFORE, This 7th day of November, in the year Nineteen Hundred and Nineteen, by the Public Service Commission of Maryland,

Ordered, 1.   That the issue by the Peninsular Light and Power Company of its Thirty-six-Year Six Per Centum First Mortgage Gold Bonds of the aggregate principal amount of Four Thousand Dollars ($4,000.00), and the sale of said bonds at not less than 89 per cent. of the par value thereof, plus accrued interest, be and the same are hereby authorized and approved.

2.   That said The Peninsular Light and Power Company shall make reports to this Commission, duly verified by affidavits, upon the issue and sale of its bonds, authorized and approved as aforesaid, or any part thereof, the fact of such issue and sale, the terms and conditions thereof, and the amount realized therefrom.

ORDER No. 5172.

In the Matter of	Before the
The Application of SALISBURY LIGHT, HEAT AND POWER COMPANY for Authority to Issue Twenty-Two Thousand Dollars, Par Value, of Its Refunding Mortgage Bonds.	Public Service Commission of Maryland. Case No. 1723.

WHEREAS, The Salisbury Light, Heat and Power Company, a corporation organized and existing under the laws of the State of Maryland, has applied to this Commission for authority to issue its Thirty-six-Year Six Per Centum Refunding Mortgage Gold Bonds of the aggregate principal amount of Twenty-two Thousand Dollers ($22,-000.00), being part of a total authorized issue of Five Hundred Thousand Dollars ($500,000.00) secured by mortgage or deed of trust dated October 1st, 1918, upon the property, rights and franchises of the said Salisbury Light, Heat and Power Company to Philadelphia Trust Company, Trustee, a copy of which mortgage or deed of trust has heretofore been filed with the Commission in Case No. 1625, and to sell said bonds at not less than 89 per cent. of the par value thereof, the proceeds from the sale of said bonds to be used for the discharge or lawful refunding of said company's obligations incurred in making betterments, improvements and additions to its plant and distributing system and for the improvement and maintenance of its service since November 1st, 1918, as more particularly set forth and described in petition herein; and

WHEREAS, The application having come on to be heard on October 28th, 1919, after due notice published in accordance with this Commission's Order No. 5136 passed October 15th, 1919, and the hearing having been continued to November 7th, 1919, upon request of the applicant, on which date the application was duly heard, and it being the opinion and finding of the Commission after investigation that the use of the capital to be secured by the issue and sale of said bonds is reasonably required for the purposes of said corporation, to wit: the discharge or lawful refunding of its obligations incurred in making expenditures for proper corporate capital purposes,

IT IS, THEREFORE, This 7th day of November, in the year Nineteen Hundred and Nineteen, by the Public Service Commission of Maryland,

Ordered, 1. That the issue by the Salisbury Light, Heat and Power Company of its Thirty-six-Year Six Per Centum Refunding Mortgage Gold Bonds of the aggregate principal amount of Twenty-two Thousand Dollars ($22,000.00), and the sale of said bonds at not less than 89 per cent. of the par value thereof, plus accrued interest, be and the same are hereby authorized and approved.

2. That the said Salisbury Light, Heat and Power Company shall make reports to this Commission, duly verified by affidavits, upon the issue and sale of its bonds, authorized and approved as aforesaid, or any part thereof, the fact of such issue and sale, the terms and conditions thereof, and the amount realized therefrom.

ORDER No. 5173.

In the Matter of

The Application of CAMBRIDGE GAS, ELEC-
TRIC LIGHT AND POWER COMPANY for
Authority to Issue Six Thousand Dollars, Par Value, of Its First and Refunding Mortgage Bonds.

Before the

Public Service Commission
of Maryland.

Case No. 1724.

WHEREAS, The Cambridge Gas, Electric Light and Power Company,
a corporation organized and existing under the laws of the State of
Maryland, has applied to this Commission for authority to issue its
Thirty-nine-Year Six Per Centum First and Refunding Mortgage
Gold Bonds of the aggregate principal amount of Six Thousand Dollars ($6,000.00), being part of a total authorized issue of Three Hun-
dred and Fifty Thousand Dollars ($350,000.00) secured by mortgage
or deed of trust dated June 1st, 1916, upon the property, rights and
franchises of the said Cambridge Gas, Electric Light and Power Company to Philadelphia Trust Company, Trustee, a copy of which mortgage or deed of trust has heretofore been filed with the Commission
in Case No. 1127, and to sell said bonds at not less than 89 per cent.
of the par value thereof, the proceeds from the sale of said bonds to
be used for the discharge or lawful refunding of said company's
obligations incurred in making betterments, improvements and additions to its plant and distributing system and for the improvement
and maintenance of its service since November 1st, 1918, as more
particularly set forth and described in petition herein; and

WHEREAS, The application having come on to be heard on October
28th, 1919, after due notice published in accordance with this Commission's Order No. 5137 passed October 15th, 1919, and the hearing
having been continued to November 7th, 1919, upon request of the
applicant, on which date the application was duly heard, and it being
the opinion and finding of the Commission after investigation that
the use of the capital to be secured by the issue and sale of said bonds
is reasonably required for the purposes of said corporation, to wit:
the discharge or lawful refunding of its obligations incurred in making
expenditures for proper corporate capital purposes,

IT IS, THEREFORE, This 7th day of November, in the year Nineteen
Hundred and Nineteen, by the Public Service Commission of Maryland,

Ordered, 1. That the issue by the Cambridge Gas, Electric Light
and Power Company of its Thirty-nine-Year Six Per Centum First
and Refunding Mortgage Gold Bonds of the aggregate principal
amount of Six Thousand Dollars ($6,000.00), and the sale of said
bonds at not less than 89 per cent. of the par value thereof, plus
accrued interest, be and the same are hereby authorized and approved.

2. That the said Cambridge Gas, Electric Light and Power Company
shall make reports to this Commission, duly verified by affidavits, upon
the issue and sale of its bonds, authorized and approved as aforesaid,
or any part thereof, the fact of such issue and sale, the terms and
conditions thereof, and the amount realized therefrom.

ORDER No. 5175.

In the Matter of

The Petition of THE UNITED RAILWAYS AND ELECTRIC COMPANY OF BALTIMORE for a Modification of Certain Orders, Now in Force, Fixing the Rates of Fare to be Charged by Said Company and for Permission to File, Publish and Put in Effect a New Schedule of Rates of Fare, Increasing Existing Rates, as Set Forth in This Petition.

Before the

Public Service Commission of Maryland.

Case No. 1682.

The above entitled matter being under consideration it is, this 7th day of November, in the year Nineteen Hundred and Nineteen, by the Public Service Commission of Maryland,

Ordered, That the time within which The United Railways and Electric Company of Baltimore shall advise the Commission whether or not it will accept and abide by Order No. 5120 of the Commission passed in this cause on September 30th, 1919, be, and the same is hereby further extended for a period of fifteen days from November 3rd, 1919.

ORDER No. 5176.

In the Matter of

The Complaint of MAYOR AND CITY COUNCIL OF HAVRE DE GRACE vs. HAVRE DE GRACE ELECTRIC COMPANY.

Before the

Public Service Commission of Maryland.

Case No. 1618.

Upon the order of the solicitor for the complainant filed herein it is, this 10th day of November, in the year Nineteen Hundred and Nineteen, by the Public Service Commission of Maryland,

Ordered, That the complaint in the above entitled matter be and the same is hereby dismissed without prejudice.

ORDER No. 5177.

In the Matter of

The Complaint of MAYOR AND CITY COUN-
CIL OF HAVRE DE GRACE *vs.* HAVRE DE
GRACE WATER COMPANY.

Before the

Public Service Commission
of Maryland.

Case No. 1586.

Upon the order of the solicitor for the complainant filed herein it is, this 10th day of November, in the year Nineteen Hundred and Nineteen, by the Public Service Commission of Maryland,

Ordered, That the complaint in the above entitled matter be and the same is hereby dismissed without prejudice.

ORDER No. 5178.

In the Matter of

The Application of THE CONSOLIDATED
GAS, ELECTRIC LIGHT AND POWER COM-
PANY OF BALTIMORE and THE CHESA-
PEAKE AND POTOMAC TELEPHONE COM-
PANY OF BALTIMORE CITY for the Approval of an Agreement, Dated September 22nd, 1919, for the Sale by the
Former to the Latter of Two Poles
Located on Wyndcrest Avenue, South
of Summit Avenue, Catonsville, Maryland, Under the Terms and Provisions
of Order No. 2954, Entered July 26th,
1911, in Case No. 1151.

Before the

Public Service Commission
of Maryland.

Case No. 1731.

The agreement or other written instrument evidencing the transaction in this case having been submitted to this Commission for the purpose of securing its consent to the consummation thereof and the Commission having determined that a hearing is unnecessary,

IT IS, THEREFORE, On this 10th day of November, in the year 1919, by the Public Service Commission of Maryland,

Ordered, That the consent of this Commission be and the same is hereby given to the disposition of the property described in said agreement, or other written instrument, evidencing the transaction in accordance with the terms outlined therein.

ORDER No. 5179.

In the Matter of

The Petition of Maryland Carriers Not Under Federal Control for Permission Under Section 15 of THE PUBLIC SERVICE COMMISSION LAW to File and Publish on Less Than Statutory Notice Supplements Canceling Tariffs Publishing Demurrage Rules of Such Carriers.

Before the

Public Service Commission of Maryland.

S. N. & R. Docket.

Case No. 579.

The above mentioned petition having been received and filed, upon consideration thereof, it is this 12th day of November, 1919, by the Public Service Commission of Maryland,

Ordered, That permission be, and is hereby given, Maryland carriers not under Federal control, shown as participating carriers in Agent J. E. Fairbanks' tariff P. S. C. Md. No. 2, effective December 1st, 1919, under concurrences filed with this Commission, to file and publish on one day's notice to the Commission and the public, supplements canceling tariffs filed by or on behalf of such individual carriers publishing demurrage rules of such carriers.

PROVIDED, Said supplements be filed with the Commission upon issuance of this Order, and published by posting as required by law, and that all copies of said supplements shall bear the following notation:

"Issued under special permission of the Public Service Commission of Maryland, Order No. 5179 of date November 12th, 1919."

ORDER No. 5181.

In the Matter of

The Investigation of the Regulations, Practices, Equipment, Appliances and Services of THE UNITED RAILWAYS AND ELECTRIC COMPANY OF BALTIMORE.

Before the

Public Service Commission of Maryland.

Case No. 1123.

WHEREAS, This Commission by its Order No. 3460 entered herein on February 6th, 1917, directed and required The United Railways and Electric Company of Baltimore, among other things, to provide one thermometer in each single-truck closed car and two thermometers in each double-truck closed car; and

WHEREAS, The railway company has now petitioned the Commission to rescind its Order No. 3460 aforesaid, for the reason that since said order was entered the railway company has installed automatic thermostats, making it unnecessary to continue the use of thermometers in order to properly regulate temperature of cars during the winter months, and that if the railway company is required to continue to provide thermometers it will entail an unnecessary expenditure of money, due to the fact that through theft and breakage it is frequently necessary to replace the thermometers. with no commensurate advantage to the railway company or its patrons; and

WHEREAS, The Chief Engineer of this Commission has recommended that Order No. 3460 aforesaid be so modified as to relieve the railway company of the requirement of installing thermometers on those cars that are equipped with thermostats, in which recommendation the Commission concurs,

IT IS, THEREFORE, This 14th day of November, in the year Nineteen Hundred and Nineteen, by the Public Service Commission of Maryland,

Ordered, That from and after November 15th, 1919, and continuing until the further order of this Commission in the premises, the requirements of this Commission's Order No. 3460 entered on February 6th, 1917, are modified and changed so as to relieve The United Railways and Electric Company of Baltimore of the requirement of installing or maintaining thermometers on such of its cars as are equipped with thermostats.

ORDER No. 5182.

In the Matter of	
The Application of THE CHESAPEAKE AND POTOMAC TELEPHONE COMPANY OF BALTIMORE CITY for Permission and Authority to File and Publish a Schedule of Rates to be Effective Upon the Return of the Petitioner's Telephone System to It by the United States Government.	Before the Public Service Commission of Maryland. Case No. 1709.

The Baltimore Chamber of Commerce, by its counsel, having filed a petition herein, wherein it asks that the hearing of the above entitled case be postponed from November 18th, 1919, to December 15th, 1919, it is, this 15th day of November, in the year Nineteen Hundred and Nineteen, by the Public Service Commission of Maryland,

Ordered, That the hearing of the above entitled matter heretofore set for November 18th, 1919, at 10.30 A. M. at the office of the Commission, Munsey Building, Baltimore, Maryland, be and it is hereby postponed until December 15th, 1919, at the same hour and place.

AND IT IS FURTHER ORDERED, That copies of the aforesaid petition of the Baltimore Chamber of Commerce and of this order be forthwith served upon the counsel or other representative of The Chesapeake and Potomac Telephone Company of Baltimore City and the Assistant General Counsel to the Public Service Commission of Maryland, and that notice of such postponement be also given by the Secretary through letter to other parties in interest who would participate in these proceedings.

ORDER No. 5183.

In the Matter of	Before the
The Complaint of CATHERINE W. HEN-NESSY vs. THE BALTIMORE COUNTY WATER AND ELECTRIC COMPANY.	Public Service Commission of Maryland. Case No. 1718.

The above cause having been previously set for hearing and having been heard on October 2nd, 1919, when both parties were represented in person or by counsel, and it being the opinion and finding of the Commission after investigation that the amount of water registered by meter and billed the complainant by the respondent actually passed through the meter and was used by said complainant or those occupying the premises to which the water was supplied by and with her permission and consent, and that for the reasons assigned the complainant is not entitled to the relief for which she has prayed,

IT IS, THEREFORE, This 17th day of November, in the year Nineteen Hundred and Nineteen, by the Public Service Commission of Maryland,

Ordered, That the complaint in the above entitled matter be, and the same is hereby dismissed.

ORDER No. 5184.

In the Matter of

The Petition of THE UNITED RAILWAYS
AND ELECTRIC COMPANY OF BALTIMORE
for a Modification of Certain Orders,
Now in Force, Fixing the Rates of Fare
to be Charged by Said Company and
for Permission to File, Publish and Put
in Effect a New Schedule of Rates of
Fare, Increasing Existing Rates, as
Set Forth in This Petition.

Before the

Public Service Commission
of Maryland.

Case No. 1682.

The above entitled matter being under consideration it is, this 17th
day of November, in the year Nineteen Hundred and Nineteen, by
the Public Service Commission of Maryland,

Ordered, That the time within which The United Railways and
Electric Company of Baltimore shall advise the Commission whether
or not it will accept and abide by Order No. 5120 of the Commission
passed in this cause on September 30th, 1919, be, and the same is
hereby further extended until November 29th, 1919.

ORDER No. 5186.

In the Matter of

The Application of THE CHESAPEAKE AND
POTOMAC TELEPHONE COMPANY OF BAL-
TIMORE CITY and CONSOLIDATED POWER
COMPANY OF BALTIMORE for the Ap-
proval of an Agreement, Dated August
4th, 1919, for the Sale by the Former
and the Purchase by the Latter of
Twenty-Two Poles and Eight Anchor
Guys Located on Charles Street Ave-
nue, South of Melvern Avenue, Balti-
more, Maryland, Under the Terms and
Provisions of Order No. 2913, Entered
June 20th, 1919, in Case No. 1131.

Before the

Public Service Commission
of Maryland.

Case No. 1734.

The agreement or other written instrument evidencing the transaction in this case having been submitted to this Commission for the
purpose of securing its consent to the consummation thereof and the
Commission having determined that a hearing is unnecessary.

IT IS, THEREFORE, On this seventeenth day of November, in the year 1919, by the Public Service Commission of Maryland,

Ordered, That the consent of this Commission be and the same is hereby given to the disposition of the property described in said agreement, or other written instrument, evidencing the transaction in accordance with the terms outlined therein.

ORDER No. 5187.

In the Matter of

The Application of CONSOLIDATED GAS, ELECTRIC LIGHT AND POWER COMPANY OF BALTIMORE for the Approval of an Agreement Between It and THE CHESAPEAKE AND POTOMAC TELEPHONE COMPANY OF BALTIMORE CITY for the Sale by the Former to the Latter of One Pole on the Northwest Corner of Fayette and Eleventh Streets, Under the Terms and Provisions of Order No. 2954, Entered July 26th, 1916, in Case No. 1151.

Before the

Public Service Commission of Maryland.

Case No. 1736.

The agreement or other written instrument evidencing the transaction in this case having been submitted to this Commission for the purpose of securing its consent to the consummation thereof and the Commission having determined that a hearing is unnecessary,

IT IS, THEREFORE, On this seventeenth day of November, in the year of 1919, by the Public Service Commission of Maryland,

Ordered, That the consent of this Commission be and the same is hereby given to the disposition of the property described in said agreement, or other written instrument, evidencing the transaction in accordance with the terms outlined therein.

ORDER No. 5197.

In the Matter of

The Discontinuance of Motor Vehicle Freight Service Between Hancock and Hagerstown, Maryland, by J. M. LEIGHTY.

Before the

Public Service Commission of Maryland.

Case No. 1701.

WHEREAS, By Order No. 5060 of this Commission entered on July 29th, 1919, the above entitled matter was set for hearing on August 1st, 1919; and

WHEREAS, Said J. M. Leighty having failed to appear at the hearing aforesaid, and it now appearing that the applicant has discontinued the operation of the motor vehicle freight line between Hancock, Maryland, and Hagerstown, Maryland, no objection to or complaint concerning which discontinuance has been made to the Commission,

IT IS, THEREFORE, This 18th day of November, in the year Nineteen Hundred and Nineteen, by the Public Service Commission of Maryland,

Ordered, That the applicant, the said J. M. Leighty, be and he is hereby authorized to abandon and discontinue the motor vehicle transportation service between Hancock, Maryland, and Hagerstown, Maryland, the Commission having determined that the continuance of said service by the applicant is no longer reasonably necessary or convenient for the public service.

ORDER No. 5200.

In the Matter of	
The Application of THE CHESAPEAKE AND POTOMAC TELEPHONE COMPANY OF BALTIMORE CITY for Permission and Authority to File and Publish a Schedule of Rates to be Effective Upon the Return of the Petitioner's Telephone System to It by the United States Government.	Before the Public Service Commission of Maryland. Case No. 1709.

Upon the separate petitions and applications of the Protective Telephone Association of Baltimore City and The Baltimore Chamber of Commerce,

IT IS *Ordered*, This 20th day of November, 1919, by the Public Service Commission of Maryland that the Chesapeake and Potomac Telephone Company of Baltimore City be and it is hereby ordered and directed, in presenting its figures for the consideration of this Commission in this cause, so to set up and present such figures that they will show, as clearly as can be reasonably shown thereby, the capital investment of the Company, both as it stood June 30th, 1914, and as additions to the same were subsequently made, segregated as between Baltimore City and the State elsewhere; and its figures as to receipts and expenditures in the operation of its property in this State, likewise segregated, so far as may be reasonably possible, as between Baltimore City and the State elsewhere.

AND IT IS FURTHER *Ordered*, That a copy of this Order be forthwith served upon the proper representatives of the said Company, and that said Company notify this Commission in writing within five days after the date of its receipt of said copy whether or not it will accept and abide by the terms of this Order.

ORDER No. 5205.

In the Matter of

The Petition of the Carriers Not Under Federal Control Named in the Official Classification, by R. N. COLLYER, Their Agent, for Permission Under Section 15 of the PUBLIC SERVICE COMMISSION LAW to File and Publish on Less Than Statutory Notice Consolidated Freight Classification No. 1.

Before the

Public Service Commission of Maryland.

S. N. & R. Docket.

Case No. 580.

The above mentioned petition having been received and filed, upon consideration thereof, it is this 24th day of November, 1919, by the Public Service Commission of Maryland,

Ordered, That permission be, and is hereby, given the carriers not under Federal control named in the Official Classification, by R. N. Collyer, their Agent, to file and publish on ten days' notice to the Commission and the public, Consolidated Freight Classification No. 1,

PROVIDED, Said Consolidated Freight Classification No. 1 be filed with the Commission upon issuance of this Order, and published by posting as required by law, and that all copies of said classification shall bear the following notation:

"Issued under special permission of the Public Service Commission of Maryland, Order No. 5205 of date November 24th, 1919."

ORDER No. 5206.

In the Matter of

The Petition of the Railroads Not Under Federal Control, Named in Uniform Storage Tariff, by J. E. FAIRBANKS, Their Agent, for Permission Under Section 15 of the PUBLIC SERVICE COMMISSION LAW to File and Publish on Less Than Statutory Notice Amended Rules and Charges Applicable to Freight Stored In or On Railroad Premises.

Before the

Public Service Commission of Maryland.

S. N. & R. Docket.

Case No. 581.

The above mentioned petition having been received and filed, upon consideration thereof, it is this 24th day of November, 1919, by the Public Service Commission of Maryland,

Ordered, That permission be, and is hereby, given the railroads not under Federal control named in Uniform Storage Tariff, by J. E. Fairbanks, their Agent, to file and publish on one day's notice to the Commission and the public, amended rules and charges applicable to freight stored in or on railroad premises, as per exhibit filed with petition herein,

PROVIDED, Tariff containing said amended rules and charges be filed with the Commission upon issuance of this Order, and published by posting as required by law, and that all copies of said tariff shall bear the following notation:

"Issued under special permission of the Public Service Commission of Maryland, Order No. 5206 of date November 24th, 1919."

ORDER No. 5208.

In the Matter of

The Application of THE EDISON ELECTRIC ILLUMINATING COMPANY OF CUMBERLAND, MARYLAND, for an Order Permitting and Approving the Exercise of a Franchise Granted by the MAYOR AND COUNCILMEN OF LONACONING and to Begin Construction Thereunder.

Before the

Public Service Commission of Maryland.

Case No. 1732.

WHEREAS, The Edison Electric Illuminating Company of Cumberland, Maryland, has applied to this Commission for an order granting the permission and approval of this Commission to the exercise of the franchise granted to said corporation by an ordinance of the Mayor and Councilmen of Lonaconing, passed July 7th, 1915, and to construction under said franchise, as in said application set forth; and

WHEREAS, After consideration of the said application and the exhibits filed therewith and after due hearing, it appears that the interests and convenience of the public will be subserved by such exercise of said franchise and by such construction under said franchise,

IT IS, THEREFORE, This 25th day of November, in the year Nineteen Hundred and Nineteen, by the Public Service Commission of Maryland,

Ordered, That the permission and approval of the Public Service Commission be and it hereby is given to the exercise by the Edison Electric Illuminating Company of Cumberland, Maryland, of the franchise granted to said corporation by the said ordinance of the Mayor and Councilmen of Lonaconing and to construction under said franchise.

ORDER No. 5217.

In the Matter of

The Joint Aplication of CAMBRIDGE GAS, ELECTRIC LIGHT AND POWER COMPANY, SALISBURY LIGHT, HEAT AND POWER COMPANY, IDLEWILD ELECTRIC LIGHT, HEAT AND POWER COMPANY OF FEDERALSBURG, MARYLAND, and THE PENINSULAR LIGHT AND POWER COMPANY for Authority to Consolidate.	Before the Public Service Commission of Maryland. Case No. 1737.

WHEREAS, Cambridge Gas, Electric Light and Power Company, Salisbury Light, Heat and Power Company, Idlewild Electric Light, Heat and Power Company of Federalsburg, Maryland, and The Peninsular Light and Power Company, all being corporations organized and existing under the laws of the State of Maryland, have applied to this Commission for the approval of an agreement of consolidation under the general laws of the State of Maryland, whereby said applicant companies are consolidated into a new corporation to be known as The Eastern Shore Gas and Electric Company of Maryland, and for authority to issue, in order to perfect said consolidation, common capital stock of said The Eastern Shore Gas and Electric Company of Maryland to the aggregate amount of Three Hundred and Fifteen Thousand Dollars ($315,000.00) par value, in exchange for common capital stock of the constituent companies of like aggregate par value; and

WHEREAS, The application having this day come on to be heard after due notice published in compliance with Order No. 5196 of the Commission passed November 18th, 1919, and the Commission being of the opinion and finding after hearing that said consolidation is convenient for the public service and that the issue of said stock is reasonably required for the purposes of said consolidated corporation prescribed by Section 34 of the Public Service Commission Law of Maryland,

IT IS, THEREFORE, This 26th day of November, in the year Nineteen Hundred and Nineteen, by the Public Service Commission of Maryland,

ORDERED, 1. That the execution of the proposed agreement of consolidation by which Cambridge Gas, Electric Light and Power Company, Salisbury Light, Heat and Power Company, Idlewild Electric Light. Heat and Power Company of Federalsburg, Maryland, and The Peninsular Light and Power Company are consolidated into a new corporation to be known as The Eastern Shore Gas and Electric Company of Maryland, be and it is hereby authorized and approved, and said The Eastern Shore Gas and Electric Company of Maryland be and it is hereby authorized and empowered to exercise the franchises and rights heretofore granted to and exercised and owned by the constituent companies, or granted to said consolidated company under the agreement of consolidation.

2. That said The Eastern Shore Gas and Electric Company of Maryland is hereby authorized to issue its common capital stock to the aggregate amount of Three Hundred and Fifteen Thousand Dollars ($315,000.00), par value, in exchange for all of the common capital stock of the constituent companies of like aggregate par value issued and outstanding.

3. That when said agreement of consolidation is executed and recorded a certified copy thereof shall be filed in these proceedings.

4. That the accounts of the consolidated company shall be so kept as to enable the Commission at any and all times to determine the capital investment, revenues and expenses of operation, and earnings of the properties of each of the several constituent companies.

ORDER No. 5218.

In the Matter of	
The Application of THE CHESAPEAKE AND POTOMAC TELEPHONE COMPANY OF BALTIMORE CITY for Permission and Authority to File and Publish a Schedule of Rates to be Effective Upon the Return of the Petitioner's Telephone System to It by the United States Government.	Before the Public Service Commission of Maryland. Case No. 1709.

WHEREAS, The Chesapeake and Potomac Telephone Company of Baltimore City has made application to this Commission for permission and authority to continue in effect the rates and charges promulgated and made effective for said The Chesapeake and Potomac Telephone Company of Baltimore City by the Postmaster General of the United States during the period of Federal control, or to charge and collect such other rates and charges as the Commission may find to be just and reasonable; and

WHEREAS, It has not been possible for the Commission to conclude its investigation concerning the reasonableness of the rates aforesaid within the four months' period after the termination of Federal control, prescribed as the time within which the rates promulgated and made effective by the Postmaster General should remain in effect by the Act of Congress approved July 11th, 1919, providing for the return of the telephone and telegraph lines of the United States to private control and operation at midnight of July 31st,

IT IS, THEREFORE, This 26th day of November, in the year Nineteen

Hundred and Nineteen, by the Public Service Commission of Maryland, **Ordered,** That the rates and charges promulgated and made effective by the Postmaster General of the United States for The Chesapeake and Potomac Telephone Company of Baltimore City during the period of Federal control, be and they are hereby extended and continued in effect as the rates of said The Chesapeake and Potomac Telephone Company of Baltimore City until such time as the Commission shall have concluded the hearings and investigations now being conducted in Case No. 1709 and shall have filed and made effective its order in said case.

ORDER No. 5219.

In the Matter of

The Application of POTOMAC EDISON COMPANY for Authority to Purchase and Acquire the Capital Stock of the WEST VIRGINIA AND MARYLAND GAS COMPANY OF MARYLAND, the NORTHERN NATURAL GAS COMPANY and the EDISON ELECTRIC ILLUMINATING COMPANY OF CUMBERLAND, MARYLAND, and Upon Acquisition of Such Capital Stock for Approval of the Transfer by Said Corporations of Their Property and Franchises to the POTOMAC EDISON COMPANY, and for Authority to Purchase and Acquire Not Less Than a Majority of the Capital Stock of the CUMBERLAND ELECTRIC RAILWAY COMPANY.

Before the

Public Service Commission of Maryland.

Case No. 1706.

WHEREAS, The Potomac Gas and Electric Company has applied to this Commission for an order authorizing and approving the acquisition by purchase by the Potomac Gas and Electric Company of all the capital stock of the West Virginia and Maryland Gas Company of Maryland, the Northern Natural Gas Company and the Edison Electric Illuminating Company of Cumberland, Maryland, and, upon such acquisition of such capital stock, the transfer to the Potomac Gas and Electric Company by the West Virginia and Maryland Gas Company of Maryland, the Northern Natural Gas Company and the Edison Electric Illuminating Company of Cumberland, Maryland, of all the respective properties and franchises of said three last mentioned corporations, and also authorizing and approving the acquisition by purchase by the Potomac Gas and Electric Company of not less than a majority of the outstanding capital stock of the Cumberland Electric Railway Company, all as in said application set forth; and

WHEREAS, The West Virginia and Maryland Gas Company of Maryland, the Northern Natural Gas Company and the Edison Electric Illuminating Company of Cumberland, Maryland, have similarly applied for an order authorizing and approving the transfer by them to the Potomac Gas and Electric Company of all their respective properties and franchises upon the acquisition by the Potomac Gas and Electric Company of all the capital stock of said three corporations; and

WHEREAS, After consideration .of the said applications and the exhibits filed therewith and thereafter, and after due hearing, it appears that the interests and convenience of the public will be subserved by .such acquisition of capital stocks and properties,

IT IS, THEREFORE, This 26th day of November, in the year Nineteen Hundred and Nineteen, by the Public Service Commission of Maryland,

ORDERED, 1. That the acquisition by purchase by the Potomac Gas and Electric Company of all the capital stock of the West Virginia and Maryland Gas Company of Maryland, the Northern Natural Gas Company and the Edison Electric Illuminating Company of Cumberland, Maryland, and, upon such acquisition of such capital stock, the transfer to the Potomac Gas and Electric Company by the West Virginia and Maryland Gas Company of Maryland, the Northern Natural Gas Company and the Edison Electric Illuminating Company of Cumberland, Maryland, of all of the respective properties and franchises of the said three last mentioned corporations, be and such acquisition and such transfer hereby are authorized and approved, and the consent, permission and·approval of the Public Service Commission is hereby given to such acquisition and transfer, the respective properties and franchises so to be transferred including—

(a) All the property, works, system and franchises of the West Virginia and Maryland Gas Company of Maryland, said franchises comprising all rights vested in said corporation under or by virtue of Section 142 of Art. 23 of the Code of Public General Laws of Maryland (Edition of 1904), or any other applicable provision of the General Laws of Maryland, and also all rights vested in said corporation under or by virtue of the following instruments, copies of which have been filed in these proceedings, to wit:

1. Ordinance No. 7 of the Mayor and Commissioners of Westernport, passed July 1st, 1907, relating to the Western Maryland Gas Company of Allegany County (the corporate name of which was subsequently changed to the West Virginia and Maryland Gas Company of Maryland). .

2. Ordinance of the Council of the Town of Midland, passed June 25th, 1907, relating to the Western Maryland Gas Company (now West Virginia and Maryland Gas Company of Maryland).

3. Ordinance of the Mayor and Council of the Town of Lonaconing,

passed October 1st, 1906, relating to the West Virginia Central Gas Company.

4. Assignment of last mentioned franchise (and others) by the West Virginia Central Gas Company to the West Virginia and Maryland Gas Company (of West Virginia) dated October 1st, 1906.

5. Assignment of last mentioned franchise by the West Virginia and Maryland Gas Company (of West Virginia) to the West Virginia and Maryland Gas Company of Maryland, dated March 21st, 1907.

6. Ordinance No. 129 of the Mayor and Councilmen of Frostburg relating to the Western Maryland Gas Company of Allegany County (now the West Virginia and Maryland Gas Company of Maryland), passed September 10th, 1906.

(b) All the property, works, system and franchises of the Northern Natural Gas Company, said franchises comprising all rights vested in said corporation under or by virtue of Section 142 of Art. 23 of the Code of Public General Laws of Maryland (Edition of 1904), or any other applicable provision of the General Laws of Maryland, and also all rights vested in said corporation under or by virtue of the following instruments, copies of which have been filed in these proceedings, to wit:

1. Ordinance of the Mayor and Common Council of the Town of Deer Park, passed April 23rd, 1909, relating to the West Virginia and Maryland Gas Company of Maryland.

2. Ordinance of the Mayor and Council of Loch Lynn Heights, passed April 23rd, 1909, relating to the West Virginia and Maryland Gas Company of Maryland.

3. Ordinance of the Mayor and Town Council of Oakland, passed April 23rd, 1909, relating to the West Virginia and Maryland Gas Company of Maryland.

4. Assignment of the three last mentioned franchises by the West Virginia and Maryland Gas Company of Maryland to the Northern Natural Gas Company, dated September 8th, 1909.

5. Agreement between the Mountain Lake Park Association of Garrett County, the Commissioners of Mountain Lake Park and the Northern Natural Gas Company, dated May 21st, 1910, and referred to in Order No. 32 of this Commission, passed July 14th, 1910, granting permission and approval to the exercise by the Northern Natural Gas Company of Maryland of the franchise thereby granted.

6. Order of the County Commissioners for Garrett County under date of March 18th, 1907, relating to the West Virginia and Maryland Gas Company (of West Virginia).

7. Assignment of last mentioned franchise by the West Virginia and Maryland Gas Company (of West Virginia) to the Northern Natural Gas Company, dated September 8th, 1909.

(c) All the property, works, system and franchises of the Edison Electric Illuminating Company of Cumberland, Maryland, said franchises comprising all rights vested in said corporation under or by virtue of any applicable provision of the General Laws of Maryland, and also all rights vested in said corporation under or by virtue of the following instruments, copies of which have been filed in these proceedings, to wit:

1. Order of the Mayor and Council of Cumberland, Maryland, passed and approved March 4th, 1884, referred to in extract from minutes of meeting held March 3rd, 1884, and set out in full in an affidavit of James A. McHenry, dated September 29th, 1919, a copy of an extract from said minutes and copy of affidavit being on file in these proceedings.

2. Franchise grant by the Road Directors for Allegany County, Maryland, to the Edison Electric Illuminating Company, dated April 7th, 1915, and referred to in Order No. 2357 of this Commission, passed June 9th, 1915, permitting and approving the exercise by the Edison Electric Illuminating Company of Cumberland, Maryland, of said franchise.

3. Ordinance of the Mayor and Councilmen of Lonaconing, passed July 7th, 1915, relating to the Edison Electric Illuminating Company of Cumberland, Maryland.

4. Ordinance No. 75 of the Mayor and City Council of Cumberland, Maryland, passed July 9th, 1900, relating to the Edison Electric Illuminating Company of Cumberland, Maryland.

2. That the acquisition by purchase by the Potomac Gas and Electric Company of not less than a majority of the outstanding capital stock of the Cumberland Electric Railway Company be and such acquisition hereby is authorized and approved and the consent, permission and approval of the Public Service Commission is hereby given to such acquisition.

PROVIDED, HOWEVER, That the consent, permission and approval hereby given to the acquisition of capital stocks shall not become operative until such acquisition shall have been approved by the Board of Directors of the Potomac Gas and Electric Company and evidence of such approval shall have been filed in these proceedings, and the consent, permission and approval hereby given to the transfer of properties and franchises shall not become operative until such transfer shall have been approved by the Board of Directors of the Potomac Gas and Electric Company and by the respective boards of directors and stockholders of the three corporations making such transfers, and evidence of such approval shall have been filed in these proceedings.

AND PROVIDED FURTHER, That nothing in this Order, or in any of the transactions on which it is based, shall hereafter be taken as committing the Public Service Commission to any valuation of the property and assets of the said purchasing Company for rate-making purposes; it being hereby expressly declared that in any future investigation or investigations of the rates of said Company the maximum rate or rates then fixed by the Commission will be based upon the value of said property and assets then used and useful in the public service regardless of the price paid for them by the said Company.

ORDER No. 5223

In the Matter of

The Petition of THE UNITED RAILWAYS
AND ELECTRIC COMPANY OF BALTIMORE
for a Modification of Certain Orders,
Now in Force, Fixing the Rates of
Fare to be Charged by Said Company
and for Permission to File, Publish and
Put in Effect a New Schedule of Rates
of Fare, Increasing Existing Rates, as
Set Forth in This Petition.

Before the

Public Service Commission
of Maryland.

Case No. 1682

Pursuant to the conclusion reached in the aforegoing opinion, it is,
this 29th day of November, in the year Nineteen Hundred and Nineteen, by the Public Service Commission of Maryland,

Ordered, That paragraph 4 of Order No. 5120 entered in this
cause by the Commission on September 30th, 1919, be and it is hereby
modified and amended so as to read as follows:

"That from and after the hour of midnight on the 30th of
September, 1920, said company's right and privilege to
charge and collect the increased fares authorized hereby
shall cease and determine and said company shall thereupon
put in force and effect, and maintain until thereafter lawfully changed, the schedule of fares operative on the 30th
of September, 1919, unless this Commission or other lawful
authority shall in the meantime have modified, extended or
superseded this order; provided, however, that if this order
has not been so extended or superseded, and there shall be
pending on September 30th, 1920, an application by said
company filed before August 31st, 1920, for a continuance
in whole or in part of the relief hereby granted or for
increased fares, then the right to collect the fares authorized by this order shall continue until the determination
by the Commission of said pending proceedings; and provided, further, that in case of any proceeding hereafter
instituted before the 30th day of September, 1920, for the
right to charge and collect fares in excess of those in effect
on the 30th of September, 1919, the burden of proving the
reasonableness of any such excess fare shall be and remain
on said company; provided, however, that nothing in this
order shall be held to affect in any way the right of the
company to proceed with the pending valuation to which
said company is a party or its right of appeal from the
finding or orders growing out of said valuation proceedings."

AND IT IS FURTHER 𝔒𝔯𝔡𝔢𝔯𝔢𝔡, That except as hereby modified and amended Order No. 5120 aforesaid shall be and remain in full force and effect.

AND IT IS FURTHER 𝔒𝔯𝔡𝔢𝔯𝔢𝔡, That a copy of this order be forthwith served upon the proper officers of The United Railways and Electric Company of Baltimore, and that said company, within ten days from the date of the service of such copy, advise this Commission in writing whether or not it will accept and abide by Order No. 5120 aforesaid as modified and amended by this order.

SUPPLEMENTARY OPINION

In the Matter of	
The Petition of THE UNITED RAILWAYS AND ELECTRIC COMPANY OF BALTIMORE for a Modification of Certain Orders, Now in Force, Fixing the Rates of Fare to be Charged by Said Company and for Permission to File, Publish and Put in Effect a New Schedule of Rates of Fare, Increasing Existing Rates, as Set Forth in This Petition.	Before the Public Service Commission of Maryland. Case No. 1682

By the Commission.   Filed November 29th, 1919.

The Commission's opinion in the above case was filed September 30th, 1919, and was accompanied by an Order No. 5120 in which it was ordered, as by law provided, that the petitioning Company should advise the Commission in writing within ten days from the date of service upon it of a copy of such order whether or not it would accept and abide by the same.

Before the expiration of said ten days the Company requested and obtained an extension of such period for the purpose of giving its representatives further opportunity to study and analyze the opinion of the Commission upon which such order was based.

On October 20th the Company filed a petition for a modification of such order and opinion. In such petition the Company alleged in substance that before, during, and since the hearing in this cause its officials had been engaged in a comprehensive study of plans for the improvement of the service and for the increase of carrying capacity of the service rendered; that its officials had hesitated to authorize large capital expenditures in view of prevailing high prices, but that in order to keep pace with and stimulate the growth of the city and in view of the seeming stabilization of prices, such officials were about to recommend to the Company's directors the purchase of from three hundred to three hundred and fifty new cars, the improvement or reconstruction of approximately forty miles of track and the expenditure of substantial sums for improvement of the power situation, all aggregating a total capital sum of several million dollars.

The Company further stated in its said petition that it was willing to continue the rates of fare established by said Order No. 5120 for a sufficient length of time to determine their adequacy or inadequacy both for the proper operation and maintenance of the property and for the establishment and maintenance of the balance to surplus which this Commission had declared in said opinion the Company was reasonably entitled to earn, but believed that no fair test of such order could be had until certain of the Commission's estimates of receipts and expenditures, particularly as to maintenance and depreciation reserves, had been corrected, and the Commission's expressions relative thereto made so clear that they could not reasonably be misinterpreted by the public.

Other orders extending the time within which the Company should signify its acceptance or rejection of Order No. 5120 were subsequently passed, and the petition finally came to a hearing on November 14th, 1919.

At this hearing counsel for the Company apparently abandoned the request that the Commission's estimates as set forth in its opinion be corrected, but contended that it should be made more abundantly clear in the opinion that such estimates were in fact merely estimates. and that if the Commission's estimates of expenditures were exceeded in actual operation without a corresponding saving in other estimates, the Company would not necessarily be penalized thereby. Great stress was laid upon the necessity of upholding the Company's credit in the eyes of the investing public in order that capital necessary to make the improvements referred to in the petition and for refinancing might the more readily be secured, and it was contended that with the opinion as originally written, such credit was more likely to be impaired than strengthened.

It was also contended that Section Four of the order should be amended in certain minor particulars.

After a careful study of the opinion in the light of the above criticisms, the Commission is unable to see wherein it is necessary that it should be corrected or modified in order to make it more abundantly clear that our estimates of probable receipts and expenditures were in fact merely estimates, and were in no sense meant to be limitations upon the Company's right to make such expenditures for the operation and maintenance of its property as might be found reasonably necessary. When the Commission states in paragraph after paragraph of an opinion that its figures are merely estimates, heads its tables with the statement that the figures therein are merely estimates, and then finally concludes that portion of its opinion with a clear statement that all of its said figures are merely estimates, and that if such estimates turn out to be materially wrong, steps will be taken at once to modify the order based upon the same, it is somewhat difficult to see how any reader of that opinion could possibly look upon such figures other than as estimates, or conceive them in any way to have been intended as limitations upon the right of the Company to expend such sums for the operation and maintenance of its property as might be found by actual experience to be reasonably necessary.

In view, however, of the fact that in the haste with which our opinion in this case was prepared in order that the new rates should go into effect by October 1st, 1919, the Commission failed to make entirely clear just what balance to surplus the Company should be permitted to earn under varying conditions in the future, we have concluded that it is desirable for us to file a supplementary opinion in which our views upon this important point will be so clearly set forth that there will be no reasonable ground for any misunderstanding as to the same.

In our original opinion in this case we stated in one place that the best interests of the public with respect to the Company required that it should earn a balance of not materially less than one and a half times its fixed charges, or $1,500,000 per annum, after the payment of operating expenses, fixed charges, taxes and the making of reasonable allowance for its accident and depreciation reserves. Subsequently in that opinion we stated that the Company was entitled to charge rates at the present time estimated to yield it a balance to surplus of approximately one million dollars after the payment of such expenses and charges and the making of such allowances. In that opinion we neglected to reconcile these two apparently conflicting statements, with the natural result that doubt has arisen as to exactly what may hereafter be our policy with respect to the rates authorized by the order passed pursuant to such opinion.

Pending the establishment of fares based upon a valuation of the Company's property or the adoption of a plan, under which fares will be more or less automatically established upon the basis of actual cost of the service rendered, it is the belief of this Commission that an earning capacity of one and a half times the fixed charges of the Company is reasonable and necessary and in the interest of the public. But we do not believe that the entire burden of earning this surplus should be placed upon the public at the present time and under existing circumstances. We feel that a portion of the responsibility for earning such balance to surplus should be placed upon the Company, and that this responsibility can and should be met by the exercise of all reasonable economies and efficiencies on its part. But the Commission is not to be understood as undertaking to establish in the future rates and fares estimated to yield such a balance to surplus of $1,500,000, or to increase existing rates in order that they may yield such amount. We merely mean that it is not our intent to refuse such earning capacity, provided the Company, by diligent, sensible economies and good service, can produce such a surplus. If, in time, the balance to surplus under any existing rate of fare should come to exceed such $1,500,000, the Commission, of its own initiative, will proceed to consider the propriety of reducing the rates of fare then in force.

Pending the institution and coming into full effectiveness of such economies and increased efficiency, it was at the date of the original opinion and is now the view of this Commission that the rates of fare authorized to be charged by the Company should be such as may reasonably be anticipated to yield a balance to surplus of approximately one million dollars ($1,000,000) after the payment of the Company's operating expenses, taxes, fixed charges, and the making of reasonable allowances for the maintenance of the property and of its accident and depreciation reserves.

In other words, if, after exercising what may seem to the Commission to be reasonable economy and efficiency in the operation of its property, it appears that the Company is unable to earn under the established rates such a balance to surplus of approximately one million dollars, the Commission stands ready, upon request of the Railways Company, to reconsider the estimates set forth in its original opinion, and also the rates of fare authorized to be charged by our Order No. 5120 passed pursuant thereto.

But in fixing $1,000,000 as the minimum balance to surplus which the Company should be permitted to earn under existing conditions, this Commission is not to be understood as undertaking to guarantee such balance to surplus at the expense of the public at any and all hazards.

It will be noted that we have conditioned our conclusion as to such balance to surplus, first, upon the exercise of reasonable efficiency in the operation of the property; second, upon the exercise of reasonable economies, and, third, upon the expenditures of no more than reasonable amounts for the maintenance of the property and of its accident and depreciation reserves.

In our original opinion in this case we had occasion to consider what, in our judgment, would constitute reasonable expenditures for the maintenance of the property and reasonable allowances for the Company's accident and depreciation reserves. This was necessary in order for us to reach a definite basis on which to establish the rates fixed by such order. We nevertheless appreciate the impossibility of determining in advance the exact amount of money to be expended upon any one item, particularly in a period of economic readjustment, such as the present. Table IV of the original opinion and our other estimates therein are not, therefore, to be construed as placing a limit upon the amount which may be spent by the Railways Company on each item, but should be understood as constituting an expression of the Commission's opinion as to the sums which would probably be necessary. It may be that actual experience will demonstrate the need of larger appropriations or expenditures for some of the items therein contained, but in any application hereafter filed for an increase in the rates prescribed by such order the Company must assume the burden of justifying any expenditures in excess of our estimates set forth in such opinion. Moreover, it is the hope of the Commission that if there should be any increased expenditures in excess of such estimates, such increases may be offset by increased income or by reductions in other items brought about by strict economy and greater efficiency in operating methods.

This Commission would not, under any circumstances, feel justified in going farther than the above in giving assurances as to what will be its future action with respect to any public utility subject to its jurisdiction. And especially would we not feel so justified in the case of this particular Company, as its monthly reports since the date of our original opinion and order have shown expenditures for maintenance and depreciation so greatly in excess of our estimates above referred to, and largely in excess of any expenditures heretofore made in like periods on account of such items. These reports have been scrutinized thoroughly by us as they have been received, and will be further scrutinized and analyzed by us in the event of an application for authority to charge fares in excess of those prescribed by our Order No. 5120. For the present we express no opinion thereon.

In view of this reluctance upon our part to commit ourselves in advance more definitely upon the specific point of a fare increase in the event of expenditures exceeding the estimates upon which our order was based, the Commission feels that both the Company and the public are entitled to a full and clear statement of the general policy which we expect to follow with respect to this particular utility during the reconstruction period upon which the world at large is now fully entered.

In our original opinion in this case we discussed at some length some of the problems of rate making before, during and since the World War.

If rates are to be based upon value, they must be based upon "fair present value," and conditions are still so far from normal that we would not feel justified at the present time in accepting present-day prices as conclusive of that fair value which should be used as the basis for the making of rates to remain effective for any considerable period in the future.

On the other hand, we would not feel justified in continuing longer to fix rates upon the "war emergency" basis, since the theory of that method of rate making was merely to preserve the *status quo ante* of the property and business during the period of the emergency created by the pendency of the war.

With the end of the war the time has come when we can no longer be satisfied merely to preserve the *status quo ante* of utilities subject to our jurisdiction. Rather has the time come for the inauguration of a truly constructive policy in the case of business enterprises of all kinds, our public utilities included.

If, before and during the war, there was any uncertainty as to
the relations which should or would continue to exist between the
public and our public utilities, now that the war is over, it is the
time, of all times, when this question should be definitely settled, in
order that both the utilities and the public should know what will
be the policy of the State with respect to such utilities in the future.
Upon no other basis than that of a full mutual understanding of the
relative rights and obligations of our public utilities and the public
can the former go ahead and do the best there is in them toward
rendering adequate service at reasonable rates to the public they have
undertaken to serve.

With respect to the particular utility whose affairs are here under
consideration, this Commission has had little or no difficulty in determining what should be its policy in the future.

Practically ever since the creation of the Public Service Commission
of Maryland in 1910, this Commission has had before it for consideration questions concerning the property, affairs and operation of the
United Railways & Electric Company of Baltimore. It is one of the
largest public utilities which are fully subject to this Commission's
jurisdiction. As we have pointed out in other of our opinions, its
continued operation is of the utmost importance to the entire community which it has undertaken to serve. The Company's property
is one of great value, and one which should not be jeopardized or
needlessly impaired in value by the adoption on the part of this
Commission of a narrow or illiberal policy with respect to its financial
affairs.

Time and again we have had occasion to consider the question of
the character of service actually rendered by the Company to the
public, and as well the character of service which the property is
susceptible of rendering with comparatively minor improvements and
additions. More recently we have noted on the part of the management of the Company what has seemed to us to be a sincere desire
so to operate the property as to render the public more adequate service than has been rendered at times in the past. This attitude
apparently has been based upon a growing recognition of the fact
that the public has rights in our public utilities which must not be
subordinated on the rights of the owners of the property.

Our consideration of the Company's affairs has extended as well
to its financial situation and requirements, and this Commission, from
time to time in the past, has passed orders authorizing the issuance of
securities of large aggregate value for the betterment of the property
and service.

With this intimate knowledge of the Company's affairs, acquired
through a period of what is now nearly ten years, this Commission
is firmly convinced that the present and future welfare of this community requires the preservation of the property of the Company
and its continued operation in the service of the public not only unim-

paired, but in a position to meet all reasonable demands incident to the growth of the city and community.

While the property of this Company nominally belongs to its stockholders, subject to mortgages held by its bondholders, the public itself is interested even to a greater extent than either the stockholders or bondholders in the continued proper operation and maintenance of such property.

In the case of operation, the public is the first to suffer from inadequate service. Inasmuch as proper service can never long be rendered in any line of business enterprise without reasonable compensation, it is incumbent upon the public to pay for the kind of service it desires, and such public cannot justly complain if it does not receive a character of service better than that for which it has paid.

But the requirements of the public will be by no means fully met merely by a satisfactory operation of the Company's present property and equipment.

The City of Baltimore is one of the most important commercial and industrial centers in the country. This growth during the past twenty years has been regular and consistent, and has kept pace fairly well with our other large cities. During this period it has been necessary for the Railways Company to add to its service equipment and property in order that it might keep up with the community which it has undertaken to serve. During the war the advantages of Baltimore as a commercial and industrial center, and as a place of residence as well, came to be appreciated to a greater extent than ever before, with the result that a new impetus was given to our city and it has now fully entered into an era of prosperity and growth the like of which it has never enjoyed at any time in the past. But the city cannot continue to grow to advantage unless its street railway system continues to grow as well and keep abreast in all respects with the community which it serves.

It appears by the petition of the Company that it now has under consideration plans for the expenditure in the near future of three or four millions of dollars in the purchase of some three hundred to three hundred and fifty new cars, the improvement or reconstruction of approximately forty miles of track, and the general improvement of service.

This money is to be expended for the benefit of the public. The surplus which the Company accumulated in pre-war times, together with the depreciation reserves which have been accumulated under more favorable conditions, has been exhausted. Therefore the Company has no funds at the present time with which to make these improvements. Hence this large sum must be borrowed, and in order to borrow the same the Company must have credit with the investing public.

It is a well-known fact that there is at the present time an almost unprecedented demand for money to meet the requirements of the business world of today. The high prices being paid for commodities of all kinds, with their resulting promise of unusually large profits, are stimulating enterprise in almost every line of business endeavor. Foreign governments as well as our own government are offering higher rates of interest for the use of money than they have paid for generations past. The securities of large and hitherto most prosperous public utilities throughout the country are being bought in the open market at abnormally low prices in order that purchasers thereof may assure themselves of an interest yield materially in excess of the return with which they were satisfied prior to the war. The daily papers are full of offers of all kinds of securities issued by business enterprises of the highest standing, and which are so much in need of money for further developments that they are willing to pay unusually high prices for the use of the same.

Companies with assets in some instances of a value several times in excess of their outstanding obligations, and with assured earnings three, four, five and six times their interest charges, are offering six and seven and in some instances as high as eight per cent. for the use of funds with which to further develop their business.

With such a demand for the use of money, investors are demanding substantial security for their loans, and are insisting that there be both a substantial equity in the property over the amount of funded securities and assured earnings largely in excess of the aggregate interest charges thereon. If less than this is offered, the investors will either decline to make the loan upon any terms whatsoever, or will insist upon an abnormally high rate of interest in order to compensate them for the additional risk taken in making the investment. This last means either that the interest rate itself must be abnormally high or that the securities be sold at a discount which will yield the desired rate.

In the case of a public utility, where securities are sold at a discount with the consent of the State regulatory body, the utility is entitled to charge the public in addition to what would otherwise be the cost of the service the amount necessary to amortize such discount during the life of the security. Where, on the other hand, the interest rate is made abnormally high with the consent of the State regulatory body, good faith requires that the purchasers of such securities be protected in their investment by the fixing of rates which will enable the utility to pay such abnormally high rate of interest.

Thus, in either event, the public is the one to suffer most where the financial credit or any of its utilities is so far impaired that it is obliged to pay abnormally high prices for the loan of funds to be used in improving its property or service for the benefit of the public.

It follows that the prospective investors shall be given reasonable assurances of earnings materially in excess of the Company's interest charges.

The present interest charges of the Railways Company amount to approximately three million dollars. It is this Commission's judgment that a balance to surplus varying from approximately one million five hundred thousand dollars as the maximum, both conditioned as hereinbefore set forth, and the latter subject to increase with increases in the Company's funded debt, would not only provide fair and reasonable compensation to the Company for the service which it expects hereafter to render the public, but would in addition give the Company such credit with the investing public as will enable it to secure upon reasonably favorable terms the capital necessary for all its corporate requirements.

For the reasons herein stated the application of the Company for a modification of the estimates contained in our original opinion will be refused, but inasmuch as it appears that the changes which the Company's representatives suggested should properly be made in Paragraph Four of our Order No. 5120, a new order will be passed embodying such changes.

ORDER No. 5224

In the Matter of

The Application of AMERICAN TELEPHONE & TELEGRAPH CO., AMERICAN TELE-PHONE & TELEGRAPH CO. OF BALTIMORE CITY and CONSOLIDATED GAS ELECTRIC LIGHT & POWER CO. OF BALTIMORE for the Approval of a Bill of Sale Dated November 15, 1919, for the Sale by the Two First-named Companies and the Purchase by the Last-named Company of Certain Poles, Together with All Anchors, Guys and Other Supports Thereto Attached, Located on the High-way in District No. 1, County of How-ard, State of Maryland.

Before the

Public Service Commission of Maryland.

Case No. 1743

The agreement of other written instrument evidencing the transaction in this case having been submitted to this Commission for the purpose of securing its consent to the consummation thereof and the Commission having determined that a hearing is unnecessary,

IT IS, THEREFORE, On this first day of December, in the year of 1919, by the Public Service Commission of Maryland,

Ordered, That the consent of this Commission be and the same is hereby given to the disposition of the property described in said agreement, or other written instrument, evidencing the transaction in accordance with the terms outlined therein.

ORDER No. 5225

In the Matter of

The Application of AMERICAN TELEPHONE
& TELEGRAPH CO., AMERICAN TELE-
PHONE & TELEGRAPH CO. OF BALTIMORE
CITY and THE CHESAPEAKE & POTOMAC
TELEPHONE COMPANY OF BALTIMORE
CITY for the Approval of a Bill of Sale
Dated November 15, 1919, for the Sale
by the Two First-named Companies
and the Purchase by the Last-named
Company of Certain Poles, Together
with All Anchors, Guys and Other
Supports Thereto Attached, Located on
the Highway in District No. 1, County
of Howard, State of Maryland.

Before the

Public Service Commission
of Maryland.

Case No. 1744

The agreement or other written instrument evidencing the transaction in this case having been submitted to this Commission for the
purpose of securing its consent to the consummation thereof and the
Commission having determined that a hearing is unnecessary.

IT IS, THEREFORE, On this first day of December, in the year of 1919,
by the Public Service Commission of Maryland,

𝔒𝔯𝔡𝔢𝔯𝔢𝔡, That the consent of this Commission be and the same is
hereby given to the disposition of the property described in said agreement, or other written instrument, evidencing the transaction in
accordance with the terms outlined therein.

ORDER No. 5226

In the Matter of

The Petition of the Railroads in the State
of Maryland for Permission Under
Section 15 of the PUBLIC SERVICE COM-
MISSION LAW to File and Publish on
Less Than Statutory Notice Tariffs
Restoring the Relationships Between
Points and Rate Groups Which Existed
Prior to June 25th, 1918, in Connection
with Railroads Not Under Federal
Control.

Before the

Public Service Commission
of Maryland.

S. N. & R. Docket

Case No. 582

The above mentioned petition having been received and filed, upon
consideration thereof, it is this 2nd day of December, 1919, by the
Public Service Commission of Maryland,

𝔒𝔯𝔡𝔢𝔯𝔢𝔡, That permission be, and is hereby given, the railroads in the State of Maryland to file and publish on one day's notice to the Commission and the public, tariffs to become effective on or before December 31st, 1919, restoring the relationships between points and rate groups which existed prior to June 25th, 1919, in connection with railroads not under Federal control.

PROVIDED, Said tariffs be filed with the Commission upon issuance of this Order, and published by posting as required by law, and that all copies of said tariffs shall bear the following notation:

> "Issued under special permission of the Public Service Commission of Maryland, Order No. 5226 of date December 2nd, 1919."

AND IT IS FURTHER 𝔒𝔯𝔡𝔢𝔯𝔢𝔡, That by passing this order the Public Service Commission is not to be taken as in any sense whatever approving any rates that may be filed under the authority of this order; all such rates being left as fully subject to investigation and correction on complaint, or on the Commission's own motion under the provisions of the Public Service Commission Law as if this order had never been passed.

ORDER No. 5228

In the Matter of	
The Application of CONSOLIDATED GAS ELECTRIC LIGHT AND POWER COMPANY OF BALTIMORE for the Approval of an Agreement Between It and THE CHESAPEAKE AND POTOMAC TELEPHONE COMPANY OF BALTIMORE CITY, for the Sale by the Former to the Latter of One Pole Located on the West Side of Harford Avenue, Forty-eight Feet North of the North Curb Line of Monument Street, Baltimore, Maryland, Under Terms and Provisions of Order No. 2954, Entered July 26th, 1916, in Case No. 1151.	Before the Public Service Commission of Maryland. Case No. 1745

The agreement or other written instrument evidencing the transaction in this case having been submitted to this Commission for the purpose of securing its consent to the consummation thereof and the Commission having determined that a hearing is unnecessary,

IT IS, THEREFORE, On this fourth day of December, in the year 1919, by the Public Service Commission,

Ordered, That the consent of this Commission be and the same is hereby given to the disposition of the property described in said agreement, or other written instrument, evidencing the transaction in accordance with the terms outlined therein.

ORDER No. 5231.

In the Matter of	
The Application of PENINSULA FERRY CORPORATION for an Order Permitting and Approving the Exercise of Its Franchise Under Its Certificate of Incorporation and for Authority to Issue $100,000.00, Par Value, of Its Preferred Stock and $150,000.00, Par Value, of Its Common Stock, Proceeds from the Sale of Said Stocks to be Used for the Purchase of Property, the Construction and Equipment of Terminal Facilities and for Other Lawful and Necessary Corporate Purposes.	Before the Public Service Commission of Maryland. Case No. 1704.

WHEREAS, The Peninsula Ferry Corporation, a body corporate organized under the laws of the State of Maryland, has applied to this Commission for an order permitting and approving the exercise of the franchise granted it by its certificate of incorporation, a certified copy of which is filed in these proceedings, which franchises include the right to operate boats or ferry boats between points in the State of Maryland, and for authority to issue eleven thousand seven hundred and fifty (11,750) shares of its common capital stock of the par value of Five Dollars ($5.00) per share, and one thousand (1,000) shares of its 7 per cent. cumulative preferred stock of the par value of one hundred dollars ($100.00) per share; and

WHEREAS, The amended application having come on to be heard on December 8th, 1919, in accordance with this Commission's Order No. 5227 passed December 4th, 1919, and it being the opinion and finding of the Commission after due hearing that the exercise of said franchises, in so far as same at this time embrace and contemplate the operation of a ferry boat or boats between Baltimore, Maryland, and Love Point, Maryland, is convenient for the public service, and that the use of the capital to be secured by the issue of said stock is reasonably required for the purposes of said corporation, to wit: the acquisition of property and the construction, completion, extension and improvement of its facilities,

IT IS, THEREFORE, This 9th day of December, in the year Nineteen Hundred and Nineteen, by the Public Service Commission of Maryland,

𝔒𝔯𝔡𝔢𝔯𝔢𝔡, (1) That the exercise by the Peninsula Ferry Corporation of the franchises granted it under its certificate of incorporation, in so far as same at this time embrace and contemplate the operation of a ferry boat or boats between Baltimore, Maryland, and Love Point, Maryland, be and the same is hereby permitted and approved.

(2) That the issue by the said Peninsula Ferry Corporation of eleven thousand seven hundred and fifty (11,750) shares of its common capital stock of the par value of Five Dollars ($5.00) per share, and one thousand (1,000) shares of its 7 per cent. cumulative preferred stock of the par value of One Hundred Dollars ($100.00) per share be and the same is hereby authorized and approved; four thousand (4,000) shares of said common capital stock to be sold for cash at not less than Two Dollars ($2.00) per share, and the remaining seven thousand seven hundred and fifty (7,750) shares of said common capital stock to be delivered to the several parties specified in the amended application in payment for a certain lease assigned to the said Peninsula Ferry Corporation and in further payment of expense of legal services and other expenses incident to the promotion and organization of the applicant company, all as more particularly set forth and described in the application herein; said 7 per cent. cumulative preferred stock to be sold for cash at not less than par with such allowance for commissions as may be necessary, provided the net amount realized by the said Peninsula Ferry Corporation shall be not less than 90 per cent. of the par value of said stock.

(3) That the said Peninsula Ferry Corporation shall make reports, duly verified by affidavits, to this Commission as follows:

(a) Upon the sale for cash of its common and preferred stock, authorized as aforesaid, or the delivery of its common capital stock, authorized to the extent above set forth, or any part thereof, the fact of such sale or sales or delivery in payment for property or services, the terms and conditions thereof, and the amount realized therefrom.

(b) At the termination of each and every period of six months from the date of this order, the disposition and use made of the proceeds of said stock, and the facts and circumstances as to the property acquired and the construction, completion, extension and improvement of its facilities.

ORDER No. 5232.

In the Matter of

The Discontinuance of the Presstman
Street Jerkwater Service by THE
UNITED RAILWAYS AND ELECTRIC COM-
PANY OF BALTIMORE.

Before the

Public Service Commission
of Maryland.

WHEREAS, The United Railways and Electric Company of Baltimore
having petitioned this Commission for an order permitting and approving the discontinuance of the operation of the line known as the
"Presstman Street Jerkwater" now operated by said company in the
City of Baltimore, and said petition having been referred to the
Transportation Expert of the Commission for investigation and report
and the Commission's Transportation Expert having reported to the
Commission that the operation of this line entails a considerable
expense to the railways company with no commensurate advantage
to the traveling public, in that the territory served by said line is
adequately provided for by means of other lines of the railways company; and

WHEREAS, It being the opinion and finding of the Commission after
due consideration that the operation of said Presstman Street Jerk-
water line is no longer reasonably necessary and convenient for the
public service,

IT IS, THEREFORE, This 9th day of December, in the year Nineteen
Hundred and Nineteen, by the Public Service Commission of Maryland,

Ordered, That the discontinuance of the operation of the Presstman Street Jerkwater line by The United Railways and Electric Company of Baltimore be and it is hereby permitted and approved, effective on and after December 14th, 1919.

ORDER No. 5234.

In the Matter of

The Petition of the Carriers Not Under
Federal Control Named in the Official
Classification, by R. N. COLLYER, Their
Agent, for Permission Under Section
15 of the Public Service Commission
Law to File and Publish on Less Than
Statutory Notice Supplement to Con-
solidated Freight Classification No. 1.

Before the

Public Service Commission
of Maryland.

S. N. & R. Docket.

Case No. 583.

The above mentioned petition having been received and filed, upon
consideration thereof, it is this 12th day of December, 1919, by the
Public Service Commission of Maryland,

Ordered, That permission be, and is hereby given, the carriers not under Federal control named in the Official Classification, by R. N. Collyer, their Agent, to file and publish on one day's notice to the Commission and the public, supplement to Consolidated Freight Classification No. 1, P. S. C. Md., O. C. No 45, to become effective December 30th, 1919, containing various changes in said Consolidated Classification No 45 authorized by the Interstate Commerce Commission on one day's notice, so far as same affect interstate traffic.

PROVIDED, Said supplement be filed with the Commission upon issuance of this Order, and published by posting as required by law, and that all copies of said supplement shall bear the following notation:

"Issued under special permission of the Public Service Commission of Maryland, Order No. 5234 of date December 12th, 1919."

ORDER No. 5235.

In the Matter of

The Application of RICHARD MACSHERRY for a Permit for the Operation of a Motor Vehicle Line Between Baltimore and Easton, Maryland, Via Annapolis and Claiborne Ferry with Feeders to Various Points.

Before the

Public Service Commission of Maryland.

Case No. 1651.

Upon the order of the applicant this day filed herein it is, this 16th day of December, in the year Nineteen Hundred and Nineteen, by the Public Service Commission of Maryland,

Ordered, That the application in the above entitled matter be and the same is hereby dismissed.

ORDER No. 5236.

In the Matter of

The Application of THE CHESAPEAKE AND POTOMAC TELEPHONE COMPANY OF BALTIMORE CITY and the COMMISSIONERS OF ST. MICHAELS for the Approval of a Bill of Sale, Dated November 18th, 1919, for the Sale by the Former to the Latter of Certain Poles, Together with All Anchor Guys and Other Supports Thereto Attached, Located on the State Road, Between St. Michaels and Easton, in Districts Numbers 1 and 2, Talbot County, Maryland.

Before the

Public Service Commission of Maryland.

Case No. 1747.

The agreement or other written instrument evidencing the transaction in this case having been submitted to this Commission for the purpose of securing its consent to the consummation thereof and the Commission having determined that a hearing is unnecessary,

IT IS, THEREFORE, On this sixteenth day of December, in the year of 1919, by the Public Service Commission of Maryland,

Ordered, That the consent of this Commission be and the same is hereby given to the disposition of the property described in said agreement, or other written instrument, evidencing the transaction in accordance with the terms outlined therein.

ORDER No. 5237.

In the Matter of

The Application of THE AMERICAN TEL-
EPHONE AND TELEGRAPH COMPANY OF
BALTIMORE CITY and THE CHESAPEAKE
AND POTOMAC TELEPHONE COMPANY OF
BALTIMORE CITY for the Approval of a
Bill of Sale, Dated November 17th,
1919, for the Sale by the Former and
the Purchase by the Latter of Certain
Poles Located on Dilley Alley in the
City of Cumberland, Allegany County,
Maryland, Under the Terms and Provi-
sions of Order No. 2913, Entered June
20th, 1916, in Case No. 1131.

Before the

Public Service Commission
of Maryland.

Case No. 1748.

The agreement or other written instrument evidencing the transaction in this case having been submitted to this Commission for the
purpose of securing its consent to the consummation thereof and the
Commission having determined that a hearing is unnecessary,

It Is, THEREFORE, On this seventeenth day of December, in the year
of 1919, by the Public Service Commission of Maryland,

Ordered, That the consent of this Commission be and the same is
hereby given to the disposition of the property described in said agreement, or other written instrument, evidencing the transaction in
accordance with the terms outlined therein.

OPINION.

In the Matter of

The Complaint of STANDARD ELECTRIC &
ELEVATOR COMPANY, INC.,

vs.

THE CHESAPEAKE AND POTOMAC TEL-
EPHONE COMPANY OF BALTIMORE CITY.

Before the

Public Service Commission
of Maryland.

Case No. 1708.

Appearances:

Charles S. Hayden, Esq., Counsel for Complainant.
Frankland Briggs, Esq., Counsel for Respondent.

By the Commission.   Filed December 18th, 1919.

The complainant is a corporation, with offices, factories and ware-
houses in Baltimore City, engaged in the business of selling and

installing elevators, electric motors, etc., and conducting a general electrical contracting and repairing business. The complaint in this case involves the rules of the respondent governing the listing of telephone subscribers in Baltimore City in the directory published by the telephone company. The complaint is most general in terms, though the points in controversy have been ultimately narrowed down to the reasonableness of the practice of the respondent company in limiting the free listing of telephone subscribers to but one heading in the classified business section of the telephone directory, and the interpretation of the respondent's rules governing listings in the alphabetical section of the directory.

In an effort to clarify the matter in controversy and if possible to reconcile the differences between the complainant and the respondent, the Commission arranged an informal conference with representatives of both parties at the Commission's offices, but was unsuccessful in its efforts to effect an amicable settlement of the matter and the case came on for hearing September 16th, 1919. At the hearing there developed a marked difference of opinion between the complainant and the respondent as to the interpretation of the rules of respondent governing the matter of directory listings, but without reviewing in detail the testimony produced at this hearing, it will suffice to say that the Commission concludes that the rules of respondent company filed with it concerning directory listings have no application to the classified business section of the directory, and that the rules covering alphabetical listings have been properly applied in the present issue of the telephone directory, so far as the listings accorded the complainant are concerned.

The practice of the telephone company at the present time is to permit but one listing in the classified section of the directory without charge, additional listings under other business designations being charged for at the rate of $6.00 per annum. The Commission is of the opinion that so long as the classified or advertising section of the directory is maintained it constitutes an integral and important part of the telephone directory and that the respondent should formulate and file with the Commission rules governing listings in such section and that when such rules have been so filed they will be and remain fully subject to the jurisdiction of the Commission, the Commission having heretofore in the complaint of the Suburban Developers' Association vs. The Chesapeake and Potomac Telephone Company of Baltimore City (P. S. C. Md. Reports, Vol. III, p. 273) asserted its jurisdiction with respect to listings and classifications in the telephone directory. The Commission is further of the opinion that free listings in the classified or advertising section of the directory should to a reasonable degree be determined on the basis of the measure of service contracted for by subscribers, and will require that such rules be filed with it for its approval. The complainant is engaged in several distinct lines of work, and despite the fact that it contracts for twelve trunk lines, with numerous stations, and pays the respondent from $200.00 to $250.00 per month for telephone service (as testified to at the hearing), the present practice restricts it to but one free listing in the classified section of the directory, regardless of the fact that there is no one business classification which embraces the several fields of its operations. The Commission recognizes the importance and desirability of keeping down the size of the directory within reasonable limits, but believes that this purpose can be accomplished without hardship by means of reasonable rules drafted along the lines indicated. The Commission finds that the present rules of the respondent filed with it governing the alphabetical listing of subscribers adequately provide for all reasonable requirements of such subscribers and at this time will require no change in such rules.

An order will be entered in accordance with these conclusions.

ORDER No. 5250.

In the Matter of	
The Complaint of STANDARD ELECTRIC & ELEVATOR COMPANY, INC.,	Before the
	Public Service Commission
vs.	of Maryland.
THE CHESAPEAKE AND POTOMAC TELEPHONE COMPANY OF BALTIMORE CITY.	Case No. 1708.

This case being at issue upon complaints and answers on file and having been duly heard and submitted by the parties and full investigation of the matters and things involved having been had, and the Commission, on the date hereof, having rendered and filed an opinion containing its findings of fact and conclusion therein, which said opinion is hereby referred to and made a part hereof,

It Is, THEREFORE, This 18th day of December, in the year Nineteen Hundred and Nineteen, by the Public Service Commission of Maryland,

Ordered, That the respondent, The Chesapeake and Potomac Telephone Company of Baltimore City, be and it is hereby directed and required to file with this Commission within twenty days of the date hereof, rules governing listings of subscribers in the classified or advertising section of said directory, which said rules shall provide free listings in said section of the telephone directory, depending upon the measure of service contracted for by subscribers, and which said rules, if approved by the Commission, shall be made applicable to the next telephone directory of Baltimore City issued after the date of such approval.

ORDER No. 5260.

In the Matter of

The Petition of F. S. DAVIS, Agent, for and on Behalf of Non-Federal Controlled Carriers and Federal Controlled Carriers in Connection with Non-Federal Controlled Carriers in the State of Maryland for Permission Under Section 15 of the Public Service Commission Law to File and Publish on Less Than Statutory Notice Exceptions to Consolidated Classification No. 1, P. S. C. Md., O. C. No. 45.

Before the

Public Service Commission of Maryland.

S. N. & R. Docket.

Case No. 584.

The above mentioned petition having been received and filed, upon consideration thereof, it is this 19th day of December, 1919, by the Public Service Commission of Maryland,

Ordered, That permission be, and is hereby given, F. S. Davis, Agent, for and on behalf of non-Federal controlled carriers and Federal controlled carriers in connection with non-Federal controlled carriers in the State of Maryland, to file and publish on one day's notice to the Commission and the public, exceptions to Consolidated Classification No. 1, P. S. C. Md., O. C. No. 45, permitting shipments of grain, grain byproducts, grain products, hay, straw, lumber, etc., to be consigned "to order" at one point and notify party located at another point, and publishing the gross ton or 2,240 pounds on the basis of net ton and minimum weights as shown in Exhibit A filed with said petition,

PROVIDED, Tariffs containing said changes be filed with the Commission upon issuance of this Order, and published by posting as required by law, and that all copies of said tariffs shall bear the following notation:

"Issued under special permission of the Public Service Commission of Maryland, Order No. 5260 of date December 19th, 1919."

ORDER No. 5261.

In the Matter of

The Petition of the Carriers Named in the Official Classification, by R. N. COLLYER, Their Agent, for Permission Under Section 15 of the Public Service Commission Law to File and Publish on Less Than Statutory Notice Supplements to and Reissues of Consolidated Classification No. 1, P. S. C. Md., O. C. No. 45, Covering Maryland Intrastate Traffic Under the Same Conditions That the Interstate Commerce Commission May Authorize Such Publication for Interstate Traffic.

Before the

Public Service Commission of Maryland.

S. N. & R. Docket.

Case No. 585.

The above mentioned petition having been received and filed, upon consideration thereof, it is this 19th day of December, 1919, by the Public Service Commission of Maryland,

Ordered, That until otherwise ordered by this Commission, permission be, and is hereby given, the carriers named in the Official Classification, by R. N. Collyer, their Agent, to file and publish supplements to and reissues of Consolidated Classification No. 1, P. S. C. Md., O. C. No. 45, covering Maryland intrastate traffic under the same conditions that the Interstate Commerce Commission may authorize such publication for interstate traffic,

PROVIDED, That all classifications and supplements issued under authority of this special permission be filed with the Commission upon issuance, and published by posting as required by law, and that all copies of said classifications and supplements shall bear the following notation:

> "Issued under special permission of the Public Service Commission of Maryland, Order No. 5261 of date December 19th, 1919."

AND IT IS FURTHER **Ordered,** That by passing this order the Public Service Commission is not to be taken as in any sense whatever approving any classifications, rates, rules or regulations that may be filed under the authority of this order; all such classifications, rates, rules and regulations being left as fully subject to investigation and correction on complaint, or on the Commission's own motion, under the provisions of the Public Service Commission Law as if this order had never been passed.

ORDER No. 5262.

In the Matter of	
The Petition of KENSINGTON RAILWAY COMPANY and SANDY SPRINGS RAILWAY COMPANY for Authority to File and Publish a Schedule of Joint and Local Rates of Fare.	Before the Public Service Commission of Maryland. Case No. 1739.

WHEREAS, The Kensington Railway Company having petitioned this Commission for a modification of the Commission's Order No. 3632 entered in Case No. 1290 on May 5th, 1917, (as heretofore modified by the Commission's Order No. 4568 entered in Case No. 1593 on December 19th, 1918) so as to permit the said Kensington Railway Company to increase its rates of fare to the extent proposed in that company's rate schedule P. S. C. Md. No. 7 submitted with said petition; and

WHEREAS, The matter having come on to be heard on December 9th, 1919, in accordance with this Commission's Order No. 5202 entered on November 21st, 1919, and it appearing that the operations of said Kensington Railway Company during the eleven months ended November 30th, 1919, have resulted in a deficit of $695.89, after providing for operating expenses, taxes, depreciation and interest on funded debt; and

WHEREAS, It being the opinion and finding of the Commission after consideration of the entire record now before it, including brief submitted by the Town of Kensington, Maryland, by W. B. Pugh, Acting Mayor, protesting against the increase in rates of fare herein sought, that the rates of fare charged by the Kensington Railway Company should properly be increased to the basis herein prayed, in order to provide more adequately for the proper corporate requirements of said company.

IT IS, THEREFORE, This 19th day of December, in the year Nineteen Hundred and Nineteen, by the Public Service Commission of Maryland, Ordered, That the petitioner, Kensington Railway Company, be and it is hereby authorized and permitted to increase the rates of fare charged by said petitioner for transportation over its line of railway on and after December 22nd, 1919, to the following basis:

Between Chevy Chase Lake and North Chevy Chase—One-way fare, 6 cents; round trip, 10 cents; 12-ride tickets, 55 cents; 50-ride tickets, $2.10.

Between Chevy Chase Lake and end of Kensington Railway—One-way fare, 7 cents; round trip, 12 cents; 12-ride tickets, 70 cents; 50-ride tickets, $2.50.

IT IS FURTHER 𝔒𝔯𝔡𝔢𝔯𝔢𝔡, That this Commission's Order No. 3632 aforesaid entered on May 5th, 1917, in Case No. 1290 (as modified by the Commission's Order No. 4586 aforesaid entered in Case No. 1593 on December 19th, 1918) be and it is hereby modified so as to permit the change in rates by first paragraph of this order authorized, and to that extent only.

ORDER No. 5270.

In the Matter of

The Petition of F. S. DAVIS, Agent, for and on Behalf of Non-Federal Controlled Carriers and Federal Controlled Carriers in Connection with Non-Federal Controlled Carriers in the State of Maryland for Permission Under Section 15 of the Public Service Commission Law to File and Publish on Less Than Statutory Notice Rules, Regulations and Charges Governing the Handling and Transportation of Live Stock.

Before the

Public Service Commission of Maryland.

S. N. & R. Docket.

Case No. 586.

The above mentioned petition having been received and filed upon consideration thereof, it is this 22nd day of December, 1919, by the Public Service Commission of Maryland,

𝔒𝔯𝔡𝔢𝔯𝔢𝔡, That permission be, and is hereby given, F. S. Davis, Agent, for and on behalf of non-Federal controlled carriers and Federal controlled carriers in connection with non-Federal controlled carriers in the State of Maryland to file and publish on one day's notice to the Commission and the public, rules, regulations and charges governing the handling and transportation of live stock, as set forth in petitioner's Exhibit "A" filed herein, the Commission also hereby waiving its tariff rules respecting supplemental requirements and the showing of symbols indicating increases and reductions in rates and charges, so far as tariffs and supplements filed with it under authority of this Order are concerned,

PROVIDED, Said tariffs and supplements be filed with the Commission upon issuance of this Order, and published by posting as required by law, and that all copies of said tariffs and supplements shall bear the following notation:

"Issued under special permission of the Public Service Commission of Maryland, Order No. 5270 of date December 22nd, 1919."

AND IT IS FURTHER **Ordered**, That by passing this Order the Public Service Commission is not to be taken as in any sense whatever approving any rules, regulations or charges that may be filed under the authority of this Order; all such rules, regulations and charges being left as fully subject to investigation and correction on complaint, or on the Commission's own motion, under the provisions of the Public Service Commission Law, as if this Order had never been passed.

ORDER No. 5302.

In the Matter of

The Application of WASHINGTON, BALTIMORE AND ANNAPOLIS ELECTRIC RAILROAD COMPANY for an Order Permitting and Approving the Construction of a Side Track Connecting with Its North-Bound Main Track South of Bell Station.

Before the

Public Service Commission of Maryland.

Case No. 1750.

WHEREAS, It appears from the petition and exhibit filed in the above entitled matter that the proposed construction of a side track is necessary and convenient for the public service, and

WHEREAS, The Commission being of the opinion that said construction is not a matter of such character as requires the same to be set for formal hearing,

IT IS, THEREFORE, This twenty-ninth day of December, 1919, by the Public Service Commission of Maryland,

Ordered, That the construction of the said side track, as set forth in said petition, be, and it is hereby permitted and approved.

OPINION

In the Matter of

THE UNITED RAILWAYS AND ELECTRIC COMPANY OF BALTIMORE for a Modification of Certain Orders Now in Force Fixing the Rates of Fare to Be Charged by Said Company and for Permission to File, Publish and Put in Effect a New Schedule of Rates of Fare, Increasing Existing Rates, as Set Forth in This Petition.

Before the

Public Service Commission of Maryland.

Case No. 1682.

Appearances:

MESSRS. JOSEPH C. FRANCE, EDWIN G. BAETJER and W. H. MALTBIE, representing The United Railways and Electric Company of Baltimore;

JOSEPH S. GOLDSMITH, ESQ., Assistant General Counsel, representing the Public Service Commission of Maryland.

By the Commission.   Filed December 31, 1919.

On October 1, 1918, all fares of The United Railways and Electric Company of Baltimore were increased one cent each, the only exception being on the Curtis Bay line of said Company, on which line the railway company had theretofore issued a three-cent continuous fare ticket, which was withdrawn on that date, with the result that persons transferring to or from this line were required to pay two cash fares of six cents each, or twelve cents for the ride formerly costing but eight cents. On January 7, 1919, the Commission filed its opinion and entered its order in Cases Nos. 1568 and 1583, in which it upheld the reasonableness of the increased fares, save the fare on the Curtis Bay line, on which line it required the railway company to restore the sale of continuous fare tickets at the rate of four cents each.

Thereafter the railway company petitioned the Commission for a further increase in fares, and on September 30, 1919, the Commission filed its opinion and entered its Order in Case No. 1682, permitting an increase in the adult cash fare from six cents to six and one-half cents when tickets or fare checks were purchased in lots of four, or seven cents cash fare. No increase was permitted in the fares charged children or commutation fares. The increase allowed by the Commission was somewhat less than that sought by the railway company, it being the contention of the company that a fare of seven and one-half cents was essential if it was to continue rendering adequate service to the public it served, and if it was to preserve its credit so that it might attract the necessary capital required to provide for additions to and improvements in its service requisite to meet the growing demands of the community which it serves.

On December 26, 1919, the railway company petitioned the Commission for a further increase in the adult cash fare to seven cents straight, and this application came on to be heard on December 30.

A complete history of the railway company and of its operations has heretofore been given in the opinions of the Commission above mentioned, and the attitude of the Commission with respect to the needs and requirements of said company has been discussed at considerable length in such opinions, as well as in supplemental opinion filed in Case No. 1682 on November 29, 1919.

The previous hearings of the Commission upon the several applications of the railway company for fare increases were most exhaustive, and the records in those cases constitute a thorough history of the financial situation of the company. Paragraphs 5 and 6 of the Commission's Order No. 5120 entered in Case No. 1682 on September 30, 1919, provide as follows:

> "That The United Railways and Electric Company of Baltimore shall furnish to this Commission accurate and complete statements under oath, and in convenient form, setting forth the number of revenue and transfer passengers carried, and the number of car miles operated, the cash receipts from operation and other sources, and the operating and other expenditures of the company, all set forth in the manner prescribed by the rules of this Commission for accounting by street railway companies, so soon as may be reasonably practicable and convenient after the end of each calendar month during the period this order remains effective, and in no event later than the last day of the next succeeding calendar month, covering the operations of the company during the next preceding month.

> "That the right of the respondent company to charge and collect the fares in this order prescribed shall be held subject at all times during the period covered by such order, or any extension thereof which may hereafter be granted as aforesaid, to the right and power of this Commission to reopen this case in the light of the facts disclosed by the monthly reports aforesaid, or of other facts otherwise coming to the attention of this Commission, and modify the rates of fare by this order authorized to be charged and collected by the respondent company."

In its opinion filed on the same day the Commission said:

> "It is to be understood by all concerned that our order passed pursuant to this opinion is so far tentative that it can be reopened at any time within such twelve months upon the evidence adduced in this and the previous case and the

, monthly reports which will be furnished under oath by the company as above stated.

"In other words, there will be no necessity during the coming year at least for any lengthy formal hearing upon applications for either the increase or decrease of the fares established by our order.

"The Commission now has before it the complete operating figures of this company for a period of approximately seven years, and there is now no necessity for further details as to such operations in the past or for further estimates of probable future operating results, except in so far as the estimates contained in this opinion may require modification from time to time by reason of actual results.

"If it should happen that the experience of several months under the new rates should demonstrate that the company is earning a larger net revenue than is anticipated by this order, and that there is a reasonable probability that such excess earnings during the course of the year would be such as to justify some reduction in the base rate of fare, the Commission will, of its own motion, require the company to show cause why such decrease should not be made.

"If, on the other hand, such reports, upon thorough investigation by the Accounting Department of the Commission and by the members of the Commission itself, should demonstrate that the company is earning materially less than we now anticipate it will earn under such rates, the company will be permitted to make an application for their increase, with the understanding that the Commission will confine the hearings upon such application, as far as it can reasonably do so under the law, to the precise issue of the rate necessary to yield approximately the net balance to surplus which we have declared a reasonable one for the company to earn during the period of the next twelve months."

The application now before the Commission is filed under the above quoted provisions of the Commission's opinion and order, and the issue is thereby confined to the question of the rate of fare necessary to provide a balance to surplus of approximately One Million Dollars during the ensuing year, which amount the Commission has heretofore found to be reasonable during such period.

The monthly reports of the company's earnings and expenses required by the Commission's Order No. 5120 have been duly filed with the Commission, the balance to surplus during October and November, 1919 (the first two months of operation under the present fare) being $18,124 and $36,991, respectively, while the average pre-war surplus during the corresponding months is shown to be $86,309 and $57,873, respectively.

The following facts are set forth in the petition of the railway company in justification of the increase in fares now sought:

1. The Commission estimated that but 70.833 per cent. of the total number of passengers would avail themselves of the privilege of buying fare checks, whereas during the first twenty-three days of December the actual figure was 89.56 per cent., which larger use of fare checks results in a shortage in income of approximately $200,000 for a year.

2. The tax rate of the City of Baltimore has been increased from the 1919 rate of $2.01 per hundred to $2.97 in 1920, with increases in the new annex and rural rates from $1.206 to $1.84 and from 67 cents to 99 cents, respectively, entailing an additional expenditure during the year upon the part of the company of $109,598.45.

3. The company paid $66,000 to the City of Baltimore for duct rentals during the year 1919, while under a pending ordinance of the Mayor and City Council of Baltimore the rental will be increased to $118,800 per annum, or $52,800 in excess of the 1919 figure.

4. An increase in the price of coal involving an additional expenditure of $20,000 per annum, with the likelihood of a further and substantial increase in the price of fuel in the near future.

5. An increase in the cost of supplies used by the company of from $75,000 to $100,000 per annum above the prices paid for similar quantities of such articles used during the current year.

6. The necessity of making some allowance to the company's platform employees for time consumed in taking cars to and from car barns, which will involve an additional payment of $91,250 per annum.

7. The need for setting aside a greater depreciation reserve than has been provided for, it having been previously shown that the cost of labor and materials used in maintenance and replacement work has increased 101 per cent. over the 1916 cost, and that if the depreciation appropriation for 1916 is increased by 101 per cent. and a reasonable depreciation allowance made on the capital additions since 1916, the depreciation reserve for 1920 will be $454,311 in excess of the Commission's estimate of $710,370 for 1919.

At the hearing upon this petition the petitioner produced its president, C. D. Emmons, as a witness to substantiate the statements of the company respecting the increased expenditures which it will be obliged to provide for during the ensuing year, as well as the need for a greater depreciation reserve, and Mr. Emmons introduced and filed with the Commission various exhibits in support of the claims of his company.

Some of these items of additional expense have already been encountered by the company, and the others are almost certain to be realized. It is impossible to foretell to what extent some of the items will still further increase, this having particular reference to the price of coal. We are all aware that a body appointed by the President of the United States is shortly to take up the question of the relations existing between the coal miners and the coal operators, and if as a result of this investigation the wages of the miners are again increased, the burden of such increase will in all probability come to be borne by the coal consuming public, including the petitioner.

The Commission is not prepared at this time to accept the claim of the railway company that its depreciation reserve should be increased in order to meet the increased cost of renewing and replacing property in kind. The contention of the railway company involves a distinct departure from the long established practice with respect to the handling of this matter, the accounting rules of this Commission, as well as the accounting rules of most other regulatory bodies (so far as the Commission is informed) providing that the difference between the original cost and the cost of renewal or replacement, where such latter cost is higher, should be charged to capital account. But the Commission does not feel that it is necessary for it in the present proceedings to pass upon the broader question of depreciation which is presented by the company's petition. Nor does the Commission find that it is necessary for the purposes of this case to attempt to indicate what, in its judgment, would be the proper amounts, or even the maximum amounts, which the railway company should be permitted to expend for maintenance, and set aside as a depreciation reserve. The conditions surrounding the cost of both wages and material are too unsettled to warrant any conclusion which might be construed to be the adoption of anything like a fixed or permanent policy with reference to either maintenance or depreciation. But dealing with the present situation with which the railway is now confronted, the Commission finds that under existing conditions, which conditions are likely to continue at least during the ensuing year, the total amount which the company claims it will require for maintenance and depreciation does not appear to be unreasonable, when consideration is given to the amount of maintenance and renewal work now being done by the company, and which it will have to continue for a considerable period of time in order to get its property in condition to render the best possible service to the community which it serves; nor does such total allowance appear unreasonable when compared with similar allowances of other railway companies, such comparison being made on a car-mile basis.

As before shown, the balance to surplus after the payment of operating expenses, taxes and fixed charges during the months of October and November aggregated $55,115, and the December balance is estimated to be about $30,000, or about $85,000 for three months' operations at the present rate of fare. The increase in the tax rate, the higher conduit rental, the known increase in the price of coal, the increase in the cost of supplies, the allowance to platform employees for time consumed in taking cars to and from car barns, and additional fixed charges of approximately $120,000 per annum, when taken together, will be sufficient to reduce the balance to surplus likely to accrue during the ensuing year at the present rate of fare to an almost negligible amount, and unless there is a material increase in traffic, will be sufficient to wipe out completely any possible surplus. The company's balance to surplus during the current year will be $161,594, using the estimated figure of $30,000 for December. This is the lowest balance to surplus earned in any of the years since 1912, as shown by the following table:

BALANCE TO SURPLUS BY YEARS

Year	Balance
1912	$678,042
1913	972,322
1914	819,368
1915	819,368
1916	1,108,124
1917	875,587
1918	332,652
1919	*161,594

*December estimated.

It is impracticable to attempt to project the earning for 1919 into 1920 on the basis of the balance to surplus shown for 1919, as the wage increase of August 17, 1919 (involving an additional expenditure of over $800,000 per annum) and the present rate of fare, which became effective on October 1, 1919, have been in effect for but a portion of the year. On the basis of the number of riders during the year 1919, the straight fare of seven cents will produce additional revenue over the present fare of seven sents each with 6½ cent tickets (90 per cent. tickets, 10 per cent. cash fares) of about $950,000 for the year, after deduction of Park Tax, and if there is an increase of 7 per cent. in the traffic of the company in the year the additional revenue produced by the increase in fare will be approximately $1,025,000, the true figure probably being somewhere between these two.

After full consideration of all of the facts which have bearing on the matter, and having made a careful estimate of income and expenses for the ensuing year, the Commission is of the opinion that while the company might possibly be able to continue its operations on a rate of fare fractionally lower than the full increase now sought (though higher than the present rate of fare) the saving to the riding public through such fractional rate of fare would be very slight, while on the other hand it might prove to be the real balance between success and failure on the part of the company. Were the Commission to prescribe a rate of fare lower than that necessary to provide for the full reasonable needs of the company, the result might easily be that the company would again be compelled to struggle along as it has struggled since 1917; barely able to meet its pressing obligations, its credit impaired, and ultimately destroyed; unable to maintain its property or give the character of service rightfully and reasonably demanded by the public.

A tabulation of the difference in revenue obtained through the sale of fare checks at fractional fares shows that a reduction under the maximum fare of seven cents as slight as that obtained through the sale of eight fare checks for 55 cents, with only 70 per cent. of the riders availing themselves of the lower fare, would aggregate approximately $200,000 for the year, and to that extent cause a shortage in the balance to surplus of approximately $1,000,000 claimed by the company, and which balance the Commission has heretofore found to be reasonably necessary for the company's purposes.

The Commission has, therefore, concluded that the interests of the entire public will be served best by allowing the company to charge a rate of fare of seven cents, and its previous orders will be modified so as to permit such change to become effective on January 1, 1920. The present fares for children, as well as the present commutation book rates, will remain unchanged. The Commission will require the railway company to continue furnishing monthly statements showing the results of its operations, so that the Commission will thereby be kept in close touch with the situation, and in a position to take any further action in the premises which may seem warranted.

The Commission has the assurance of the railway company that a straight fare of seven cents will enable it to meet its financial requirements, secure needed equipment, get its roadbed and equipment in good operating condition and meet every reasonable demand for adequate service, and the Commission in permitting the increase prayed for is taking the company at its word, and will require the company to fulfill promptly its promise of improved service.

An order will be passed in accordance with the conclusions herein.

ORDER No. 5327.

In the Matter of

The Petition of THE UNITED RAILWAYS
AND ELECTRIC COMPANY OF BALTIMORE
for a Modification of Certain Orders,
Now in Force, Fixing the Rates of
Fare to be Charged by Said Company,
and for Permission to File, Publish and
Put in Effect a New Schedule of Rates
of Fare, Increasing Existing Rates, as
Set Forth in This Petition.

Before the

Public Service Commission
of Maryland.

Case No. 1682.

Pursuant to the conclusions reached in the aforegoing opinion, it is, this 31st day of December, in the year Nineteen Hundred and Nineteen, by the Public Service Commission of Maryland,

Ordered, 1. That except as to paragraph (1) thereof, Order No. 5120 entered by this Commission on September 30th, 1919, as modified and amended by Order No. 5223 entered on November 29th, 1919, be and it is hereby annulled and rescinded.

2. That on and after January 1st, 1920, and until midnight of December 31st, 1920, and for no longer, unless such period be extended for a further period as hereinafter provided, or this order be earlier modified or abrogated by further order of this Commission, The United Railways and Electric Company of Baltimore shall be permitted to charge and collect for the transportation of persons over its several street railway lines, in Baltimore City and vicinity, the following rates, fares and charges, to wit:

a) Seven cents fare for the conveyance of each passenger over twelve years of age, and four cents for each child between the ages of four and twelve years, on any of its lines between the points designated under the first general caption in its schedule P. S. C. Md. No. 8, filed with this Commission August 28th, 1918, effective October 1st, 1918, or between intermediate points, in either direction, on any of such lines, except in the case of its Curtis Bay line, on which line The United Railways and Electric Company of Baltimore shall issue transfers entitling the holder to a continuous ride on such line as such transfers were issued on and prior to September 30th, 1918, except that the charge for such transfers shall be four cents instead of three cents, as theretofore.

(b) Full-fare and half-fare continuous trip tickets, good as fare on connecting lines, to be sold on the lines and between the points, on the Company's Gorsuch Avenue, East Monument Street (Orangeville), Third and Eighth Streets, Union Avenue, South Charles Street, Walbrook-Hillsdale, Shore line and Ferry Bar lines, as designated in said schedule P. S. C. Md. No. 8, otherwise the regular fare to be collected between the points so designated.

(c) Four and one-half cents when paid by commutation tickets sold for use on the first county fare zone between the points so designated in the schedule P. S. C. Md. No. 8, aforesaid, and five cents when paid by commutation tickets sold for use on second and third county fare zones between the points so designated in said schedule, said commutation tickets to be sold in the manner and subject to the conditions set forth in said schedule with respect thereto, the full fare in each of said cases otherwise to be paid.

(d) Four and one-half cents between Sparrows Point and Dundalk and four and one-half cents between Dundalk and Highlandtown when paid by employee's tickets from 20-trip books sold in lots to the Maryland Steel Company for distribution; five cents between Dundalk and Highlandtown and five cents between Highlandtown and city points, when paid by strip tickets sold in lots to the Central Foundry Company for distribution; and two and one-half cents on the Lakeside line when paid by tickets from 200-trip books sold to the landowners along such line, all such tickets to be subject to the conditions printed thereon and to the rules of the Company governing the use thereof, the full fare in each of said cases otherwise to be paid.

3. That from and after the hour of midnight on the 31st of December, 1920, said company's right and privilege to charge and collect the increased fares authorized hereby shall cease and determine and said company shall thereupon put in force and effect, and maintain until thereafter lawfully changed, the schedule of fares operative on the 31st of December, 1919, unless this Commission or other lawful authority shall in the meantime have modified, extended or superseded this order; provided, however, that if this order has not been so extended or superseded, and there shall be pending on December 31st, 1920, an application by said company filed before November 30th, 1920, for a continuance in whole or in part of the relief hereby granted or for increased fares, then the right to collect the fares authorized by this order shall continue until the determination by the Commission of said pending proceedings; and provided, further, that in case of any proceeding hereafter instituted before the 31st day of December, 1920, for the right to charge and collect fares in excess of those in effect on the 31st of December, 1919, the burden of proving the reasonableness of any such excess fare shall be and remain on said company; provided, however, that nothing in this order shall be held to affect in any way the right of the company to proceed with the pending valuation to which said company is a party or its right of appeal from the finding or orders growing out of said valuation proceedings.

4. That the United Railways and Electric Company of Baltimore shall furnish to this Commission accurate and complete statements under oath, and in convenient form, setting forth the number of revenue and transfer passengers carried, and the number of car-miles

operated, the cash receipts from operation and other sources, and the operating and other expenditures of the Company, all set forth in the manner prescribed by the rules of this Commission for accounting by street railway companies, so soon as may be reasonably practicable and convenient after the end of each calendar month during the period this Order remains effective, and in no event later than the last day of the next succeeding calendar month, covering the operations of the Company during the next preceding month.

5. That the right of the respondent Company to charge and collect the fares in this order prescribed shall be held subject at all times during the period covered by such order, or any extension thereof which may hereafter be granted as aforesaid, to the right and power of this Commission to reopen this case in the light of the facts disclosed by the monthly reports aforesaid, or of other facts otherwise coming to the attention of this Commission, and modify the rates of fare by this order authorized to be charged and collected by the respondent Company.

AND IT IS FURTHER Ordered, That a copy of this order be forthwith served upon the proper officers of the respondent, The United Railways and Electric Company of Baltimore, and that said Company, within ten days from the date of the service of such copy, advise this Commission in writing whether or not it will accept and abide by the same.

ORDER No. 5328.

In the Matter of

The Petition of THE BALTIMORE TRANSIT COMPANY for Permission Under Section 15 of the Public Service Commission Law to File and Publish on Less Than Statutory Notice a Schedule of Rates Changing Its Rate of Fare from Six and One-Half Cents when Tickets or Fare Checks are Purchased, or Seven Cents Cash Fare, to Straight Fare of Seven Cents.

Before the

Public Service Commission of Maryland.

S. N. & R. Docket.

Case No. 587.

WHEREAS, The Baltimore Transit Company, a corporation organized under the laws of the State of Maryland and operating a line of passenger motor busses for the public use in the City of Baltimore, having petitioned this Commission for permission under Section 15 of the Public Service Commission Law to file and publish on less than statutory notice of thirty days a schedule of rates changing its rate of fare from six and one-half cents when tickets or fare checks are purchased in lots of four, or seven cents cash fare, to straight fare of seven cents; and

WHEREAS, It appears from statement filed with said petition that during the months of October, November and December, 1919, under the present rate of fare, the total operating revenues of petitioner were $35,286.50 and the total operating expenses, exclusive of fixed charges and taxes, but inclusive of an allowance for depreciation reserve, were $35,135.90, leaving a balance of $150.60, from which balance must be deducted interest and discount of $4,002.31 and taxes of $1,351.80 during said period, making the deficit for the three months in question $5,203.51; and

WHEREAS, This Commission by its Order No. 5327 this day entered in Case No. 1682 having permitted The United Railways and Electric Company of Baltimore, which company owns practically all of the capital stock of the petitioner, to increase its base adult fare from six and one-half cents when tickets or fare checks are purchased in lots of four, or seven cents cash fare, to straight fare of seven cents, which increased fare becomes effective January 1st, 1920; and

WHEREAS, It is not desirable to have a rate of fare on the line of the petitioner lower than the rate of fare contemporaneously in effect on the lines of The United Railways and Electric Company of Baltimore, the car lines of which company parallel the route of the petitioner's motor bus line, in that such lower fare would tend unduly to divert traffic to the bus line and result in severe over-crowding of said company's busses; and

WHEREAS, It being the opinion and finding of the Commission, in view of the aforegoing, that the petitioner should be permitted to file and publish on less than the statutory notice of thirty days a schedule changing its rate of fare to the extent prayed,

IT IS, THEREFORE, This 31st day of December, in the year Nineteen Hundred and Nineteen, by the Public Service Commission of Maryland,

Ordered, That permission be and is hereby given to The Baltimore Transit Company to file and publish a schedule changing its rate of fare from six and one-half cents when tickets or fare checks are purchased, or seven cents cash fare, to straight fare of seven cents; such increased fare to become effective January 1st, 1920,

PROVIDED, Said schedule be filed with the Commission upon issuance of this order and published by posting as required by law, and that all copies of said schedule should bear the following notation:

> "Issued under special permission of the Public Service Commission of Maryland, Order No. 5328 of date December 31st, 1919."

PROVIDED FURTHER, That this Commission by passing this order is not to be taken or construed as in any sense whatsoever passing upon the reasonableness of the rate of fare contained in schedule filed hereunder, such rate of fare being left as fully subject to investigation and correction upon complaint or upon the Commission's own motion as if this order had never been passed.

ORDER No. 5829.

In the Matter of

The Application of THE CHESAPEAKE AND POTOMAC TELEPHONE COMPANY OF BALTIMORE CITY for the consent of the PUBLIC SERVICE COMMISSION OF MARYLAND to the Sale of the Property Located at the Northeast Corner of Dark Lane and Love Grove Alley, in the City of Baltimore, Under the Terms and Provisions of Order 2913 of the Said Commission Entered June 20, 1916, in Case No. 1131.

Before the

Public Service Commission of Maryland.

Case No. 1751.

The agreement or other written instrument evidencing the transaction in this case having been submitted to this Commission for the purpose of securing its consent to the consummation thereof and the Commission having determined that a hearing is unnecessary,

IT IS, THEREFORE, On this thirty-first day of December, in the year 1919, by the Public Service Commission of Maryland,

Ordered, That the consent of this Commission be and the same is hereby given to the disposition of the property described in said agreement, or other written instrument evidencing the transaction in accordance with the terms outlined therein.

APPENDIX III

OPINIONS FILED BY COUNSEL TO COMMISSION

(375)

Right to Compel an Electric Corporation to Furnish New Mechanical Devices When Changes are Made in the Style or Type of Current Furnished.	January 8, 1919.

Public Service Commission,
Munsey Building, Baltimore, Md.

Gentlemen:

I have received your communication of the 7th inst., which was accompanied by a letter, dated the 4th inst., from M. L. Veasey to you. Mr. Veasey maintains a vacuum cleaner system in his dwelling at Pocomoke City, and he complains that the Electric & Ice Manufacturing Co. has converted its electric current from a direct to an alternating current without furnishing him with a new motor suitable for alternating current; and that consequently his vacuum cleaner system is useless to him. Mr. Veasey also asks whether the Electric & Ice Manufacturing Co. has a right to alter its charges for current without giving notice to its customers.

I find that the tariff schedule filed by the Electric & Ice Manufacturing Co. with the Commission is entirely silent as to the kind of current that is to be furnished to its customers; and I therefore assume that the contract between Mr. Veasey and the company is silent upon this subject too. I cannot see, therefore, that the company is under any contractual obligation to supply Mr. Veasey with any particular kind of current, or to refrain from supplying him with a special kind of current which requres the addition of a motor to his vacuum cleaner system. In other words, no evidence is before me to show that the contract between the parties was made subject to the condition that the company should furnish current that would not necessitate any mechanical change in Mr. Veasey's vacuum cleaner system. Even if this reasoning on my part is incorrect, all the company would have to do to get rid of its contract with Mr. Veasey would be to file a new tariff schedule with the Commssion expressly limited to an alternating current. Such contracts are necessarily subject to the control of the Police Power of the State. Yeatman *vs.* Public Service Commission, 126 Md., 513, 518.

As to notice to the customer of a change of rate, let me say that rate changes of gas and electric companies are regulated by Order No. 246 of the Commission, passed on April 19, 1911. This order simply provides that, unless the Commission otherwise orders, no change shall be made in any rate or charge, or rule or regulation forming a part of the rate or charge, which shall have been filed with the Commission, except after thirty days' notice to the Commission; and that the new schedule shall plainly state the changes proposed to be made in the schedule then in force, and the time when the changed rate, charge or regulation will go into effect; and that all proposed changes shall be shown by printing, filing and publishing new schedules, or shall be plainly indicated upon the schedules in force at the time kept open to public inspection. In my judgment, this language does not contemplate any notice to the consumer other than that given to him by the filing and publishing of the new schedule; in other words, I do not think that a special notice of the rate change has to be given to each customer of a gas or electric company, though I think that, as a matter of courtesy and sound business policy, such a company might well give such a special notice to each.

Truly yours,
WM. CABELL BRUCE,
General Counsel.

---

(376)

Jurisdiction of The Commission in the Matter of Establishing or Re-establishing a Station on an Interstate Railroad.	January 20, 1919.

Public Service Commission,
    Munsey Building, Baltimore, Md.

Gentlemen:

Pursuant to your communication to me of December 12th last, I duly considered the question submitted to me thereby; and on December 18th last, wrote to the Director General of Railroads, referring to the President's Proclamation of December 26, 1917, which declared that any order, general or special, thereafter made by the Director General of Railroads should have paramount authority, and asked him whether there was any general or special order of his which revoked, or modified the power of the Public Service Commission of

Maryland to order railroad companies in the State of Maryland to establish or re-establish such a station as Ashland on the Northern Central Railway. To this letter I received a reply, under date of January 3, 1919, from Mr. R. Walton Moore, Assistant General Counsel of the Director General of Railroads.. This reply I enclose herewith. After receiving it, I addressed a letter, under date of January 6, 1919, asking him to kindly refer me to the specific provisions contained in Congressional Legislation and Executive Proclamations in regard to the Director General, which, in his judgment, negatived the idea that until its authority was superseded by some general or special order of the Director General, the Public Service Commission of Maryland had the power to require the Pennsylvania Railroad Company, as the lessee of the Northern Central Railway Company, to re-establish the station at Ashland. To this letter I received a reply from Mr. Moore, under date of January 18, 1919, which I herewith enclose. Mr. Moore's letters make it very clear, in my judgment, that if the Commission attempts to re-establish the station at Ashland its action will be strenuously antagonized by the Director General of Railroads, even to the extent, if necessary, of passing a special order requiring the abandonment of the station if re-established by the Commission.

Under the circumstances, I think it would be a mistake for the Commission to pâss an order attempting to re-establish the station at Ashland. And I ask the Commission to be so kind as to return to me the enclosures which accompany this letter.

Truly yours,
WM. CABELL BRUCE,
General Counsel.

---

(877)

Right of	
The Commission to Enforce Its Order in Connection with Freight Movements Which Occurred Prior to Federal Control.	February 8, 1919.

Public Service Commission,
  Munsey Building, Baltimore, Md.

Gentlemen:

I have received your communication of the 7th inst., in which you ask me whether the Commission can require the Penna. R. R. Co. to amend 17 freight bills, which it has made out at its 6-cent class rate per 100 pounds against the consignor of certain movements of structural steel from Calvert Station to the new Poole Engineering and

Machine Co. plant at Woodberry, so as to make them harmonize with the order of the Commission of May 31, 1912, which prescribed a switching rate of $5.00 per car for such movements. These bills have already been the subject of earnest and detailed consideration by the Commission, its Rate Clerk and myself, and now, if I am not mistaken, the fact is brought for the first time to the attention of the Commission, its Rate Clerk and myself that the movements evidenced by the bills all occurred before the railroads, owing to the exigencies of the great war, were taken over by the general government.

It is immaterial, under the circumstances, it seems to me, to ask whether the Commission has the power to order the Penna. R. R. Co. to amend the bills, seeing that they have never yet been paid; but should it endeavor in any manner to collect the amounts of the bills, as now made out at its 6-cent class rate per 100 pounds instead of at the switching rate of $5.00 per car, prescribed by the order of the Commission above mentioned, I do not doubt the right of the Commission to vindicate the authority of its order by an application to the Courts for an injunction, or by a penal action as provided by Section 28 of the Public Service Commission Law.

But it is only fair to the Penna. R. R. Co. to say that I think it not improbable that when its attention, too, is pointedly called to the fact that the movements in question took place before the enactment of the Congressional Legislation and the promulgation of the Executive Proclamations by which the control of the Federal Government over the railroads was established, it will, of its own accord, correct the bills.

Truly yours,

WM. CABELL BRUCE,

General Counsel.

---

(378)

Right of

The MAYOR & COUNCIL OF CRISFIELD to Annul or Revoke Franchise Granted to a Public Service Corporation Pending the Hearing of a Rate Controversy by the Commission.

February 28, 1919.

Public Service Commission,
Munsey Building, Baltimore, Md.

Gentlemen:

I have received your communication of the 27th inst., which was accompanied by a letter to you from the Crisfield Light & Power Co., dated the 26th inst., enclosing a letter from the Mayor and Council of Crisfield to the Light & Power Co., dated the 25th inst., in which the Mayor and Council of Crisfield threatens to revoke the franchise granted by it to the Light & Power Co. should the latter charge for its gas a rate in excess of $1.25 per thousand cubic feet.

From what the Mayor and Council of Crisfield say in their letter, I infer that one of the conditions, or terms, upon which the franchise was granted by it to the Light & Power Co. was that the latter should maintain a fixed rate of $1.25 per thousand cubic feet for its gas. The correspondence submitted to me does not disclose the date upon which the franchise was granted, and I am therefore not advised as to whether the grant was made before or after the enactment of the Public Service Commission Law on April 5, 1910. But this is immaterial, in my judgment, for it is well settled that contracts between individuals, whether made before or after the passage of such a law, are necessarily subject to the control of the Police Power of the State, whenever such contract relates to the matters which are, or may be, subject to the exercise of this power; and this whether the power is exercised by the Legislature directly or committed by it to a Board or Commission. Manifestly, when the General Assembly of Maryland conferred upon the Public Service Commission of Maryland the authority to fix gas and electric rates, its action was an exercise of the Police Power; and to this power, in my judgment, the rate for gas prescribed by the Mayor and Council of Crisfield when it granted the franchise to the Crisfield Light & Power Co. must yield.

Yeatman vs. P. S. C. of Md., 126 Md., 513, 517, 518.

Manigault vs. Spring, 199 U S., 473.

Armour Packing Co. vs. U. S., 209 U. S., 56.

L. & N. Ry. Co. vs. Mottley, 219 U. S., 467.

Nor, in my opinion, does the fact that the contract entered into between the Town of Crisfield and the Light & Power Co. when the franchise was granted has been superseded by the jurisdiction and authority of the Public Service Commission, so far as the fixed rate of $1.25 for gas is concerned, work an annulment of the franchise or give the Mayor and Council of Crisfield the right to annul it. The franchise stands, though the rate, owing to the exercise of an authority paramount to that of the contracting parties, is gone. (L. & N. Ry. Co. vs. Mottley, supra.)

If the Mayor and Council of Crisfield should undertake to carry out the threat it has made before the rate controversy between it and the Light & Power Co. now pending before the Public Service Commission is determined, it could, in my opinion, be restrained by injunction on the application of the Light & Power Co. to the Circuit Court for Somerset County. If the Commission should pass an order in the rate controversy fixing a maximum rate higher than $1.25 per thousand cubic feet of gas, and the Mayor and Council of Crisfield were to disregard or violate it in any manner, the Commission would have the power under Section 38 of the Public Service Commission Law, (Chapter 180 of the Acts of 1910), to sue out an injunction against the Mayor and Council of Crisfield for so doing.

Truly yours,

WM. CABELL BRUCE,

General Counsel.

---

(379)

In the Matter of

The Complaints of MRS. J. M. HORNER and REV. S. M. ENGLE

vs.

PENNSYLVANIA RAILROAD COMPANY.

March 21, 1919.

Case No. 1606

Public Service Commission,
Munsey Building, Baltimore, Md.

Gentlemen:

I have received your communication of the 20th inst. Paragraph 1 of General Order No. 58 of the United States Railroad Administration, dated February 20, 1919, expressly declares,

> "That transportation systems under Federal control shall continue subject to the lawful Police Regulations of the several States which were and are applicable to privately operated transportation systems in such matters as * * * the establishment, maintenance and sanitation of station facilities * * * and all other matters of local service, safety and equipment."

And that,

> "It will be the policy of the Director General to cause the orders of the State Commissions in those matters to be carried out."

In view of these provisions of the above mentioned order, I see no legal reason why the Commission could not now proceed to re-establish the station at Ashland on the Northern Central Railway.

Truly yours,

WM. CABELL BRUCE,

General Counsel.

(880)

March 22, 1919.

Public Service Commission,
Munsey Building, Baltimore, Md.

Gentlemen:

Pursuant to the request of your Chairman, made to me this morning, I submit the following opinion:

By Chapter 708 of the Acts of 1918, the State Roads Commission was authorized and directed in their discretion to provide a suitable steamer or steamers to connect the Town of Claibourne with the City of Annapolis or some adjoining suburb, and to provide wharf facilities at each terminal and to make such trips across the bay as might be justified, and to charge such rates therefor as might be established by the Public Service Commission of Maryland. In my opinion, this act authorized the State Roads Commission to either operate a ferry between the termini in question with a steamer or steamers purchased by itself and with its own employees, or to let the function out to contract.

By the City Charter, it was provided that there should be a Superintendent of Lamps and Lighting, appointed by the Mayor, and that he should have "under his charge and supervision the lighting of the City of Baltimore." Commenting on this language, the Court of Appeals said:

> "It is plain that he can have this charge and exercise this supervision as well whether the actual work is done under a contract with an independent contractor as when it is done by men employed by him."
>
> (Am. Lighting Co. *vs.* McCuen, 92 Md., pages 703, 708.)

Were the State Roads Commission to operate a ferry with a steamer or steamers purchased by it and with employees of its own, it is very clear that the enterprise would not be subject to the jurisdiction and authority of the Public Service Commission, notwithstanding the fact that if a private corporation were to engage in the same business it would undoubtedly be a common carrier, within the purview of Sections 1 and 3 of the Public Service Commission Law of Maryland. A body politic of the State of Maryland, whether the State of Maryland itself or one of its municipal corporations, engaged in the business of furnishing a public service commodity or service, is not subject to the jurisdiction of the Public Service Commission in the absence of some express enactment making it so. That this is true was recognized by the Legislature when it passed a special enactment after the passage of the Public Service Commission Law in 1910, declaring that every municipal corporation of the State of Maryland engaged in the business of manufacturing and supplying or supplying gas or electricity for other than municipal purposes should be included within the terms "gas corporation" and "electrical corporation," as defined in Section 1 of the Public Service Commission Law, and should be subject, as other gas and electrical corporations are, to the provisions of that law. (Pub. Serv. Com. Law, Sec. 1½.)

Agreeably with the powers conferred upon it by the Act of 1916 above mentioned, the State Roads Commission entered into a contract dated March 14, 1919, with Frank E. McNamee and Hampden D. Mepham, of New York City, in which the latter agreed to furnish a steamer and to operate the ferry between Annapolis and Claibourne for a period of three years, at certain rates mentioned in the agreement, provided that these rates were approved by the Public Service Commission. Afterwards, the charter of the Claibourne-Annapolis Ferry, Inc., a corporation incorporated under the general incorporation laws of the State of Maryland, was so amended at their instance as to authorize the company to establish and maintain an automobile, passenger, freight and express service between Claibourne, Maryland, and Annapolis, Maryland, and to enter into or assume contracts with the State Roads Commission of Maryland for the operation of such ferry service. By its charter, the company is also authorized to own and operate vessels, wharves, docks, etc., generally, but it does not propose to exercise any of these additional powers at the present time, and the stock and bond issues which it contemplates are to be issued for the purpose of obtaining money that is to be applied solely to the needs of the ferry that the State Roads Commission desires to establish. In other words, the company has no immediate expectation whatever of exercising any powers conferred upon it by its charter except those conferred upon it for the purpose of enabling it to perform the duty delegated to it by the contract between the State Roads Commission and Messrs. McNamee and Mepham above mentioned, which is about to be assigned by the latter to it with the consent of the State Roads Commission.

Under these conditions, it seems to me that the company should be regarded as merely a State agency which the State of Maryland, through its State Roads Commission, has caused to be created for the purpose of exercising on its behalf a State function which the State Roads Commission could exercise directly and immediately were it to see fit to do so. I do not think, therefore, that the Public Service Commission should attempt to assert any authority over the proposed issues of stocks and bonds, or to subject the operation of the company to its general jurisdiction and authority at the present time. Its one power, at present, in relation to the company, is to establish the rates at which the ferry service shall be rendered by the company. This it is empowered to do, and this it is its duty to do under the provisions of Chapter 708 of the Acts of 1916. If the rates mentioned in the agreement between the State Roads Commission and Messrs. McNamee and Mepham are just and reasonable in its judgment, it can, after an investigation and hearing in the usual manner, approve them. If they are not such in its judgment, it can reject them and establish whatever rates it may believe to be just and reasonable.

Should the Claibourne-Annapolis Ferry, Inc., ever proceed to exercise any of the general powers of transportation with which it is endowed by its charter, it would have to obtain an order from the Commission approving their exercise, and it would become subject in every respect as regards such of its general powers as it proposed to exercise, to the full jurisdiction and authority of the Public Service Commission over common carriers.

Truly yours,   .

WM. CABELL BRUCE,

General Counsel.

---

(381)

R. E. DUVALL & COMPANY	
vs.	March 26, 1919.
HAGERSTOWN & FREDERICK RAILWAY CO.	Case No. 1640.

Public Service Commission,

Munsey Building, Baltimore, Md.

Gentlemen:

In compliance with your request, I submit herewith my opinion as to the jurisdiction of the Commission in the above entitled case.

It appears, from the papers in the case, that on August 27, 1918, two cars, which were loaded with railroad ties at a siding near Frederick, Maryland, were placed in charge of the Hagerstown & Frederick Railway Company for transportation to Carroll Switch, Baltimore, Maryland, a siding on the Baltimore & Ohio Railroad. Bills of lading for the shipment were issued, on the above mentioned date, to the consignor. The consignee was intended to be the United Railways and Electric Company of Baltimore, but the name was erroneously entered on the bills of lading as the United States Railway and Electric Company. When the cars reached the point at which they should have been transferred to the Baltimore & Ohio Railroad, they were held up there because of the fact that the railroad company was permitted to carry only a limited quantity of such material as constituted the shipment, and in each case it was necessary to secure a special permit. The cars were held at the said junction point until September 13, when, for the first time, the consignor was notified by telegraph of the fact that the cars were so held, subject to demurrage charges. Subsequently, one car was sent forward, subject to demurrage charges of $100 and a war tax of $3.00. The other car was held somewhat longer, and then, without the knowledge of the consignor, was unloaded, and the consignor does not now know where the railroad ties are.

It appears to me that there is a question involved in this case which the Public Service Commission ought to investigate. It is not clear to me, from the facts presented in the papers in the case, that the railroad company had the right to subject the cars to demurrage charges, under the rules which had been adopted by the company and are on file with this Commission. Rule 1 states specifically when demurrage may be charged. The rule is as follows:

"Cars held for or by consignors or consignees for loading, unloading, forwarding directions, or for any other purpose, are subject to these demurrage rules except as follows."

(We are not concerned with the exceptions.)

I interpret this rule, which says demurrage charges are applicable when cars are held "for or by consignors or consignees," to mean that such charges can be made only when the transportation is delayed or interrupted, or delivery is delayed because of something which the consignor or consignee is required to do, but has failed to do in time to avoid delay.

As stated above, bills of lading had been issued for the above mentioned cars, and under ordinary conditions, when bills of lading have been issued, the shipment is in the absolute custody of the railroad company until delivered to the consignee. In this case, however, a question arises which cannot be answered from what appears in the papers in the case. Permits were necessary to enable the railroad company to accept the cars and carry them to their destination. If the duty to secure such permits rested upon the consignor or consignee, then the cars may be regarded as having been held for the consignor and, in my judgment, demurrage might have been properly charged. If it was the duty of the initial carrier, before issuing the bills of lading, to provide itself with permits and see that the way was clear, then, in my judgment, the failure of the initial carrier to perform its duty in that respect did not give it the right to charge demurrage.

It is stated in one of the letters that the consignor erroneously advised the Hagerstown & Frederick Railway Company that the shipment was intended for the United States Government, and if such a statement was made, the employees of the railway company might readily have been misled, because of the fact that the consignee is given the name United States Railway & Electric Company. If it was the duty of the railway company to secure the necessary permits, it is my opinion that the misstatement of fact above mentioned, if it was made, would not justify the demurrage charge, but that any remedy which the railway company might be entitled to because of the erroneous statement would have to be sought in another tribunal.

In brief, it appears to me that the Commission should inquire into the facts, so as to ascertain whether or not the cars were held for or by the consignor or consignee, so that the charge for demurrage would be justifiable. I think the Commission should take cognizance of the fact that the charge was made, if made contrary to the demurrage rules.

Very truly yours,
JOSEPH S. GOLDSMITH,
Asst. General Counsel.

(382)

March 31, 1919.

Public Service Commission,
  Munsey Building, Baltimore, Md.

Gentlemen:

I return herewith the proposed form of order in Case No. 1645, (The Claibourne-Annapolis Ferry Matter). I see no substantial objection to the mere form of the order, but I do to its substance.

Chapter 708 of the Acts of 1916 imposes upon the Commission the positive duty to "establish" the ferriage rates for the ferry, and this language necessarily implies, in my opinion, full investigation, valuation, and the ascertainment of the proper return to the Company under the circumstances—in other words, a real exercise of the discretion required of the Commission by the Act. Of course, I do not know what testimony was elicited at the hearing in this case, but from the recitals in the proposed order I should infer that the essentials above mentioned have not been gratified. The Commission would seem simply to have accepted the rates suggested to it by the Company at their face value, and by an express reservation to have left it to time to determine whether they are excessive or not. This does not seem to me to be an adequate execution of the intent of the Act. The proper course, in my judgment, would be for the Commission to call in testimony of its own, expert and otherwise, (in addition to the testimony, if any, brought forward by the Company), for the purpose of valuing the property and assets of the Company, estimating its probable receipts and expenditures, and fixing the return to which it is fairly entitled under the circumstances. When this had been done, it could then very properly in its order reserve the right to modify the rates established by it should experience show that they were either inadequate or excessive. If expert testimony is invoked, I can not see that there should be any difficulty at all about valuing the property and assets of the Company. This, of course, I can not say as to the estimation of the probable receipts and expenses of the Company, but is there not always more or less difficulty about forecasting the probable receipts and expenditures of any new public service enterprise? Yet is such difficulty ever assigned as a reason why a public service commission should not at least do its best to form an independent judgment of its own? Very unfortunate, indeed, in my opinion, would be the precedent set by a declaration from the Commission that no accurate estimate of the prospective receipts and expenses of a public service corporation can be made because the corporation is of recent origin, and such an estimate must, in the nature of things, be to some extent conjectural.

Truly yours,

WM. CABELL BRUCE,
General Counsel.

(383)

April 3, 1919.

Public Service Commission,
Munsey Building, Baltimore, Md.

Gentlemen:

I have received your communication of the 31st ultimo, and the copy of the letter dated the 27th ultimo from the Lovettsville Lighting Company to you, by which it was accompanied. As I read the letter of the company, it states that it is a corporation, incorporated, organized and existing under the laws of the State of Virginia, which desires to obtain a supply of current at Brunswick, Maryland, through the agency of a line which it proposes to establish over the Potomac River, between its domicile in Virginia and Brunswick.

Being a foreign corporation, it will not be subject to the jurisdiction of the Public Service Commission of Maryland, except to a limited extent. It would not have to file tariff schedules with the Commission, unless it expects to furnish customers in Maryland with current, which I do not understand to be the case; nor would it have to apply to the Commission for the approval of bond and stock issues made by it; but it could not operate its proposed line between the Potomac River and Brunswick without obtaining the necessary local franchises in Maryland to do so. Before, therefore, it could begin the construction of the line just mentioned, or exercise any such local franchises within the State of Maryland, it would have to secure the permission and approval of the Commission.

As to whether it would have to pay any foreign corporation franchise taxes or charges, it should apply for information to the Secretary of State at Annapolis; and as to the taxes, State and local, which it would have to pay within the State of Maryland, it should apply for information to the County Commissioners of Frederick County. The Public Service Commission is not clothed with any powers of assessment of taxation, and is, therefore, not the source from which any such information should be sought. Nor has the Public Service Commission the authority to entertain any application for the condemnation of a right of way for the Lovettsville Lighting Company over the tracks of the Baltimore and Ohio Railroad Company. The condemnation of private property, whether belonging to corporations or individuals, is regulated by the constitution and general statutes of the State of Maryland, and turns, in the main, doubtless upon principles of law as familiar to the constitution and laws of the State of Virginia as to the constitution and laws of the State of Maryland.

Truly yours,

WM. CABELL BRUCE,
General Counsel.

(384)

April 3, 1919.

Public Service Commission,
Munsey Building, Baltimore, Md.

Gentlemen:

I have received your communication of the 2nd instant, together with the letter dated the 28th ultimo from James B. Walker, the Secretary of the National Association of Railway and Utilities Commissions. The following statutory provisions are in force in this State: By Section 280 of Article 23 of the Public General Laws of Maryland (Bagby's Annotated Code) it is provided that every railroad company organized under that article shall be required to erect, at all points where its road shall cross any public road, at a sufficient elevation from such public road to admit of the free passage of vehicles of every kind, a sign with large and distinct letters placed thereon to give notice of the proximity of the railroad, and warn persons of the necessity of looking out for the cars; and that any company neglecting and refusing to erect such sign shall be liable to damages for all injuries occurring to persons or property from such neglect and refusal.

By Section 303 of the same Article, it is further provided that whenever the several railroads of Maryland operated by steam shall cross any public highway at grade outside the corporate limits of cities, and any such highways shall be believed to be of such a character as to render the passage of locomotives and trains thereon dangerous to life and property, it shall be the duty of the Commissioners of the county in which such point of crossing shall be located, after according the hearing prescribed by the same section, in case they shall determine that such protection is necessary, to notify the railroad company through its superintendent or ticket agent in such county that within 60 days thereafter said railroad company shall either place a flagman at said crossing, whose duty it shall be to give timely notice to all persons using said crossing of the approach of locomotives or trains, or a system of electric alarm bells to give such notice at the approach of trains, or shall erect safety gates at said crossing which shall be closed not less than one-half minute before the passage and during the passage of every railroad train or locomotive across the highway; or shall change the said grade crossing so as to pass said highway with an under or over-grade crossing, in which case neither a flagman nor safety gate shall be required.

By Section 304 of the same Article, it is provided that if any railroad company shall neglect or refuse to comply with the requirements of the said County Commissioners as provided for by Section 303, said railroad company shall be liable to a fine of $25.00 per day for each and every day it shall neglect or refuse so to do.

By Section 314 of the same Article, every Maryland railroad company is empowered to provide at its own cost and expense that a public highway which makes a dangerous crossing, in its judgment, shall be carried across its tracks, either overhead by a bridge, or under by a tunnel.

Truly yours,
WM. CABELL BRUCE,
General Counsel.

(385)

April 11, 1919.

Public Service Commission,
  Munsey Building, Baltimore, Md.

Gentlemen:

I reply to your communication of the 9th inst., which was accompanied by a copy of a letter from Edgar P. Wine, of Waynesboro, Pa., to you, dated the 7th inst., in which the writer inquires of the Commission what he should do to authorize him to operate "a motor truck service between Waynesboro, Pa., and Hagerstown, Md., for the purpose of hauling express, freight and produce between these points, and also collecting and delivering the same at the villages and farms along the route."

By Section 1 of Chapter 304 of the Acts of the General Assembly of Maryland for the year 1918, it is provided as follows:

"It shall be the duty of each owner of a motor vehicle to be used in the public transportation of merchandise or freight, operating over State, State Aid, improved County roads, and streets and roads of incorporated towns and cities in the State of Maryland, to secure a permit from the Public Service Commission of Maryland to operate over said roads and streets, and present same to the Motor Vehicle Commissioner annually at the time and according to the method and provisions prescribed by law for owners of all other motor vehicles, to make an application in writing for registration with the Commissioner of Motor Vehicles, and to state in said application besides the other matters by law provided, the carrying capacity as given by the manufacturer of such motor vehicles, the route on which said motor vehicle is to be used, whether reserve or substitute cars are maintained by the applicant to be used only in emergencies, and if so, the number of such reserve and substitute cars and a complete description of each, and when in use same to be designated by a special marker to be furnished by the Commissioner of Motor Vehicles, the length of the route in miles on State, State Aid, improved County roads, and streets and roads of incorporated towns and cities under which it shall operate during the ensuing year."

These provisions are followed in the same section by other provisions classifying motor vehicles according to tonnage weight, and prescribing the license fee based upon a charge of one-fifth cent or more for each ton mile, according to the class of motor vehicle to which the particular motor vehicle belongs multiplied by the total number of miles that the applicant shows will be traveled by such motor vehicle over State, State Aid, improved County roads, and streets and roads of incorporated towns and cities in the State of Maryland during the year for which the certificate is issued.

For the other steps necessary to qualify foreign corporations generally to do business of any kind in this State, I respectfully refer Mr. Wine to the Secretary of State at Annapolis.

The drift of some of Mr. Wine's inquiries are quite obscure, and I am at a loss to know therefore just how to answer them. As I do not know whether he has yet taken out a charter, either in Pennsylvania or Maryland, to operate the proposed motor truck service, and, if he has, what its contents are, I cannot well tell him what such a charter as he speaks of would permit him to do in this State. As to what he should do to take out a charter in this State, if he has not already taken one out in either Pennsylvania or Maryland, and it is his intention to take one out, he should consult some lawyer. Corporate charters are not lodged, under the Laws of Maryland, with the Public Service Commission.

Truly yours,
WM. CABELL BRUCE,
General Counsel.

---

(386)

Jurisdiction of
The Commission Over the C. & P. TEL. Co., While Under Federal Control.

April 21, 1919.

Public Service Commission,
Munsey Building, Baltimore, Md.

Gentlemen:

I have received your communication of the 16th inst. asking me whether the Chesapeake & Potomac Telephone Company can lawfully increase its rates within the State of Maryland, as it proposes to do, without the consent of the Public Service Commission of Maryland; and also, if it can, whether these increased rates would automatically cease and be succeeded by those heretofore established by the Commission, upon the termination of the present Federal control of the telephone lines of the United States.

This control originated in the Joint Resolution adopted by Congress on July 16, 1918, which reads as follows:

"Resolved by the Senate and House of Representatives of the United States of America in Congress assembled, That the President during the continuance of the present war is authorized and empowered, whenever he shall deem it necessary for the national security or defense, to supervise or to take possession and assume control of any telegraph, telephone, marine cable, or radio system or systems, or any part thereof, and to operate the same in such manner as may be needful or desirable for the duration of the war, which supervision, possession, control or operation shall not extend beyond the date of the proclamation by the President of the exchange of ratifications of the treaty of peace: Provided, that just compensation shall be made for such supervision, possession, control, or operation, to be determined by the President; and if the amount thereof, so determined by the President, is unsatisfactory to the person entitled to receive the same, such person shall be paid seventy-five per centum of the amount so determined by the President and shall be entitled to sue the United States to recover such further sum as, added to said seventy-five per centum, will make up such amount as will be just compensation therefor, in the manner provided for by section twenty-four, paragraph twenty, and section one hundred and forty-five of the Judicial Code: Provided further, That nothing in this Act shall be construed to amend, repeal, impair, or affect existing laws or powers of the States in relation to taxation or the lawful police regulations of the several States, except wherein such laws, powers, or regulations may affect the transmission of Government communications, or the issue of stocks and bonds by such system or systems."

The power conferred by this Resolution upon the President was exercised by an Executive Proclamation on July 22, 1918, whereby he announced that he did thereby take possession and assume control and supervision of each and every telegraph and telephone system, and every part thereof within the jurisdiction of the United States, including all equipment thereof, and appurtenances thereto, whatsoever, and all materials and supplies; and whereby he directed that the supervision, possession, control and operation of such telegraph and telephone systems thus undertaken should be exercised by and through the Postmaster General, Albert S. Burleson, who might perform the duties so imposed upon him so long as, and to such extent, and in such manner, as he should determine, through the owners, managers, boards of directors, receivers, officers and employees of said telegraph and telephone systems; and that until, and except so far as, said Postmaster General should from time to time by general or special orders otherwise provide, the owners, managers, boards of directors, receivers, officers and employees of the various telegraph and telephone systems should continue the operation thereof in the usual and ordinary course of the business of said systems, in the names of their respective companies, associations, organizations, owners or managers as the case might be. And the Proclamation of the President further declared that from and after 12 o'clock midnight on July 31, 1918, all the telegraph and telephone systems included in it should conclusively be deemed within the possession and control and under the supervision of the Postmaster General without further act or notice.

And on August 1, 1918, this Proclamation was followed by a bulletin in which the Postmaster General declared that, pursuant to the Proclamation, he had assumed possession, control and supervision of the telegraph and telephone systems of the United States, and that until further notice the telegraph and telephone systems taken over by him should continue operation in the ordinary course of business through regular channels; that regular dividends theretofore declared and maturing, and interest on bonds, debentures and other obligations might be paid in due course, and that the telephone companies might renew or extend their maturing obligations, unless otherwise ordered by the Postmaster General; and that all officers, operators and employees of these companies should continue in the performance of their existing duties; reporting to the same officers as theretofore, and on the same terms of employment. Thus, agreeably with the Joint Resolution of Congress, and the Proclamation of the President, the Postmaster General *did* actually seize the telegraph and telephone systems of the United States; and, in the management of the lines of the Chesapeake & Potomac Telephone Co., has now approved the proposed increase of rates by it, above mentioned, which is to become effective May 1st, 1919.

In my opinion, the adoption of the Joint Resolution of July 16, 1918, by Congress was in every respect a valid exercise of constitutional power.

By Section 8 of Article 1 of the Federal Constitution, the authority to declare war, and, subject to a few minor reservations, all legislative authority to provide for its effective prosecution are committed to Congress. By Section 2 of Article 2 of the same Constitution, it is declared that the President shall be the Commander-in-chief of the Army and Navy of the United States and of the militia of the several States, when called into the actual service of the United States. By Section 8 of Article 2, it is also provided that Congress shall have the power to make all laws which shall be necessary and proper for carrying into execution the several powers conferred upon it by that Section; and by Article 6 of the Federal Constitution, it is declared that the Constitution and the Laws of the United States, which shall be made in pursuance thereof, and all treaties made, or which shall

be made under the authority of the United States, shall be the supreme
law of the land. When the telephone lines of the country were seized
by the Postmaster General war between the United States and Germany was flagrant, and I entertain no doubt that the control and
operation of the telephone lines of the United States, interstate and
intrastate, in time of war fall within the purview of the provisions of
the Federal Constitution, which clothe Congress with plenary authority
to do whatever may be necessary to be done to secure military victory,
or to avert military disaster when the honor, the permanent welfare,
or even the life of the nation is at stake. Nor can I doubt that few
things may be more essential to the successful prosecution of modern
warfare by a people than the complete dominion of its agents over
all private telephonic and telegraphic channels of communication,
whether for the purpose of keeping domestic disaffection in check,
accelerating the transportation of soldiers or military supplies, or
keeping the Government in sensitive touch with the movement of its
own armies and fleets and of those of its enemies. Whatever may be
the extent of the pecuniary waste or general inefficiency produced
by the governmental control of telephonic and telegraphic lines of
communication under normal conditions, Congress might well deem
it fully compensated for in time of war by the enhanced facility and
secrecy of communication which result, so far as the Government
is concerned, from the unity of administration and exemption from
the ordinary responsibilities of management that attend the control
of a public utility by the Government. Nor, as I see it, can it be
justly contended that the Joint Resolution of July 16, 1918, involved
any undue delegation by Congress to the President of its own constitutional authority. There is no legal objection to the delegation by the
legislature to a subordinate agency of a part of its own powers,
provided the grant is made subject to some fixed or definite legislative
standard, in accordance with which the discretion reposed must be
exercised. Such a standard, it seems to me, is to be found in the very
nature, if not in the express terms of the Joint Resolution itself, when
properly construed in the light of the exigencies which evoked it and
were to surround its execution. So construed it is tantamount to an
express statement by Congress that in its judgment the emergencies of
the pending war were such that at any time between the date of the
adoption of the Resolution and the date of the Proclamation by the
President of the exchange of ratifications of the treaty of peace it
would be such a reasonable and proper thing for the President, for
the sake of the national security or defense, to take over any telephone line, interstate or intrastate, and to operate the same in such
manner as might be needful or desirable for the duration of the war
that he might do so whenever he might deem it necessary to do so.
Therefore it cannot be justly said, under the circumstances, it appears
to me, that the power given to the President by the Resolution to
seize the telephone lines of the country was left wholly to the personal
discretion of the President, without any standard for his guidance in

its exercise beyond what might be suggested by the arbitrary or capricious impulses of his own will. But even if this were not so, a limitation upon the exercise of his discretion could well be implied from the powers with which the Chief Executive of the United States is invested by the provisions of the Federal Constitution. By that Constitution, he is made the Commander-in-chief of the Army and Navy of the United States and the militia of the several States when called into the actual service of the United States, and there is no reason to think that the powers granted by the Resolution to the President were granted to him otherwise than as such. They are exercisable, in consequence, by him in that capacity only, and are subject to every defect or qualification of authority that belongs to him in that capacity. As Commander-in-chief of the army and navy he would have no right to seize the telephone lines of the country except for some purpose directly or reasonably tributary to the success of our arms; and that Congress might justly believe that its war powers might, through the agency of the President, be wisely and effectively applied to such purposes is, I think, too plain for further discussion.

This view is in accord with the opinion rendered on June 10, 1919, by Judge Chatfield of the District Court of the United States for the Southern District of New York, in the cases of the Commercial Cable Co. and Commercial Pacific Cable Co., respectively, *vs.* Albert S. Burleson *et al.*, now pending on appeal in the Supreme Court of the United States. The Joint Resolution of July 16, 1918, Judge Chatfield held, simply placed in the President's hands as Chief Executive and the head of the army and navy an instrumentality essential both for military and naval operations, and the negotiation of peace.

I am also of the opinion that the control of the telephone lines of the Chesapeake & Potomac Telephone Co. by the Government did not end with the armistice reached by the United States and its allies with Germany, on November 11, 1918. Whatever may have been the actual sequels, that pact, considered as a convention, was an armistice merely, and as such was intended to work only a suspension of hostilities and not to bring the war to an unconditional end. To go no further, the fact that it is not deemed even by the United States to have finally terminated the war and to have established a status of real peace between the warring parties to it is abundantly demonstrated by the circumstance that the condition of Europe is still so unsettled and the possibility of war being resumed between Germany and the United States so credible that the United States still deems it necessary to maintain a force of a million and a half of soldiers in France and Germany.

Assuming that there was a distinct military advantage to be secured by the United States in taking over the control of the telephone lines of the country, (and it is enough to say that Congress thought there was), it would certainly seem unduly precipitate for it to surrender this control now and to hazard the necessity of another seizure of the lines and a fresh reorganization of the control, in advance of anything short of the complete and final consummation of peace; especially as this welcome event would appear to be very close at hand.

In view of these considerations, it is hardly material for me to call attention to the fact that by its express terms the Joint Resolution of Congress did not limit the control that might be taken by the Government of the telephone lines of the country to the declaration of an armistice, but to "the date of the proclamation by the President of the exchange of ratifications of the treaty of peace." The conviction I have formed as to the effect of the armistice of November 11, 1918, likewise coincides with the opinion of Judge Chatfield in the cases which I have just cited.

In the recent case of the Commonwealth of Pennsylvania *ex rel.* Schaffer, Attorney General, *vs.* The Bell Telephone Co. of Penna., decided on April 2, 1919, it was held by the Court of Common Pleas of Dauphin County, Pa., sitting in equity, that an increase of telephone rates without the approval of the Public Service Commission of Pennsylvania was an unwarranted interference with the police powers of the State of Pennsylvania, because the Joint Resolution of Congress of July 16, 1918, expressly provided that nothing therein should be construed to amend, repeal, impair or affect the existing laws or powers of the States in relation to the lawful police regulations of the several States, except wherein such laws, powers or regulations might affect the transmission of Government communications, or the issue of stocks and bonds by telephone systems. The same conclusion had been previously reached on January 31, 1919, by the Public Service Commission of Massachusetts *in Re* New England Telephone and Telegraph Co. *et al.*, (Public Utility Reports Annotated, issue of March 27, 1919),—a case which involved an increase in telephone rates ordered by the Postmaster General of the United States. But I cannot concur with this construction of the Joint Resolution of Congress. It is manifest that the Resolution, the Proclamation of the President and the Bulletin of the Postmaster General, to which I have referred, contemplated complete and unqualified control by the Government of the telephone lines, interstate and intrastate, of the United States, and I am slow to believe that with such a sweeping intent as this Congress could have intended to withhold from the Government the most essential of all the powers necessary to the unified control and operation which it had in mind—that is to say, the power to fix telephone rates. The lawful police regulations of the several States spoken of in the Joint Resolution are, in my opinion, merely such lawful police regulations relating to telephone and telegraph companies as are police regulations in the narrower sense— that is to say, police regulations of a criminal or penal character, such as are called for by the graver abuses attendant upon the operations of public utilities. This belief is strengthened by the fact that Congress adopted exactly the same saving clause in its

Act of March 21, 1918, providing for Government control during the war of common carriers; notwithstanding the fact that by this Act it expressly conferred upon the President the power to initiate rates, fares, charges, classifications, regulations and practices of common carriers by filing the same with the Interstate Commerce Commission. (See Barnes Federal Code 1919, Sections 10170 and 10163.) It is perfectly true that, in the broader sense, State regulations in relation to transportation or telephone rates may be termed police regulations, but such regulations do not, in my judgment, fall within the class of police regulations contemplated by the Joint Resolution of Congress of July 16, 1918. The language in that Resolution which excepts from the saving clause relating to the lawful police regulations of the several States such police regulations as might affect the transmission of Government communications, or the issue of stocks and bonds by telephone systems, was used simply out of an abundance of caution by Congress to exempt the Government even from police regulations of the States, in the more limited sense, that might tend to unduly hamper it in expediting its own messages, or issuing stocks and bonds for telephone purposes. For illustration, there are many statutory provisions of a penal or perhaps even criminal nature enacted by the different States of the Union in connection with stock or bond issues or railroad combinations which the Government might think too constrictive of its freedom in time of war.

In my judgment, Government control of intrastate telephone operations, including the establishment of rates, will come to an end when the President proclaims the exchange of the ratifications of the treaty of peace, as forecast by the Joint Resolution of Congress. But I do not think that such telephone rates of the Chesapeake & Potomac Telephone Co. as shall then be in force will automatically come to an end along with that control. In other words, the control will cease, but not the existing consequences of this control resulting from its past exercise. Any other conclusion would lead to the conclusion that everything which is actually done by Congress, or its delegated agents in the exercise of authority, justifiable only on the ground of military exigency, passes away with the passing of the crisis or emergency that brought it about, and that whether the thing so done was the emancipation of a race, the acquisition of foreign territory, or the establishment of a telephone rate. When, under the stress of war, the power of the States to regulate telephone rates is completely displaced by Federal authority, pursuant to the provisions of the Federal Constitution, what is done by Federal authority during the period of displacement is not done temporarily or provisionally, unless so done with that express intent, properly manifested, but is done as amply and unconditionally as if done by the superseded State authority itself. With the cessation of Government control of the telephone, the jurisdiction of the Public Service Commission of Maryland over the rates of the Chesapeake & Potomac Telephone Co. will revive, just as a State insolvent system revives with the repeal of a

Federal Bankrupt Law. (Butler *vs.* Goreley, 146 U. S. 303-314.) But this will not be true of the rates of the Chesapeake & Potomac Telephone Co. established by the Public Service Commission of Maryland before the adoption of the Joint Resolution of Congress of July 16, 1918. To the extent that they conflict with the rates about to be put in force by the Chesapeake & Potomac Telephone Co. they will be wholly supplanted by those rates, and the substitution thus operated will continue until peace is proclaimed by the President and the Public Service Commission of Maryland, on the complaint of the citizen or of its own motion, prescribes other rates for the Telephone Co.

How far the continued control of the telephone lines of the country by the Government is expedient, in the light of its past results or of existing conditions, is a matter, of course, as to which I might well have my own opinion as a citizen; but I have no right, I hardly need say, to approach the questions you have submitted to me except as your legal adviser, charged with the duty of frankly and fearlessly stating my conclusions on the legal points involved in them, however repugnant these conclusions may be to my own ideas of public policy or public necessity.

Truly yours,
WM. CABELL BRUCE,
General Counsel.

---

(387)

Jurisdiction of	April 25, 1919.
Commission in a Demurrage Controversy.	Case No. 1640

Public Service Commission,
Munsey Building, Baltimore, Md.

Gentlemen:

I have examined, at your request, the papers, including the testimony, in the matter of the complaint of R. E. Duvall & Co. *vs.* The Hagerstown & Frederick Railway Co., Case No. 1640, and, so far as I can see, the controversy involved therein is merely a judicial controversy, and therefore not one cognizable by the Commission.

The demand for the refund of demurrage in this case originated in the fact that the goods affected by the claim for demurrage were erroneously billed to the United States Railway and Electric Co. at Carroll Switch, Baltimore Md., instead of to the United Railways and Electric Co., and to the further fact that a war embargo permit was not necessary at the time for a shipment to the National Government or one of its agents, but was necessary for a shipment to a private company. Because of the misnomer of the consignee, and the failure to obtain a permit for the shipment before it was made, the goods were suspended so long *in transitu* as to become subject to a large amount of demurrage. The consignee claims that the carrier is responsible for the misnomer, and the delay occasioned by the lack of the permit, and the converse of this claim is made by the carrier. So far as I can see, it is not alleged by the consignee that the order of the Commission of July 17, 1913, in the matter of demurrage on cars of railroad companies in Maryland in relation to free time, has been violated, or that the carrier, assuming that it is not responsible for the delay in the delivery of the goods, has charged the consignee at a rate in excess of its just demurrage charges. It is only where a carrier has charged demurrage in violation of some order of the Commission, or of its own published tariff, that the Commission has the right to sue out an injunction against the carrier, or to bring a penal action against it, or to have its agents arrested as for a misdemeanor, or to pursue such other particular mode of redress as may be allowed by the Public Service Commission Law or the General Laws of the State of Maryland. Where a claim for reparation is based upon conflicting testimony and resolves itself, as the present does, merely into a claim for money had and received, the proper forum for redress is not the Commission but a court of common law.

Truly yours,

WM. CABELL BRUCE,

General Counsel.

---

(388)

Electric Rates: |

Right of the Commission to Fix Same for Sale of in Virginia. | April 25, 1919.

Public Service Commission,
Munsey Building, Baltimore, Md.

Gentlemen:

I have received your communication of the 25th inst., which was accompanied by a letter from the Secretary of the Lovettsville Lighting Co., a Virginia corporation, in which he asks the Commission whether the Commission has the power to establish rates for electric current generated by the Harpers Ferry Electric & Power Co., a West Virginia corporation, in West Virginia, and conducted by its transmission lines through the State of Maryland, via Weverton and Brunswick, to a point on the boundary line between the State of Maryland and the State of Virginia, and there delivered to the Lovettsville Lighting Co. for distribution in Virginia.

I answer no. As respects the State of Maryland, the current distributed in Virginia never loses its character as an interstate commodity.

Truly yours,

WM. CABELL BRUCE,

General Counsel.

(389)

Jurisdiction of

Commission in Matter of Taxicabs.   May 19, 1919.

Public Service Commission,
   Munsey Building, Baltimore, Md.

Gentlemen:

I acknowledge the receipt of the letter, dated the 13th inst., from Whiting & Eppler, attorneys at law, of Cumberland, Md., to you, which was left at my office by two members of the Commission on Saturday last. The letter, in effect, asks you whether the Commission has jurisdiction and authority to prescribe rates for taxicabs operated in the City of Cumberland.

In my opinion, the Commission has, in view of the provisions of Section 1½ of the Public Service Commission Law, which were enacted by Chapter 445 of the Acts of 1914, and declare that the term "common carrier" when used in the Public Service Commission Law shall likewise include all automobile transportation companies and all persons, or associations of persons, whether incorporated or not, operating automobiles or motor cars or motor vehicles for public use in the conveyance of persons or property within the State of Maryland. The term "motor vehicle" would certainly seem to be broad enough to include taxicabs. The only distinction recognized by Section 1½, in my judgment, is that between motor vehicles used merely for the personal convenience of the owner and motor vehicles operated for hire for the use, in some way, of the public. It is true that a taxicab patron usually stipulates, expressly or impliedly, for the exclusive use of the vehicle, but, as the use on these terms is offered to the whole traveling public indistinguishably, a taxicab can, I think, be aptly and properly said, within the meaning of Section 1½ of the Public Service Commission Law, to be operated "for public use in the conveyance of persons."

Truly yours,
WM. CABELL BRUCE,
General Counsel.

(390)

Jurisdiction of   ⎫
                                         ⎪
The Commission Over Controversy Be-   ⎬   June 18, 1919.
tween Land Owner and R. R. Co. as to   ⎪
the Location of a Fence.   ⎭

Public Service Commission,
      Munsey Building, Baltimore, Md.

Gentlemen:

I have received your communication of the 2nd inst., which was accompanied by a letter to you, dated May 29, 1919, from William S. Jones, who complains that the tracks of the Pennsylvania R. R. Co. encroach on his lot to such an extent that he cannot erect a fence on one of the lines of this lot.

The Commission has no jurisdiction to entertain actions of eject-ment or trespass *quare clausum fregit*, and Mr. Jones should resort to the courts for redress.

Truly yours,
WM. CABELL BRUCE,
General Counsel.

---

(391)

Rules of   ⎫
                                         ⎪
Pleading Before the Commission in the   ⎬   June 18, 1919.
Matter of the FAWN LIGHT & POWER   ⎪
COMPANY.   ⎭

Public Service Commission,
      Munsey Building, Baltimore, Md.

Gentlemen:

I have received your letter of the 17th inst., accompanied by a letter to you dated the 16th inst., from Thomas Mackenzie, attorney at law, in which the writer asks whether the Fawn Grove Light & Power Co. and certain individuals, who obtained from the Commission the right to exercise a franchise granted to them by the County Com-missioners of Harford County, could unite in a common petition, under the circumstances more fully set forth in the letter, for an order of the Commission approving the assignment by the petitioners of their respective franchise rights to the Fawn Light & Power Co.

As the Commission is not bound by any strict rules of pleading, I see no legal objection to such a consolidated petition.

Truly yours,
WM. CABELL BRUCE,
General Counsel.

(392)

Jurisdiction of

Commission in the Matter of Co-operative Bus Line.

July 21, 1919.

Public Service Commission,
Munsey Building, Baltimore, Md.

Gentlemen:

I have received your communication of the 18th inst., asking me
to answer certain questions put to you by Henry W. Summer, of
Fullerton, Md., in his letter to you, dated the 15th inst. I answer the
questions seriatim:

1. In my opinion, a co-operative bus company is a company which
maintains its service, not for the accommodation of the public at
large, but merely for the mutual accommodation of its own share-
holders or members; or a company which does not seek to obtain from
the public at large hire sufficient to enable it to defray its running
expenses, including depreciation and to earn a net profit distributable
in the form of dividends to its share-holders or members, but which
collects from its own share-holders or members, in the form of fixed
contributions or ordinary fares, in return for the service it renders
them an aggregate sum sufficient only to defray its expenses, including
depreciation.

2. In my opinion, there is no reason why the passenger privilege
of a share-holder or member should not include his wife and children.

3. In my opinion, there is no reason why the passenger privilege
of the share-holder or member should not include his guests, if bona
fide guests.

4. In my opinion, there is no reason why such a company should not
prescribe a special contribution or rate for children of share-holders
or members en route to or from school.

5. In my opinion, if the operations of such a company were carried
on in good faith it could have no motive to accumulate a surplus
applicable to dividends in the ordinary sense. Any such surplus
would merely represent an amount contributed by the share-holders
or members in the form of fixed contributions or fares in excess of
the actual expenses of the company, including depreciation, and to
distribute it in the form of dividends, in the ordinary sense, would
be simply taking money out of one pocket and putting it in another.

6. In my opinion, such a company can be either an incorporated or
unincorporated company, but should such a company, if unincorporated, not be evidenced by formal articles of association, duly signed
by all its members and by other unmistakable tokens of honesty and
good faith, there would be substantial grounds for suspecting that

it was a mere colorable device for the purpose of defrauding the State of its just revenue and circumventing the jurisdiction and supervision of the Public Service Commission of Maryland; especially would this be true were it to undertake, under any pretext, to distribute as dividends any real or pretended surpluses.

Truly yours,
WM. CABELL BRUCE,
General Counsel.

---

(893)

In the Matter of   }
                            }   July 31, 1919.
Maryland Intrastate Telegraph Rates. }

Public Service Commission,
  Munsey Building, Baltimore, Md.

Gentlemen:

Referring to the application of the Western Union Telegraph Company asking you for leave to continue the Intrastate Telegraph Rates fixed by the Postmaster General, pursuant to the authority conferred upon him by the Resolution of Congress of July 16, 1918, I beg leave to say that, in my opinion, no order by you, or waiver of the thirty days' notice required by Sections 15 and 41 of the Public Service Commission Law, is necessary to authorize the continuance of these rates. All that the Western Union Telegraph Co. has to do is to file them with the Commission, whereupon they will become subject to the jurisdiction of the Commission as other rates are.

It is true that it is provided in the Act of Congress passed during the present month that the toll and exchange telephone rates fixed by the Postmaster General pursuant to the Resolution of Congress of July 18, 1918, shall continue in force for a period not to exceed four months after July 31, 1919, unless sooner modified or changed by the public authorities, State, municipal, or otherwise. But this Act does not contain any such limitation in regard to telegraph rates. Consequently, in harmony with the opinion which I rendered you on April 21, 1919, touching the effect of the above mentioned Resolution of Congress on Intrastate Toll and Exchange Telephone Rates, I think that, while the Act of Congress just mentioned repeals the Resolution, it does not annul the telegraph rates fixed by the Postmaster General thereunder. They have simply become subject to the provisions of the Public Service Commission Law of Maryland, which forbid any rates except such as are evidenced by tariff schedules filed with the Commission, and clothe both the citizen and the Commission with the right to attack rates believed to be excessive.

Truly yours,
WM. CABELL BRUCE,
General Counsel.

(394)

Question of

Jurisdiction of Commission Over Rates of   July 31, 1919.
C. & P. TEL. CO.

Public Service Commission,
Munsey Building, Baltimore, Md.

Gentlemen:

I have received your communication of the 28th inst., submitting to me an application of the C. & P. Telephone Co. of Baltimore City to you, in which the applicant prays that it may be permitted to file certain rates with the Commission, and, pending the decision of the Commission as to the reasonableness of these rates, to charge and collect the rates fixed by the Postmaster General pursuant to the Resolution of Congress of July 16, 1918.

In my judgment, your permission is not necessary to authorize the applicant to charge and collect the rates last mentioned until December 1, 1919; for, by a recent Act of Congress, passed on the 11th day of the present month, it was provided that the existing toll and exchange telephone rates established or approved by the Postmaster General on or prior to June 6, 1919, pursuant to the Resolution of Congress of July 16, 1918, should continue in force for a period not to exceed four months after the Act took effect, which, by its terms, was July 31, 1919. To lawfully continue its existing rates until December 1, 1919, all that the applicant has to do is to file with the Commission a tariff schedule embodying the rates now being charged and collected by it, in conformity with Federal authority.

By the express terms of the Act of Congress of July 11, 1919, these rates may, even before December 1, 1919, be modified or changed by the Commission; and after December 1, 1919, they will éxpire by limitation. Thereupon the rates of the C. & P. Tel. Co. filed with the Commission, and in force at the time that the Resolution of Congress of July 16, 1918, was adopted, would revive, and as they were established by the Commission in a controverted case would remain in force until modified or changed by the Commission. Seeing, however, that the rates which are now being charged by the C. & P. Tel. Co. of Baltimore City pursuant to Federal authority are, by the express terms of the Act of Congress of July 11, 1919, made subject to modification or change by the Commission, I know of no reason why the Commission should not, even before December 1, 1919, entertain jurisdiction of an application by the C. & P. Telephone Co. of Baltimore City for a general readjustment of its rates.

Truly yours,
WM. CABELL BRUCE,
General Counsel.

(395)

Right of ⎫
⎪
Town to Charge Motor Vehicle Fees ⎬   July 31, 1919.
Other Than Those Prescribed by ⎪
Statute. ⎭

Public Service Commission,
Munsey Building, Baltimore, Md.

Gentlemen:

I have received your communication of the 25th inst., which was accompanied by a letter, dated the 24th inst., from Benj. B. F. Graves, Acting Manager, to you, asking you whether the Town Council of North Beach, in Calvert County, is lawfully empowered to adopt a license ordinance requiring every public conveyance carrying passengers or freight, as a regular business, within the corporate limits of North Beach to pay a license fee of $10.00, in addition to such fee as it is required to pay for the purpose of registration to the Commissioner of Motor Vehicles. I assume, as I think I can safely do, that the public conveyances mentioned in Mr. Graves' letter are altogether automobiles, or motor cars, or motor vehicles within the purview of Section 1½ of the Public Service Commission Law as amended by the Acts of 1914, Chapter 445.

In my opinion, the Town Council of North Beach has no lawful right to impose such a license fee. It is provided by the Public General Laws of the State, (Section 133, of Art. 56, of the Annotated Code of Maryland, Vol. 4), that no City, County or other municipal subdivision of the State shall have the right to make or authorize any local ordinance or regulation which shall require any registration or licensing of motor vehicles or operators thereof, in addition to the registration and licensing prescribed in Article 56, Sub-title Motor Vehicles, or impose upon the owner or operator of any motor vehicle any tax, registration fee, license fee, assessment or charge of any kind for the use of a motor vehicle upon any public highway or highways of Maryland.

Truly yours,
WM. CABELL BRUCE,
General Counsel.

(396)

Validity of ⎱

Franchise Rate of the UNITED RAILWAYS ⎰   August 2, 1919.
& ELECTRIC CO.

Public Service Commission,
   Munsey Building, Baltimore, Md.

Gentlemen:

I have received your communication of the 28th inst., asking me to submit an opinion to you covering the question submitted to you by Mr. Yellott, the Special Counsel in the United Railways & Electric Co. rate investigation case, in his letter to you of the 25th inst.

The inquiry suggested by Mr. Yellott is as to what effect should be given by the Commission to the special provisions in regard to rates contained in Ordinance No. 44 of the Mayor & City Council of Baltimore of March 28, 1859; and in Chapter 71 of the Acts of the General Assembly of Maryland for the year 1862 by which Ordinance No. 44 was approved.

The ordinance granted to the original promoters of the Baltimore City Passenger Railway Company, the successor in interest of these promoters, and one of the corporate entities of which The United Railways & Electric Co. of Baltimore is the consolidated result, certain valuable franchises in Charles, Read and Calvert Streets and other public highways in the City of Baltimore, and provided that the price for transporting passengers in the cars which were to be operated over the streets or highways in which the franchises were to be exercised should, for transit from any one part of the City to any other on the lines established on these streets or highways, not exceed the sum of 5 cents per passenger. Subsequently, by Chapter 71 of the Acts of 1862 all the rights and privileges granted by Ordinance No. 44 were conferred upon the Baltimore City Passenger Railway Co., save where the provisions of the Ordinance were inconsistent with the Act; the company having, in the meantime, taken over the rights of the original promoters. Still later, by Chapter 170 of the Acts of the General Assembly of Maryland for the year 1864, it was provided, after a recital setting forth the fact that the 5 cent fare prescribed by the Ordinance had proved insufficient for running the road of the Baltimore City Passenger Railway Co., that it should be authorized to charge and collect 6 cents as the fare from each passenger from any one part of the City of Baltimore to any other part on the line of the said railway without charge for transfer tickets. And still later, by Chapter 100 of the Acts of the General Assembly of Maryland for the year 1865, it was provided that the fares of the Baltimore City Passenger Railway Co. should be 6 cents for each passenger and a charge of 4 cents for transfer tickets. And still later, by legislation which afterwards came to be embodied in Section 796 of the Baltimore City Charter (Weeks' Compilation, p. 429), it was provided that the United Railways & Electric Co. of Baltimore, into which the Baltimore City Passenger Railway Co. had in the meantime been merged, its successors and assigns, should charge 5 cents and no more as a fare for the conveyance of each passenger over 12 years of age, and 3 cents and no more for each child between the ages of 4 and 12 years from any point on any of its lines to any other point on such lines within the City of Baltimore; provided that such company should give a free transfer when the same should be requested upon the payment of each cash fare, which transfer should be good at all points of intersection of lines of said railway for a continuous ride, except at such points on said lines where such form a route so as to permit a passenger to return in the same general direction of the line upon which the transfer was issued; the privilege of transfer, however, not to apply to the terminus of any line or route. These provisions, as embodied in Section 796 of the Baltimore City Charter, were also accompanied by the further proviso that nothing in them should be construed to affect any of the interests of the Mayor and City Council of Baltimore in the United Railways & Electric Company of Baltimore or any of the railways consolidated under the corporate name.

Thus the matter of fares that could be charged on the Baltimore City Passenger Railway lines of the United Railways & Electric Co. of Baltimore stood at the time of the passage of the Public Service Commission Law on April 5, 1910; by which law full power was conferred upon the Public Service Commission to regulate the fares of all street railways in the State of Maryland, including the Baltimore City Passenger Railway lines of the United Railways & Electric Co. of Baltimore.

From the above statement of facts, it is manifest that the original 5 cent fare prescribed by Ordinance No. 44 as one of the conditions of the franchise which the Ordinance granted was repeatedly, even before the passage of the Public Service Commission Law, modified at pleasure by the General Assembly of Maryland. Nor was this the only respect in which that Ordinance was so modified by the General Assembly. By Section 14 of the Ordinance, the promoters of the Baltimore City Passenger Railway Co. were peremptorily required to pay into the hands of the City Register of Baltimore City quarterly one-fifth of the gross receipts accruing from the passenger travel upon the roads located within the City limits under the Ordinance, or upon any extension of said limits which might be determined upon thereafter. It is a matter of common knowledge, of course, that subsequently this requirement was by the General Assembly of Maryland replaced by a tax of 9 per cent. upon the gross receipts of the several passenger street railways companies in Baltimore City, payable in quarterly installments to the Mayor and City Council of Baltimore, (Baltimore City Charter, Section 797, Weeks' Compilation, p. 429).

Having for years acquiesced in the modifications of the original 5 cent fare fixed by Ordinance No. 44 which were operated by successive Acts of the General Assembly of Maryland, as well as in the modification of the Gross Receipts Tax fixed by Ordinance No. 44; and having year after year settled with the United Railways & Electric Co. of Baltimore and its corporate predecessors in accord with these statutory modifications, it would seem plain that even if the effect of Ordinance No. 44 was to create a binding contract between the original promoters of the Baltimore City Passenger Railway Co. and their assignees and the City of Baltimore, this contract was, even before the passage of the Public Service Commission Law, waived or abandoned by the City of Baltimore, and that though it were assumed that the General Assembly of Maryland did not have the constitutional power to alter the original 5 cent rate prescribed by Ordinance No. 44. It is true, as we have seen, that the above mentioned legislation in force at the time the Public Service Commission Law was passed provided that nothing in that legislation should be construed to affect any of the interests of the Mayor and City Council of Baltimore in the United Railways & Electric Co. of Baltimore or any of the railways consolidated under the corporate name, but it is obvious that these reservations, following as they do immediately upon legislative provisions declaring in the clearest and most pointed manner what the fares of the United Railways & Electric Co., its successors and assigns, should be, had and could have no application to any franchise-made fare that its own terms superseded.

The question, therefore, that has been submitted to me resolves itself purely, it appears to me, into the question as to whether all previous rates for the United Railways & Electric Co. of Baltimore or any of its predecessors, including the Baltimore City Passenger Railway Co., were by necessary implication repealed by the State-wide police jurisdiction and authority over street railroad rates conferred upon the Public Service Commission by the Public Service Commission Law; to say nothing of Section 31½ of that Law, which expressly revoked all Acts, or parts of Acts, that prescribed or limited the price at which any corporation subject to the Public Service Commission Law might furnish, sell or dispose of its product or utility.

In view of what the Court of Appeals decided in this connection in the case of Gregg vs. Laird et al., 121 Md., 1, and the case of Yeatman vs. Towers, 126 Md., 513; and in view of what the Supreme Court of the United States decided in Manigault vs. Spring, 199 U. S., 473, Armour Packing Co. vs. U. S., 209 U. S., 56, and L. & N. R. R. Co. vs. Mottley, 219 U. S., 467, all of which cases, both State and Federal, I have repeatedly had occasion to call to the attention of the Commission as authorizing the principle that contracts, even as between individuals, when entered into are necessarily subject to the control of the police power of the State whenever germane to that power, is a question that I cannot answer but in one way.

The power to regulate rates is a police power and is one which may be exercised by the Legislature directly, or its exercise may be committed by the Legislature to a Board or Commission. (Yeatman vs. Towers, 126 Md., 517.) When, therefore, the General Assembly of Maryland created the Public Service Commission, and clothed it with the authority to regulate street railroad rates, and expressly repealed all Acts, or parts of Acts, by which special street railroad rates were prescribed, all pre-existing street railroad rates within the State of Maryland, whether franchise-made rates or otherwise, were, in my judgment, annulled.

I can see no reason in principle why the special water rate which Yeatman was enjoying by virtue of a binding contract at the time that the Public Service Commission Law went into effect should have been abrogated by the passage of that Law, as was held in Yeatman vs. Towers, supra, that would not be equally applicable to a Maryland municipality which prior to the passage of the same Law granted a franchise in its streets to a street railroad company subject to the condition that the company should not charge a fare in excess of a certain amount. Nor can I see anything in the case of the Columbus Railway & Power Co. vs. the City of Columbus, 39 Supreme Court Reporter, 340, to which you have been referred by Mr. Yellott, to affect this conclusion. All that the Court said in that case was that an ordinance which grants a franchise in the streets of a city to a street railroad company, and prescribes a fixed fare as one of the conditions of the grant, is a valid and binding contract between the city and the company which the city is powerless to cancel. Of course, that is just what the Court of Appeals of Maryland long before the decision in the Yeatman case, supra, decided in the case of the C. & P. Tel Co. of Baltimore City, 89 Md., 689, with respect to Ordinance No. 41 of the Mayor and City Council of Baltimore, afterwards ratified by the General Assembly of Maryland, which gave the C. & P. Tel. Co. the right to construct conduits under the streets of Baltimore upon certain conditions which had been faithfully performed by the Company. But while the Court held that a valid contract was created by the passage of this Ordinance and its acceptance by the Company, and that this contract could not be rescinded by the Mayor & City Council of Baltimore under ordinary circumstances, it distinctly recognized the principle that if the safety, health or morals of the public should require the rescission or modification of such a contract, it might be rescinded or modified under the police power of the State, or even of the City where the City had been vested with such power (p. 711). And moreover, even under the circumstances as actually presented to it, it declined to say whether it was competent for the General Assembly to repeal the legislation by which it had approved the rights and privileges conferred upon the company by Ordinance No. 41. The State, it said, had not attempted such repeal and until it did so it would be premature and unauthorized to pass upon its right and power to do so. (716.) And this, it should be borne in mind, was a case in which the power to regulate the rates of public service corporations, an unquestionable branch of the police jurisdiction of the State, was not involved at all. But since the decision of Yeatman vs. Towers, *supra*, what the Court would have said in this connection, if the power to regulate rates had been involved in the C. & P. Telephone Co. case, is too obvious to admit of any doubt. Cases can undoubtedly be found in which Public Service Commissions have reached a conclusion different from my own, though it is observable that as late as December 23, 1918, it was held by the Pennsylvania Public Service Commission, in the case of the Borough of Warren vs. Warren Street Railway Co., P. U. R. Annotated, 1919-B, p. 619, that the Commission had jurisdiction to fix reasonable rates, notwithstanding a franchise-made fare. The same thing was held in *Re* Central Illinois Public Service Commission, No. 8290, January 7, P. U. R., 1919-B, and *Re* Bridgeton Electric Co., No. 14, 1918 (New Jersey). But it is a matter of secondary importance, I think, to ask what the conclusions of the different Public Service Commissions of the country touching the question have been; for, as I see the matter, it has been finally determined for us by decisions of the Supreme Court of the United States and our own Court of Appeals.

Truly yours,
WM. CABELL BRUCE,
General Counsel.

---

(397)

In the Matter of

The Complaint of R. B. B. CHEW, JR., } .August 25, 1919.
vs.
PENNA. R. R. CO.

Public Service Commission,
Munsey Building, Baltimore, Md.

Gentlemen:

I have received your communication of the 22nd inst., in the matter of the complaint of Mr. R. B. B. Chew, Jr., that the Penna. R. R. Co. has removed a siding at Chew Station, on the Pope's Creek Branch of the Penna. R. R. Co., which is alleged by the complainant to be a matter of importance to him.

Paragraph 1, of General Order No. 58, of the United States Railroad Administration, dated February 20, 1919, expressly declares,

"That transportation systems under Federal control shall continue subject to the lawful Police Regulations of the several States which were and are applicable to privately operated transportation systems in such matters as * * * the establishment, maintenance and sanitation of station facilities * * * and all other matters of local service, safety and equipment."

And that,

"It will be the policy of the Director General to cause the orders of the State Commissions in these matters to be carried out."

In view of these provisions of the above mentioned order, I see no legal reason why the Commission could not now proceed, with due notice to the Penna R. R. Co., to re-establish the siding in question.

Truly yours,
WM. CABELL BRUCE,
General Counsel.

---

(898)

MAYOR & CITY COUNCIL OF LONACONING vs. LONACONING WATER COMPANY.	September 4, 1919. Case No. 1616.

Public Service Commission,
Munsey Building, Baltimore, Md.

Gentlemen:

I have received your communication of the 3rd inst., together with the letter from Mr. D. L. Sloan, attorney at law, Cumberland, Md., to the Commission, dated the 30th ult., which accompanied it.

I answer the inquiries of Mr. Sloan by saying that re-hearings by the Public Service Commission are regulated by Section 11 of the Public Service Commission Law, (Ch. 180 of the Acts of 1910). Under the provisions of this Section, any party interested in an order of the Commission may apply for a re-hearing in respect to any matter determined therein; and the Commission may grant and hold such a re-hearing if in its judgment sufficient reason therefor be made to appear; and if the re-hearing shall be granted the same shall be determined by the Commission within 30 days after the same shall have been finally submitted. But, by this same Section, it is also expressly declared that any application for such a re-hearing shall not excuse any public service corporation subject to the jurisdiction of the Commission from complying with or obeying any order or any requirement of any order of the Commission, or operate in any manner to stay or postpone the enforcement thereof; except as the Commission may by order direct.

Truly yours,
WM. CABELL BRUCE,
General Counsel.

(399)

In the Matter of.

"Jitney" Between Flohrville and Sykesville.

October 7, 1919.

Public Service Commission,
   Munsey Building, Baltimore, Md.

Gentlemen:

I have just received your letter of the 6th inst., which was accompanied by a letter from Mr. M. S. H. Unger, Superintendent of the Board of Education of Carroll County, dated the 6th inst., in which the writer combats the right of Mr. Wickes, the Transportation Expert of the Commission, to refuse a permit to the owner of a touring car who is holding himself out as a common carrier to the general public, but has entered into an undertaking with the Board of Education of Carroll County to give up to them, for the purposes of two round trips each day between Flohrville and Sykesville, the exclusive use of his cars. The object of the Board in securing this contract right is to provide for the speedy transportation of 22 school children to and fro between the two points just mentioned, so as to obviate an existing shortage of teachers. The children pay no fee or charge and ride or walk as they choose, and, under the circumstances, the Board believes that the car, so far as it is employed for the purposes of the two round trips, is not engaged in the public transportation of passengers for hire over a State, State Aid, or improved County road, or an urban road or street, within the meaning of Chapter 610 of the Acts of 1916 as amended by Chapter 199 of the Acts of 1918, but merely in what the Board terms "private service."

There is a case now pending in the Court of Appeals of Maryland— namely, the case of Wildason *vs.* the Public Service Commission—which will be argued in a few days, and which will probably be decisive of the question submitted to me. In view of this fact, my advice for the present to the Commission is to withhold a permit from the owner of the car mentioned in the letter of the Board to you, but to refrain likewise from an application for an injunction to restrain the continued execution of the undertaking mentioned in that letter.

Truly yours,
·WM. CABELL BRUCE,
General Counsel.

(400)

In Re

Right of the Commission to Grant a
Bridge Co. Permission to Charge Re-
duced Rates for Transportation of   October 8, 1919.
Freight Over Its Bridge Co. to the
State of Virginia.

Public Service Commission,
Munsey Building, Baltimore, Md.

Gentlemen:

I have received your communication of the 7th inst. and the accompanying letter, dated the 6th inst., from H. D. Baker, President of
the Berlin & Lovettsville Bridge Co., to you, in which the writer asks
you whether his company can lawfully permit the Virginia State
Highways Commission, a political agency of the State of Virginia, to
transport free of charge across its bridge at Brunswick stone for the
resurfacing of the road leading from Lovettsville, in the State of
Virginia, to Brunswick.

By Section 16 of the Public Service Commission Law, it is provided
that no common carrier (which term is, by Section 1¾ of the same
law, made broad enough to cover the bridge at Brunswick) shall
directly or indirectly issue or give any free tickets, free pass, or free
transportation for passengers or property between points within this
State, except certain persons and certain classes of service which are,
by the express terms of the same section, exempted from its operation. Without stopping to ask the legal effect of the term "between
points within this State," it is enough for me to say that among the
kinds of service so exempted is "the carriage free or at reduced rates
of persons or property for the United States, State or Municipal Governments." This language, in my opinion, is sufficiently comprehensive to warrant the Commission in answering the question of Mr.
Baker in the affirmative.

Truly yours,

WM. CABELL BRUCE,
General Counsel.

APPENDIX IV

Summaries for Twelve Months Ended
September 30, 1919

METER TESTS
Gas, Electric, Water and Proportional

GAS TESTS AND ANALYSES

ACCIDENTS
Personal Accident Reports

TRANSPORTATION AND UTILITY COMPANIES

SUMMARY OF GAS METER TESTS FOR THE YEAR ENDED SEPTEMBER 30, 1919.

Size Lt.	Company	New			Old			Complaint			Totals			Totals	Company Totals
		O. K.	Fast	Slow	O. K.	Fast	Slow	O. K.	Fast	Slow	O. K.	Fast	Slow		
2	American Street Lighting Company							1			1			1	1
3	Annapolis Public Utilities Company				119	6	31				119	6	31	156	
5	"	61	2	12	70	6	14		2		131	10	26	167	
20	"	3			1						4			4	327
3	Cambridge Gas Electric Light & Power Co.				20		4				20		4	24	24
3	Chestertown Gas Co.				1		1				1		1	2	
5	"				3	2					3	2		5	7
3	Citizens Gas Co.				46	9	17				46	9	17	72	
5	"				11	12	8				11	12	8	31	
10	"				1						1			1	
20	"				1		2				1		2	3	107
2	Consolidated Gas Electric Light & Power Co.				295	1	65				295	1	65	361	
3	"				15		9				15		9	24	
5	"	2,249	71	502	12,448	780	3,245	2	3	1	14,699	854	3,748	19,301	
10	"	53	1	8	316	7	80				369	8	88	465	
20	"	160	4	27	203	3	47				363	7	74	444	
25	"				1						1			1	
30	"	97		19	156	2	22				253	2	41	296	
45	"			3	43		6				43		9	52	
60	"	23		11	45	2	4				68	2	15	85	
80	"				11		1				11		1	12	
100	"				27	3					27	3		30	
160	"				17	6					17	6		23	
200	"				24	1	15				24	1	15	40	
230	"	3									3			3	21,137
3	Consolidated Public Utilities Co.				12	1	1				12	1	1	14	
5	"				1						1			1	
20	"				1						1			1	16
3	Crisfield Light & Power Co.				4		1				4		1	5	
5	"	9		1	5		1				14		2	16	21

Easton Light & Fuel Co.	3									0	1	2			
	5									0					15
Elkton Gas Co.	3							5		5			2	2	7
Hagerstown Light & Heat Co.	3	40	1	9	255	44	87	255	45	87	387	722
	5				161	39	69	201	40	78	319	
	10				6	1	3	6	1	3	10	
	30								1		1	
	45				1	1		1	1		1	
	60				1	1	1	1	1		2	
	100				1	1		1	1	1	1	
	250										1	
Hagerstown & Frederick Railway Co.	3	19		6	272	13	62	291	13	68	372	722
	5	23		6	30	1	8	53	2	14	69	
	10			1	1		1	5		2	7	
	20	4		1	3					1	2	
Hyattsville Gas & Electric Co.	5	84		21	48	14	8	132	14	29	175	450
	10	1		1	1			1		1	2	
West Virginia & Maryland Gas Co.	5	114	27	57	507	110	240	621	137	297	1,055	177
	10				1	1	1	4	1	1	6	
	20				1			1			1	
	30				4	1	2	3		2	7	
	60				3			3			3	
	100											
Totals		2,943	107	684	15,211	1,067	4,060	18,157	1,181	4,746	24,084	1,073
												24,084

Total new gas meters tested.................... 3,734
Total old gas meters tested.................... 20,338
Total complaint gas meters tested.............. 12
Grand total, gas meters........................ 24,084

SUMMARY OF ELECTRIC METER TESTS FOR THE YEAR ENDED SEPTEMBER 30, 1919.

Size Amps.	Company	New	Old	Complaint O. K.	Complaint Fast	Complaint Slow	Totals	Company Totals
5	Annapolis Public Utilities Co.............	101	....	....	....	1	102	
10	"	24	....	....	....		24	
15	"	3	....	....	....	1	4	
25	"	5	....	....	....		5	
50	"	5	....	....	....		5	
75	"	2	....	....	....		2	142
5	Antietam Electric Light & Power Co.	....	3	....	....		3	
25	"	....	1	....	....		1	
50	"	....	1	....	....		1	5
5	Bel Air Electric Co.	....	1	....	....		1	
10	"	29	6	....	....		35	
25	"	1	....	....	....		1	37
5	Calvert Building & Construction Co...	1	....	....	....		1	
50	"	1	1	....	....		2	3
5	Cambridge Gas Electric Light & Power Co....	....	....	....	....	2	2	2
5	Centreville Electric Plant...................	15	....	....	....		15	15
5	Chestertown Electric Light & Power Co......	18	5	....	....		23	
10	"	1	6	....	....		7	
15	"	....	1	....	....		1	
50	"	....	1	....	....		1	32
3	Consolidated Gas Electric Light & Power Co..	....	50	....	....		50	
5	"	5,235	1,731	....	....		6,966	
7½	"	....	30	....	....		30	
10	"	401	485	....	....		886	
15	"	124	285	....	....	1	410	
20	"	....	10	....	....		10	
25	"	97	201	....	....		298	
40	"	2	6	....	....		8	
50	"	84	138	....	....		222	
75	"	28	57	....	....		85	
80	"	....	2	....	....		2	
100	"	26	28	....	....		54	
120	"	....	1	....	....		1	
150	"	18	28	....	....		46	
160	"	....	1	....	....		1	
200	"	16	12	....	....		28	
300	"	15	12	....	....		27	
400	"	1	8	....	....		9	
450	"	....	1	....	....		1	
600	"	2	10	....	....		12	
800	"	1	4	....	....		5	
1200	"	2	....	....	....		2	9,153
5	Consolidated Public Utilities Co.............	19	3	....	....		22	
10	"	11	3	....	....		14	
25	"	11	....	....	....		11	
50	"	....	1	....	....		1	
600	"	1	....	....	....		1	49
5	Consumers Ice Co.......................	....	16	....	....		16	
10	"	....	1	....	....		1	
25	"	3	....	....	....		3	
100	"	1	....	....	....		1	21
30	Crown, Cork & Seal Co....................	....	1	....	....		1	1
10	Dobler, John S............................	....	....	....	....	1	1	
25	"	....	....	....	....	1	1	2
	Forward..........................	6,304	3,151	....	....	7	9,462	9,462

SUMMARY OF ELECTRIC METER TESTS FOR THE YEAR ENDED SEPTEMBER 30, 1919
—Continued.

Size Amps.	Company	New	Old	Complaint O. K.	Fast	Slow	Totals	Company Totals
	Forward.............................	6,304	3,151	....	.....	7	9,462	9,462
5	Eastern Shore Gas & Electric Co.............	106	295	....	.....	.....	401	
10	"	11	96	....	.....	.....	107	
15	"	.....	44	....	.....	.....	44	
20	"	....	3	....	.....	.....	3	
25	"	20	28	....	.....	.....	48	
40	"	.....	2	....	.....	.....	2	
50	"	5	27	....	.....	.....	32	
75	"	.....	3	....	.....	.....	3	
100	"	3	7	....	.....	.....	10	
150	"	.....	1	....	.....	.....	1	
200	"	.....	1	....	.....	.....	1	
300	"	.....	1	....	.....	.....	1	
								653
2	Easton Utilities Commission...............	2	....	....	.....	.....	2	
5	"	12	....	....	.....	.....	12	
								14
3	Edison Electric Illuminating Co............	.....	1	....	.....	.....	1	
5	"	134	37	....	.....	.....	171	
10	"	6	29	....	.....	.....	35	
15	"	.....	7	....	.....	.....	7	
25	"	.....	11	....	.....	.....	11	
50	"	.....	4	....	.....	.....	4	
								229
100	Emerson Hotel Co...........	.....	1	....	.	.....	1	
								1
5	Frederick Gas & Electric Co................	111	59	....	.....	.....	170	
10	"	5	8	....	.....	.....	13	
15	"	9	....	....	.....	.....	9	
25	"	21	5	....	.....	.....	26	
50	"	7	3	....	.....	.....	10	
75	"	9	....	....	.....	.....	9	
120	"	.....	1	....	.....	.....	1	
150	"	.....	1	....	.....	.....	1	
								239
100	General Elevator Co........................	.....	....	....	.....	1	1	
								1
5	Hagerstown Municipal Electric Plant........	447	80	....	.....	.....	527	
10	"	22	18	....	.....	.....	40	
15	"	4	2	....	.....	.....	6	
20	"	2	5	....	.....	.....	7	
25	"	9	10	....	.....	.....	19	
30	"	3	4	....	.....	.....	7	
40	"	.....	2	....	.....	.....	2	
50	"	11	1	....	.....	.....	12	
60	"	1	4	....	.....	.....	5	
75	"	5	1	....	.....	.....	6	
80	"	.....	2	....	.....	.....	2	
100	"	2	2	....	.....	.....	4	
120	"	1	....	....	.....	.....	1	
200	"	.....	2	....	.....	.....	2	
300	"	2	2	....	.....	.....	4	
								644
5	Hagerstown & Frederick Railway Co........	248	57	....	.....	.....	305	
10	"	1	18	....	.....	.....	19	
15	"	.....	14	....	.....	.....	14	
20	"	.....	1	....	.....	.....	1	
25	"	3	23	....	.....	.....	26	
40	"	.....	1	....	.....	.....	1	
50	"	2	11	....	.....	.....	13	
60	"	.....	2	....	.....	.....	2	
75	"	.....	1	....	.....	.....	1	
80	"	.....	2	....	.....	.....	2	
100	"	1	3	....	.....	.....	4	
								388
	Forward.............................	7,529	4,094	....	.....	8	11,631	11,631

SUMMARY OF ELECTRIC METER TESTS FOR THE YEAR ENDED SEPTEMBER 30, 1919
—Concluded.

Size Amps.	Company	New	Old	Complaint O. K.	Fast	Slow	Totals	Company Totals
	Forward.........	7,529	4,094	.....	.....	8	11,631	11,631
5	Harpers Ferry Electric Light & Power Co.....	47	6	.....	.....	.....	53	
10	"	1	1	.....	.....	.....	2	
15	"	17	3	.....	.....	.....	20	
								75
5	Havre de Grace Electric Co...............	74	3	.....	.....	.....	77	
10	"	3	1	.....	.....	.....	4	
20	"	.....	1	.....	.....	.....	1	
25	"	1	.....	.....	.....	.....	1	
40	"	1	.....	.....	.....	.....	1	
50	"	1	.....	.....	.....	.....	1	
100	"	1	.....	.....	.....	.....	1	
								86
5	Home Manufacturing Light & Power Co......	29	22	.....	.....	.....	51	
15	"	.....	1	.....	.....	.....	1	
25	"	1	4	.....	.....	.....	5	
50	"	1	.....	.....	.....	.....	1	
								58
50	Industrial Building Co......................	.....	1	.....	.....	.....	1	
								1
5	Maryland Electric Railway Co..............	.....	1	.....	.....	.....	1	
40	"	.....	1	.....	.....	.....	1	
								2
1500	Mt. Vernon Cotton Duck Co.................	.....	1	.....	.....	.....	1	
								1
50	Potomac Electric Power Co.................	.....	.....	.....	1	.....	1	
								1
5	St. Michaels Utilities Commission...........	8	25	.....	.....	.....	33	
50	"	1	.....	.....	.....	.....	1	
								34
5	Severn Apartment......................	.....	1	.....	.....	.....	1	
								1
5	Severna Park Co.......	.....	3	.....	.....	.....	3	
10	"	.....	1	.....	.....	.....	1	
								4
5	Snow Hill Electric Light & Power Co........	.....	1	.....	.....	.....	1	
								1
5	Swentsel, Mrs. H. C.....................	.....	.....	.....	1	.....	1	
								1
	Totals............................	7,715	4,171	.....	2	8	11,896	11,896

```
Total new electric meters tested..............  7,715
Total old electric meters tested...............  4,171
Total complaint electric meters tested.........    10
                                                 _____
       Grand total..........................  11,896
```

GRAND SUMMARY OF METER TESTS.

Company	Gas	Electric	Totals
American Street Lighting Co.	1		1
Annapolis Public Utilities Co.	327	142	469
Antietam Electric Light & Power Co.		5	5
Bel Air Electric Co.		37	37
Calvert Building & Construction Co.		3	3
Cambridge Gas Electric Light & Power Co.	24	1	25
Centreville Electric Plant		15	15
Chestertown Electric Light & Power Co.		32	32
Chestertown Gas Co.	7		7
Citizens Gas Co., Salisbury	107		107
Consolidated Gas Electric Light & Power Co., Baltimore	21,137	9,153	30,290
Consolidated Public Utilities Co.	16	49	65
Consumers Ice Co.		21	21
Crisfield Light & Power Co.	21		21
Crown, Cork & Seal Co.		1	1
Dobler, John S.		2	2
Eastern Shore Gas & Electric Co.		654	654
Easton Light & Fuel Co.	15		15
Easton Utilities Commission		14	14
Edison Electric Illuminating Co.		229	229
Elkton Gas Co.	7		7
Emerson Hotel		1	1
Frederick Gas & Electric Co.		239	239
General Elevator Co.		1	1
Hagerstown Light & Heat Co.	722		722
Hagerstown Municipal Electric Plant		644	644
Hagerstown & Frederick Railway Co.	450	388	838
Harpers Ferry Electric Light & Power Co.		75	75
Havre de Grace Electric Co.		86	86
Home Manufacturing Light & Power Co.		58	58
Hyattsville Gas & Electric Co.	177		177
Industrial Building Co.		1	1
Maryland Electric Railways Co.		2	2
Mt. Vernon Cotton Duck Co.		1	1
Potomac Electric Power Co.		1	1
St. Michaels Utilities Commission		34	34
Severn Apartment House		1	1
Severna Park Co.		4	4
Swentsel, Mrs. H. C.		1	1
Snow Hill Electric Light & Power Co.		1	1
West Virginia & Maryland Gas Co.	1,073		1,073
Totals	24,084	11,896	35,980

SUMMARY OF TESTS OF COMPLAINT METERS.

	1911	1912	1913	1914	1915	1916	1917	1918	1919
GAS METERS:									
Total number tested	24	57	26	22	23	18	12	7	12
Total over 2% fast	1	8	1	4	3	2	6	1	1
ELECTRIC METERS:									
Total number tested	24	30	10	4	8	12	13	7	10
Total over 4% fast	2	1	0	0	0	0	2	1	0
WATER METERS:									
Total number tested	2	3	18	13	20	17	13	11	25
Total over 4% fast	1	1	1	1	0	0	1	0	1
STEAM METERS:									
Total number tested	0	0	0	1	0	1	0	5	10
Total over 4% fast	0	0	0	1	0	0	0	2	1

All records since the organization of the Commission have been checked and discrepancies adjusted to September 30, 1919.

COMPLAINT GAS METER TESTS—FOR YEAR ENDED SEPTEMBER 30, 1919.
CONSOLIDATED GAS ELECTRIC LIGHT AND POWER COMPANY OF BALTIMORE

Date Test	Card No.	Size Lt.	Applicant	RESULTS			Paid by
				O. K.	% Fast	% Slow	
10-15-18	204	5	Meyer S. Rosenblatt..........		1.0	......	App.
11-18-18	205	5	Mrs. Margaret C. Parker...... .	......	......	4.8	"
1-16-19	207	5	Miss Vena M. Harpold..............	......	2.0	......	"
2- 1-19	209	20	Simon Berkowits..................	......	......	2.9	"
2-25-19	210	10	J. T. Wentworth..................	......	1.4	......	"
2-25-19	211	5	Joseph Hoffman Jacobs.............	O. K.	......	......	"
2-28-19	212	5	Andrew Manigault....................	O. K.	......	......	"
8-18-19	215	5	F. Pettingell.......................	......	4.2	......	Co.
			Totals........................	2	4	2	

Total number tested............................. 8
Total number over 2% fast...................... 1

COMPLAINT ELECTRIC METER TESTS—FOR YEAR ENDED SEPTEMBER 30, 1919.
CONSOLIDATED GAS ELECTRIC LIGHT AND POWER COMPANY OF BALTIMORE.

Date Test	Card No.	Size Amp.	Applicant	RESULTS			Paid by
				O. K.	% Fast	% Slow	
12-11-18	108	15	Robert J. Auer.....................	.. ...	....	0.6	App.

COMPLAINT WATER METER TESTS FOR THE YEAR ENDED SEPTEMBER 30, 1919.

Date Test	Card No.	Size Inch	Applicant and Company	O. K.	% Fast	% Slow	Paid by
10–18–18	104	¾	George C. Heidelbach, Baltimore Co. Water & Electric Co..			7.58	App.
10–18–18	105	¾	George V. McGowan, Baltimore Co. Water & Electric Co..			1.08	"
10–17–18	106	⅝	Mrs. A. Moore, Artesian Water Company		1.01		"
10–14–18	107	⅝	W. F. Ludwig, Artesian Water Company		1.20		"
10–17–18	108	⅝	George Schneider, Artesian Water Company			20.20	"
11–12–18	109	⅝	H. B. Hasenbalg, Suburban Water Company		5.27		Co.
11–19–18	110	¾	Edwin McColgan, Baltimore Co. Water & Electric Co.			0.56	App.
12– 2–18	111	¾	H. G. Kiefer, Baltimore Co. Water & Electric Co.		0.29		"
12–13–18	112	½	Estate of William L. Russell, Artesian Water Co.			5.60	"
1– 7–19	113	½	Charles O. D. Adams, Baltimore Co. Water & Electric Co.			0.53	"
1–14–19	114	⅝	T. A. Deakins, Artesian Water Co.		1.0		"
1–15–19	115	¾	Lucian Duke, Baltimore Co. Water & Electric Co.		1.3		"
1–14–19	116	½	B. Shapiro, Artesian Water Co.			0.40	"
1–17–19	118	⅝	Sallie A. Beelér, Artesian Water Co.			5.00	"
1–17–19	119	⅝	A. Burker, Artesian Water Co.		0.30		"
1–30–19	120	¾	Mrs. Louise Frantz, Baltimore Co. Water & Electric Co.			19.53	"
2–20–19	121	⅝	Mrs. Anna M. Pollack, Baltimore Co. Water & Electric Co.			0.5	"
2–24–19	122	¾	R. N. Brown, Baltimore Co. Water & Electric Co.			0.03	"
3– 3–19	123	½	B. Cavalier, Artesian Water Co.			7.53	"
4– 9–19	124	½	Jonas Herman, Baltimore Co. Water & Electric Co.			0.10	"
4–10–19	125	½	McCauley & Co., Dorchester Water Co.			12.53	"
4–15–19	126	¾	Thomas F. McHugh, Baltimore Co. Water & Electric Co.			0.17	"
5– 5–19	127	½	H. S. Davis, Artesian Water Co.			2.22	"
6– 3–19	128	½	J. P. Brandau, Artesian Water Co.			34.86	"
8– 8–19	129	¾	M; Mahoney, Baltimore Co. Water & Electric Co.		2.90		"
			Totals	0	8	17	

Total number tested............................ 25
Total over 4% fast............................ 1

COMPLAINT STEAM METER TESTS.
FOR THE YEAR ENDED SEPTEMBER 30, 1919.

Date Test	Card No.	Size No.	Applicant and Company	O. K.	% Fast	% Slow	Paid by
12-26-18	8	....	R. W. Gray, John J. Carlin Heating Co..............		4.53	....	Co.
12-26-18	9	....	Edmund L. Bossle, John J. Carlin Heating Co....			12.30	App.
12-26-18	10	....	E. M. Alexander,* John J. Carlin Heating Co.............			100	Fee Retd.
12-26-18	11	....	E. H. Stewart.* John J. Carlin Heating Co.			100	Fee Retd.
12-26-18	12	....	R. E. Driver, John J. Carlin Heating Co.....		3.90	....	App.
1-15-19	13	....	U. S. Marine Corps, Terminal Freezing & Heating Co.....			2.4	"
3-11-19	14	2	R. Bers, John J. Carlin Heating Co..........	O. K.			"
3-18-19	15	2	E. J. Feltser, John J. Carlin Heating Co..........			9.26	"
3-19-19	16	6	Park Bank Building Co., Terminal Freezing & Heating Co.....			1.72	"
5-21-19	17	2	Mrs. V. J. Sieck, John J. Carlin Heating Co..........		3.6	....	"
			Totals........................	1	3	6	

```
Total number tested.............................10
Total over 4% fast............................. 1
*Would not register............................. 2
```

SUMMARY OF GAS TESTS AND ANALYSES.
CONSOLIDATED GAS ELECTRIC LIGHT AND POWER COMPANY OF BALTIMORE.

DATE	CANDLE POWER			B. T. U. TOTAL HEATING VALUE		
	High	Low	Ave.	High	Low	Ave.
October, 1918........................	18.7	14.7	16.5	569	541	554
November, 1918........................	18.8	14.3	16.1	567	541	552
December, 1918........................	17.5	13.7	15.4	556	541	549
January, 1919.................... ...	17.4	13.8	15.4	567	528	549
February, 1919........................	16.0	12.4	13.7	576	540	550
March, 1919...........................	16.5	13.5	14.9	568	535	549
April, 1919............................	18.5	16.4	17.5	575	541	555
May, 1919.............................	17.9	15.9	16.9	565	531	550
June, 1919............................	19.8	15.4	16.6	570	529	550
July, 1919.	18.7	16.4	17.7	561	530	550
August, 1919.........................	18.9	15.4	17.4	561	538	551
September, 1919.......................	18.2	15.2	16.8	564	542	551

	RANGE IN AVERAGE	
	Candle Power	Heating Value
Maximum..............................	17.7	555
Minimum..............................	13.7	549

PRIVATE ELECTRIC METERS TESTED.

FOR YEAR ENDED SEPTEMBER 30, 1919.

Date Test	Card No.	Size Amp.	Applicant	RESULTS			Paid by
				O. K.	% Fast	% Slow	
10-23-18	106	10	John S. Dobler, Baltimore....................	....	....	0.3	App.
10-29-18	107	100	General Elevator Co., Baltimore....................	....	....	100	"
1-21-19	110	5	Mrs. H. C. Swintsel, Tuscany Apartments Co..............	....	0.30	......	"
2- 4-19	111	25	John S. Dobler, Baltimore....................	....	....	2.15	"
			Totals........................	0	1	3	

Total number tested............................. 4

Total over 4% fast............................. 0

COMPLAINT ELECTRIC METER TESTS OUTSIDE OF BALTIMORE.

FOR THE YEAR ENDED SEPTEMBER 30, 1919.

Date Test	Card No.	Size Lt.	Applicant	RESULTS			Paid by
				O. K.	% Fast	% Slow	
12- 3-18	109	5	D. Weintrob, Eastern Shore Gas & Electric Company, Cambridge.................	......	....	0.6	App.
2-10-19	112	50	Mrs. E. S. Ewing, Potomac Electric Power Co........	....	0.60	......	"
2-24-19	113	5	Max Snyder, Annapolis Public Utility Co.........	....	....	1.01	"
7-15-19	115	15	Mrs. S. M. Smith, Annapolis Public Utility Co.........	....	....	0.22	"
9-11-19	116	5	C. A. Heagy, Cambridge General Electric Light & Power Co.....................	....	....	0.30	No Fee
			Totals........................	0	1	4	

Total number tested............................. 5

Total over 4% fast............................. 0

COMPLAINT GAS METER TESTS OUTSIDE OF BALTIMORE.

FOR THE YEAR ENDED SEPTEMBER 30, 1919.

Date Test	Card No.	Size Lt.	Applicant	RESULTS			Paid by
				O. K.	% Fast	% Slow	
1-13-19	206	5	R. J. Duval, Annapolis Public Utility Co.........	....	1.0	....	App.
2-13-19	208	3	T. L. Brodie, Hagerstown Light & Heating Co.....	....	0.76	....	"
3- 3-19	213	5	P. H. Magruder, Annapolis Public Utility Co.........	....	0.5	....	"
			Totals........................	0	3	0	

Total number tested.. 3
Total over 2% fast.. 0

PRIVATE GAS METER TESTS FOR THE YEAR ENDED SEPTEMBER 30, 1919.

Date Test	Card No.	Size Lt.	Applicant	RESULTS			Paid by
				O. K.	% Fast	% Slow	
5-19-19	214	2	American St. Lighting Co............. Baltimore, Md..................	O. K.	....	....	App.

INTERRUPTIONS TO POWER SUPPLY—ELECTRIC RAILWAYS, SUMMARY OF REPORTS UNDER COMMISSION'S ORDER No. 792.

Company	Oct., 1918	Nov.	Dec.	Jan., 1919	Feb.	Mar.	Apr.	May	June	July	Aug.	Sept.	Total Time Off	Average per Month
	h. m.	h. m.	h. m.	h. m.	h. m.	h. m.	h. m.	h. m.	h. m.	h. m.	h. m.	h. m.	h. m.	h. m. s.
Capital Traction Co., Washington, D. C.						0.49		1.20		0.7			2.52	0 14.20
Cumberland Electric Railway Co., Cumberland, Md.	0.45	0.30	2.50	1.85		0.35	0.27		1.25	1.35			9.42	0.45.30
United Railways & Electric Co., Baltimore, Md.	11.51	14.37	7.01	4.53		17.33	3.85	0.21	1.53	3.01	1.59		73.44	6.08.40
Maryland Electric Railways Co., Annapolis, Md.	1.03	0.05	0.16	0.19		0.36	1.34		0.16	0.33	0.47		6.31	0.32.35
Hagerstown & Frederick Railway Co., Frederick, Md.	5.55	1.37	0.38	0.15			0.81		2.10	1.54	3.25		21.54	1.49.30
Washington, Baltimore & Annapolis Electric Railway Co., Baltimore, Md.	3.47	9.39	14.25	7.46		18.47	26.49	7.49	9.20	11.31	16.39		134.01	11.10.05
Washington Railway & Electric Co., Washington, D. C.	23.04	1.36	5.33	5.57		2.45	4.53	4.23	2.42	10.34	4.00		80.14	6.41.10
Cumberland & Westernport Electric Railway Co., Cumberland, Md.	00.20	2.55	2.00			1.20	1.10		3.15	4.00			17.00	1.25.00
Towson & Cockeysville Electric Railway Co., Belair, Md.	No Interruptions.													
Chambersburg, Greencastle & Waynesboro Street Railway Co. (Blue Ridge Ry.), Waynesboro, Pa.	No Interruptions.													
Washington & Great Falls Railway & Power Co., Washington, D. C.	Not reporting.													
Baltimore & Belair Electric Railway, Belair, Md.	No Interruptions.													
Ke..ton Railway Co., Kensington,														

SUMMARY OF PERSONAL ACCIDENT REPORTS OF ALL TRANSPORTATION COMPANIES IN THE STATE OF MARYLAND, OCTOBER 1, 1918, TO SEPTEMBER 30, 1919.

Class of Person	Baltimore & Ohio Railroad Co.		Pennsylvania Railroad Co.		Western Maryland Railway Co.		Minor Steam Railroad Cos.		Total	
	Killed	Injured	Killed	Injured	Killed	Injured	Killed	Injured	Killed	Injured
Public:										
On right of way	16	9	16	14	7	5	3	2	42	30
Passengers		18	3	29		1		1	3	49
Carried under contract				2						3
Others not trespassing	6	7	9	22		2	3	11	18	42
Total public	22	34	28	67	7	8	6	15	63	124
Employees:										
Trainmen	1	138	8	61	4	52	1	17	14	268
Trainmen in yards	3	47	1	4		8		6	4	65
Yard trainmen	4	81	2	31		95		2	6	139
Trackmen and bridgemen	3	1	2	1	1				6	2
Other employees	5	5	2	9	1	2	1	7	7	23
Employees not on duty										
Total employees	16	272	13	106	6	87	2	32	37	497
Grand total	38	306	41	173	13	95	8	47	100	621

SUMMARY OF PERSONAL ACCIDENT REPORTS OF THE MINOR GAS AND ELECTRIC COMPANIES IN MARYLAND.
OCTOBER 1, 1918—SEPTEMBER 30, 1919.

Class of Person.	October, 1918. Killed.	October, 1918. Injured.	November. Killed.	November. Injured.	December. Killed.	December. Injured.	January, 1919. Killed.	January, 1919. Injured.	February. Killed.	February. Injured.	March. Killed.	March. Injured.	April. Killed.	April. Injured.	May. Killed.	May. Injured.	June. Killed.	June. Injured.	July. Killed.	July. Injured.	August. Killed.	August. Injured.	September. Killed.	September. Injured.	Total. Killed.	Total. Injured.
PUBLIC:																										
Street or stations													1												1	
Consumers' premises																										
Other place																										
Total public													1												1	
EMPLOYEES:																										
Construction																										
Operation																	2								2	
Consumers' premises																										
Other places																										
Total employees																	2								2	
Grand total													1				2								3	

Details of Above Table:

April 24, 1919......Joseph Adams, a non-employee of the Perryville Electric Company, is said to have been electrocuted at the Company's power house by coming in contact with an outside wire.

June 21, 1919......Ted Forbes, signal maintainer, electrocuted by high tension transformer hanging down. C. V. R. R.

June 10, 1919......Lineman Magee came in contact with live wire on pole south of Pumphrey Station. Died upon arriving at hospital.

SUMMARY OF PERSONAL ACCIDENT REPORTS OF ALL UTILITY COMPANIES IN THE STATE OF MARYLAND, OCTOBER 1, 1918—SEPTEMBER 30, 1919.

Class of Person	Chesapeake & Potomac Telephone Co.		United Railways and Electric Co.		All Other Electric Railways		Consolidated Gas Electric Light and Power Co.		All Other Gas and Electric Companies		Total	
	Killed	Injured	Killed	Injured	Killed	Injured	Killed	Injured	Killed	Injured	Killed	Injured
Public:												
On street or stations	....	6	23	726	14	7	....	1	1	....	38	740
Consumers' premises or Company's territory	....	2	7	5,196	3	18	....	....	....	....	10	5,216
Vehicles and other places	....	5	8	393	3	15	....	....	....	....	11	413
Total public	....	13	38	6,315	20	40	....	1	1	....	59	6,369
Employees:												
Cars or construction	1	66	3	875	....	14	....	6	....	....	4	961
Track or operation	....	....	....	172	....	....	1	67	....	....	1	239
Consumers' premises or Company's territory	....	98	....	373	....	....	1	5	....	....	1	476
Others	....	26	1	200	1	2	2	18	2	....	6	246
Total employees	1	190	4	1,620	1	16	4	96	2	....	12	1,922
Grand total	1	203	42	7,935	21	56	4	97	3	....	71	8,291

TRANSPORTATION COMPANIES.
PERSONS KILLED.
OCTOBER 1, 1918, TO SEPTEMBER 30, 1919.

Company	Public	Employees	Total
Baltimore & Ohio Railroad Co.	22	16	38
The Pennsylvania Railroad Co.	28	13	41
Western Maryland Railway Co.	7	6	13
Minor steam railroad companies in Maryland	6	2	8
Total	63	37	100

TRANSPORTATION COMPANIES.
PERSONS INJURED.
OCTOBER 1, 1918, TO SEPTEMBER 30, 1919.

Company	Public	Employees	Total
Baltimore & Ohio Railroad Co.	34	272	306
The Pennsylvania Railroad Co.	67	106	173
Western Maryland Railway Co.	8	87	95
Minor steam railroad companies in Maryland	15	32	47
Total	124	497	621

SUMMARY OF PERSONAL ACCIDENT REPORTS OF THE BALTIMORE & OHIO RAILROAD COMPANY, OCTOBER 1, 1918, TO SEPTEMBER 30, 1919.

Class of Person	October, 1918		November		December		January, 1919		February		March		April		May		June		July		August		September		Total	
	Killed	Injured	Killed	Injured	Killed	Injured	Killed	Injured	Killed	Injured	Killed	Injured	Killed	Injured	Killed	Injured	Killed	Injured	Killed	Injured	Killed	Injured	Killed	Injured	Killed	Injured
Public:																										
On right of way	3	1	2		2				1	1	1	1	2		1	1		2		1	3		1	1	16	9
Passengers				1		5				1						1		3		1				2		18
Carried under contract																										
Others not trespassing					1	1		2			1	1	2		1	2							1	1	6	7
Total public	3	1	2	1	3	6		2	1	2	2	2	4	1	2	4		5		2	3	4	2	4	22	34
Employees:																										
Trainmen		13		11		16		12		13		5		8		11		8		12		17		12	2	138
Trainmen in yards		2		5		8		9		3		8		5		1		4		5		1		3	3	47
Yard trainmen		8		7		9		9		2		8		6		6		8		5		8		10	3	81
Trackmen and bridgemen																										
Other employees			1							1						1						1		1	8	1
Employees not on duty		1			1		1						1	2	1				1		1		1	1	5	5
Total employees	2	24	3	23	1	33	2	30		17		11	3	19	2	19		20	2	22	1	27	2	27	16	272
Grand total	5	25	5	24	4	40	2	32	1	19	2	13	7	20	3	23		25	2	23	4	31	3	31	38	306

SUMMARY OF PERSONAL ACCIDENT REPORTS OF THE WESTERN MARYLAND RAILWAY COMPANY, OCTOBER 1, 1918, TO SEPTEMBER 30, 1919.

Class of Person	October, 1918 Killed	October, 1918 Injured	November Killed	November Injured	December Killed	December Injured	January, 1919 Killed	January, 1919 Injured	February Killed	February Injured	March Killed	March Injured	April Killed	April Injured	May Killed	May Injured	June Killed	June Injured	July Killed	July Injured	August Killed	August Injured	September Killed	September Injured	Total Killed	Total Injured
Public:																										
On right of way	2	1	1		1		1	1	1			1		1		2					1				7	6
Passengers																										
Carried under contract																										
Others not trespassing																						1		1		2
Total public	2	1	1		1		1	1	1			1		1		2					1	1		1	7	8
Employees:																										
Trainmen	1	4		6	1	6	1	10		4	1			2		2		4		5		4		5	4	52
Trainmen in yards				7				1								2		1								8
Yard trainmen		2				3		2		2		3		1		2		1		2		1		2		25
Trackmen and bridgemen			1																						1	
Other employees		1																								1
Employees not on duty											1			1								1			1	2
Total employees	1	7	1	13	1	9	1	13		6	2	3		4		6		6		7		6		7	6	87
Grand total	3	8	2	13	2	9	2	14	1	6	2	4		5		8		6		7	1	7		8	13	95

SUMMARY OF PERSONAL ACCIDENT REPORTS OF THE PENNSYLVANIA RAILROAD COMPANY, OCTOBER 1, 1918, TO SEPTEMBER 30, 1919.

Class of Person	October, 1918 Killed	October, 1918 Injured	November Killed	November Injured	December Killed	December Injured	January, 1919 Killed	January, 1919 Injured	February Killed	February Injured	March Killed	March Injured	April Killed	April Injured	May Killed	May Injured	June Killed	June Injured	July Killed	July Injured	August Killed	August Injured	September Killed	September Injured	Total Killed	Total Injured
Public:																										
On right of way	3	1			2	2	2	1		1	1	1	1	2	1	2	3		1	2	1	2	2		17	14
Passengers		1		3	1	2		1		4	1	2		3		2	1	3		2		3		3	3	29
Carried under contract																		1						1		2
Others not trespassing		5		1	2	2		3		2		1	4			1		2				4	3	1	9	22
Total public	3	7		4	5	6	2	5		7	2	4	5	5	1	5	4	6	1	4	1	9	5	5	29	67
Employees:																										
Trainmen	4	5		3	2	5		9	1	4	1	3		2		2		6		8		7		7	8	61
Trainmen in yards	1	1		1																				2	1	4
Yard trainmen	1	1		3	1	7		3		3		2		3		4		3		1				1	2	31
Trackmen and bridgemen																										
Other employees									1										1	1					2	1
Employees not on duty								1				2		1		1		1		2				1		9
Total employees	6	7		7	3	12		13	2	7	1	7		6		7		10	1	12		7		11	13	106
Grand total	9	14		11	8	18	2	18	2	14	3	11	5	11	1	12	4	16	2	16	1	16	5	16	42	173

SUMMARY OF PERSONAL ACCIDENT REPORTS OF THE CHESAPEAKE AND POTOMAC TELEPHONE COMPANY OF BALTIMORE CITY, OCTOBER 1, 1918—SEPTEMBER 30, 1919.

Class of Person	Oct. 1918 Killed	Oct. 1918 Injured	Nov. Killed	Nov. Injured	Dec. Killed	Dec. Injured	Jan. 1919 Killed	Jan. 1919 Injured	Feb. Killed	Feb. Injured	Mar. Killed	Mar. Injured	Apr. Killed	Apr. Injured	May Killed	May Injured	June Killed	June Injured	July Killed	July Injured	Aug. Killed	Aug. Injured	Sept. Killed	Sept. Injured	Total Killed	Total Injured
PUBLIC:																										
Street or stations		2						1		1				1		1										6
Subscribers' premises										1				1												2
Other places		1				1		1		1				1												5
Total public		3				1		2		3				3		1										13
EMPLOYEES:																										
Construction		9		7		8		7		3		8		2		4	1	13		13		8		8	1	66
Subscribers' premises		3		3		2				1		2		2		3		2		2		4		2		42
Exchanges		6		2		6		8		2		7		3		10		4		6		2		6		56
On street								2		1		4		1		1		2						1		26
Total employees		18		12		16		17		7		21		8		18	1	21		21		14		17	1	190
Grand total		21		12		17		19		10		21		11		19	1	21		21		14		17	1	203

SUMMARY OF PERSONAL ACCIDENT REPORTS OF THE CONSOLIDATED GAS ELECTRIC LIGHT & POWER COMPANY OF BALTIMORE, OCTOBER 1, 1918—SEPTEMBER 30, 1919.

Class of Person.	Oct. 1918 Inj.	Oct. Kld.	Nov. Inj.	Nov. Kld.	Dec. Inj.	Dec. Kld.	Jan. 1919 Inj.	Jan. Kld.	Feb. Inj.	Feb. Kld.	Mar. Inj.	Mar. Kld.	Apr. Inj.	Apr. Kld.	May Inj.	May Kld.	June Inj.	June Kld.	July Inj.	July Kld.	Aug. Inj.	Aug. Kld.	Sept. Inj.	Sept. Kld.	Total Inj.	Total Kld.
PUBLIC:																										
Street or stations															1										1	
Consumers' premises																										
Other places																										
Total public															1										1	
EMPLOYEES:																										
Construction					1		2				1												2		6	
Operation	5		6		10		8		11	1	10		7				1		2		3		4		67	1
Consumers' premises							2		1		2		1			1	1		2		1				5	1
Other places										1	5										7	1	1		18	2
Total employees	5		6		11		12		12	2	18		8			1	2		4		11	1	7		96	4
Grand total	5		6		11		12		12	2	18		8		1	1	2		4		11	1	7		97	4

SUMMARY OF PERSONAL ACCIDENT REPORTS OF THE UNITED RAILWAYS & ELECTRIC COMPANY OF BALTIMORE, OCTOBER 1, 1918, TO SEPTEMBER 30, 1919.

Class of Person	Oct. 1918 Killed	Oct. 1918 Injured	Nov. Killed	Nov. Injured	Dec. Killed	Dec. Injured	Jan. 1919 Killed	Jan. 1919 Injured	Feb. Killed	Feb. Injured	Mar. Killed	Mar. Injured	Apr. Killed	Apr. Injured	May Killed	May Injured	June Killed	June Injured	July Killed	July Injured	Aug. Killed	Aug. Injured	Sept. Killed	Sept. Injured	Total Killed	Total Injured
Public:																										
Struck by cars		42	5	72	5	80	5	61	2	77	1	55	1	69	2	66		60	1	48	1	47		49	23	726
Boarding cars		100		111		140		166		159		141		148		123		155		122		132		113	1	1,610
Alighting from cars		117		127		167		130		105		98		129		103		173		146		162		140	1	1,598
Leaving front platform		39		46	1	54		61		61		60		60		61		64		58		52	1	59	2	675
Falling in cars		8		12		14		15		20		17	1	11		13		13		14		12		10	1	169
On cars		46		47		81		82		88		89		75		83		88		96		106		72	1	953
Collisions		28		28		15		28		21		8		9		10		13		14		16		20	1	201
In vehicles	1	49		59		44		35		20		18		20		22		22		38	2	36		30	8	393
Other																										
Total public	1	427	8	500	9	595	5	573	3	551	1	486	3	521	2	481		588	2	536	3	504	1	493	38	6,315
Employees:																										
On cars		61	3	108		90		71		60		58		65		52		68		87		78		77	3	875
On track		11		9		6		10		18		18		12		9		18		16		18		27		172
In shops and barns		19		25		28		33		24		29		24		34		38		47		39		34		373
Other		17		13		15		23	1	11		15		19		15		18		14		18		22	1	200
Total employees		108	3	155		139		136	1	113		120		120		110		142		164		163		160	4	1,620
Grand total	1	535	11	655	9	734	5	709	4	664	1	606	3	641	2	591		730	2	700	3	717	1	653	42	7,935

SUMMARY OF PERSONAL ACCIDENT REPORTS OF THE MINOR STEAM RAILROAD COMPANIES IN MARYLAND, OCTOBER 1, 1918, TO SEPTEMBER 30, 1919.

Class of Person	October, 1918		November		December		January, 1919		February		March		April		May		June		July		August		September		Total	
	Killed	Injured	Killed	Injured	Killed	Injured	Killed	Injured	Killed	Injured	Killed	Injured	Killed	Injured	Killed	Injured	Killed	Injured	Killed	Injured	Killed	Injured	Killed	Injured	Killed	Injured
Public:																										
On right of way			1					1	1		1					1									3	2
Passengers																			1							1
Carried under contract														1												1
Others not trespassing			2	3		1															1	5		2	3	11
Total public			3	3		1		1	1		1			1		1		1			1	5		2	6	15
Employees:																										
Trainmen				1		7		2						2		1		1		2	1	1			1	17
Trainmen in yards		1						1		1										1		1		1		6
Yard trainmen																2										2
Trackmen and bridgemen																										
Other employees												1										6				7
Employees not on duty							1																		1	
Total employees		1		1		7	1	3		1		1		2		3		1		3	1	8		1	2	32
Grand total		1	3	4		8	1	4	1	1	1	1		3		4		2		3	2	13		3	8	47

SUMMARY OF PERSONAL ACCIDENT REPORTS OF THE MINOR ELECTRIC RAILWAYS COMPANIES IN MARYLAND. OCTOBER 1, 1918, TO SEPTEMBER 30, 1919.

Class of Person	October, 1918.		November		December.		January, 1919.		February.		March.		April.		May.		June.		July.		August.		September.		Total.	
	Killed.	Injured.	Killed.	Injured.	Killed.	Injured.	Killed.	Injured.	Killed.	Injured.	Killed.	Injured.	Killed.	Injured.	Killed.	Injured.	Killed.	Injured.	Killed.	Injured.	Killed.	Injured.	Killed.	Injured.	Killed.	Injured.
Public:																										
Pedestrians	2	1	3		1		2		4	2	1	2	1			4		3	1			1		1	14	7
Passengers		3						3				1				3		3		1		3	2		3	18
In vehicles										1				1			1			5			2	2	3	15
Total public	2	4	3		1		2	3	4	3	1	3	1	1		7	1	6	1	6		4	4	3	20	40
Employees:																										
On cars		1						2				1		2				1		1		2		4		14
On track																										
In shops and barns																										
Others																				2			1		1	2
Total employees		1						2				1		2				1		3		2	1	4	1	16
Grand total	2	5	3		1		2	5	4	3	1	4	1	3		7	1	7	1	9		6	5	7	21	56

SUMMARY OF PERSONAL ACCIDENT REPORTS OF THE PUBLIC MOTOR VEHICLES OPERATING IN MARYLAND, OCTOBER 1, 1918, TO SEPTEMBER 30, 1919.

Cause	PUBLIC								EMPLOYEES						Grand Total	
	Passengers		Pedestrians		Other Persons		Total Public		Operators		Other Employees		Total Employees			
	Killed	Injured	Killed	Injured	Killed	Injured	Killed	Injured	Killed	Injured	Killed	Injured	Killed	Injured	Killed	Injured
Struck by buses		1		8				9								9
Boarding buses		1						1								1
Alighting from buses		5						5								5
Falling from buses									1				1		1	
Injured on buses		8						8								8
Collisions		1						1								1
Miscellaneous		12				5		17		3		3		6		23
Total		28		8		5		41	1	3		3	1	6	1	47

Date	Company	Public or Private Crossing and Protection	Location	Pedestrians				Remarks
				Killed	In-jured	Killed	In-jured	
Oct. 11, 1918	Md. Elec. Rys. Co.	Public; watchman	Maryland Ave., Westpt.	1				Struck by electric train.
Oct. 24, 1918	Penna. R. R. Co.	Public; watchman	Fleet St., Baltimore				6	Electric car struck by shifting engine.
Oct. 29, 1918	United Rys. & Elec. Co.	Public; no protection	York Road and McCabe Ave., Baltimore			1		Auto struck by electric car.
Nov. 2, 1918	B. & O. R. R. Co.	Public; watchman	Hyattsville			2	2	Auto struck by passenger train.
Nov. 9, 1918	B. C. & A. Ry. Co.	Public; no protection	East of Parsonsburg			2	2	Auto struck by passenger train.
Nov. 14, 1918	Penna. R. R. Co.	Public; no protection	Chesapeake Mills	1				Struck by passenger train.
Nov. 18, 1918	Cumb. & Penna. R.R. Co.	Public; signs	Lafferty's, Eckhart Junction				1	Auto collided with freight train.
Nov. 20, 1918	Western Md. Ry. Co.	Public; watchman	Oak Hill Ave., Hagerstown				1	Auto collided with freight train.
Nov. 21, 1918	B. & O. R. R. Co.	Public; sign	East of Mt. Airy				1	Auto struck by train.
Dec. 7, 1918	Penna. R. R. Co.	Public; bell and signals	Near Chattolanee Station				1	Auto truck struck by passenger train.
Dec. 12, 1918	Penna. R. R. Co.	Public; signs	Showell			2		Auto struck by express train.
Dec. 21, 1918	Cumb. Valley R. R. Co.	Public; watchman	Church St., Hagerstown				1	Auto struck by passenger train.
Dec. 21, 1918	Western Md. Ry. Co.	Public; watchman	Washington St., Hagerstown		1			Watchman struck by auto.
Dec. 22, 1918	Cumb. Valley R. R. Co.	Public; watchman	Washington St., Hagerstown				14	Motor bus struck by engine.
Dec. 30, 1918	B. & O. R. R. Co.	Public; watchman	Virginia Lane, Cumberland				1	Auto struck by passenger train.
Jan. 1, 1919	Western Md. Ry. Co.	Public; bell	Kemp's					Auto struck by train.
Jan. 3, 1919	Penna. R. R. Co.	Public; bell	Goldsboro St., Easton				2	Auto struck by passenger train.
Jan. 6, 1919	B. & O. R. R. Co.	Public; watchman	Baltimore St., Cumberland		1			Struck by freight engine.
Jan. 9, 1919	B. & O. R. R. Co.	Public; watchman	Baltimore St., Cumberland		1			Struck by passenger engine.
Jan. 9, 1919	Western Md. Ry. Co.	Public; watchman	Antietam St., Hagerstown				1	Auto collided with motor car.
Jan. 15, 1919	Penna. R. R. Co.	Public; bell	Loretto				1	Auto truck struck by passenger train.
Feb. 8, 1919	B. & O. R. R. Co.	Public; bell	West of Catoctin					Team struck by train.
Feb. 22, 1919	Wash. Ry. & Elec. Co.	Public; no protection	Bladensburg				1	Auto struck by electric car.

Date	Company	Protection	Location			Remarks
Feb. 28, 1919	Penna. R. R. Co.	Public; bell	Sparks		2	Auto collided with freight engine.
Mr. 7, 1919	B. & O. R. R. Co.	Public; watchman	William St., Cumberland		1	Auto struck by engine.
Mr. 7, 1919	B. & O. R. R. Co.	Public; gates and watchman	Fort Ave., Baltimore	1 1		Struck by engine.
Mar. 27, 1919	Western Md. Ry. Co.	Public; watchman	Washington St., Hagerstown		1	Auto struck by train.
Mar. 28, 1919	B. & O. R. R. Co.	Public; bell	Dorsey	1		Auto struck by passenger train.
Apr. 3, 1919	Baltimore & Belair Elec. Ry. Co.	Public; no protection	Harford Rd. at German La.		2	Team struck by electric car.
Apr. 4, 1919	B. & O. R. R. Co.	Public; bell, watchman, sign	Singerly	2		Auto collided with passenger train.
Apr. 25, 1919	Penna. R. R. Co.	Public; bell	Sparks	4		Auto struck by passenger train.
May 6, 1919	B. & O. R. R. Co.	Public; watchman	Virginia Lane, Cumberland		1	Auto struck by yard engine.
May 7, 1919	Penna. R. R. Co.	Public; no protection	Guilford and Pleasant Sts., Baltimore		1	Tractor struck by electric car.
May 15, 1919	Penna. R. R. Co.	Public; sign	Airey		1	Team struck by work train.
May 22, 1919	B. & O. R. R. Co.	Public; watchman	Baltimore St., Cumberland		1	Struck by yard engine.
May 28, 1919	Western Md. Ry. Co.	Public; no protection	Kendalls		1	Electric car struck by yard engine.
June 6, 1919	Penna. R. R. Co.	Public; no protection	Boston and Chester Sts., Baltimore		1	Electric car collided with engine.
June 14, 1919	Western Md. R. R. Co.	Public; flagman	Washington St., Hagerstown		1	Auto struck by train.
June 14, 1919	Western Md. R. R. Co.	Public; sign	West of Hancock		1	Auto struck by train.
June 15, 1919	Hag. & Fredk. Ry. Co.	Public; no protection	Funkstown	1	3	Auto struck by electric car.
June 21, 1919	Penna. R. R. Co.	Public; sign	Salisbury		1	Auto struck by passenger train.
July 3, 1919	Western Md. Ry. Co.	Public; no protection	Main St., Smithburg			Auto struck by train.
July 10, 1919	Hag. & Fredk. Ry Co.	Public; no protection	Thurmont		4	Auto struck by electric car.
July 13, 1919	Western Md. Ry. Co.	Public; sign	Kemp's		2	Auto struck by engine.
Ag. 10, 1919	W. B. & A. Elec. R. R. Co.	Public; no protection	Linthicum Heights		3	Auto struck by electric train.
Aug. 17, 1919	Chesapeake Beach Ry. Co.	Public; signs	Marlboro	1	5	Auto collided with train.
Ag. 21, 1919	Western Md. Ry. Co.	Public; bell	Cranberry		1	Truck struck by train.
Aug. 26, 1919	Penna. R. R. Co.	Public; signs	Harmony Grove		4	Auto struck by freight train.
Aug. 27, 1919	Penna. R. R. Co.	Public; gates	Timonium	1		Struck by passenger train.
Aug. 29, 1919	Western Md. Ry. Co.	Public	McGinnis			Team struck by engine.

GRADE CROSSING ACCIDENTS, OCTOBER 1, 1918, TO SEPTEMBER 30, 1919—Concluded.

Date	Company	Public or Private Crossing and Protection	Location	Pedestrians		In Vehicles		Remarks
				Killed	In-jured	Killed	In-jured	
Sep. 13, 1919	Penna. R. R. Co.	Public; signs	Westover			3		Auto tak by train.
Sep. 15, 1919	Norfk. & West. R. R. Co.	Public; bell	South of Antietam				2	Wagon struck by train.
Sep. 17, 1919	W. B. & A. Elec. R. R. Co.	Private; no protection	Camp Parole			2		Truck struck by train.
Sep. 17, 1919	B. & O. R. R. Co.	Public; watchman	Baltimore St. Crossing, Cumberland					Eltric car struck by engine.
Sep. 18, 1919	B. & O. R. R. Co.	Public; no protection	Crossing of Curtis Bay Chemical Co.				1	Electric car struck by train.
Totals				3	5	21	73	

	Killed	Injured	Totals
Baltimore & Ohio Railroad Co.	6	9	15
Pennsylvania Railroad Co.	10	21	31
Western Maryland Railway Co.	0	8	8
Miscellaneous Steam Railroads	3	25	28
Miscellaneous Electric Railways	5	15	20
Total deaths and injuries	24	78	102

APPENDIX V

PRELIMINARY STATEMENT.

The corporations named below are operated as parts of other systems:

STEAM RAILROADS.

CORPORATIONS NOT OPERATING.	CORPORATIONS OPERATING.
Baltimore Belt R. R. Co.	Baltimore & Ohio R. R. Co.
Baltimore & Ohio R. R. Co. in Pa.	Baltimore & Ohio R. R. Co.
Confluence & Oakland R. R. Co.	Baltimore & Ohio R. R. Co.
Lancaster, Cecil & Southern R. R. Co.	Baltimore & Ohio R. R. Co.
Metropolitan Southern R. R. Co.	Baltimore & Ohio R. R. Co.
Washington County R. R. Co.	Baltimore & Ohio R. R. Co.
Delaware R. R. Co.	Phila., Balto. & Wash. R. R. Co.
Delaware, Md. & Va. R. R. Co.	Phila., Balto. & Wash. R. R. Co.
Md. & Pa. Terminal Ry. Co.	Maryland & Pennsylvania R. R. Co.
York, Hanover & Fredk. R. R. Co.	Pennsylvania R. R. Co.

ELECTRIC RAILROADS.

CORPORATIONS NOT OPERATING.	CORPORATIONS OPERATING.
Balto., Sparrow's Pt. & Ches. Ry. Co.	United Railways & Electric Co.
Balto., Halethorpe & Elk. Ry. Co.	United Railways & Electric Co.
Loraine Electric Ry. Co.	United Railways & Electric Co.
Blue Ridge Ry. Co.	Cham., Green. & Waynesboro Ry. Co.
Sandy Springs Ry. Co.	Kensington Ry. Co.
Washington & Glen Echo R. R. Co.	Washington Ry. & Electric Co.
Washington, Berwyn & Laurel Elec. Ry. Co.	Washington Ry. & Electric Co.

ELECTRIC LIGHT COMPANIES.

CORPORATIONS NOT OPERATING.	CORPORATIONS OPERATING.
Baltimore Electric Light Co.	Con. Gas Electric Light & Power Co.
Baltimore County Electric Co.	Con. Gas Electric Light & Power Co.
Mt. Washington E. L. & P. Co.	Con. Gas Electric Light & Power Co.
Patapsco Elec. & Mfg. Co. of Md.	Con. Gas Electric Light & Power Co.
Patapsco Elec. & Mfg. Co. of Del.	Con. Gas Electric Light & Power Co.
Roland Park Electric & Water Co.	Con. Gas Electric Light & Power Co.

FRAGMENTARY REPORTS

The following abstracts are from reports of various corporations which were rendered in such incomplete or otherwise defective form as to furnish little or no material for the statistical tables. Where inconsistencies were shown in the figures given, or where information called for was not given, the reporting corporation was notified, but failed to correct the figures or supply the information required.

1—BLUE RIDGE WATER COMPANY.

Capital Stock $28,120. Plant cost $29,020. Revenue, $3,513. Expenses, $4,211. Has one reservoir 150,000 gallons capacity, 3 wells, 2 pumps, 1 boiler 100 H. P., 1 gas engine 50 H. P., and 96 meters.

2—CENTREVILLE ELECTRIC LIGHT PLANT.

Plant owned by the Town of Centreville. Plant cost $36,275. Funded Debt,$22,500. Revenue, $14,233. Expenses, $19,284. Depreciation, $1,000. Has 2 boilers, total H. P. 285; 2 engines 250 H. P., 2 generators 175 K. W. capacity, 24 transformers, 196 meters, and 240 consumers.

3—CHESTER RIVER STEAMBOAT COMPANY.

Capital Stock, $100,000. Owned by the Maryland, Delaware & Virginia Ry. Co. The company ceased operating in 1905.

4—CUMBERLAND & PENNSYLVANIA RAILROAD COMPANY.

Telephone line for railroad operations, but as a convenience to the public allows the use of its lines at published rates. Plant cost $4,223. Has 35½ miles of pole lines and 286.43 miles of aerial wire.

5—DENMORE PARK WATER, LIGHT & HEATING COMPANY.

Private Plant—cost $7,157. Revenue, $3,221. Expenses, $2,456. Has 3 artesian wells, 3 pumps, 3 gas engines; 1 standpipe, 15,000 gallons capacity; 2 miles 1 to 3 inch mains, and 325 consumers.

6—EVERGREEN WATER COMPANY.

Private plant operated in connection with a suburban development. Plant cost $25,315. Revenue, $1,787. Expenses, $2,893. Has 2 artesian wells, 2 pumps, 2 gas engines, 1 standpipe, 55,000 gallons capacity, 146 meters, and 146 consumers.

7—FROSTBURG-GRAHAMTOWN WATER COMPANY.

A co-operative water company. Capital stock, $1,250. Plant cost $1,500. Revenue, $416. Expenses, $314. Dividends paid, $225. Has 59 consumers.

8—GILPIN'S FALLS ELECTRIC COMPANY.

Plant value, $100,000. Revenue, $16,192. Expenses, $2,285. Has 1 water wheel 325 H. P., 1 generator 200 K. W. capacity, 70 transformers, 314 meters, and 335 consumers.

9—GLEN BURNIE ELECTRIC LIGHT & POWER COMPANY.

Capital Stock, $680. Plant value, $680. Revenue, $1,391. Expenses, $1,202.

10—LINTHICUM HEIGHTS WATER COMPANY.

Plant operated in connection with a suburban development. Plant cost $10,000. Revenue, $674. Expenses, $1,279. Has 3 standpipes and 2 pumps.

11—LYNCH RURAL TELEPHONE COMPANY.

A small country plant having 4 miles of pole lines. Capital stock, $600. Plant cost $324. Has 6 subscribers. Revenue, $6. Expenses, $43.

12—NEW WINDSOR ELECTRIC LIGHT & WATER COMPANY.

Capital Stock, $4,900. Plant cost $6,476. Revenue, $2,921. Expenses, $2,633.

13—OVERLEA REALTY COMPANY.

Operates water plant costing $10,288. Revenue, $1,369. Expenses, $792. Has 2 wells, 3 standpipes, total capacity 28,000 gallons; 1 gas engine 4 H. P., 1 electric motor 2 H. P., and 92 consumers. 2 pumps.

14—N. L. RIGGIN & CO.

Owner of power boat valued at $7,000. Wharf property, $3,000.

15—RINGGOLD TELEPHONE CO. OF WASHINGTON COUNTY.

Small farmers' telephone line having a capital stock of $500.

16—ROUZERVILLE WATER COMPANY.

Operates principally in Pennsylvania. Plant cost $7,856. Revenue, $955. Expenses, $1,543. Has 60 consumers in Maryland. Has 2 reservoirs 175,000 gallons capacity, 2 pumps, 1 water wheel, and 1 gasoline engine.

17—SUSQUEHANNA POWER COMPANY.

Sold under foreclosure. Purchased by Frank J. Hoen for $300,-000. Subject to $150,000 underlying 6 per cent. bonds, sale ratified by court May 2, 1914. On account of litigation reorganization plans have not been perfected.

18—STOCKTON ELECTRIC LIGHT COMPANY.

Partnership investment, $7,155. Plant cost $7,110. Revenue, $2,465. Expenses, $1,754. Has 2 engines 75 H. P., 1 generator 25 K. W. capacity, 6 transformers, 50 meters, and 155 consumers.

19—THE SEVERNA COMPANY.

Operates electric plant costing $5,100. Electric Revenue, $1,260. Electric Expenses, $1,089. Also operates water plant costing $12,000. Water Revenue, $680. Water Expenses, $867. Has 2 reservoirs, 1 pump, 1 electric motor, 23 meters, and 24 consumers.

20—TERMINAL HEATING & FREEZING COMPANY.

Capital Stock, Common, $794,400. Capital Stock, Preferred, $675,000. First Mortgage 5% 20-year gold bonds outstanding, $398,000. Collateral Trust 6% notes outstanding, $35,000. Revenue from steam heating, $118,363. Operating Expenses, $100,654. Taxes, $4,991. Interest, $5,459. Income from operation, $7,260. .

21—UNION TRANSFER COMPANY.

Incorporated under the laws of the State of Pennsylvania in February, 1867. Investment in State of Maryland, $65,057. Operating Revenue in Maryland, $47,363. Operating Expenses in Maryland, $60,799. Deficit from operation, $13,436.

22—WEEMS STEAMBOAT COMPANY.

Capital Stock, $600,000. Owned by the Maryland, Delaware & Virginia Ry. Co. The Company ceased operating in 1905.

23—WESTERN UNION TELEGRAPH CO. OF BALTIMORE CITY.

Operated as part of the Western Union Telegraph Company System. Capital Stock, $60,000. Has 1,091 miles of pole lines, 18,375 miles of aerial wires, 1,236 miles of underground wires and 9½ miles of submarine wires. Revenue from intrastate business, $42,410. Expenses in Maryland not separated in system accounts.

CORPORATIONS NOT REPORTING

STEAM RAILROADS.

Baltimore & Virginia Railroad Company.
Preston Railroad Company.
Washington, Potomac & Chesapeake Railway Company.
Washington, Westminster & Gettysburg Railroad Company.

ELECTRIC RAILWAYS.

North Beach Railway Company.
Washington & Great Falls Electric Railway Company.
Washington, Berwyn & Laurel Electric Railway Company.

ELECTRIC COMPANIES.

Crisfield Ice Manufacturing Company.
Electric & Ice Company.
Mayor & City Council of Laurel, Maryland.

ELECTRIC & GAS COMPANIES.

Receivers of Easton Gas & Fuel Company.

WATER COMPANIES.

Delmar Water Company.
Ellicott City Water Company.
Emmitsburg Water Company.
Mountain Lake Water & Light Company.
Port Deposit Water Company.
Salisbury Water Company.

ALPHABETICAL LIST OF CORPORATIONS REPORTING, SHOWING TOTAL CAPITALIZATION, FUNDED DEBT AND INTEREST ACCRUED ON SAME, AND CAPITAL STOCK AND DIVIDENDS DECLARED ON CAPITAL STOCK, SO FAR AS REPORTED.

Marginal Number.	Title of Corporation.	Capital Stock. 1	Funded Debt. 2	Total Capitalization. 3	Interest Accrued on Funded Debt. 4	Dividends Declared on Capital Stock. 5
32	Antietam Electric Light & Power Co.	$11,500	$14,000	$25,500	$770	
232	Annapolis Public Utilities Co.	172,700	177,000	349,700	10,715	
72	Artesian Water Co.	155,050	85,000	240,050		
82	Adams Express Co.	10,000,000	19,733,000	29,733,000	417,230	
82	American Express Co.	17,182,000		17,182,600		$516,474
2	Baltimore & Ohio Railroad Co.	210,808,824	452,371,078	663,179,902	19,060,885	9,191,964
6	Baltimore & Ohio Railroad Co. in Penna.	204,987	42,311,500	816,487		
6	Baltimore Belt Railroad Co.	3,500,000	6,000,000	9,500,000		
2	Baltimore, Chesapeake & ...ic Railway	2,500,000	1,290,000	3,790,000	64,500	
12	Baltimore & Sparrow's Point Railroad Co.			150,000		
12	Baltimore & Bel Air Electric Railway Co	46,250		46,250		43,000
16	Bare, Haletborpe & ...ke Ry. Co.	10,000		10,000		2,775
16	Baltimore, Spa... 's Point & ... Ry. Co.	400,000	2,000,000	2,400,000	90,000	
16	Blue Ridge Railway Co.	15,000		15,000		
36	Baltimore Electric C... ...ny of Balti...nre City	3,500,000	3,721,000	7,221,000	186,050	5000
36	Baltimore ...ity Electric Company	150,000	221,000	371,000		
32	Bel Air Electric Co.	44,400	13,000	57,400	2,280	
72	Brooklyn & ...uffis Bay Water Co.	100,000	50,000	150,000		
72	...hire ...fity Wer & Electric Co.	390,00	893,000	1,283,000	44,694	19,500
72	Bel Air Water & Light Co.	49,500	48,300	98,300	2,470	
72	Boonsboro Water Co.	10,000	10,000	20,000	500	300
72	Ble Ridge Water Co.	28,120		2820		
72	...ck Heights Water Co.	8,500		18,000		
72	Burl...uville Water Co.	2,110	9,500	2,110	570	
92	Baltimore & Philadelphia Steamboat Co.	281,400		281,400		28,140
2	Chesapeake Beach Railway Co.	1,000,000	1,000,000	2,000,000	5000	
6	Confluence & Oakland Railway Co.	200,000	128,500	328,500		
2	Cumberland & Pennsylvania Railroad Co.	1,500,000	681,000	2,181,000	53,483	62,267
2	...land ...alley Railroad Co.	5,333,550		5,333,550		426,676
2	Canton Railroad Co.	200,000		200,000		
12	City & Suburban Railway ...G. Washington.	1,750,000	1,750,000	3,500,000	87,500	16,000
12	...land Electric Railway Co.	200,000	100,000	300,000	5,000	
12	Capital ...n Co. of Washington.	12,000,000	5,606,000	17,606,000	280,300	720,000
12	Chambersburg, Greencastle & Waynesboro ...et Railway Co.	600,000	793,400	1,383,400	39,670	15,000
12	...nd & Westernport Electric Railway Co.	625,000	655,000	1,280,000	32,750	
32	Chestertown Electric Light & Power ...o.	15,000	22,000	37,...	1,320	
232	Consolidated ...G Electric Light & Power Co.	14,423,900	37,752,217	52,176,147	1,762,090	1,151,575
232	Consolidated ...olidated Power Co. ...G. Electric & ...G.	100	5,468,000	5,468,100	318,460	
232	Consolidated Public Utilities Co., Elect. & ...G.	35,540	50,000	85,540	2,500	
	Public Utilities Co. ...Wer De...t	102,000	78,000	180,000	3,120	

22	Citizens Gas Co.	65,000	120,000	85,000		7,200
22	Chestertown Gas Co.	15,000	20,000	35,000		1,000
32	Crisfield Ice Manufacturing Co.	50,000		50,000		
52	Chesapeake & Potomac Telephone Co. of Balto. City	10,000		10,000		600,000
52	Cumberland Valley Telephone Co.	138,800	1,500	138,800		
52	Cecil Farmers' Telephone Co.	13,525		15,025		75
94	Chester River Steamboat Co.	100,000	8,000	100,000		
32	Cannon, Everett C.	5,000		13,000		480
6	Delaware Railroad Co.	987,275	448,000	5,435,275	21,330	398,982
6	Delaware, Maryland & Virginia Railroad Co.	164,700	1,043,979	1,498,679	37,909	
32	Delmarvia Utilities Co.	76,000	10,000	86,000	600	
32	Delta Electric Power Co.	2,500	23,500	5,500	1,180	
72	Delmar Water Co.	35,000	30,000	65,000	1,800	
78	Dorchester Water Co.	103,970		103,970		
78	Denmore Park Water, Light & Heating Co.	7,158		7,158		279
2	Emmitsburg Railroad Co.	50,000	485,000	5000		1,000
32	Edison Electric Illuminating Co.	275,000	6,000	760,000	24,312	5,500
22	Elkton Gas Light Co.	18,527		24,527	360	
32	Emmitsburg Electric Co.	7,500	30,000	7,500		600
32	Easton Utilities Co. Electric Dept.	1,900		30,000	1,500	960
72	Emmitsburg Water Co.			12,000		
72	Evergreen Water Co.	25,315		25,315		
232	Easton Light & Fuel Co.	50,000	50,000	100,000	3,000	
72	Ellicott City Water Co.	25,000	20,000	45,000	1,200	
32	Electric & Ice Manufacturing Co.	26,900	15,000	41,900		
72	Frostburg Water Co.	9,950		9,950		225
72	Frostburg-Grahamtown Water Co.	250		1,250		
22	Georgetown Gas Light Co. of Montgomery Co.	10,000	10,000	10,000		
38	Gilpin's Falls Electric Co.	100,000	100,000	100,000		
52	Garret County Telephone Co.	16,700		16,700		13,412
38	Glen Burnie Electric Light & Power Co.	680	700	680	42	
12	Hagerstown & Frederick Railway Co.	2,355,450	919,000	5,374,450	168,065	12,640
22	Hagerstown Light & Heat Co.	200,000	325,000	525,000	14,550	20,000
32	Havre de Grace Electric Co.	50,000		50,000		
32	Home Manufacturing Light & Power Co.	8,800	43,400	52,000	434	6,880
22	Hyattsville Gas & Electric Co.	84,000		80,000		
22	Havre de Grace Gas Co.	50,000	50,000	100,000	2,500	
32	Home Electric Light Co.	13,825	19,800	33,625	1,188	
32	Harper's Ferry Light & Power Co.	49,900		49,900		
32	Hagerstown Municipal Electric Light Plant.	45,000	45,000	45,000	1,840	
72	Havre de Grace Water Co.	75,000	50,000	125,000	2,000	
102	Havre de Grace & Perryville Bridge Co.	500,000		500,000		40,000
32	Idlewild Electric Light, Heat & Power Co.	17,000	33,000	50,000	1,080	
12	Kensington Railway Co.	25,000	35,000	0,600	1,750	
6	Lancaster, Cecil & Southern Railway Co.	200,000	200,000	400,000		
16	Loraine Electric Railway Co.	5,000		5,000		

ALPHABETICAL LIST OF CORPORATIONS REPORTING—Continued.

Marginal Number	Title of Corporation	Capital Stock. 1	Funded Debt. 2	Total Capitalization. 3	Interest Accrued on Funded Debt. 4	Dividends Declared on Capital Stock. 5
72	Lonaconing Water Co.	$70,000	$25,500	$95,500	$1,607	$2,100
52	Lynch Rural Telephone Co.	600		600		
6	Maryland, Delaware & Virginia Railway Co.	3,000,000	2,000,000	5,000,000	100,000	
2	Maryland & Pennsylvania Railroad Co.	1,602,500	2,326,450	3,928,950	65,690	
2	Maryland & Pennsylvania Terminal Railway Co.	200,000	200,000	400,000	10,000	
6	Metropolitan Southern Railroad Co.	1,200,000	1,200,000	2,400,000		
2	Maryland Electric Railways Co.	1,164,000	6,109,928	7,273,928	307,875	
32	Midland Electric Light Co.	5,000		5,000		1,000
32	Mayor & City Council of Laurel, Maryland	83,260		83,260		
36	Mount Washington Electric Light & Power Co.	5,380		5,380		
22	Manchester Lighting & Heating Co.	9,500		9,500		
72	Mechanicstown Water Co.	42,500	13,000	55,500	780	1,330
72	Mountain Lake Water & Light Co.	41,500	23,500	65,000	1,175	
72	Midland-Elk Lick Water Co.	1,000,000		1,000,000		
72	Maryland Telephone Co. of Baltimore	11,120		11,120		
52	Maryland & Delaware Telephone & Telegraph Co.	11,800		11,800		
32	Mt. Airy Electric & Ice Co.					
2	New York, Philadelphia & Norfolk Railroad Co.	2,500,000	3,737,000	6,237,000	152,706	2,166,172
2	Northern Central Railway Co.	27,077,200	7,092,081	34,169,281	356,882	9,357,102
12	Norfolk & Western Railway Co.	143,566,700	90,390,500	233,957,200	3,956,501	
32	North Beach Railway Co.	28,300	13,000	41,300	650	
42	New Windsor Electric Light & Power Co.	4,900		4,900		
32	Northern Natural Gas Co.	100,000		100,000		8,000
32	Northern Virginia Power Co.	600,000	415,000	1,015,000	22,430	39,000
72	Overlea Realty Co. (Water)	10,288		10,288		576
2	Philadelphia, Baltimore & Washington Railroad Co.	26,437,000	25,969,146	52,406,146	1,051,943	1,586,220
36	Patapsco Electric & Manufacturing Co. of Maryland	200,000		200,000		
38	Patapsco Electric & Manufacturing Co. of Delaware	225,000		225,000		
38	Perryville Electric Co.	20,755		20,755		
32	Port Deposit Electric Co.	8,125		8,125		
32	Peninsular Light & Power Co.	75,000		75,000		1,875
32	Potomac Electric Power Co.	6,000,000	9,391,000	15,391,000	437,350	660,000
72	Perryville Water Co.	10,200		10,200		
72	Port Deposit Water Co.	10,000	5,000	15,000		
52	Poolesville Telephone Co.	3,930		3,930		
52	Princess Anne Telephone Co.	1,000		1,000		
66	Postal Telegraph-Cable Co.	50,000		50,000		
92	Pullman Co.	120,000,000		120,000,000		9,544,016
36	Roland Park Electric & Water Co.	25,000	300,000	325,000	15,000	
72	Roland Park Water Co.	50,000	165,000	215,000	8,433	7,500

No.	Company					
98	Rock Creek Steamboat Co.	13,250		13,250		1,325
98	Riggin Co., N. L.	10,000		10,000		
72	Roguel Heights Water Co.	15,000	15,000	30,000	750	
32	Salisbury Light, Heat & Power Co.	100,000	29,500	129,500	2,294	3,750
33	Snow Hill Electric Light & Power Co.	12,000		12,000		
33	Stockton Electric Light Co.	7,155		7,155		
33	Susquehanna Transmission Co.	500		500		
52	South Dorchester Telephone Co.	3,470	1,906,000	1,909,500	5,520	
72	Suburban Water Co.	100,000	92,000	192,000		
82	Southern Express Co.					
72	Severna Park Water Co.	12,000		12,000		
32	Susquehanna Power Co.	300,000	150,000	450,000		
32	St. Michaels Utilities Commission.		22,500	22,500		
98	Stony Creek Steamboat Co.	20,000		20,000		
12	Towson & Cookeyville Electric Railway Co.	36,400		36,400	210	456,750
92	Tolchester Beach Improvement Co.	253,000		253,000	24,300	22,770
92	Terminal Freezing & Heating Co.	1,469,400	470,000	1,948,400		
2	Union Railroad Co.	2,100,000	5,812	2,105,812	232	456,750
12	United Railways & Electric Co.	20,484,200	58,639,000	79,123,200	2,557,677	819,368
72	Union Bridge Water Co.	11,745	10,000	21,745	600	705
52	Union Telephone Co.	6,500		6,500		325
32	Union Bridge Electric Co.	25,000		25,000		
6	Washington County Railroad Co.	982,680	194,000	1,176,680		
2	Washington, Westminster & Gettysburg Railroad Co.	579,800		579,800		
2	Western Maryland Railway Co.	77,167,198	61,978,462	139,145,660	2,669,607	492,345
2	Washington, Baltimore & Annapolis Electric Railroad Co.	4,455,750	5,239,000	9,694,750	258,179	
14	Washington & Glen Echo Railroad Co.	200,000	250,000	450,000		
12	Washington Railway & Electric Co.	15,000,000	17,465,350	32,465,350	709,227	750,000
12	Washington & Rockville Railway Co.	275,000	185,000	460,000	9,250	
12	Washington Interurban Railway Co.	50,000	150,000	200,000	7,500	
12	Washington & Great Falls Railway & Power Co.	300,350	500,000	800,350		
12	Washington & Maryland Railway Co.	10,100	96,000	106,100	5,760	600
22	Washington Gas Light Co. of Montgomery County.	10,000		10,000		
42	West Virginia Gas Co. of Maryland.	20,000		20,900		
42	West Virginia & Maryland Gas Co. of West Virginia.	2,000,000		2,000,000	6,750	
66	Walkersville Water Co.	20,000		20,000		1,000
66	Western Union Telegraph Co. of Baltimore.	60,000		60,000		
94	Weems Steamboat Co.	600,000		600,000		
98	Woodill & Welch Freighting Co.	12,000		12,000		
82	Wells Fargo & Co. Express.	23,967,400		23,967,400		
82	Waynesboro Electric Light & Power Co.	50,000		50,000		719,022
32	Washington, Berwyn & Laurel Electric Railway Co.	250		250		
6	York, Hanover & Frederick Railroad Co.	525,000	150,000	675,000	6,000	

KEY TO MARGINAL NUMBERS

Class of Corporation.	Operating.	Not Operating.	Operated Under Lease or Agreement.	Individual.
Steam Railroad Co.	2	4	6	8
Street or Electric Railroad Co.	12	14	16	18
Gas Co. (coal or water gas only)	22	24	26	28
Electrical Co.	32	34	36	38
Gas and Electrical Co.	232	234	236	238
Natural Gas Co.	42	44	46	48
Telephone Co.	52	54	56	58
Telegraph Co.	62	64	66	68
Water Co.	72	74	76	78
Express Co.	82	84	86	88
Steamboat Co., etc.	92	94	96	98

TABLES.

STEAM RAILROAD CORPORATIONS.

1. Consolidated statement of assets, liabilities, surplus and income.
2. Assets, with classification.
3. Liabilities, with classification.
4. Securities of all classes outstanding.
5. Funded debt and capital stock, with rate of interest on debt and dividends on stock.
6. Cost of road and equipment and cost per mile of road.
7. Income account and profit and loss account.
*8. Railway operating revenues.
*9. Railway operating expenses.
*10. Mileage of road operated.
*11. Description of equipment.
*12. Statistics of rail operations.
*13. Statistics of rail operations, continued.
*14. Revenue freight carried.

ELECTRIC RAILROAD CORPORATIONS.

15. Consolidated statement of assets, liabilities, surplus and income.
16. Assets, with classification.
17. Liabilities, with classification.
18. Securities of all classes outstanding.
19. Funded debt and capital stock, with rate of interest on debt and dividends on stock.
20. Cost of road and equipment.
21. Income account and profit and loss account.
22. Railway operating revenues.
23. Railway operating expenses.
24. Mileage of road operated and description of equipment.
25. Mileage, traffic and miscellaneous statistics.

ELECTRIC LIGHT CORPORATIONS.

26. Consolidated statement of assets, liabilities, surplus, gross income. deductions from gross income and net income.
27. Assets, liabilities and surplus, with classification.
28. Gross income, with deductions, payments, etc.
29. Funded debt and capital stock, with rate of interest on debt and dividends on stock.
30. Operating statistics, for year ended December 31, 1918.
31. Operating statistics, for year ended December 31, 1918.
32. Casualties, classified as to employees and others.

GAS AND ELECTRICAL CORPORATIONS.

33. Consolidated statement of assets, liabilities, surplus, gross income, deductions from gross income and net income.
34. Assets, liabilities and surplus, with classification.
35. Gross income, with deductions, payments, etc.
36. Funded debt and capital stock, with rate of interest on debt and dividends on stock.
37. Operating statistics, for year ended December 31, 1918.
38. Casualties, classified as to electrical and gas corporation employees and others.

WATER CORPORATIONS.

39. Consolidated statement of assets, liabilities, surplus, gross income, deductions from gross income and net income.
40. Assets, liabilities and surplus, with classification.
41. Gross income, with deductions, payments, etc.
42. Funded debt and capital stock, with rate of interest on debt and dividends on stock.
43. Supply and service, classification of, for year ended December 31, 1918.
44. Casualties, classified as to employees and others.

TELEPHONE AND TELEGRAPH CORPORATIONS.

45. Consolidated statement of assets, liabilities, surplus, gross income, deductions from gross income and net income.
46. Assets, liabilities and surplus, with classification.
47. Gross income, with deductions, payments, etc.
48. Funded debt and capital stock, with rate of interest on debt and dividends on stock.
49. Operating statistics for year ended December 31, 1918.
50. Casualties, classified as to employees and others.

EXPRESS CORPORATIONS.

51. Assets, with classification.
52. Liabilities, with classification.
53. Income account and profit and loss account.
54. Operating revenues, with distribution.
55. Operating expenses, with distribution.

PULLMAN COMPANY.

56. Assets and liabilities.
57. Income account and profit and loss account.
*58. Operating revenues, with distribution.
*59. Operating expenses, with distribution.
*60. Operating statistics.

OTHER CORPORATIONS.

61. Assets and liabilities.
62. Income account.

TAB

SHOWING FOR EACH OF THE STEAM RAILROAD CORPORATIONS NAMED THEREIN THE TOTAL AMOUNTS OF ASSET
FROM GROSS REVENUE AND THE NET INCOME FROM THE OPERATIONS OF THE Y

	TOTALS.			
	ASSETS.		LIABI	
TITLE OF CORPORATION.	Total Amount December 31, 1918.	Increase Over Preceding Year.	Total Amount December 31, 1918.	I P
	1	2	3	
1 (a) Baltimore Belt R. R. Co................	$12,848,632	$163,688	$10,348,632	$163,
2 Baltimore, Chesapeake & Atlantic Ry. Co........	4,513,273	138,450	5,362,146	601,
3 Baltimore & Ohio R. R. Co................	817,248,743	46,306,420	789,953,908	50,970,
4 (a) Baltimore & Ohio R. R. Co. in Pennsylvania......	46,313,214	1,662,426	46,313,348	1,662,
5 Baltimore & Sparrow's Point R. R. Co............	394,089	45,547	226,632	40,
6 Canton R. R. Co................	1,135,463	155,918	1,380,382	218,
7 Chesapeake Beach Ry. Co................	2,655,367	36,489	4,604,288	114,
8 (a) Confluence & Oakland R. R. Co................	331,279	....	331,638	
9 Cumberland & Pennsylvania R. R. Co..........	7,067,599	80,938	5,936,456	2
10 Cumberland Valley R. R. Co..........	16,831,017	1,885,977	8,732,630	1,152,
11 (a) Delaware R. R. Co................	8,293,729	46,792	6,012,336	333
12 (a) Delaware, Maryland & Virginia R. R. Co.....	2,186,886	39,225	4,387,020	209
13 Emmitsburg R. R. Co................	91,720	565	54,321	
14 (a) Lancaster, Cecil & Southern R. R. Co............	402,694	....	402,694	
15 Maryland, Delaware & Virginia Ry. Co..........	5,225,227	104,260	6,708,395	228
16 Maryland & Pennsylvania R. R. Co............	4,637,236	204,930	4,343,475	180
17 (a) Maryland & Pennsylvania Terminal Ry. Co......	434,690	....	437,564	
18 (a) Metropolitan Southern R. R. Co............	2,697,438	....	2,697,438	
19 New York, Philadelphia & Norfolk R. R. Co......	17,447,788	2,513,402	10,106,760	730
20 Northern Central Ry. Co................	54,161,924	2,129,279	43,470,975	2,028
21 Norfolk & Western Ry. Co................	372,200,072	31,417,940	307,372,905	24,479
22 Philadelphia, Baltimore & Washington R. R. Co....	110,912,829	5,063,211	73,859,937	4,765
23 Union R. R. Co................	5,086,797	177,264	2,920,608	98,
24 (a) Washington County R. R. Co................	1,191,650	....	1,501,148	
25 Western Maryland Ry. Co................	148,782,251	4,558,311	147,088,706	4,417,
26 (a) York, Hanover & Frederick R. R. Co............	906,963	33,875	1,413,764	8,

(a) Denotes that the Company is operated by another Company, and its revenues and expenses are inclu
in the report of the operating Company. See "Preliminary Statement."

* Not Comparable.

NOTE—Deficit, loss and other reverse items on this table are printed in bold type.

No. 1

Liabilities and of Surplus, on December 31, 1918, and the Total Amount of Gross Revenue, the Ended December 31, 1918, and the Increases or Decreases from the Preceding Year.

Totals—Continued.

Surplus or Deficit.		Gross Revenue.		Deductions from Gross Revenue.		Net Inco Opera
Total Amount December 31, 1918.	Increase Over Preceding Year.	Total Amount December 31, 1918.	Increase Over Preceding Year.	Total Amount December 31, 1918.	Increase Over Preceding Year.	Total Amount December 31, 1918.
5	6	7	8	9	10	11
$2,500,000						
848,373	$462,632	$98,515	*	$252,805	*	$154,290
27,294,835	4,664,302	32,945,691	*	21,920,288	*	11,025,403
134						
167,457	4,863	56,674	*	12,173	*	44,501
224,919	62,685	267,599	*	330,283	*	62,684
1,946,921	78,382	150,081	$36,756	228,421	$14,101	78,340
359						
1,131,143	78,139	371,705	*	243,197	*	128,508
8,098,387	733,808	1,386,134	*	240,017	*	1,146,117
2,281,393	286,642					
2,290,134	170,653					
57,399	996	20,181	372	20,168	3,581	13
1,483,168	124,509	51,392	*	156,483	*	105,091
293,761	24,156	615,720	70,553	590,471	92,823	25,249
2,874						
7,341,028	1,783,266	1,088,180	*	264,648	*	823,532
8,690,949	100,356	2,526,357	2,050	359,989	1,212	2,166,368
64,827,167	6,938,015	21,634,302	*	5,829,775	*	15,804,527
37,052,892	297,844	2,695,421	*	1,107,816	*	1,587,605
2,166,189	275,397	181,615	*	263	*	181,352
309,498						
1,693,545	140,476	3,209,991	*	3,107,854	*	102,137
506,901	25,575					

SHOWING FOR EACH OF THE STEAM RAILROAD CORPORATIONS NAMED

TITLE OF CORPORATION.	ASSETS.	
	Total Assets December 31, 1918.	Increase Over Preceding Year.
	1	2
1 Baltimore Belt R. R Co....	$12,848,632	$163,688
2 Baltimore, Chesapeake & Atlantic Ry. Co....	4,513,273	138,450
3 Baltimore & Ohio R. R. Co....	817,248,743	46,306,420
4 Baltimore & Ohio R. R. Co. in Penna....	46,313,214	1,662,426
5 Baltimore & Sparrow's Point Railroad Co....	394,089	45,547
6 Canton R. R. Co....	1,135,463	155,918
7 Chesapeake Beach Ry. Co....	2,655,367	36,489
8 Confluence & Oakland R. R. Co....	331,279	....
9 Cumberland & Pennsylvania R. R. Co....	7,067,599	80,938
10 Cumberland Valley R. R. Co....	16,831,017	1,885,977
11 Delaware R. R. Co....	8,293,729	**46,792**
12 Delaware, Maryland & Virginia R. R. Co....	2,186,886	39,225
13 Emmitsburg R. R. Co....	91,720	**565**
14 Lancaster, Cecil & Southern R. R. Co....	402,694	....
15 Maryland, Delaware & Virginia Ry. Co....	5,225,227	104,260
16 Maryland & Pennsylvania R. R. Co....	4,637,236	204,930
17 Maryland & Pennsylvania Terminal Ry. Co....	434,690	....
18 Metropolitan Southern R. R. Co....	2,697,438	....
19 New York, Philadelphia & Norfolk R. R. Co....	17,447,788	2,513,402
20 Northern Central Ry. Co....	54,161,924	2,129,279
21 Norfolk & Western Ry. Co....	372,200,072	31,417,940
22 Philadelphia, Baltimore & Washington R. R. Co....	110,912,829	5,063,211
23 Union R. R. Co....	5,086,797	**177,264**
24 Washington County R. R. Co....	1,191,650	....
25 Western Maryland Ry. Co....	148,782,251	4,558,311
26 York, Hanover & Frederick R. R. Co....	906,963	33,875

TITLE OF CORPORATION.	Notes of Non-Affiliated Companies.	Miscellaneous, in Non-Affiliated Companies.	I
	12	13	
1 Baltimore Belt R. R. Co....	....	....	
2 Baltimore, Chesapeake & Atlantic Ry. Co....	....	....	
3 Baltimore & Ohio R. R. Co....	$152,729	$714,730	
4 Baltimore & Ohio R. R. Co. in Penna....	....	....	
5 Baltimore & Sparrow's Point R. R. Co....	....	....	
6 Canton R. R. Co....	....	....	
7 Chesapeake Beach Ry. Co....	....	....	
8 Confluence & Oakland R. R. Co....	....	....	
9 Cumberland & Pennsylvania R. R. Co....	....	....	
10 Cumberland Valley R. R. Co....	....	....	
11 Delaware R. R. Co....	....	....	
12 Delaware, Maryland & Virginia R. R. Co....	....	....	
13 Emmitsburg R. R. Co....	....	....	
14 Lancaster, Cecil & Southern R. R. Co....	....	....	
15 Maryland, Delaware & Virginia Ry. Co....	....	....	
16 Maryland & Pennsylvania R. R. Co....	....	....	
17 Maryland & Pennsylvania Terminal Ry. Co....	....	....	
18 Metropolitan Southern R. R. Co....	....	....	
19 New York, Philadelphia & Norfolk R. R. Co....	....	....	
20 Northern Central Ry. Co....	....	....	
21 Norfolk & Western Ry. Co....	....	375	
22 Philadelphia, Baltimore & Washington R. R. Co....	500,000	2	
23 Union R. R. Co....	....	....	
24 Washington County R. R. Co....	....	....	
25 Western Maryland Ry. Co....	16,500	....	
26 York, Hanover & Frederick R. R. Co....	....	....	

NOTE—Deficit, loss and other reverse items on this table are printed in bold type.

No. 2.

AMOUNT OF ASSETS ON DECEMBER 31, 1918, AND THE CLASSIFICATION OF SUCH ASSETS.

INVESTMENTS—Continued.

Sinking Funds and Deposits for Property Sold.	Miscellaneous Physical Property.	Stocks of Affiliated Companies.	Bonds of Affiliated Companies.	Notes of Affiliated Companies.	Advances to Affiliated Companies.	Stocks of Non-Affiliated Companies.	C
4	5	6	7	8	9	10	
	$336	$2,503					
$905,445	8,784,707	61,051,703	$204,457,980	$512,288	$60,980,377	$22,672,763	$1
807,976							
	9,827	245,963	1,042,086		544,006	185,491	
447,384		164,508	160,750		232,786		
		7,068				1,002	
	1,966	50,500			40,744		
1,006,119		7,708		1	1,367	3,253	
	8,510	2,126,677	269,109			205,575	
7,627	2,746,816	1,985,362	354,673		5,715,285	4,806	10
	227,573	7,342,364	584,722	203,001	234,298	1,001	
			173,984				
111,164	638,312	932,012	1		10,895,589	38,257	

CURRENT ASSETS.

Cash.	Demand Loans and Special Deposits.	Loans and Bills Receivable.	Traffic and Car Service Balances, Receivable.	Due by Agents and Conductors.	Miscellaneous Accounts Receivable.	Materials and Supplies.	In D Re
15	16	17	18	19	20	21	
		$88,420			$93,200		
$3,560,660	$729,464	6,022	$771,744		6,092,360		
89,144					58,133		
203,950			11,870	$144,461	28,872	$7,788	
43,330		1,770		1,784	23,258	5,083	
	5,425				9,518		
38,838		760,312			1,250,269		
21,926	213,278						
	37,884				2,934		
4,974	11,000						
					76,871		
190,332	13,861		7,930	33,219	18,931	83,072	
67							
	60				1,058,592		
98,194		1,933,501					
933,861		10,050			153,750		
2,268,507	11,400				1		
1,965,740					360,294		
159,535	8,255		5,832		136,149		

TABLE N

TITLE OF CORPORATION.	CURRENT A		W
	Rents Receivable and Other Current Assets.	Total Current Assets.	Ad
	23	24	
1 Baltimore Belt R. R. Co...............	....	....	
2 Baltimore, Chesapeake & Atlantic Ry. Co..................	....	$181,620	
3 Baltimore & Ohio R. R. Co................	$7,343	11,152,907	$1
4 Baltimore & Ohio R. R. Co. in Penna....	....	....	
5 Baltimore & Sparrow's Point R. R. Co....	....	147,277	
6 Canton R. R. Co..................	....	398,088	
7 Chesapeake Beach Ry. Co....	....	75,225	
8 Confluence & Oakland R. R. Co....	....	....	
9 Cumberland & Pennsylvania R. R. Co....	....	14,943	
10 Cumberland Valley R. R. Co....	5	2,068,499	
11 Delaware R. R. Co....	....	238,018	
12 Delaware, Maryland & Virginia R. R. Co....	....	40,818	
13 Emmitsburg R. R. Co....	....	15,974	
14 Lancaster, Cecil & Southern R. R. Co....	....	....	
15 Maryland, Delaware & Virginia Ry. Co....	....	76,871	
16 Maryland & Pennsylvania R. R. Co....	5,709	353,055	
17 Maryland & Pennsylvania Terminal Ry. Co....	....	1,733	
18 Metropolitan Southern R. R. Co....	....	....	
19 New York, Philadelphia & Norfolk R. R. Co....	....	1,058,652	
20 Northern Central Ry. Co....	1,122,364	3,154,059	
21 Norfolk & Western Ry. Co....	....	1,111,067	
22 Philadelphia, Baltimore & Washington R. R. Co....	2,437	2,282,346	
23 Union R. R. Co....	84,030	2,410,064	
24 Washington County R. R. Co....	....	....	
25 Western Maryland Ry. Co....	1,815,048	2,124,819	
26 York, Hanover & Frederick R. R. Co....	....	....	

NOTE—Deficit, loss and other reverse items on this table are printed in bold type.

ontinued.

	DEFERRED ASSETS—Continued.		UNADJUSTED DEBITS.				
oe ter .	Other Deferred Assets.	U. S. Government Deferred Assets.	Rents and Insurance Paid in Advance.	Discount on Capital Stock.	Discount on Funded Debt.	Other Unadjusted Debits.	Total Unadj Deb
	27	28	29	30	31	32	3:
$4,120		$214,639	$468			$791	$1
507,354	$7,838	71,972,248	8,335			1,229,043	1,237,
		12,674					
	52,167		3,842				3
	6,057	371,833				78,411	78,4
33,295	19,451	1,760,698				121,107	121,1
				$20,500			20,5
		129,421		1,800,000	$248,500	350	2,048,8
6,228			347		8,389	8,938	17,6
82,264		1,778,939	90			164,154	164,
65,000	39,342,909	20,634,142	8,539		1,641	136,522	146,7
	561					8,573	8,5
		7,777					
		3,160,862	1,432			1,287,621	1,289,0

Showing for Each of the Steam Railroad Corporations Named Therein

		Liabilities.	
Title of Corporation.		Total Liabilities December 31, 1918.	Increase Over Preceding Year.
		1	2
1	Baltimore Belt Railroad Co.	$10,348,632	$163,688
2	Baltimore, Chesapeake & Atlantic Railway Co.	5,362,146	601,082
3	Baltimore & Ohio Railroad Co.	789,953,908	50,970,722
4	Baltimore & Ohio Railroad Co. in Pennsylvania	46,313,348	1,662,426
5	Baltimore & Sparrow's Point Railroad Co.	226,632	40,684
6	Canton Railroad Co.	1,360,382	218,603
7	Chesapeake Beach Railway Co.	4,604,288	114,871
8	Confluence & Oakland Railroad Co.	331,638	....
9	Cumberland & Pennsylvania Railroad Co.	5,936,456	2,799
10	Cumberland Valley Railroad Co.	8,732,630	1,152,169
11	Delaware Railroad Co.	6,012,336	333,434
12	Delaware, Maryland & Virginia Railroad Co.	4,387,020	209,878
13	Emmitsburg Railroad Co.	54,321	421
14	Lancaster, Cecil & Southern Railroad Co.	402,694	....
15	Maryland, Delaware & Virginia Railway Co.	6,708,395	228,760
16	Maryland & Pennsylvania Railroad Co.	4,343,475	180,774
17	Maryland & Pennsylvania Terminal Railway Co.	437,564	....
18	Metropolitan Southern Railroad Co.	2,697,438	....
19	New York, Philadelphia & Norfolk Railroad Co.	10,106,760	730,136
20	Northern Central Railway Co.	45,470,975	2,028,923
21	Norfolk & Western Railway Co.	307,372,905	24,479,925
22	Philadelphia, Baltimore & Washington Railroad Co.	73,859,937	4,765,367
23	Union Railroad Co.	2,920,608	98,133
24	Washington County Railroad Co.	1,501,148	....
25	Western Maryland Railway Co.	147,088,706	4,417,835
26	York, Hanover & Frederick Railroad Co.	1,413,764	8,300

		Current Liabilities—Con	
Title of Corporation.		Dividends Matured, Unpaid.	Funded Debt Matured, Unpaid.
		12	13
1	Baltimore Belt Railroad Co.	....	....
2	Baltimore, Chesapeake & Atlantic Railway Co.	$12	....
3	Baltimore & Ohio Railroad Co.	65,864	$18,800
4	Baltimore & Ohio Railroad Co. in Pennsylvania	....	....
5	Baltimore & Sparrow's Point Railroad Co.	....	....
6	Canton Railroad Co.	....	....
7	Chesapeake Beach Railway Co.	....	....
8	Confluence & Oakland Railroad Co.	....	....
9	Cumberland & Pennsylvania Railroad Co.	....	4,000
10	Cumberland Valley Railroad Co.	106,944	....
11	Delaware Railroad Co.	10,147	203,131
12	Delaware, Maryland & Virginia Railroad Co.	....	650,000
13	Emmitsburg Railroad Co.	559	....
14	Lancaster, Cecil & Southern Railroad Co.	....	....
15	Maryland, Delaware & Virginia Railway Co.	....	....
16	Maryland & Pennsylvania Railroad Co.	....	....
17	Maryland & Pennsylvania Terminal Railway Co.	....	....
18	Metropolitan Southern Railroad Co.	....	....
19	New York, Philadelphia & Norfolk Railroad Co.	....	....
20	Northern Central Railway Co.	1,048	....
21	Norfolk & Western Railway Co.	11,425	6,000
22	Philadelphia, Baltimore & Washington Railroad Co.	....	140,150
23	Union Railroad Co.	84,000	....
24	Washington County Railroad Co.	....	....
25	Western Maryland Railway Co.	....	....
26	York, Hanover & Frederick Railroad Co.	....	....

Note—Deficit, loss and other reverse items on this table are printed in bold type.

No. 3.

OF LIABILITIES ON DECEMBER 31, 1918, AND THE CLASSIFICATION OF SUCH LIABILITIES.

FUNDED DEBT—Continued.			CURRENT LIABILITIES.			
Funded Debt, Unmatured.	Non-Negotiable Debt to Affiliated Companies.	Total Long Term Debt.	Loans and Bills Payable.	Traffic and Car Service Balances, Payable.	Audited Accounts and Wages, Payable.	Miscellaneous Accounts, Payable.
4	5	6	7	8	9	10
$6,000,000	$848,632	$6,848,632				
1,290,000		1,290,000	$913,062		$601	$6,774
452,371,078		452,371,078	33,881,428	$136,744	285,581	1,838,642
42,811,500	1,496,860	44,308,360			12	17,419
			455,000	51,176	309,090	
1,000,000		1,000,000	133,375	10,387	6,459	578
128,500	3,138	131,638				
681,000	2,792,261	3,473,261			9	72
				22,748	3,727	275,749
448,000		448,000				360,584
1,043,979		1,043,979				1,187,785
200,000	2,694	202,694				
2,000,000		2,000,000	1,014,819		553	6,765
2,326,450		2,326,450	194,610	32,917	14,335	10,875
200,000	35,897	235,897				
1,200,000	297,438	1,497,438				
3,737,000		3,737,000			144,592	26,881
7,092,081		7,092,081				6,101,458
90,390,500		90,390,500	4,500,000		47,715	11,569
25,969,145		25,969,145	7,227,773			10,229,116
5,812		5,812				23,350
194,000	15,207	209,207				309,261
61,978,462		61,978,462	113,000	10,547	3,454	60,694
150,000		150,000				608,330

CURRENT LIABILITIES—Continued.			DEFERRED LIABILITIES.				UNADJUSTED C
Accrued Interest and Rents, Not Due.	Other Current Liabilities.	Total Current Liabilities.	Provident Funds.	Other Deferred Liabilities.	U. S. Government Deferred Liabilities.	Tax Liability.	
15	16	17	18	19	20	21	
$21,561		$924,460			$106,065		
2,896,985	$65,414	46,867,931	$2,775,034	$193,027	48,200,425	$242,215	
		17,431			34,621	12,210	
		963,470				1,572	
	789,056	2,593,577					
8,333		13,840			34,570	6,918	
		409,168		439	1,610,250	236,608	
		573,862		28,591		3,198	
12,560		2,775,464		37,884			
		559					
41,831		1,085,823			107,138		
15,684	1,415	269,837	6,228	11,059		7,852	
1,667		1,667					
21,333		248,946			1,362,936	124,244	
37,578		7,314,530					
1,250,203		6,529,467	65,000	39,946,156		1,750,553	
166,556		17,863,165					
		107,349			2,601	704,845	
		309,261					
702,754		985,278		45,499	233,347	238,553	
1,000		738,329				435	

	Title of Corporation.	Unadji	
		Operating Reserves.	Accrued Depreciation, Road and Equipment.
		23	24
1	Baltimore Belt Railroad Co............................		
2	Baltimore, Chesapeake & Atlantic Railway Co............		$519,501
3	Baltimore & Ohio Railroad Co.........................		25,434,412
4	Baltimore & Ohio Railroad Co. in Pennsylvania.........		
5	Baltimore & Sparrow's Point Railroad Co...............		12,202
6	Canton Railroad Co...................................		72,118
7	Chesapeake Beach Railway Co..........................		10,711
8	Confluence & Oakland Railroad Co.....................		
9	Cumberland & Pennsylvania Railroad Co................		822,250
10	Cumberland Valley Railroad Co........................	$9,383	1,059,057
11	Delaware Railroad Co.................................		
12	Delaware, Maryland & Virginia Railroad Co............		2,934
13	Emmitsburg Railroad Co..............................		3,762
14	Lancaster, Cecil & Southern Railroad Co..............		
15	Maryland, Delaware & Virginia Railway Co.............		514,684
16	Maryland & Pennsylvania Railroad Co.................		119,120
17	Maryland & Pennsylvania Terminal Railway Co..........		
18	Metropolitan Southern Railroad Co...................		
19	New York, Philadelphia & Norfolk Railroad Co.........	63,917	1,975,928
20	Northern Central Railway Co..........................		3,987,164
21	Norfolk & Western Railway Co.........................	279,360	18,405,829
22	Philadelphia, Baltimore & Washington Railroad Co......	255,446	3,295,161
23	Union Railroad Co....................................		
24	Washington County Railroad Co.......................		
25	Western Maryland Railway Co..........................	37,000	325,498
26	York, Hanover & Frederick Railroad Co................		

Note—Deficit, loss and other reverse items on this table are printed in bold type.

No. 3—Continued.

UNADJUSTED CREDITS—Cont.	CORPORATE SURPLUS OR DEFICIT.				
Total Unadjusted Credits.	Additions to Property Through Income and Surplus.	Sinking Fund and Other Reserves.	Appropriated Surplus Not Specifically Invested.	Profit and Loss.	Corporate Surplus or Deficit.
26	27	28	29	30	31
....	....	....	....	$2,500,000	$2,500,000	....
$523,621	$146,552	....	....	996,425	848,873	..
28,737,587	7,155,370	....	....	20,139,465	27,294,835	4
....	....	....	....	134	134	....
24,579	27,880	....	....	139,577	167,457	
196,913	....	....	....	224,919	224,919	
10,711	....	....	....	1,948,921	1,948,921	
....	....	....	....	350	350	....
829,199	....	$1,126,976	$4,166	....	1,131,143	
1,351,070	3,652,239	....	....	4,446,148	8,098,387	7
3,198	326,492	990,384	....	964,517	2,281,393	
2,934	203,211	....	....	2,403,345	2,200,134	
3,762	25,746	....	11,000	653	37,399	
515,434	38,840	....	....	1,522,006	1,483,166	
127,400	243,283	....	50,500	22	293,761	
....	32,956	....	....	35,830	2,874	
2,257,878	2,531,656	1,269,119	....	3,540,252	7,341,028	1,
3,987,164	5,025,061	....	....	3,665,888	8,690,949	
26,875,081	38,150,836	....	....	26,676,331	64,827,167	6,
3,588,701	23,258,964	....	....	13,793,928	37,052,892	
704,845	230,554	....	....	1,935,636	2,166,189	
....	....	....	....	309,498	309,498	....
866,969	....	....	....	1,693,545	1,693,545	
435	60,616	....	....	567,417	506,801	

SHOWING IN DETAIL FOR EACH OF THE STEAM RAILROAD CORPORATIONS NAMED THEREIN THE FUND

TITLE OF CORPORATION.	Tor ALL C — Amount Outstanding December 31, 1918.
	1
1 Baltimore Belt Railroad Co.	$9,500,000
2 Baltimore, Chesapeake & Atlantic Ry. Co.	3,790,000
3 Baltimore & Ohio Railroad Co.	663,179,902
4 Baltimore & Ohio R. R. Co. in Pennsylvania	44,816,487
5 Baltimore & Sparrow's Point Railroad Co.	150,000
6 Canton Railroad Co.	200,000
7 Chesapeake Beach Railway Co.	2,000,000
8 Confluence & Oakland Railroad Co.	328,500
9 Cumberland & Pennsylvania Railroad Co.	2,181,060
10 Cumberland Valley Railroad Co.	5,333,550
11 Delaware Railroad Co.	5,435,275
12 Delaware, Maryland & Virginia Railroad Co.	1,570,737
13 Emmitsburg R. R. Co.	50,000
14 Lancaster, Cecil & Southern Railroad Co.	400,000
15 Maryland, Delaware & Virginia Railway Co.	5,000,000
16 Maryland & Pennsylvania Railroad Co.	3,928,950
17 Maryland & Pennsylvania Terminal Ry. Co.	400,000
18 Metropolitan Southern Railroad Co.	2,400,000
19 New York, Philadelphia & Norfolk R. R. Co.	6,237,000
20 Northern Central Railway Co.	34,169,281
21 Norfolk & Western Railway Co.	233,957,200
22 Philadelphia, Baltimore & Washington R. R. Co.	52,408,070
23 Union Railroad Co.	2,105,812
24 Washington County Railroad Co.	1,176,680
25 Western Maryland Ry. Co.	139,145,660
26 York, Hanover & Frederick Railroad Co.	675,000

DETAILS O
—Co

FUND
—Co

TITLE OF CORPORATION.	Collateral Trust Bonds.
	11
1 Baltimore Belt Railroad Co.	
2 Baltimore, Chesapeake & Atlantic Ry. Co.	
3 Baltimore & Ohio Railroad Co.	$63,493,8
4 Baltimore & Ohio R. R. Co. in Pennsylvania	
5 Baltimore & Sparrow's Point Railroad Co.	
6 Canton Railroad Co.	
7 Chesapeake Beach Railway Co.	
8 Confluence & Oakland Railroad Co.	
9 Cumberland & Pennsylvania Railroad Co.	
10 Cumberland Valley Railroad Co.	
11 Delaware Railroad Co.	
12 Delaware, Maryland & Virginia Railroad Co.	
13 Emmitsburg R R. Co.	
14 Lancaster, Cecil & Southern Railroad Co.	
15 Maryland, Delaware and Virginia Railway Co.	
16 Maryland & Pennsylvania Railroad Co.	300,000
17 Maryland & Pennsylvania Terminal Ry. Co.	
18 Metropolitan Southern Railroad Co.	
19 New York, Philadelphia & Norfolk R. R. Co.	
20 Northern Central Railway Co.	
21 Norfolk & Western Railway Co.	
22 Philadelphia, Baltimore & Washington R. R. Co.	
23 Union Railroad Co.	
24 Washington County Railroad Co.	
25 Western Maryland Railway Co.	5,000,
26 York, Hanover & Frederick Railroad Co.	

NOTE—Deficit, loss and other reverse items on this table are printed in bold type.

o. 4.

PITAL STOCK SECURITIES OUTSTANDING ON DECEMBER 31, 1918, AND THE CLASSIFICATION OF THE SAME.

TOTALS—Continued.				DETAILS OF SECURITIES.			
FUNDED DEBT.		STOCKS.		FUNDED DEBT.			
Amount Outstanding December 31, 1918.	Increase Over Preceding Year.	Amount Outstanding December 31, 1918.	Increase Over Preceding Year.	Equipment Obligations.	Increase Over Preceding Year.	Mortgage Bonds.	I₁
3	4	5	6	7	8	9	
$6,000,000	....	$3,500,000	....	....	....	$6,000,000	....
1,290,000	....	2,500,000	....	....	....	1,250,000	....
452,371,078	$11,430,245	210,808,824	$27	$22,813,000	$3,887,000	229,679,380	$70
42,811,500	599,000	2,004,987	....	....	....	42,811,500	599,
....	....	150,000					
1,000,000	....	1,000,000	....	....	....	1,000,000	....
....	....	200,000					
128,500	....	200,000	....	....	....	128,500	....
681,000	172,000	1,500,000	....	....	76,000	681,000	96
....	....	5,333,550					
448,000	52,000	4,987,275	....	....	....	448,000	52,
1,013,979	....	526,758	....	....	....	1,043,979	....
....	....	50,000					
200,000	....	200,000	....	....	....	200,000	....
2,000,000	....	3,000,000	....	....	....	2,000,000	....
2,326,450	8,500	1,602,500	....	27,000	8,500	1,099,450	....
200,000	....	200,000	....	....	....	200,000	....
1,200,000	....	1,200,000	....	....	....	1,200,000	....
3,737,000	171,000	2,500,000	....	400,000	100,000	2,600,000	....
7,002,081	29,480	27,077,200	....	....	....	6,820,000	....
90,390,500	1,121,000	143,566,700	129,500	6,000,000	992,000	83,226,500	....
25,969,145	556,000	26,438,925	....	....	....	19,717,000	53,
5,812	....	2,100,000					
191,000	7,000	982,680	....	....	....	194,000	7,
61,978,462	177,808	77,167,198	....	6,769,936	282,074	50,176,100	26,
150,000	....	525,000	....	....	....	150,000	....

DETAILS OF SECURITIES—Continued.

| FUNDED DEBT—Continued. | | | | STOCKS. | | | |
| Income Bonds. | Increase Over Preceding Year. | Miscellaneous Obligations. | Increase Over Preceding Year. | Common Stock. | Increase Over Preceding Year. | Preferred Stock. | Incr Ov Pre Year. |
13	14	15	16	17	18	19	20
....	....	....	....	$3,500,000	....	$1,500,000	....
....	....	$40,000	....	1,000,000	....	58,863,275	....
....	....	66,384,868	$125	151,945,549	$69		
....	....	....	....	2,004,987	....		
....	....	....	....	150,000	....		
....	....	....	....	200,000	....		
....	....	....	....	1,000,000	....		
....	....	....	....	200,000	....		
....	....	....	....	1,500,000	....		
....	....	....	....	4,848,650	....	484,900	....
....	....	....	....	4,987,275	....		
....	....	....	....	526,758	....		
....	....	....	....	50,000	....		
....	....	....	....	200,000	....		
....	....	....	....	1,500,000	....	1,500,000	....
....	....	....	....	1,602,500	....		
....	....	....	....	200,000	....		
$900,000	....	....	....	1,200,000	....		
....	....	....	....	2,500,000	....		
737,000	$71,000	....	....	27,077,200	....		
....	....	272,081	29,480	120,574,400	129,000	22,992,300	....
....	....	1,164,000	129,000	26,438,925	....		
....	....	6,252,146	503,000	2,100,000	....		
....	....	5,812	....	982,680	....		
....	....	32,425	13,418	49,426,098	....	27,741,100	....
....	....	....	....	525,000	....		

TABLE

EACH OF THE STEAM RAILROAD CORPORATIONS NAMED THEREIN THE TOTAL FUNDED DEBT AND
AS ARE HELD BY THE ISSUING CORPORATION), THE RATE PER CENT. AND DATES OF PAYMENT OF

TITLE OF CORPORATION.	FUNDED DEBT.			
	PRINCIPAL.			
	Description of Bonds.	Date.	Date of Maturity.	Amount Outstanding.
	1	2	3	4
Belt Railroad Co.	1st Mortgage...	1890	1990	$6,000,000
, Chesapeake & Atlantic Railway Co.	1st Mortgage...	1894	1934	1,250,000
	Real Estate.....	1909	1919	40,000
& Ohio Railroad Co.	Prior Lien....	1898	1925	74,910,175
	1st Mortgage...	1898	1948	81,995,705
	Convertible....	1913	1933	63,250,000
	Refunding......	1915	1995	60,000,000
	Real Estate....	Various	Various	1,111,310
	Ground Rents...	Various	Various	2,023,557
	Equipment.....	1912	1922	4,000,000
	Equipment.....	1913	1923	5,000,000
	Equipment.....	1916	1926	4,000,000
	Equipment.....	1917	1927	9,000,000
'nnati, Hamilton & Dayton Railway Co.	Equipment.....	1910	1920	348,000
	1st & Refunding.	1909	1959	182,000
	General........	1892	1942	3,000,000
	2nd Mortgage...	1887	1937	2,000,000
ge's Creek Coal & Iron Co.	Car Trust.....	1905	1920	20,000
n Coal & Coke Co.	Equipment.....	1911	1921	145,000
	Equipment.....	1916	1921	300,000
h Western Division.	Coll. Trust.....	1899	1925	44,991,630
sburgh Junction & Middle Division.	1st Mortgage...	1898	1925	6,124,500
sburgh, Lake Erie & West Virginia System.	Refunding......	1901	1941	43,000,000
tral Ohio Railroad Co.	Con'd 1st Mtge.	1886	1930	1,009,000
eland, Loraine & Wheeling Railway Co.	General........	1896	1936	890,000
	Con'd Refunding	1900	1930	950,000
	1st Consol.....	1893	1933	5,000,000
veland Terminal & Valley Railroad Co.	1st Mortgage...	1895	1995	3,301,000
ood Short Line Railroad Co.	1st Mortgage...	1892	1922	300,000
tington & Big Sandy Railroad Co.	1st Mortgage...	1892	1922	303,000
pshire Southern Railroad Co.	1st Mortgage...	1909	1934	5,000
ongahela River Railroad Co.	1st Mortgage...	1889	1919	700,000
& Little Kanawha Railroad Co.	1st Mortgage...	1900	1950	228,000
River Railroad Co.	1st Mortgage...	1886	1936	2,000,000
	General........	1887	1937	2,941,000
ua & Troy Branch Railroad.	1st Mortgage...	1900	1939	7,000
sburgh Junction Railroad Co.	1st Mortgage...	1882	1922	934,000
	2nd Mortgage...	1894	1922	243,000
burgh, Cleveland & Toledo Railroad Co.	1st Mortgage...	1882	1922	441,000
enswood, Spencer & Glendale Railway Co.	1st Mortgage...	1890	1920	361,000
ylkill River & East Side Railroad Co.	1st Mortgage...	1903	1935	5,000,000
do-Cincinnati Division.	Refunding Mtge.	1917	1959	11,002,200
	Gold Notes.....	1917	1919	7,500,000
t Virginia & Pittsburgh Railroad Co.	1st Mortgage...	1890	1990	3,854,000
& Ohio Railroad Co. in Penna.	1st Mortgage...	1913	1963	40,000,000
	Refunding......	1915	1995	2,811,500
e & Sparrow's Point Railroad Co.				......
Railroad Co.				......
ake Beach Railway Co.	1st Mortgage...	1898	1923	1,000,000
ce & Oakland Railroad Co.	1st Mortgage...	1890	1914	120,000
	Refunding......	1916	1995	8,500
land & Pennsylvania Railroad Co.	1st Mortgage...	1891	1921	681,000
land Valley Railroad Co.				......
e Railroad Co.	General........	1892	1932	448,000
o. Maryland & Virginia Railroad Co.	1st Mortgage...	1913	1922	658,979
ction & Breakwater Railroad Co.	1st Mtge. Extd.	1867	1932	185,000
akwater & Frankford Railroad Co.	1st Mtge. Extd.	1879	1932	200,000
burg Railroad Co.				......
er, Cecil & Southern Railroad Co.	1st Mortgage...	1895	1925	200,000

No. 5.

CAPITAL STOCK OUTSTANDING ON DECEMBER 31, 1918 (EXCLUSIVE OF SUCH FUNDED DEBT AND CAPIT INTEREST ON FUNDED DEBT AND THE RATE PER CENT. AND AMOUNT OF DIVIDENDS DECLARED.

FUNDED DEBT—Cont.		CAPITAL STOCK.				
INTEREST.		COMMON.			PREFERRED.	
Rate Per Cent.	Dates When Payable.	Amount Outstanding.	Dividends Declared During Year.	Rate Per Cent.	Amount Outstanding.	Dividends Declared During Year.
5	6	7	8	9	10	11
5	M. & N.	$3,500,000				
5	M. & S.	1,000,000			$1,500,000	
5	J. & J.					
3½	J. & J.....	151,945,549	$6,837,432	4.5	58,863,275	$2,354,531
4	A. & O....					
4½	M. & S.					
5	J. & D.					
Various	Various					
Various	Various					
4½	F. & A.					
4½	A. & O.					
4½	M. & N.					
4½	A. & O.					
5	J. & D.					
4	J. & J.					
5	J. & D.					
4½	J. & J.					
4½	J. & D.					
5	M. & N.					
4½	M. & N.					
3½	J. & J.					
3½	M. & N.					
4	M. & N.					
4½	M. & S.					
5	J. & D.					
4½	J. & J.					
5	A. & O.					
4	M. & N.					
5	J. & D.					
6	J. & J.					
5	J. & J.					
5	F. & A.					
5	M. & S.					
5	J. & D.					
5	A. & O.					
4	M. & N.					
6	J. & J.					
5	J. & J.					
6	A. & O.					
6	F. & A.					
4	J. & D.					
4	J. & J.					
5	J. & J.					
4	A. & O.					
5	J. & J.	2,004,987	43,000	28 2-3		
5	M. & S.					
		150,000				
		200,000				
5	J. & J.	1,000,000				
5	M. & N.	200,000				
5	J. & D.					
5	M. & N.	1,500,000	62,267	4.15		
		4,848,650	387,884	8	484,900	38,792
4½	J. & J.	4,987,275	398,982	8		
4	M. & N.	526,758				
3	J. & J.					
3	J. & J.					
		50,000	1,000	2		
5	M. & S.	200,000				

TA

Showing for Each of the Steam Railroad Corporations Named Therein the Total Cost of Road and
Per

| TITLE OF CORPORATION. | TOTALS. | | Dis |
| | Cost of Road and Equipment. | Increase Over Preceding Year. | In in Jul 1! |
	1	2	
1 Baltimore Belt Railroad Co..........................	$12,848,632	$163,688	$12,
2 Baltimore, Chesapeake & Atlantic Ry. Co...................	4,108,796	**38,383**	2,
3 Baltimore & Ohio Railroad Co.........................	370,620,339	7,826,991	
4 Baltimore & Ohio Railroad Co. in Pennsylvania..............	46,313,214	1,662,426	:
5 Baltimore & Sparrow's Point Railroad Co....................	234,138	17,709	
6 Canton Railroad Co...................................	741,217	58,339	
7 Chesapeake Beach Railway Co............................	2,527,975	6,075	2,
8 Confluence & Oakland Railroad Co.......................	331,279	....	
9 Cumberland & Pennsylvania Railroad Co..................	5,788,378	**43,845**	3,
10 Cumberland Valley Railroad Co.........................	10,291,085	481,008	3,
11 Delaware Railroad Co..................................	7,050,282	653,707	5,
12 Delaware, Maryland & Virginia Railroad Co.................	2,146,068	38,981	1,
13 Emmitsburg Railroad Co...............................	55,246	....	
14 Lancaster, Cecil & Southern Railroad Co..................	402,694	....	
15 Maryland, Delaware & Virginia Railway Co.................	2,962,015	2,077	1,
16 Maryland & Pennsylvania Railroad Co.....................	4,165,551	11,809	3,
17 Maryland & Pennsylvania Terminal Ry. Co.................	432,956	....	
18 Metropolitan Southern Railroad Co......................	2,607,438	1,049	2,
19 New York, Philadelphia & Norfolk R. R. Co...............	13,345,241	1,688,686	4,
20 Northern Central Railway Co...........................	48,396,969	2,025,784	22,
21 Norfolk & Western Railway Co..........................	289,446,708	13,515,118	151,
22 Philadelphia, Baltimore & Washington R. R. Co.............	98,748,364	9,696,967	59,
23 Union Railroad Co....................................	2,494,972	14,145	2,
24 Washington County Railroad Co.........................	1,191,650	....	1,
25 Western Maryland Railway Co........................•....	126,702,357	2,129,949	'
26 York, Hanover & Frederick Railroad Co....................	906,963	8,300	'

(a) Cost per mile of road and equipment, exclusive of floating equipment.

(*) The asterisk in this table denotes that the required figures were not furnished in the report.

NOTE—Deficit loss and other reverse items on this table are printed in bold type.

No. 6.

MENT, AND THE DISTRIBUTION OF SAME ON DECEMBER 31, 1918, AND THE AVERAGE INVESTMENT IN ROAD AND E
ROAD OWNED.

vestment Equipment June 30, 1907.	Investment From July 1, 1907 to June 30, 1914.	Investment From July 1, 1914 to December 31, 1918.	Total Investment.	Length of Road Owned, Miles.	In
4	5	6	7	8	
....	$449,309	$130,252	$12,848,632	7.24	
$1,038,127	613,222	149,591	4,108,796	87.61	
*	295,467,449	75,152,890	370,620,339	*	
*	42,900,156	3,413,058	46,313,214	267.87	
....	32,549	51,589	234,138	5.43	
3,358	249,919	239,086	741,217	*	
66,370	3,746	37,895	2,527,974	28.32	
....	752	1,103	331,279	19.70	
418,662	1,578,177	607,583	5,788,377	50.98	
1,596,481	3,155,744	2,266,707	10,291,085	108.03	
....	566,140	1,045,281	7,050,282	245.15	
1,671	75,997	201,905	2,146,068	97.64	
....	12,240	1,584	55,245	7.30	
....	132	....	402,694	4.06	
1,269,420	22,682	12,166	2,962,015	77.43	
213,230	403,699	149,578	4,165,551	80.18	
....	176,436	33	432,956	2.45	
....	293,593	3,845	2,697,438	6.68	
2,632,474	4,298,125	1,646,613	13,345,241	121.57	
10,413,658	7,748,334	7,515,395	48,396,969	144.45	
24,383,021	73,512,713	40,110,228	289,446,808	2,073.40	
8,206,456	11,932,366	18,872,980	98,748,364	408.31	
....	159,746	126,720	2,494,972	8.25	
....	17,243	172,388	1,191,650	27.40	
*	*	126,702,857	126,702,357	617.09	
*	818,926	88,037	906,963	61.14	

Showing for Each of the Operating Steam Railroad Corporations Named T

		Operating Income.		
Title of Corporation.		Railway Operating Revenues.	Railway Operating Expenses.	Net Revenue From Railway Operations.
			2	3
1	*Baltimore, Chesapeake & Atlantic Railway Co.........			
2	*Baltimore & Ohio Railroad Co.....			
3	*Baltimore & Sparrow's Point Railroad Co..............			
4	Canton Railroad Co.....	$263,658	$229,821	$33,837
5	Chesapeake Beach Railway Co.	140,862	118,414	22,448
6	*Cumberland & Pennsylvania Railroad Co.		13,135	13,135
7	*Cumberland Valley Railroad Co.			
8	Emmitsburg Railroad Co.	19,901	18,866	1,035
9	*Maryland, Delaware & Virginia Railway Co.....			
10	Maryland & Pennsylvania Railroad Co.....	606,167	472,718	133,449
11	*New York, Philadelphia & Norfolk Railroad Co.			
12	*Northern Central Railway Co.			
13	*Norfolk & Western Railway Co.			
14	*Phila., Balto. & Wash. R. R. Co.			
15	Union Railroad Co. (Jan. 1, 1918, to March 31, 1918)..			
	*Union Railroad Co. (April 1, 1918, to Dec. 31, 1918)...			
16	*Western Maryland Railway Co.....		22,746	22,747
17	*York, Hanover & Frederick Railroad Co.............			

		Non-Operating Income Contin		
Title of Corporation.		Miscellaneous Rents.	Miscellaneous Non-Operating Physical Property.	Separately Operated Properties, Profit.
		14	15	16
1	*Baltimore, Chesapeake & Atlantic Railway Co.........	$4,626	$48	
2	*Baltimore & Ohio Railroad Co.....	792,051	81,393	$396,487
3	*Baltimore & Sparrow's Point Railroad Co.	101		
4	Canton Railroad Co.			
5	Chesapeake Beach Railway Co.		12	
6	*Cumberland & Pennsylvania Railroad Co.	127		
7	*Cumberland Valley Railroad Co.	9,457	98	
8	Emmitsburg Railroad Co.			
9	*Maryland, Delaware & Virginia Railway Co.....	827		
10	Maryland & Pennsylvania Railroad Co.....			
11	*New York, Philadelphia & Norfolk Railroad Co.	1,601		
12	*Northern Central Railway Co.			
13	*Norfolk & Western Railway Co.	190,095	29,855	
14	*Phila., Balto. & Wash. R. R. Co.			
15	Union Railroad Co. (Jan. 1, 1918, to March 31, 1918)..	726		
	*Union Railroad Co. (April 1, 1918, to Dec. 31, 1918)...			
16	*Western Maryland Railway Co.	19,601	85	53,254
17	*York, Hanover & Frederick Railroad Co.............	1,047		

*Properties operated by United States Railroad Administration.

Note—Deficit, loss and other reverse items on this table are printed in bold type.

o. 7.

COMB ACCOUNT FOR THE YEAR AND THE PROFIT AND LOSS ACCOUNT ON DECEMBER 31, 1918.

OPERATING INCOME—Continued.				NON-OPERATING INCOME.				
ncollectible tailway venues.	Railway Operating Income.	Miscellaneous Operating Income.	Total Operating Income.	Hire of Freight Cars. Credit Balance.	Rent from Locomotives.	Rent from Passenger Cars and Other Equipment.	Joint Facility Rent Income.	Lease of Roads.
κ	6	7	8	9	10	11	12	13
				..				$86,
								27,760,
								55,
$58	$12,049		$12,049	..				
1	28 188		28,188					
	18,967		18,967			$9,085		
...i....	20,063		20,063					255,
	142,702		142,702					1,228,
	280		280					
								49,
92	112,745		112,745		$6,602			
	105,605		105,605					
								996,
								2,526,
6	1,716,006		1,716,006					20,634,
								2,694,
	106,205		106,205					346,
								168,
	140,347	$2,642	142,989					3,075,
								19,

N-OPERATING INCOME—Continued.					DEDUCTIONS FROM GROSS INCOME.			
ncome from ided and nfunded curities.	Income from Reserve Funds.	Miscellaneous Income.	Total Non-Operating Income.	Gross Income.	Hire of Freight Cars. Debit Balance.	Rent for Locomotives.	Rent for Passenger Cars and Other Equipment.	Joint Facilit Rents
18	19	20	21	22	23	24	25	26
$6,799	$280		$98,515	$98,515				
,947,542	15,874	$9,332	32,945,691	32,945,691				
1,053			56,674	44,625				
3,941			3,941	32,129	$41,371	$26,010		
122			9,219	28,186	1,180			
53,209		62,677	371,705	351,652				
133,963	856	21	1,386,134	1,243,432				
280			280	560	547			
942			51,392	51,392				
2,951			9,553	122,299	17,141			
31,005	59,092		1,088,180	982,575				
			2,526,357	2,526,357				
659,580		118,970	21,634,302	19,918,295				
		1,384	2,695,421	2,695,421				
1,957			349,625	241,420				
13,352			181,615	181,615				
4,618	4,873	18,645	3,209,991	3,067,002				
			17,998	17,998				

TABL

Title of Corporation.	Rent for Leased Roads. 27	Miscella- neous Rents. 28	Miscella- neous Tax Accruals. 29	Separately Operated Properties, Loss. 30
1 *Baltimore, Chesapeake & Atlantic Railway Co....		$35,348		
2 *Baltimore & Ohio Railroad Co.................	$324,643	499,646	$501,778	$56,635
3 *Baltimore & Sparrow's Point Railroad Co........				
4 Canton Railroad Co..............				
5 Chesapeake Beach Railway Co............		1		
6 *Cumberland & Pennsylvania Railroad Co........				
7 *Cumberland Valley Railroad Co........	65,209	140		....
8 Emmitsburg Railroad Co..............				
9 *Maryland, Delaware & Virginia Railway Co.....		41,561		
10 Maryland & Pennsylvania Railroad Co........	10,000	1,319		
11 *New York, Philadelphia & Norfolk R. R. Co....				
12 *Northern Central Railway Co........				
13 *Norfolk & Western Railway Co............		915		500
14 *Phila., Balto. & Wash. R. R. Co.				
15 Union Railroad Co. (Jan. 1, 1918, to Mar. 31, 1918)		1	148	
*Union Railroad Co. (April 1, 1918, to Dec. 31, 1918)				
16 *Western Maryland Railway Co.................	65,130	4,219		
17 *York, Hanover & Frederick Railroad Co........		1,392		

Title of Corporation.	Income Balance Transferred to Profit and Loss. 41	Credit Balance at Beginning of Year. 42	Balance Transferred from Income. 43
		CREDITS.	
1 *Baltimore, Chesapeake & Atlantic Railway Co.........	$154,570		
2 *Baltimore & Ohio Railroad Co.................	5,600,500	$24,853,880	$5,600,500
3 *Baltimore & Sparrow's Point Railroad Co........	1,501	134,987	1,501
4 Canton Railroad Co..............	62,685		
5 Chesapeake Beach Railway Co.............	78,340		
6 *Cumberland & Pennsylvania Railroad Co........	50,299		50,299
7 *Cumberland Valley Railroad Co............	713,201	3,712,339	713,201
8 Emmitsburg Railroad Co...........	13	5,920	13
9 *Maryland, Delaware & Virginia Railway Co........	105,091		
10 Maryland & Pennsylvania Railroad Co...........	4,254	3,161,854	4,254
11 *New York, Philadelphia & Norfolk Railroad Co.......	455,480	3,161,854	455,480
12 *Northern Central Railway Co...........	196	3,565,531	196
13 *Norfolk & Western Railway Co..................	14,884,834	19,738,317	14,884,834
14 *Phila., Balto. & Wash. R. R. Co.............	1,385	13,500,160	1,385
15 Union Railroad Co. (Jan. 1, 1918, to March 31, 1918)..	241,248	1,964,562	241,248
*Union Railroad Co. (April 1, 1918, to Dec. 31, 1918)...	181,352	2,211,034	181,352
16 *Western Maryland Railway Co.............	102,137	1,553,069	102,137
17 *York, Hanover & Frederick Railroad Co.............	25,576		

* Properties operated by United States Railroad Administration.

NOTE—Deficit, loss and other reverse items on this table are printed in bold type.

—Continued.

	DEDUCTIONS FROM GROSS INCOME—Continued.				DISPOSITION OF NET INCOME.				
Interest on Unfunded Debt.	Miscellaneous Income Charges.	Total Deductions from Gross Revenue.	Net Income.	Applied to Sinking and Other Reserve Funds.	Dividend Appropriations of Income.	Investments in Physical Property.	Miscellaneous.	A
32	33	34	35	36	37	38	39	
$52,907	$100,050	$252,805	$154,290	$280				
1,229,788	246,912	21,920,288	11,025,403	31,514	$5,393,389			
	124	124	44,501		43,000			
	133	94,814	62,684					
55,346		105,526	78,340					
150,809	18,851	223,144	128,508	78,209				
	15,997	97,315	1,146,117	856	426,676		$5,383	
		547	13					
14,116	805	156,483	105,091					
110	2,833	97,050	25,249			$20,926	31	
324	6,011	159,043	823,532	68,052	300,000			
	3,106	359,989	2,166,368		2,166,172			
15,465	140,887	4,113,768	15,804,527		919,692			
54,523	1,350	1,107,816	1,587,605		1,586,220			
		172	241,248					
	53	263	181,352					
9	225,900	2,964,865	102,137					
	185	7,578	25,576					

Miscellaneous Credits.	Debit Balance at Beginning of Year.	Balance Transferred from Income.	Dividend Appropriation from Surplus.	Debt Discount Extinguished Through Surplus.	Loss on Retired Road and Equipment.	Miscellaneous Debits.	Credit Balance Carried to Balance Sheet.
45	46	47	48	49	50	51	52
$1,518	$532,792	$154,570			$114	$309,466	
281,243			$3,798,575	$277	91,677	6,705,857	$20,139,465
12,947					36	9,822	139,577
	162,234	62,685					
	1,870,539	78,340				42	
11,967			62,266				
32,811						12,203	4,446,148
			1,000			4,000	653
	1,397,499	105,091			638	18,780	
	3,284				768	324	
						77,082	3,549,252
100,161							3,665,888
553,773			8,437,410		48,887	14,643	26,676,331
299,502						7,119	13,793,928
7,777						2,553	2,211,034
			456,750				1,935,636
40,147					86	1,722	1,693,545
	541,841	25,576					

TABLE No. 15.

OF THE ELECTRIC RAILROAD CORPORATIONS NAMED THEREIN THE TOTAL AMOUNTS OF ASSETS, OF LIABILITIES AND OF SURPLUS, ON DECEMBER 31, 1918, AND THE TOTAL OF GROSS INCOME, THE DEDUCTIONS FROM GROSS INCOME AND THE NET INCOME FROM THE OPERATIONS OF THE YEAR ENDED DECEMBER 31, 1918, AND THE INCREASES OR DECREASES FROM THE PRECEDING YEAR.

TOTALS.

CORPORATION.	ASSETS.		LIABILITIES.		SURPLUS OR DEFICIT.		GROSS INCOME.		DEDUCTIONS FROM GROSS INCOME.		NET INCOME.	
	Total Amount Dec. 31, 1918.	Increase Over Preceding Year.	Total Amount Dec. 31, 1918.	Increase Over Preceding Year.	Total Amount Dec. 31, 1918.	Increase Over Preceding Year.	Total Amount Dec. 31, 1918.	Increase Over Preceding Year.	Total Amount Dec. 31, 1918.	Increase Over Preceding Year.	Total Amount Dec. 31, 1918.	Increase Over Preceding Year.
	1	2	3	4	5	6	7	8	9	10	11	12
...el Air Electric Ry. Co...	$63,968	$3,116	$57,676	$126	$6,292	$3,242	$19,935	$1,813	$17,586	$3,040	$2,349	$1,227
...horpe & Elkridge Ry. Co.	119,227	332	146,496	2,650	27,269	2,318	15,762	1,742	18,081	5,706	2,319	7,450
...w's Pt. & Ches. Ry. Co.	3,037,567	105,040	3,037,567	105,040	37							
...ailway Co.	14,963		15,00									
...ion Co. of Washington..	19,523,755	555,259	19,026,262	387,313	497,493	167,946	3,543,535	743,735	2,655,446	652,176	888,089	91,559
..., Greencastle & Waynes- Co.	1,465,040	20,231	1,421,508	9,961	43,532	10,270	130,871	12,532	113,601	10,356	17,270	2,176
...ian Ry. Co. of Washington	3,895,006	38,123	3,785,618	32,780	109,388	5,343	707,384	166,990	704,041	128,412	3,313	38,588
...Electric Railway Co....	542,402	2,354	423,040	1,129	119,362	1,225	143,209	18,773	125,984	16,053	17,225	2,720
...Westernport Elec.Ry.Co.	1,642,263	22,680	1,389,260	18,371	253,003	4,309	207,484	31,639	187,000	37,058	20,484	5,419
...Frederick Ry. Co....	6,649,152	561,778	6,444,533	535,887	204,619	25,891	506,162	56,702	467,592	79,785	38,570	23,063
...ailway Co....	60,307		77,727	4,611	17,420	4,644	8,337	1,731	12,981	1,458	4,644	3,189
...rie Railway Co....	45,113		87,352	4,786	42,239	4,786	2,173	158	6,959	769	4,786	811
...ctric Railways Co....	9,260,500	279,665	9,893,319	241,816	632,819	37,849	751,533	171,022	708,205	132,561	43,328	38,461
...ays & Electric Co....	88,045,185	232,127	87,485,615	468,086	559,570	700,213	12,012,762	1,355,825	11,680,110	1,898,759	332,652	542,934
...& Annapolis Elec.R.R.Co.	11,994,484	1,107,727	166,166	1,195,263	428,318	87,636	3,047,156	1,448,563	2,552,620	1,416,678	494,536	31,885
...- Glen Echo Railroad Co.	369,899	715	671,152	1,024	301,253	1,739	1,739		1,739	20	1,739	20
...terurban Railway Co....	214,631	3,594	250,026	22,077	35,395	18,483	21,504	1,162	39,987	6,997	18,483	5,835
...ailway & Electric Co....	34,994,361	1,153,688	34,240,252	1,183,070	745,109	29,382	3,920,223	902,306	3,207,797	697,859	712,426	204,447
...Rockville Railway Co...	631,623	45,206	653,653	59,113	29,030	13,907	95,191	19,030	109,098	15,915	13,907	3,115
...Maryland Ry. Co....	118,438		176,489		58,031	97	2,591		6,545		3,954	*

by another company.

denotes absence of required figures on report.

...cit, loss and other reverse items on this table are printed in bold type.

TA

SHOWING FOR EACH OF THE ELECTRIC RAILROAD CORPORATIONS NAMED THEREIN THE TOTAL

TITLE OF CORPORATION.	TOTALS.	
	Total Assets December 31, 1918.	In Yea
	1	2
1 Baltimore & Bel Air Electric Railway Co.............................	$63,968	
2 Baltimore, Halethorpe & Elkridge Railway Co.......................	119,227	
3 Baltimore, Sparrow's Point & Chesapeake Railway Co..............	3,037,567	1
4 Blue Ridge Railway Co..	14,963	....
5 Capital Traction Co. of Washington................................	19,523,755	
6 Chambersburg, Greencastle & Waynesboro Street Railway Co.......	1,465,040	
7 City & Suburban Railway Co. of Washington........................	3,895,006	
8 Cumberland Electric Railway Co....................................	542,402	
9 Cumberland & Westernport Electric Railway Co....................	1,642,263	
10 Hagerstown & Frederick Railway Co................................	6,649,152	
11 Kensington Railway Co...	60,307	....
12 Loraine Electric Railway Co..	45,113	....
13 Maryland Electric Railways Co.....................................	9,260,500	
14 United Railways & Electric Co......................................	88,045,185	
15 Washington, Baltimore & Annapolis Electric Railroad Co...........	11,994,484	1,1
16 Washington & Glen Echo Railroad Co..............................	369,899	
17 Washington Interurban Railway Co................................	214,631	
18 Washington Railway & Electric Co.................................	34,994,361	1,1
19 Washington & Rockville Railway Co................................	634,623	
20 Washington & Maryland Railway Co...............................	118,458	*

DETAILS OF
—Contint

TITLE OF CORPORATION.	Other Investments.	To Invest
	11	1
1 Baltimore & Bel Air Electric Railway Co.............................	$463	
2 Baltimore, Halethorpe & Elkridge Railway Co.......................	....	
3 Baltimore, Sparrow's Point & Chesapeake Railway Co..............	....	3,
4 Blue Ridge Railway Co...	....	
5 Capital Traction Co. of Washington................................	34,506	18,
6 Chambersburg, Greencastle & Waynesboro Street Railway Co.......	8,750	1,
7 City & Suburban Railway Co. of Washington........................	834	3,
8 Cumberland Electric Railway Co....................................	7,500	
9 Cumberland & Westernport Electric Railway Co....................	1,301	1,
10 Hagerstown & Frederick Railway Co................................	725	6,
11 Kensington Railway Co...	....	
12 Loraine Electric Railway Co..	....	
13 Maryland Electric Railways Co.....................................	....	6,
14 United Railways & Electric Co......................................	200,030	75,
15 Washington, Baltimore & Annapolis Electric Railroad Co...........	290,000	11,
16 Washington & Glen Echo Railroad Co..............................	....	
17 Washington Interurban Railway Co................................	....	
18 Washington Railway & Electric Co.................................	11,434	32,
19 Washington & Rockville Railway Co................................	....	
20 Washington & Maryland Railway Co...............................	....	

NOTE—Deficit, loss and other reverse items on this table are printed in bold type.
Asterick * denotes required figures not given on report.

No. 16.

or Assets and the Deficit on December 31, 1918, and the Classification of Such Assets.

Totals—Continued.			**Details of Assets.**					
			Investments.					
Corporate Deficit.	Increase Over Preceding Year.	Road and Equipment.	Miscellaneous Physical Property.	Stocks of Affiliated Companies.	Bonds of Affiliated Companies.	Notes of Affiliated Companies.	Ac C
3	4	5	6	7	8	9	
$27,269	$2,318	$59,965					
....	....	119,227					
37	....	3,037,567					
....	....	14,963					
....	....	18,151,008	$101,677				
....	....	1,180,674	19,642	$72,120			
....	....	3,823,956					
....	....	506,406					
....	....	1,564,184					
....	....	5,343,201		910,955			
17,420	4,644	60,000	307				
42,239	4,786	43,484		5			
632,819	37,849	6,719,250	5	5			
....	....	72,474,123	6,813	67,372	$65,175	$51,996	
....	....	10,743,093		173,200		93,000	
301,253	1,739	369,843					
35,395	18,483	212,050					
....	....	32,551,673	5,783	34,773	160,000	67,524	
29,030	13,907	491,388		110,000			
58,031	*	95,519					

Details of Assets—Continued.

Current Assets.

Cash.	Special Deposits.	Loans and Notes Receivable.	Miscellaneous Accounts Receivable.	Materials and Supplies.	Interest, Dividends and Rents Receivable.	Other Current Assets.	T
13	14	15	16	17	18	19	
$3,540							
....	....	....	....	....	....	....	
....	....	....	....	....	....	....	
42,674	$432,590	....	$26,942	$143,010	....	$7,333	
13,100	37,912	....	2,173	6,787	....	....	
51,142	1,050	....	15,811	....	....	....	
11,945	....	....	371	16,180	....	....	
27,193	....	....	21,569	18,060	....	100	
29,481	....	$900	166,998	104,073	....	3,607	
....	....	....	....	....	....	....	
4	....	35	....	1,590	....	....	
53,130	....	15,000	98,312	26,804	....	....	
274,807	145,597	4,000	343,126	1,217,038	$1,895	....	..,
275,049	....	....	133,184	125,873	....	....	
....	....	....	50	....	....	....	
989	....	....	1,383	....	....	....	
715,847	42,273	104,500	521,807	289,798	25,120	25,266	1,
5,804	4,625	....	75	....	21,875	....	
....	....	6,217	6,593	....	....	....	

TABL

Details of Assets—Co

	Deferred Assets	
TITLE OF CORPORATION.	Insurance and Other Funds.	Other Deferred Assets.
	21	22
1 Baltimore & Bel Air Electric Railway Co..........................		
2 Baltimore, Halethorpe & Elkridge Railway Co.....................		
3 Baltimore, Sparrow's Point & Chesapeake Railway Co.............		
4 Blue Ridge Railway Co..		
5 Capital Traction Co. of Washington..............................	$554,942	
6 Chambersburg, Greencastle & Waynesboro Street Railway Co.......		
7 City & Suburban Railway Co. of Washington.......................		
8 Cumberland Electric Railway Co...................................		
9 Cumberland & Westernport Electric Railway Co....................		
10 Hagerstown & Frederick Railway Co..............................		
11 Kensington Railway Co...		
12 Loraine Electric Railway Co.....................................		
13 Maryland Electric Railways Co...................................	(a)1,811,762	
14 United Railways & Electric Co..................................		$6,012,239
15 Washington, Baltimore & Annapolis Electric Railroad Co.........		
16 Washington & Glen Echo Railroad Co.............................		
17 Washington Interurban Railway Co...............................		
18 Washington Railway & Electric Co...............................		21,850
19 Washington & Rockville Railway Co..............................		
20 Washington & Maryland Railway Co..............................		

(a) General sinking fund for first mortgage 5% bonds, $724,164; special sinking fund, $1,087,597

(b) Includes $468,700, discount on bonds sold to pay for property leased to The United Railways Company.

(c) Includes $3,920,000, past due coupons on income bonds for which same amount of 5% fundin in 1936 have been issued and are outstanding.

ed.

DETAILS OF ASSETS—Continued.

UNADJUSTED DEBITS.

Discount on Stock.	Discount on Funded Debt.	Property Abandoned Chargeable to Operating Expenses.	Other Unadjusted Debits.	Total Unadjusted Debits.	Total Assets.	Grand Total.
25	26	27	28	29	30	31
....	....	....	....	....	$63,968	$63,968
....	....	....	....	....	119,227	146,496
....	....	....	....	....	3,037,567	3,037,567
....	....	....	....	....	14,963	15,000
....	....	$18,497	....	$29,071	19,523,755	19,523,755
....	$1,300	....	$500	2,187	1,465,040	1,465,040
....	....	1,046	....	2,212	3,895,006	3,895,006
....	....	....	....	....	542,402	542,402
....	....	....	....	9,855	1,642,263	1,642,263
....	46,728	....	42,372	89,211	6,649,152	6,649,152
....	....	....	....	....	60,307	77,727
....	....	....	....	....	45,113	87,352
....	(b) 533,600	....	646	536,231	9,260,500	9,893,319
$2,730,600	205,684	....	(c)4,180,567	7,141,029	88,045,185	88,045,185
....	83,226	....	36,025	122,231	11,994,484	11,994,484
....	....	....	....	6	369,899	671,152
....	....	....	198	207	214,631	250,026
....	389,780	....	16,404	416,711	34,994,361	34,994,361
....	358	....	835	855	634,623	663,653
....	27	....	10,100	10,127	118,458	176,489

TA

| | TITLE OF CORPORATION. | TOTALS. | |
| | | Total Liabilities December 31, 1918. | Increase Y |
		1	2
1	Baltimore & Bel Air Railway Co....	$57,676	
2	Baltimore, Halethorpe & Elkridge Railway Co....	146,496	
3	Baltimore, Sparrow's Point & Chesapeake Railway Co....	3,037,567	1
4	Blue Ridge Railway Co.	15,000	....
5	Capital Traction Co. of Washington....	19,026,262	
6	Chambersburg, Greencastle & Waynesboro Street Railway Co....	1,421,508	
7	City & Suburban Railway Co. of Washington....	3,785,618	
8	Cumberland Electric Railway Co....	423,040	
9	Cumberland & Westernport Electric Railway Co....	1,389,260	
10	Hagerstown & Frederick Railway Co....	6,444,533	
11	Kensington Railway Co....	77,727	
12	Loraine Electric Railway Co....	87,352	
13	Maryland Electric Railways Co....	9,893,319	
14	United Railways & Electric Co....	87,485,615	
15	Washington, Baltimore & Annapolis Electric Railroad Co....	11,566,166	1,1
16	Washington & Glen Echo Railroad Co....	671,152	
17	Washington Interurban Railway Co....	250,026	
18	Washington Railway & Electric Co....	34,249,252	1,1
19	Washington & Rockville Railway Co....	663,653	
20	Washington & Maryland Railway Co....	176,489	*

DETAILS OF LIABILITI —Continued.

CURRENT LIABILITIE —Continued.

| | TITLE OF CORPORATION. | Miscellaneous Accounts Payable. | Ma In Divi and Un |
		11	12
1	Baltimore & Bel Air Railway Co....	....	....
2	Baltimore, Halethorpe & Elkridge Railway Co....	$566	....
3	Baltimore, Sparrow's Point & Chesapeake Railway Co....	3,567	
4	Blue Ridge Railway Co....		
5	Capital Traction Co. of Washington....	3,859	$2
6	Chambersburg, Greencastle & Waynesboro Street Railway Co....	227	
7	City & Suburban Railway Co. of Washington....	55,022	
8	Cumberland Electric Railway Co....		
9	Cumberland & Westernport Electric Railway Co....		
10	Hagerstown & Frederick Railway Co....	10,918	
11	Kensington Railway Co....	12,700	
12	Loraine Electric Railway Co....	2,728	
13	Maryland Electric Railways Co....	7,427	
14	United Railways & Electric Co....		1
15	Washington, Baltimore & Annapolis Electric Railroad Co....	212,936	2
16	Washington & Glen Echo Railroad Co....	819	1
17	Washington Interurban Railway Co....	22,076	
18	Washington Railway & Electric Co....	4,950	
19	Washington & Rockville Railway Co....	64,945	
20	Washington & Maryland Railway Co....	634	....

(a) First Mortgage Bonds matured June 1st, 1916.

Asterisk (*) denotes absence of required figures.

NOTE—Deficit, loss and other reverse items on this table are printed in bold type.

No. 17.

F LIABILITIES AND THE SURPLUS ON DECEMBER 31, 1918, AND THE CLASSIFICATION OF SUCH LIABILITIES.

TOTALS—Continued.		DETAILS OF LIABILITIES.						
			LONG-TERM DEBT.				CURRENT LIABILITIES	
Corporate Surplus.	Increase Over Preceding Year.	Capital Stock.	Funded Debt, Unmatured.	Non-Negotiable Debt to Affiliated Companies.	Total Long-Term Debt.	Loans and Notes Payable.	Audi Accou and W Payab
3	4	5	6	7	8	9	10
$6,292	$3,242	$46,250	....	....	....	....	....
....	....	10,000	....	....	....	$136,000	....
....	....	400,000	$2,000,000	....	$2,000,000	634,000	....
....	....	15,000	....	....	....	....	....
497,493	167,946	12,000,000	5,606,000	....	5,606,000	200,000	3
43,532	10,270	600,000	793,400	....	793,400	....	10,
109,388	5,343	1,750,000	1,750,000	$89,909	1,839,909	....	12,
119,362	1,225	200,000	100,000	....	100,000	10,000	....
253,003	4,309	625,000	655,000	....	655,000	72,744	9,
204,619	25,891	2,355,450	3,019,000	13,000	3,032,000	800,000	111,
....	....	25,000	35,000	....	35,000	450	....
....	....	5,000	....	....	....	49,462	....
559,570	700,213	1,164,000	6,109,928	....	6,109,928	526,026	31,
428,318	87,536	20,484,200	58,639,000	....	58,639	....	679,
....	....	4,455,750	5,239,000	93,000	5,332,000	....	117,
....	....	200,000	50,000	22,061	72,061	....	...
....	....	50,000	150,000	4,258	154,258	....	....
745,109	29,382	15,000,000	17,465,350	....	17,465,350	246,200	235,
....	....	275,000	185,000	....	185,000	90,055	....
....	....	10,100	96,000	....	96,000	60,500	....

DETAILS OF LIABILITIES—Continued.

CURRENT LIABILITIES—Continued.					UNADJUSTED CREDITS.		
Matured Funded Debt Unpaid.	Accrued Interest, Dividends and Rents Payable.	Other Current Liabilities.	Total Current Liabilities.	Deferred Liabilities.	Tax Liability.	Insurance and Casualty Reserves.	Operati Reserv
13	14	15	16	17	18	19	20
....	....	$226	$226	....	....	....	....
....	....	....	136,566	....	$69	....	....
....	....	....	637,567	....	....	....	....
....	$23,358	....	451,453	$2,949	180,863	$194,150	$6,
....	7,032	....	3,966	....	1,915	1,709	....
....	36,458	....	106,504	....	12,557	....	....
....	1,250	....	11,250	....	....	....	....
....	6,052	1,868	89,873	....	2,587	$60	....
....	48,395	....	970,868	653	301	74	....
....	104	....	13,254	....	....	....	....
....	....	....	82,352	....	....	....	....
....	86,851	....	700,378	1,811,762	12,901	460	21,
....	759,739	....	1,584,847	6,323,573	203,383	....	....
....	88,368	....	665,368	....	449,622	....	55,
(a)$200,000	....	....	398,319	....	43	....	....
....	3,125	....	44,202	....	....	....	1,
118	118,477	....	647,868	14	91,084	....	14,
....	2,632	....	158,573	11	....	....	....
....	3,900	5,355	70,389	....	....	....	....

TABLE N

	TITLE OF CORPORATION.	Accrued Depreciation, Road and Equipment.	Un Credi
		21	22
1	Baltimore & Bel Air Railway Co.	$11,200	
2	Baltimore, Halethorpe & Elkridge Railway Co.		
3	Baltimore, Sparrow's Point & Chesapeake Railway Co.		
4	Blue Ridge Railway Co.		
5	Capital Traction Co. of Washington.	554,793	
6	Chambersburg, Greencastle & Waynesboro Street Railway Co.	16,749	
7	City & Suburban Railway Co. of Washington.	73,876	
8	Cumberland Electric Railway Co.	111,790	
9	Cumberland & Westernport Electric Railway Co.	17,660	
10	Hagerstown & Frederick Railway Co.	82,874	
11	Kensington Railway Co.	4,472	
12	Loraine Electric Railway Co.		
13	Maryland Electric Railways Co.	44,592	
14	United Railways & Electric Co	188,919	
15	Washington, Baltimore & Annapolis Electric Railroad Co.	571,402	
16	Washington & Glen Echo Railroad Co.	729	
17	Washington Interurban Railway Co.	60	
18	Washington Railway & Electric Co.	911,968	1
19	Washington & Rockville Railway Co.	36,069	
20	Washington & Maryland Railway Co.		

NOTE—Deficit, loss and other reverse items on this table are printed in bold type.

—Continued.

DETAIL OF LIABILITIES—Continued.

Unadjusted Credits— Continued.		Corporate Surplus.					
Total Unadjusted Credits.	Total Liabilities.	Additions to Property Through Surplus.	Sinking Fund Reserves.	Total Appropriated Surplus.	Profit and Loss.	Corporate Surplus.	Gr To
23	24	25	26	27	28	29	3
$11,200	$57,676				$6,292	$6,292	$63
69	146,496				27,269	27,269	119
	3,037,567						3,037
	15,000						15
965,859	19,026,262				497,493	497,493	19,523
20,642	1,421,508				43,532	43,532	1,465
89,205	3,785,618				109,388	109,388	3,895
111,790	423,040		$6,500	$6,500	112,862	119,362	542
19,386	1,389,260				253,003	253,003	1,642
85,562	6,444,533				204,619	204,619	6,649
4,472	77,727				17,420	17,420	60
	87,352				42,239	42,239	45
107,251	9,893,319				632,819	632,819	9,260
453,994	87,485,615		197,200	197,200	362,370	559,570	88,045
1,113,048	11,566,166	$136,400		136,400	291,918	428,318	11,994
772	671,152				301,253	301,253	369
1,566	250,026				35,395	35,395	214
1,136,020	34,249,252		1,991	1,991	743,118	745,109	34,994
36,069	663,653				29,030	29,030	634
	176,489				58,031	58,031	118

Showing for Each of the Electric Railroad Corporations Named Therein the Amount of
Corporation), and a Classificati

	TITLE OF CORPORATION.	TOTALS.	
		ALL CLASSE	
		Amount Outstanding December 31, 1918.	
		1	
1	Baltimore & Bel Air Electric Railway Co.	$46,250	.....
2	Baltimore, Halethorpe & Elkridge Railway Co.	10,000	
3	Baltimore, Sparrow's Point & Chesapeake Railway Co.	2,400,000	.....
4	Blue Ridge Railway Co.	15,000	
5	Capital Traction Co. of Washington	17,606,000	
6	Chambersburg, Greencastle & Waynesboro Street Railway Co.	1,393,400	
7	City & Suburban Railway Co. of Washington	3,500,000	
8	Cumberland Electric Railway Co.	300,000	
9	Cumberland & Westernport Electric Railway Co.	1,280,000	
10	Hagerstown & Frederick Railway Co.	5,374,450	
11	Kensington Railway Co.	60,000	.....
12	Loraine Electric Railway Co.	5,000	
13	Maryland Electric Railways Co.	7,273,928	
14	Towson & Cockeysville Electric Railway Co.	36,400	
15	United Railways & Electric Co.	79,123,200	
16	Washington, Baltimore & Annapolis Electric Railroad Co.	9,694,750	
17	Washington & Glen Echo Railroad Co.	250,000	.....
18	Washington Interurban Railway Co.	200,000	
19	Washington Railway & Electric Co.	32,465,350	
20	Washington & Rockville Railway Co.	460,000	.....
21	Washington & Maryland Railway Co.	106,100	.....

	TITLE OF CORPORATION.	DETAILS OF FUND —Continued	
		Collateral Trust Bonds.	Inco
		9	
1	Baltimore & Bel Air Electric Railway Co.	....	.....
2	Baltimore, Halethorpe & Elkridge Railway Co.	....	.....
3	Baltimore, Sparrow's Point & Chesapeake Railway Co.	....	.....
4	Blue Ridge Railway Co.	....	.....
5	Capital Traction Co. of Washington.	....	.....
6	Chambersburg, Greencastle & Waynesboro Street Railway Co.	....	.....
7	City & Suburban Railway Co. of Washington.	....	.....
8	Cumberland Electric Railway Co.	....	.....
9	Cumberland & Westernport Electric Railway Co.	....	.....
10	Hagerstown & Frederick Railway Co.	....	.....
11	Kensington Railway Co.	....	.....
12	Loraine Electric Railway Co.	....	.....
13	Maryland Electric Railways Co.	....	.....
14	Towson & Cockeysville Electric Railway Co.	....	.....
15	United Railways & Electric Co.	....	$
16	Washington, Baltimore & Annapolis Electric Railroad Co.	....	.....
17	Washington & Glen Echo Railroad Co.	....	.....
18	Washington Interurban Railway Co.	....	.....
19	Washington Railway & Electric Co.	....	.....
20	Washington & Rockville Railway Co.	....	.....
21	Washington & Maryland Railway Co.	....	.....

NOTE—Deficit, loss and other reverse items on this table are printed in bold type.

No. 18.

or Securities Outstanding on December 31, 1918 (Exclusive of Any Such as are Held by the Securities Between Funded Debt and Stocks.

Totals—Continued.

	Funded Debt.		Stocks.		Details of Funded	
Amount Outstanding December 31, 1918.	Increase Over Preceding Year.	Amount Outstanding December 31, 1918.	Increase Over Preceding Year.	Equipment Obligations.	Mo Bo
3	4	5	6	7	
		$46,250			
		10,000			
$2,000,000		400,000			$2,
		15,000			5,
5,606,000		12,000,000			
793,400		600,000			
1,750,000		1,750,000			1,
100,000		200,000			
655,000		625,000			
3,019,000	$65,000	2,355,450			2,
35,000		25,000			
		5,000			
6,109,928	36,000	1,164,000		$163,928	5,
		36,400			34,
58,639,000		20,484,200			5,
5,239,000	95,000	4,455,750			
50,000		200,000			
150,000		50,000			17,
17,465,350	999,000	15,000,000			
185,000		275,000			
96,000		10,100			

Details of Stocks.

Details of Funded Debt—Continued.	Common.			Preferred.	
Miscellaneous Obligations.	Amount Outstanding December 31, 1918.	Increase Over Preceding Year.	Amount Outstanding December 31, 1918.	In (Year.
11	12	13	14	15
	$46,250			
	10,000			
	400,000			
	15,000			
	12,000,000			
	300,000		$300,000	
	1,750,000			
	200,000			
	625,000			
$880,000	1,512,950		842,500	
	25,000			
	5,000			
	1,164,000			
	36,400			
9,670,000	20,461,200		23,000	
	3,000,000		1,455,750	
	200,000			
	50,000			
	6,500,000		8,500,000	
	275,000			
	10,100			

TABLE

R EACH OF THE ELECTRIC RAILROAD CORPORATIONS NAMED THEREIN THE FUNDED DEBT AND CAPITAL ISSUING CORPORATION), DESCRIPTION OF SAME, RATE PER CENT, THE AMOUNT OF INTEREST ACCRUING

TITLE OF CORPORATION.	FUNDED DEBT.			
	PRINCIPAL.			
	Description of Bonds.	Date.	Date of Maturity.	Amount Outstanding.
	1	2	3	4
re & Bel Air Electric Railway Co.				
re, Halethorpe & Elkridge Ry. Co.				
re, Sparrow's Point & Chesapeake Ry. Co.	1st Mortgage.	1903	1953	$2,000,000
dge Railway Co.				
Traction Co., Washington, D. C.	1st Mortgage.	1907	1947	5,606,000
rsburg, Greencastle & Waynesboro Street Railway Co.	1st Mortgage.	1903	1933	300,000
	2nd Mortgage.	1908	1938	299,500
	1st Refunded	1911	1941	163,900
	1st Refunded	1914	1941	30,000
Suburban Ry. Co., Washington, D. C.	1st Mortgage.	1898	1948	1,750,000
d Electric Railway Co.	1st Mortgage.	1903	1923	100,000
d & Westernport Electric Ry. Co.				
urg. Elkhart & Cumberland Ry. Co.	1st Mortgage.	1901	1926	230,000
ning, Midland & Frostburg Ry. Co.	1st Mortgage.	1901	1926	200,000
nport & Lonaconing Ry. Co.	1st Mortgage.	1903	1928	225,000
& Frederick Railway Co.	1st Mortgage.	1914	1944	1,324,000
	Gold Notes.	1917	1927	600,000
	Collat. Trust.	1917	1932	280,000
wn & Boonsboro Ry. Co.	1st Mortgage.	1902	1922	110,000
rstown & Myersville Ry. Co.	1st Mortgage.	1904	1924	120,000
rstown & Northern Ry. Co.	1st Mortgage.	1907	1927	200,000
rick & Middletown R. R. Co.	1st Mortgage.	1905	1935	126,000
cacy Valley Ry. Co.	1st Mortgage.	1908	1925	30,000
rick Gas & Electric Co.	1st Mortgage.	1904	1929	179,000
burg Illuminating & Manufacturing Co.	1st Mortgage.	1899	1929	50,000
n Railway Co.	1st Mortgage.	1902	1922	15,000
	Consolidated	1909	1934	20,000
Electric Railway Co.				
d Electric Railways Co.	1st Mortgage.	1906	1931	4,946,000
	Equipment.	1910	1911–1919	10,928
	Equipment.	1913	1914–1924	153,000
to. & Annapolis Short Line R. R. Co.	1st Mortgage.	1906	1946	1,000,000
Railways & Electric Co.	1st Mortgage.	1899	1949	26,450,000
	Income.	1899	1949	13,977,000
	Funding.	1906	1936	3,920,000
	Notes.	1916	1921	1,244,000
	Con.Gold Notes	1917	1922	1,506,000
	Con.Gold Notes	1917	1922	3,000,000
tral Railway Co.	1st Mortgage.	1892	1932	692,000
	Exp. & Imp.	1897	1932	600,000
& Suburban Ry. Co.	1st Mortgage.	1892	1922	2,000,000
imore Traction Co.	1st Mortgage.	1899	1929	5,500,000
th Baltimore Passenger Ry. Co.	1st Mortgage.	1892	1942	750,000
e Roland Elevated Ry Co.	1st Mortgage.	1892	1942	000,000
n, Balto. & Annapolis Electric R. R. Co.	1st Mortgage.	1911	1941	144,000
n & Glen Echo Railroad Co.	2nd Mortgage.	1898	1918	50,000
n & Great Falls Ry. & Power Co.	1st Mortgage.	1912	1937	500,000
n Interurban Railway Co.	1st Mortgage.	1916	1946	150,000
n Railway & Electric Co.	Consolidated.	1902	1951	11,642,350
	Gen'l Mortgage.	1918	1925	2,000,000
politan R. R. Co.	1st Mortgage.	1895	1925	850,000
a & Potomac R. R. Co.	1st Mortgage.	1899	1949	979,000
n & Rockville Railway Co.	1st Mortgage.	1915	1965	185,000
n & Maryland Railway Co.	Gen'l Mortgage.	1917	1947	96,000

No. 19.

STOCK OUTSTANDING ON DECEMBER 31, 1918 (EXCLUSIVE OF SUCH FUNDED DEBT AND CAPITAL STOCK AS ARE HE ON FUNDED DEBT AND THE AMOUNT OF DIVIDENDS DECLARED ON CAPITAL STOCK DURING THE YEAR.

FUNDED DEBT—Cont.		STOCKS.					
INTEREST.		COMMON.			PREFERRED.		
Rate Per Cent.	Dates When Payable.	Amount Outstanding.	Dividends Declared During Year.	Rate Per Cent.	Amount Outstanding.	Dividends Declared During Year.	Rate Per Cent.
5	6	7	8	9	10	11	12
....	....	$46,250	$2,775	6	....	....	....
....		10,000	....				
4½	F. & A.	400,000	....				
....		15,000	....				
5	J. & D.	12,000,000	720,000	6	....	....	....
5	J. & J.	300,000	....		$300,000	$15,000	
5	A. & O.						
5	A. & O.						
5	A. & O.						
5	F. & A.	1,750,000	....				
5	A. & O.	200,000	16,000	8	0	....	
		625,000					
5	J. & D.						
5	J. & D.						
5	J. & J.						
6	A. & O.	1,512,950	....		842,500	12,637	
6	M. & N.						
5	M. & S.						
5	F. & A.						
5	J. & J.						
5	F. & A.						
5	J. & D.						
5	J. & J.						
5	J. & J.						
5	Mch. Quart'y	25,000					
5	Mch. Quart'y.	5,000					
....	A. & O.	1,164,000					
5	F. & A.						
6	J. & D.						
5	F. & A.						
4	M. & S.	20,461,200	818,448	4	23,000	920	
4	J. & D.						
5	J. & D.						
5	F. & A.						
5	F. & A.						
6	F. & A.						
5	M. & N.						
5	M. & S.						
5	J. & D.						
5	M. & N.						
5	J. & D.						
5	M. & S.						
5	M. & S.	3,000,000	405,000	13½	1,455,750	87,360	
6	M. & N.	200,000					
5	J. & D.	300,350					
5	F. & A.	50,000					
4	J. & D.	6,500,000	325,000	5	8,500,000	425,000	
6	J. & D.						
5	F. & A.						
5	A. & O.						
5	M. & N.	275,000					
6	J. & J.	10,100					

TABLE No. 20.

Showing for Each of the Electric Railroad Corporations Named Therein the Investment in Road and Equipment on December 31, 1918.

Title of Corporation.	Investment in Road and Equipment.			Average Cost Per Mile.			
	Cost of Road and Equipment June 30, 1914.	Invested Since June 30, 1914.	Total Cost of Road and Equipment Dec. 31, 1918.	Length of Road Owned. Miles.	Average Investment Per Mile.	Length of Track Owned. Miles.	Average Investment Per Mile.
	1	2	3	4	5	6	7
1 Baltimore & Bel Air Electric Railway Co.	$57,927	$2,038	$59,965	3.22	$16,346	3.28	$16,047
2 Baltimore, Halethorpe & Elkridge Railway Co.	113,274	5,953	119,227	2.84	41,981	3.05	39,078
3 Baltimore, Sparrow's Point & Chesapeake Railway Co.	2,864,372	173,195	3,037,567	17.63	172,246	34.27	88,615
4 Blue Ridge Railway Co.	14,963		14,963	1.60	9,352	1.60	9,352
5 Capital Traction Company of Washington	17,658,961	492,047	18,151,008	30.16	647,232	64.00	304,030
6 Chambersburg, Greencastle & Waynesboro St. Railway Co.	619,972	560,702	1,180,674	30.00	39,356	31.00	38,086
7 City & Suburban Railway Co. of Washington	3,806,700	17,256	3,823,956	25.50	149,959	41.41	92,344
8 Cumberland Electric Railway Co.	440,059	66,347	506,406	7.87	64,346	8.64	58,611
9 Cumberland & Westernport Electric Railway Co.	1,417,358	146,826	1,564,184	25.00	62,567	25.50	61,344
10 Hagerstown & Frederick Railway Co.	3,738,166	272,193	4,010,359	82.30	48,728	86.80	46,202
11 Kensington Railway Co.	60,000		60,000	2.50	24,000	2.60	23,07
12 Loraine Electric Railway Co.	43,484		43,484	1.12	38,824	1.12	38,824
13 Maryland Electric Railways Co.	5,509,073	1,210,177	6,719,250	30.16	222,787	42.66	157,507
14 United Railways and Electric Co.	68,008,087	4,466,036	72,474,123	180.18	402,232	378.82	191,316
15 Washington, Baltimore & Annapolis Electric R. R. Co.	9,452,248	1,290,845	10,743,093	54.95	195,506	103.43	103,869
16 Washington & Glen Echo Railroad Co.	369,938	95	369,843	7.54	49,051	7.54	49,051
17 Washington Interurban Railway Co.		212,050	212,050	8.03	26,407	8.26	25,072
18 Washington Railway and Electric Co.	31,984,924	566,749	32,551,673	53.61	607,194	103.25	315,270
19 Washington & Rockville Railway Co.	381,504	109,884	491,388	13.26	37,058	14.44	34,030
20 Washington & Maryland Railway Co.			95,519	3.57	26,756	3.57	26,756

Note—Deficit, loss and other reverse items on this table are printed in bold type.

TAB

SHOWING FOR EACH OF THE ELECTRIC RAILROAD CORPORATIONS NAMED THEREIN

	TITLE OF CORPORATION.	OPERATING INCOME.			
		Railway Operating Revenues.	Railway Operating Expenses.	Net Revenue, Railway Operations.	R A Operati
		1	2	3	4
1	Baltimore & Bel Air Electric Railway Co.............	$19,935	$17,415	$2,520	....
2	Baltimore, Halethorpe & Elkridge Railway Co..........	15,762	10,987	4,775	....
3 (a)	Baltimore, Sparrow's Point & Chesapeake Railway Co....				
4 (b)	Blue Ridge Railway Co.				
5	Capital Traction Co. of Washington...............	3,529,854	2,083,060	1,446,794	
6	Chambersburg, Greencastle & Waynesboro Street Ry.,Co.	127,221	80,831	46,390	
7	City & Suburban Railway Co. of Washington............	707,068	573,409	133,659	
8	Cumberland Electric Railway Co.	143,209	115,059	28,150	
9	Cumberland & Westernport Electric Railway Co.......	197,605	142,113	55,492	
0	Hagerstown & Frederick Railway Co.	369,066	276,649	92,417	(c)$103,
1	Kensington Railway Co.	8,337	10,926	2,589	
2	Loraine Electric Railway Co.	2,173	2,641	467	
3	Maryland Electric Railways Co.	476,800	334,944	141,856	
4	United Railways & Electric Co.	11,929,701	7,436,307	4,493,394	
5	Washington, Baltimore & Annapolis Electric Railroad Co.	2,902,014	1,740,281	1,161,733	(d) 127,
6	Washington & Glen Echo Railroad Co.		170	170	
7	Washington Interurban Railway Co.	21,504	31,144	9,640	
8	Washington Railway & Electric Co.	3,217,451	2,291,822	925,629	
9	Washington & Rockville Railway Co.	84,691	90,966	6,275	
	Washington & Maryland Railway Co.	2,591	2,645	54	

	TITLE OF CORPORATION.	NON-OPERATING INCOME —Continued.			DEDUCTI FROM GROSS INCO
		Miscellaneous Income.	Total Non-Operating Income.	Gross Income.	Rent fo Leased Roads.
		14	15	16	17
1	Baltimore & Bel Air Electric Railway Co............			$2,349	
2	Baltimore, Halethorpe & Elkridge Railway Co........			4,378	
3 (a)	Baltimore, Sparrow's Point & Chesapeake Railway Co....				
4 (b)	Blue Ridge Railway Co.				
5	Capital Traction Co. of Washington........	$4,771	$13,680	1,173,484	
6	Chambersburg, Greencastle & Waynesboro Street Ry. Co.	657	3,650	44,040	
7	City & Suburban Railway Co. of Washington.........		316	99,457	
8	Cumberland Electric Railway Co.			23,025	
9	Cumberland & Westernport Electric Railway Co........	8,658	9,879	56,789	
0	Hagerstown & Frederick Railway Co.	13,592	33,437	229,513	
1	Kensington Railway Co.			2,594	
2	Loraine Electric Railway Co.			467	
3	Maryland Electric Railways Co.		274,732	391,508	
	United Railways & Electric Co.	8,412	83,061	3,416,003	435,
	Washington, Baltimore & Annapolis Electric Railroad Co..	5,424	17,953	783,448	
	Washington & Glen Echo Railroad Co.			416	
	Washington Interurban Railway Co.			10,727	
	Washington Railway & Electric Co.	2,906	702,772	1,457,125	
	Washington & Rockville Railway Co.			1,285	
	Washington & Maryland Railway Co.		10,500	54	

(a) Road operated by The United Railways & Electric Co.
(b) Road operated by The Chambersburg, Greencastle & Waynesboro St. Railway Co.
(c) Net Income from Gas and Electric operations.
(d) Net Income from Power Contracts.
(e) Includes Taxes, $14,050.

NOTE—Deficit, loss and other reverse items on this table are printed in bold type.

No. 21.

INCOME AND THE PROFIT AND LOSS ACCOUNT FOR THE YEAR ENDED DECEMBER 31, 1918.

OPERATING INCOME—Continued.   NON-OPERATING INCOME.

Net Operating Revenue.	Taxes Assignable to Railway Operations.	Operating Income.	Miscellaneous Rent Income.	Dividend Income.	Income from Funded Securities.	Income from Unfunded Securities and Accounts.	Income from Reserve Funds.	o
5	6	7	8	9	10	11	12	
$2,520	$171	$2,349						
4,775	396	4,378						
1,446,794	286,990	1,159,804			$2,852	$5,866		
46,390	6,000	40,389	$1,600	$150		1,243		
133,659	34,518	99,141				316		
28,149	5,124	23,025						
55,492	8,582	46,910	425			796		
196,076		196,076	152	19,617			$75	
2,589	305	2,894						
467		467						
141,856	25,081	116,775	272,510			841		
4,493,394	1,160,452	3,332,942	2,570		24,992	43,810	3,277	
1,288,921	523,426	765,495	2,571			9,958		
170	246	416						
9,640	1,087	10,727						
925,629	171,276	754,353		660,000	8,000	31,757	109	
6,275	2,939	9,214				10,500		
54		54						

PROFIT AND LOSS.

DEDUCTIONS FROM GROSS INCOME—Continued.

CREDITS.

Interest on Funded Debt.	Interest on Unfunded Debt.	Amortization of Discount on Funded Debt.	Miscellaneous Debits.	Total Deductions from Gross Income.	Net Income Transferred to Profit and Loss.	Credit Balance at Beginning of Year.	Balance Transferred from Income.
18	19	20	21	22	23	24	25
					$2,349	$9,534	$2,349
	$6,697			$6,697	2,318		
$280,300			$4,809	285,395	888,089	329,547	888,089
26,470		$300		26,770	17,270	33,262	17,270
87,500	5,394		1,220	94,114	5,343	104,045	5,343
5,000	800			5,800	17,225	111,637	17,225
32,750	3,555			36,305	20,484	248,694	20,484
166,115	5,657	2,027	(e) 17,143	190,942	38,570	178,727	38,570
1,750				1,750	4,644		
	4,318				4,786		
307,876	37,858		2,445	348,179	43,329		43,329
2,530,431	32,512	39,410	45,769	3,083,351	332,652	1,066,988	332,652
257,078	15,394	2,984	11,344	288,912	494,536	456,853	494,536
	1,324			1,324	1,740		
7,500	256			7,756	18,483		
709,227	15,109	10,754	9,607	744,698	712,426	772,856	712,426
9,250	5,444	8	490	15,192	13,907		
	3,900			3,900	3,964		

TABLE No. 2

	PROFIT AND LOSS—Continued.			
	CREDITS—Continued.		DEBITS.	
TITLE OF CORPORATION.	Miscellaneous Credits.	Total Credits.	Debit Balance at Beginning of Year.	Bala from Income.
	27	28	29	30
Baltimore & Bel Air Electric Railway Co....	....	$11,883	....	
Baltimore, Halethorpe & Elkridge Railway Co......	....	....	$24,951	$2,3
(a) Baltimore, Sparrow's Point & Chesapeake Railway Co....	....	....	37	
(b) Blue Ridge Railway Co..................	....	....	....	
Capital Traction Co. of Washington...........	$48	1,217,684	....	
Chambersburg, Greencastle & Waynesboro Street Ry. Co.	12,500	63,032	....	
City & Suburban Railway Co. of Washington..........	....	109,388	....	
Cumberland Electric Railway Co.....	....	128,862	....	
Cumberland & Westernport Electric Railway Co..........	....	269,178	....	
Hagerstown & Frederick Railway Co..................	41	217,256	....	
Kensington Railway Co...................	....	....	12,775	4,
Loraine Electric Railway Co...................	....	....	37,453	4,
Maryland Electric Railways Co..................	....	43,329	670,668	......
United Railways & Electric Co..................	15,325	1,426,465	....	
Washington, Baltimore & Annapolis Electric Railroad Co.	1,137	952,526	....	
Washington & Great Falls Railway & Power Co..........	....	....	299,513	1,
Washington Interurban Railway Co..........	....	....	16,912	18,
Washington Railways & Electric Co................	985	1,497,393	....	
Washington & Rockville Railway Co..................	....	....	15,123	13,
Washington & Maryland Railway Co..................	....	....	52,534	3,

NOTE—Deficit, loss and other reverse items on this table are printed in bold type.

' ued.

PROFIT AND LOSS—Continued.

DEBITS—Continued.

ds	Dividend Appropriations From Surplus.	Surplus Invested in Physical Property.	Debt Discount Extinguished Through Surplus.	Miscellaneous Appropriations of Surplus.	Delayed Income Debits.	Miscellaneous Debits.	Total Debits.	Credit Balance Carried to Balance Sheet.	Debit Balance Carried to Balance Sheet.
	32	33	34	35	36	37	38	39	40
...	$2,775					$2,816	$5,691	$6,292	
...							27,269		$27,269
...									37
...	720,000					191	720,191	497,493	
...	15,000				$2,500	2,000	19,500	43,532	
...								109,388	
75	16,000						16,000	112,862	
...							16,175	253,003	
...	12,637						12,637	204,619	
...							17,420		17,420
...							42,239		42,239
...			$2,902			2,578	676,148		632,819
...	819,368			$17,000		227,727	1,064,095	362,370	
...	582,345	$77,400				864	660,609	291,917	
...							301,253		301,253
...							85,395		85,395
...	750,000					3,915	754,274	743,118	
...							29,030		29,030
...						1,543	58,031		58,031

SHOWING FOR EACH OF THE ELECTRIC RAILROAD CORPORATIONS NAMED THEREI

	TITLE OF CORPORATION.	TOT Revenue for Year Ended Dec. 31, 1918. 1	I
1	Baltimore & Bel Air Electric Railway Co.	$19,935	
2	Baltimore, Halethorpe & Elkridge Railway Co.	15,762	
3 (a)	Baltimore, Sparrow's Point & Chesapeake Railway Co.		
4 (a)	Blue Ridge Railway Co.		
5	Capital Traction Co. of Washington	3,529,854	
6	Chambersburg, Greencastle & Waynesboro Street Railway Co.	127,221	
7	City & Suburban Railway Co. of Washington	707,068	
8	Cumberland Electric Railway Co.	143,209	
9	Cumberland & Westernport Electric Railway Co.	197,605	
10	Hagerstown & Frederick Railway Co.	369,066	
11	Kensington Railway Co.	8,337	
12 (a)	Loraine Electric Railway Co.	2,173	
13	Maryland Electric Railways Co.	476,800	
14	United Railways & Electric Co.	11,929,701	
15	Washington, Baltimore & Annapolis Electric Railroad Co.	2,902,014	
16 (b)	Washington & Glen Echo Railroad Co.		
17	Washington Interurban Railway Co.	21,504	
18	Washington Railway & Electric Co.	3,217,451	
19	Washington & Rockville Railway Co.	84,691	
20	Washington & Maryland Railway Co.	2,591	

	TITLE OF CORPORATION.	REVENUE FROM TATION Miscellaneous Transportation Revenue. 11	
1	Baltimore & Bel Air Railway Co.		
2	Baltimore, Halethorpe & Elkridge Railway Co.	$96	
3 (a)	Baltimore, Sparrow's Point and Chesapeake Railway Co.		
4 (a)	Blue Ridge Railway Co.		
5	Capital Traction Co. of Washington		
6	Chambersburg, Greencastle & Waynesboro Street Railway Co.		
7	City & Suburban Railway Co. of Washington		
8	Cumberland Electric Railway Co.		
9	Cumberland & Westernport Electric Railway Co.		
10	Hagerstown & Frederick Railway Co.		
11	Kensington Railway Co.		
12 (a)	Loraine Electric Railway Co.		
13	Maryland Electric Railways Co.	1,190	
14	United Railways & Electric Co.	10,938	
15	Washington, Baltimore & Annapolis Electric Railroad Co.	5	
16 (b)	Washington & Glen Echo Railroad Co.		
17	Washington Interurban Railway Co.		
18	Washington Railway & Electric Co.		
19	Washington & Rockville Railway Co.		
20	Washington & Maryland Railway Co.		

(a) Road operated by another company.

(b) Inactive corporation.

NOTE—Deficit, loss and other reverse items on this table are printed in bold type.

No. 22.

OPERATING REVENUES FOR THE YEAR ENDED DECEMBER 31, 1918, AND THE DISTRIBUTION THEREOF.

REVENUE FROM TRANSPORTATION.

Passenger Revenue.	Baggage Revenue.	Special Car Revenue.	Mail Revenue.	Express Revenue.	Milk Revenue.	Freight Revenue.
3	4	5	6	7	8	9
$19,760			$175			
15,666						
3,490,699			507			
120,068	$4,877	$40	735		$1,086	$117
698,919		120	59			
139,799						2,908
180,736	1,817		250			14,801
265,211	683	1,148	2,053	$5,269	7,064	73,611
8,267						20
2,173						
377,871	420	15	3,840	11,538		59,704
11,623,258		6,176	31,856			
2,665,519	1,711	611	838	28,350	2,603	148,535
21,504						
2,637,975		218	625			4,035
81,689		37	55	1,301		
2,591						

REVENUE FROM OTHER RAILWAY OPERATIONS.

Station and Car Privileges.	Parcel Room Receipts.	Demurrage.	Rent of Tracks and Facilities.	Rent of Equipment.	Rent of Buildings and Property.	Sale of Power.	Miscellaneous.
13	14	15	16	17	18	19	20
$11,895				$657	$420	$25,676	
297							
3,000				4,021	949		
300							
769					425	7,847	$42
829	$52	$3,577			894		8
50							
414	27	6,520		67	345	3,238	216
52,236	267			725	2,525	200,253	1,466
4,687	5,324	2,634	$19,576		8,021	2,784	10,093
11,100			5,468	29,752	40,386	466,719	
445				1,164			

SHOWING FOR EACH OF THE ELECTRIC RAILROAD CORPORATIONS NAMED THE

	TITLE OF CORPORATION.	TOTALS.		DISTRIBUTION EXPE
		Operating Expenses, Year Ended December 31, 1918.	Increase Over Preceding Year.	Maintenance of Way and Structures.
		1	2	3
1	Baltimore & Bel Air Electric Railway Co......	$17,415	$3,274	$2,241
2	Baltimore, Halethorpe & Elkridge Railway Co.	10,987	6,432	950
3 (a)	Baltimore, Sparrow's Point & Chesapeake Ry. Co.	....	....	....
4 (a)	Blue Ridge Railway Co...........	....	....	....
5	Capital Traction Co. of Washington.........	2,083,060	549,730	222,176
6	Chambersburg, Greencastle & Waynesboro Street Railway Co...........	80,831	....	10,744
7	City & Suburban Railway Co. of Washington...	573,409	125,789	63,711
8	Cumberland Electric Railway Co...........	115,059	15,609	16,088
9	Cumberland & Westernport Electric Ry. Co.....	142,113	31,911	23,707
10	Hagerstown & Frederick Railway Co...........	275,649	52,898	41,477
11	Kensington Railway Co...........	10,926	1,453	3,153
12 (a)	Loraine Electric Railway Co...........	2,641	380	....
13	Maryland Electric Railways Co...........	331,944	132,177	51,159
14	United Railways & Electric Co...........	7,436,307	(c) 1,640,870	1,148,240
15	Washington, Baltimore & Annapolis El. R. R. Co.	1,740,281	1,001,685	458,132
16 (b)	Washington & Glen Echo Railroad Co...........	170	....	5
17	Washington Interurban Railway Co	31,144	6,963	3,979
18	Washington Railway & Electric Co...........	2,291,822	636,319	239,763
19	Washington & Rockville Railroad Co...........	90,966	14,021	12,622
20	Washington & Maryland Railway Co...........	2,645	....	25

	TITLE OF CORPORATION.	Maintenance of Buildings, Fixtures and Grounds.	Depreciation of Way and Structures.	Equalisation, Way and Structures.
		12	13	14
1	Baltimore & Bel Air Electric Railway Co......		....	....
2	Baltimore. Halethorpe & Elkridge Railway Co...	$53	....	....
3 (a)	Baltimore, Sparrow's Point & Chesapeake Ry. Co.		....	....
4 (a)	Blue Ridge Railway Co.		....	....
5	Capital Traction Co. of Washington...........	7,209	$120,991	....
6	Chambersburg, Greencastle & Waynesboro Street Railway Co...........	437	....	....
7	City & Suburban Railway Co. of Washington...	1,274	2,124	....
8	Cumberland Electric Railway Co...........	1,260	7,416	....
9	Cumberland & Westernport Electric Ry. Co.....	482	....	....
10	Hagerstown & Frederick Railway Co...........	1,976	....	....
11	Kensington Railway Co...........		1,130	....
12 (a)	Loraine Electric Railway Co...........		....	....
13	Maryland Electric Railways Co...........	2,630	....	$10,732
14	United Railways & Electric Co...........	33,933	596,485	....
15	Washington, Baltimore & Annapolis El. R. R. Co.	16,039	261,024	....
16 (b)	Washington & Glen Echo Railroad Co...........		....	....
17	Washington Interurban Railway Co	21	1,126	....
18	Washington Railway & Electric Co...........	4,720	20,971	....
19	Washington & Rockville Railway Co...........	222	....	....
20	Washington & Maryland Railway Co...........		....	....

(a) Road operated by another company.

(b) Inactive corporation.

(c) Includes depreciation on ways and structures and equipment. $536,485.

NOTE—Deficit, loss and other reverse items on this table are printed in bold type.

No. 23.

OPERATING EXPENSES FOR THE YEAR ENDED DECEMBER 31, 1918, AND THE DISTRIBUTION THEREOF.

DISTRIBUTION OF OPERATING EXPENSES—Continued.

I

WAY AND STRUCTUI

Production of Power.	Conducting Transportation.	Traffic Expenses.	General Expenses.	Superintendence.	Maintenance of Way.	Mainte of Ele Lin
5	6	7	8	9	10	11
$2,180	$7,339	....	$5,655	....	$1,333	
3,041	6,454	....	542	....	682	
381,357	967,399	$954	296,691	$5,284	80,373	
21,598	18,553	1,509	15,458	855	7,057	
83,389	257,931	745	86,429	4,989	50,814	
18,326	43,688	492	20,705	425	5,848	
45,029	39,599	1,580	14,646	3,404	16,229	
77,165	87,536	5,203	33,148	2,719	30,521	
1,004	3,800	....	2,139	500	1,292	
925	1,402					
61,795	85,122	4,687	87,469	4,146	31,474	
1,073,045	3,518,311	16,561	963,913	43,724	398,217	7
201,104	486,502	17,643	261,562	17,983	117,857	4
			8			
5,698	12,765	4	7,332	137	3,997	
486,200	968,813	1,244	272,863	17,886	162,200	
16,272	33,162	307	14,441	810	8,282	
425	1,030	....	1,060	....		

DETAILS OF OPERATING EXPENSES—Continued.

EQUIPMENT—Continued.

Maintenance of Cars.	Maintenance of Electrical Equipment.	Maintenance of Locomotives.	Miscellaneous Equipment Expenses.	Depreciation of Equipment.	Equipment Retired.	Equaliss Equipm
16	17	18	19	20	21	22
$78,316	$43,077		$13,751	$73,397		
4,193	2,415	....	222	4,800		
35,340	25,056	....	7,049	10,314		
7,256	1,527	....	319	3,147	$2,536	
605	14,330	$2,616	....			
13,393	3,055	1,814	1,161	11,050	5	
164	306	....		360		
315						
14,286	6,919	3,156	1,505	7,143		$1
355,798	260,556	....	82,539			
90,417	79,841	....	10,868	125,755		
				162		
477	419	....	852	21		
116,958	97,787	758	24,976	73,526		
5,787	5,122	....	1,057	1,185		
50	55	....				

TABL

	TITLE OF CORPORATION.	DETAILS OF OPE		
		POWER.		
		Superintendence.	Power Plant Buildings and Grounds.	Maintenance of Power Equipment.
		23	24	25
1	Baltimore & Bel Air Electric Railway Co......			
2	Baltimore, Halethorpe & Elkridge Railway Co...			
3 (a)	Baltimore, Sparrow's Point & Chesapeake Ry. Co.			
4 (a)	Blue Ridge Railway Co.			
5	Capital Traction Co. of Washington.	$3,342	$1,361	$22,113
6	Chambersburg, Greencastle & Waynesboro Street Railway Co.......		31	749
7	City & Suburban Railway Co. of Washington...	979	131	901
8	Cumberland Electric Railway Co...			
9	Cumberland & Westernport Electric Ry. Co....	484		2,463
10	Hagerstown & Frederick Railway Co..........	3,742	412	10,245
11	Kensington Railway Co...			
12 (a)	Loraine Electric Railway Co.			
13	Maryland Electric Railways Co...			2,955
14	United Railways & Electric Co....	14,500	4,705	21,585
15	Washington, Baltimore & Annapolis El. R. R. Co.	1,008	54	10,460
16 (b)	Washington & Glen Echo Railroad Co....			
17	Washington Interurban Railway Co...			
18	Washington Railway & Electric Co...	2,957	520	3,094
19	Washington & Rockville Railway Co..........	971	110	321
20	Washington & Maryland Railway Co.			

	TITLE OF CORPORATION.	DETAILS OF OPE		
		CONDUCTING TRANSPORTATION—Cont.	TRAFFIC.	G M
		Miscellaneous Transportation Expenses.	Traffic Expenses.	General Expenses.
		34	35	36
1	Baltimore & Bel Air Electric Railway Co.....			$2,964
2	Baltimore, Halethorpe & Elkridge Railway Co...	$82		
3 (a)	Baltimore, Sparrow's Point & Chesapeake Ry. Co.			
4 (a)	Blue Ridge Railway Co...			
5	Capital Traction Co. of Washington.	108,814	$954	104,416
6	Chambersburg, Greencastle & Waynesboro Street Railway Co.......	2,506	1,509	11,662
7	City & Suburban Railway Co. of Washington...	42,910	745	22,519
8	Cumberland Electric Railway Co....	2,358	492	16,867
9	Cumberland & Westernport Electric Ry. Co....	5,142	1,580	8,684
10	Hagerstown & Frederick Railway Co....	6,247	5,203	15,517
11	Kensington Railway Co...			760
12 (a)	Loraine Electric Railway Co...			
13	Maryland Electric Railways Co....	41,896	4,687	26,985
14	United Railways & Electric Co....	425,866	16,561	386,198
15	Washington, Baltimore & Annapolis El. R. R. Co.	225,458	17,643	109,997
16 (b)	Washington & Glen Echo Railroad Co....			3
17	Washington Interurban Railway Co...	519	4	805
18	Washington Railway & Electric Co....	168,154	1,244	95,705
19	Washington & Rockville Railway Co....	6,761	307	3,916
20	Washington & Maryland Railway Co....	270		625

(a) Road operated by another company.

(b) Inactive corporation.

NOTE—Deficit, loss and other reverse items on this table are printed in bold type.

ed.

DETAILS OF OPERATING EXPENSES—Continued.

	Power—Continued.				Conducting Transportation.	
	Fuel for Power.	Other Power Supplies and Expenses.	Power Purchased.	Other Operations. Cr.	Superin-tendence.	Conductors, Motormen and Trainmen.
	28	29	30	31	32	33
	....	....	$2,180	....	....	$7,339
	....	....	3,041	....	....	6,372
	....	....	....	....	....	....
2	$258,642	$12,340	5,194	....	$97,619	760,966
	....	1,557	19,260	....	149	15,897
	....	7,540	73,122	....	23,417	191,604
	....	....	18,326	....	972	40,358
5	26,529	2,607	....	....	2,102	32,355
1	133,951	13,535	1,841	$115,472	*7,902	63,387
	....	....	1,003	....	500	3,300
	....	....	925	....	....	1,401
	....	4,062	54,777	....	6,734	36,493
	365,878	71,792	446,982	....	266,882	2,825,563
	....	20,360	192,448	74,304	23,306	237,738
	....	....	5,698	....	339	11,906
	376,881	30,055	22,002	....	91,795	708,864
	....	2,814	12,056	....	3,580	22,821
	....	....	425	....	....	760

DETAILS OF OPERATING EXPENSES—Continued.

	General and Miscellaneous—Continued.					Ratio of Operating Expenses to Operating Revenue. Per Cent.
	Insurance.	Stationery and Printing.	Store, Garage and Stable Expenses.	Rent of Tracks and Facilities.	Rent of Equipment.	
	39	40	41	42	43	44
1	$142	....	....	....	$1,928	87.36
	....	....	....	....	434	69.71
	....	....	....	....	....	....
	9,178	$24,157	$8,486	$3,360	....	59.01
	780	1,147	4	....	50	63.54
	777	5,507	4,798	....	18,967	81.10
	1,094	269	96	....	....	80.34
	2,098	648	816	....	....	71.92
	2,050	3,945	1,750	....	8,026	74.96
	....	30	....	1,350	....	131.06
	....	....	....	....	....	121.55
	531	3,856	752	37,730	6,787	70.24
	56,210	71,496	61,005	....	....	62.33
	2,275	12,620	2,126	82,528	9,119	59.96
	5	....	....	....	....	100.00
	6	318	227	....	4,884	144.84
	6,557	23,937	18,021	....	....	71.23
	108	1,035	724	110	2,033	107.41
	....	25	....	....	410	102.08

SHOWING FOR EACH OF THE ELECTRIC RAILROAD CORPORATIONS NAMED

TITLE OF CORPORATION.	ROAD OWNED—MILES.		
	Miles of Road.	Second Track.	All Other Main Track.
	1	2	3
1 Baltimore & Bel Air Electric Railway Co.	3.22		
2 (a) Baltimore, Halethorpe & Elkridge Railway Co.	2.84		
3 (a) Baltimore, Sparrow's Point & Chesapeake Ry. Co.	17.63	14.81	
4 (a) Blue Ridge Railway Co.	1.60		
5 Capital Traction Co. of Washington.	30.65	26.67	
6 Chambersburg, Greencastle & Waynesboro St. Ry. Co.	30.59		
7 City & Suburban Railway Co. of Washington.	26.26	15.18	
8 Cumberland Electric Railway Co.	7.87		
9 Cumberland & Westernport Electric Railway Co.	25.00		
10 Hagerstown & Frederick Railway Co.	87.00		
11 Kensington Railway Co.	2.50		
12 (a) Loraine Electric Railway Co.	1.12		
13 Maryland Electric Railways Co.	24.90		
14 United Railways & Electric Co.	180.18	177.81	
15 Washington, Baltimore & Annapolis Electric R. R. Co.	54.95	37.27	
16 (b) Washington & Glen Echo Railroad Co.	7.54		
17 Washington Interurban Railway Co.	8.03		
18 Washington Railway & Electric Co.	53.62	44.03	
19 Washington & Rockville Railway Co.	13.25	0.50	
20 Washington & Maryland Railway Co.	3.57		

EQUIPMENT, OWNED OR LE

PASSENGER CARS.

TITLE OF CORPORATION.	Closed Passenger Cars.	Closed Passenger Cars with Electrical Equipment.	Open Passenger Cars.	Open Passenger Cars with Electrical Equipment
	14	15	16	17
1 Baltimore & Bel Air Electric Railway Co.		2		
2 (a) Baltimore, Halethorpe & Elkridge Railway Co.				
3 (a) Baltimore, Sparrow's Point & Chesapeake Ry. Co.	110			110
4 (a) Blue Ridge Railway Co.				
5 Capital Traction Co. of Washington.	91	317	119	100
6 Chambersburg, Greencastle & Waynesboro Street Railway Co.		5		5
7 City & Suburban Railway Co. of Washington.		40		
8 Cumberland Electric Railway Co.		14		3
9 Cumberland & Westernport Electric Ry. Co.		16		
10 Hagerstown & Frederick Railway Co.		24		16
11 Kensington Railway Co.		3		
12 (a) Loraine Electric Railway Co.				
13 Maryland Electric Railways Co.	2	12		
14 United Railways & Electric Co.	149	209		407
15 Washington, Baltimore & Annapolis Elec. R. R. Co.	56	59		
16 (b) Washington & Glen Echo Railroad Co.				
17 Washington Interurban Railway Co.		1		
18 Washington Railway & Electric Co.	31	364	143	50
19 Washington & Rockville Railway Co.		5		
20 Washington & Maryland Railway Co.				

(a)   Road operated by another company.
(b)   Inactive.

No. 24.

EQUIPMENT IN SERVICE AND THE NUMBER OF MILES OF ROAD OPERATED ON DECEMBER 31, 1918.

ROAD OWNED—MILES —Continued.		ROAD OPERATED—MILES—SINGLE TRACK.					
Track in Car Houses, Shops, Etc.	Total Road Owned.	Main Line.	Branches and Spurs.	Lines of Proprietary Companies.	Lines Operated Under Lease.	Lines Operated Under Contract, Etc.	Lines Operated Under Trackage Rights.
5	6	7	8	9	10	11	12
....	3.28	3.22	....	....	....	....	....
....	3.05	2.84	0.21	....	....	....	....
....	34.27	....	....	....	....	....	....
....	1.60	....	....	....	....	....	....
6.14	65.15	64.09	....	....	....	3.37	2.11
0.05	31.73	29.40	....	....	....	....	....
0.68	43.00	39.62	1.78	....	....	....	1.60
0.27	8.64	8.64	....	....	....	....	....
....	25.50	25.00	0.50	....	....	....	....
2.50	91.50	82.30	4.50	....	4.70	....	....
....	2.60	2.50	0.10	....	1.00	....	....
....	1.12	....	....	....	....	....	....
....	37.40	23.60	1.30	....	....	....	1.70
14.71	378.82	357.98	20.83	....	54.71	....	0.82
0.17	101.97	54.95	11.04	....	....	6.97	....
....	7.54	....	....	....	....	....	....
....	8.26	8.26	....	....	....	....	....
5.02	106.53	102.33	0.92	....	....	....	3.28
14.43	14.44	....	....	....	....	....	....
3.57	....	....	....	....	....	....	....

EQUIPMENT, OWNED OR LEASED—Continued.

PASSENGER CARS —Continued.		OTHER CARS.							
Combination Passenger Cars with Electrical Equipment.	Total Passenger Cars.	Freight.	Mail and Express.	Work.	Snow Plows.	Sweepers.	Miscellaneous.	Total All Classes of Cars.	Locomotives, Electric.
19	20	21	22	23	24	25	26	27	28
....	2	....	....	....	....	....	....	2	....
....	220	....	....	....	....	....	....	220	..
....	627	....	....	27	....	9	14	677	....
....	10	1	....	7	....	....	3	21	....
....	40	....	....	1	1	2	10	54	....
....	17	....	....	1	2	....	....	20	....
....	16	2	....	1	....	1	1	21	....
....	40	62	4	3	1	....	....	110	4
....	3	....	....	1	....	....	....	4	....
....	14	47	....	....	....	....	....	61	1
1,021	1,786	....	12	45	10	38	22	1,913	....
....	115	19	....	20	....	....	4	158	....
....	1	....	....	....	....	....	1	2	....
....	588	....	1	6	2	18	15	630	2
....	5	....	....	....	....	....	....	5	....
....	....	....	....	....	....	....	....	....	....

TAB

SHOWING FOR EACH OF THE ELECTRIC RAILROAD CORPORATIONS NAMED THEREIN MILEAGE, TRAFFIC
REQ

TITLE OF CORPORATION.	Passenger Car Mileage.	Freight, Mail and Express Car Mileage.	Total Car Mileage.	Passenger Car Hours.
	1	2	3	4
1 Baltimore & Bel Air Electric Railway Co.	126,416		126,416	9,
2 Baltimore, Halethorpe & Elkridge Railway Co.	101,378		101,378	8,
3 Capital Traction Co. of Washington	8,362,128		8,362,128	971,
4 Chambersburg, Greencastle & Waynesboro Street Ry. Co.	360,800	520	361,320	28,
5 City & Suburban Railway Co. of Washington	2,437,535		2,437,535	266,
6 Cumberland Electric Railway Co.	408,800		408,800	52,
7 Cumberland & Westernport Electric Railway Co.	435,216	33,600	468,816	41,
8 Hagerstown & Frederick Railway Co.	1,082,868	166,285	1,249,153	98,
9 Kensington Railway Co.	54,750		54,750	6,
0 Maryland Electric Railways Co.	802,740	59,168	861,908	30,
1 United Railways & Electric Co.	32,569,906	199,569	32,769,475	3,926,
2 Washington, Baltimore & Annapolis Electric R. R. Co.	4,695,364	221,526	4,916,890	*
3 Washington Interurban Railway Co.	162,805		162,805	15,
4 Washington Railway & Electric Co.	8,350,839	16,741	8,367,580	1,006,
5 Washington & Rockville Railway Co.	395,483	10,200	405,683	81,

TITLE OF CORPORATION.	Average Fare, Revenue Passengers.	Average Fare, All Passengers.	Total Revenue from Transportation.	Revenue from Transportation, per Car Mile.	per Ho
	14	15	16	17	1
	Cents.	Cents.	Dollars.	Cents.	Dol
1 Baltimore & Bel Air Electric Railway Co.	4.905	4.905	19,935	15.631	2.
Baltimore, Halethorpe & Elkridge Railway Co.	4.792	4.782	15,762	15.548	1.
Capital Traction Co. of Washington	4.408	3.472	3,491,206	41.750	3.
Chambersburg, Greencastle & Waynesboro St. Ry. Co.	5.300	5.400	126,924	35.128	4.
City & Suburban Railway Co. of Washington	4.312	3.506	699,098	28.680	2.
Cumberland Electric Railway Co.	4.868	*	142,909	34.958	2.
Cumberland & Westernport Electric Railway Co.	5.018	5.018	197,605	45.420	4.
Hagerstown & Frederick Railway Co.	7.300	7.300	363,706	29.000	3.
Kensington Railway Co.	4.423	4.423	8,287	15.136	1.
Maryland Electric Railways Co.	27.575	27.575	465,974	54.063	13.
United Railways & Electric Co.	5.124	3.765	11,672,228	35.619	2.
Washington, Baltimore & Annapolis Electric R. R. Co.	4.482	4.482	2,848,896	57.730	*
Washington Interurban Railway Co.	4.400	3.175	21,504	13.208	1.
Washington Railway & Electric Co.	4.408	3.395	2,664,026	31.837	2.
5 Washington & Rockville Railway Co.	3.823	3.823	83,082	20.479	2.

o. 25.

ISCELLANEOUS STATISTICS FOR THE YEAR ENDED DECEMBER 31, 1918. THE ASTERISK (*) DENOTES ABSENCE OF IURES.

eight, il and xpress Hours.	Total Car Hours.	Regular Fare Passengers Carried.	Revenue Transfer Passengers Carried.	Total Revenue Passengers Carried.	Free Transfer Passengers Carried.	Total Passengers Carried.	Employes and Others Carried Free.	
5	6	7	8	9	10	11	12	13
....	9,815	402,861	....	402,861	....	402,861	1,152	19,7
....	8,824	326,942		326,942	.661	327,603	7,235	15,
....	971,451	78,314,377	871,630	79,186,007	21,329,003	100,515,010	....	3,490,
100	28,320	2,265,433	1,311	2,266,744		2,266,744	21,850	120,
....	266,044	16,104,076	103,025	16,207,101	3,730,317	19,937,418	91,181	698,
....	52,560	2,871,302		2,871,302	*	2,871,302	22,691	139,
5,431	46,917	3,601,940		3,601,940		3,601,940	11,716	180,
*	98,038	3,629,461		3,629,461	*	3,629,461	48,890	265,
	6,710	184,628		184,628		184,628	*	8,
5,425	35,595	1,370,322		1,370,322		1,370,322	70,537	377,
32,364	3,958,932	225,269,335	1,565,193	226,834,528	81,879,968	308,714,496	3,174,014	11,623,
*		5,946,697		5,946,697		5,946,697	286,988	2,665,
	15,834	488,706		488,706	188,574	677,280	2,794	21,
1,287	1,007,902	59,634,760	206,704	59,841,464	17,855,962	77,697,426	368,275	2,637,
1,273	32,468	2,130,990		2,130,990		2,130,990	22,832	81,

ie er y ns.	Revenue from Other Railway Operations, per Car Mile.	Revenue from Other Railway Operations, per Car Hour.	Total Operating Revenues.	Operating Revenues, per Car Mile.	Operating Revenues, per Car Hour.	Total Operating Expenses.	Operating Expenses, per Car Mile.	Operati Expens per Ca Hour.
20	21	22	23	24	25	26	27	
Dollars.	Cents.	Cents.	Dollars.	Cents.	Dollars.	Dollars.	Cents.	Do
....	....	....	19,935	4.948	2.03	17,415	4.323	1.
			15,762	15.548	1.78	10,987	10.838	1.
38,649	0.462	3.980	3,529,854	42.210	3.63	2,083,060	24.910	2.
297	0.321	0.150	127,221	35.211	4.492	80,831	22.370	2.
7,970	0.327	2.996	707,068	29.007	2.66	573,409	23.524	2.
300	0.073	0.570	143,209	35.031	2.72	115,059	28.146	2.
9,083	2.703	1.672	206,689	44.008	4.405	142,123	30.318	3.
5,361	0.400	0.054	369,067	30.000	3.760	276,649	22.000	2.
50	0.091	0.745	8,337	15.227	1.242	10,927	19.957	1.
10,826	1.256	30.416	476,800	55.319	13.395	334,944	38.860	9.
257,472	0.786	6.503	11,929,701	36.405	3.013	7,436,307	22.693	1.
53,118	1.080	*	2,902,015	58.801	*	1,740,282	25.373	*
....	....	....	21,504	13.208	1.358	31,145	19.130	1.
553,425	6.614	54.908	3,217,451	38.451	3.192	2,291,822	27.389	2.
1,609	0.397	4.956	84,691	20.876	2.608	90,967	22.423	2.

TOTALS.

Title of Corporation.	Assets.		Liabilities.		Surplus or Deficit.		Gross Income.		Deductions from Gross Income.		Net Income.	
	Total Amount Dec. 31, 1918.	Increase Over Preceding Year.	Total Amount Dec 31, 1918.	Increase Over Preceding Year.	Total Amount Dec. 31, 1918.	Increase Over Preceding Year.	Total Amount Dec. 31, 1918.	Increase Over Preceding Year.	Total Amount Dec. 31, 1918.	Increase Over Preceding Year.	Total Amount Dec. 31, 1918.	Increase Over Preceding Year.
	1	2	3	4	5	6	7	8	9	10	11	12
(a) Antietam Electric Light Co.	$52,480	$11,592	$44,049	$9,624	$8,431	$1,968	$10,159	$2,066	$7,398	$549	$2,761	$1,517
(a) Baltimore County Electric Co.	371,000	40,188	371,000	40,188	6,719							
(a) Baltimore Elec. Co. of Baltimore City	7,753,278		7,746,559		15,225	1,684	13,598	508	12,845	988	758	1,496
Bel Air Electric Co.	115,436	2,435	100,211	751	722	1,595	12,800	1,826	14,395	1,003		733
Chestertown Electric L. & P. Co.	47,203	605	47,925	2,200	1,067	276	8,739	226	8,590	1,501	149	1,235
Delmarvia Utilities Co.	90,800	208	91,957	68	21,907	676	2,643	961	961	1,200	676	248
Delta Electric Power Co.	61,766	999	83,573	1,675	901	4,127	29,399	8,537	25,786	1,194	3,613	4,731
Easton Utilities Commission	59,635	1,312	58,734	2,815	48,667	5,960	294,214	58,423	268,303	72,200	25,911	13,777
Edison Elec. Illuminating Co.	1,024,072	21,550	975,405	27,500	3,249	185	4,616	213	3,600	232	1,016	445
Emmitsburg Electric Co.	13,400	650	10,151	835	325	65	17,335	1,120	14,810	24	2,525	1,096
Harper's Ferry Electric L. & P. Co.	58,895	17,129	58,570	17,194	2,309	840	38,554	14,027	39,394	14,700	840	673
Havre de Grace Electric Co.	113,063	9,712	111,356	10,552	9,152	3,873	17,364	3,120	12,291	2,759	5,073	361
Home Electric Light Co.	61,626	742	52,474	3,131	4,486	1,684	19,221	5,741	12,758	2,313	6,463	3,428
Home Manufacturing L. & P. Co.	61,650	907	66,136	777	2,425	1,979	27,772	3,594	21,489	1,570	2,283	2,024
Idlewild Electric L., H. & P. Co.	59,187	5,810	56,762	3,831	6,019	101	5,518	197	4,417	74	1,101	271
Midland Electric Light Co.	11,019	101	5,000		116	473	7,809	4,011	6,574	2,459	1,235	1,552
Mt. Airy Ice & Electric Co.	16,368	221	16,252	252								
(a) Mt. Washington Elec. L. & P. Co.	236,251	2,743	88,700	2,743	199,551	10,510	111,013	3,662	92,402	2,299	18,611	5,051
Municipal Elec. L. P. of Hagerstown	299,549	17,996	110,415	7,486	179,133	90,636	265,290	960	219,003	36,062	46,287	37,022
Northern Virginia Power Co.	689,047	91,205	1,752,504	181,931	63,457							
(a) Patapsco Elec. & Man. Co. of Del	225,000		225,000									
(a) Patapsco Elec. & Man. Co. of Md.	200,000		200,000									
Peninsular Light & Power Co.	121,682	2,655	91,256	5,001	30,426	2,346	24,796	1,374	22,321	2,212	1,475	636
Perryville Electric Co.	20,914	727	22,874	16	1,960	711	4,115	1,162	3,404	843	711	319
Port Deposit Electric Co.	17,517	406	8,145	20	9,402	387	4,832	613	4,445	1,949	387	2,562
(a) Potomac Electric Power Co.	20,237,995	3,388,015	20,116,147	3,459,235	171,848	91,220	3,071,814	432,227	2,145,458	562,819	926,356	130,592
Roland Park Electric & Water Co.	336,845	32,287	336,067	46,159	353		67,724	9,790	72,135	23,653	4,411	13,863
Salisbury Light, Heat & Power Co.	269,845	439	258,020	485	11,825	46	6,316	217	6,362	252	46	34
Snow Hill Elec. L. & P. Co.	16,984	409	15,050	464	1,934	873	7,114	5,757	7,887	6,293	773	536
St. Michaels Utilities Commission	21,616	66,720	22,726	93,320	1,110	26,600	61,629	14,932	61,629	14,932		
Susquehanna Trans. Co. of Md.	1,723,866		1,914,766		190,900							
Union Bridge Electric Man. Co.	35,007		35,242		235		7,713		7,948		235	
Waynesboro Electric Co.	214,726	41,642	196,392	52,497	18,334	10,858						

(a) Operated by Consolidated Gas Electric Light & Power Co. of Baltimore.
* Denotes required figures not given.
Note—Deficit, loss and other reverse items on this table are printed in bold type.

TITLE OF CORPORATION.	Total Amount Dec. 31, 1918.	Increase Over Preceding Year.	Total Amount Dec. 31, 1918.
	1	2	3
1 Antietam Electric Light & Power Co.	$52,480	$11,592	$44,049
2(a) Baltimore County Electric Co.	371,000		371,000
3(a) Baltimore Elec. Co. of Baltimore City	7,753,278	40,188	7,746,559
4 Bel Air Electric Co.	115,436	2,435	100,211
5 Chestertown Electric Light & Power Co.	47,203	605	47,925
6 Delmarvia Utilities Co.	90,890	208	91,957
7 Delta Electric Power Co.	61,766	999	83,573
8 Easton Utilities Commission.	59,635	1,312	58,734
9 Edison Electric Illuminating Co.	1,024,072	21,550	975,405
10 Emmitsburg Electric Co.	13,400	650	10,151
11 Harper's Ferry Electric Light & Power Co.	58,895	17,129	58,570
12 Havre de Grace Electric Co.	113,665	9,712	111,356
13 Home Electric Co.	61,626	742	52,474
14 Home Manufacturing Light & Power Co.	61,650	907	66,136
15 Idlewild Electric Light, Heat & Power Co.	59,187	5,810	56,762
16 Midland Electric Light Co.	11,019	101	5,000
17 Mt. Airy Ice & Electric Co.	16,368	221	16,252
18(a) Mt. Washington Electric Light & Power Co.	286,251	2,743	86,700
19 Municipal Electric Light Plant of Hagerstown.	289,549	17,996	110,415
20 Northern Virginia Power Co.	1,689,047	91,295	1,752,504
21(a) Patapsco Electric & Manufacturing Co. of Delaware.	225,000		225,000
22(a) Patapsco Electric & Manufacturing Co. of Maryland.	200,000		200,000
23 Peninsular Light & Power Co.	121,682	2,655	91,256
24 Perryville Electric Co.	20,914	727	22,874
25 Port Deposit Electric Co.	17,547	406	8,145
26 Potomac Electric Power Co.	20,287,995	3,368,015	20,116,147
27(a) Roland Park Electric & Water Co.	336,420		336,067
28 Salisbury Light, Heat & Power Co.	269,845	32,287	258,020
29 Snow Hill Electric Light & Power Co.	16,984	↑439	15,050
30 St. Michaels Utilities Commission.	21,616	↑409	22,726
31 Susquehanna Transmission Co. of Maryland.	1,723,866	66,720	1,914,766
32 Union Bridge Electric Manufacturing Co.	35,007	*	35,242
33 Waynesboro Electric Co.	214,726	41,642	196,392

TITLE OF CORPORATION.	DETAILS OF ASSETS—Continued.		DETAILS OF
	Unextinguished Discount on Securities.	Sundries.	Capital Stock.
	14	15	16
1 Antietam Electric Light & Power Co.		$85	$11,500
2(a) Baltimore County Electric Co.	$16,486		150,000
3(a) Baltimore Electric Co. of Baltimore City	8,750		3,500,000
4 Bel Air Electric Co.			50,000
5 Chestertown Electric Light & Power Co.	1,980		15,000
6 Delmarvia Utilities Co.			76,000
7 Delta Electric Co.			29,500
8 Easton Utilities Commission.			
9 Edison Electric Illuminating Co.	40,134	444	275,000
10 Emmitsburg Electric Co.			7,500
11 Harper's Ferry Electric Light & Power Co.			49,900
12 Havre de Grace Electric Co.			50,000
13 Home Electric Light Co.	35		13,825
14 Home Manufacturing Light & Power Co.	5,880	7,822	8,600
15 Idlewild Electric Light, Heat & Power Co.	3,103		17,000
16 Midland Electric Light Co.			5,000
17 Mt. Airy Ice & Electric Co.			11,800
18(a) Mt. Washington Electric Light & Power Co.			83,260
19 Municipal Electric Light Plant of Hagerstown.		172	
20 Northern Virginia Power Co.			600,000
21(a) Patapsco Electric & Manufacturing Co. of Delaware.			225,000
22(a) Patapsco Electric & Manufacturing Co. of Maryland.			200,000
23 Peninsular Light & Power Co.			75,000
24 Perryville Electric Co.		655	20,755
25 Port Deposit Electric Co.			8,125
26 Potomac Electric Power Co.	410,014	57,239	6,000,000
27(a) Roland Park Electric & Water Co.	25,000		25,000
28 Salisbury Light, Heat & Power Co.	171	629	100,000
29 Snow Hill Electric Light & Power Co.			12,000
30 St. Michaels Utilities Commission.			
31 Susquehanna Transmission Co. of Maryland.			500
32 Union Bridge Electric Manufacturing Co.			25,000
33 Waynesboro Electric Co.		1,000	50,000

(a) Operated by Consolidated Gas Electric Light & Power Co. of Baltimore.
Asterick * denotes required figures not given.

No. 27.

AMOUNT OF LIABILITIES AND THE SURPLUS ON DEC. 31, 1918, AND THE CLASSIFICATION OF SUCH ASSETS AND LIA

TOTALS—Cont.		DETAILS OF ASSETS.					
Surplus or Deficit.							
Total Amount Dec. 31, 1918.	Increase Over Preceding Year.	Cost of Plant.	Cash.	Bills and Accounts Receivable.	Materials and Supplies.	Investments.	Sinking Fund and Optional Reserves.
5	6	7	8	9	10	11	12
$8,431	$1,968	$50,610	$121	$238	$1,425	....	....
....	....	303,756	....	50,757	....	....	....
6,719	....	5,959,654	....	279,315	....	$1,155,000	$350,559
15,225	1,684	105,012	505	2,018	436	5,600	1,865
722	1,595	42,600	2,622	....	....	....	....
1,067	276	90,890	....	....	....	....	....
21,807	676	61,374	19	185	225	....	....
901	4,127	45,644	1,040	9,760	3,191	....	....
48,667	5,960	892,389	7,858	60,417	15,109	7,720	....
3,249	185	11,100	520	747	32	....	....
325	65	58,190	325	380	....	....	....
2,309	840	100,995	548	7,484	4,637	....	....
9,152	3,875	53,552	517	5,472	2,050	....	....
4,486	1,684	38,334	4,471	4,470	659	....	....
2,425	1,979	41,684	295	14,032	....	....	....
6,019	101	9,030	264	1,562	162	....	....
116	473	16,000	79	42	247	....	....
199,551	....	265,065	....	21,187	....	....	....
179,133	10,510	260,207	12,166	15,436	1,566	....	....
63,457	90,636	1,619,688	851	36,240	18,467	....	....
....	....	213,180	....	11,820	....	....	....
....	....	179,746	....	20,254	....	....	....
30,426	2,346	102,695	384	8,085	....	10,126	....
1,960	711	19,189	109	960	....	....	....
9,402	387	8,000	955	462	1,704	6,425	....
171,848	91,220	14,628,085	116,251	10,080,010	425,142	1,713,878	1,130,734
353	....	311,420	....	....	....	....	....
11,825	13,872	248,905	2,303	17,024	....	....	....
1,934	46	14,289	460	2,160	75	....	....
1,110	873	19,379	679	682	....	....	....
190,900	26,600	1,723,865	....	....	....	....	....
235	....	33,415	34	927	....	....	....
18,334	10,855	181,662	12,049	10,706	....	9,000	....

DETAILS OF LIABILITIES—Continued.

Taxes Accrued and Unpaid.	Interest Accrued on Funded Debt.	Interest Accrued on Unfunded Debt.	Bills and Accounts Payable.	Dividends Payable.	Consumers' Deposits.	Sinking Fund and Optional Reserves.	Reserves for Amortizations and Depreciation.	S
18	19	20	21	22	23	24	25	
$312	....	....	$9,875	....	....	....	$8,362	...
....	....	....	....	....	....	....	....	...
....	....	....	175,000	....	....	....	350,559	...
273	$375	....	11,321	....	$122	$119	....	...
....	$375	....	10,550	....	....	....	....	...
189	....	$840	4,718	$210	....	....	....	...
....	75	....	30,498	....	....	....	....	...
....	750	....	20,879	....	....	....	7,105	...
....	6,062	....	53,000	....	4,191	11,637	125,514	...
....	....	....	1,650	....	....	....	....	...
....	....	....	8,670	....	....	....	....	...
....	....	....	61,271	....	85	....	....	...
....	1,200	....	14,698	....	....	....	2,400	...
48	434	....	5,841	....	....	....	....	...
593	....	....	5,614	....	4	379	172	...
....	....	....	....	....	....	....	....	...
700	252	....	....	....	....	....	3,440	...
....	....	....	....	....	....	....	65,417	...
....	....	....	135,000	....	....	....	....	...
....	....	....	....	....	....	....	....	...
123	....	....	7,187	....	....	294	8,651	...
....	....	....	2,119	....	....	....	....	...
20	....	....	....	....	....	....	....	...
222,052	7,083	14,884	747,647	....	115,758	1,745,215	1,310,411	...
....	....	....	11,067	....	....	....	....	...
569	194	....	78,673	....	355	6,195	5,598	...
187	....	....	1,489	....	....	....	....	...
....	....	....	22,727	....	....	....	....	...
....	....	....	5,266	....	....	....	....	...
....	....	....	8,907	....	....	1,335	....	...
301	13,200	....	124,467	....	....	893	7,200	...

	TITLE OF CORPORATION.	Gross Income from all Sources.	Deductions from Gross Income.	Net Income.
		1	2	3
1	Antietam Electric Light & Power Co.	$10,159	$7,398	$2,761
2	Bel Air Electric Co.	13,598	12,845	753
3	Chestertown Electric Light & Power Co.	12,800	14,395	1,595
4	Delmarvia Utilities Co.	8,739	8,590	149
5	Delta Electric Power Co.	2,643	3,319	676
6	Easton Utilities Commision.	29,399	25,786	3,613
7	Edison Electric Illuminating Co.	294,214	268,303	25,911
8	Emmitsburg Electric Co.	4,616	3,600	1,016
9	Harper's Ferry Elec. Lt. & Power Co.	17,335	14,810	2,525
10	Havre de Grace Electric Co.	38,554	39,394	840
11	Home Electric Light Co.	17,364	12,291	5,073
12	Home Manufacturing Lt. & Power Co.	19,221	12,758	6,463
13	Idlewild Elec. Light Heat & Power Co.	27,772	21,489	2,283
14	Midland Electric Light Co.	5,518	4,416	1,101
15	Municipal Elec. Lt. Plant of Hagerstown.	111,013	92,402	18,611
16	Mt. Airy Electric & Ice Co.	7,809	6,574	1,235
17	Northern Virginia Power Co.	265,290	219,003	46,287
18	Peninsular Light & Power Co.	24,796	23,321	1,475
19	Perryville Electric Co.	4,115	3,404	711
20	Port Deposit Electric Co.	4,832	4,445	387
21	Potomac Electric Power Co.	3,071,814	2,145,458	926,356
22	Salisbury Light, Heat & Power Co.	67,724	72,135	4,411
23	Snow Hill Electric Light & Power Co.	6,316	6,362	46
24	St. Michaels Utilities Commision.	7,114	7,887	773
25	Susquehanna Transmission Co. of Md.	61,629	61,629	
26	Union Bridge Electric Mfg. Co.	7,713	7,948	235

	TITLE OF CORPORATION.	DEDUCTIONS FROM GROSS INCO		
		OPERATING EXPENSES —Continued.		
		Commercial and New Business.	General.	Taxes.
		11	12	13
1	Antietam Electric Light & Power Co.	$40	$326	$290
2	Bel Air Electric Co.	368	2,659	420
3	Chestertown Electric Light & Power Co.	7	3,234	470
4	Delmarvia Utilities Co	232	95	237
5	Delta Electric Power Co.		380	116
6	Easton Utilities Commission.		2,161	
7	Edison Electric Illuminating Co.	9,706	31,384	13,895
8	Emmitsburg Electric Co.		1,315	378
9	Harper's Ferry Electric Light & Power Co.		2,352	417
10	Havre de Grace Electric Co.		4,106	1,378
11	Home Electric Light Co.	263	1,795	508
12	Home Manufacturing Lt. & Power Co.	134	1,756	280
13	Idlewild Elec. Lt., Heat & Power Co.	1,830	4,808	599
14	Midland Electric Light Co.	432	125	413
15	Municipal Electric Lt. Plant of Hagerstown.	8,029	162	
16	Mt. Airy Electric & Ice Co.	2,290	139	43
17	Northern Virginia Power Co.	*	187,731	7,255
18	Peninsular Light & Power Co.	2,126	3,352	1,331
19	Perryville Electric Co.		410	120
20	Port Deposit Electric Co.		50	397
21	Potomac Electric Power Co.	149,665	207,593	244,835
22	Salisbury Light, Heat & Power Co.	7,296	12,845	3,301
23	Snow Hill Electric Light & Power Co.		460	152
24	St. Michaels Utilities Commission.		1,367	
25	Susquehanna Transmission Co. of Md.			
26	Union Bridge Electric Mfg. Co.		1,026	315

* Denotes absence of required figures.

NOTE—Deficit, loss and other reverse items on this table are printed in bold type.

No. 28.

THE DEDUCTIONS FROM GROSS INCOME, THE NET INCOME, THE APPROPRIATIONS FROM NET INCOME AND THE 8
YEAR ENDED DECEMBER 31, 1918.

TOTALS—Cont.	DISTRIBUTION OF INCOME.				
Surplus or Deficit.	Operating Revenue.	Non-Operating Revenue.	Production.	Distribution.	Utilisatio
5	6	7	8	9	10
$1,968	$9,648	$511	$4,271	$1,522	
1,684	13,208	390	4,512	1,531	
1,595	12,761	39	7,379	1,266	
276	8,739	....	6,598	816	....
678	2,643	....	2,152	....	....
4,127	29,399	....	21,147	978	....
5,950	293,880	334	138,492	8,483	
185	4,603	13	1,452	312	
65	17,335	....	4,765	4,983	
340	38,554	....	28,413	1,708	
3,873	17,311	53	5,189	2,135	
1,684	19,221	....	8,052	1,712	
1,979	23,362	410	9,568	1,938	
101	5,518	....	2,700	716	
10,510	110,966	47	68,037	14,616	
473	7,809	....	3,852	....	
90,837	265,290	....	*	*	*
2,346	24,796	....	14,681	1,437	
711	4,115	....	2,874	....	
387	4,832	....	2,708	1,290	
91,220	3,032,869	38,945	770,503	242,292	
13,871	67,724	....	41,260	1,175	
46	6,316	....	5,599	46	
873	4,816	2,298	3,351	313	....
....	61,629	....	....	61,629	
235	4,672	3,041	4,810	....	

DEDUCTIONS FROM GROSS INCOME—Continued.			APPROPRIATIONS FROM INCOME.			
OTHER DEDUCTIONS—Continued.						
Interest on Funded Debt.	Interest on Unfunded Debt.	Miscellaneous.	Amortisations and Depreciation of Plant.	Sinking Fund and Optional Reserves.	Dividends Declared.	8
15	16	17	18	19	20	
....	$846	....	$793	....	....	
$2,280	619	....	931	....	....	
1,299	....	$250	....	....	....	
600	12	....	....	....	....	
150	520	....	....	....	....	
1,500	....	....	2,712	....	....	
24,312	2,000	20,960	21,498	$4,862	$5,500	
....	90	....	....	305	600	
....	474	....	735	....	....	
....	3,352	....	....	....	....	
1,066	933	138	1,200	....	....	
434	156	....	8,923	....	....	
2,082	....	82	304	....	....	
....	....	....	....	....	1,000	
1,840	....	283	8,101	....	....	
252	....	....	....	....	....	
22,430	1,586	....	92,432	....	39,000	
....	64	....	1,620	....	1,875	
....	....	....	....	....	....	
417,350	29,294	....	249,173	106,000	660,000	
2,294	2,257	100	4,210	1,500	3,750	....
....	84	....	....	....	....	
....	717	2,140	100	....	....	

#	Title of Corporation	Descr. (1)	Date (2)	Term of (3)	Amount On (4)	Rate P (5)	Dates Payable (6)	Amount On (7)	Divi (8)	Rate Per (9)	Amount On (10)	Divid Dann (11)	Rate Per (12)
1	Antietam Electric L. & P. Co.	Mortgage	1911	40	$14,000	5½	Quarterly	$11,600					
2	Baltimore County Electric Co.	1st Mortgage	97	40	221,000	5	J. & D.	150,000					
3	Baltimore Elec. Co. of Balto. City	1st Mortgage	90	50	3,721,000	5	J. & D.	2,500,000			$1,000,000	$50,000	5
4	Bel Air Electric Co.	1st Mortgage	96	1 to 15	25,000	6	A. & O.	25,000			19,400		
		Notes	92	Various	13,000	5	A. & O.						
5	Centreville Electric Light Plant	Series 1.	94	Various	18,500	5	A. & O.						
		Series 2.											
6	Chestertown Elec. Lt. & P. Co.	1st Mortgage	96	20	4,000	6	F. & A.	15,000			6,000	420	7
7	Delmarvia Utilities Co.	Mortgage	97	3	22,000	6	J. & J.	70,000					
8	Delta Electric Power Co.	1st Mortgage	97	30	10,000	5	April	29,500					
		Real Estate			23,000								
					500								
9	Easton Utilities Commission	1st Mortgage	1914	20	30,000	5	J. & J.	275,000	$5,500	2			
10		1st Mortgage			485,000	5	A. & O.	7,500	600	8			
11								100,000	13,412	13.41			
12								49,900					
13								50,000					
14	Co.												
15	Home Electric Light Co.	1st Mortgage	1913	10	19,800	6	J. & D.	13,825					
16	Home Mfg. Light & Power Co.	1st Mortgage	91 6	10 to 30	43,400	6	M. & N.	8,800					
17	Idlewild Elec. L., H. & P. Co.	1st Mortgage	91 6	40	33,000	6	J. & D.	17,000	1,000	20			
18	Midland Electric Light Co.							5,000					
19	Mt. Airy Ice & Electric Co.	Mortgage	1915	Various	3,500	6	J. & L.	11,800					
20	Mt. Washington Elec. L. & P. Co.	Municipal	1900	20	45,000			83,280					
21	Municipal E. L. P. of Hagerstown	1st Mortgage	94	20	150,000	4	J. & J.	600,000	39,000	6¼			
22	Northern Virginia Power Co.	1st Mortgage	96	20	66,000	5	D. & J.						
	Cacapon Power Co.	1st Mortgage	93	13	38,000	6	F. & A.						
	Cacapon Power Co.	1st Mortgage	96	20	115,000	5	F. & A.						
	Winchester & Wash. Co. Ry. Co.	1st Mortgage	98	20	56,000	6	M. & N.						
	Northern Virginia Power Co.												
23	Patapsco El. & Mfg. Co. of Del.	1st Mortgage	94	25	1,700,000	5	J. & D.	225,000	1,875	2½			
24	Patapsco El. & Mfg. Co. of Md.	Consolidated	96	30	4,841,000	5	J. & J.	200,000					
25		Debenture	97	10	2,100,000	6	J. & J.	75,000					
26		General Mtge.	98	5		6	J. & J.	20,755					
27	Peninsular Light & Power Co.	1st Mortgage	97	30	300,000	5	F. & A.	8,125					
28	Potomac Electric Power Co.	1st Mortgage	90 1	20	29,500	5	J. & D.	5,750,000	652,500	11			
29	Roland Park Elec. & Water Co.	1st Mortgage	1911	20	1,000,000	5	J. & J.	25,000			250,000	27,500	11
30	Salisbury Lt., Ht. & P. Co.					5	J. & J.	100,000					
31	Snow Hill Elec. Light & Power Co.					6	J. & J.	12,000	3,750	3¾			
32	Susquehanna Trans. Co. of Md.					6	F. & A.	500					
33	Union Bridge Electric Mfg. Co.	1st Mortgage				5	J. & D.	25,000					
34	Waynesboro Electric Co.							50,000					

TABLE No. 30.

Showing for Each of the Electric Light Corporations Named Therein Various Operating Statistics for the Year Ended December 31, 1918. The Characters Shown in this Table Indicate as Follows: 0—None; *—Absence of Required Figures.

	Stations						Plant							
	Number and Capacity				1000 K.W. Hours. Made and Sold.									
Title of Corporation.	Generating Stations.	Capacity in K. W.	Sub-Stations.	Capacity in K. W.	Total Station Output.	Total Sold	Number of Boilers.	Rated Horse Power.	Number of Engines.	Rated Horse Power.	Number of Water Wheels.	Rated Horse Power.	Number of Generators.	Total K. W.
	1	2	3	4	5	6	7	8	9	10	11	12	13	14
1 Antietam Electric Light & Power Co....	1	150	0	0	*	*	1	125	1	125	2	360	2	150
2 Baltimore Electric Co. of Balto. City.	1	6,000	1	8,500	*	*	8	4,000	3	8,040	0	0	3	6,000
3 Bel Air Electric Co....	1	210	0	0	144	110	0	25	1	25	0	0	8	210
4 Consolidated Gas Elec. L. & P Co....	1	55,500	9	39,820	427,422	393,573	28	23,908	8	74,085	6	3,558	11	55,500
5 Consolidated Public Utilities Co....	2	350	0	0	422	380	2	350	2	650	0	0	2	350
6 Centreville Electric Light Plant...	1	175	0	0	99	98	2	285	2	250	0	0	1	175
7 Chestertown Electric Light & Power Co.	1	125	0	0	108	86	2	180	2	142½	0	0	3	125
8 Delmarvia Utilities Co....	1	177½	0	0	*	46	3	325	3	370	0	0	1	177½
9 Delta Electric Power Co....	1	350	0	0	413	*	2	300	2	350	2	600	2	350
10 Easton Utilities Commission...	1	250	1	3,000	13,285	9,309	11	3,892	4	5,956	0	0	4	250
11 Edison Electric Illuminating Co....	0	4,000	1	0	55	45	0	0	0	0	0	0	0	4,400
12 (c) Emmitsburg Electric Co....	1	0	0	0	*	*	0	0	0	0	0	0	0	0
13 Hagerstown & Frederick Ry. Co., Electric Department...	1	10,250	8	3,550	17,400	9,920	4	2,800	3	10,250	0	0	3	10,250
14 (a) Harper's Ferry Elec. L. & P. Co....	1	325	0	0	654	548	4	525	3	458	0	0	4	325
15 Havre de Grace Electric Co....	1	435	0	0	282	236	4	0	3	0	0	0	0	435
16 (c) Home Electric Light Co....	0	0	2	220	322	222	0	0	0	0	0	0	0	0
17 (c) Home Manufacturing Light & Power Co.	0	0	0	0	385	385	0	0	0	0	0	0	0	0
18 (c) Midland Electric Light Co....	1	35	0	0	*	*	2	180	1	57	0	0	1	35
19 Mt. Airy Ice & Electric Co....	1	2,330	1	0	4,529	3,082	6	1,800	3	3,250	5	4,700	3	2,330
20 Municipal Elec. L. Plant of Hagerstown	2	8,650	1	0	*	*	4	2,650	3	8,400	3	160	8	8,650
21 Northern Virginia Power Co....	1	427½	2	0	507	439	1	150	2	470	0	0	4	427½
22 Peninsular Light & Power Co....	0	0	0	0	555	*	0	0	0	0	0	0	0	0
23 Perryville Electric Co....	0	0	0	0	34	34	0	0	0	0	0	0	0	0
24 Port Deposit Electric Co....	0	0	3	0	0	*	0	0	0	0	0	0	0	0
25 (b) Potomac Electric Power Co....	0	0	3	1,700	1,187	1,821	0	0	0	0	3	200	0	0
26 Salisbury Light, Heat & Power Co....	1	675	1	0	*	*	2	710	3	760	0	0	3	675
27 Snow Hill Electric Light & Power Co...	1	120	0	0	*	*	1	125	2	215	0	0	4	120
28 Union Bridge Electric Mfg. Co....	1	75	1	0	*	*	0	0	1	75	0	0	1	75
29 Waynesboro Electric Co....	1	0	1	1,500	*	*	4	1,000	0	0	0	0	0	0

TABLE No. 31.

SHOWING FOR EACH OF THE ELECTRIC LIGHT CORPORATIONS NAMED THEREIN VARIOUS OPERATING STATISTICS FOR THE YEAR ENDED DECEMBER 31, 1918. THE CHARACTERS SHOWN IN THIS TABLE INDICATE AS FOLLOWS: 0—NONE; *—ABSENCE OF REQUIRED FIGURES.

		STREET LIGHTING.						COMMERCIAL Inc.		
		Arc Lamps.			Incandescent Lamps.					
TITLE OF CORPORATION.	On What Schedule.	Number of Enclosed.	Watts at Lamp.	Price Per Lamp Per Year.	Number of Lamps.	Candle Power.	Price Per Lamp Per Year.	Number of Consumers.	Number of Meters in Service.	Number of Transformers in Service.
	1	2	3	4	5	6	7	8	9	10
1 Antietam Electric Light & Power Co.	All Night	0	0	0	59	60	$23.33	365	267	73
2 Bel Air Electric Co.	Midnight	0	0	0	52	60	13.33	0	0	0
3 Consolidated Gas Elec. Light & Power Co.	Various	3,738	80.86	$0.86	83	40-400	18.00-75.00	286	289	97
4 Consolidated Public Utilities Co.	Moonlight	49	30	6000	6,798	16-400	6.00-75.00	56,106	57,758	5,364
5 Centreville Electric Light Plant	Philadelphia	0	0	0	31	40	18.00	332	332	24
6 Chestertown Electric Light & Power Co.	Moonlight	0	0	0	92	50-100	20.00-100.00	240	197	34
7 Delmarvia Utilities Co.	On Meter	0	0	0	101	32	18.00	260	251	24
8 Delta Electric Power Co.	0	0	0	0	*	*	*	217	215	18
9 Easton Utilities Commission		0	0	0	0	0	*	24	25	20
10 Edison Electric Illuminating Co.	Freund System	38	495-500	35.90	637	50-600	3.96-26.85	419	419	39
11 Emmitsburg Electric Co.	Dusk to Dawn	0	0	0	38	40	12.00	3,714	4,170	212
12 Hagerstown & Frederick Railway Co.	2400 Hours	0	0	0	0	0	0	148	164	7
13 Harper's Ferry Electric Light & Power Co.	0	0	0	0	188	100	9.00-12.00	3,677	3,927	586
14 Havre de Grace Electric Co.	All Night	8	750	70.00	120	40-60	17.50-22.50	475	747	88
15 Home Electric Light Co.	*	0	0	0	90	0	0	750	475	*
16 Home Manufacturing Light & Power Co.	Mid. 0	0	0	0	163	25-40	12.00-16.00	263	739	*
17 Idlewild Electric Light, Heat & Power Co.	Sunset to Rise	0	0	0	37	32-250	10.09-13.20	*	229	42
18 Midland Electric Light Co.	Dusk to Dawn	0	0	0	55	60	15.00-18.00	360	*	58
19 Mt. Airy Ice & Electric Co.	Sunset to Rise	0	0	0	200	45-400	18.00-25.00	126	103	7
20 Municipal Elec. Light Plant of Hagerstown	All night	210	660	50.00	107	240-400	25.00-41.50	3,861	3,960	326
21 Northern Virginia Power Co.	All	0	0	0	40	80	15.00	*	*	12
22 Peninsular Light & Power Co.	On Mr.	0	0	0	*	*	*	207	202	67
23 Perryville Electric Co.	All Night	0	0	0	15	32	18.00	107	107	11
24 Port Deposit Electric Co.	All Night	0	0	0	51	32	20.00	131	89	18
25 Potomac Electric Power Co.	Dark to 1.30 A. M.	0	0	0	767	20-60	12.908.11	3,591	3,899	795
26 Salisbury Light, Heat & Power Co.	All Night	0	0	0	*	40-250	12.00-30.50	*	*	*
27 St. Michaels Utilities Commission	Sunset to Sunrise	0	0	0	59	40-80	*	96	96	8
28 Snow Hill Electric Light & Power Co.	3000 Hours	0	0	0	67	16	12.17	178	132	78
29 Union Bridge Electric Manufacturing Co.	All Night	0	0	0	20	100	26.50	166	146	22
30 Waynesboro Electric Co.	Moonlight	0	0	0	0	0	0	67	67	9

TABLE No. 32.

Showing for Each of the Electric Light Corporations Named Therein the Casualties, Classified as to Employees and Others, for the Year Ended December 31, 1918. The Character Shown in This Table Indicates as Follows: 0—None.

Title of Corporation	Power House Killed (1)	Power House Injured (2)	Line Killed (3)	Line Injured (4)	Shop Killed (5)	Shop Injured (6)	Other Killed (7)	Other Injured (8)	Total Employees Killed (9)	Total Employees Injured (10)	Persons Other Than Employees Killed (11)	Persons Other Than Employees Injured (12)	Total all Persons Killed (13)	Total all Persons Injured (14)
1 Antietam Electric Light & Power Co	0	0	0	0	0	0	0	0	0	0	0	0	0	0
2 Bel Air Electric Co	0	0	0	0	0	0	0	0	0	0	0	0	0	0
3 Centreville Electric Light Plant	0	0	0	0	0	0	0	0	0	0	0	0	0	0
4 Chestertown Electric Light & Power Co	0	0	0	0	0	0	0	0	0	0	0	0	0	0
5 Delmarvia Utilities Co	0	0	0	0	0	0	0	0	0	0	0	0	0	0
6 Delta Electric Power Co	0	0	0	0	0	0	0	0	0	0	0	0	0	0
7 Easton Utilities Commission	0	0	0	0	0	0	0	0	0	0	0	0	0	0
8 Edison Electric Illuminating Co	0	1	0	0	0	0	0	0	0	1	0	0	0	1
9 Emmitsburg Electric Co	0	0	0	0	0	0	0	0	0	0	0	0	0	0
10 Harper's Ferry Electric Light & Power Co	0	0	0	1	0	0	0	0	0	1	0	0	0	1
11 Havre de Grace Electric Co	0	0	0	0	0	0	0	0	0	0	0	0	0	0
12 Home Electric Light Co	0	0	0	0	0	0	0	0	0	0	0	0	0	0
13 Home Manufacturing Light & Power Co	0	0	0	1	0	0	0	0	0	1	0	0	0	1
14 Idlewild Electric Light, Heat & Power Co	0	0	0	0	0	0	0	0	0	0	0	0	0	0
15 Midland Electric Light Co	0	0	0	0	0	0	0	0	0	0	0	1	0	1
16 Mt. Airy Ice & Electric Co	0	0	0	1	0	0	0	0	0	1	0	0	0	1
17 Municipal Electric Light Plant of Hagerstown	0	0	0	0	0	0	0	0	0	0	0	0	0	0
18 Northern Virginia Power Co	0	0	0	0	0	0	0	0	0	0	0	0	0	0
19 Peninsular Light & Power Co	0	0	0	0	0	0	0	0	0	0	0	0	0	0
20 Perryville Electric Co	0	0	0	0	0	0	0	0	0	0	1	0	1	0
21 Port Deposit Electric Co	0	0	0	0	0	0	0	0	0	0	0	0	0	0
22 Potomac Electric Power Co	0	0	0	0	0	0	0	0	0	0	0	0	0	0
23 Salisbury Light, Heat & Power Co	0	0	0	0	0	0	0	0	0	0	0	0	0	0
24 Snow Hill Electric Light & Power Co	0	0	0	0	0	0	0	0	0	0	0	0	0	0
25 St. Michaels Utilities Commission	0	0	0	0	0	0	0	0	0	0	0	0	0	0
26 Susquehanna Transmission Co. of Maryland	0	0	0	0	0	0	0	5	0	5	0	0	0	5
27 Union Bridge Electric Manufacturing Co	0	0	0	0	0	0	0	0	0	0	0	0	0	0
28 Waynesboro Electric Co	0	0	0	0	0	0	0	0	0	0	0	0	0	0

TABLE No. 33.

Each of the Electric Light and Gas Corporations Named Therein the Total Amount of Assets, of Liabilities and of Surplus, on December 31, 1918, and Total Amount of Gross Income, the Deductions from Gross Income and the Net Income from the Operations of the Year Ended December 31, 1918, and the Increases or Decreases from the Preceding Year.

	TOTALS.											
Title of Corporation.	Assets.		Liabilities.		Surplus or Deficit.		Gross Income.		Deductions from Gross Income.		Net Income.	
	Total Amount Dec. 31, 1918.	Increase Over Preceding Year.	Total Amount Dec. 31, 1919.	Increase Over Preceding Year.	Total Amount Dec. 31, 1918.	Increase Over Preceding Year.	Total Amount Dec. 31, 1918.	Increase Over Preceding Year.	Total Amount Dec. 31, 1918.	Increase Over Preceding Year.	Total Amount Dec. 31, 1918.	Increase Over Preceding Year.
	1	2	3	4	5	6	7	8	9	10	11	12
Public Utilities Co.	$489,226	$18,158	$492,638	$22,705	$3,412	$4,547	$111,303	$30	$109,918	$23,908	$1,385	$8,878
G. Electric Light & Power Co.	358,872	12,748	335,347	7,916	23,525	4,832	84,756	14,044	75,806	6,272	8,950	7,772
wn Gas Co.	75,162	2,940	91,276	6,239	16,114	3,398	14,417	7,304	17,815	8,634	3,398	1,304
Gas Co.	191,575	2,675	191,575	2,675			46,689	6,253	43,466	10,937	3,223	484
ted Gas Electric Light & Power Co.	61,478,730	1,034,125	59,879,711	1,401,056	1,599,019	366,931	12,134,433	2,584	9,585	2,876,477	2,159,248	8,886
ated Power Co.	12,286,318	967,055	12,286,318	967,055								
ated Public Hies Co.	141,624	8,466	141,624	8,466			34,584	6,994	30,139	10,199	4,445	3,204
Light & Power Co.	76,732	541	78,136	2,273	1,404	1,732	15,660	7,499	17,392	10,185	1,732	2,696
as Light Co.	26,531	396	26,531	396			7,576	1,420	7,523	2,075	53	655
wn Gas Light G. of Montgomery Co.	106,671	1,871	108,902	1,628	2,231	245	32,085	7,113	31,850	5,065	245	2,048
wn Light & Heat G.	596,968	1,728	584,061	25,895	12,907	24,813	125,091	34,460	125,424	45,770	333	11,310
e Grace Gas Co.	116,521	2,724	136,763	3,210	262	486	16,387	4,792	15,873	3,152	486	1,640
lle Gas & Electric Co.	219,911	5,049	188,683	17,144	31,228	12,096	61,656	10,269	66,414	21,774	4,758	11,505
ter Lighting & Heating Co.	6,423	85	6,230	100	190	15	854	38	828	24	26	14
ton Gas Light Co. of Montgomery Co.	25,795	1,496	22,130	1,420	3,665	66	15,525	3,381	14,858	3,958	666	577
Md Gas Co.	201,013	3,978	189,794	1,750	11,219	5,737	40,468	10,290	38,171	9,952	2,297	338
gnia & Maryland G. of Md.	256,358	6,713	263,780	33,820	7,421	27,107	87,454	32,117	114,561	38,498	27,107	6,381
ginia & Maryland Gas Co. of W, &	3,701,597	68,812	3,815,118	51,031	113,521	17,781	534,088	202,367	551,860	191,415	17,781	10,952

ural Gas Companies.

x—Deficit, loss and other reverse items in this table are printed in bold type.

SHOWING FOR EACH OF THE ELECTRIC LIGHT AND GAS CORPORATIONS NAMED THEREIN THE TOT
OF 9

TITLE OF CORPORATION.	TOTALS.		
	Assets.		]
	Total Amount Dec. 31, 1918.	Increase Over Preceding Year.	Total Amount Dec. 31, 1918.
	1	2	3
1 Annapolis Public Utilities Co.	$489,226	$18,158	$492,638
2 Cambridge Gas, Electric Light & Power Co.	358,872	12,748	335,347
3 Chestertown Gas Co.	75,162	2,840	91,276
4 Citizens Gas Co.	191,575	2,675	191,575
5 Consolidated Gas Electric Light & Power Co.	61,478,730	1,034,125	59,879,711
6 Consolidated Power Co.	12,286,318	967,055	12,286,318
7 Consolidated Public Utilities Co.	141,624	8,466	141,624
8 Crisfield Light & Power Co.	76,732	541	78,136
9 Elkton Gas Light Co.	26,531	396	26,531
10 Georgetown Gas Light Co. of Montgomery Co.	106,671	1,871	108,902
11 Hagerstown Light & Heat Co.	596,968	1,728	584,061
12 Havre de Grace Gas Co.	116,521	2,724	136,753
13 Hyattsville Gas & Electric Co.	219,911	5,049	188,683
14 Manchester Lighting & Heating Co.	6,423	85	6,230
15 Washington Gas Light Co. of Montgomery Co.	25,795	1,486	22,130
16 †Northern Natural Gas Co.	201,013	3,976	189,794
17 †West Virginia & Maryland Gas Co. of Maryland.	256,358	6,713	263,780
18 †West Virginia & Maryland Gas Co. of West Virginia.	3,701,597	68,812	3,815,118

TITLE OF CORPORATION.	DETAILS OF ASSETS—Continued.		
	Unextinguished Discount on Securities.	Reacquired Securities.	Sundries.
	14	15	16
1 Annapolis Public Utilities Co.		$34	$857
2 Cambridge Gas, Electric Light & Power Co.	$3,721		
3 Chestertown Gas Co.			66
4 Citizens Gas Co.			
5 Consolidated Gas Electric Light & Power Co.	949,893		3,714,804
6 Consolidated Power Co.	283,049		a6,468,000
7 Consolidated Public Utilities Co.		250	
8 Crisfield Light & Power Co.			
9 Elkton Gas Light Co.			
10 Georgetown Gas Light Co. of Montgomery Co.			
11 Hagerstown Light & Heat Co.	33,272		34,000
12 Havre de Grace Gas Co.			
13 Hyattsville Gas & Electric Co.			
14 Manchester Lighting & Heating Co.			
15 Washington Gas Light Co. of Montgomery Co.			50
16 †Northern Natural Gas Co.			3,502
17 †West Virginia & Maryland Gas Co. of Maryland.			6,538
18 †West Virginia & Maryland Gas Co. of West Virginia.			124,227

† Natural Gas Companies.

(a) Certified 1st mortgage 5 per cent 20-year bonds in treasury.

NOTE—Deficit, loss and other reverse items in this table are printed in bold type.

No. 34.

OF ASSETS, THE TOTAL AMOUNT OF LIABILITIES AND THE SURPLUS ON DECEMBER 31, 1918, AND THE CLA
AND |LIABILITIES.

TOTALS—Continued.

DETAILS OF ASSETS.

SURPLUS OR DEFICIT.		DETAILS OF ASSETS.					
Total Amount Dec. 31, 1918.	Increase Over Preceding Year.	Cost of Plant.	Cash.	Bills and Accounts Receivable.	Materials and Supplies.	Investments.	Sinking Fund and Optional Reserves.
5	6	7	8	9	10	11	12
$3,412	$4,547	$407,170	$9,686	$26,628	$12,416		$29,375
23,525	4,832	307,390	956	46,382			
16,114	3,398	72,170	50	912	1,963		
		175,664	1,182	7,928	6,800		
1,599,019	366,931	47,981,305	1,991,599	1,537,881	1,332,296	$2,825,826	534,017
		4,527,029	100	425,000			
		121,662	7,273	7,287	5,015		
1,464	1,732	71,429	3	2,368	2,931		
		25,150		996	384		
2,231	245	103,610	6	3,025			
12,907	24,113	488,098	3,894	12,393	20,544		
20,232	486	111,998	584	678	3,066		
31,228	12,095	196,529	1,706	14,289	6,929		
190	15	5,380	153		40		850
3,665	66	20,770	3,355	1,620			
11,219	5,737	194,082	2,349	1,080			
7,421	27,107	248,475		1,345			
113,521	17,781	3,168,477	70,611	108,282		230,000	

DETAILS OF LIABILITIES—Continued.

Funded Debt.	Taxes Accrued and Unpaid.	Interest Accrued on Funded and Other Debt.	Bills and Accounts Payable.	Dividends Payable.	Consumers' Deposits.	Sinking Fund and Optional Reserves.	Reserve for Depreciation and Amortisation.
18	19	20	21	22	23	24	25
$198,500	$1,668	$3,864	$43,994		$4,127	$55,700	$12,089
161,000	677		57,318		4,186	1,424	10,742
20,000			56,271				
120,000		810	2,542				3,223
37,752,247		842,917	3,584,589	$288,428	53,717	974,000	1,956,101
11,468,000			818,218				
50,000		912	19,579		40		35,553
30,000		900	7,236				
6,000			2,004				
			95,015		3,888		
325,000	770	6,084	28,691		9,735	1,425	12,810
50,000		10,196	26,557				
	786	119	97,979		4,685	2,275	
						850	
			11,645		485		46,356
			8,811		274	34,353	135,065
			33,339		2,325	73,050	1,009,623
			770,138		24,016	11,341	

SHOWING FOR EACH OF THE ELECTRIC LIGHT AND GAS CORPORATIONS NAMED THEREIN THE AMO
NET INCOME AND THE SURPL

TITLE OF CORPORATION.	TOTALS.		
	Gross Income from all Sources.	Deductions from Gross Income.	Net Income.
	1	2	3
1 Annapolis Public Utilities Co....................	$111,303	$109,918	$1,385
2 Cambridge Gas, Electric Light & Power Co..............	84,756	75,806	8,950
3 Chestertown Gas Co........................	14,417	17,815	3,398
4 Citizens Gas Co........................	46,689	43,466	3,223
5 Consolidated Gas Electric Light & Power Co............	12,134,433	9,975,185	2,159,248
6 Consolidated Public Utilities Co................	34,584	30,139	4,445
7 Crisfield Light & Power Co..................	15,660	17,392	1,732
8 Elkton Gas Light Co.....................	7,576	7,523	53
9 Georgetown Gas Light Co. of Montgomery Co...........	32,095	31,850	245
10 Hagerstown & Frederick Ry. Co. (Electric and Gas Depts.).	349,564	312,469	37,095
11 Hagerstown Light & Heat Co................	125,091	125,424	333
12 Havre de Grace Gas Co..................	15,387	15,873	486
13 Hyattsville Gas & Electric Co..............	61,656	66,414	4,758
14 Manchester Lighting & Heating Co............	854	828	26
15 Washington Gas Light Co. of Montgomery Co........	15,525	14,858	666
16 †Northern Natural Gas Co................	40,468	38,171	2,297
17 †West Virginia & Maryland Gas Co. of Maryland........	87,454	114,561	27,107
18 †West Virginia & Maryland Gas Co. of West Virginia.......	534,088	551,869	17,781

TITLE OF CORPORATION.	DEDUCTIONS FROM GROSS INCO		
	OPERATING EXPENSES, GAS—C		
	Transmission and Distribution.	Commercial.	General.
	14	15	16
1 Annapolis Public Utilities Co.....................	$1,699	$2,440	$2,363
2 Cambridge Gas, Electric Light & Power Co..............	1,055	1,041	3,179
3 Chestertown Gas Co........................	11		
4 Citizens Gas Co........................	1,796	205	7,339
5 Consolidated Gas Electric Light & Power Co...........	303,658	212,019	259,485
6 Consolidated Public Utilities Co................	907		1,164
7 Crisfield Light & Power Co..................	1,244	1,016	1,787
8 Elkton Gas Light Co.....................	75	337	18
9 Georgetown Gas Light Co. of Montgomery Co...........	3,079	1,087	2,359
10 Hagerstown & Frederick Ry. Co. (Electric and Gas Depts.).	2,841	1,610	3,073
11 Hagerstown Light & Heat Co................	5,675	6,950	16,288
12 Havre de Grace Gas Co..................	888	367	1,509
13 Hyattsville Gas & Electric Co..............	2,362	5,188	5,006
14 Manchester Lighting & Heating Co............			
15 Washington Gas Light Co. of Montgomery Co........	776	684	1,521
16 †Northern Natural Gas Co................	8,841		3,107
17 †West Virginia & Maryland Gas Co. of Maryland........	36,572		13,577
18 †West Virginia & Maryland Gas Co. of West Virginia.......	150,612		31,784

† Natural Gas Companies.

NOTE—Deficit, loss and other reverse items in this table are printed in bold type.

No. 35.

INCOME FROM ALL SOURCES, THE DEDUCTIONS FROM GROSS INCOME, THE NET INCOME, THE APPROPRIATIONS OPERATIONS OF THE YEAR ENDED DECEMBER 31, 1918.

TOTALS —Continued.	DISTRIBUTION OF INCOME.			DEDUCTIONS F				O E
				OPERATING EXPENSES, ELECTRIC.				
Surplus or Deficit.	Operating Revenue, Electric.	Operating Revenue, Gas.	Non-Operating Revenue.	Production.	Transmission and Distribution.	Utilisation and Commercial.	General.	Pro
5	6	7	8	9	10	11	12	
$4,547	$60,877	$50,426	....	$34,136	$1,586	$3,022	$2,318	
4,832	64,256	20,500	....	29,054	3,772	3,974	7,096	
3,398	....	14,417	....	....	....	....	....	
....	....	46,689	....	....	....	....	....	
366,932	7,284,398	4,817,540	$32,495	2,691,114	522,211	235,550	316,498	2,
....	21,118	13,294	172	6,998	986	519	1,892	
1,732	....	15,660	....	....	....	....	....	
53	....	7,576	....	....	....	....	....	
245	....	32,095	....	....	....	....	....	
37,095	276,114	40,014	33,436	133,607	15,010	16,301	18,244	
24,113	....	124,791	300	....	....	....	....	
486	....	15,387	....	....	....	....	....	
12,095	....	61,656	....	....	....	....	....	
14	....	854	....	....	....	....	....	
66	....	15,456	69	....	....	....	....	
5,703	....	40,368	100	....	....	....	....	
27,107	....	87,054	400	....	....	....	....	
17,781	....	526,552	7,536	....	....	....	....	A

DEDUCTIONS FROM GROSS INCOME—Continued.

OTHER DEDUCTIONS—Continued.

APPROPRIATIONS FROM NET INCOME.

Uncollectible Bills.	Interest on Funded Debt.	Interest on Unfunded Debt	Miscellaneous.	Amortisation and Depreciation of Plant.	Sinking Fund and Optional Reserves.	Dividends Declared.	Su
18	19	20	21	22	23	24	
....	$10,715	$1,042	$237	$4,164	$1,786	....	
$364	9,660	2,218	100	$3,369	....	$750	
7	1,275	3,568	....	....	....	....	....
....	7,200	471	....	3,223	....	....	
17,457	2,005,981	157,420	....	1,125,000	250,000	1,151,180	
....	2,500	861	128	4,445	....	....	
204	1,800	227	....	....	....	....	
....	360	67	....	....	....	....	
23	....	4,350	....	....	....	....	
317	14,550	646	....	3,780	....	20,000	
3	2,500	28	....	....	....	6,880	
300	....	5,135	15	....	....	....	
....	....	16	....	....	....	600	
....	....	780	....	9,528	....	8,000	....
....	....	2,687	....	23,264	....	....	....
....	6,750	45,339	....	191,305	....	....	

TABLE No. 36.

Showing for Each of the Electric Light and Gas Corporations Named Therein the Total Funded Debt and Capital Stock Outstanding on December 31, 1918 (Exclusive of Such Funded Debt and Capital Stock as are Held by the Issuing Corporation), the Rate Per Cent. and Dates of Payment of Interest on Funded Debt, and the Rate Per Cent. and Amount of Dividends Declared on Capital Stock.

	Title of Corporation.	1 Description.	2 Date.	3 Term of Years.	Funded Debt — 4 Amount Outstanding.	5 Rate Per Cent.	Interest — 6 Dates Payable.	Common Stock — 7 Amount Outstanding.	8 Dividends Declared During Year.	9 Rate Per Cent.	Preferred Stock — 10 Amount Outstanding.	11 Dividends Declared During Year.	12 Rate Per Cent.
1	Annapolis Public Utilities Co.	1st Mortgage	1891	30	$57,500	6	J. & J.	$172,700	0	0	0	0	0
2	Cambridge Gas, Electric Lt. & Power Co.	1st Cons'd	1903	50	119,500	5	A. & O.	100,600	0	0	0	0	0
3	Chestertown Gas Co.	1st & Ref'd'g	1916	30	161,000	6	J. & D.	15,000	750	5	0	0	0
4	Citizens Gas Co.	1st Mortgage	1912	35	20,000	6	A. & O.	85,000	0	0	0	0	0
5	Consolidated Gas Electric Lt. & P. Co.	1st Mortgage	1915	50	120,000	6	J. & J.	14,423,900	1,150,869	8	0	0	0
		Gen'l Mtge.	1905	30	15,000,000	4½	M. & N.						
		Debentures	1913	0	397,747	4½	M. & N.						
		Gold Notes	1916	5	8,455,500	5	J. & J.						
	Consolidated Gas Co.	Consol's	1889	50	3,400,000	5	J. & J.	0	0	0	0	0	0
		General	1904	50	6,100,000	4½	A. & O.						
6	United Electric Light & Power Co.	1st Mortgage	1899	30	4,428,000	4½	M. & N.	0	0	0	0	0	0
	Consolidated Power Company	Gold Notes	1917	5	5,000,000	6	F. & A.	100	0	0	0	0	0
7	Consolidated Public Utilities Co.	Notes	1918	3	468,000	6	Quarterly	35,540	0	0	0	0	0
8	Crisfield Light & Power Co.	1st Mortgage	1908	30	30,000	5	A. & O.	0	0	0	0	0	0
9	Elkton Gas Light Co.	1st Mortgage	1904	20	20,000	5	J. & J.	40,000	0	0	0	0	0
10	Georgetown G. Lt. Co. of Montgomery Co.	Gen'l Mtge.	1911	20	30,000	6	J. & D.	18,527	0	0	0	0	0
			1915	5	6,000	6							
11	Hagerstown Light & Heat Co.	0	0	0	0	0	0	10,000	0	0	0	0	0
12	Havre de Grace Gas Co.	1st Mortgage	1912	50	291,000	5	F. & A.	200,000	20,000	10	0	0	0
13	Hyattsville Gas & Electric Co.	1st Mortgage	1908	30	50,000	5	M. & S.	50,000	0	0	0	0	0
14	Manchester Lighting & Heating Co.	0	0	0	0	0	0	86,000	6,880	8	0	0	0
15	Washington G. Lt. Co. of Montgomery Co.	0	0	0	0	0	0	5,380	600	6	0	0	0
16	*Northern Natural Gas Co.	0	0	0	0	0	0	10,000	8,000	8	0	0	0
17	*W. Va. & Md. Gas Co. of Md.	0	0	0	0	0	0	100,000	8,000	8	0	0	0
18	*W. Va. & Md. Gas Co. of W. Va.	0	0	0	0	0	0	2,000,000	0	0	0	0	0

* Natural Gas Companies.

Showing for Each of the Electric Light and Gas Corporations Named Therein Various Ope
0—None;

Title of Corporation.	Production Pla		
1 Annapolis Public Utilities Co.	6	36	0
2 Cambridge Gas, Electric Light & Power Co.	3	17	0
3 Citizens' Gas Co.	0	0	2
4 Consolidated Gas Electric Light & Power Co.	0	0	12
5 Consolidated Public Utilities Co.	3	12	0
6 Crisfield Light & Power Co.	0	0	1
7 Elkton Gas Light Co.	2	6	0
8 (a) Georgetown Gas Light Co. of Montgomery Co.	0	0	0
9 Hagerstown & Frederick Ry. Co. (Elec. & Gas Depts.)	0	0	2
10 Hagerstown Light & Heat Co.	0	0	2
11 Havre de Grace Gas Co.	0	0	1
12 Hyattsville Gas & Electric Co.	4	24	0
13 (b) Manchester Lighting & Heating Co.	0	0	0
14 (a) Washington Gas Light Co. of Montgomery Co.	0	0	0
15 †Northern Natural Gas Co.	0	0	0
16 †West Virginia & Maryland Gas Co. of Maryland	0	0	0
17 †West Virginia & Maryland Gas Co. of West Virginia.	0	0	0

Title of Corporation.	Quantities Mad The		
	Coal Gas, M. Cub. Ft.	Water Gas, M. Cub. Ft.	Mixed Gas, M. Cub. Ft.
	13	14	15
1 Annapolis Public Utilities Co.	26,244	0	0
2 Cambridge Gas, Electric Light & Power Co.	•	•	•
3 Citizens' Gas Co.	0	28,007	0
4 Consolidated Gas Electric Light & Power Co.	0	0	7,133,471
5 Consolidated Public Utilities Co.	6,882	0	0
6 Crisfield Light & Power Co.	0	9,446	0
7 Elkton Gas Light Co.	3,089	0	0
8 (a) Georgetown Gas Light Co. of Montgomery Co.	32,095	0	0
9 Hagerstown & Frederick Ry. Co. (Elec. & Gas Depts.)	0	24,791	0
10 Hagerstown Light & Heat Co.	0	102,070	0
11 Havre de Grace Gas Co.	0	•	0
12 Hyattsville Gas & Electric Co.	0	34,074	0
13 (b) Manchester Lighting & Heating Co.	0	0	0
14 (a) Washington Gas Light Co. of Montgomery Co.	16,260	0	0
15 †Northern Natural Gas Co.	0	0	0
16 †West Virginia & Maryland Gas Co. of Maryland	0	0	0
17 †West Virginia & Maryland Gas Co. of West Virginia.	0	0	0

(a) Distributing Company, does not manufacture.

(b) Makes acetylene gas.

† Natural Gas Companies.

No. 37.

stics for the Year Ended December 31, 1918. The Characters Shown in This Table Indicate as F
of Required Figures.

Production Plant, Etc. —Continued.	Daily Capacity of Plant.		Quantities Made, Bought and Sold During the Ye				
			Made.			Bought.	
Capacity of Holders, Cub. Ft.	Coal Gas, M. Cub. Ft.	Water Gas, M. Cub. Ft.	Coal Gas, M. Cub. Ft.	Water Gas, M. Cub. Ft.	Natural Gas, M. Cub. Ft.	Coal Gas, M. Cub. Ft.	Natu M.
5	6	7	8	9	10	11	
85,000	300	0	35,731	0	0	0	
30,000	75	0	*	*	*	*	
60,000	0	300	0	30,030	0	0	
13,400,000	0	34,000	0	5,290,163	0	2,141,268	
33,000	0	0	*	0	0	0	
20,000	24	50	0	10,485	0	0	
15,000	35	0	*	0	0	0	
0	0	0	0	0	0	32,095	
46,424	0	150	0	30,365	0	0	
330,000	0	930	0	117,330	0	0	
20,000	0	100	0	*	0	0	
60,000	180	0	36,836	0	0	0	
0	0	0	0	0	0	16,260	
0	0	0	0	0	0	0	2
0	0	0	0	0	0	0	9
0	0	0	0	0	0	0	
0	0	0	0	0	0	0	

Transmission and Distribution Mains, Length in Feet.					Consumers.	
Above 12 Inches in Diameter.	Above 4 Inches but not above 12 Inches.	Above ½ Inch but not above 4 Inches.	Number of Street Lamps.	Price Per Year.	Number of Private Consumers.	Num Me Se
17	18	19	20	21	22	2
0	1,798	57,413	0	0	1,547	
0	2,450	215,346	0	0	*	
0	8,278	145,770	0	0	1,563	
627,082	1,389,609	2,372,886	12,501	6.50	140,239	
0	3,000	22,000	0	0	601	
0	0	49,692	0	0	566	
0	140	17,076	0	0	312	
0	53,505	49,328	0	0	496	
0	10,036	61,156	0	0	1,464	
0	54,889	116,179	0	0	4,148	
0	2,610	23,126	0	0	540	
0	35,743	98,257	0	0	1,501	
0	0	6,600	31	*	55	
0	9,236	20,632	0	0	413	
0	79,857	68,898	0	0	723	
0	80,698	352,100	0	0	3,368	
0	153,908	362,332	0	0	6,011	

TABLE No. 38.

SHOWING FOR EACH OF THE ELECTRIC LIGHT AND GAS CORPORATIONS NAMED THEREIN THE CASUALTIES OCCURRING DURING THE YEAR ENDED DECEMBER 31, 1918. THE CHARACTER SHOWN IN THIS TABLE INDICATES AS FOLLOWS: 0—NONE.

	Electric Employes.								Gas Employes.								Total Employes.		Persons Other Than Employes.		All Persons.	
Title of Corporation.	Power House.		Line.		Shop.		Other.		Works.		Street Dept.		Shop.		Other.							
	Killed.	Injured.	Killed.	Injured.	Killed.	Injured.	Killed.	Injured.	Killed.	Injured.	Killed.	Injured.	Killed.	Injured.	Killed.	Injured.	Killed.	Injured.	Killed.	Injured.	Killed.	Injured.
	1	2	3	4	5	6	7	8	9	10	11	12	13	14	15	16	17	18				
1 Annapolis Public Utilities Co.	0	0	0	0	0	0	0	0	0	0	0	0	0	0	0	0	0	0	0	0	0	0
2 Cambridge Gas, Elec. Lt. & P. Co.	0	0	0	0	0	0	0	0	0	0	0	0	0	0	0	0	0	0	2	1	2	1
3 Chestertown Gas Co.	0	0	0	0	0	0	0	0	0	0	0	0	0	0	0	0	0	0	0	0	0	0
4	0	0	0	0	0	0	0	0	0	0	0	0	0	0	0	0	0	0	0	0	0	0
5 Consol. Gas Elec. Lt. & P. Co.	2	185	0	34	0	93	0	0	0	40	0	50	0	6	0	54	2	462	0	19	2	481
6 Consolidated Public Utilities Co.	0	0	0	0	0	0	0	0	0	0	0	0	0	0	0	0	0	0	0	0	0	0
7 Crisfield Light & Power Co.	0	0	0	0	0	0	0	0	0	0	0	0	0	0	0	0	0	0	0	0	0	0
8 Elkton Gas Light Co.	0	0	0	0	0	0	0	0	0	0	0	0	0	0	0	0	0	0	0	0	0	0
9 Georgetown Gas Lt. Co. of Mfg'y Co.	0	0	0	0	0	0	0	0	0	2	0	0	0	0	0	0	0	2	0	0	0	2
10 H'g'st'n & Fred'k Ry. Co. (E. & G. D.)	0	0	0	0	0	0	0	0	0	0	0	0	0	1	0	0	0	1	0	0	0	1
11 Hagerstown Light & Heat Co.	0	0	0	0	0	0	0	0	0	0	0	0	0	0	0	0	0	0	0	0	0	5
12 Ha'vre de Grace Gas Co.	0	0	0	0	0	0	0	0	0	0	0	0	0	0	0	0	0	0	0	0	0	0
13 Hyattsville Gas & Electric Co.	0	0	0	0	0	0	0	0	0	0	0	2	0	0	0	0	0	2	0	0	0	0
14 Manchester Lighting & Heating Co.	0	0	0	0	0	0	0	0	0	0	0	0	0	0	0	0	0	0	0	0	0	0
15 Washington Gas Lt. Co. of Mfg'y Co.	0	0	0	0	0	0	0	0	0	0	0	0	0	0	0	0	0	0	0	0	0	0
16 *Northern Natural Gas Co.	0	0	0	0	0	0	0	0	0	0	0	0	0	0	0	0	0	0	0	0	0	0
17 *W. Va. & Md. Gas Co. of Md.	0	0	0	0	0	0	0	0	0	0	0	0	0	0	0	0	0	0	0	0	0	0
18 *W. Va. & Md. Gas Co. of W. Va.	0	0	0	0	0	0	0	0	0	0	0	0	0	0	0	0	0	0	0	0	0	0

* Natural Gas Companies.

TABLE No. 39.

WING FOR EACH OF THE WATER CORPORATIONS NAMED THEREIN THE TOTAL AMOUNTS OF ASSETS, OF LIABILITIES AND OF SURPLUS, ON DECEMBER 31, 1918, AND THE TOTAL AMOUNT OF GROSS INCOME, THE DEDUCTIONS FROM GROSS INCOME AND THE NET INCOME FROM THE OPERATIONS OF THE YEAR ENDED DECEMBER 31, 1918.

TOTALS.

TITLE OF CORPORATION.	ASSETS. Total Amount Dec. 31, 1918.	ASSETS. Increase Over Preceding Year.	LIABILITIES. Total Amount Dec. 31, 1918.	LIABILITIES. Increase Over Preceding Year.	SURPLUS OR DEFICIT. Total Amount Dec. 31, 1918.	SURPLUS OR DEFICIT. Increase Over Preceding Year.	GROSS INCOME. Total Amount Dec. 31, 18.	GROSS INCOME. Increase Over Preceding Year.	DEDUCTIONS FROM GROSS INCOME. Total Dec. 31, 1918.	DEDUCTIONS FROM GROSS INCOME. Increase Over Preceding Year.	NET INCOME. Total Amount 1918.	NET INCOME. Increase Over Preceding Year.
	1	2	3	4	5	6	7	8	9	10	11	12
Artesian Water Co.	$256,534	$1,697	$251,108	$59	$5,426	$1,756	$9,982	$730	$6,250	$121	$3,732	$851
Baltimore County Water & Electric Co.	2,786,282	142,196	2,297,964	123,204	488,318	18,992	253,656	45,087	184,611	37,071	69,045	8,015
Bel Air Water & Light Co.	593	16	108,243	780	7,870	705	7,809	1,334	8,604	1,995	795	661
Boonsboro Water Co.	32,694	232	30,241	49	2,353	183	2,038	35	1,821	351	217	370
Braddock Heights Water Co.	27,266	345	24,921	530	2,345	185	2,001	173	2,046	277	95	104
Brooklyn & Curtis Bay L. & W. Co.	195,848	1,424	182,664	1,320	13,184	104	36,848	10,430	36,444	14,319	104	5
Burkittsville Water Co.	3,299	135	2,618	6	651	141	165	13	70	18	95	6
Consolidated Public Utilities Co. W. D.	213,230	5,051	228,419	13,277	15,189	7,326	19,194	5,051	25,274	9,253	6,090	4,202
Dorchester Water Co.	119,683	1,257	119,649	126	34	1,131	27,615	4,814	23,429	5,130	4,186	316
Frostburg Water Co.	16,749	138	11,950		4,799	1,188	1,417	38	1,334	34	83	4
Havre de Grace Water Co.	135,725	3,223	126,167	500	9,558	2,728	14,864	5,107	11,542	2,280	3,322	2,827
Lonaconing Water Co.	137,829	779	110,287	988	27,542	1,767	9,876	122	7,866	2,516	2,010	2,638
Mechanicstown Water Co.	21,522	712	12,750	279	8,772	433	3,737	252	1,474	461	2,263	209
Midland-Elk Lick Water Co.	73,320	345	70,703	300	2,617	45	4,165	18	3,619	165	546	147
Perryville Water Co.	31,072	506	10,210	3	20,862	503	3,906	575	2,856	928	1,050	353
Rognel Heights Water Co.	31,846	687	30,675	165	1,171	-522	3,677	1,932	3,004	1,792	673	140
Roland Park Water Co.	267,539	388	261,480	5,002	6,059	5,890	38,663	*	29,933	2,052	8,730	2,725
Suburban Water Co.	206,650	4,424	204,012	1,301	4,638	3,123	27,220	*	22,360	*	4,860	*
Union Bridge Water Co.	28,159	490	24,448	610	3,711	3,120	3,505	13	2,320	29	1,185	16
Walkersville Water Co.	22,070	221	23,122	233	182	12	1,843	415	582	256	1,261	59

NOTE—Deficit, loss and other reverse this on this title are printed in bold type.

* Asterisk denotes absence of required figures.

Showing for Each of the Water Corporations Named Therein the Total Amo
Classifica

		TOTALS.		
		Assets.		Liabi
TITLE OF CORPORATION.	Total Amount Dec. 31, 1918.	Increase Over Preceding Year.	Total Amount Dec. 31, 1918.
	1	2	3
1 Artesian Water Co.	$256,534	$1,697	$251,108
2 Baltimore County Water & Electric Co.	2,786,282	142,196	2,297,964
3 Bel Air Water & Light Co.	100,373	15	108,243
4 Boonsboro Water Co.	32,594	232	30,241
5 Braddock Heights Water Co.	27,266	345	24,921
6 Brooklyn & Curtis Bay Light & Water Co.	195,848	1,424	182,664
7 Burkittsville Water Co	3,269	135	2,618
8 Consolidated Public Utilities Co., Water Dept.	213,230	5,951	228,419
9 Dorchester Water Co.	119,683	1,257	119,649
10 Frostburg Water Co.	16,749	138	11,950
11 Havre de Grace Water Co.	135,725	3,228	126,167
12 Lonaconing Water Co.	137,829	779	110,297
13 Mechanicstown Water Co.	21,522	712	12,750
14 Midland-Elk Lick Water Co.	73,320	345	70,703
15 Perryville Water Co.	31,072	506	10,210
16 Rognel Heights Water Co	31,846	687	30,675
17 Roland Park Water Co.	267,539	388	261,480
18 Suburban Water Co.	208,650	4,424	204,012
19 Union Bridge Water Co.	28,159	490	24,448
20 Walkersville Water Co.	22,970	221	23,122

| | Details of Assets —Continued. | | Det Liai |
| TITLE OF CORPORATION. | Unextinguished Discount on Securities. | Sundries. | Capital Stock. |
	14	15	16
1 Artesian Water Co.			$155,050
2 Baltimore County Water & Electric Co.	$54,910	$34,297	390,000
3 Bel Air Water & Light Co.			49,500
4 Boonsboro Water Co.			10,000
5 Braddock Heights Water Co.		8	8,500
6 Brooklyn & Curtis Bay Light & Water Co.			100,000
7 Burkittsville Water Co.			2,110
8 Consolidated Public Utilities Co., Water Dept.			102,000
9 Dorchester Water Co.			103,970
10 Frostburg Water Co.			9,950
11 Havre de Grace Water Co.			7,500
12 Lonaconing Water Co.	28		70,000
13 Mechanicstown Water Co.			9,500
14 Midland-Elk Lick Water Co.	22,714		41,500
15 Perryville Water Co.			10,200
16 Rognel Heights Water Co.			15,000
17 Roland Park Water Co.		552	50,000
18 Suburban Water Co.			100,000
19 Union Bridge Water Co.			11,745
20 Walkersville Water Co.			20,000

Note—Deficit, loss and other reverse items on this table are printed in bold type.

No. 40.

THE TOTAL AMOUNT OF LIABILITIES, THE TOTAL AMOUNT OF SURPLUS ON DECEMBER 31, 1918, AND THE ASSETS AND LIABILITIES.

TOTALS—Continued.

SURPLUS OR DEFICIT.		DETAILS OF ASSETS.						
Total Amount Dec. 31, 1918.	Increase Over Preceding Year.	Cost of Plant.	Cash.	Bills and Accounts Receivable.	Materials and Supplies.	Invest-ments.	Sinking Funds.	
5	6	7	8	9	10	11	12	
$5,426	$1,756	$224,229	$3,456	$8,774	....	....	....	
488,138	18,992	2,337,661	37,833	98,059	$3,257	$210,731	$569	
7,870	795	100,205	64	....	103	....	....	
2,353	183	25,545	5	444	....	5,850	750	
2,345	185	27,165	46	24	....	....	....	
13,184	104	187,419	953	6,336	1,140	....	....	
651	141	2,947	162	159	....	....	....	
15,189	7,326	212,535	11,668	4,960	63	7,250	....	
34	1,131	110,091	695	8,897	....	....	....	
4,799	138	15,000	257	1,417	75	....	....	
9,558	2,728	126,435	842	8,148	300	....	....	
27,542	1,767	130,219	221	1,983	377	5,000	....	
8,772	433	17,833	1,341	645	202	1,500	....	
2,617	45	46,097	270	768	144	3,325	....	
20,862	503	29,105	1,445	521	....	....	....	
1,171	522	30,754	849	....	242	....	....	
6,059	5,390	250,277	2,806	4,813	2,232	6,332	429	
4,638	3,123	197,623	....	7,353	1,100	....	2,422	
3,711	120	26,326	511	621	....	....	700	
152	12	22,821	140	289	....	....	....	

DETAILS OF LIABILITIES—Continued.

Accrued Interest on Funded and Other Debt.	Taxes Accrued.	Bills and Accounts Payable.	Customers' Deposits.	Dividends Payable.	Sundries.	Sinking Fund and Optional Reserves.
18	19	20	21	22	23	24
....	....	$8,163	$792	....	....	$102
$8,358	....	197,291	35,265	$11,700	$31,138	406,985
734	....	9,209	....	....	....	....
....	....	10,241	....	....	....	....
194	....	6,727	....	....	....	....
5,296	....	9,397	10,970	....	....	....
....	....	507	....	....	....	....
1,047	....	23,129	....	....	....	225
....	....	15,678	....	....	....	....
....	....	2,000	....	....	....	....
667	....	....	....	....	....	....
788	....	....	....	....	....	....
....	....	....	....	....	....	....
450	....	800	....	....	....	....
....	....	....	....	....	....	....
125	$139	....	....	....	....	....
687	350	5,729	1,127	....	2,197	....
1,840	....	6,172	....	....	....	1,000
....	....	....	....	30	....	....
....	....	140	....	....	....	....

Showing for Each of the Water Corporations Named Therein the Gross Income from
Surplus from the Operations of the Year Ended December 31, 1918. The

	TITLE OF CORPORATION.	TOTALS.		
		Gross Income from All Sources.	Increase Over Preceding Year.	Deductions from Gross Income.
		1	2	3
1	Artesian Water Co...................	$9,982	$730	$6,250
2	Baltimore County Water & Electric Co.............	253,656	45,087	184,611
3	Bel Air Water & Light Co.....................	7,809	1,334	8,604
4	Boonsboro Water Co.....................	2,038	35	1,821
5	Braddock Heights Water Co.............	2,001	173	2,086
6	Brooklyn & Curtis Bay Light & Water Co...........	36,548	10,430	36,444
7	Burkittsville Water Co.............	165	13	70
8	Consolidated Public Utilities Co., Water Dept......	19,194	5,051	25,274
9	Dorchester Water Co..................	27,615	4,814	23,429
10	Frostburg Water Co..................	1,417	38	1,334
11	Havre de Grace Water Co.............	14,864	5,107	11,542
12	Lonaconing Water Co..................	9,876	122	7,866
13	Mechanicstown Water Co..............	3,737	252	1,474
14	Midland-Elk Lick Water Co.............	4,165	18	3,619
15	Perryville Water Co..............	3,906	575	2,856
16	Rognel Heights Water Co..............	3,677	1,932	3,004
17	Roland Park Water Co..............	38,663	673	29,933
18	Suburban Water Co..............	27,220	*	22,360
19	Union Bridge Water Co..............	3,505	13	2,320
20	Walkersville Water Co..............	1,843	415	582

DEDUCTIONS FROM GROSS INCO

	TITLE OF CORPORATION.	OPERATING EXPENSES.		
		Collecting and Pumping Systems.	Distribution.	Repairs.
		13	14	15
1	Artesian Water Co...................	$2,917	0	$543
2	Baltimore County Water & Electric Co...........	57,896	$1,481	17,489
3	Bel Air Water & Light Co..............	2,091	480	89
4	Boonsboro Water Co.............	13	2	214
5	Braddock Heights Water Co.............	485	84	250
6	Brooklyn & Curtis Bay Light & Water Co...........	23,739	911	747
7	Burkittsville Water Co.............	0	0	0
8	Consolidated Public Utilities Co., Water Dept......	13,519	483	493
9	Dorchester Water Co..............	12,911	214	821
10	Frostburg Water Co.............	0	0	115
11	Havre de Grace Water Co.............	5,410	0	710
12	Lonaconing Water Co.............	136	897	982
13	Mechanicstown Water Co.............	0	0	83
14	Midland-Elk Lick Water Co.............	75	154	556
15	Perryville Water Co.............	23	0	132
16	Rognel Heights Water Co.............	1,238	0	0
17	Roland Park Water Co.............	11,210	1,260	1,532
18	Suburban Water Co.............	9,939	0	1,028
19	Union Bridge Water Co.............	983	37	255
20	Walkersville Water Co.............	0	211	0

NOTE—Deficit, loss and other reverse items on this table are printed in bold type.

No. 41.

THE DEDUCTIONS FROM GROSS INCOME, THE NET INCOME, THE APPROPRIATIONS FROM NET INCOME, AND SHOWN IN THIS TABLE INDICATE AS FOLLOWS: 0—NONE; *ABSENCE OF REQUIRED FIGURES.

		TOTALS—Continued.				REVENUE.	
Net Income.	Increase Over Preceding Year.	Appropriations from Net Income.	Increase Over Preceding Year.	Surplus or Deficit.	Increase Over Preceding Year.	Operating Revenue.	No Opera Reve
5	6	7	8	9	10	11	12
$3,732	$851	$1,976	$1,924	$1,756	$1,875	$9,982	0
69,045	8,016	50,053	5,184	18,992	2,832	242,361	$1
796	661	0	0	796	661	7,809	0
217	379	400	168	183	211	1,750	
85	104	100	100	185	204	1,968	
104	3,889	0	0	104	3,889	36,510	
95	5	46	62	141	57	165	0
6,080	4,202	1,246	1,248	7,326	5,448	18,879	
4,186	316	3,055	3,173	1,131	2,857	27,573	
83	4	55	55	138	59	1,417	0
3,322	2,827	594	594	2,728	2,233	14,079	
2,010	2,638	3,777	177	1,767	2,815	9,876	0
2,263	299	1,830	95	433	114	3,737	0
546	147	500	47	45	194	4,165	0
1,050	353	547	1,577	503	1,224	3,903	
673	140	151	104	522	36	3,677	0
8,730	2,725	14,120	6,407	5,390	9,132	38,145	
4,860	*	3,000	*	1,860	*	27,220	0
1,185	16	1,305	352	120	368	3,495	0
1,261	159	1,272	272	12	113	1,843	0

DEDUCTIONS FROM GROSS INCOME—Continued.

NON-OPERATING EXPENSES.

APPROPRIATIONS FROM NET INCOME.

Taxes.	Uncollectible Bills.	Interest on Funded and Other Debt.	Miscellaneous.	Depreciation of Plant.	Sinking Fund and Optional Reserves.	Dividends.	Oth Deduc
17	18	19	20	21	22	23	24
$462	0	0	0	$2,000	0	0	
15,273	$1,198	$47,583	0	29,118	0	$19,500	
305	0	3,002	0	0	0	0	0
67	24	1,087	$4	0	$100	300	0
78	0	938	0	100	0	0	0
1,026	0	3,300	0	0	0	0	0
0	0	40	14	0	0	0	
1,127	0	4,033	1,858	472	0	0	
2,892	564	933	0	976	0	2,079	0
46	0	120	42	0	0	0	
826	0	2,140	0	500	0	0	
739	296	1,625	0	1,500	0	2,100	
672	0	0	0	500	0	1,330	
269	90	1,259	0	500	0	0	0
559	0	0	0	276	0	0	0
202	76	750	0	151	0	0	0
1,192	0	8,486	200	7,944	0	7,500	
674	0	6,043	0	3,000	0	0	0
223	0	600	0	600	0	705	0
293	0	0	0	272	0	1,000	0

TABLE No. 42.

SHOWING FOR EACH OF THE WATER CORPORATIONS NAMED THEREIN THE TOTAL FUNDED DEBT AND CAPITAL STOCK OUTSTANDING ON DECEMBER 31, 1918. (EXCLUSIVE OF SUCH FUNDED DEBT AND CAPITAL STOCK AS ARE HELD BY THE ISSUING CORPORATION), THE RATE PER CENT. AND DATES OF PAYMENT OF INTEREST ON FUNDED DEBT, AND THE RATE PER CENT. AND AMOUNT OF DIVIDENDS DECLARED ON CAPITAL STOCK.

	TITLE OF CORPORATION.	FUNDED DEBT.				INTEREST.		COMMON STOCK.			PREFERRED STOCK.
		Description.	Date.	Term of Years.	Amount Outstanding.	Rate Per Cent.	Dates When Payable.	Amount Outstanding.	Dividends Declared During the Year.	Rate Per Cent.	Amount Outstanding.
		1	2	3	4	5	6	7	8	9	10
1	Artesian Water Company	1st Mtge.	1915	30	$85,000	6	J. & J.	$155,050	$19,500	5	
2	Baltimore County Water & Electric Company	1st Mtge.	906	40	893,000	5	M. & N.	390,000			
3	Bel Air Water & Light Company	1st Mtge.	1891	30	21,400	5	M. & S.	49,500			
		2nd Mtge.	1914	30	2400	5	A. & O.				
		Notes	1911	3	2,800	5	F. & J.				
4	Boonsboro Water Company	Mortgage	1908	20	1000	6	J. & J.	10,000	300	3	
5	Braddock Heights Water Company	Mortgage	1914	10	9,500	6	A. & O.	8,500			
6	Brooklyn & Curtis Bay Light & Water Company	Mortgage	1914	5	5000	8	June 15	100,000			
7	Burkittsville Water Company							2,110			
8	Consolidated Public Utilities Company, Water Department.										
	Westminster Water Company.	1st Mtge.	1902	30	45,000	4	F. & A.	60,000			
	Citizens Water & Power Company.	1st Mtge.	1905	40	40,000	4	A. & O.	400	2,079	2	
		1st Mtge.	1913	20	30,000	0	J. & J.	35,000			
								970			
9	Delmar Water Company	1st Me.	1916	3	8,500	6	Sean.	25,000			
10	Dorchester Water Company	2nd Me.	1900	3	5,500	6	Quart.				
11	Ellicott City Water Company	3rd Me.	909	2	6,000	6	Quart.				
12	Emmitsburg Water Company							12,000	960	8	
13	Frostburg Water Company							9,950			
14	Havre de Grace Water Company	1st Mtge.	1903	20	50,000	4	M. & R.	75,000	2,100	3	
15	Lonaconing Water Company	1st Mtge.	1915	20	25,500	6	F. & A.	70,000	1,330	14	
16	Mechanicstown Water Company							9,500			
17	Midland-Elk Lick Water Company	1st Mtge.	1904	20	23,500	5	M. & S.	41,600			
18	Mountain Lake Water & Light Company	1st Me.	1911	11	13,000	6	J. & J.	42,500			
19	Perryville Water Company							10,200			
20	Port Deposit Water Company	1st Mtge.	1897	20	5,000	6	M. & S.	10,000			
21	Rognel Heights Water Company	1st Me.	1917	40	15,000	5	M. & N.	15,000			
22	Roland Park Water Company	1st Me.	1912	25	165,000	6	J. & D.	50,000	7,500	15	
23	Suburban Water Company	1st Me.	1911	40	92,000	6	M. & S.	100,000			
24	Union Bridge Water Company	1st Me.	1916	20	10,000	6	A. & O.	11,745	705	6	

TABLE No. 42.

SHOWING FOR EACH OF THE WATER CORPORATIONS NAMED THEREIN THE TOTAL FUNDED DEBT AND CAPITAL STOCK OUTSTANDING ON DECEMBER 31, 1918, (EXCLUSIVE OF SUCH FUNDED DEBT AND CAPITAL STOCK AS ARE HELD BY THE ISSUING CORPORATION), THE RATE PER CENT. AND DATES OF PAYMENT OF INTEREST ON FUNDED DEBT, AND THE RATE PER CENT. AND AMOUNT OF DIVIDENDS DECLARED ON CAPITAL STOCK.

	TITLE OF CORPORATION.	FUNDED DEBT.				Interest.		COMMON STOCK.			PREFERRED STOCK.
		Description.	Date.	Term of Years.	Amount Outstanding.	Rate Per Cent.	Dates When Payable.	Amount Outstanding.	Dividends Declared During the Year.	Rate Per Cent.	Amount Outstanding.
		1	2	3	4	5	6	7	8	9	10
1	Artesian Water Company	1st Mtge.	1915	30	$85,000	6	J. & J.	$155,050	$19,500	5	
2	Baltimore County Water & Electric Company	1st Mtge.	1906	40	893,000	5	M. & N.	390,000			
3	Bel Air Water & Light Company	1st Mtge.	1891	30	21,400	5	M. & S.	40,500			
		2nd Mtge.	1914	30	24,600	5	A. & O.				
		Notes	1911		2,800	6	F. & A.				
4	Boonsboro Water Company	Mortgage	1908	20	10,000	5	J. & J.	10,000	300	3	
5	Braddock Heights Water Company	Mortgage	1914	10	9,500	6	A. & O.	8,500			
6	Brooklyn & Curtis Bay Light & Water Company	Mortgage	1914	5	50,000	6	June 15	100,000			
7	Burkittsville Water Company							2,110			
8	Consolidated Public Utilities Company, Water Department.										
	Westminster Water Company	1st Mtge.	1902	30	45,000	4	F. & A.	60,000			
9	Citizens Water & Power Company	1st Mtge.	1905	40	40,000	4	A. & O.	42,000			
		1st Mtge.	1913	20	30,000	6	J. & J.	35,000	2,079	2	
10	Delmar Water Company							103,970			
11	Dorchester Water Company	1st Mtge.	1916	3	8,500	6	Semi-An.	25,000			
		2nd Mtge.	1900	3	5,500	6	Quart.				
	Ellicott City Water Company	3rd Mtge.	1909	2	6,000	6	Quart.				
12	Emmitsburg Water Company.							12,000	960	8	
13	Frostburg Water Company							9,950			
14	Havre de Grace Water Company	1st Mtge.	1903	20	50,000	4	M. & R.	75,000			
15	Lonaconing Water Company	1st Mtge.	1915	20	25,500	6	F. & A.	70,000			
16	Mechanicstown Water Company							9,500	2,100	3	
17	Midland-Elk Lick Water Company	1st Mtge.	1904	20	23,500	5	M. & S.	41,500	1,330	14	
18	Mountain Lake Water & Light Company	1st Mtge.	1911	11	13,000	6	J. & J.	42,500			
19	Perryville Water Company							10,200			
20	Port Deposit Water Company	1st Mtge.	1897	20	5,000	6	M. & S.	10,000			
21	Rognel Heights Water Company	1st Mtge.	1917	40	15,000	5	M. & N.	15,000			
22	Roland Park Water Company	1st Mtge.	1912	25	165,000	6	J. & D.	50,000	7,500	15	
23	Suburban Water Company	1st Mtge.	1911	40	92,000	6	M. & D.	100,900			
24	Union Bridge Water Company	1st Mtge.	1916	20	10,000	6	A. & O.	11,745	705	6	

. SHOWING FOR EACH OF THE WATER CORPORATIONS NAMED THEREIN VARIOUS STATISTICS RELA
THIS TABLE INDICATE AS FOLLOWS

TITLE OF CORPORATION.	SUPPLY SYSTEM.	
	Number of Reservoirs and Stand Pipes.	Capacity in Gallons.
	1	2
1 Artesian Water Co.	1	50,000
2 Baltimore County Water & Electric Co.	10	95,363,000
3 Bel Air Water & Light Co.	2	3,000,000
4 Boonsboro Water Co.	2	225,000
5 Braddock Heights Water Co.	5	478,000
6 Brooklyn & Curtis Bay Light & Water Co.	3	480,000
7 Burkittsville Water Co.	2	40,000
8 Consolidated Public Utilities Co., Water Dept.	4	2,180,000
9 Dorchester Water Co.	1	143,000
10 Frostburg Water Co.	1	200,000
11 Havre de Grace Water Co.	1	2,500,000
12 Lonaconing Water Co.	3	7,000,000
13 Mechanicstown Water Co.	2	200,000
14 Midland-Elk Lick Water Co.	1	3,000,000
15 Perryville Water Co.	1	3,000,000
16 Rognel Heights Water Co	6	168,500
17 Roland Park Water Co.	4	1,446,278
18 Suburban Water Co.	3	170,000
19 Union Bridge Water Co.	1	420,000
20 Walkersville Water Co.	1	500,000

TITLE OF CORPORATION.	PUMPING SYSTEM—Cor	
	Number of Water Wheels.	Rated Horse Power.
	12	13
1 Artesian Water Co.	0	0
2 Baltimore County Water & Electric Co.	2	400
3 Bel Air Water & Light Co.	0	0
4 Boonsboro Water Co.	0	0
5 Braddock Heights Water Co.	0	0
6 Brooklyn & Curtis Bay Light & Water Co.	0	0
7 Burkittsville Water Co.	0	0
8 Consolidated Public Utilities Co., Water Dept.	1	15
9 Dorchester Water Co.	0	0
10 Frostburg Water Co.	0	0
11 Havre de Grace Water Co.	0	0
12 Lonaconing Water Co.	0	0
13 Mechanicstown Water Co.	0	0
14 Midland-Elk Lick Water Co.	0	0
15 Perryville Water Co.	0	0
16 Rognel Heights Water Co	0	0
17 Roland Park Water Co.	0	0
18 Suburban Water Co.	0	0
19 Union Bridge Water Co.	0	0
20 Walkersville Water Co.	0	0

No. 43.

Y AND SERVICE OF THE SAME, FOR THE YEAR ENDED DECEMBER 31, 1918. THE CHARACTERS SHOWN ...ENCE OF REQUIRED FIGURES.

| | PLY SYSTEM—Cont. | | | PUMPING SYSTEM. | | | |
| | Purification System Used. | Number of Pumps. | Rated Daily Capacity, Gallons. | Number of Boilers. | Rated Horse Power. | Number of Steam or Gas Engines. | Rated Horse Po... |
4	5	6	7	8	9	10	11
*	0	7	126,900	0	0	5	
325	Sand & Chem.	6	21,000,000	5	750	3	
7	0	0	0	0	0	1	
2	0	0	0	0	0		0
*	Chlorine	2	300,000	0	0	1	
*	0	2	100,000	2	300	2	
*	0	0	0	0	0	0	0
*	Slow Sand	4	1,800,000	2	180	1	
*	0	4	1,500,000	1	80	1	
2	0	0	0	0	0	0	0
0	Chlorine	4	*	2	165	0	0
10	0	1	72,000	1	20	1	
0	0	0	0	0	0	0	0
4	0	0	0	0	0	0	0
6	Chemical	0	0	0	0	0	0
0	0	1	221,760	0	0	2	
0	0	5	1,042,560	0	0	1	
0	Chemical	5	*	0	0	4	
0	Chemical	2	120,000	0	0	2	
*	0	0	0	0	0	0	0

DISTRIBUTION SYSTEM.

| h of ..., ... | Sizes of Mains, Inches. | Number of Main Pipe Valves. | Number of Fire Hydrants. | Number of Consumers. | Number of Services. | Number of Meters. | Num Fou and |
	16	17	18	19	20	21	
7.75	2 to 6	56	21	392	392	390	0
151.94	½ to 20	944	451	11,031	11,031	4,996	
8.00	4 to 12	48	48	357	357	357	
3.90	2 to 8	15	20	121	121	0	0
2.65	2 to 6	20	19	75	75	73	
14.58	4 to 8	65	73	974	974	974	
.80	4	5	0	18	18	0	0
19.63	1 to 10	131	91	1,014	1,014	555	
*	1 to 10	67	48	1,991	1,991	79	
17.84	½ to 8	14	1	160	145	0	0
12.50	4 to 10	*	58	659	*	257	0
3.60	4 to 12	46	34	817	*	43	0
4.00	2 to 6	*	29	217	212	4	0
6.18	1 to 10	17	11	438	*	8	0
4.40	4 to 12	17	11	202	136	4	0
.55	4	26	4	76	74	74	0
18.34	½ to 10	260	120	1,083	1,083	1,071	0
9.70	2 to 6	*	19	1,349	1,349	1,349	0
*	4 to 8	21	16	450	450	4	0
6.00	4 to 8	*	27	625	125	25	0

TABLE No. 44.

SHOWING FOR EACH OF THE WATER CORPORATIONS NAMED THEREIN THE CASUALTIES, CLASSIFIED AS TO EMPLOYEES AND OTHERS, OCCURRING DURING THE YEAR ENDED DECEMBER 31, 1918. THE CHARACTER SHOWN IN THIS TABLE INDICATES AS FOLLOWS: 0—NONE.

	TITLE OF CORPORATION.	Collecting System.		Pumping System.		Distribution System.		Total Employees.		Persons Other Than Employees.		All Persons.	
		Killed.	Injured.	Killed.	Injured.	Killed.	Injured.	Killed.	Injured.	Killed.	Injured.	Killed.	Injured.
		1	2	3	4	5	6	7	8	9	10	11	12
1	Artesian Water Co.	0	0	0	0	0	0	0	0	0	0	0	0
2	Baltimore County Water & Electric Co.	0	0	0	0	0	0	0	0	0	0	0	0
3	Bel Air Water & Light Co.	0	0	0	0	0	0	0	0	0	0	0	0
4	Boonsboro Water Co.	0	0	0	0	0	0	0	0	0	0	0	0
5	Braddock Heights Water Co.	0	0	0	0	0	0	0	0	0	0	0	0
6	Brooklyn & Curtis Bay Light & Water Co.	0	0	0	0	0	0	0	0	0	0	0	0
7	Burkittsville Water Co.	0	0	0	0	0	0	0	0	0	0	0	0
8	Consolidated Public Utilities Co., Water Dept.	0	0	0	0	0	0	0	0	0	0	0	0
9	Dorchester Water Co.	0	0	0	0	0	0	0	0	0	0	0	0
10	Frostburg Water Co.	0	0	0	0	0	0	0	0	0	0	0	0
11	Havre de Grace Water Co.	0	0	0	0	0	0	0	0	0	0	0	0
12	Lonaconing Water Co.	0	0	0	0	0	0	0	0	0	0	0	0
13	Mechanicstown Water Co.	0	0	0	0	0	0	0	0	0	0	0	0
14	Midland-Elk Lick Water Co.	0	0	0	0	0	0	0	0	0	0	0	0
15	Perryville Water Co.	0	0	0	0	0	0	0	0	0	0	0	0
16	Rognel Heights Water Co.	0	0	0	0	0	0	0	0	0	0	0	0
17	Roland Park Water Co.	0	0	0	0	0	0	0	0	0	0	0	0
18	Suburban Water Co.	0	0	0	0	0	0	0	0	0	0	0	0
19	Union Bridge Water Co.	0	0	0	0	0	0	0	0	0	0	0	0
20	Walkersville Water Co.	0	0	0	0	0	0	0	0	0	0	0	0

TABLE No. 45.

Each of the Telephone and Telegraph Corporations Named Therein the Total Amounts of Assets, of Liabilities and of Surplus, on December 31, 1918, and the Total Amount of Gross Income, the Deductions from Gross Income and the Net Income from the Operations of the Year Ended December 31, 1918, and the Increase or Decrease from the Preceding Year.

Names of Corporation.	Assets — Total Amount Dec. 31, 1918. (1)	Assets — Increase Over Preceding Year. (2)	Liabilities — Total Amount Dec. 31, 1918. (3)	Liabilities — Increase Over Preceding Year. (4)	Surplus or Deficit — Total Amount Dec. 31, 1918. (5)	Surplus or Deficit — Increase Over Preceding Year. (6)	Gross Income — Total Amt Dec. 31, 18. (7)	Gross Income — Increase Over Preceding Year. (8)	Deductions from Gross Income — Total Amt Dec. 31, 1918. (9)	Deductions — Increase Over Preceding Year. (10)	Net Income — Total Amount Dec. 31, 1918. (11)	Net Income — Increase Over Preceding Year. (12)
rmers' Telephone Co.	$31,502	$1,978	$26,351	$767	$5,151	$1,211	$8,271	$1,368	$6,924	1,528	$1,346	$390
ake & Potomac Tel. Co.	18,494,408	2,124,157	17,836,923	2,526,175	657,485	402,018	4,826,523	424,337	4,068,244	7205	757,979	296,468
land Valley Telephone Co.	139,831	1,879	138,600	20	1,231	1,859	3,312	3,440	3,316	2,060	4	1,390
County Telephone Co.	23,375	188	17,842	237	5,533	49	4,537		4,488		49	*
d Telephone Co. of Balto.	2,557,213	741	8,454,495	61,922	897,282	62,663	25,318	630	87,981	57,062	62,963	56,432
d & Del. Tel. & Tel. Co.	14,298		13,991		295	51	1,989	259	1,990	90	51	349
lle Telephone Co.	9,335	835	7,665	520	1,670	315	2,579	96	1,864	243	715	339
elegraph-Cable Co.	2,040,209	785,663	2,039,219	778,796	990	11,867	2,181,595	301,615	1,703,827	13054	477,768	139
Anne Telephone Co.	465	368	2,553	259	1,932	100	1,343	290	1,234	192	109	98
orchester Telephone Co.	388		4,548	*	2,285	*	2,351	*	1,881	*	970	*
elephone Co.	8,861	1,042	8,959		96	384	2,078	6	2,187	925	59	920

(*) denotes absence of required figures.

Deficit, loss and other reverse items on this table are printed in bold type.

TABLE No. 44.

SHOWING FOR EACH OF THE WATER CORPORATIONS NAMED THEREIN THE CASUALTIES, CLASSIFIED AS TO EMPLOYEES AND OTHERS, OCCURRING DURING THE YEAR ENDED DECEMBER 31, 1918. THE CHARACTER SHOWN IN THIS TABLE INDICATES AS FOLLOWS: 0—NONE.

TITLE OF CORPORATION.	Collecting System.		Pumping System.		Distribution System.		Total Employees.		Persons Other Than Employees.		All Persons.	
	Killed.	Injured.	Killed.	Injured.	Killed.	Injured.	Killed.	Injured.	Killed.	Injured.	Killed.	Injured.
	1	2	3	4	5	6	7	8	9	10	11	12
1 Artesian Water Co.	0	0	0	0	0	0	0	0	0	0	0	0
2 Baltimore County Water & Electric Co.	0	0	0	0	0	0	0	0	0	0	0	0
3 Bel Air Water & Light Co.	0	0	0	0	0	0	0	0	0	0	0	0
4 Boonsboro Water Co.	0	0	0	0	0	0	0	0	0	0	0	0
5 Braddock Heights Water Co.	0	0	0	0	0	0	0	0	0	0	0	0
6 Brooklyn & Curtis Bay Light & Water Co.	0	0	0	0	0	0	0	0	0	0	0	0
7 Burkittsville Water Co.	0	0	0	0	0	0	0	0	0	0	0	0
8 Consolidated Public Utilities Co., Water Dept.	0	0	0	0	0	0	0	0	0	0	0	0
9 Dorchester Water Co.	0	0	0	0	0	0	0	0	0	0	0	0
10 Frostburg Water Co.	0	0	0	0	0	0	0	0	0	0	0	0
11 Havre de Grace Water Co.	0	0	0	0	0	0	0	0	0	0	0	0
12 Lonaconing Water Co.	0	0	0	0	0	0	0	0	0	0	0	0
13 Mechanicstown Water Co.	0	0	0	0	0	0	0	0	0	0	0	0
14 Midland-Elk Lick Water Co.	0	0	0	0	0	0	0	0	0	0	0	0
15 Perryville Water Co.	0	0	0	0	0	0	0	0	0	0	0	0
16 Roqnel Heights Water Co.	0	0	0	0	0	0	0	0	0	0	0	0
17 Roland Park Water Co.	0	0	0	0	0	0	0	0	0	0	0	0
18 Suburban Water Co.	0	0	0	0	0	0	0	0	0	0	0	0
19 Union Bridge Water Co.	0	0	0	0	0	0	0	0	0	0	0	0
20 Walkersville Water Co.	0	0	0	0	0	0	0	0	0	0	0	0

TABLE No. 45.

EACH OF THE TELEPHONE AND TELEGRAPH CORPORATIONS NAMED THEREIN THE TOTAL AMOUNTS OF ASSETS, OF LIABILITIES AND OF SURPLUS, ON DECEMBER 31, 1918, AND THE TOTAL AMOUNT OF GROSS INCOME, THE DEDUCTIONS FROM GROSS INCOME AND THE NET INCOME FROM THE OPERATIONS OF THE YEAR ENDED DECEMBER 31, 1918, AND THE INCREASES OR DECREASES FROM THE PRECEDING YEAR.

NAME OF CORPORATION.	ASSETS. (TOTALS)		LIABILITIES.		SURPLUS OR DEFICIT		GROSS INCOME. (TOTALS)		DEDUCTIONS FROM GROSS INCOME.		NET INCOME.	
	Total Amount Dec. 31, 1918.	Increase Over Preceding Year.	Total Amount Dec. 31, 1918.	Increase Over Preceding Year.	Total Amount Dec. 31, 1918.	Increase Over Preceding Year.	Total Amount Dec. 31, 1918.	Increase Over Preceding Year.	Total Amount Dec. 31, 1918.	Increase Over Preceding Year.	Total Amount Dec. 31, 1918.	Increase Over Preceding Year.
	1	2	3	4	5	6	7	8	9	10	11	12
rmers' Telephone Co....	$31,502	$1,978	$26,351	$767	$5,151	$1,211	$8,271	$1,368	$6,924	$1,728	$1,346	$360
ake & Potomac Tel. Co.	18,494,408	2,124,157	17,836,923	2,526,175	657,485	402,018	4,826,223	424,337	4,068,244	720,805	757,979	206,468
land Valley Telephone Co.	139,831	1,879	188,000	20	1,231	1,859	3,312	3,440	3,316	2,060	4	1,380
County Telephone Co.	23,375	188	17,842	237	5,533	49	4,537	*	4,488	*	49	*
d Telephone Co. of Balto.	2,557,213	741	3,454,495	61,922	897,282	62,663	25,318	630	87,981	57,062	62,663	56,432
d & Del. Tel. & Tel. Co.	11,286	......	13,991	51	295	51	1,030	259	1,990	90	51	349
lle Telephone Co.	9,335	835	7,665	520	1,670	315	2,579	96	1,864	243	715	339
elegraph-Cable Co.	2,040,209	785,663	2,039,219	773,796	1,867	11,867	2,181,595	301,615	1,703,827	301,754	477,768	139
Anne Telephone Co.	4,485	308	2,653	259	1,932	109	1,343	280	1,234	192	109	88
orchester Telephone Co.	6,853	*	2,548	*	2,285	*	2,351	*	1,381	*	970	*
elephone Co.	8,861	1,042	8,950	658	98	384	2,078	5	2,137	925	59	920

k (*) denotes absence of required figures.

Deficit, loss and other reverse items on this table are printed in bold type.

TAB

		Totals.		
		Assets.		Liab
TITLE OF CORPORATION.		Total Amount Dec. 31, 1918.	Increase Over Preceding Year.	Total Amount Dec. 31, 1918.
		1	2	3
1	Cecil Farmers' Telephone Co...............	$31,502	$1,978	$26,35
2	Chesapeake & Potomac Telephone Co........	18,494,408	2,124,157	17,836,
3	Cumberland Valley Telephone Co............	139,	1,579	138,
4	Garrett County Telephone Co...............	23,531	198	17,
5	Maryland Telephone Co. of Baltimore.......	2,557,275	741	3,454,
6	Maryland & Delaware Telephone & Telegraph Co...	14,266	....	13,
7	Poolesville Telephone Co...................	9,335	835	7,
8	Postal Telegraph-Cable Co.................	2,040,209	785,663	2,039,
9	Princess Anne Telephone Co................	4,485	368	2,
10	South Dorchester Telephone Co.............	6,833	*	4,
11	Union Telephone Co.......................	8,861	1,042	8,

		Details of Assets—Cont.		
TITLE OF CORPORATION.		Sinking Fund and Optional Reserves.	Special Deposits and Pre-payments.	Sundri
		12	13	14
1	Cecil Farmers' Telephone Co...............	....	....	....
2	Chesapeake & Potomac Telephone Co........	....	$29,058	$13,
3	Cumberland Valley Telephone Co............	....	....	....
4	Garrett County Telephone Co...............	....	....	....
5	Maryland Telephone Co. of Baltimore.......	....	13	....
6	Maryland & Delaware Telephone & Telegraph Co...	*	....	....
7	Poolesville Telephone Co...................	....	4,096	....
8	Postal Telegraph-Cable Co.................	....	....	....
9	Princess Anne Telephone Co................	....	....	....
10	South Dorchester Telephone Co.............	$1,078	....	....
11	Union Telephone Co.......................	....	....	....

* Denotes required figures not given.

Note—Deficit, loss and other reverse items on this table are printed in bold type.

No. 46.

Assets, the Total Amount of Liabilities and the Surplus on December 31, 1918, and the Class and Liabilities.

	TOTALS—Cont.			DETAILS OF ASSETS.				
LIABILITIES —Cont.	SURPLUS OR DEFICIT.							
Increase Over Preceding Year.	Total Amount Dec. 31, 1918.	Increase Over Preceding Year.	Cost of Plant.	Cash.	Bills and Accounts Receivable.	Materials and Supplies.	In
4	5	6	7	8	9	10	
$767	$5,151	$1,211	$28,108	$1,376	$1,585	$433	....
2,526,175	657,485	402,018	17,072,955	125,356	709,314	544,284	.
29	1,231	1,889	135,449	25	200	157	
237	5,533	49	19,143	4,911	4,182	....	.
61,922	897,222	62,663	2,473,196	479	2	83,520	....
51	295	51	14,286	....	....	....	....
520	1,670	315	3,930	282	1,027	....	....
773,796	990	11,867	50,000	107,055	1,880,170	2,984	....
259	1,932	109	3,801	28	656	....	....
•	2,285	•	4,290	1,315	....	150	....
658	98	384	7,014	930	800	116	....

DETAILS OF LIABILITIES.

Capital Stock.	Funded Debt.	Interest Accrued on Funded and Other Debt.	Taxes Accrued and Unpaid.	Bills and Accounts Payable.	Subscribers' Deposits.	Dividends Payable.	Sinking Fund and Optional Reserves.	
15	16	17	18	19	20	21	22	
$13,525	$1,500	....	....	$4,059		....	$319,736	3,
10,000	....	....	$335,092	13,833,641	$9,215	....	....	
138,600	....	....	....	....	....	....	....	..
16,000	....	....	....	1,842	....	....	....	..
1,000,000	....	....	17	2,454,478	....	....	....	..
11,120	....	....	....	2,871	....	....	....	
3,930	....	....	....	120	....	....	....	
50,000	....	....	....	613,619	....	....	....	1,
1,000	....	....	314	840	....	....	....	
3,470	....	....	....	....	....	....	....	
6,500	....	....	....	459	....	....	....	

TA

SHOWING FOR EACH OF THE TELEPHONE AND TELEGRAPH CORPORATIONS NAMED THEREIN THE GROSS
INCOME AND THE SURPLUS FROM THE O

		TOTALS.		
TITLE OF CORPORATION.		Gross Income from all Sources.	Deductions from Gross Income.	Net In
		1	2	3
1	Cecil Farmers' Telephone Co.	$8,271	$6,924	$
2	Chesapeake & Potomac Telephone Co.	4,826,223	4,068,244	75
3	Cumberland Valley Telephone Co.	3,312	3,316	
4	Garrett County Telephone Co.	4,537	4,488	
5	Maryland Telephone Co. of Baltimore	25,318	87,981	
6	Maryland & Delaware Telephone & Telegraph Co.	1,939	1,990	
7	Poolesville Telephone Co.	2,579	1,864	
8	Postal Telegraph-Cable Co.	2,181,595	1,703,827	4
9	Princess Anne Telephone Co.	1,343	1,234	
10	South Dorchester Telephone Co.	2,351	1,381	
11	Union Telephone Co.	2,078	2,137	

		DEDUCTIONS FROM GROSS INCO		
TITLE OF CORPORATION.		General Expense.	Taxes.	Unco B
		11	12	
1	Cecil Farmers' Telephone Co.	$549	$452	
2	Chesapeake & Potomac Telephone Co.	445,861	361,024	1
3	Cumberland Valley Telephone Co.	67	339	
4	Garrett County Telephone Co.	14	118	....
5	Maryland Telephone Co. of Baltimore	3,167	404	....
6	Maryland & Delaware Telephone & Telegraph Co.	26	46	....
7	Poolesville Telephone Co.	34	153	....
8	Postal Telegraph-Cable Co.	93,497	46,099	....
9	Princess Anne Telephone Co.	70	146	
10	South Dorchester Telephone Co.	....	236	....
11	Union Telephone Co.	144	109	....

NOTE—Deficit, loss and other reverse items on this table are printed in bold type.

No. 47.

FROM ALL SOURCES, THE DEDUCTIONS FROM GROSS INCOME, THE NET INCOME, THE APPROPRIATIONS FROM
OF THE YEAR ENDED DECEMBER 31, 1918.

TOTALS—Cont.		REVENUE.		DEDUCTIONS FROM GROSS INCOME.		
Appropriations from Net Income.	Surplus or Deficit.	Operating Revenue.	Non-Operating Revenue.	Traffic Expense.	Repairs.	Co E
4	5	6	7	8	9	
$135	$1,211	$8,271	....	$3,046	$2,236	
1,159,997	402,018	4,799,000	$27,223	1,341,690	586,208	
1,855	1,859	3,312	....	1,141	1,241	
....	49	4,537	....	2,140	1,852	
....	62,633	25,227	90	225	140	
400	51	1,939	....	....	1,918	....
475,000	315	2,579	....	900	657	
....	2,768	1,739,024	442,571	1,290,649	270,718	....
....	109	1,343	....	807	199	
325	970	2,351	....	590	565	
	384	2,078	....	478	1,406	....

DEDUCTIONS FROM GROSS INCOME—Cont.			APPROPRIATIONS FROM NET INCOME.			
Interest on Funded Debt.	Interest on Unfunded Debt.	Sundries.	Depreciation of Plant.	Sinking Fund and Optional Reserves.	Dividends Declared.	Sun
14	15	16	17	18	19	20
$38	$100	$309	$136	....	....	
....	730,678	3,595	558,892	....	$600,000	
....	....	....	1,855	....	....	
....	48	....	....	....	....	
....	84,041	....	....	....	....	
....	....	....	....	....	....	
....	....	....	400	....	....	
....	....	....	475,000	....	....	
....	....	....	....	....	....	
....	....	....	....	....	....	
....	....	....	....	....	325	....

TABLE No. 48.

Showing for Each of the Telephone and Telegraph Corporations Named Therein the Total Funded Debt and Capital Stock Outstanding on December 31, 1918 (Exclusive of Such Funded Debt and Capital Stock as are Held by the Issuing Corporation), the Rate Per Cent. and Dates of Payment of Interest on Funded Debt, and the Rate Per Cent. and Amount of Dividends Declared on Capital Stock.

Title of Corporation	Funded Debt				Interest		Common Stock			Preferred Stock
	Description	Date	Term of Years	Amount Outstanding	Rate Per Cent.	Dates Payable	Amount Outstanding	Dividends Declared During Year	Rate Per Cent.	Amount Outstanding
	1	2	3	4	5	6	7	8	9	10
1 Cecil Farmers' Telephone Co.	Mortgage	1917	5	$1,500	5	J. & D.	$18,525	600,000	6,000	
2 Chesapeake & Potomac Telephone Co.							10,000			
3 Cumberland Valley Telephone Co.							138,600			
4 Garrett County Telephone Co.										16,000
5 Maryland Telephone Co. of Baltimore							1,000,000			
6 Maryland & Delaware Telephone & Tel. Co.							11,120			
7 Poolesville Telephone Co.							8,980			
8 Postal Telegraph-Cable Co.							50,000			
9 Princess Anne Telephone Co.							1,000			
10 South Dorchester Telephone Co.							8,470	325	5	
11 Union Telephone Co.							6,500			

T

TITLE OF CORPORATION.	STATIONS.		E
	Exchange Stations.	Private Branch Stations.	
	1	2	
1 Cecil Farmers' Telephone Co.	379	0	
2 Chesapeake & Potomac Telephone Co.	81,870	23,461	
3 Cumberland Valley Telephone Co.	172	0	
4 Garrett County Telephone Co.	440	0	
5 Maryland Telephone Co. of Baltimore.	0	0	
6 Maryland & Delaware Telephone & Telegraph Co.	0	0	
7 Poolesville Telephone Co.	0	0	
8 Postal Telegraph-Cable Co.	0	0	
9 Princess Anne Telephone Co.	86	0	
10 South Dorchester Telephone Co.	1	0	
11 Union Telephone Co.	130	0	

TITLE OF CORPORATION.	PLANT MILES	
	Miles of Underground Wire.	
	Exchange.	Toll.
	13	14
1 Cecil Farmers' Telephone Co.	0	0
2 Chesapeake & Potomac Telephone Co.	194,012	10,774
3 Cumberland Valley Telephone Co.	0	0
4 Garrett County Telephone Co.	0	0
5 Maryland Telephone Co. of Baltimore.	0	0
6 Maryland & Delaware Telephone & Telegraph Co.	0	0
7 Poolesville Telephone Co.	0	0
8 Postal Telegraph-Cable Co.	0	0
9 Princess Anne Telephone Co.	0	0
10 South Dorchester Telephone Co.	0	0
11 Union Telephone Co.	0	0

o. 49.

ITISTICS FOR THE YEAR ENDED DECEMBER 31, 1918. THE CHARACTERS SHOWN IN THIS TABLE INDICATE A ENCE OF REQUIRED FIGURES.

	STATIONS—Cont.				PLANT MILEAGE.			
Total Owned.	Service Stations.	Private Line Stations.	Connected Stations.	Total All Stations.	Miles of Poles.		Miles of Aerial	
					Exchange.	Toll.	Exchange.	T
4	5	6	7	8	9	10	11	
397	0	0	0	397	31	9	373	
117,228	2,182	1,382	898	121,690	3,386	1,740	94,361	25,
172	0	0	0	172	17	77	469	
440	0	0	0	440	35	0	500	0
0	0	3	0	3	63	123	698	69
0	14		0	14	55	0	116	0
0	0	0	0	0	338	0	5,079	0
89	90	0	0	179	30	0	73	0
1	0	0	57	58	45	0	45	0
130	0	0	0	130	68	0	295	0

MILE—Cont.	NUMBER OF EXCHANGES.						
files of bmarine Wire.	Having Over 5,000 Stations.	Having From 1,000 to 5,000.	Having From 500 to 1,000.	Having From 300 to 500.	Having From 100 to 300.	Having Less than 100.	Total.
Toll.							
16	17	18	19	20	21	22	23
0	0	0	0	1	0	0	
360	1	10	13	14	58	21	11
0	0	0	0	0	1	0	
0	0	0	0	0	1	11	1
0	0	0,	0	0	0	0	
0	0	0	0	0	0	0	
0	0	0	0	0	1	0	
0	0	0	0	0	0	0	
0	0	0	0	0	1	1	
0	0	0	0	0	1	0	

TABLE No. 50.

SHOWING FOR EACH OF THE TELEPHONE AND TELEGRAPH CORPORATIONS NAMED THEREIN, THE CASUALTIES, CLASSIFIED AS TO EMPLOYEES AND OTHERS, FOR THE YEAR ENDED DECEMBER 31, 1918. THE CHARACTER SHOWN IN THIS TABLE INDICATES AS FOLLOWS: 0—NONE.

TITLE OF CORPORATION.	Exchange Lines.		Toll Lines.		Exchange Operator and Clerks.		Other Employees.		Persons Other Than Employees.		All Persons	
	Killed.	Injured.	Killed.	Injured.	Killed.	Injured.	Killed.	Injured.	Killed.	Injured.	Killed.	Injured.
	1	2	3	4	5	6	7	8	9	10	11	12
1 Cecil Farmers' Telephone Co	0	0	0	0	0	0	0	0	0	0	0	0
2 Chesapeake & Potomac Telephone Co	2	117	1	33	0	32	0	87	0	27	3	296
3 Cumberland Valley Telephone Co	0	0	0	0	0	0	0	0	0	0	0	0
4 Garrett County Telephone Co	0	0	0	0	0	0	0	0	0	0	0	0
5 Maryland Telephone Co. of Baltimore	0	0	0	0	0	0	0	0	0	0	0	0
6 Maryland & Delaware Telephone & Telegraph Co	0	0	0	0	0	0	0	0	0	0	0	0
7 Poolesville Telephone Co	0	0	0	0	0	0	0	0	0	0	0	0
8 Postal Telegraph-Cable Co	0	0	0	0	0	0	0	0	0	0	0	0
9 Princess Anne Telephone Co	0	0	0	0	0	0	0	0	0	0	0	0
10 South Dorchester Telephone Co	0	0	0	0	0	0	0	0	0	0	0	0
11 Union Telephone Co	0	0	0	0	0	0	0	0	0	0	0	0

TA

SHOWING FOR EACH OF THE EXPRESS CORPORATIONS NAMED THEREIN THE

TITLE OF CORPORATION.	INVESTMENT.			
	Real Property and Equipment.	Miscellaneous Physical Property.	Stocks of Other Companies.	Bond; Oth Com
	1	2	3	
1 *Adams Express Company..................	$10,339,362	$11,042	$17,933,569	$21,162
2 *American Express Company...............	19,531,947	2,051,078	3,876,873	9,784
3 *Southern Express Company...............	2,534,327	31,998	179,200	183
4 *Wells Fargo & Company..................	11,702,134	843,326	5,696,620	12,443
5 †American Railway Express Company, Inc....	29,708,351	....	....	2,100

TITLE OF CORPORATION.	CURRENT ASSETS—Continued.			
	Miscellaneous Accounts Receivable.	Materials and Supplies.	Interest, Rents and Dividends Receivable.	Oth
	13	14	15	
1 *Adams Express Company..................	$1,480,357	$233,935	$230,594	$341
2 *American Express Company...............	6,212,300	629,493	199,668	84
3 *Southern Express Company...............	360,197	73,432	44,192	
4 *Wells Fargo & Company..................	1,741,586	355,781	221,095	453
5 †American Railway Express Company, Inc....	11,811,776	1,506,926	46,786	137

* Report of separate companies for 6 months ended June 30, 1918.
† Report of American Railway Express Company, Inc., for 6 months ended December 31, 1918.

1.

	Investment—Continued.			Current Assets.			
of r 'es.	Advances to Affiliated Companies.	Total Investment.	Cash.	Special Deposits.	Loans and Notes Receivable.	Traffic Balances Receivable.	Net Balances Due from Agents and Messengers.
	6	7	8	9	10	11	12
202	$467,316	$50,654,026	$4,679,785	$28,158	$65,000	$918,118	$4,816,741
273	....	36,354,160	3,391,535	242,772	5,321	108,637	10,711,153
....	....	2,929,325	2,677,491	....	1,450,000	186,818	2,269,549
996	....	32,258,162	8,205,645	....	564,130	388,982	3,636,809
....	....	31,808,886	20,801,312	129,014	....	139,205	13,397,045

As- nt.	Deferred and Unadjusted Debits.						
t	Insurance and Other Reserve Funds.	Advance Payments on Contracts.	Rent and Insurance Premiums Paid in Advance.	Taxes Paid in Advance.	Other Deferred and Unadjusted Debits.	Total Deferred and Unadjusted Debits.	Total Assets.
	18	19	20	21	22	23	24
1	....	....	$51,998	....	$33,410	$85,408	$63,533,477
64	$438,168	....	36,606	$110,553	1,064,118	1,649,445	59,589,170
23	....	....	9,237	....	8,030	17,266	10,008,315
74	....	$1,046,666	36,709	....	162,017	1,245,392	49,070,629
:61	....	....	265,260	33,236	3,125,008	3,423,503	83,201,750

TABLE

SHOWING FOR EACH OF THE EXPRESS CORPORATIONS NAMED THEREIN THE AMOUNT OF

TITLE OF CORPORATION.	Capital Stock.	Funded Debt.	CURRENT LIABILITIES. Loans and Notes Payable.
	1	2	3
press Company	$10,000,000	$19,733,000	$5,450,000
Express Company	17,182,600		8,000
Express Company			
go & Company	23,967,400		1,500,000
Railway Express Company, Inc.	34,719,548		

TITLE OF CORPORATION.	CURRENT LIABILITIES —Cont. Other Current Liabilities.	DEFERRED LIABILITIES AND UNADJUSTED CREDITS. Liability on Account of Provident Funds.	Liability on Account of Fidelity and Indemnity Funds.
	12	13	14
press Company	$1,079,126	$23,099,791	
Express Company			$52,296
Express Company	197,433	13,379	49,641
& Company	456,798		
y Express Company, Inc.	3,229,568		

of separate companies for 6 months ended June 30, 1918.
of American Railway Express Company, Inc., for 6 months ended December 31, 1918.

o. 52.

s on DECEMBER 31, 1918, AND THE CLASSIFICATION OF SUCH LIABILITIES.

CURRENT LIABILITIES—Continued.

Traffic Balances Payable.	Audited Accounts and Wages Unpaid.	Miscellaneous Accounts Payable.	Matured Interest, Dividends and Rents Unpaid.	Unpaid Money Orders, Cheques and Drafts.	Express Privilege Liabilities.	Estimated Tax Liability.	Unma Interest, Dividends and Rents Payable.
4	5	6	7	8	9	10	11
$439,725	$2,191,169	$101,811	$44,008	$1,599,146	$11,894,811	$109,508	$190,
377,355	1,869,362	8,980,216	32,342	11,407,430	6,717,640	203,377	269,7
46,015	446,339	219,139	....	1,069,229	1,924,901	86,228	....
48,540	3,653,118	....	21,285	4,070,576	7,717,286	254,996	371,0
273,970	11,674,744	3,334,202	....	....	21,111,935	362,429	....

DEFERRED LIABILITIES AND UNADJUSTED CREDITS—Continued. | CORPORATE SURPLUS.

Operating Insurance Reserves.	Accrued Depreciation, Buildings.	Accrued Depreciation, Equipment.	Other Deferred and Unadjusted Credits.	Reserves from Income and Surplus.	Profit and Loss Balance.	Corporate Surplus.	Total Liabilities.
15	16	17	18	19	20	21	22
1,996,799	$279,071	$2,888,231	$58,732	$2,690,992	$1,904,564	$4,595,556	$63,533,47
1,101,657	2,105,651	3,968,475	590,924	....	4,718,091	4,718,091	59,589,17
555,226	254,634	786,643	7,034	....	4,380,471	4,380,471	10,008,31
1,496,580	358,960	2,544,154	62,115	....	2,547,782	2,547,782	49,070,6
7,302,640	134,968	1,055,196	2,548	....	....	....	83,201,7

TABLE

SHOWING FOR EACH OF THE EXPRESS CORPORATIONS NAMED THEREIN THE INCOME ACCOUNT

	OPERATING INCOME.				
ITLE OF CORPORATION.	Charges for Transportation.	Express Privileges. Dr.	Revenue from Transportation.	Revenue from Operations Other Than Transportation.	Total Operating Revenues.
	1	2	3	4	5
Express Company.............	$29,876,163	$14,941,755	$14,934,408	$272,717	$15,207,125
Express Company............	43,508,142	21,671,059	21,837,083	1,712,811	23,549,894
Express Company............	11,480,661	5,871,798	5,608,863	189,359	5,798,222
rgo & Company.............	33,812,974	17,834,525	15,978,449	601,504	16,579,953
n Railway Express Co., Inc.....	128,128,620	64,237,727	63,890,893	2,538,592	66,429,845

	OTHER INCOME—Continued.				
TLE OF CORPORATION.	Dividend Income.	Income from Funded Securities.	Income from Unfunded Securities and Accounts.	Income from Reserve Funds.	Miscellaneous Income.
	14	15	16	17	18
Express Company.............	$109,155	$418,772	$47,034	....	....
n Express Company............	81,932	243,806	40,622	$9,789	$29,507
Express Company............	4,800	3,744	37,691	....	15
rgo & Company.............	154,461	288,795	78,377	....	56,734
n Railway Express Co., Inc.....	....	22,060	170,591	....	107,093

	DEDUCTIONS FROM GROSS INCOME—Cont.		DISPOSITION OF NET INCOME.		PROFIT AND LOSS, CREDITS.
ITLE OF CORPORATION.	Total Deductions from Gross Income.	Net Income.	Dividends Declared.	Income Balance Transferred to Profit and Loss.	Balance at Beginning of Year.
	27	28	29	30	31
Express Company.............	$723,879	$6,122,562	....	$6,122,562	$8,015,005
n Express Company............	162,387	982,126	....	982,126	6,213,917
a Express Company............	4,449	53,344	....	53,344	3,892,153
rgo & Company.............	105,692	901,306	$719,022	1,620,328	4,122,785
n Railway Express Co., Inc.....	22,324	9,591,855	....	9,591,855	....

t of separate companies for 6 months ended June 30, 1918.

of American Railway Express Co., Inc., for 6 months ended December 31, 1918.

Deficit, loss and other reverse items on this table are printed in bold type.

No. 53.

FOR THE YEAR AND THE PROFIT AND LOSS ACCOUNT ON DECEMBER 31, 1918.

			OPERATING INCOME—Continued.			OTHER INCOME.		
Operating Expenses. Dr.	Net Operating Revenue.	Uncollectible Revenue from Transportation.	Express Taxes. Dr.	Operating Income.	Rent from Real Property and Equipment Used Jointly.	Income from Miscellaneous Physical Property.	Sep O Pr
6	7	8	9	10	11	12	
$21,011,119	$5,303,993	$25,275	$150,905	$5,980,173	$5,612	$600	.....
24,516,171	966,275	19,032	280,447	1,285,754	9,665	30,693	.....
5,602,556	195,666	2,192	194,129	656	11,477	722	.....
17,667,159	1,087,206	20,755	280,264	1,388,225	2,291	11,952	.....
75,527,594	9,097,689	6,927	765,700	9,870,316	1,039	325	.....

OTHER INCOME —Continu°d.			DEDUCTIONS FROM GROSS INCOME.					
Total Other Income.	Gross Income.	Rent for Real Property and Equipment Used Jointly.	Miscellaneous Rents.	Miscellaneous Taxes.	Interest on Funded Debt.	Interest on Unfunded Debt.	M I I
19	20	21	22	23	24	25	
$581,490	$5,396,683	$11,148	$291	$450	$417,230	$116,063	
446,015	819,739	5,259	18,392	14,523	....	124,073	
58,450	57,793	3,851	102	78	....	321	
592,612	795,613	5,307	40,386	27,631	....	31,791	
300,785	9,569,531	100	22,214	....	....	10	.....

PROFIT AND LOSS—Continued.							
CREDITS—Continued.				DEBITS.			
Credit Balance Transferred from Income.	Delayed Income Credits.	Unrefundable Overcharges.	Miscellaneous Credits.	Dividend Appropriations of Surplus.	Delayed Income Debits.	Miscellaneous Debits.	C B Ca. B S
32	33	34	35	36	37	38	
$6,122,562	....	$2,281	$44,042	....	....	$34,202	$1,
962,126	....	1,364	33,597	$516,474	....	32,186	4,
53,344	$28,637	355	438,702	....	....	32,719	4,
1,620,328	....	23,192	23,527	....	....	1,394	2,
9,591,855	....	8,379	9,583,950	....	....	474	.....

T

Title of Corporation.	Transportation.		
	Express, Domestic.	Express, Foreign.	
	1	2	3
1 *Adams Express Company	$29,817,642	$34,437	$24
2 *American Express Company	43,428,976	62,557	16
3 *Southern Express Company	11,470,342	9,838	
4 *Wells Fargo & Company	33,715,607	90,686	6
5 †American Railway Express Company, Inc.	128,115,574		13

Title of Corporation.	Operations Other Than Tran tion—Continued.		
	C. O. D. Cheques.	Limited and Unlimited Cheques.	
	11	12	13
1 *Adams Express Company	$150,144	$169	$
2 *American Express Company	277,311	10,560	1
3 *Southern Express Company	141,201		
4 *Wells Fargo & Company	252,250	71	
5 †American Railway Express Company, Inc.	810,662		

* Report of separate companies for 6 months ended June 30, 1918.

† Report of American Railway Express Company, Inc., for 6 months ended December 31, 1918.

No. 54.

REVENUE FOR THE YEAR ENDED DECEMBER 31, 1918, AND THE DISTRIBUTION THEREOF.

	TRANSPORTATION—Continued.			OPERATIONS OTHER THAN TRANSPORTATION.		
Total Transportation.	Express Privileges, Dr.	Revenue from Transportation.	Customs Brokerage Fees.	Order and Commission.	Rents of Buildings and Property.	Money O
4	5	6	7	8	9	10
$29,876,163	$14,941,755	$14,934,408	$31,348	$278	$4,259	$5
43,506,142	21,671,059	21,837,083	58,325	3,238	138,627	
11,450,661	5,871,798	5,608,863	836	3	6,024	
33,812,974	17,834,535	15,978,449	17,923	3,472	81,800	
128,128,620	64,237,727	63,890,893	42,244	2,708	125,223	......

			OPERATIONS OTHER THAN TRANSPORTATION—Continued.			
Telegraph and Cable Transfers.	Letters of Credits	Foreign Postal Remittances.	Profit on Exchange and Other Financial Revenue.	Miscellaneous.	Total Other Than Transportation.	To Oper Reve
14	15	16	17	18	19	2
$13	....	$849	$6,170	$25,367	$272,717	$15,
90,631	$837	5,016	349,174	531,726	1,712,811	23,
....	....	....	....	2,318	189,359	5,
1,463	....	....	14,975	100,692	601,504	16,
....	....	....	1,261,360	256,751	2,538,592	66,

ITLE OF CORPORATION.	MAINTENANCE.			
	Superintend-ence.	Repairs of Buildings.	Depreciation and Retirement of Buildings.	Repairs of Cars.
	1	2	3	4
Express Company............	$1,756	$23,792	$28,330	....
n Express Company..........	22,909	105,628	96,481	$6,445
Express Company..........	421	20,800	11,368	....
rgo Express Company........	17,187	70,149	31,186	15,704
ı Railway Express Co., Inc.....	68,925	246,229	137,041	56,133

ITLE OF CORPORATION.	MAINTENANCE—Continued.				
	Repairs of Office Furniture and Equipment.	Deprecia-tion and Retirement of Office Furniture and Equipment.	Repairs of Line Equipment.	Deprecia-tion and Retirement of Line Equipment.	Miscella-neous Repairs.
	13	14	15	16	17
xpress Company............	$27,622	$18,125	$10,077	$7,555	$3,451
Express Company..........	36,774	49,140	15,816	8,241	5,419
Express Company..........	14,528	15,051	2,455	4,781	234
go & Company............	24,792	44,178	2,654	17,194	56
Railway Express Co., Inc.....	93,243	106,940	22,224	34,584	2,480

ITLE OF CORPORATION.	TRANSPORTATION—Continued.				
	Commissions.	Office Supplies and Expenses.	Rent of Local Offices.	Vehicle Employes.	Stable and Garage Employes.
	26	27	28	29	30
xpress Company............	$831,798	$405,516	$440,336	$2,387,896	$260,239
Express Company..........	1,498,162	551,176	586,057	3,144,901	307,761
Express Company..........	679,169	115,954	122,640	320,890	21,405
go & Company............	1,378,796	355,825	468,840	2,035,834	213,884
Railway Express Co., Inc.....	5,383,467	1,503,125	1,777,709	9,910,814	1,008,973

ITLE OF CORPORATION.	GENERAL.				
	Salaries and Expenses, General Officers.	Salaries and Expenses, Clerks and Attendants.	General Office Supplies and Expenses.	Law Expenses.	Insurance and Fidelity Bond Premiums.
	39	40	41	42	43
xpress Company............	$54,792	$400,483	$31,128	$84,332	$128,861
Express Company..........	88,122	672,935	131,456	52,549	508,193
Express Company..........	35,124	210,587	11,412	22,540	15,746
go & Company............	62,285	519,696	23,947	136,904	142,256
Railway Express Co., Inc.....	149,906	1,248,489	121,186	79,765	458,693

of separate companies for 6 months ended June 30, 1918.
of American Railway Express Co., Inc., for 6 months ended December 31, 1918.
Deficit, loss and other reverse items on this table are printed in bold type.

FOR THE YEAR ENDED DECEMBER 31, 1918, AND THE DISTRIBUTION THEREOF.

MAINTENANCE—Continued.

t	Repairs of Automobiles.	Depreciation and Retirement of Automobiles.	Repairs of Wagons, Sleighs and Harness.	Depreciation and Retirement of Wagons, Sleighs and Harness	Depreciation and Retirement of Horses.	Repairs of Trucks.	Depreciation and Retirement of Trucks.
	6	7	8	9	10	11	12
..	$331,716	$174,388	$157,039	$25,422	$72,900	$30,908	$11,987
2	286,790	223,346	173,435	31,752	107,840	45,378	29,387
.	35,333	36,244	30,097	10,462	15,152	19,328	8,946
7	89,725	65,860	161,261	50,794	120,047	36,432	20,160
	805,109	487,449	644,049	106,705	289,490	154,652	71,299

NCE—Continued. | TRAFFIC | TRANSPORTATION.

on t.	Other Expenses.	Superintendence.	Advertising.	Stationery and Printing.	Other Expenses.	Superintendence.	Office Employes.
	19	20	21	22	23	24	25
	$2,104	$32,348	$2,249	$5,473	....	$337,460	$6,337,486
	....	66,876	52,691	5,542	$14	760,772	7,159,694
	34	19,424	12,120	4,873	4	182,820	1,567,986
	....	61,434	20,185	7,898	....	729,154	4,657,423
	202	56,105	15,938	111,413	....	2,351,966	25,149,426

TRANSPORTATION—Continued.

e	Drayage.	Train Employes.	Train Supplies and Expenses.	Stationery and Printing.	Loss and Damage.	Injuries to Persons.	Other Expenses.
	32	33	34	35	36	37	38
5	$1,292,666	$727,894	$21,066	$215,184	$4,598,674	$64,703	$79,277
8	1,502,240	1,114,253	87,692	386,114	2,714,334	98,716	66,832
9	101,688	521,623	13,108	.107,947	1,030,067	18,000	12,728
9	622,598	1,165,704	57,046	281,623	2,291,014	280,609	26,951
3	3,495,876	4,488,374	215,250	1,080,074	8,765,427	171,862	18,157

L—Continued. | RECAPITULATION.

	Other Expenses.	Maintenance.	Traffic.	Transportation.	General.	Total Operating Expenses.	Ratio Operating Expenses to Operating Revenue.
	45	46	47	48	49	50	51
5	$18,438	$929,737	$40,070	$19,293,112	$748,199	$21,011,119	138.17
1	55,890	1,262,839	125,123	21,534,922	1,593,286	24,516,171	104.10
	11,499	225,510	36,422	5,028,716	311,908	5,602,556	96.63
	76,976	786,285	89,517	15,793,431	997,926	17,667,159	106.56
	145,925	3,370,773	183,456	69,611,043	2,362,261	75,527,594	113.70

TABLE No. 56.

THE PULLMAN COMPANY.

COMPARATIVE BALANCE SHEET—DECEMBER 31, 1918.

Assets:		Assets.	Liabilities.
Investments:			
Cost of Property and Equipment.........		$163,089,906	
Stocks Owned............................	$1,812,745		
Funded Debt Owned......................	6,402,582	8,215,327	
Land Owned.............................		6,651	
Total Investments......................		$171,311,884	
Current Assets:			
Cash....................................	$712,255		
Bills Receivable........................	1,000,000		
Due from Agents and Conductors........	....		
Due from Solvent Cos. and Individuals....	682,072		
Other Cash Assets......................	6,427,286		
Total Current Assets...................		8,821,614	
Other Assets:			
Equipment Trusts.......................	$5,872,247		
Materials and Supplies.................	1,311,599		
Sinking, Insurance and Other Funds......	473,763		
Sundries...............................	1,186,021		
Total Other Assets.....................		8,843,630	
U. S. Government Deferred Assets........		23,723,430	
U. S. Government Standard Return.......	12,323,595		
Less Advances on Account..............	1,200,000		
Liabilities:		11,123,595	
Capital Stock..........................			$120,000,000
Current Liabilities:			
Audited Vouchers and Accounts..........		$2,457,407	
Wages and Salaries.....................		23,195	
Dividends not called for................		21,424	
Miscellaneous..........................		716,576	
Total Current Liabilities...............			3,218,602
Other Liabilities:			
Dividends accrued on Capital Stock.......		$1,590,669	
Depreciation on Cars...................		13,651,156	
Reserve for Accrued Depreciation on Equipment.........................		40,498,241	
Reserve for Accrued Depreciation on Buildings, etc........................		747,366	
Deferred Repairs.......................		1,750,000	
Insurance and Other Reserve Funds......		624,657	
Total Other Liabilities.................			58,862,089
U. S. Government Deferred Liabilities.....			22,190,073
Profit and Loss........................			19,553,439
Grand Totals......................		$223,824,203	$223,824,203

TABLE No. 57.

THE PULLMAN COMPANY.

SHOWING THE INCOME ACCOUNT FOR THE YEAR AND THE PROFIT AND LOSS ACCOUNT ON DECEMBER 31, 1918.

INCOME ACCOUNT.

OPERATING INCOME:

Sleeping Car Revenues....................................	....	
Sleeping Car Expenses...................................	$120,342	
Net Sleeping Car Deficit.................................	**$120,342**	
Net Deficit from Auxiliary Operations....................	**3,700**	
Total Net Revenue.......................................	**$124,042**	
Taxes Accrued...	2,285,478	
Operating Deficit..		**$2,409,520**

OTHER INCOME:

Hire of Equipment—Credit Balance.......................	$310	
*Miscellaneous Rents Receivable.........................	12,323,595	
Dividends on Stocks Owned..............................	97,506	
Interest on Other Securities, Loans and Accounts...........	774,873	
**Miscellaneous Income................................	1,285,407	
Total Other Income......................................		11,930,877
Gross Corporate Income.................................		$9,521,357

DEDUCTIONS FROM GROSS INCOME:

Hire of Equipment—Debit Balance.......................	....	
Interest..	$500	
***Other Deductions....................................	764,483	
Total Deductions..		764,983
Net Corporate Income...................................		$8,756,374

DISPOSITION OF NET INCOME:

Dividends Declared......................................	$9,544,016	
Appropriations to Reserve...............................	....	9,544,016
Balance Carried to Debit of Profit and Loss...............		**$787,642**

PROFIT AND LOSS ACCOUNT:

Credit Balance January 1, 1918...........................		$17,719,722
Credit Balance from Manufacturing Plants.................		2,676,897
Unrefundable Overcharges..............................		4,956
Miscellaneous Credits....................................		9,715
Debit Balance from Income Account.......................	**$787,642**	
Uncollectible Sleeping Car Revenues.....................	**502**	
Miscellaneous Debits.....................................	**69,707**	
Balance Credit, Carried to Balance Sheet.................	19,553,439	
Totals...	$20,411,290	$20,411,290

* Standard Return from U. S. Government as certified by the Interstate Commerce Commission.
** Overlap Revenue Items.
*** Overlap Expense Items.
NOTE—Deficit, loss and other reverse items on this table are printed in bold type.

TABL

Showing for Each of the Corporations Named Therein the Amount of Assets, the Amount

TITLE OF CORPORATION.	TOTALS.			
	ASSETS.		LIABILITIES.	
	Total Amount December 31, 1918	Increase Over Preceding Year.	Total Amount December 31, 1918.	Increa Over P Year
	1	2	3	4
Baltimore & Philadelphia Steamboat Co.	$691,098	$4,498	$411,392	$1,
Rock Creek Steamboat Co.	12,703	1,081	13,250	....
Stony Creek Steamboat Co.	32,415	2,875	29,500	5,
Tolchester Beach Improvement Co.	343,041	9,001	253,000	8,
Woodall & Welch Freighting Co.	12,000	....	12,000	

TITLE OF CORPORATION.	DETAILS OF ASSETS—Continued.		
	Sinking Fund and Other Reserves.	Special Deposits and Prepayments.	Sundries.
	12	13	14
Baltimore & Philadelphia Steamboat Co.	$50,932	....	$5,
Rock Creek Steamboat Co.			
Stony Creek Steamboat Co.			
Tolchester Beach Improvement Co.			
Woodall & Welch Freighting Co.			

NOTE—Deficit, loss and other reverse items in this table are printed in bold type.

No. 61.

LIABILITIES AND THE SURPLUS ON DEC. 31, 1918, AND THE CLASSIFICATION OF SUCH ASSETS AND LIABILITIES.

Total Amount December 31, 1918.	Increase Over Preceding Year.	Real Property and Land Equipment.	Marine Equipment	Cash.	Bills and Accounts Receivable.	M St
5	6	7	8	'9	10	
$279,706	$2,834	415,571	$199,000	$15,694	$4,900	
547	1,081	180	10,000	2,338	184	
2,915	2,125	....	31,500	915	....	
90,041	17,001	129,407	195,000	18,634	....	
....	....	....	12,000	....	....	

DETAILS OF LIABILITIES.

Capital Stock.	Funded Debt.	Bills and Accounts Payable.	Salaries and Wages Unpaid.	Interest, Dividends and Rents Accrued.	Sinking Fund and Other Reserves.	Su
15	16	17	18	19	20	
$281,400	....	$75,000	....	....	$50,932	
13,250	....	....	....	....	....	
20,000	....	9,500	....	....	....	
253,000	....	....	....	....	....	
12,000	....	....	....	....	....	

T

SHOWING FOR EACH OF THE CORPORATIONS NAMED THEREIN THE GROSS INCOME FROM ALL So

		TOTALS.	
TITLE OF CORPORATION.	Gross Income From All Sources.	Increase Over Preceding Year.	
	1	2	
1 Baltimore & Philadelphia Steamboat Co..............	$506,073	$79,649	
2 Rock Creek Steamboat Co...........................	10,283	3,360	
3 Stony Creek Steamboat Co.........................	33,550	*	
4 Tolchester Beach Improvement Co.	360,121	79,718	
5 Weedall & Welch Freighting Co.....................	16,568	3,376	

	DETAILS OF INCOME—Cont.	DEDUCTIONS FROM	
TITLE OF CORPORATION.	Miscellaneous.	Maintenance and Depreciation	To Ligh
	11	12	1
1 Baltimore & Philadelphia Steamboat Co..............	$5,725	$62,938	
2 Rock Creek Steamboat Co...........................	2,095	571	
3 Stony Creek Steamboat Co.........................	14,067	2,650	
4 Tolchester Beach Improvement Co..................	83,748	36,367	....
5] Weedall & Welch Freighting Co...................	....	1,047	....

* Asterisk denotes figures not furnished.

NOTE—Deficit, loss and other reverse items in this table are printed in bold type.

No. 62.

DEDUCTIONS FROM INCOME AND THE NET INCOME FROM THE OPERATIONS OF THE YEAR ENDED DECEMBER 31, 1

	TOTALS—Continued.			DETAILS OF INCOME.			
Increase Over Preceding Year.	Surplus or Deficit.	Increase Over Preceding Year.	Passenger Traffic.	Freight Traffic.	Rents.		In Di
4	5	6	7	8	9		10
$69,449	$21,011	$10,200	$57,161	$433,142	$5,045		
1,024	2,236	2,336	7,562	561			
	5,616		12,024	12,519			
40,403	39,771	39,315	95,785	115,588			
697	4,183	4,183		10,508			

DEDUCTIONS FROM INCOME—Continued.

Transportation.	Tolls and Rents.	Interest on Funded and Other Debt.	Taxes.	Insurance.	Dividends.	Miscel
14	15	16	17	18	19	20
$301,454	$46,325	$4,888	$16,204	$7,574	$28,140	
6,519	49	5	165	300	1,325	
14,565		819	855	1,182		
195,446		583	15,094	11,070	22,770	
5,678			100			

INDEX

Lightning Source UK Ltd.
Milton Keynes UK
UKHW010803110119

335238UK00008B/752/P